The Palgrave Handbook of Posthumanism in Film and Television

The Palgrave Handbook of Posthumanism in Film and Television

Edited by

Michael Hauskeller
University of Exeter, UK

Thomas D. Philbeck
World Economic Forum, Switzerland

Curtis D. Carbonell
Khalifa University of Science, Technology and Research, UAE

Selection and editorial matter © Michael Hauskeller, Thomas D. Philbeck and Curtis D. Carbonell 2015
Individual chapters © Respective authors 2015

All rights reserved. No reproduction, copy or transmission of this publication may be made without written permission.

No portion of this publication may be reproduced, copied or transmitted save with written permission or in accordance with the provisions of the Copyright, Designs and Patents Act 1988, or under the terms of any licence permitting limited copying issued by the Copyright Licensing Agency, Saffron House, 6–10 Kirby Street, London EC1N 8TS.

Any person who does any unauthorized act in relation to this publication may be liable to criminal prosecution and civil claims for damages.

The authors have asserted their rights to be identified as the authors of this work in accordance with the Copyright, Designs and Patents Act 1988.

First published 2015 by
PALGRAVE MACMILLAN

Palgrave Macmillan in the UK is an imprint of Macmillan Publishers Limited, registered in England, company number 785998, of Houndmills, Basingstoke, Hampshire RG21 6XS.

Palgrave Macmillan in the US is a division of St Martin's Press LLC, 175 Fifth Avenue, New York, NY 10010.

Palgrave Macmillan is the global academic imprint of the above companies and has companies and representatives throughout the world.

Palgrave® and Macmillan® are registered trademarks in the United States, the United Kingdom, Europe and other countries.

ISBN 978–1–137–43031–1

This book is printed on paper suitable for recycling and made from fully managed and sustained forest sources. Logging, pulping and manufacturing processes are expected to conform to the environmental regulations of the country of origin.

A catalogue record for this book is available from the British Library.

A catalog record for this book is available from the Library of Congress.

Contents

Preface ix

Notes on Contributors xv

1 Posthumanism in Film and Television 1
   Michael Hauskeller, Thomas D. Philbeck and Curtis D. Carbonell

Part I Paving the Way to Posthumanism: The Precursors

2 From DelGuat to ScarJo 11
   William Brown

3 'Self-Immolation by Technology': Jean Baudrillard and the Posthuman in Film and Television 19
   Jon Baldwin

4 Derrida on Screen 28
   Stefan Herbrechter

5 Bruno Latour: From the Non-Modern to the Posthuman 37
   T. Hugh Crawford

6 Friedrich Nietzsche and the Posthuman/Transhuman in Film and Television 45
   Babette Babich

Part II Varieties of People-to-Come: Posthuman Becomings

7 Terminated: The Life and Death of the Cyborg in Film and Television 57
   Rhys Owain Thomas

8 Of Iron Men and Green Monsters: Superheroes and Posthumanism 66
   Dan Hassler-Forest

9 Growing Your Own: Monsters from the Lab and Molecular Ethics in Posthumanist Film 77
   Anna Powell

10 Post-Singularity Entities in Film and TV 88
   David Roden

11 Chimeras and Hybrids: The Digital Swarms of the Posthuman Image 99
   Drew Ayers

Part III Rise of the Machines: Posthuman Intellects

12 Androids and the Posthuman in Television and Film 111
    Kevin LaGrandeur

13 'Change for the Machines'? Posthumanism as Digital Sentience 120
    Sherryl Vint

14 Alive in the Net 130
    Jeff Menne and Jay Clayton

15 Autonomous Fighting Machines: Narratives and Ethics 141
    Dónal P. O'Mathúna

Part IV Body and Soul: Posthuman Subjectivities

16 A Contest of Tropes: Screened Posthuman Subjectivities 153
    Curtis D. Carbonell

17 Desire and Uncertainty: Representations of Cybersex in Film
    and Television 163
    Hilary Wheaton

18 At Home In and Beyond Our Skin: Posthuman Embodiment in Film
    and Television 172
    Joel Krueger

19 Constructed Worlds: Posthumanism in Film, Television and Other
    Cosmopoietic Media 182
    Ivan Callus

20 Games, Gamers and Posthumanism 192
    Tanya Krzywinska and Douglas Brown

Part V Better Humans: Posthuman Capacities

21 'Life's a bitch, and then you *don't* die': Postmortality in Film and
    Television 205
    Michael Hauskeller

22 A New Lease on Life: A Lacanian Analysis of Cognitive
    Enhancement Cinema 214
    Hub Zwart

23 *Limitless*? There's a Pill for That: Filmic Representation as Equipment
    for Living 225
    Kyle McNease

24 Posthumans and Democracy in Popular Culture 235
    James J. Hughes

25 Negative Feelings as Emotional Enhancement in Cinema: The Case
    of Ulrich Seidl's *Paradise* Trilogy 246
    Tarja Laine

Part VI Creating Difference and Identity: Posthuman Communities

26 Biopleasures: Posthumanism and the Technological Imaginary in
    Utopian and Dystopian Film 259
    Ralph Pordzik

27 Of Posthuman Born: Gender, Utopia and the Posthuman in Films
    and TV 269
    Francesca Ferrando

28 Sharing Social Context: Is Community with the Posthuman
    Possible? 279
    David Meeler and Eric Hill

29 Our Posthuman Skin Condition 289
    Teodora Manea

30 Muddy Worlds: Re-Viewing Environmental Narratives 299
    John Bruni

Part VII Us and Them: Posthuman Relationships

31 Executing Species: Animal Attractions in Thomas Edison and
    Douglas Gordon 311
    Anat Pick

32 The Sun Never Set on the Human Empire: Haunts of Humanism in
    the *Planet of the Apes* Films 321
    Phil Henderson

33 Uncanny Intimacies: Humans and Machines in Film 330
    Alexander Darius Ornella

34 Posthumanous Subjects 339
    Steen Christiansen

35 Identity: Difficulties, Discontinuities and Pluralities of Personhood 349
    James DiGiovanna

Part VIII More Human than Human: Posthuman Ontologies

36 The Final Frontier? Religion and Posthumanism in Film and
    Television 361
    Elaine Graham

37 The Ghost in the Machine: Humanity and the Problem of Self-Aware Information 371
Brett Lunceford

38 'Trust a Few, Fear the Rest': The Anxiety and Fantasy of Human Evolution 380
Pramod K. Nayar

39 Onscreen Ontology: Stages in the Posthumanist Paradigm Shift 391
Thomas D. Philbeck

40 Object-Oriented Ontology 401
Graham Harman

Bibliography 410

Index of Films and TV Shows 436

General Index 443

Preface

This handbook is structured in eight parts.

Part I – Paving the Way to Posthumanism: The Precursors

This section focuses on some of the intellectual influences that have paved the way for the posthumanist discourse.

William Brown begins with posthumanism's most referenced theorists, Deleuze and Guattari. Brown highlights the often-cited idea of 'bodies without organs' and 'desiring machines' as critical to understanding Deleuzian posthumanism. These decentring concepts of the human, leading away from a grounded, circumscribed, individuated entity, challenge simplistic transhumanist notions of the self, allowing Brown a critique of cinema from a posthuman/Deleuzian perspective, in which he argues that cinema has always represented a world 'teeming with life' to the point where humans have little or no control.

Jon Baldwin follows with a look into media theorist Baudrillard and his thinking that the digital world reduces us to the inhuman. Baldwin focuses on how alterity may be lost in our posthuman moment, in particular how virtual reality is represented as a space in science fiction (SF) for the eradication of difference. The copy and the clone become the hyperreal, or the new real, and the posthuman experience divorces us from ourselves.

Stefan Herbrechter wades into the difficult work of deconstruction theorist Derrida, arguing that 'Derrida is both a "proto-posthumanist" and a "media philosopher"', and that posthumanism and contemporary media would not even exist without Derridean deconstruction. Herbrechter teases apart Derrida as both someone screened and someone who comments on moving pictures such as film and television, and on visual media in general.

T. Hugh Crawford provides an examination of Latour's critique of modernity and how it relates to posthumanism. Crawford notes that Latour's critical approach undermines the notion of the posthuman because, as with being modern, we have never been human in the naïve Enlightenment sense. Latour's focus on the non-human provides a 'theatre of proof', whereby scientists like Pasteur were able to foreground certain dramatic elements in their experiments, thus making an impact in much the same mode as cinema.

Babette Babich ends this section with an overview of Nietzsche's Zarathustra 2.0, detailing how the philosopher's notion of the *Übermensch* relates to Singularitarian ideas of posthumanity, and how the popular imagination skews Nietzsche's idea towards posthuman supermen.

Part II – Varieties of People-to-Come: Posthuman Becomings

This second part deals with the various different ways we imagine the posthuman and the transhuman to be; that is, what we may one day be and what we are already in the process of becoming.

Rhys Owain Thomas starts the section off with a look at the cyborg in film and television. Thomas locates the postmodern cyborg within the discourse of critical theory so that its posthuman inflections are noted, namely, those of subject creation and identity. The screened versions reflect shared anxieties of the technologized human.

Dan Hassler-Forest applies ideas from critical theory to screened superheroes, according to which posthuman bodies are discursive processes being written today by technology. He sees the posthuman as providing a necessary tension for the superhero paradigm in its quest to overcome the body's limitations.

Anna Powell provides a Deleuzian reading of how the posthuman monstrous is comprised of processes of 'becoming, assemblages, anomalies'. She moves through examples of screened cloning texts, slowing down with a detailed reading of *Casshern*, a film with multiplicities of narrative, style and content that imagine posthumans as Deleuzian neo-sapiens.

David Roden tackles posthumanism within the context of the technological singularity as seen in film and television, attempting to understand how we will know that we have entered a truly post-singularity world.

Drew Ayers ends this section with a unique look into how swarm technology in digital media provides a metaphor for understanding posthumanism. For Ayers, the combination of digital and analogue elements forms a hybrid synonymous with our posthuman condition.

Part III – Rise of the Machines: Posthuman Intellects

Artificial intelligence (AI) is the focus of the third section.

It begins with *Kevin LaGrandeur*'s examination of androids as a cinematic trope wherein anxieties over the human losing control of its creation appear again and again, from outright enslavement to more subtle, nuanced representations of android/human interaction.

Sherryl Vint provides a comment on digital sentience, or 'supercomputers, distributed network AIs', to show that real-world posthumanism in this context is about the fusing of the human and the digital, while film and TV attempt to represent anxieties about such integrations.

Jeff Menne and *Jay Clayton* examine two foundational representations of AI: centralized, self-contained intelligences that grow in size and power, and those that come into being via networks. They examine how the counterculture of the 1960s and 1970s does not appear in the movies until much later than expected. Even more recent is the exploration of the posthuman.

Finally, *Dónal P. O'Mathúna* looks into autonomous fighting machines and how they reflect our current posthuman moment. Mining both contemporary realist film and television, as well as standards from SF, O'Mathúna sees, in modern technology like weaponized drones, a central mechanism for understanding how AI leads to posthumanism. For him, these fictions provide extrapolative scenarios with didactic lessons we should heed.

Part IV – Body and Soul: Posthuman Subjectivities

Focusing on virtual reality, this section explores the reality of the virtual and the virtuality of the real, and how both require and complement each other.

Curtis D. Carbonell argues that a contest of tropes exists in the most interesting representations of posthumanism in SF and fantasy. For him, examples of screened posthumans are telling illustrations of subject formation reflective of our highly technologized realities.

Hilary Wheaton examines how cybersex in film and television emerges at the intersection of technology and virtual space. The posthuman angle, for her, recognizes that these virtual interactions require us to reconcile the physical body with our understanding of desire and technology, before we can fully embrace what it means to be posthuman.

Joel Krueger shifts focus from the virtual to the embodied world by discussing some of the ways that transformative relations between embodiment and technology have been explored in film and television. Krueger concludes that 'these onscreen portrayals of posthuman embodiment remind us that to be an embodied subject is to be always in some way *transcending* that embodiment'.

Ivan Callus explores the resonances between the constructed worlds found in posthumanist fictions and possible worlds theory. Those fictions 'allow the contemporary imagination to play with degrees of (im)probability and the varying scales of pragmatic response to speculation on what could occur suddenly, imminently, gradually, fantastically or inexorably, given where humanity stands in the world(s) it has contrived', which in turn helps to define our actual world.

Tanya Krzywinska and *Douglas Brown* discuss the presence of the posthuman in SF-based games and in the way that film and television represents virtual reality, games and gamers. They argue that, although games do not only often represent posthuman concepts and imagery, they are also posthumanist in the way they are constructed, and usually serve a decidedly humanist agenda.

Part V – Better Humans: Posthuman Capacities

This section addresses human enhancement by considering representations in film and television of the various ways in which we imagine humans to become better through technological modification, as well as the outcomes of such practices.

Michael Hauskeller starts the section off with an exploration of radical life extension and post-mortality, arguing that it is the filmic representation of the vampire that shows most clearly not only the urgency of the human desire for immortality, but also the price that has to be paid for it.

Hub Zwart looks into a Lacanian understanding of posthuman cognitive enhancement. He views the broadening of our cognitive capabilities as providing a reflexive understanding of ourselves as limited human beings, often seen in film and television via neural implants or pharmaceuticals. Rather than providing a reading of the usual suspects, Zwart engages in a focused Lacanian reading of *Limitless*, wherein cognitive enhancers illuminate understandings of standard categories like masculine gender roles.

Kyle McNease also focuses on *Limitless* as a key cinematic text reflecting the problematic notion of human enhancement. He deftly steps through art criticism, philosophy and critical theory, viewing in the film a reminder to be wary of transhumanist promises.

James J. Hughes views popular culture as a contested site of subject formation, one with potential to further democratic pluralism. In particular, he moves through a variety of screened texts in which posthuman 'modalities' run the gamut from the extreme 'other' to sympathetic persons. He ultimately argues that the progressive trajectory from viewing the posthuman as monstrous to democratically agential persons can be seen clearly in SF film and television.

Finally, *Tarja Laine* discusses Ulrich Seidl's *Love*, *Faith* and *Hope* trilogy and argues that, contrary to the hopes of some transhumanists, emotional enhancement does not mean eradicating negative feelings. She sees in film a mechanism for viewers to work through negative emotions. Even more, she applies theories of critical posthumanism to the films, engaging in an ethical project 'aimed at altering our project of looking'.

Part VI – Creating Difference and Identity: Posthuman Communities

What kind of communities are possible and/or desirable in a posthumanist world? This section addresses this question by engaging with the social dimension of posthumanism, asking how we can and will live together in a community with other humans, non-humans and posthumans.

Ralph Pordzik explores how utopian and dystopian film reimagines the boundaries between the human and its varieties of often-extrapolated opposites, ultimately seeing dystopian inflections 'carve out a potential for debate' wherein stable humanist categories open themselves up to transformation.

Francesca Ferrando follows with an intriguing look into screened utopian SF as 'seeds of the future', focusing on difference as a key mechanism in articulating the posthuman through gender and sexuality, through the category of race, through the identity of the cyborg as other and through their acceptance as chimeras and hybrids deserving of love.

David Meeler and *Eric Hill* examine the notion of governance as a missing concept in most screened representations of the posthuman. They see such narratives as driven by a struggle between humans and posthumans, rather than a focus on 'shared communities'. They ultimately question if true governance can be represented between posthuman and human communities.

Teodora Manea focuses on skin as the element we most encounter between ourselves and the other. She provides 'epidermal readings' in her examination of 'our posthuman skin condition'. Moving through close readings of a wide range of screened texts, she foregrounds skin as a mechanism for challenging normative identity.

John Bruni ends this section with a unique view of environmental posthumanism, or 'muddy worlds', eschewing the usual suspects in SF and fantasy, for contemporary realist film and TV like *Zabriskie Point* and *Treme*. These texts can be used to imagine a truly post-anthropocene environment in which humanity has been displaced by a posthuman reality of scarcity and challenge.

Part VII – Us and Them: Posthuman Relationships

This section grounds the previous one, beginning with *Anat Pick*'s admission that screened animals have more narrative importance than usually admitted. In fact, her Deleuzian and Latourian understanding sees cinema as an assemblage of reflections in which animals feature prominently as dominated elements. She highlights the 'cinematic animal' as a 'new kind of being'. The posthuman context, here, works along the trajectory of valuing the non-human animal in an increasingly complex parliament of things.

Phil Henderson follows with an examination of the latest *Planet of the Apes* films as highly humanist, even in their most posthuman inflections. He sees these posthuman narratives as advocating a challenge to the traditional human/animal dichotomy, while still reinforcing a fundamental humanism.

Alexander Darius Ornella steps away from the human/animal dichotomy towards themes of human/machine relationships wherein SF film and TV represent a 'return to an (idealized) nature, erotic encounters, social robots, and cybernetics'.

Steen Christiansen playfully offers the 'posthumanous' as a way to rethink the posthuman beyond terms of the life/death dichotomy. He foregrounds how the dividing line between life and death is 'inherently unstable and problematic'. Thus, 'we need a posthumanous subject to articulate the liminality of life'.

James DiGiovanna ends with the important subject of personhood as a posthuman category. He sees SF as keenly situated to ask philosophical questions about identity, functioning as a type of thought experiment through which future posthuman realities may be constructed.

Part VIII – More Human than Human: Posthuman Ontologies

This final section turns towards the examination of how it is that we construct and work through frameworks and structures to reconnoitre our conception of human being. The authors evidence the ontological foundations of the posthumanist framework through the use of SF examples, influences and themes.

Elaine Graham sees in SF film and TV a shift to both a post-secular and posthumanist world, viewing their conjunction through a religious frame. She shows that SF today, while still retaining its core 'elevation of scientific enquiry and secular humanist values', is also 'post-secular' in that religious elements exist in a vibrant tension with secular humanist elements.

Brett Lunceford follows with an important question from the philosophy of mind, whether we are truly 'thinking machines' that 'can be reduced to their own information processing'. His focus on sentient machines as a trope in SF film and TV relies on the notion that memory and emotions are key to defining our humanity and, even with technological interventions into the posthuman, very fundamental human categories remain.

Pramod K. Nayar examines how superhero and dystopic films exhibit a dialectic between the evolved superhuman and 'species cosmopolitanism'. Nayar reads this dialectic as providing either a contracting of discursive properties for the former or a broadening for the latter. He sees, ultimately, 'a significant posthumanist strain in them, and that is the possibility of trans-species yet human morality and ethics'.

Thomas D. Philbeck uses the way our relationship to technology is represented in film and television to trace the paradigm shift that has occurred during the last half century, leading us from a broadly humanist paradigm that takes the separation between technology and humanity and the self-containment of human agency for granted to a posthumanist paradigm that acknowledges the distributed nature of our collective subjectivity.

Graham Harman ends the final section with a description of object-oriented ontology wherein he teases out the differences between speculative realism, posthumanism, transhumanism and materialism. He relates these to film and art theory, seeing in cinema, theatre and live television an encounter between objects and viewers that suggests a complex relationship of posthuman viewpoints.

Contributors

Drew Ayers researches, teaches and writes on the subjects of cinema, visual culture, digital technology, visual effects and non-human theory. Since finishing degrees from Carleton College, the University of Texas at Austin and Georgia State University, he has taught at Northeastern University, Antioch University and Santa Barbara City College. His work has appeared in *Animation*, *Film Criticism*, *Configurations*, *Scope* and *In Media Res*, and an essay will appear in a forthcoming British Film Institute anthology on special effects. He is currently at work on a manuscript that explores the digital logic and 'vernacular posthumanism' of hybrid images in contemporary film, media and visual culture.

Babette Babich is Professor of Philosophy at Fordham University in New York City. She is the author of numerous books, including *The Hallelujah Effect: Philosophical Reflections on Music, Performance Practice and Technology* (2013), *La fin de la pensée? Philosophie analytique contre philosophie continentale* (2012), *Nietzsches Wissenschaftsphilosophie* (2010), *Eines Gottes Glück, voller Macht und Liebe* (2009), *Words in Blood, Like Flowers* (2007), *Nietzsche e la Scienza* (1996) and *Nietzsche's Philosophy of Science* (1994). Her two most recent edited collections include the 2013–2014 special issue of *New Nietzsche Studies: Nietzsche and Kant* and, co-edited with Dimitri Ginev, *The Multidimensionality of Hermeneutic Phenomenology* (2014).

Jon Baldwin teaches at the London Metropolitan University and is the author of *The Financial Crash and Hyper-Real Economy*. He has published widely on film and media, continental philosophy, poetics and culture. He is contributing editor of the collections 'Baudrillard and Politics' and 'Baudrillard and Film-Philosophy'. He is on the editorial boards of *Film-Philosophy*, *Subject Matters* and the *International Journal of Baudrillard Studies*.

Douglas Brown is Head of Games and Animation at Falmouth University, Cornwall, UK, where he teaches and researches digital games. He has previously written on games and adaptation in the context of Hollywood movies and the *Lord of the Rings* franchise. His research interests encompass games and narrative, and he is currently working on a book looking into how the suspension of disbelief operates in digital games.

William Brown is Senior Lecturer in Film at the University of Roehampton, London. He is the author of *Supercinema: Film-Philosophy for the Digital Age* (2013) and, with Dina Iordanova and Leshu Torchin, and of *Moving People, Moving Images: Cinema and Trafficking in the New Europe* (2010). He is the editor, with David Martin-Jones, of *Deleuze and Film* (2012) and, with Jenna P-S Ng, of a Special

Issue of *Animation: An Interdisciplinary Journal* on *Avatar* (2012). He has written numerous essays for journals and edited collections, with his research specializing in film-philosophy, cognitive film theory and digital cinema. Furthermore, he has directed seven zero-budget and often experimental feature films, *En Attendant Godard* (2009), *Afterimages* (2010), *Common Ground* (2012), *China: A User's Manual (Films)* (2012), *Selfie* (2014), *The New Hope* (2015) and *Ur: The End of Civilization in 90 Tableaux* (2015).

John Bruni teaches in the School of Communication at Grand Valley State University. He is the author of *Scientific Americans: The Making of Popular Science and Evolution in Early-Twentieth-Century U.S. Literature and Culture* (2014). Currently he is working on a book-length project on systems theory and the films of John Cassavetes. His research interests include biopolitics and ecocriticism.

Ivan Callus is associate professor at the Department of English, University of Malta, where he teaches courses in contemporary fiction and literary theory. He has co-edited special issues on posthumanism for the journals *Subjectivity* and *EJES*, and co-founded the 'Critical Posthumanisms' book series with Brill and the Critical Posthumanism Network (http://www.criticalposthumanism.net). With Stefan Herbrechter he is the co-editor, among other books, of *Cy-Borges: Memories of the Posthuman in the Work of Jorge Luis Borges* (2009) and *Posthumanist Shakespeares* (Palgrave Macmillan 2013). His current research is on genealogies of the posthuman.

Curtis D. Carbonell teaches English at Khalifa University to engineering students. He is interested in how the humanities have to work within the technosocial sphere. He has published on the two cultures debate, as well as in SF studies. He is currently working on how posthumanism is emerging in fantasy and SF.

Steen Christiansen is Associate Professor of English at Aalborg University, Denmark. His research interests include visual culture, popular film and SF, with a particular emphasis on questions of embodiment and sensation. He is currently working on two book projects, one on post-vitalist SF and the other on action cinema in the 21st century. His recent publications include 'Violence and Constraint in Nicolas Winding Refn's *Only God Forgives*', 'Hyper Attention Blockbusters' and 'Terminal Films'.

Jay Clayton is William R. Kenan, Jr. Professor of English and Director of the Curb Center for Art, Enterprise, and Public Policy at Vanderbilt University. He is author of a number of books, including, most recently, *Charles Dickens in Cyberspace*. He has written frequently on SF, film and new media, and online gaming.

T. Hugh Crawford is Associate Professor of Science, Technology, and Culture Studies at Georgia Institute of Technology. He holds a PhD in American Literature from Duke University. He is the author of *Modernism, Medicine, and William Carlos*

Williams, along with articles on Bruno Latour and science studies. A past president of the Society for Literature, Science, and the Arts, he also edited their journal *Configurations* for many years. An avid long-distance hiker, he is currently writing a book on walking.

James DiGiovanna is Assistant Professor of Philosophy at John Jay College, CUNY, and was formerly the award-winning film critic for *The Tucson Weekly*. His philosophical publications include 'Knowledge, Understanding and Pedagogy' in *Teaching Philosophy* (2014), 'You Are and Are Not the Person I Once Knew: Eclecticism and Context in Continuity of Identity' in *Appraisal: A Journal of Constructive and Post-Critical Philosophy and Interdisciplinary Studies* (2012) and 'Identity, Memory and Continuity' in *Watchmen and Philosophy* (2009). His fiction has appeared in *Blue Moon Review*, *20X18* and *SporkPress*. His philosophical writings focus on personal identity, personhood, the epistemology of understanding and the nature of fictional worlds.

Francesca Ferrando teaches Philosophy at New York University, as an adjunct faculty member of the Program of Liberal Studies. She holds a PhD in Philosophy from the University of Roma Tre (Italy). For her doctoral dissertation she received the Philosophical Prize 'Vittorio Sainati' (2014), with the acknowledgment of the President of the Italian Republic. She has published extensively on the topic of the posthuman in academic journals and anthologies. She is also a TEDx speaker and one of the founders of the NY Posthuman Research Group. She is actively involved in the posthumanist scene as a visionary thinker and organizer.

Elaine Graham is Grosvenor Professor of Practical Theology at the University of Chester, UK. She has written extensively in areas such as practical theology, technology and popular culture, media and religion, and religion and politics. Her current research interest concerns the future of public discourse on religion in a post-secular and pluralistic society. She is the author of *Making the Difference: Gender, Personhood and Theology* (1995), *Transforming Practice: Pastoral Theology in an Age of Uncertainty* (1996), *Representations of the Post/Human* (2002), *Words Made Flesh: Writings in Pastoral and Practical Theology* (2009) and *Between a Rock and a Hard Place: Public Theology in a Post-Secular Age* (2013).

Graham Harman is a distinguished university professor at the American University in Cairo. He is the author of 12 books, most recently *Bells and Whistles: More Speculative Realism* (2013) and *Bruno Latour: Reassembling the Political* (2014). He is a founding member of the Speculative Realism and Object-Oriented Ontology movements, and edits the Speculative Realism book series at Edinburgh University Press and (with Bruno Latour) co-edits the New Metaphysics series at Open Humanities Press.

Dan Hassler-Forest was born in New York and now resides in the Netherlands, where his lifelong addiction to film, television and books currently finds a welcome outlet in his position as Assistant Professor of English Literature at the University of Amsterdam. In his work, he struggles to align his passion for pop culture with his dedication to radical Marxism, the results of which are published from time to time in international journals and edited collections. His own books include the monograph *Capitalist Superheroes*, and an edited collection on comics and graphic literature.

Michael Hauskeller is Professor of Philosophy at the Department of Sociology and Philosophy, University of Exeter, UK. He specializes in moral philosophy, but has also worked in various other areas, including the philosophy of mind, the philosophy of art and beauty, phenomenology and the philosophy of human enhancement. His important recent publications include *Biotechnology and the Integrity of Life* (2007), *Better Humans? Understanding the Enhancement Project* (2013) and *Sex and the Posthuman Condition* (Palgrave Macmillan, 2014).

Phil Henderson received his Bachelor's degree (Political Science) from the University of Western Ontario in 2014. Master's studies are ongoing at the University of Victoria (Cultural, Social and Political Thought) and are anticipated to conclude in 2016. Henderson's thesis intends to bring a focus on the sense of *ressentiment* that poverty, resulting from neoliberal policies, has induced in Canadian rural communities. This work is meant to be tied into a larger literature on white settler societies, ultimately highlighting the impasse that neoliberalism has created against the decolonizing project.

Stefan Herbrechter is an independent scholar and Privatdozent at Heidelberg University, Germany. Until 2014, he was Reader in Cultural Theory and Postgraduate Programme Manager (Media) at Coventry University, UK, where he remains an honorary research fellow. He is the author of a number of volumes and edited collections, and many articles on critical and cultural theory, English and comparative literature, and media and cultural studies. His most recent volume is *Posthumanism: A Critical Analysis* (2013). He is also a translator of Derrida, general editor of the monograph series Critical Posthumanisms and director of the Critical Posthumanism Network.

Eric Hill is a graduate student in Winthrop University's Masters of Liberal Arts programme on Political and Civic Engagement. His research focuses on what constitutes humanity in the face of governance, including analyses of humanity, the relationship between the governor and the governed, and whether conventional conceptions of humanity remain intact when viewed through the lens of the body politic.

James J. Hughes is Executive Director of the Institute for Ethics and Emerging Technologies, a technoprogressive think tank. A bioethicist and sociologist, he teaches health policy and serves as Director of Institutional Research and Planning at Trinity College in Hartford Connecticut. He is author of *Citizen Cyborg:*

Why Democratic Societies Must Respond to the Redesigned Human of the Future, a fellow of the World Academy of Arts and Sciences, and a member of Humanity+, the American Society of Bioethics and Humanities and the Working Group on Ethics and Technology at Yale University. He serves on the State of Connecticut Regenerative Medicine Research Advisory Committee.

Joel Krueger is Lecturer in Philosophy at the University of Exeter, UK. He works on various issues in phenomenology, philosophy of mind and cognitive science, with a particular focus on emotions and social cognition. He also works on philosophy of music, Asian and comparative philosophy, and pragmatism. His work has appeared in journals such as *Behavioral and Brain Sciences, Consciousness and Cognition, Phenomenology and the Cognitive Sciences, Philosophy East and West* and *Inquiry*.

Tanya Krzywinska is professor with the Academy of Innovation and Research at Falmouth University, Cornwall, UK, where she leads a research and PhD programme in digital games. She is editor of the journal *Games and Culture* and the author of many books and articles on games design, cinema and transmedial culture. She is currently writing a book that investigates uses of the gothic in digital games, and has recently published work on games and weird fiction.

Kevin LaGrandeur is Professor and Director of Technical Writing Programs at the New York Institute of Technology (NYIT), and a fellow of the Institute for Ethics and Emerging Technology. He has written many articles and conference presentations on digital culture, AI and ethics, and literature and science. His publications have appeared in journals such as *Computers & Texts, Computers and the Humanities* and *Science Fiction Studies*, as well as in popular publications such as United Press International news agency, where he recently published an Op-Ed piece titled 'The Mars Landing and Artificial Intelligence', which discusses future ethical protocols for developing AI. His most recent book, titled *Androids and Intelligent Networks in Early Modern Literature and Culture* (2013), is about the premodern cultural history of AI. It was awarded the 2014 Science Fiction and Technoculture Studies Prize.

Tarja Laine is Assistant Professor of Film Studies at the University of Amsterdam, and Adjunct Professor of Film Studies at the University of Turku (Finland), as well as visual artist-in-training at Wackers Academy, Amsterdam. She is the author of *Bodies in Pain: Emotion and the Cinema of Darren Aronofsky* (2015), *Feeling Cinema: Emotional Dynamics in Film Studies* (2011) and *Shame and Desire: Emotion, Intersubjectivity, Cinema* (2007). Her research interests include cinematic emotions, film aesthetics and film phenomenology.

Brett Lunceford is a rhetorician who focuses on the intersections between the body, sexuality and technology. He holds a PhD from Pennsylvania State University, USA. He is the author of the book *Naked Politics: Nudity, Political Action, and the Rhetoric of the Body* and more than 30 journal articles and book chapters. His work has appeared in such journals as *Communication Law Review, ETC: A Review of General Semantics, Explorations in Media Ecology, Journal of Contemporary Rhetoric, Review of Communication* and *Theology & Sexuality*. He is the current editor of the *Journal of Contemporary Rhetoric* and serves as Vice-President Elect of the Media Ecology Association.

Kyle McNease is a doctoral student in Communication and Bioethics at Florida State University. As a Rogerian therapist, he has expertise working with marginalized groups, those experiencing psychological distress brought about by illness, suffering and loss. His research focuses on existential suffering, meaning-making and the political economy of biotechnology. Recent publications include *Brij Mohan: Person, Pioneer and Professor* (2010) and *Soma, Sema, Sacred: Prolegomena to an Ethics of Suffering* (2014).

Teodora Manea studied Philosophy at the 'Al. I. Cuza' University of Iasi, Romania. Between 2000 and 2009 she was Senior Lecturer in History of Philosophy and Hermeneutics at the same university. Since 2010 she has been teaching Medical Humanities at the University of Exeter's Medical School. Her research interests encompass bioethics, hermeneutics, ethics of care, postmodern philosophy and enhancement. Her publications in German, Romanian and English include *The Recovery of Categories in Contemporary Philosophy* (2004), *On the Way with Hippocrates: Romanian Medical Migration* (co-edited, 2013) and *Bocca de la Verita* (co-edited, 2004), as well as many articles and book chapters.

David Meeler is Associate Professor of Philosophy and Director of the interdisciplinary Legal Studies programme at Winthrop University, South Carolina. His primary research interests include posthumanism and human rights, the role guidelines and rules play in shaping institutional culture, appropriate methods for selecting political leaders, public political discourse, corporate social responsibility, legal and moral conceptions of privacy, theories of punishment, and human rights and intervention in international affairs.

Jeff Menne is Assistant Professor and programme director of Screen Studies at Oklahoma State University. He is completing *Art's Economy: Post-Fordist Cinema and Hollywood Counterculture, 1962–1975*, a study of Hollywood's vanguard role in the changing political economy of the postwar era. His study *Francis Ford Coppola* came out recently, followed by his co-edited collection *Film and the American Presidency*.

Pramod K. Nayar teaches at the Department of English, the University of Hyderabad, India. Besides posthumanism, his other interests include colonial writings on India and the graphic narrative, celebrity studies and postcolonial studies. His recent books includes *Citizenship and Identity in the Age of Surveillance* (2015), *Posthumanism* (2014), the edited five-volume *Women in Colonial India: Historical Documents and Sources* (2014), *Frantz Fanon* (2013), *Colonial Voices: The Discourses* *of Empire* (2012) and *Writing Wrongs: The Cultural Construction of Human Rights in India* (2012). He is currently working on a book on human rights and literary studies and a book on the Indian graphic narrative.

Dónal P. O'Mathúna is Senior Lecturer in Ethics, Decision-Making and Evidence in the School of Nursing and Human Sciences at Dublin City University, Ireland. His primary research interests are in bioethics, particularly related to emerging technologies, disasters and narrative ethics. He also conducts research in evidence-based health-care practice and research ethics. He is the co-editor of *Disaster Bioethics: Normative Issues When Nothing Is Normal* (2014), the author of *Nanoethics: Big Ethical Issues with Small Technology* (2009) and co-author of *Alternative Medicine: The Christian Handbook* (2007). He has published over 50 peer-reviewed articles and more than 30 book chapters.

Alexander Darius Ornella is Lecturer in Religion at the School of Social Sciences, University of Hull, UK. He received his doctorate in Catholic Theology from the University of Graz (Austria). His research interests include religion and popular culture/film/media, religion and body, religion and technology, and CrossFit and sports and religion. His recent publications include *Fascinatingly Disturbing: Interdisciplinary Perspectives on Michael Haneke's Cinema* (co-edited, 2010) and *Commun(icat)ing Bodies: Body as Medium in Religious Symbol Systems* (co-edited, 2014).

Thomas D. Philbeck is Global Leadership Fellow at the World Economic Forum in Geneva. He previously served as Assistant Dean of the College of Arts and Sciences for the New York Institute of Technology, and holds a PhD from Florida State University and MBA from HEC Paris. His areas of interest are in philosophy of technology, especially the roles of phenomenology and ontology. He enjoys science, technology and the question 'Where are we going?'

Anat Pick is Senior Lecturer in Film at Queen Mary, University of London. She is the author of *Creaturely Poetics: Animality and Vulnerability in Literature and Film* (2011) and co-editor of *Screening Nature: Cinema beyond the Human* (2013). She works at the intersection of continental philosophy, film and animal ethics.

Ralph Pordzik studied English and American Studies at Free University Berlin, where he received his doctoral degree in 1995. He obtained his post-doctoral degree (Habilitation) 2000 from Duisburg-Essen University. A senior lecturer at Würzburg University since 2004, he has published widely in magazines and journals. Recent publications include *Futurescapes: Space in Utopian and Science Fiction Discourses* (ed., 2009) and *Victorian Wastelands: Apocalyptic Discourse in Nineteenth-Century Poetry* (2012).

Anna Powell has recently retired as Reader in Film and English Studies to become research fellow at Manchester Metropolitan University. Her research interests include gothic, film/philosophy and affect in film and literature, experimental film and video. Her other research interest is Deleuze, and she was the founding director of *A/V* web journal and is a member of the editorial board of *Deleuze Studies*. Her books include *Deleuze and the Horror Film*, *Deleuze, Altered States and Film*, and *Psychoanalysis and Sovereignty in Popular Vampire Fiction*. She also co-authored *Teaching the Gothic* with Andrew Smith, and has published a wide range of articles and chapters on diverse topics, most recently on steampunk culture. She is currently researching Algernon Blackwood's occult fiction.

David Roden is Lecturer in Philosophy at the Open University. He is author of *Posthuman Life: Philosophy at the Edge of the Human* (2014). His research has addressed posthumanism, philosophical naturalism, interpretation-based accounts of meaning, computer music and the metaphysics of sound. Recent articles include 'The Disconnection Thesis' in *The Singularity Hypothesis: A Scientific and Philosophical Assessment* and 'Nature's Dark Domain: An Argument for a Naturalized Phenomenology' in the *Royal Institute of Philosophy Supplement: Phenomenology and Naturalism*.

Rhys Owain Thomas received his doctoral degree from the University of East Anglia in 2015. His thesis charts the emergence of specific liminal constructs – characters he has termed 'the unliving' – within 21st-century American SF television. He is co-editor (with Christine Cornea) of *Dramatising Disaster: Character, Event, Representation* (2013). He is also co-editor (with Sophie Halliday) of an MeCCSA *Networking Knowledge* special issue on American telefantasy (2012). His work on reality television, meanwhile, has appeared in the journal *Celebrity Studies* (2011).

Sherryl Vint is Professor of Science Fiction Media Studies at the University of California, Riverside, where she co-directs the Science Fiction and Technoculture Studies programme. She is the author of *Bodies of Tomorrow* (2007), *Animal Alterity* (2010), *The Wire* (2013) and *Science Fiction: A Guide to the Perplexed* (2014), and co-author of *The Routledge Concise History of Science Fiction* (2011). She co-edits the journals *Science Fiction Film and Television* and *Science Fiction Studies*.

Hilary Wheaton is an honorary research fellow at the University of Exeter in the College of Social Sciences and International Studies. She is also a member of the Editorial and Advisory Board for the Centre for Media and Celebrity Studies and an editorial board member for the newly established WaterHill Publishing. She completed her doctorate, titled 'Sexuality and the Internet: Conceiving Sex and the Body in Computer-Mediated Interaction', at Curtin University in Perth, Western Australia, in 2013. Her research interests relate primarily to sexuality and the human body, as well as those contexts on the Internet that cater to sexual expression and interaction. However, her interests extend to technology and society, celebrity studies, Marxist theory and broader cultural studies.

Hub Zwart is Full Professor of Philosophy at the Faculty of Science, Radboud University Nijmegen. In 2004, he established the Centre for Society and the Life Sciences (CSG) at his department, and in 2005 he became Director of the Institute for Science, Innovation and Society (ISIS). He is a member of the Human Genome Organisation (HUGO) ethics committee and editor-in-chief of the journal *Life Sciences, Society and Policy*. In his research and teaching he addresses scientific developments such as genomics, synthetic biology, brain research and nanomedicine from a continental philosophical perspective, using dialectics (Hegel), phenomenology (Heidegger) and psychoanalysis (Lacan) as sources of inspiration. Special attention is given to the role of genres of the imagination (novels, poetry, drama) in philosophical reflection on contemporary science.

1
Posthumanism in Film and Television

Michael Hauskeller, Thomas D. Philbeck and Curtis D. Carbonell

Cary Wolfe begins his widely known book *What Is Posthumanism?* (2010) by announcing the results of a Google search. He reports that at the time of his writing (summer 2008) the search word 'humanism' yielded 3,840,000 hits, while the word 'posthumanism' gave him only 60,200. Wolfe concludes from these data that, apparently, 'humanism is alive and well' (2010, xi). When we repeated the experiment six years later, in December 2014, 'humanism' came up with 9,030,000 results and 'posthumanism' with 294,000, which is still considerably less, but almost five times as many as six years ago. You do, however, get *many* more results if you search for 'posthuman' (3,250,000), 'transhumanism' (2,310,000) or even (a term that is, outside academia, little known or used) 'transhuman' (484,000). So even though humanism may still be alive and well today, the idea of the posthuman and what it signifies, namely the surpassing of the human condition, is rapidly catching up and has now secured a well-established place in our cultural imagination. Clearly, an evolving posthumanist narrative has taken shape in popular culture, providing a new context for what it means to be human and challenging long-held assumptions about the human condition. Yet this narrative did not arrive fully formed. It was first prophesied and then dissected in academic spheres for many years before reaching a level of diffusion large enough to impact popular consciousness.

In 1977, the literary theorist Ihab Hassan published a paper in which he envisaged the arrival of a posthumanist culture that would heal the 'inner divisions of consciousness and the external divisions of humankind' (1977, 833). What we need to understand, claimed Hassan, is:

> *That the human form – including human desire and all its external representations – may be changing radically, and thus must be re-visioned. We need to understand that five hundred years of humanism may be coming to an end, as humanism transforms itself into something that we must helplessly call posthumanism.*
>
> (Hassan 1977, 843)

While we ourselves change in the wake of new technological developments and possibilities, traditional boundaries between the human and the non-human, the natural and the artificial, the organic and the machinic, as well as the spiritual and the material, become increasingly brittle and unconvincing. Moreover, the way we think about our place in the world also must adapt to the changing human form. 'Humanism' is here understood as an outlook that stands and falls with a particular ontological condition, a particular way of being in the world that has long defined what it means to be human. However, it may no longer define us in future, or may indeed have already ceased to do so. Thus, our current human nature informs how we understand and position ourselves, that is, the humanist framework that guides our thinking and actions, so if the former changes (to something that is no longer human as we used to understand it, and thus to something posthuman), the latter must too (to a posthumanism). For Hassan, the change manifesting itself in a merging of the sciences and the arts will eventually lead to a 'dematerialization of life and the conceptualization of existence' (835) through the 'expansion of human consciousness' to the whole cosmos. Such an expansion of human consciousness is obviously an idea that is rooted in a particular kind of humanism (i.e., the conviction that our human destiny is to transform the world in our image, which is ultimately the image of God) and is echoed in current transhumanist ambitions and visions of our imminent posthuman future, popularized by Ray Kurzweil (2005, 21) and others.

There is an ambiguity here that would eventually lead to a diversification of the posthumanist discourse into incommensurable, but equally posthumanist standpoints. On the one hand, Hassan is well aware that common predictions of the impending 'end' of humanity, like the notorious final paragraph of Michel Foucault's *The Order of Things*, in which Foucault contemplates the possibility that 'man' might 'be erased, like a face drawn in the sand at the edge of the sea' (1970, 387), are not to be taken literally. They instead invoke 'the end of a particular image of us', which casts us as a 'hard Cartesian Ego' (Hassan 1977, 845) radically distinct from the world. On the other, Hassan envisages a real change in the human condition beyond just a change of a particular image. The human species is transforming in a continuing process of becoming that Hassan aptly calls the 'transhumanisation of the human', as we increasingly become aware of new 'staggering' possibilities of evolution (1977, 849). Hassan associates those possibilities with the development of artificial intelligence (AI), prompting him to recall the supercomputer HAL in Stanley Kubrick's *2001*, whom he finds 'so strangely human, that is, at once so sinister and pathetic in every circuit and bit' (1977, 845). Yet whatever this development will bring, whether it leads to a transformation or a replacement of the human, it is sure to alter 'the image of man, the concept of the human' (1977, 845).

We might not be quite there yet, but we have certainly moved considerably further towards the posthumanist culture that Hassan described. Although the early 21st century has much in common with the 1970s in terms of technological proliferation and its effects on society, our relationship with technology is quite different in important ways. Forty years ago the dominant narrative still saw technology mainly as a deterministic force working alongside humanity for good or ill. In contrast, the early 21st century has adopted the view that we are, deep down, inseparable from our technologies. We have lost our fear, or if not exactly lost it, found a way to accept the beneficial sides of this merger and its hopeful prospects. For example, we promote challenging the limits of our bodies through prosthetic and biological enhancement. We also seek to transcend our mental limitations through new arrangements and ensembles of technological devices, chemicals and knowledge resources, resulting in a distributed form of conscious engagement with the world. In the process of this transformation, we have acknowledged the challenges to the long-held foundation of Enlightenment humanism that has undergirded our views and given shape to what it means to be human.

And rightly so: the limitations of Enlightenment humanist categories are visible everywhere posthumanism spreads, from the philosophical problematic of self and agency in which technology exerts its own influence on our corporeal identities, to the political concern that affects a variety of categories, such as gender and sexuality, in both the scientific and cultural spheres. This last aspect of political posthumanism is of key importance, since modern technology has been problematizing the humanist framework for nearly two hundred years. Long-standing technological challenges to selfhood and agency, combined with the political evolution of the social sphere, have helped people accept the challenges to selfhood that technology has posed since our Pleistocene past. These two areas, technology and politics, have reciprocally buoyed each other, revealing fissures in humanism's rigid foundations.

While critical theory and cultural studies have focused on posthumanism and its political application, the key factor in the appearance and development of posthumanism as an interdisciplinary discourse is the underlying claim that technology is the missing ingredient in Enlightenment humanism's recipe for what constitutes being human. Modern 'technology' and its artefacts have exposed the ontological problems with Enlightenment humanism's metaphysical assumptions about the human condition. Technology, or rather technoscience, provides a material means to challenge social categories. It also forces the philosophical discussion towards an inherently existential stance wherein technology plays a critical role in our constitution. Thus, posthumanism's foundation combines the philosophy of technology with the sociological critique of science, especially how artefacts and objects influence the network of relations that define the human world. By investigating the outcomes of science and technology via the discourse of critical and philosophical posthumanism, the ontological frameworks for the constitution of technology and human beings have been foregrounded through a dissection of the natural versus cultural (artefactual) world.

Luckily, one need not be a scholar to observe how this paradigm shift is affecting humanity, since much of the narrative is reflected in Western popular culture, and perhaps, more than anywhere else, in film and television. Indeed, this collection reinforces the idea that the shift in popular consciousness is due to arts that mirror and disseminate visions of our possible futures. Such a process is, indeed, a matter of art mimicking life and life mimicking art. And technology is transforming both life and art into a new set of opportunities. The medium of moving pictures is particularly well suited to reflect this transformation, not only by providing thought experiments for possible transformations of the human, but also by creating concrete, visual representations. Screened representations translate concepts into moving images, living pictures, and thus make them immediate in a way that an abstract and thus dead (or more precisely not-yet-living) concept could never be. Here, more than anywhere else, and especially in films that belong to the science fiction (SF) genre, we find literally the image of the human transformed into images of the posthuman. As a result, we learn to see ourselves differently. We can debate endlessly about the meaning of proposed changes in the human condition, but it is the visual images and the stories that are being told with them that bring the point home. Moreover, the predictive element involved in the representations or the creative licenses taken in SF film and television series is not what is most important. Much has been made of the influence of *Star Trek* on the public consciousness and on technological advancement (e.g., flip phones and hypodermic injections, tricorders), but SF does much more. As leading SF studies theorist Istvan Csicsery-Ronay Jr writes in *The Seven Beauties of Science Fiction*, the ludic aspect of SF film separates it from written forms as a unique and valuable mode that emphasizes 'perception at the expense of reflection' (2008, 11). These cinematic spectacles ask us to play with the world, with reality, to see what it can be. Through trial and error and serendipitous cross-pollination of thoughts and influences, play fuses lateral thinking and quirky recombinations, working like selection pressures in evolution to produce much debris and a few true insights into our human condition. Screened SF allows us to play with our possible selves. At the same time, however, it also demands a serious response, because what it plays with, what it enacts, is what our own lives might one day turn out to be, and it does so at a time when we are all fully aware that things are changing quickly, and that more drastic changes are likely to occur during our own lifetime, affecting what we are, how we think of ourselves and how we look at each other.

A trajectory can be charted in SF's representation of posthumanist concepts through film and television over the last century. In SF films, early 'posthumans' were monsters in horror films – *Frankenstein* for example. Later, posthumans and transhumans were villains that challenged human society in one way or another. Even later, posthumans became ambiguous in terms of their status as moral creatures, like the Terminator played by Arnold Schwarzenegger in *Terminator 2: Judgment Day* or the Cylons in *Battlestar Galactica*. The most recent incarnations are fantasy figures and heroes such as the X-Men's Wolverine, Tony Stark as Ironman and Will Caster in *Transcendence*, who sacrifices himself for the world as a technological Christ. This trajectory from monsters to heroes is evidence of a change in social consciousness concerning what we consider acceptable posthuman attributes. Clearly, the discourse surrounding the transformation of technology's place in our world has been with us for some time. However, the discourse on the transformation of *our* place in a technological world began in earnest in an atmosphere of technological determinism in the 20th century. Despite an initial optimism regarding technology's ability to help us remodel the world (Th. Hughes 2004), we started to feel, at a pervasive social level, galvanized by the warning voices of Martin Heidegger ('The Question Concerning Technology', 1954/1977), Jacques Ellul (*The Technological Society*, 1954/1967), Günther Anders (*The Obsolescence of Man*, 1956) and others, that technology might get the upper hand to autonomously undermine, overpower or destroy us. Since the 1980s, with nuclear power, robotic manufacturing and the introduction of computers at the household level, many SF films of this era, such as *War Games*, *The Terminator*, *RoboCop* and so on, played with these difficult scenarios, framing technology as a false friend, something of which to be wary.

And some of us still are anxious, while a growing number of others see only the wonderful opportunities that a thoroughly technologized world might bring. The fear and wonder of the posthumanist turn continues in a trajectory that was once only hypothetical, being explored through the magnifying lens of SF. Yet as SF increasingly becomes reality, an amorphous future looms over our fragmented but reified identities. We clutch them as we do notions of a nation state, sovereign and inviolable, even though we know that, like a nation state, our identities are a composition of abstract concepts and/or components. In essence, they are a tradition that we participate in (Hauskeller 2009). In regard to individual identity, we use our history to contextualize ourselves. We might even say that we actually *are* traditions, each and every one of us reified beings that stabilize ourselves (or have learned to do so) through the retelling of our stories and the construction of behaviours. These traditions make our individual notions of self and collective notions of society function by handling the practical question of agency. Such juggling demands attention at every turn of social intercourse involving interaction with technology.

We, the protagonists of our own historical drama, have been slowly demoted from the leading role of creators and masters of technology to that of technological co-dependents and co-agents. This recasting is ongoing. Indeed, the role of slave-to-technology (or perhaps even worse, of 'obsolete bystander'[1]) is intimated as waiting just over the horizon, and technology's role cannot be separated from the drama. Whether the objective is to transform people into cyborgs, create new biological or disembodied beings, dissolve humanist categories that reinforce biased values of gender or race, or critique our assumptions about human 'nature', technology is the key ingredient in the long running discourse on *being* human. Technology has evolved far past the Aristotelian notion of a *poietic* eruption, dependent on human origin, and is becoming independent, intellectually superior, self-replicating and possibly sentient. More importantly, while we are being recast as dependents, technology is being recast as a saviour that transforms us into something else entirely.

We may have never been modern, as Latour professes (1993), or we may have, as Hayles describes (1999), become posthuman decades before we realized it, but we are now, a decade and a half into the 21st century, beginning to understand our place beyond the old humanist categories. The popular narrative of the relationship between human beings and technologies has been filled with cognitive biases, blind spots and wishful thinking. We have long considered ourselves masters of technology, makers of tools and givers of purpose to inanimate material.

Egocentrism, metaphysical beliefs and the resulting ontological categories distorted any other form of consideration. We have now come to accept that we are no longer the centre of the universe and (for most of us) that we are no longer the centre of the natural kingdom. Now, we are on the cusp of realizing that we are no longer the ontological rational intentional centre of the world either. We have learned to look at ourselves as one object among others, even if we can't quite escape our subjectivity (and thus humanism). We must ask, as Bruce Mazlish does in *The Fourth Discontinuity* (1995), if the intersection of humans and machines is also forcing us to rethink who we are in the world. Advancing technology recontextualizes us to discover, comprehend and investigate more about the world and our own attributes. As we engage ourselves in a techno-social narrative, whereby technology and humans are increasingly integrated, the resulting ontological consequences are rewriting and recasting what being human entails. We are no longer the beings we thought we were. Maybe, as some scholars have been saying, we never were.

This handbook is intended to provide an essential resource for those interested in film and television, posthumanism and how the latter is reflected (and possibly also practised) in the former. It acknowledges that posthumanism has developed into a major intellectual force influencing our culture. It affects research agendas, economic developments, social policies, philosophical theories, and ultimately the way we look at ourselves and our world. This handbook provides a comprehensive overview of the various aspects of posthumanism and how they are represented, discussed and exemplified in the cultural medium of film and television. We have not tried to impose a particular view of posthumanism on the contributors, as a wide spectrum of ideas and worldviews are all called posthumanist in academic and popular discourse.

For the purpose of this handbook, posthumanism should be understood broadly as any critical engagement with the possibility that what we have always considered to be *the* human condition (which is *both* a particular way of being in the world *and* a particular way of positioning ourselves in this world) is no longer a given, that it is more fluid than we once thought, and that we are free (or will soon be free, or are becoming increasingly freer) to remould our identities. Thus, the posthumanism represented in this handbook is a reflection on the malleability of the human condition. Naturally, this reflection emerges in different forms, ranging from: (a) an enthusiastic embrace of new 'anthropo-technologies' (Sloterdijk 2014) and the many new freedoms that they may bring us (known as *popular* or *liberal* posthumanism, or simply *trans*humanism), over (b) the embrace of those technologies' potential to dissolve ossified humanist pretensions of the human and the non-human (known as *critical*, *cultural* or *radical* posthumanism), (c) the insistence on the ubiquity of other, non-human forms of agency, which reframes the human as just one among many players in the game that is our life, and thus strips us of the exceptionalism that once set us apart from the rest of the world (*methodological* posthumanism), to, finally, (d) a deep scepticism regarding the desirability of all the changes in our condition that are already taking place or are being envisaged for the near future (*dystopian* posthumanism, or, rather disparagingly, *bioconservatism*). A very useful, convincing mapping of those different strands of posthumanism on several axes has recently been proposed by Tamar Sharon (2014). There are still others, of course, for instance Jaime de Val and Stefan Sorgner's *metahumanism* (2011) (which intends to bridge the gap between transhumanism and critical posthumanism), David Roden's (2014) *speculative* posthumanism or Sharon's (2014) very own *mediated* posthumanism. All these versions of posthumanism provide alternative takes on the same issue, which is the ongoing transformation of the human image.

Note

1. Pieter Bonte's term, used in a personal communication.

Part I

Paving the Way to Posthumanism: The Precursors

2
From DelGuat to ScarJo

William Brown

In this chapter, I want to offer an overview of how/why Gilles Deleuze and Félix Guattari have been influential on posthumanist thought before looking at how posthumanism is increasingly operating as a framework through which to consider film (and the media more generally) and before, in turn, looking at how Deleuze and Guattari influence such posthumanist readings of film. Finally, I should like briefly to offer a reading of various films from 2013 to 2014 that feature Scarlett Johansson in order to draw out some of the seeming contradictions surrounding posthumanism, namely that posthumanism remains a very human (if not humanist) way of thinking and, perhaps, of being in, or, better, with, the world.

Deleuze, Guattari and posthumanism

Deleuze and Guattari only merit one brief mention in the main body of N. Katherine Hayles' classic text *How We Became Posthuman* (they also feature in two endnotes). Nonetheless, the reference is a useful point for us to start thinking about the links between Deleuze and Guattari and posthumanist thought. Hayles enumerates various discourses that have sought to subvert what she terms the 'liberal humanist subject' – or the belief that the human stands free from, and in many respects against, nature, and that the human is unique and distinct from the rest of life on earth because the human has a brain separate from the body, a brain endowed with consciousness, with consciousness itself being the phenomenon that allows the human to become a 'subject' in the first place. Feminist theorists have challenged the 'liberal humanist subject' for being shorthand for the 'white European male', while postcolonial theorists have challenged its universalist claims along similar lines, especially for being European. Postmodern theorists, meanwhile, of whom Deleuze and Guattari are, for Hayles, exemplary, 'have linked it [the liberal humanist subject] with capitalism, arguing for the liberatory potential of a dispersed subjectivity distributed among diverse desiring machines they call "body without organs"' (Hayles 1999, 4).

The 'body without organs' is a concept that recurs consistently in the work of Deleuze and Guattari, particularly in their two-volume treatment of *Capitalism and*

Schizophrenia, namely *Anti-Oedipus* (2000) and *A Thousand Plateaus* (1987). Broadly speaking, the body without organs is an 'uninterrupted limit', it is 'immanence', an 'immanent limit'; the body without organs is 'the *field of immanence* as desire, the *plane of consistency* specific to desire' (Deleuze & Guattari 1987, 154). What Deleuze and Guattari mean by this is that the body without organs has no fixed location in space and/or time (it is 'immanent', or, in Hayles' terms, 'dispersed'); furthermore, the body without organs exists as a state of potential, in that being everywhere and everywhen ('immanent'), means that it is not concrete and fixed, but in a state of possibly being/becoming; and finally, being in a state of potential, the body without organs is thus permanently becoming, in that this potential is consistently realized as we lead our lives – we consistently become fixed in a specific time and place – rendered as a subject with a specific identity.

In comparison with the body without organs, Deleuze and Guattari develop the concept of desiring machines. For Deleuze and Guattari, everything is a machine; a mouth, for instance, is a machine for eating, as well as a machine for vomiting and various other things (kissing, for example). It is in desiring food that the mouth becomes an eating machine, while in desiring the rejection of food it becomes a vomiting machine, and in desiring another mouth, the mouth becomes (in accordance with a much more commonplace sense of the term 'desire') a kissing machine. This may sound strange, then, but it is only in becoming a machine of one sort or another (eating, vomiting, kissing) that the mouth takes on an identity; in-between these moments of desire, the mouth exists on a plane of pure potential – it could, in a certain sense, become anything. Rather than having/being a fixed definition, then (the mouth as an organ/a specific machine), at these moments 'between' desire, the mouth is a sort of body without organs. Perhaps the same applies also to human beings: I exist as a human that could, in some senses, be anything, and yet at different moments in my life I become different, specific things (a child, a student, a journalist, a teacher, a filmmaker, a parent, a dead body). Desiring machines, then, 'make us an organism' – in that they bring organization to our lives, and they turn our bodies into organs (that have a purpose and that are productive, especially of things that are useful for the running of a capitalist society). For this reason, Deleuze and Guattari say that 'the body *suffers* from being organized' (my emphasis) and that the body without organs (the disorganized body?) is 'the unproductive, the sterile, the unengendered, the unconsumable' (Deleuze & Guattari 2000, 8). If the body without organs has no fixed purpose, no fixed identity, and is not organized, then it is perhaps defined as 'schizophrenic', hence the title of Deleuze and Guattari's tomes, *Capitalism and Schizophrenia*. In this way, when Deleuze and Guattari proclaim that 'the self and the non-self, outside and inside, no longer have any meaning whatsoever' (2000, 2), and that 'we make no distinction between man and nature' (4), they are suggesting that the body without organs is a 'true' version of ourselves, whereby we do not exist as subjects (with jobs/functions/identities – in short, as machines), but instead that subjectivity/identity is, as Hayles says, dispersed. It is a condition of potential, one that is open for/to all manner of possible becomings.

Deleuze and Guattari's appeal to, and influence on, posthumanist thought, then, is as follows: posthumanism stands in contrast to humanism in arguing that humans are not the epicentre of existence, in suggesting that there is indeed no distinction between man and nature, and in positing that humans do not exist as individuals isolated from the world, but are in fact part of the world (the self and the non-self no longer have any easy distinction). It is a seeming paradox that humans have in part come to realize simultaneously their diminished centrality in and their entangled nature with the universe as a result of technological innovations. This functions on at least three levels, one of which is, as I shall argue, flawed, but which nonetheless historically – *as an idea* – has perhaps had an important role to play in the development of posthumanist thought. Firstly, there is the possibility that humans might develop artificial intelligence (AI). For, if humans could develop life that was equally as conscious and autonomous as themselves, then not only might humans be replaced by machines (a kind of literal, but also hysterical, definition of 'posthumanism'), but (more soberly) humans would also have to admit their non-central role in the universe (as well as, concomitantly, the supposed fact that we were assigned a central role in the universe by a deity); with AI as a manmade construct, humans would realize that they themselves are not impossibly special beings, but something that even a human could create. Secondly, if humans could upload their consciousness into a computer, such that they no longer needed their body, then not only might we face a second 'hysterical' version of posthumanity (we all exist in the computer ether), but we would also realize that our being extends beyond our bodies and that our 'selves' as such are distributed. This second approach, endorsed by the likes of Hans Moravec (1988), is, for me, flawed, for we will always need a body to exist as humans (that uploaded consciousness could not be 'me', for it would not have a body; posthumanism here signals not so much the end of humanity, then, but an evolution in how humanity understands its *embodied* place within the universe – as I shall discuss in greater detail shortly). Finally, that humans use technology at all, technology that is both inside and outside of us (from hammers and spectacles to medicine and artificial limbs, let alone computers), suggests that we do not exist in isolation from the world – but that the self extends into the world as the world extends into the self.

Even though, as Ella Brians (in an excellent essay) attests, Deleuze and Guattari did not write about cyberculture specifically (see Brians 2011, 117), Deleuze and Guattari's provocative argument that everything is a machine perhaps attests already to these combined meanings of the role that technology (in particular digital technology in the first two 'levels' mentioned) plays in human existence. For, in saying that everything is a machine, Deleuze and Guattari speak of the constructed, rather than God-given nature of humanity and of the universe; they speak of an inability to separate the manmade from the natural; and thus they speak of an inability to separate man from nature. That said, it perhaps seems paradoxical that humans have realized increasingly that they are not the paragon of existence and that they are not inseparable from the world via their use of technology, because humans often consider themselves to be the only species to make and to use technology (thereby making them different from nature/the rest of the world). However, it is not just on the technological level that posthumanist thought has recently gathered steam. Indeed, the case for posthumanist thought is bolstered by discoveries in/from numerous disciplines. Take, for example, breakthroughs in our understanding of biology. Frans de Waal (2009) argues not only that species other than humans use technology (meaning that it is not really paradoxical that technology reveals to humans their enworlded, posthuman condition), but that species other than humans have empathy, an understanding of other minds, and thus of how they also are in the world – thereby reducing the prominence of man as set apart from other species, and increasing our understanding of man as simply another species on the planet. Neuroscience also reveals that the human mind, long since considered to be separate from the body via Cartesian dualism, is in fact wholly embodied, that our 'higher' thoughts in fact depend upon our 'lower' body/bodily functions (meaning that, *pace* Moravec, we cannot 'upload' ourselves into a computer, since we cannot survive without our bodies), and that our bodies are also dependent on the world (see Damasio 1994). Neuroscience therefore also suggests both that the brain and the body are co-dependent, and that the body and the world are co-dependent; that is, humanity consists of more than just our minds, or rather that our conscious minds, that which supposedly sets us apart from nature/the rest of the world, are tied to our bodies, and that humanity is thus not separate from nature. Finally, physics also would seem to suggest that humans are 'entangled' with nature, and that we evolve with it as much as it evolves with us (Barad 2007).

In other words, in twinning Deleuze and Guattari as 'postmodern' and alongside feminist and postcolonial scholars in challenging the 'liberal humanist subject', Hayles points to the political nature of posthumanist thought; that is, posthumanism is the next in a series of *-isms* that seek to undermine the hegemony of white, male, European/North American capitalists. However, developments in biology, neuroscience and physics suggest that posthumanism functions not just on a political, but also on an ontological level: it is not that we 'should' understand that white, male, European capitalists are not the be-all and end-all; it is that humans *are not* the be-all and end-all at all. Who we are is not limited uniquely to our bodies, even if our bodies are necessary (but not sufficient) for our existence; our technology, the characteristics that we share with other species, the embodied nature of our brains and the simple fact that we need oxygen, carbon, water and sunlight to exist, all make clear that the entire universe extends into us as we extend into it.

Even if Deleuze and Guattari's concept of the body without organs merits a mention in Hayles' classic text on posthumanism (as it does in the work of Cary Wolfe 2010, xxiv; and as does their concept of the 'machinic phylum' in the work of Robert Pepperell 2003, 2), their thought is, however, not so much central to posthumanist thought as an important precursor lingering in the background (brief references here and there). Conversely, I would suggest that posthumanist thought has had a more overt influence on Deleuzian scholars rather than the other way round. This is made clear by the way in which Deleuzian scholars like Patricia MacCormack (2012) and Rosi Braidotti (2013) have turned their attention to posthumanism, rather than posthumanist scholars turning their attention specifically to Deleuze and Guattari. Braidotti in particular reconciles posthumanist thought with Deleuze and Guattari's concepts of becoming animal, becoming machine and her own concept of becoming earth in order to elaborate the way in which 'as embodied and embedded entities, we are all part of nature, even though academic philosophy continues to claim transcendental grounds for human consciousness' (i.e., that humans 'transcend', or are apart from nature/the world in general; Braidotti 2013, 66). With a turn that distinctly fits into the 'ecological' thinking of the early 21st century, Braidotti suggests that in the 'anthropocene', the age in which humans are the biggest influential factor in shaping the planet, it is urgent that humans come to realize their enworlded, rather than separate, nature.

Posthumanism and film theory

I have argued elsewhere that posthumanism is perhaps a rich lens through which to consider much of contemporary cinema (Brown 2009). In that essay I considered the way in which Hollywood routinely tells stories about the end of humanity, be that via alien invasion or via ecological disaster, suggesting both that humans are frail, and also that they are not as dominant or technologically advanced as they think they are. I also made mention of the growing number of non-human protagonists in mainstream cinema, from mutants to aliens to fantastic creatures. Furthermore, I considered the way in which (virtual) camera movement can also suggest an enworlded human. For, when a (virtual) camera passes into and out of a human without so much as a cut, as happens in the opening moments of *Fight Club* (David Fincher, USA, 1999) as the 'camera' tracks from the fear centre of the brain of the protagonist (Edward Norton) and out on to his scalp, down his face and along the barrel of a gun, then the (virtual) camera movement arguably suggests not a separation of man from nature (as might be heralded by a cut from inside to outside of a human), but that both inside and outside lie on the same continuum of space – that, to reiterate the words of Deleuze and Guattari, 'the self and the non-self, outside and inside, no longer have any meaning whatsoever'.

However, there are significant other ways in which contemporary cinema might be considered posthuman. This is not simply a case of cinemas other than Hollywood beginning to look at the end of humanity, as evidenced in, say, *Melancholia* (Lars von Trier, Denmark/Sweden/France/Germany, 2011) and *A torinói ló/The Turin Horse* (Béla Tarr, Hungary/France/Germany/Switzerland/USA, 2011). It is also evidenced in numerous films that adopt what might be called a 'slow' style (films comprised of long takes that themselves feature little action and which are often filmed in long shot). For such techniques, broadly speaking, invite the viewer not just to witness events unfolding according to a more 'geological' rather than 'human' pace, but also invite us (in particular via the long shot) to see how humans are not set against, but are embedded within nature/the world. Furthermore, it is also evidenced in various films that have turned their attention away from the human, and which instead focus on animals (e.g., Andrea Luka Zimmerman's *Taşkafa, Stories from the Street*, Turkey, 2013, which is about street dogs in Istanbul) and/or perhaps on the rhythms of nature itself (such as the films of James Benning; for a Deleuzian consideration of his work as 'cinema beyond the human', see Panse 2013).

While such films point to a rise in posthumanist thought among filmmakers, and while both the special effects shots of *Fight Club* and the extended takes of various 'slow' films are enabled by digital technology (suggesting, once again, that technological developments seem to draw us towards posthumanist thinking), posthumanism is perhaps better understood as a framework through which to consider all cinema, rather than as a set of qualities that pertain to a specific body of contemporary films. As I have also argued elsewhere, cinema has always shown us not just humans, but also other species that inhabit our planet, the technologies that extend our sense of being from beyond ourselves and outwards, towards the rest of the world (Brown 2013). While cinema has often, perhaps always, been anthropocentric, in that it has featured human figures carrying out heroic deeds, it has also always captured the environments in which those figures act (or rather, with which those figures interact), as well as the other humans and species with which those figures interact. We see an active nature in films like *The Wind* (Victor Sjöström, USA, 1928), and we see the presence of nature in the long shots and long takes of a filmmaker like Yasujiro Ozu – all long before the advent of digital technology and its effects on filmmaking. Cinema, perhaps by its very nature, has always only ever shown us a view of the world that is not specifically our own (even if we can only look at films through our own eyes) – thereby meaning that cinema has always made us aware of other perspectives. And cinema has perhaps always shown us a world, even a universe, that is teeming with life – even if not all films have used techniques ('virtual' camera movements, long takes, long shots, a relatively 'still' and natural *mise-en-scène*) that invite us to see such things. In this respect, Deleuze returns as an important precursor in helping us to understand cinema in this posthumanist way, even if Deleuze does not himself use the term posthumanism. For, especially in his consideration of *The Time-Image* (2005), Deleuze identifies the ways in which certain cinemas (starting with Italian neorealism) place an emphasis on real-world locations, on the breakdown between inside and outside (figured in particular in films in which it becomes hard to separate reality from fantasy), and on the way in which humans do not have so much control over their environment as their environment in fact shapes them.

The persistence of the human: Scarlett Johansson

However, for all the grand claims of posthumanism (humanity is not the centre of the universe), the posthuman remains, as Braidotti states, 'all too human' (Braidotti 2013, 194–197). Even if we live in a world of seemingly ever-greater human achievements (Usain Bolt running faster than any recorded human before him), and in which sheep are cloned and humans are enhanced by technology (Braidotti mentions Oscar Pistorius, the South African 'blade runner', who himself has, subsequent to the publication of Braidotti's book, proved his very humanity by becoming embroiled in a murder trial), we nonetheless still live in, or, better, with, a world where humans have bodies – and for all the congratulation that we as humans might give ourselves for our achievements, there are still many areas in which we might improve. Indeed, as humanity faces possible/impending ecological disaster, the ongoing inequalities of human societies and continued cruelty towards other species that almost certainly do feel pain and trauma as a result of our actions towards them, posthumanism functions as a call for humans to develop an ethics that pays respect to fellow humans, to other species and to the planet/nature as a whole – as MacCormack's Deleuze-inspired work (2012) makes clear. While humans like to boast about their technological prowess, technology perhaps does not make humans any 'better' or more ethical inhabitants of their planet; technology might on one level help us to see the world in a 'posthumanist' fashion, but it does not *necessarily* help us to do so. And several recent films, all featuring Scarlett Johansson, all explore these very ideas in different ways – as I shall briefly explore now.

In *Don Jon* (Joseph Gordon Levitt, USA, 2013), Johansson plays Barbara Sugarman, the seeming object of the affections of porn-addicted Jon Martello (Gordon-Levitt), who is dumped by her after discovering his addiction for porn. In *Her* (Spike Jonze, USA, 2013), Johansson voices Samantha, the artificially intelligent operating system bought by Theodore Twombly (Joaquin Phoenix), with which Theodore falls in love, but which eventually abandons him to go live with other AIs. In *Under the Skin* (Jonathan Glazer, UK, 2013), Johansson is an unnamed alien that abducts and kills men from Glasgow and its environs, before being hunted down by a man in a forest who at first wants to rape, and who then, upon discovering that under her skin she is a black alien, decides to kill her. And in *Captain America: The Winter Soldier* (Anthony and Joe Russo, USA, 2014), Johansson plays Black Widow (real name, Natasha Romanoff), a deadly former Russian assassin now working for SHIELD (Strategic Homeland Intervention, Enforcement, Logistics Division), who teams up with Captain America (Chris Evans) to thwart a plot, originated from within SHIELD, to kill numerous humans for having a genetic make-up that suggests future crimes against the state.

From these descriptions, it is hopefully clear that all four films deal with themes that are relevant to posthumanist thought, in particular technology and the role that it plays in the contemporary world. *Don Jon*, *Her* and *The Winter Soldier* all take a relatively dim view of technology (despite being, in various ways, the results of technologically advanced filmmaking apparatuses): in the former, the Internet and ubiquitous porn prevent humans from having genuine relationships (Jon desires images of women and cannot connect with a real woman, Barbara, whom he wishes was an image); *Her* sees Theodore desire a computer programme that ultimately leaves him; and *The Winter Soldier* suggests that total surveillance – including the ability to see future crimes – is an infringement on civil liberties. Meanwhile, *Under the Skin* offers us an intriguing look at how an alien might view our world – in a detached, curious fashion, as in one scene when the alien allows humans to drown at sea and a baby to be abandoned without showing any emotion whatsoever. All four, then, suggest a highly technologized society that does not improve humans' relationship with the world per se, but which rather distances humans, including those who dwell in contemporary Glasgow (*Under the Skin*) from each other. Furthermore, all four films depict male desire in a problematic fashion, as I shall discuss presently.

Jon is addicted to pornography and as a result cannot connect with a real woman (and when he does, with Esther, played by Julianne Moore, the relationship is not a loving, but more of a sexual, relationship). Similarly, Theodore loves a computer programme – together, perhaps, with his memories of ex-partner Catherine (Rooney Mara) – more than he does any humans, as is clear from the muted ending when Theodore may or may not get together with his neighbour, Amy (Amy Adams). In *The Winter Soldier*, Black Widow is obviously the object of Captain America's desire, and yet their partnership is seemingly impossible because, as an action heroine, Black Widow cannot be with a man. And, finally, all men want to sleep with the alien in *Under the Skin*, including the man who finally kills it, having tried to rape it/(what he thinks is a) her. In all four films, then, Johansson is deemed as an impossible woman, rendered other by being beyond reach of all men – as well as ultimately cruel for not staying with Jon and Theodore in *Don Jon* and *Her*, and for luring men to their deaths in *Under the Skin*. This is the old-fashioned sexual politics of mainstream cinema, as established so emphatically (if using a different framework) by Laura Mulvey nearly 40 years ago (Mulvey 1975): woman is by turns impossible, out of reach, a machine, an alien, a killer – anything but human.

And yet Scarlett Johansson, who plays all four roles, is, of course, a human. The films demonstrate that, in a technologized world, new forms of desire (humans wanting to mate with images, AI, superheroines and aliens) are immanent. And yet the (all too) human limitations remain: humans, or more specifically men, cannot connect with their conspecifics. This may make Johansson a star (rather than a human being), but if, as outlined at the outset of this chapter via N. Katherine Hayles, feminism was one of several discourses, including posthumanism, designed to make humans view their enworlded and connected nature (women and men are not different species), then a posthumanist discourse, as well as a feminist one, are required not only to reflect the contemporary world, but also to critique the representations of it which are presented in (these) films.

Without wishing to offer too superficial an analysis of these four films (*Under the Skin* in particular merits a more nuanced reading, as, probably, does *Her*), it seems that the old human issues remain: that the world is a patriarchal, controlling and predominantly white society that struggles to put into practise the 'liberatory potential' that a Deleuze-inspired and posthumanist framework might help to bring about. In other words, posthumanism must still do political work – perhaps especially because humans continue to ignore the ontological nature of our human posthumanism/our posthuman humanity, even if digital technology features very prominently in these films.

3
'Self-Immolation by Technology': Jean Baudrillard and the Posthuman in Film and Television

Jon Baldwin

The 'decentring of the human' by its imbrication in technical, medical, informatic and economic networks 'is increasingly impossible to ignore' (Wolfe 2010, 121). In simple terms, and in recent times, 'it has become increasingly difficult to separate the human from the technological' (Bukatman 1993, 2). In this context, the posthuman 'refers to the experience of the subject in the age of digital media' (Scheer 2012, 25). For Jean Baudrillard this presents a problem. He was apprehensive about the technological excitement around the digital, cloning, virtual reality, virtual bodies and so on. The human, in this posthuman scenario, becomes a prosthesis to technology and information systems. Baudrillard is critical of the ever-improving operational efficiency of technological systems such that the human becomes irrelevant to the process. In digital reduction we witness the supersession, in Baudrillard's terms, of the symbolic, alterity and singularity of the human by the semiotic, simulation and technological. The posthuman here becomes the inhuman. This resonates with the familiar poststructuralist concentration and concern with the heterogeneous over the homogeneous. For Baudrillard, the universe of simulation aims at 'a virtual universe from which everything dangerous and negative has been expelled' (Baudrillard 2005, 202). In this case, alterity, synonymous with otherness, difference and negativity in their radical forms, will be its victim. Especially with the onslaught of virtual reality, the human may be likened, in Lyotard's words, to a 'poor binarized ghost' (Lyotard 1991, 17).

In the light of recent innovations in robotics, prosthetic technologies, neuroscience, nanotechnology, biogenetic capital and so on, the posthuman condition 'urges us to think critically and creatively about who and what we are actually in the process of becoming' (Braidotti 2013, 11). Baudrillard contributes to this critique by attempting to think beyond the pragmatism of the technoscientists and neoliberalists, and consider the alterity that is being lost in the posthuman process. One popular and creative forum for consideration of the posthuman would be through the science fiction (SF) film. I shall outline Baudrillard's anxiety about virtual reality and the posthuman, and then discuss how anxieties around the posthuman manifest themselves in the SF films of Andrew Niccol.

Much of Baudrillard's later work is concerned with issues that may be deemed posthuman – cloning, artificial intelligence (AI), transsexuality,[1] mediated reality, virtuality and increased networks.[2] The specific concern is that the human is slowly but surely eradicating all ambiguity and radical otherness from themselves. This is part of what Baudrillard has identified as the process of simulation. The ambiguous and enigmatic real is eradicated and superseded by the copy and the clone. The fullest engagement with Baudrillard's work and the notion of the posthuman is made in a book by Kim Toffoletti. She uses Baudrillard's work to explore a variety of sites of 'posthuman imagery'. The Barbie doll is declared the 'posthuman prototype', insofar as it offers the potential to be read and used as a 'transformative plastic figuration' challenging any 'truth' about female identity (Toffoletti 2007, 67). The persona of Marilyn Manson is posited as 'neither male nor female, organism nor machine, human nor animal', and this subsequently confuses 'the role of the image as either reflecting the self or representing an Other' (Toffoletti 2007, 83). A TDK electronics digitalized advertising image features a baby with large ears, square eyes that appear adapted to computer screens, and a smiling mouth profile that could receive a CD. For Toffoletti, this image exemplifies the nature of immersion of the body in communication forms to the extent that any distinction between the body and communication media and technology appears eradicated. The biotechnology of cloning is considered as a posthuman form collapsing the distinctions of natural and artificial, real and virtual. These performative events, acts and figures of the posthuman, Toffoletti argues, allow for creative and transgressive potentialities that offer new possibilities for human subjectivities and a 'post-gender' experience. The rigid dichotomous constructions of identity, in particular gender identity, might be challenged, called into question, and reformulated by the fluidity and mutability of a subjectivity exposed to the implosive forces of hyperreality and 'simulation culture'.

This is clearly aligned with enthusiasts of the posthuman such as Donna Haraway and Sadie Plant as a means of furthering the cause of their particular brand of (post-)feminism. The cyborg, as a hybrid of machine and organism, offers the possibility to 'recraft' our bodies: 'The cyborg is a kind of disassembled and reassembled, postmodern collective and personal self. This is the self feminists must code' (Haraway 1991, 163). However, this notion of the possibilities and potentials of the posthuman, as presented by Toffoletti, has been challenged by Victoria Grace. She points out that Baudrillard critiques rather than celebrates the posthuman condition, and he cannot be held to 'advocate simulation': 'Nowhere does Baudrillard invoke hyperreal simulation for its "challenging" propensities for "contestation" or to "enable re-thinking" or "offer new possibilities" for "new imaginings"' (Grace 2008). On the contrary, Baudrillard in fact despairs at the effect of posthuman and hyperreal subjectivities which further remove us from the possibility of symbolic and singular selves. As Sim suggests, 'cyborgism will seem a very high price to pay for liberation from gender inequality' (Sim 2001, 66).

This contrast between the hyperreal and semiotic self on the one hand, and the singular and symbolic self on the other, is an important dichotomy in Baudrillard's theories. Understanding his work, in the broadest sense, is helped by what Baudrillard has called the 'double spiral' of his thought and writing. This typically involves two antagonistic paradigms that cannot be reconciled or subjected to a higher synthesis. On the one hand are concepts associated with the semiotic, such as political economy, production, hyperreality, simulation and the virtual. On the other, are the themes associated with the symbolic, such as potlatch, duality, expenditure, symbolic exchange and seduction. Baudrillard's theoretical target is the semiotic, which reduces the symbolic and thwarts experience of the real. Self-referential semiotic sign systems, or simulation, obscures the symbolic and replaces the real. Baudrillard's concept of the symbolic resonates with the Lacanian real, and what he often targets as 'reality' is largely equivalent with the Lacanian symbolic. In this sense, the 'real' is just as much a form of simulation as the hyperreal. The fundamental distinction is not between the real and the virtual, 'but between the symbolic and the successive attempts to neutralise it – the real, the hyper-real and the virtual' (Pawlett in Smith 2010, 238). Simulation is also interrupted by the symbolic in singular acts and events. Smith summarizes, 'the double spiral traces the destruction of the symbolic by the semiotic and the ironic eruption of the former in the latter' (Smith 2010, 58). In terms of the posthuman and digital technology we are presented with the two antagonistic paradigms of virtual reality and singularity.

One can see how digital media and virtual reality link with Baudrillard's key idea around simulation. The virtual is the 'fourth order' or highest stage of simulation. The virtual real is that without origin, referent or representation of the real. Baudrillard's notion of simulation concerns sign systems becoming divorced from the real or the referent. They become self-referential and hyperreal. For instance, the economic sphere becomes a self-referential system divorced from real wealth, resulting in a hyperreal economy (Baldwin 2013). The hyperreal comes to dictate matters, and finally the map does indeed precede the territory. This further distances one from the possibility of singularity, symbolic exchange, alterity and duality. The characteristics of Baudrillard's conception of the virtual are high definition (1996, 29), high fidelity, immersion, immanence and immediacy (2005, 31). It is distinct from the notion of the spectacle, which still left room for a possible critical consciousness and demystification (Baudrillard 1996, 27). The virtual is complicit with hyperreality, the space of the screen, mental space and so on. In previous times the virtual was intended to become actual, and actuality was its destination. Today, the function of the virtual is to proscribe the actual (Baudrillard 2000, 50). Indeed, the virtual dimension monopolizes all the other worlds today, and totalizes the real by evacuating any imaginary alternative (Baudrillard 1998, 50). With the virtual we enter not only upon the era of the liquidation of the real and the referential, but that of the extermination of the other (Baudrillard 1996, 107). Baudrillard's critique of the virtual is based upon this loss of singularity, the imaginary and alterity.

Everyday life and culture is increasingly reliant upon networks of communication and information, and the human is immersed within digital circuits of information technologies allowing for little critical distance from cyberspace. The virtual is developing into a dimension that will never become actual, or even exist parallel to the real, but which will take the place of the real. Humans become nodes and fit, or are capable of being absorbed, into a networked totality. They become exchangeable rather than singular. The 'neo-individual' or posthuman is 'an interactive, communicational particle, plugged into the network, getting continuous feedback' (Baudrillard 2001, 106). In posthuman–technology relations, individuals have become 'terminals of multiple networks' (Baudrillard 1998, 16). In this scenario, the posthuman is becoming the virtual reality of the machine (Baudrillard 2002, 178), and at a certain level of immersion in the machinery of the virtual, the man/machine distinction no longer exists (Baudrillard 2005, 80). We are no longer actors of the real, but double agents of the virtual. The posthuman emerges as a prosthesis, an addition and application, to digital technology and the virtual. Generations steeped in the virtual, Baudrillard claims, will never have known the real (Baudrillard 2006, 55). The lack of distinction between the real and the virtual is the obsession of our age (Baudrillard 2006, 92). In essence: 'The human gives way to the post-human when the virtual replaces the actual as the primary mode by which we conceptualise and experience reality' (Toffoletti in Smith 2010, 16).

One antidote to this would be the notion of the singularity and singularities. In a posthuman world that wants to be universal, digital, productive and cleansed of all ambiguity, a 'culture of equivalence and calculation' (Baudrillard 1997, 128), the singularity stands as, and valorizes, the unique, uncertain, unpredictable, incalculable, unrepresentable, untranslatable and unproductive. It threatens the drive towards a posthuman globalized, secure, neutralized sameness with a radical otherness. In this sense, a singularity is analogous to the concepts offered by Baudrillard as antidotes to simulation, globalization, monoculture and the principle of equivalence, namely symbolic exchange, seduction, radical alterity, negativity and death – 'the most singular of singularities' (Baudrillard 2002, 68). Baudrillard speaks of the possible singularity of events, beings and things (1998, 69). A singularity might take an ethnic, religious, linguistic or individual form (Baudrillard 1998, 13). Singularity is valorized as an existential attitude. Existence under the aegis of singularity is preferred to identity (and identity politics): 'each person should have an unyielding singularity' (Baudrillard 1997, 8). Singularity is sovereignty, a fight for glory, adventure, a mastery of existence, because in 'a totalised, centred, concentric universe, only eccentric possibilities are left' (Baudrillard 1997, 9). On the other hand, identity is security, a mere reference, 'an existence label' (Baudrillard 1998, 49) in a 'bloodless and undifferentiated world' (Baudrillard 2002, 65). This is a singular existence against, or in antagonism, with a virtual existence.

There is another use of the term 'singularity' from science – the technological singularity. This is the possibility of a future point that occurs during a phase of unprecedented technological progress, sometime after the creation of a superintelligence. This event of intelligence explosion could see the machine surpass human intellect and improve its design into far greater intelligences. The intelligence of man would be left far behind. Vernor Vinge proposed that drastic changes in society would occur following such an intelligence explosion and technological singularity. This anxiety is often reflected in the SF literature of Isaac Asimov, Greg Bear, Phillip K. Dick, William Gibson, and in popular film and TV such as *Terminator*, *The Matrix* and *Battlestar Galactica*. It is a staple of contemporary SF film, most recently *Transcendence*.

Baudrillard suggests that ambitions and anxieties around technology and virtual reality are an obsession of our age, and are reflected and constructed in film. Commenting on *The Matrix*, he notes that 'there have been other films that treat the growing indistinction between the real and the virtual: *The Truman Show*, *Minority Report*, or even *Mulholland Drive*, the masterpiece of David Lynch' (Baudrillard 2004b, n.p.). The writer of *The Truman Show* (1998) is Andrew Niccol and it could be argued that his films, particularly *S1m0ne*, are more reflective of Baudrillardian themes than, for instance, the much discussed *The Matrix* trilogy. Niccol wrote *The Truman Show* and was writer and director of *Gattaca* (1997), *S1m0ne* (2002) and *In Time* (2011). These popular genre films share Baudrillard's concern around the themes of virtual reality, cloning and the perfection of the same over the ambiguity of otherness.

Gattaca is an SF genetic engineering, biopolitical dystopia which foregrounds anxiety around 'the not-too-distant future' possibility of cloning and eugenics in the form of conceiving 'improved' children by genetic manipulation. The film's title is based on the first letters of guanine, adenine, thymine and cytosine, the four nucleobases of DNA. The film can be seen to pose ethical questions around the concept of the human and genetic determinism in its conception of the use of biometrics to construct the ideal human and the elimination of otherness by way of the eradication of 'in-valids' susceptible to genetic 'disorders'.

In Time is an SF genetic engineering dystopia, whereby when someone turns 25 they stop aging. They are engineered to live only one further year, when they will 'time-out' and die. However, in a mirror of neoliberal economic inequality, this engineered time can be bought and sold. The rich attain decades at a time while the poor beg, borrow or steal just enough hours to make it through another day. As a time-rich character states, 'For a few to be immortal, many must die' – the neoliberal analogy is the 'for a few to be rich, many must be poor'. The film plays with the fantasy of mastering and ordering time, and treads the same ground as recent films such as *Inception*, *Source Code* and *Looper*. In *In Time* time becomes a universal currency – 'time is money' – and can extend youth and immortality. This is the posthuman and cryogenic fantasy of immortality. It is an attempt to eradicate the ambiguity and singularity of death, and eradicate the ambiguity and singularity of the human, all too human.

The Truman Show, famously, explores the virtual real, and the simulation of reality. Truman, unknowingly, lives on a film set where 5,000 cameras carry the events of his life to a television audience. The film satirizes our media-saturated world and anticipates developments in reality television and virtual reality. For the film's visual style, and cloning of the real, director Peter Weir was influenced by hyperrealist painter Norman Rockwell. Specifically, the 'idealization' of Rockwell's renderings of an America that had already vanished by the time the artist created them. The film therefore presents a nostalgic copy of a nostalgic copy which had no original. The majority of the simulated town was actually filmed in Seaside, Florida, chosen for its 'too-perfect' look, and which itself was already a form of simulation as a designed, gated and controlled environment, a 'master-planned community'. The soundstage that functions as Truman's home is Baudrillard's conception of Disneyland writ large – a place which is nothing more than an immense script and a perpetual motion picture. Product placement and overt advertising is incorporated into the actors' scripts as they communicate with Truman. This performance of the human envisions the neoliberal posthuman as first and foremost a consumer in a promotional culture and marketing society.

S1m0ne is self-reflective upon the filmmaking process and the possibilities of film and virtual reality. Al Pacino plays Viktor Taransky (a clear allusion to Victor Frankenstein), a washed-up film director. Taransky has become disillusioned with filmmaking after having difficulties with the star of his new film. The actress is a demanding diva, eternally late, and eventually walks out of the film. Upon hearing this threat to the completion of the film, Taransky is visited by a 'mad professor' type called Hank Aleno. In a representation of posthuman film theory, Aleno (an anagram of 'alone') reminds Taransky that they previously met at 'The Future of Film conference' in San Jose. Niccol's script has him say: 'I was keynote speaker. You must remember my speech, "Who Needs Humans?"'[3] Viktor faintly recognizes this: 'That's right. You were booed off the stage.' However, who needs humans when, as Aleno claims, he has a computer program which can create 'synthespians'. These are virtual actors that the film calls 'vactors'. Viktor protests: 'I need flesh.' 'Flesh is weak', Aleno replies. The trope of the posthuman is made apparent insofar as the messiness, unpredictability and uniqueness of the human actress can be replaced by the perfect, ordered, controllable posthuman virtual actress. This is a simulated clone with all otherness eradicated.

Taransky can now use a computer-generated 'synthespian' to replace the movie's leading actress. The program is titled Simulation One, which is shortened and combined to name the virtual actress Simone. In the film title there is the use of the 1 and 0 of binary code to result in 'S1m0ne'. Here Simone is without origin, reality or referent. As with virtual images produced by digital visual technologies there are no real-life referents. The virtual actress is deemed by critics and the public to give a flawless performance in the film and more is demanded. Taransky duly obliges, marketing her as a real person, and subsequent performances result in an Academy Award for Best Actress. She appears in simulated interviews and as a hologram in a stadium performance. The machinery of celebrity celebration goes into spin without a real celebrity. Developments around the posthuman and technology are entwined with political economy. Viktor exclaims, 'See beyond that irrational allegiance to flesh and blood. See that with the rise in price of a real actor and the fall in price of a fake, the scales have tipped in favour of the fake.'

The key piece of dialogue of the film in terms of exemplifying anxiety around virtual reality is when Viktor excitedly says to Simone, 'Do you have any idea what this means, Simone? Our ability to manufacture fraud now exceeds our ability to detect it.' Simone replies, 'I am the death of real.' This is Baudrillard's thesis in a nutshell. If virtual reality could speak, it would say precisely this: 'I am the death of real.' Another core exchange is an interview with Simone on a screen in a television studio. The interviewer asks the screen, 'Who are you really?' Simone replies, 'That's a good question. As Nietzsche said, "Whenever a man strives long and hard to appear someone else, he ends up finding it is difficult to be himself again."' The warning, albeit blunt, is the warning of the film and the warning of the virtual. By immersing ourselves in the virtual and the digital, by becoming posthuman and inhuman, we may not finally find our way back to the real and back to the human.

The film begins to conclude when tabloid reporters begin to get suspicious of the lack of real-life appearances of Simone. The creation begins to get out of Taransky's control. He decides to end Simone by using a computer virus to erase her. Viktor kills her off but is then suspected of her murder as there is no actual body. The only way to save himself is to resurrect Simone and explain her 'death' away as a tasteless publicity stunt. 'Who says the only bad publicity is your obituary?' Simone says. The film resolves with an attempt to recover the real after letting loose the virtual. In the film the real and the virtual can be differentiated and the virtual is deemed false. This is a departure from Baudrillard's work where it is increasingly difficult to discern the real from the virtual.

SF in Niccol's films follows Suvin's defining characteristic of the genre as producing an 'alternate reality logically necessitated by and proceeding from the narrative kernel of the novum' (Suvin 1979, 75). The novum is typically a scientific or technological cognitive innovation. As in Niccol's case, the novum are posthuman issues such as virtual reality, cloning, genetic engineering, biopower, the technological singularity and so on. Badmington has linked the SF film and posthumanism by suggesting that concomitant with the philosophical anti-humanism of the 1950s was the anxiety of the crisis in humanism expressed and explored in popular culture: 'Humanism was in trouble – Hollywood knew this but took refuge in denial' (Badmington 2000, 8). In classic SF films such as *Invasion of the Body Snatchers* (1956), *Them!* (1954), *The War of the Worlds* (1953) and *The Blob* (1958), man faced a variety of threats from an inhuman other. Man's position at the centre was at risk from an alien other ready to take over, invade, and occupy man. In a scenario mirrored in many SF cinema of the contemporary age, this posthuman anxiety was the remedy of humanism: 'the aliens were always defeated, frequently by a uniquely "human" quality' (Badmington 2000, 7).

The films of Niccol function in such a way. They are, of course, restricted by genre conventions, audience expectations, filmic limitations, the political economy of Hollywood and so on. They share a concern around the drive towards a sense of human perfectibility – the genetically perfect, the perfect virtual world, the perfect virtual actress and thus towards the eradication of otherness – the 'in-valid', the time-poor, the ambiguities of the real world and real people. The anxieties that are explored and raised are resolved by human qualities. There is a recourse to the human as a solution to the problems posed by the posthuman in the form of love, family relations, authenticity and something seemingly tangible and real. Despite their contemporary themes and futuristic settings, the films are actually quite traditional and conservative. In these films there remains a sense of the real (in the form of the in-valid, the poor, the television audience or human love) to be discerned behind the virtual real.

This mirrors how Baudrillard had read SF literature in 1981. Writers such as Phillip K. Dick are said to 'revitalize, reactualize, requotidianize fragments of simulation' in order 'to reinvent the real' (Baudrillard 1994, 124). On the other hand, writers such as J. G. Ballard often eschew such reinventions and restorations of the simulated real, and hence Ballard's *Crash* is deemed 'the first great novel of the universe of simulation' (Baudrillard 1994, 119). Ballard, for example, takes SF beyond its usual coordinates of imaginary future universes and turns towards our current world as hyperreal (Baudrillard 1994, 125). In this sense, SF becomes theory and theory becomes SF. It is understandable that Baudrillard is often praised, or dismissed, for being 'as skilled a fiction writer as Ballard, Dick, or Stanislaw Lem. More than describe the implosion into simulation, his works enact it' (Hayles 1991, 323). Compared with the utopian resolutions offered to the posthuman condition by Niccol, Baudrillard's SF is decidedly dystopian.

In summation, Baudrillard's work places his concept of singularity against the technological singularity. He often celebrates the interruption of alterity and singularities and stands against their violent incorporation and simulation. His work challenges the implications and pursuit of a technological singularity, cloning, AI, virtuality, networks and simulation. This technological posthuman goal is inhuman, against the human: 'in a world that wants absolutely to cleanse everything, to exterminate death and negativity [thought must] remain humanist, concerned for the human' (Baudrillard 2003, 92). Theory itself,[4] to resist the artificial double, to resist assimilation, must be akin to a singularity, for 'in its singularity thought may be able to protect us' (Baudrillard 2000, 29). One can finally say of Baudrillard that which has been said of Lyotard, and could be said of Foucault, Derrida and others: that we 'see the glimmerings of a new form of humanism in [the] later writings' (Sim 2001, 25). This might be 'a post-humanist humanism' (Sim 2001, 65). For Baudrillard, without the symbolic, alterity and singularity we might be said to have lost the human. Just as for Lyotard, without difference, 'we have lost the human' (Sim 2001, 29). This potential loss becomes all the more important as we slip irrecoverably into the 'future primitive society of the digital'.[5]

Notes

1. In an article 'We are all Transsexuals Now' (1987), which may just as well be 'We are all Posthuman Now', Baudrillard anticipates and warns against the virtual identity that 'social' media phenomena such as Facebook facilitate: 'We no longer have the time to seek out an identity in the historical record, in memory, in a past, nor indeed in a project or a future. We have to have an instant memory which we can plug in to immediately – a kind of promotional identity which can be verified at every moment' (Baudrillard 2002, 11). The upshot here on identity is 'all that remains is to perform an appearing act, without bothering to be, or even to be seen. It is not: "I exist, I'm here", but "I'm visible, I'm image – look, look!"... Being oneself becomes an ephemeral performance, with no lasting effects, a disenchanted mannerism in a world without manners' (Baudrillard 2002, 11–12).

2. The problem with the Internet as a network would be in thwarting otherness, the event, the new, a singularity, and instead being another simulation, obeying a code, a form of virtual reality: 'And is there really any possibility of discovering something in cyberspace? The Internet merely simulates a free mental space, a space of freedom and discovery. In fact, it merely offers a multiple, but conventional, space, in which the operator interacts with known elements, pre-existent sites, established codes. Nothing exists beyond these search parameters. Every question has its anticipated response. You are the automatic questioner and, at the same time, the automatic answering device of the machine. Both coder and decoder – in fact your own terminal, your own correspondent. That is the ecstasy of communication. There is no "Other" out there and no final destination. And so the system goes on, without end and without purpose' (Baudrillard 2002, 179).
3. http://www.dailyscript.com/scripts/Simone_Andrew_Niccol.html (Accessed 11 May 2014).
4. The parallel with Lyotard is pronounced. Thought should remain enigmatic and open to otherness. Thought would take time: 'I do not like this haste. What it hurries, and crushes, is what after the fact I find that I have always tried, under diverse headings – work, figural, heterogeneity, dissensus, event, thing – to reserve: the unharmonizable' (Lyotard 1991, 2).
5. This closing suggestion and the chapter title is from here: 'On the pretext of immortality, we're moving towards slow extermination...Human beings can't bear themselves, they can't bear their otherness, this duality...They can't bear failing the world by their very existence, nor the world failing them...It's now become a major undertaking, an enterprise of self-immolation by technology. [Welcome to] the future primitive society of the digital' (Baudrillard 2007, 35–36).

4
Derrida on Screen

Stefan Herbrechter

> *I watch a lot of television, both because it fascinates me (...) but also because I try, at the same time, to analyse this fascination and to know what is going on on the other side.*
>
> (Derrida & Stiegler 2002, 137)
>
> *The specter is also, among other things, what one imagines, what one thinks one sees and which one projects – on an imaginary screen where there is nothing to see. Not even the screen sometimes, and a screen always has, at bottom, in the bottom or background that it is, a structure of disappearing apparition.*
>
> (Derrida 1994, 100–101)

Some may be surprised to see a chapter on Derrida in a *Handbook on Posthumanism in Film and Television*. There are two reasons for this. One lies in the fact that Jacques Derrida (1930–2004) is not usually related to posthumanism, even though he has certainly influenced a number of writers who do own up to that label, most notably Cary Wolfe (2010), Neil Badmington (2000) and myself (2013). The other reason is that Derrida's relationship with film and television – despite his undeniable influence on film and media studies more generally – is anything but straightforward. This chapter will argue, however, that Derrida is both, a 'proto-posthumanist' and a 'media philosopher'; in fact, it will aim to show that neither posthumanism nor the media today would be thinkable without Derridean deconstruction. In order to spell out the relationship between posthumanism, the media and deconstruction I will proceed by looking at 'Derrida on screen' at three levels: at the level of Derrida screened (i.e., Derrida's appearances on screen, and film in particular); Derrida on being screened (Derrida's comments on becoming a subject to screening, or on being filmed, mediated, etc.); and Derrida on screens (or his thinking about the 'televisual' and mediated representation more generally). At each level, the implication for a very specific understanding of posthumanism in Derridean deconstruction should become apparent.

Apart from numerous television interviews, YouTube clips, seminars and conferences, photographs and portraits, Jacques Derrida appeared as a 'character' (playing himself) in three films: *The Ghost Dance* (1983), *D'Ailleurs Derrida* [Derrida's Elsewheres, 1999], and *Derrida* (2002). 'Derrida screened' refers to the kind of dynamic that partakes of Derrida as a subject of the media, as someone, a 'media philosopher' who has been 'produced' and has therefore also produced 'himself' on film and television. In all these appearances Derrida foregrounds the self-reflexivity of 'being screened', or of what it means to become a subject of and subjected to the (televisual) media. While *D'Ailleurs Derrida* is an almost lyrical film that characterizes Derrida as a modern Marrano Jew on his autobiographic journey 'back' from France to Algeria, his birthplace (a journey that traces what he calls his *'nostalgérie'*), Amy Ziering Kofman and Kirby Dick's 2002 biopic tries to picture Derrida, the 'great philosopher' in his everyday routine. Derrida is shown and interviewed in his house, at work and on his travels around the world. Here, he literally is and plays with the role of being the subject of film. He foregrounds the 'spectrality' that the photographic inscription produces – a theme that goes back to Roland Barthes' work on the relationship between photography and death in *Camera Lucida*, where he shows that the subject of a photograph (very much like the author of any text) is always already 'dead' (if not literally, then at least 'structurally'), since the photograph (and the text) signifies the absence of its subject.

This idea of spectrality is linked to the question of autobiography more generally, which Derrida foregrounds in *Derrida*, from the beginning. The story I tell myself – my identity – is a form of inscription that is designed, on the one hand, to insure my singular presence and a kind of ownership over my 'experience'; on the other hand, it is necessarily taking 'my' place – it is designed to be able to speak of 'me' and for 'me' (even in my absence). So, in making myself appear to others, I am at the same time giving up my control over my story, which thus becomes subject to interpretation and will have to be countersigned or acknowledged by others (who will necessarily see things differently). I am thus the subject of my autobiography only in the form of a spectre – an absent presence that comes back to haunt me, constantly. The same is true of the lives of others, of course, and especially the ones who have already disappeared, died, but whose influence can still be felt. This is our 'inheritance' which constantly demands to be heard, according to Derrida's reading of Shakespeare's *Hamlet* in *Specters of Marx*, in which he creates an analogy between the impossible contemporaneity of Marxist legacy and Hamlet being haunted by his murdered father's ghost. It is also a rereading of Freudian psychoanalysis and the unconscious as a haunted 'archive'. Memory, despite its material inscription of events, knowledge and information cannot dispense with immaterial, psychic or mental processes that are supposed to guarantee truth and order, but, at the same time, expose their relativity and disjointedness ('the time is out of joint', as Hamlet says). The bad news is thus that truth is never established once and for all, while the good news is that the spectrality of being necessarily creates a radical opening for a future that is unpredictably other (as Derrida says in *Ghost Dance*: 'The future belongs to ghosts').

Derrida's more general claim would be that actually all subjectivity works according to this logic of spectrality, which is why, in *Specters of Marx*, he coins the word 'hauntology' – a serious pun that signifies that the entire tradition of ontology (philosophy of 'being') is haunted by the spectral, by the 'ghosts' it continues to repress. And here is thus the first aspect of a Derridean posthumanism in the context of the media: 'our' media – from language to new and hypermedia – have always been 'spectralizing', because of the necessarily 'teleological' character of communication (of their message-sending and destinatory logic). The reason why Derrida could therefore be called a media philosopher and, even more specifically, a thinker of *televisual* media, is closely linked to this idea of a spectral absent presence of a trace or of *différance*, as Derrida calls it, on which 'Western metaphysics' (or, in other words, philosophy and thinking as we know it) is based. In *The Post Card* – itself a symptomatic 'medium' of what Derrida refers to as the 'postal epoch' – he develops nothing less than a deconstruction of the teleological structure of all (media) communication. Since communication (visual, symbolic, oral, written, etc.) is always 'destined' or 'sent', there must be necessarily the possibility of a message not arriving at its destination, of letters, postcards and messages in general, going astray. At the same time, the only assurance of a letter arriving at its destination is some form of feedback to the sender. This relay situation is what Derrida refers to as the postal principle:

> *As soon as there is [a postal principle], there is différance (and this does not await language, especially human language, and the language of Being, only the mark and the divisible trait), and there is postal maneuvering, relays, delay, anticipation, destination, telecommunicating network, the possibility, and therefore the fatal necessity of going astray, etc.*
>
> (Derrida 1987, 66)

It may be the case that today we are moving away from a lettered and paper-based material support culture towards a computerized, digital culture. However, what the new teletechnological situation of email, instant messaging, video and mobile media does not mean is the end, but rather the acceleration and intensification, of the postal as such. As Deborah Cook explains:

> *The postal era, the era of love letters, literature, metaphysics, history, etc., is coming to an end. The Post, or the Postal Principle, however, will endure, living on transformed, transferred, and translated as the trace... The Postal Principle is the über, meta, trans, and tele of all epochs.*
>
> (Cook 1987, 293)

In *Ghost Dance* Derrida is interviewed in his office by a student (played by Pascale Ogier, who died shortly after the film was completed). She asks him whether he believes in ghosts, and he explains that this is a somewhat difficult question because, right here, right now, she is speaking to a ghost (in the sense outlined earlier in this chapter, namely Derrida's filmic presence relying on his physical absence). At the end of the scene, after Derrida's little lecture on films producing ghosts, Derrida returns the question to Ogier and she answers, in a close-up looking straight into the camera: 'Yes, now I believe in ghosts.' Years later, after her death, and upon rewatching this scene, Derrida is struck by its temporal spectrality, as he explains in one of the transcribed television interviews with Bernard Stiegler, 'Spectographies' (Derrida & Stiegler 2002, 120):

> *Suddenly I saw Pascale's face, which I knew was a dead woman's face, come onto the screen. She answered my question: 'Do you believe in ghosts?' Practically looking me in the eye, she said to me again, on the big screen: 'Yes, now I do, yes'. Which now? Years later in Texas. I had the unnerving sense of the return of her specter, the specter of her specter coming back to say to me – to me here, now: 'Now...now...now, that is to say, in this dark room on another continent, in another world, here, now, yes, believe me, I believe in ghosts.'*

This is, of course, more than just the eerie personal experience of Derrida, the individual subject of a film. It is the experience of film (and all writing – Derrida here exploits the near homophony in French of *écrit* and *écran* (Derrida & Stiegler 2002, 130)) in general. As Laurence Simmons elegantly puts it:

> *To watch a film is to be in the presence of spectres, the already-dead or the soon-to-be-dead, and it is also to be watched by them as they look back at us and see that we, too, shall die. The spectrality of cinema transforms the spectator of the film into a spectre who can no longer maintain the distance between subject and object, seer and seen, the living and the dead. The film spectator becomes caught up in the becoming spectres of the characters on screen. We the audience can no longer retain a distance, and collapse into the spectral relation.*
>
> (Simmons 2011, 136)

And this spectral relation, arguably, is at work in all forms of visual and non-visual media representation. It is at work in representation and communication as such, in the form of a

> *trace that marks the present with an absence in advance. The spectral logic is de facto a deconstructive logic. It is in the element of haunting that deconstruction finds the place most hospitable to it, at the heart of the living present, in the quickest heartbeat of the philosophical. Like the work of mourning, in a sense, which produces spectrality, and like all work produces spectrality.*
>
> (Derrida & Stiegler 2002, 117)

Here, once more, lies the first important nexus between Derridean deconstruction, media and posthumanism: even though the 'spectral' has always been a necessary part of the 'human', modernity, or the time of the televisual mass medium is characterized by an increasing proliferation of this 'logic of spectrality' to an extent where it has become difficult to ignore the mutual penetration (Donna Haraway (1985) would call it 'cyborgization') of human and teletechnological forms of representation. As Derrida explains in an interview entitled 'Specters of Media':

> *There is no doubt that the extraordinary technological development of the media has to do with the unprecedented, unheard of possibilities of spectrality, and that teletechnology is a way of producing, handling, organizing, making profit out of some spectrality. The structure of television, the structure of computerization, has everything to do with spectrality. This has deeply transformed the public space, that is, the political space, not only nationally but also through what is called globalization, mondialisation. For that reason, of course, the power and thus the responsibilities of the media are enormous. There is nothing in the world, and certainly no political or economic power, which could avoid being dependent on the media.*
> (Derrida 2001b, 45)[1]

So, as a first summary, we can say that there is in Derrida's work a kind of phenomenological critique of the experience of media subjectivity which involves a reinterpretation of the 'televisual', or of 'being-screened', 'being-on-screen' driven by the unattained and unattainable ideal of 'telepathy' (of instant, self-present, communication without loss across distances, without spectres, etc.).[2] However, what happens in 'televisual' mass media (and arguably even more today and in future through digital media) is a proliferation and increasing autonomy of spectral images. The proliferation of posthuman figures – ghosts, zombies, cyborgs and so on – might therefore be seen in the context of this general spectralization, as one aspect of our own intensifying engagement with and loss of control over our media representations. This posthumanising trend would thus be closely linked to a form of 'cyborgization' that, on the one hand, produces human–machine and, on the other hand, human–media assemblages.

So, if one agrees with Derrida that media spectralization has always contributed to the *decentring* of the human subject and continues to do so, this could in itself be seen as a 'posthumanist' scenario or potential. Digitalization, a further spectre raised by Derrida (2001b) in the previous quotation ('computerization'), in a sense is merely upping the ante in this respect. More specifically, digitalization and the changes it produces in, amongst other things, our relation to images, also have a fundamental effect on (human) memory and the archive. In *Archive Fever*, Derrida (1996) develops an argument about the necessarily political structure of every archive and the double imperative every process of archivization has to obey: on the one hand, there is the question of power (and very often of state politics and national sovereignty), including who the archivists or archiving institutions should be. On the other hand, the question is what to archive and how to regulate the access to this externalized public memory. This becomes especially complex in a situation where there is, today, due to digitalization and decentralization of archiving possibilities, a proliferation of archives, as well as a huge increase in information, and thus an increased instability of 'data' and very often a lack of verifiability. The creation of a 24/7, online, mediated, social and increasingly global public memory that is always 'telepresent' to itself is not necessarily 'good news', because it also produces a generalization of the 'conundrum' of the archive that Derrida refers to as the *mal d'archive*, namely the structural aporia that underlies any archival desire. Derrida specifically refers to the Freudian archive and to psychoanalysis as an institution in his text to demonstrate the paradox of memory. On the one hand, memory needs externalization (e.g., an archive, but also other techniques and technologies of remembering, and, by implication, all technological prostheses, and especially writing and all forms of inscription) and, on the other that process depends on repression (wilful forgetting), which makes a politics of memory at once almost impossible (because it would have to involve the individual and collective 'unconscious') but at the same time absolutely necessary (because archives are not only about the preservation of the past, but must also contain all possible futures). As Derrida explains, in *Echographies*:

> *Whoever is in a position to access this past or to use the archive should know concretely that there was a politics of memory, a particular politics, that this politics is in transformation, and that it is a politics. We must awaken to critical vigilance with regard to the politics of memory: we must practice a politics of memory and, simultaneously, in the same movement, a critique of the politics of memory.*
>
> (Derrida & Stiegler 2002, 63)

Again, here we find at work a deconstructive logic that has always contained a posthumanist potential and which, under current teletechnological, digitalized conditions, stresses the relativization of 'humanity's' control over its own memory and archivization processes. And it also poses the question of democracy and the role of the (new) media, of course.

Even more problematically, the question of memory raises the question of technology, media and the human more generally. As Cary Wolfe – one of the chief proponents of a deconstructive posthumanism – explains:

> *Indeed, the 'human' is itself a prosthetic being, who from day one is constituted as human by its co-evolution with and co-constitution by external archival technologies of various kinds – including, of course, language itself as the 'first' archive and prosthesis.*
>
> (Wolfe 2008, 90)

Wolfe builds here on the work of two other thinkers heavily influenced by Derrida's work – Bernard Stiegler's *Technics and Time* (1998) in which he develops the history of humans' 'originary technicity'; and David Wills' *Prosthesis* (1995) and *Dorsality* (2008). To understand the history of humanity as a process of hominization that depends on the originary supplement of the technical (from language to hypermedia) means to look at intensification and increasing technicization. But it also bears the critique of this long-term view and therefore a certain relativization of human 'cyborgization' and the idea of the 'posthuman'. On the one hand, technology ironically is what made us human in the first place, on the other hand this 'technological condition' has triggered a metaphysical process that threatens the human with extinction. Here is what Derrida says about the inextricability of this 'bodily condition':

> *There is no natural originary body: technology has not simply added itself, from the outside or after the fact, as a foreign body. Or at least this foreign or dangerous supplement is 'originarily' at work and in place in the supposedly ideal interiority of the 'body and soul'. It is indeed at the heart of the heart.*
>
> (Derrida 1995, 244–245)

The history and future of technology and media is therefore closely linked with human self-understanding in the form of an externalization (of memory) and a prosthesization that produces what might be called 'culture' in the widest sense (including science as a human practice and institution). This is because the originary prosthesis is that of 'auto-affection'. Deconstruction shares with psychoanalysis an idea of identity formation that is based on a desire of the other. The 'of' in this phrase plays on the ambiguity of this other having aspects both of auto- and hetero-affection. In other words, an 'I' needs an 'other' who precedes it, at the same time this 'other' serves for identification and thus auto-affection purposes, and fires the desire to 'become who I think I am'. This 'other' who is neither real nor fictional (if anything he/she/it is 'virtual') is thus necessary but also uncontrollable. The 'price' for auto-affective 'self'-identity is therefore also an auto-immunitarian defence mechanism (Derrida 2003a). This is true for all significant others – be they humans, non-humans, objects, ideas or institutions.

And this is where another nexus between deconstruction, media and posthumanism can be identified, namely in the fact that the auto-affection and auto-immunity mechanism is necessarily 'mediated' by an otherness that gives rise to desire but always escapes it – be that at an individual or a social level. In this insight lies the potential for a posthumanism that takes the relativization of human agency and a non-anthropocentric understanding of communication and human–environment interaction as its starting point. However, it also connects quite problematically to the history of technicization and media in the sense that contemporary forms of teletechnological and computerized media raise the stakes of auto-affective and auto-immunitarian practices so to speak.

At the same time, they also lead to an extension of the realm of the 'virtual'. Derrida's response to this is the coining of the words 'artifactuality' and 'actuvirtuality', which are connected to a call for a heightened responsibility of the media in the light of their increased virtualizing power (Derrida & Stiegler 2002, 3). There is thus in Derrida also an analysis of the screen as such, of the process of representation involved in the mediated 'message'. In this sense, Derrida is a media critic, who sees the crucial political stake for the media in their relation to and their implication in the archivization of the 'event'. How can the dynamics of spectralization and thus virtualization of (hyper)media continue to guarantee the 'event-ness of the event'? In other words, how can 'we' continue to take responsible decisions in the absence of trustworthy media representations (which, arguably, is the question that ultimately underlies all forms of 'media studies' and 'media critique')? Derrida formulates this problem in *Specters of Marx*, by linking it back to his idea of the ghost, spectrality and hauntology:

> *If we have been insisting so much since the beginning on the logic of the ghost, it is because it points toward a thinking of the event that necessarily exceeds a binary or dialectical logic, the logic that distinguishes or opposes effectivity or actuality (either present, empirical, living – or not) and ideality (regulating or absolute non-presence). This logic of effectivity or actuality seems to be of a limited pertinence. The limit, to be sure, is not new; it has always been leaving its mark on anti-Marxist idealism as well as on 'dialectical materialism'. But it seems to be demonstrated today better than ever by the fantastic, ghostly, 'synthetic', 'prosthetic', virtual happenings in the scientific domain and thus the domain of the techno-media and thus the public or political domain. It is also made more manifest by what inscribes the speed of a virtuality irreducible to the opposition of the act and the potential in the space of the event, in the event-ness of the event.*
>
> (Derrida 1994, 63)

The awareness of the media's 'construction' of actuality, of the virtual and therefore entirely political nature of the mediated event, raises the question of the media's responsibility and also calls for a media pedagogical emphasis on critique. The 'task' (for the philosopher, but also any subject of or to the media, today) is thus the following:

> *Today, a philosopher who 'thinks his time' must, among other things, be attentive to the implications and consequences of this virtual time [of 'actuality' or the 'event']. To the innovations in its technical implementation, but also to what the new recalls of much more ancient possibilities.*
>
> (Derrida & Stiegler 2002, 6)

Derrida, as a media philosopher, thus clearly sees the potential but also the dangers of the increasing and intensifying mediation of (human and non-human) life on this planet, and, maybe most importantly, he also sees the necessity for a critique that does not neglect the long term, a critique that does not forget to 'inherit' in the face of teletechnological acceleration and globalization:

> *A new ethics and a new law or right, in truth, a new concept of 'hospitality' are at stake. What the accelerated development of teletechnologies, of cyberspace, of the new topology of the 'virtual' is producing is a practical deconstruction of the traditional and dominant concepts of the state and citizen (and thus of 'the political') as they are linked to the actuality of a territory. I say 'deconstruction' because, ultimately, what I name and try to think under this word is, at bottom, nothing other than this very process, its 'taking-place' in such a way that its happening affects the very experience of place and the recording (symptomatic, scientific, or philosophical) of this 'thing', the trace that traces (inscribes, preserves, carries, refers, or defers) the différance of this*

event which happens to place [qui arrive au lieu] – which happens to take place, and to taking-place *[qui arrive à l'avoir-lieu].*

(Derrida & Stiegler 2002, 36)

Deconstruction – and its powerful and critical commentary in Derrida's work – thus bears the closest possible affinity with the analysis of the interlinked processes of mediatization and hominization. In this sense, deconstruction has always been (proto-)posthumanist. The important thing, however, is that it stresses both the continuity *and* the complexification, the inheritance *and* the newness of today's situation (with its specific potentials and dangers). So, even though Derrida died before the advent of the so-called 'new media' and Web 2.0, his work leaves many threads to be taken up.[3] In terms of an understanding of posthumanism, however, Derridean deconstruction also teaches us that the one humanism that we will not be able to escape here is the one of auto-hetero-affection contained in this very work with the proper name 'Derrida'. This work may not often be cited today, either in connection with (new) media studies or with techno-media-centred theories of posthumanism, but without this inheritance (and the inheritance before it) our responsibility in the face of new and ever greater challenges seems frightfully limited. Deconstruction has in fact always happened, with and without humans. Derridean deconstruction 'taking place' continues to haunt our increasingly mediated selves, environments, bodies and socialities, as we are beginning to see ourselves, from imagined post-anthropocentric futures, as 'posthumans'.

Notes

1. On the relationship between religion, media and globalization see e.g. Derrida (2001a), and Naas (2012).
2. For a more detailed discussion on telepathy see Derrida (1988), and Royle (2008).
3. On an early link between the work of Derrida to digitalization and the database see Bennington (1993).

5
Bruno Latour: From the Non-Modern to the Posthuman

T. Hugh Crawford

In *We Have Never Been Modern* (1991, 62), Bruno Latour announces that there 'is only one positive thing to be said about the postmoderns: after them there is nothing. Far from being the last word, they mark the end of ends.' Clearly, he does not embrace the nihilistic irony of some forms of postmodernity, but his relation to the posthuman is much more complex and nuanced. Latour's ongoing critique of modernity, carried out through numerous empirical studies of scientific and technological practices as well as his investigation of the politics of nature (developed in a book of that title), is perhaps best articulated in *We Have Never Been Modern* and his recent *An Inquiry into Modes of Existence*. In the first he lays a clear foundation for his 'non-modern constitution' and the second creates a place for a positive posthumanist position. Although his work does not touch directly on film or television, Latour has long examined the visual arts and, through the figure of 'The Theatre of Proof', creates a powerful way to critique the production of objectivity in the sciences and in public discourse.

To understand the broad contours of his work, both as critique and as positive contribution, it is best to start with his unpacking of the idea of an accomplished modernity. Initially trained as an anthropologist, first doing fieldwork on the Ivory Coast and later at the Salk Institute in La Jolla, Latour learned early in his career to question modernity, which for him entails the radical separation of subject and object while at the same time, beneath the official notice of knowledge producers/protectors, strange hybrids – what he calls quasi-objects, quasi-subjects – proliferate. Under the influence of his friend Isabelle Stengers, Latour adopted Alfred North Whitehead's critique of the 'bifurcation of nature', which initially is the division between an object's primary and secondary qualities, but ultimately leads to the birth of modern subjectivity. One must suppose Latour would reject the term 'posthuman', echoing his critique of modernity by claiming that we have never been fully human. That is, an accomplished humanism would be the result of a fundamental break with the things that authorize being. He notes that

> Modernity is often defined in terms of humanism, either as a way of saluting the birth of 'man' or as a way of announcing his death. But this habit itself is modern, because it remains asymmetrical. It overlooks the simultaneous birth of 'nonhumanity' –

things, or objects, or beasts – and the equally strange beginning of a crossed-out God, relegated to the sidelines.

(1993, 13)

What I propose to do first is explore some of his earlier work in science studies on what could be called the birth of the non-human, as well as his discussion of the human in *We Have Never Been Modern*, turning then to his appropriation of the work of Étienne Souriau to frame his more recent *An Inquiry into Modes of Existence*.

Much of his early empirical work consisted of the development of the often contentious discipline of 'Science Studies'. *Laboratory Life* (in collaboration with Steve Woolgar) was probably the first anthropology of a Western scientific laboratory. There he encountered the patient but difficult birth of the scientific object – the isolation of a brain peptide. Characteristically, he gropes for terms to help his readers gain perspective on ways to understand the processes through which non-humans can be seen for what they are – the co-emergent products of very complicated practices. For a time, he adopted the explanatory notion of the theatre, an interesting strategy, harking back as it does to one of the founding documents of Western modernity, Francis Bacon's 'Four Idols'. There the theatre is an impediment to scientific understanding, even though, only a few years later, Robert Boyle was to recast scientific proof of objective knowledge in the Royal Society as the presentation of a material object in front of competent witnesses (cf. Shapin 1988; Shapin & Schaffer 1985).

Latour deploys this term in 'Give Me a Laboratory and I will Raise the World' where he examines Louis Pasteur's anthrax trials:

The Pouilly le Fort field trial is the most famous of all the dramatic proofs that Pasteur staged in his long career. The major mass media of the time were assembled on three successive occasions to watch the unfolding of what was seen as Pasteur's prediction. "Staging" is the right word because, in practice, it is the public showing of what had been rehearsed many times in his laboratory.

(1983, 151)

Like Pasteur's notion of theatre, Latour's notion here is 19th century, for Pasteur was able to rehearse over and over, though trial after trial, testing the efficacy of his therapy before opening night when all came to bear witness to the scientific truth of his vaccine's efficacy. In *The Pasteurization of France* – itself an odd hybrid of biography, methodology and philosophy – Latour also takes up theatre. He notes,

Pasteur's genius was in what might be called the theatre of proof. Having drawn the attention of others to the only place where he knew that he was the strongest, Pasteur invented such dramatized experiments that the spectators could see the phenomena he was describing in black and white. Nobody really knew what an epidemic was; to acquire such knowledge required a difficult statistical knowledge and long experience. But the differential death that struck a crowd of chickens in the laboratory was something that could be seen 'as in broad daylight'.

(1988, 85; cf. Crawford 2012)

The goal of Latour's analysis is to understand the emergence, stabilization and acceptance of a scientific fact, but his theatrical metaphor is charged. The Latour/Pasteur theatre is a technology designed to reveal simple but significant differentials, and at the same time, to produce truth, or at least to compel assent. Its narrative is a series of observable transformations, actually three tableaux (again, how very 19th century). Unlike its namesake, the theatre of proof is not a darkened, curtained space where the audience perhaps expects to be thrilled by a seemingly illusory or at least ephemeral set of images, sounds or actions. This theatre produces enlightenment, truth 'in broad daylight', and thus suppresses its own theatricality, apparently removing the impediment of Bacon's idol to stabilize objects and to make facts.

While this is an interesting appropriation of the metaphorics of the theatre, it does not directly lead to a posthuman cinema. What it does, is chart out the emergence of the non-human in what Latour call the 'modern parenthesis' (2011, 304), and, consequently, the co-emergence of the modern human. From that perspective, his next text, the slight volume called *We Have Never Been Modern* is a logical progression. On the surface, he seems to have moved abruptly from laboratory studies or the careful articulation of a science studies' methodology (in *Science in Action*) to speculative philosophy. But as part of an ongoing critique of modernity and the Enlightenment subject, his move from the theatrical presentation of a seemingly unmediated object to a critique of liberal humanism is perfectly coherent.

Introducing *An Inquiry into Modes of Existence*, he characterizes *We Have Never Been Modern* as essentially negative, a critique that his more recent work is meant to take in a positive direction. Nevertheless, it is important to understand that negative argument. According to Latour, at some point roughly in the 17th century in the West, modern science emerged, and with it modernity: a radical repudiation of the past, an affirmation of the human as subject and nature as object, and studious blindness to all the hybrid subject–objects that proliferate beneath, behind or beyond the obvious notice of the modernisers.

A first move in this critique with implications for the notion of the posthuman is his problematization of time. Latour does not claim that modernity is atemporal, just that it depends on a radical break with its past. Modern science is necessarily not just objective, but also free of the contaminants of a misguided, overly rational, non-empirical and probably superstitious historical mentality. As he says in *We Have Never Been Modern*:

> *The asymmetry between nature and culture then becomes an asymmetry between past and future. The past was the confusion of things and men; the future is what will no longer confuse them.* (71)

His principle of symmetry here is taken from the Edinburgh School of science studies, which argued for symmetrical explanations of scientific success and failure. Essentially, they objected to those who explained the failure of scientific theories through human foibles, while attributing success to an accurate presentation of natural objective knowledge, the world as it actually is. They insisted that there should be a social explanation for both. Latour proposed a double rule of symmetry – that there should be a 'natural' explanation to both success and failure. Viewed from some distance, this should probably be seen as a precursor to his attitude – which emerges clearly later in his critique of the bifurcation of nature – that the subject/object distinction is deeply flawed and part of the problem produced by modernity, not a marker of accomplishment. But the key here is the asymmetry between past and future. For Latour, modernity is a repudiation of a past that mixes humans and things, one that cannot be part of a modern state that polices those boundaries carefully.

Of course, he is not celebrating this atemporality. Rather, *We Have Never Been Modern* questions the achievement of such a break. With that, the connection between a theatre of proof that presents and stabilizes atemporal or eternal objects and this modern temporal break becomes clear. And with that, one can see the technological history of early cinema as straight out of Pasteur's desire to present an objectified nature seemingly without subjective intervention. After all, Étienne-Jules Marey was a physiologist intent on capturing dynamic processes for clear and careful analysis. As François Dagognet argues, Marey was not interested in creating the illusion of movement with his sequential photographic studies. Rather, he wanted to produce clear, isolated marks: single moments separated from the flow of time (1992, 153–154). In the 'modern constitution' outlined by Latour, the modernisers continually try to produce and stabilize those moments.

But it is not just the modern repudiation of time that Latour wants to rectify, it is also the bifurcation of nature that, on one level, is the separation of the world into primary and secondary qualities, but also makes the subject/object distinction, and ultimately the Cartesian mind/ body duality. In *We Have Never Been Modern*, this bifurcation comes under scrutiny, though he offers no real way out except the simple assertion that 'we have never been modern'. This implies that all we would need to do is embrace the hybrids that already compose our world: 'So long as humanism is constructed through the contrast with the object that has been abandoned to epistemology, neither the human nor the nonhuman can be understood' (136). His position is not that, at some point in the Enlightenment, the human emerged from millennia of backward, superstitious idiocy. Rather, the object – the natural phenomenon that becomes the object of epistemology – produces the human, the subject nearly capable of knowing said object. This contrast, the Whiteheadian bifurcation of nature, is the basis of the modernist parenthesis, and the way into understanding Latour's pre-posthumanist position. He goes on to note that: 'Modern humanists are reductionists because they seek to attribute action to a small number of powers, leaving the rest of the world with nothing but simple mute forces. (...) The human is in the delegation itself, in the pass, in the sending, in the continuous exchange of forms' (138). *We Have Never Been Modern* attempts to dispose of modernity and the human in one stroke.

He waited a number of years before attempting to explicate these moves in *An Inquiry into Modes of Existence*. A key to this renewed effort is his reading of the work of Étienne Souriau, particularly his *Les différents modes d'existence*, but it is also important to note Souriau's later work on aesthetics and his development of filmology, a practice that Christian Metz lauds as precursor to film semiology. Souriau was a broad-ranging thinker, and the concepts Latour adopts for *An Inquiry into Modes of Existence* are fundamental. In an essay primarily on Souriau, published in a volume of essays about speculative realism, Latour lays out the philosophical basis for *An Inquiry into Modes of Existence*. He turns first to William James, whose radical empiricism

> wants to put experience (and not the severely amputated experience found among the first empiricists) at the centre of philosophy by posing a question that is both very ancient and very new: if relations (prepositions in particular) are given to us in experience, where then are they leading us? Could their deployment allow us a total rephrasing of the question of knowledge? Can the bifurcation of nature be brought to an end?
>
> (2011, 306)

Although it is impossible to recapitulate the argument of his nearly 500-page *An Inquiry into Modes of Existence*, its entry point is this notion of pre-positions constructing relations. In brief, a philosophy concerned with subjects and objects along with forms of predication misses the plurality of modes of being given in experience, those that could be called pre-positional, if by pre-position one means the construction of a context to pre-position, and the felicity conditions necessary for recognition that enable different modes of existence. In Latour's hands, this very proliferation of modes ends up running roughshod over the modern bifurcation of nature and an Enlightenment notion of the human. In other words, he actively produces the posthuman.

He starts with Souriau on James:

> We know how much William James valued, in his description of the stream of consciousness, what he called 'a feeling for or, a feeling for because'. Here we would be in a world where *the* or rather, *or the* because of, *the* for, *and above all the* and then, and thus, *would be true existences* (...). *This would be a sort of grammar of existence, which we would thus decode piece by piece.*
>
> (2011, 308)

In essence, Souriau wants to start before subject/object distinctions, in the pre-positional modes, where, as Latour then comments, the 'essential point is that the ontology of prepositions immediately takes us away from the all-too-familiar sorts of inquiry in the philosophies of being' (2011, 308). But the question remains, what do these multiple modes take us towards? Ever the playful philosopher, Latour invokes one of the very bifurcating sciences he is critiquing in an attempt to articulate the pre-positional aggregate:

> *To risk a chemical metaphor, if we note humans as h and nonhumans as nh, it is as if we were now following long chains of polymers: nh-n-nh-nh-h-h-nh-n-nh-h-h-h-nh,*

in which we could sometimes recognize segments that look more like 'social relations' (h-h), others that look more like aggregates of 'objects' (nh-nh), but where attention would be focused on the transitions (h-nh or nh-h).

(2013, 423)

But he also comments quite soberly,

The essential point is that the ontology of prepositions immediately takes us away from the all-too-familiar sorts of inquiry in the philosophies of being. Here, the preposition indicates neither an ontological domain, nor a region, territory, sphere, or material. The if or the and has no region. But as its name perfectly suggests, the preposition prepares the position that has to be given to what follows, giving the search for meaning a definite inflection that allows one to judge its direction or vector.

(2011, 308–309)

He then asks,

can one carry out serious research on relations, as one has for so long on sensations, without requiring them immediately to align themselves in one and only one direction leading either towards the object (and thus away from the subject) or towards the subject (and thus away from the object)?

(2011, 309)

His answer is *An Inquiry into Modes of Existence*, but can also be paralleled by some of the elements of Souriau's filmology.

A figure who draws this complex together – Latour, Souriau, James – is Gilles Deleuze, whose work Latour has engaged throughout his career, either directly or in a form mediated by Isabelle Stengers. Deleuze's last published essay, 'Pure Immanance' (2001), argues for a 'transcendental empiricism' closely aligned to the pre-positional stance Latour sets up in opposition to the modern subject/object. Deleuze opens with devastating precision:

What is a transcendental field? It can be distinguished from experience in that it doesn't refer to an object or belong to a subject (empirical representation). It appears therefore as a pure stream of a-subjective consciousness, a pre-reflexive impersonal consciousness, a qualitative duration of consciousness without a self. It may seem curious that the transcendental be defined by such immediate givens: we will speak of a transcendental empiricism in contrast to everything that makes up the world of the subject and the object. There is something wild and powerful in this transcendental empiricism that is of course not the element of sensation (simple empiricism), for sensation is only a break within the flow of absolute consciousness.

(2001, 25)

Of course, Deleuze's engagement with the concept of transcendental empiricism runs all the way back to *Difference and Repetition* (2001a), and the possible worlds it produces runs through his cinema books, but here we find an articulation of almost precisely the pre-positional stance. More poignantly, it is a full frontal assault on the modernity Latour is at great pains to undermine.

But how does one encounter this 'wild and powerful' transcendental empiricism? One way is through the second term Latour adopts from Souriau – instauration:

> not only should we differentiate research on prepositions from research on substances or foundations, but we should also look for a term that allows us to link questions of language to the question of being, and this despite the demand that they be distinguished. This is Souriau's most important innovation in philosophy. He devoted his whole career to it, giving it the wonderful name of instauration.
>
> (2011, 309)

There are multiple ways to articulate this term, but, in essence, instauration is the act of making, of bringing into existence, not through the imposition of form on compliant matter – what Deleuze and Guattari critique as the hylomorphic model in *Nomadology* (1986). As Latour puts it in *An Inquiry into Modes of Existence*,

> This is why we had to be so suspicious of the concept of 'action on matter', which threatened to place the point of departure in the depths of a human subject instead of waiting for this human subject to emerge from his works – though the possessive adjective is quite unwarranted, because the human subject does not master 'his' works any more than he possesses them. (230)

To instaurate is to instantiate in cooperation with, and in humble awareness of, the multiple modes of existence demanded by all the human and non-human entities present in the emergent collective, along with the range of affordances each participant brings. Instauration is the bringing into existence of beings that are not reducible to the simple binarisms form/matter or subject/object. Combining pre-position with instauration produces a multi-realism that, according to Latour, would 'explore rather different modes of existence than the sole action of saying several things about the same being. Its whole aim is that there be several ways of being' (2011, 312). The key here is that multiple modes include complicated amalgams of non-humans with humans, or, to be more precise, they are posthuman. If the human is 'in the pass', the posthuman is enacted as instauration. In *An Inquiry into Modes of Existence*, Latour goes on to work out a methodology for the recognition and articulation of 15 modes of existence, but also makes it clear it is possible to explore others. Souriau's later work also articulates a number of specific technical aesthetic modes. As Latour notes though, Souriau should not be read as an aesthetician, but instead as 'a metaphysician who always operates on the privileged "field" (if I may say so) of the reception of the artwork, all the better to grasp his key idea of instauration' (2011, 309). It is in this nexus of both terms and attitudes that Latour's posthuman philosophy links directly to cinema studies.

In his 'Profile of Étienne Souriau', Christian Metz exclaims, 'What moves is not exactly the camera, the movement of which is only one of the means of executive operation. It is the point of view that moves. How many theoretical, semiological, and psychoanalytical analyses have their roots in this simple remark!' (1984, 6). There are a number of ways to unpack this claim, but from a Latourian perspective, Metz is firmly within the pro-positional. The moving point of view technologically instantiated in cinema is an excellent way to understand that pre-position is not just a grammatical concept. As argued throughout *An Inquiry into Modes of Existence*, pre-position creates both a stance or perspective and it sets the felicity conditions necessary to recognize the emergence of a mode of existence. Although this is not the place for a discussion of Souriau's seven levels of filmic reality (cf. Buckland 2007, 4), it is clear that they destabilize subject/object distinctions and the objectifying strategies of the theatre of proof. Latour's Pasteur necessarily sought to suppress any suspicion of theatrical manipulation apart from his single simple show: competent witnesses, live chickens, dead chickens. Souriau's Afilmic, Profilmic, Filmographic, Filmophanic, Diegetic, Spectatorial and Creational 'realities' are modes of filmic existence. They are both pre-positional and specific instaurations, and their very proliferation erases many, but not all, traces of the human. There is no simple auteur, spectator nor object in this crazily proliferating collective. Through Latour and Souriau, film becomes a Deleuzian transcendental empiricism, 'a pure stream of a-subjective consciousness, a pre-reflexive impersonal consciousness, a qualitative duration of consciousness without a self' (Deleuze & Boyman 2001, 178).

Although he is discussing networks and not film, Latour's claim, as follows, characterizes the basis of a posthuman cinema:

> *Its* patuity, *to borrow Souriau's term, its particular form of presence, does not make it any more visible, for it appears in the form of an ever-lengthening list of beings through which it is necessary to pass in order to subsist. But this time it is not a matter of the risk taken by lines of force or lineages in order to insist, maintain themselves, pass, reproduce, endure; what appears is the surprising series of detours necessary to* attach quasi subjects and quasi objects *and* make them hold together in a lasting way.

(2013, 423)

Cinema's patuity, its form of presence, foregrounding as it does Metz's moving point of view, Souriau's modes of filmic reality, Latour's pre-positional and instauration, and ultimately Deleuze's transcendental empiricism, is fundamentally posthuman. Its multiplicity resists the clear differentials of Pasteur's theatre, and instead celebrates all those quasi-objects and quasi-subjects that had been silenced in modernity but which now populate the posthuman world.

6
Friedrich Nietzsche and the Posthuman/Transhuman in Film and Television

Babette Babich

> *That which doesn't kill you makes you stronger.*
> John Milius, *Conan the Barbarian* (1982)

If any philosopher is identified with posthumanism in film or television it would seemingly have to be Nietzsche, whose Zarathustra proclaimed the doctrine of the *Übermensch*, the overhuman, traditionally transmitted to the English dramatic world via George Bernard Shaw in his 1903 play in four acts, *Man and Superman* (rendered in 1982 for television and starring Peter O'Toole), and thus the association with Superman, the posthuman. Of course, and this too is not surprising, the association is a caricature and a dangerous one, embracing the various instaurations of transhumanism in the celebration of Nazi eugenics in Leni Riefenstahl's (1935) *Triumph des Willens*, to the variously padded and coifed versions of *Superman* in film and in a range of television series, including the teenage transhuman Clark Kent in television's *Smallville* (2001–2011).

Arguably the omnipresent nostalgia for empowering bodily enhancements may be traced to adolescence: the original inspiration for transhuman advantages transpiring spontaneously, aided, to be sure, by the Dionysian, in our era that is to say: sex, alcohol and lifestyle drugs. The adolescent ideal precludes, as Nietzsche points out, 'death, change, age, as well as procreation and growth', as 'objections to life' corresponding to the philosophical resentment of life (and of the body 'impudent enough to behave as if it actually existed!'), as this is also found in religious fantasies of salvation and the scientific versions of the same.

Post the similarly eugenics-driven biopunk science fantasy of the 1997 film *Gattaca*, directed by Andrew Niccol and starring Ethan Hawke and Uma Thurman, and post the 'add-mechanicals-and-stir', combo biomedical technology, with its celebration of scanning the body for illness – as if diagnostic technologies were simultaneously cures, à la *Star Trek* – in the 2013 Matt Damon vehicle starring a maleficent Jodie Foster, *Elysium*, the ideal of posthumanism can be at least loosely connected with the figure of Nietzsche (although transhumanism might better be connected to the 2007 *Transformers* film series based on the toys of the same name).

The tech geek documentary film (or infomercial) on Ray Kurzweil, *Transcendent Man* (2009), repeats the underestimation of the scientific, technological problems involved with Kurzweil's surprisingly literal filmic vision of the technological singularity. Thus the 1966 Raquel Welch film *Fantastic Voyage*,[1] down to the technical notion of sending small spaceships into the body, adumbrates Kurzweil's vision, updated as 'nanobots' sent to make 'repairs' on the body's failing systems.[2]

The point of Kurzweil's Singularity™ (in the culture industry it will never do to forget the ™ trademark) is its new age Hegelian and ergo non-Nietzschean dimension. The inattention to technological details, like Marxist materialism or Deepak Chopra-like automaticism, is no accident: the singularity to come will transpire through itself, like adolescence, all by itself.

If its original coinage in science fiction (SF) is part and parcel of this notion, it also corresponds to the Holy Grail (and the nightmare) of artificial intelligence (AI) in the Steven Spielberg film *A.I. Artificial Intelligence*, which plays on the old fairy-tale dream of an artefact that comes to life, here a late 20th-century robot longing to be human. The technological singularity, otherwise expressed, is *the* problem of robots-becoming-conscious for Stanislaw Lem, as indeed for Isaac Asimov. The desire is fraught, and known since Milton's *Paradise Lost*, where to rule (if not in heaven?), and the problem solved by the efficient Asimov was rule or code-driven (i.e., the so-called law of robotics).[3] Indeed, the San Diego computer scientist Vernor Vinge (via John von Neumann) can claim that he has predicted 'the end of the human era' (and we should add other names here as such claims are routine enough among pulp SF authors), but Kurzweil owns the trademark.

The technological singularity as depicted in film reflects the conflict between the human and the machine. Scholars note this alliance in the 1999 film *The Matrix*, starring Keanu Reeves, but it already appears in Ridley Scott's 1982 *Blade Runner*, which was itself a dark quotation rather than a remake of the 1956 (so-called 'B') horror film, the black-and-white SF *Invasion of the Body Snatchers*, directed by Don Siegel, itself duly remade in 1978 and directed by Philip Kaufman, starring Donald Sutherland as well as Jeff Goldblum and Leonard Nimoy. Stanley Kubrick's 1968 film, *2001: A Space Odyssey*, drew on one Cold War fantasy after another: international violence given iconic lip-service to be sure, but turning, as all SF films ultimately do, on the relationship between man and machine and towards a life lived on mechanical terms, including, in the case of *2001*, the iconic fantasy projection of an intractable and controlling computer unbrained, decognitivized by the expedient of unplugging it – a Turing machine running backwards. It is a short step, albeit without a Nietzsche or cryptographic connection, to the recent AI sex fantasy, directed by Spike Jonze, the 2013 *Her*.

As the plausibility of the Joaquin Phoenix phone-sex film, in which Scarlett Johansson gives her voice to a Siri-style computer operating system, thereby hugely improving Siri, suggests more in its easy realism than its unremarkably fantastic aspects, have our machines not *already* 'woken up'? What do we do these days that is not done mediatedly, via machines? The question belongs to every sorcerer's apprentice involved in a certain transfiguration (in the olden days involving roses and an ass and then in Goethe's cautionary fairy tale, a broom and a bucket) or an array of body parts in the old transhumanist projection of a body on a slab robbed from the grave, exposed to lightning and old technologies as dramatized in the film version – electricity being the life force of choice for the late 17th and early 18th century, for Mary Shelley in 1818, and lasting into the 20th century with the iconic 1931 version starring Boris Karloff. We may add, if we like, Mel Brooks' 1974 *Young Frankenstein,* or any of the several television instaurations. The question of how to control the work of our hands if we create life happens to correspond to the question of how to control our machines, our servants, if (and when) they 'become' conscious.

Thereby, we overlook the difficulty of making a decently functional prosthesis much beyond the technology for contact lenses. The same notion has been revised in the fashion of product updates, so that one may speak of Zarathustra 2.0 to match the sociological entrepreneur's *Humanity 2.0*.[4] Technologically stipulated in this way and with a clear reference to the marketing strategies of technological products at all levels, the posthuman is the human once again on the progressive way to the 'more than human'.

Thus, futurist utopian articles date back in the popular literature to the postwar enthusiasms of the 1950s and 1960s, then engendering less the technologies that 'eliminate aging' in Nick Bostrom's terms than serial television cartoons like *The Jetsons,* motion pictures like *Fantastic Voyage* and regular television programmes like *Lost in Space* and *Star Trek.*

A seemingly tailor-made SF tale in David Simpson's self-rendered (i.e., self-published) e-novel *Post-Human* (2009) speaks to us in the bad-future genre style that we know from films like *Blade Runner,* or *Mad Max* or the sequel *Road Warrior,* or indeed the original *RoboCop.* Simpson's *Post-Human* begins by depicting everyday life in the ultra-longevity lifestyle paradise created by nanotechnology, which the author, to show his harmless familiarity with this technology, speaks of as so many fairy beings called 'nans', a paradise which is then undone by nans, whereby in the predictable ('I hope the screenplay version gets made as a movie before this book disappears from Kindle radar' sense of predictable) course of events, the devastation is revealed to be the fault of the usual caricature evil-doer, only to end with a new world made by nans, in this case good ones.

Man and Superman: Parsing the Nietzschean *Übermensch*

For the popular mind, Nietzsche remains a stock character, his name alone fulfilling Nietzsche's ambition expressed at the conclusion of his extended array of aphorisms, 'Expeditions of an Untimely Man', confessing his 'ambition to say in ten sentences what everyone else says – what everyone else *does not say* in a book'. But there are liabilities, and Ricky Gervais' YouTube Hitler–Nietzsche gag awkwardly illustrates the shadow influence of Nietzsche on television and film, corresponding to his influence on popular culture overall – and, like much pop cultural influence, there is a good deal of free association and license.

Nietzsche, who famously insisted in his *Ecce Homo,* 'I will not be misunderstood!' would seem to have the market on being misunderstood. It doesn't hurt for film and television that Nietzsche, moustache and all, is one of the most physically identifiable thinkers we have. He is instantly recognizable in the 1972 Monty Python sketch, *The Philosopher's Football Match*, and Nietzsche's name alone admits of caricature as well, owing to his association with nihilism and dark, vaguely existentialist themes. Woody Allen, no slouch when it comes to negative vibes, foregrounds Nietzsche's nihilism in a key voiceover to one of his most autobiographical films, the 1986 *Hannah and Her Sisters*. Indeed, here the director takes the direct expedient or shortest doppelgänger route to transhumanism (transplanting brains into new bodies will be the next big thing) by casting himself as Michael Caine (much to Caine's own discomfiture, who recalls the awkward character of the substitution in a later interview), substituting the tall, blond and abundantly curly-haired actor for himself as Mia Farrow's husband in the film, sex scenes and all, and, as if that were not enough, having Caine play the philanderer to boot.

For, and this is a posthuman technique, why on earth not? At the time, Michael Caine was a mere two decades advanced and hence relatively fresh from his 1966 *Alfie* days (longevity matters when it comes to posthumanism), well before Caine's Alfred the Butler days of more recent *Batman* fame. Thus, one posthuman ideal dramatizes body doubles, not Patty Duke and her 'British' cousin (herself), but ideally improved and, by contrast with the time–date vulnerable replicants in *Blade Runner*, via the effectively deathless Schwarzenegger android, complete with operating system in the 1984 *Terminator* (and sequels/updates) or, less recognizably human, but more special-effects friendly, in James Cameron's *Avatar*.

Nietzsche's name suffices for most purposes, not only in quotes associated with military and masculinist and untrammelled or barbarian violence,[5] as in the case of the various versions of Robert E. Howard's *Conan the Barbarian*, including, in Milius' initial film version, the palimpsest for the eventual corruption or decadence of evil turning into itself in James Earl Jones' portrayal of the decadent oriental king Thulsa Doom on his way to the voice of Darth Vader in the 1977 *Star Wars*. Hence the wildly popular (and by definition there is only the 'wildly popular' in capitalist movies – or HBO-land: think of the short-lived *Carnivale*) HBO series *The Sopranos*, as this dramatized the emergence into puberty of the troubled young son of Tony Soprano by mentioning Nietzsche's name with a screenshot of the cover of *The Will to Power*. Nietzsche is a symbol of subversion. The illustrative device, showing a book cover on film, had already been used in a Woody Allen film, but the philosopher was Martin Heidegger and the book was Heidegger's *Introduction to Metaphysics*. The difference has everything to do with posthumanism.

By contrast with Heidegger, a mention of Nietzsche requires neither reading nor thinking. Indeed, the popular mind's tendency to favour a one-dimensional characterization of Nietzsche affects even scholars of his thought who write on Nietzsche and transhumanism.[6] It is no stretch to connect the 'transhuman' or the 'posthuman', understood not as Nietzsche's Zarathustra offered the image of the Overhuman as a parable and model and even a mockery of the human, all-too-human, desires of the crowd (echoes here of the contradictory notion of the 'genius' of the crowd mind for Nietzsche, who mocked the general run of humanity even in himself), but proclaimed as the coming or future superior human being. The ideal dates back to Plato's programme for selective breeding, today designated by way of some technical admixture of transgenics associated in the academic mind with the human genome project and which works so much better in practice in film or television fantasies, utopian or dystopian. Thus the 2014 season of the AMC series *The Walking Dead* features, as a plot teaser hints of a US government research project gone wrong in the form of a runaway bioweapon designed to take out large swathes of the 'enemy' population (though in today's day of rampant human overpopulation who would not qualify as the enemy?). The manufactured virus is more deadly than AIDS/Ebola in the nicely self-replicating, just a bite will do it, and all-too-literally posthumous (Nietzsche's word) power of the zombie.

Television's fondness for vampires à la *True Blood* goes so far as to feature a seemingly Nietzsche-style 'blond beast' in the blond-haired and personally superior style of the obviously named, for Aryan tastes, Erik Northman. The eponymous 'True Blood' itself referred to the technological advance of untrue blood, suited for the undead, a synthetic human blood that made it possible for the posthuman (qua dead) transhumans (qua vampires) to associate with the non-undead and all too human (never mind that Sookie, the most human of them all, was herself a fairy and hence her charms for vampires transcended more than a southern accent and a uniform of white T-shirts and short shorts).

A monotone view of strength oppressing weakness or indeed simple self-assertion or even self-aggrandisement would lead Ayn Rand to insist upon Nietzsche's influence in King Vidor's 1949 film version of her 1943 novel *The Fountainhead*, starring the quintessential actors Gary Cooper and Patricia Neal. Hence, and in this same respect, this genre of film could also be regarded under the rubric of the trans- or the posthuman in film. In the same vein, a certain finance industry Nietzscheanism rules the recent *The Wolf of Wall Street* along with *The Great Gatsby*, at least in versions starring Leonardo DiCaprio. The need to emphasize Leonardo DiCaprio is significant for sheer associative force. Arguably, even the film *Titanic* could be said to exemplify Nietzschean themes, American style, albeit more Horatio Alger meets Shakespeare's *Romeo and Juliet*: transhuman love being the essence of life affirmation, a key Nietzschean theme, here encountering another key Nietzschean theme in the indomitable will meeting the world will itself. Cameron's *Titanic* is all Schopenhauer, all Nietzschean marine monstrosity and visceral excess in the form of the iceberg and the cold dark of the night sea. The world of the frozen sea wins/loses at the same time. Speaking with television's Charlie Rose, Slavoj Žižek repeats his interpretation of *Titanic* in good Lacanian fashion as a misogynist's revenge on women, via deliberate misprision, claiming that Kate shoves Leo into the brink, deciphering the sinking of a frozen corpse not as a burial at sea but a deliberate letting go, pushing Leo away while claiming 'never' to let go. The scandal for Žižek is that the lady, wealthy and spoiled, has the temerity to save herself. That, and the fact that her lover has already sacrificed all his vitality. No Wagnerian love death here. For Žižek, Leo posthuman, already dead, is irrelevant (shades of Lacan's famous exchange with Luce Irigaray regarding Bernini's St Theresa: men see what they like). Women – this remains the key Freudian trope, French or otherwise – do not get a break.

Still, *Titanic* is replete with instances of Žižekian pushing, if not, contra Slavoj's insistence, on the bit of flotsam where Kate and dead Leo find themselves under the starry heavens of the real, revealed (this is the imaginary after all) as all too real. But shoving and overreaching desperation, as Nietzsche describes at an emigrant's seaport in *The Gay Science*, appears in Cameron's film in the details of the capitalist symbolic order (and this includes Žižek's homoerotic vitality), ordered by money and class, Brit style: counting from the first-class cabin down the levels of the ship and the doomed layers of the lower cabin classes.[7] Nietzsche's 'Thought of Death' matters because the Overhuman tells the truth of the 'posthuman' condition of our day. Nietzsche means this as he tells us, as a posthumous insight – 'be true to the earth' – almost in an Ash Wednesday voiceover: *remember man, that you are dust, and unto dust you shall return*. The locus mentioned in *The Gay Science* is the Port of Genoa, not unlike the port from which the original Titanic took its leave, as Nietzsche himself also departed from such a port for his voyage to Messina, about which scholars pretend to know everything, as revealing – this is the secret of *Zarathustra's Secret* – Nietzsche's fancied homosexuality and so on.

Associations with death are inevitable for Nietzsche, given the tragedy of his own death and the protracted end of his life, contra his idealization in *Thus Spoke Zarathustra* and the unmistakably named *Twilight of the Idols* of 'dying at the right time'. Nietzsche himself was not to have that same grace. Another motor of today's posthumanity, modern drugs or their late 19th-century versions, accompanied his life, directing its every expression for the last ten years, from psychopharmaceuticals, to nootropics, the entire chemical panoply of remedies, including physician-prescribed mercury, in the form of a skin salve for his genitalia, was at hand.

In the spirit of chemical enhancements, Nietzsche is the subject of at least one film on madness, not counting Liliana Cavani's surrealist 1977 *Al di là del bene e del male*: Pinchas Perry's 2007 *When Nietzsche Wept*, a perhaps calculatedly kitsch style film on Nietzsche and the inventors of psychoanalysis, setting Freud and Jung in *fin de siècle* Vienna and fancifully including Nietzsche. The 'fancy' works because Lou von Salomé was a collaborator of Freud's, an association augmented by the salacious, taking us back to all the Nietzschean secrets (Did he have sex with Lou? Did he not have sex with Lou? Was he gay? Or was he merely, as Wagner reports, an inveterate onanist?), the complexities of Nietzsche's supposed syphilis, the drama of his unluckiness at love, along with his inordinate enthusiasm for, and so his association with, Wagner, who supposedly dispatched Nietzsche on shopping trips to buy Wagner's underwear, silk underwear, to be ordered at certain stores, all to the embarrassment of the sensitive young professor.[8]

What is biography? And what is history? Complex questions indeed and Nietzsche's philosophical perspective can be difficult to untangle from such questions, not least because Nietzsche is also associated with Hitler, owing to an important visit Hitler paid to the Nietzsche Archives, a visit immortalized in a photograph showing Hitler in profile looking at a bust, full on, of the philosopher.

If almost no film or television documentary illustrates the story of the classicist Nietzsche's reflections on tragedy or music, much less his important reflections on the pitch or stress ictus as this aided his reconstruction of Greek prosody,[9] or his reflections on statues and antiquities and so on, the popular vision of the Nietzschean political strongman is viscerally dramatized in Bruno Ganz's proclamation of Nietzsche's name in his portrayal of Hitler in the 2004 German film *Downfall* – Oliver Hirschbiegel's *Der Untergang*. The association of Nietzsche with Hitler is about as strong a connection as it gets and it persists despite the fact that Nietzsche himself could never have taken part in the political movement known as National Socialism. Still, Nazi politics deliberately sought to adopt Nietzsche, and in the case of film his name remains, if only because, once again, of Riefenstahl's *Triumph of the Will*, a film that arguably continues to set the bar for commercial television and even sports programming to this day, and that echoes the title of Nietzsche's own *The Will to Power*, a book compiled from Nietzsche's notes by his sister.

Yet the Frankfurt School theorist, Max Horkheimer reminds us to put just this constellation in the context of the culture industry itself, including the contradictions of Western, Hollywood-style capitalism, reminding us that:

> *The consummate superman, against whom no one has warned more than Nietzsche himself, is a projection of the oppressed masses, King Kong rather than Cesare Borgia. The hypnotic spell that such counterfeit superman as Hitler have exercised derives not so much from what they think or say or do as from their antics, which set a style of behavior for men, who stripped of their spontaneity by the industrial processing, need to be told how to make friends and influence people.*[10]

To this extent, according to Horkheimer (and Adorno), the popular image of the Nietzschean 'superman' is a projective overcompensation serving mass culture. But if, as suggested with the reference to Zizek and Leo, Christian Bale's *Dark Knight Rising*, as the culmination of Christopher Nolan's Batman trilogy, spells out such an 'overcompensation' in a Zizekian schema – Imaginary-Symbolic-Real – the dead actor (life imitating art), that is Heath Ledger's Joker in the second of Nolan's Batman trilogy, *The Dark Knight*, brings a negative Nietzschean superman, like the Bizarro Superman. The distorted, dwarf, fool or clown, is played by Ledger with an uncanny combination of levity and grim gravity. The lightness matters in the dark and we cannot forget that Zarathustra's dwarf leaps constantly, whether springing over the tightrope walker at the start of *Thus Spoke Zarathustra* or else springing to Zarathustra's shoulder to weigh him down as he attempts his own ascent: dripping lead thoughts (like printed letters) into his brain.

Film fantasies on Nietzsche's eternal return and superman

Woody Allen's *Hannah and Her Sisters* features another kind of posthumanism, better than a replicant in *Blade Runner* or *Invasion of the Body-Snatchers* or the more literalized gaming avatar fantasy like a suit of clothes or an iPhone in the

2009 *Surrogates*, starring Bruce Willis, simply, as we have seen, by exploiting a Catfish-style, movie-star version, of the director. To be sure, the thought of eternal recurrence does not mean, as Allen's own morose voiceover here implies, that Woody (or anyone else) will be condemned to having to endure the *Ice Capades* (again and again). Nor, rather in the same way, is another film typically taken to illuminate the thought of eternal recurrence on target either, that is, the 1993 film directed by the late Harold Ramis, *Groundhog Day*, starring Bill Murray.[11]

Popular statements of the eternal return miss the central point of the thought for Nietzsche: eternal recurrence of the same entails that there would be no sense of repetition. One loses – this is what makes this thought of Nietzsche's most difficult – the new, even the iteratively new, and thereby one loses boredom *and* the future, and, of course, for the Nietzsche who taught the death of God, one loses any possibility of redemption.[12]

Yet film qua film, television qua television, exemplifies the Nietzschean idea of the eternal return of the self-same: What else is a rerun? To this extent, even the video artist Nam June Paik may be said to replicate Nietzschean ideas. Thematically, and more mainstream, the same idea is featured in Terry Gilliam's *12 Monkeys*. If the idea of eternal recurrence does not give us the transhuman per se, the imaginary ideal image of Nietzsche may stand behind any triumphant filmic vision, even *Lawrence of Arabia*, and if one takes that line one can either claim Nietzsche as the inspiration for *Apocalypse Now* (rather than, as is more technically or literally precise, Conrad's *Heart of Darkness*) or find him in a series of Westerns. The main character in the 1953 film *Shane*, for instance, can be seen as the Nietzschean ideal vision of the *Übermensch*, that is to say the ideal of the superman, as Nietzsche himself speaks of this as a combination of genius and saint. We see the extraordinary importance of the cleverness that characterizes a true hero who is always on top of any turn of event, ideally in advance or at least with a ready back-up plan B. This is Bale's Batman in *The Dark Knight Rises*, not only physically resourceful in the face of personal catastrophe after personal catastrophe, but expert in finance and coding as well.

Here we can recall the quote we began with, from *Conan the Barbarian*, although Schwarzenegger's hero is rather simple-minded. Steve Reeve in the masterful *Thief of Baghdad*, searching for a blue rose for his lady and looking to prove and transform himself before the Sultan, has resplendently higher human qualities: genial and honest (for a thief), clever and resourceful (because he is a thief) and possessed of the famous honour among thieves which gives him an advantage over palace intrigues and palace guards and the stock grand vizier. In the same way, we had cause to begin by invoking the eponymous Action Comics cartoon hero *Superman* in his various instaurations, including his physiologically transhuman splendour in the television series *Smallville*, which shows the close beauty and fragility of the young individual, the young beautiful soul, that is, once again: the teenager.

If the figure of Superman counts as Nietzsche's posthuman or overhuman, then the career of the television shows featuring Superman, particularly George Reeves' depiction in its television form, *Adventures of Superman* from 1951 to 1958, echoes Nietzsche's own emphasis on death and downgoing, here in the tragedy of the actor's suicide (or murder). This downgoing would be echoed with the paralyzing fall of Christopher Reeve, who depicted Superman in a series of films that were at the time heralded for a more realistic portrayal of flight. The number and versions of Superman on screen and as a character in a television series shows little sign of coming to an end, and we would still not be done if we did not neglect the Saturday morning and daytime children's characters.

Where the 2009 film comic book realization *Watchmen* featured an obviously transhuman naked blue giant, like the naked Schwarzenegger in the first *Terminator*, the 2012 film *Prometheus* (or, as the video trailer/prelude still available online indicates the title: *Prometheus Now*)[13] features the same thematic of transhuman superman, not dissimilar to Tony Stark (the name is almost eponymous) *Iron Man* plus sequels, which themselves draw on the anthropomorphically enhanced *RoboCop*, where the original (1987), far more than the 2014 *RoboCop* remake, is redemptive. But what makes all the difference is Iron Man's transhumanism embedded in, and thus, like his nuclear reactor heart, inseparable from the human, all too human.

The eternal return of the ideal of the superman retains its dark side. And if this dark side may be argued to connect Batman and Superman as well as the vampire (on the high side) and the zombie (on the low), there is still the dark political danger of the transhuman fantasy for profit and political advantage, a conflict illustrated not only for ever more in Riefenstahl's *Triumph of the Will* but in the space of the imaginary, as this always collides, as Žižek reminds us, with the Real: an ongoing collision illustrated by Simon Temple's 2009 film, *Übermensch* with its poster of a pensive young Superman, chest emblazoned with a swastika.

Notes

1. This reference to the 1966 film *Fantastic Voyage* is more than apt: the earlier instauration of Kurzweil's contributions on this theme is the health-oriented (and there is nothing wrong with being health-oriented) book he co-authored with a physician (Kurzweil & Grossman 2004).
2. I discuss this further, including additional references, in Babich (2013).
3. See for references, again: Babich (2013).
4. Again, references listed in Babich (2013).
5. For a discussion of this masculinist project in the Conan films, see David Smith (1996).
6. See Sorgner (2012), in addition to supporting contributions by Keith Ansell-Pearson and Paul S. Loeb and my own critical essay (Babich 2012).
7. British Air to this day counts up to four layers of class seating.
8. See Babich (2008).
9. See, for discussion and further references, the last chapters of Babich (2013a).
10. Max Horkheimer, *Eclipse of Reason* (London: Continuum 2004), 113.
11. I explain this further with specific reference to just these films in Babich (2014). Maurizio Ferraris adds *Mickey's Magical Christmas* (Ferraris 2013, 156).
12. See Babich (2013b).
13. http://www.projectprometheus.com/discover/.

Part II

Varieties of People-to-Come: Posthuman Becomings

7
Terminated: The Life and Death of the Cyborg in Film and Television

Rhys Owain Thomas

As an amalgam of the words 'cybernetic' and 'organism', the term 'cyborg' effectively evokes the figure's defining characteristic: the fusing of electronic, mechanical or robotic components with a living creature. Ever since the term was coined in 1960 by Manfred E. Clynes and Nathan S. Kline in an article in *Astronautics* magazine (Clynes & Kline 1960), the popularity of the cyborg has grown exponentially, and the figure quickly became synonymous with the science fiction (SF) genre. Cyborgs are created either through the (often brutal) insertion of machine components into a previously wholly organic entity, as in the case of the *Star Trek* franchise's horrific Borg,[1] or are designed from the outset as a synthesis of the organic and the artificial, such as Arnold Schwarzenegger's quintessential cyborg villain/hero in the *Terminator* movies. Technically, cyborgism is not limited to humans, but most examples found within film and television narratives involve the blending of (wo)man and machine.[2]

Regardless of specifics, the figure of the cyborg has enthralled film and television audiences, critics and academic theorists alike for over half a century, and this chapter provides a brief survey of this fascinating archetype as it has appeared in popular film and television. It begins with a general overview of the way in which the cyborg has been conceptualized as a particularly postmodern construct, before presenting an examination of the ways in which the figure has been used to embody various social, political and cultural concerns over the past 50 years. Margaret Lock notes that 'when claims about the epistemological neutral status of nature and its rigorous separation from society are challenged by the existence of...ambiguous, technologically created entities – neither alive nor dead, both dead and alive – moralizing runs wild' (Lock 2002, 41). Lock is referring to real-world 'patient-cadavers',[3] but her assertion also neatly summarizes the often complex responses engendered by the cyborg (both real and fictional). Lock's assertion stresses how, considered in light of the widespread belief in an individual's inherently holistic human identity, the insertion of 'artificial' technology into a 'natural' human body is an act of great personal significance, which often challenges established social norms. The blending of humans with machines produces contentious figures imbued with social, political, cultural and even religious meaning. Furthermore, as an essentially 'unnatural' entity, the cyborg can never simply 'be' – its very existence signals some *intent*, and its presence understandably invites the question of 'why?' What is the cyborg *for*? Therefore, the presence of a cyborg in a fictionalized narrative is, in itself, an invitation to question its inclusion, and what it represents.

As a literal embodiment of the blending of the technological and the organic, the cyborg has, unsurprisingly, often been understood as a conduit for the articulation of discourses regarding the impact of new technologies on established notions of self-identity and subjectivity. These anxieties focus especially on the telecommunications revolution of the late 20th century and its impact on fundamental conceptions of selfhood. Indeed, the fear of losing one's humanity is at the heart of cyborg narratives. As J. P. Telotte (1991, 1992, 1995, 1995a) has persuasively maintained, these narratives use the figure of the cyborg to explore our understanding of both the possibilities suggested by emergent technologies and the effect they have on notions of human identities and contemporary subjectivities. Furthermore, seemingly 'inherent' human attributes are questioned and are exposed as essentialist assumptions. The wide range of subjectivities exhibited by cyborg characters as diverse as Alex Murphy (Peter Weller/Joel Kinnaman) in *RoboCop* (Paul Verhoeven, 1987/José Padilha, 2014), Alex (Olivier Gruner) in *Nemesis* (Albert Pyun, 1992), Seven of Nine (Jeri Ryan) in *Star Trek: Voyager* (1995–2001), Doctor Octopus (Alfred Molina) in *Spider-Man 2* (Sam Raimi, 2004) and Kiera Cameron (Rachel Nichols) in *Continuum* (2012–) suggest that one can never be sure where the line dividing the 'natural' and the 'unnatural' lies, whether it even exists in any real sense, or whether there are, in its stead, a variety of different permutations and subject positions. This absence of a definite boundary, separating the natural from the unnatural, evokes the defining quality of postmodernity: a fragmentation of subjectivity to such an extent that the concept of subjectivity itself becomes unfeasible. When the natural/organic and the unnatural/inorganic become a single entity, the line demarcating the one from the other becomes arbitrary, even illusionary.

Despite the blending of separate organic and technological constituents, the cyborg is not simply a copy of an 'original'. Unlike the android duplicate, another artificial humanoid figure which recurs in SF and with which the cyborg is often mistaken, the cyborg is not simply a derivative of another. It has no referent and is not a simulation. It is, in Jean Baudrillard's terms, a simulacrum. Indeed, Baudrillard's definition of the simulacrum almost reads as an account of cyborg representation:

> *The real is produced from miniaturised units, from matrices, memory banks and command models – and with these it can be reproduced an indefinite number of times. It no longer has to be rational, since it is no longer measured against some ideal or negative instance. It is nothing more than operational. In fact, since it is no longer enveloped by an imaginary, it is no longer real at all. It is hyperreal, the product of an irradiating synthesis of combinatory models in a hyperspace without atmosphere.*
>
> (Baudrillard 1983, 3)

The cyborg is SF's most formidable herald of hyperreality, and the scene in *Terminator: Salvation* (McG, 2009) wherein the eponymous killing machines mass-produce even more Terminators on a factory assembly line is simply Baudrillard's portentous theory made flesh (and metal).

The cyborgs of SF film and television narratives have, predominantly, been figures of abject horror, their hybridized nature and 'disturbed' corporeality the contemporary equivalent of Dr Frankenstein's monster. The robot, the favoured synthetic humanoid of the modern era, traditionally portrayed as a useful machine, created in order to assist humanity (at least, initially), was quite evidently portrayed as an 'other' and posed no threat to the integrity of the human body. The cyborg, meanwhile, its postmodern equivalent, represents the fear of corporeal corruption, an intrusive infiltration by technology, perverting the perceived harmonious and synergetic relationship between mind and body. As Janice Hocker Rushing and Thomas S. Frentz have noted, 'the mind/body dichotomy of modernism gives way to the postmodern trichotomy of mind/body/machine, and the mind and body, once fighting a Cartesian battle for preeminence, are now both vulnerable to annexation by technology' (Rushing & Frentz 1995, 14).

More recent academic engagement with the cyborg has attempted to reverse the tendency to portray the cyborg in purely negative terms, exploring how such a being could enable a shift away from unfavourable modes of classifying social, political or cultural groups. Most notably, Donna J. Haraway has argued that cyborgism should be celebrated as a means of circumventing traditional methods of designating personal identity based on outmoded notions of gender, the fragmentation inherent to the cyborg allowing an alternative to the regressive and repressive male/female binary. Haraway asserts that:

> *Cyborg imagery can suggest a way out of the maze of dualisms in which we have explained our bodies and our tools to ourselves ... It is an imagination of a feminist speaking in tongues to strike fear into the circuits of the supersavers of the new right. It means both building and destroying machines, identities, categories, relationships, space stories. Though both are bound in the spiral dance, I would rather be a cyborg than a goddess.*
>
> (Haraway 1991, 181)

Surveying the landscape of film and television SF of the last 50 years, it becomes apparent that representations of the cyborg have tended towards the negative associations of technological anxieties more than they have to Haraway's idealistic figurations. However, the cyborg is not an ahistoric creature, and its portrayal has reflected changes in social attitudes regarding technology, personal identity, social subjectivities and the shifting relationship between all three throughout the decades. This is evident from two of the most popular SF television programmes of the 1970s, which also featured two of the earliest, most positive and most enduring portrayals of cyborgism – *The Six Million Dollar Man* (1974–1978) and its spinoff, *The Bionic Woman* (1976–1978). *The Six Million Dollar Man* was based on the 1972 novel *Cyborg* by Martin Caidin, whilst *The Bionic Woman* was, to all intents and purposes, a remake of the parent programme, with the protagonists of both shows, Steve Austin (Lee Majors) and Jaime Sommers (Lindsay Wagner), undergoing cybernetic enhancement after being involved in an accident, and ending up working as agents for the same secret American government agency, the Office of Scientific Intelligence (OSI). These may not have been the earliest depictions of the cyborg but they have, arguably, become two of the most recognizable.[4] This is, in part, due to their being indelibly linked with the era in which they first appeared – the mid-1970s being a flashpoint for several radical social and cultural forces in the United States. Most notably, these included second-wave feminism and a growing popular technophilia fuelled by unparalleled advances in technoscience. With their remarkable physical and technological prowess, Steve Austin, an astronaut, and Jaime Sommers can be read as physical embodiments of an attempt to deflect fears of the United States trailing behind Russia in scientific matters in general (and, despite their earlier success in putting the first man on the moon, the 'Space Race' in particular). They also represent contemporary optimism regarding the essentially beneficial and life-enriching nature of emergent technologies. Explaining the initial conceptualizing of the character of Steve Austin, the producer (and occasional writer/director) of both programmes, Harve Bennett, noted how he 'took this fascinating character, a cowboy with a bionic capability, and said, "How would he be? What will he do? How can he help us?"' (Gross 2011, 114). It is apparent that, for Bennett at least, the technological possibilities represented by emergent cyborg identities were not just positive, they were needed. Given the socio-political climate at that time, perhaps this is unsurprising. Austin and Jamie projected a healthy, wholesome and potent image of the United States, in direct opposition to the corruption and disappointment associated with the scandal and embarrassment of Watergate and the Vietnam War.

Despite the initial disgust felt towards the bionic implants by their protagonists, by emphasizing the beneficial effects of bionics both programmes attempted to promote an optimistic outlook of human enhancement. Indeed, Steve and Jaime's life-saving bionic surgery proposes the possibility that technology may even facilitate a means of evading death itself. In this manner, the narratives of *The Six Million Dollar Man* and *The Bionic Woman* attempt to constrain potentially disquieting discourses around life/death liminality, whilst promoting positive discourses regarding the relationship between technology and humanity. However, both programmes also suggest the existence of the more recognizable negative discourse between technology, the human body and personal subjectivity, often signalling the existence of a rather more complex and negative relationship between these concepts that lies just outside the confines of the narrative. As Tricia Jenkins notes:

> In an impassioned speech to a senator, Jaime explains that since receiving her bionic implants, she has continually feared the loss of her humanity, but the senator's attempts to lock her in a human zoo suggests that politicians operating out of fears

about national security run an even greater risk of losing their humanity as they jeopardize the civil liberties of others.
(Jenkins 2011, 101)

The complex relationship between cyborgian subjectivities and human identities was very much a part of the cyborg movie cycle of the 1980s, which included *RoboCop*, *Cyborg* (Albert Pyun, 1989), *Hardware* (Richard Stanley, 1990), *RoboCop 2* (Irvin Kershner, 1990), *Terminator 2: Judgment Day* (James Cameron, 1991), *Nemesis*, *Universal Soldier* (Roland Emmerich, 1992) and *RoboCop 3* (Fred Dekker, 1993). All these movies, to lesser or greater extents, were meditations on the ethics of using technology to 'enhance' the human race. Despite the perceived benefits of cyborgism, the effects of such enhancements on the recipients' identities were problematic, often cruel and sometimes devastating. The films themselves articulated conflicting viewpoints on the benefits/disadvantages of being a cyborg as well as *how* cyborgism impacts on personal subjectivity. As Samantha Holland has noted:

Clearly, the 'mind-body problem' is a central issue in the cyborg film, whose narrative tends to reassert an essentially mental, Cartesian 'self' over any materialist conception of selfhood. And while various devices operate to align the audience with the Cartesian rather than materialist position, the centrality of the body in these films tends to undermine the narrative emphasis on the disembodied 'self,' rendering the films' own position riddled with ambiguity and uncertainty.
(Holland, 'Descartes Goes to Hollywood', in Johnston 2001, 27)

Meanwhile, despite the success of *The Six Million Dollar Man* and *The Bionic Woman*, cyborg characters on television were few and far between in the years following the simultaneous cancellation of both programmes in 1978. It wasn't until the introduction of the Borg in the 1989 *Star Trek: The Next Generation* episode 'Q Who' (2.16) that cyborgs became a perceptible presence on television once more. The Borg quickly became iconic adversaries in the *Star Trek* universe, and their success not only helped to cement the popularity of the revived *Star Trek* at a time when it looked as though it was destined to remain in the shadow of its far more feted forbearer but turned the Borg into the most high-profile and recognizable examples of the cyborg in any media since the original *Terminator* movie in 1984. As their name suggests, the Borg are a race of cyborgs, consisting of unwillingly 'upgraded' individuals from various organic species, technologically enhanced, and intent on 'assimilating' all other species whose biological and technological distinctiveness they consider worth adding to their own Collective. All traces of individuality are erased and subsumed within a central 'hive' mind, which is administered/regimented by a single individual, the Borg Queen (Alice Krige/Susanna Thompson), who directs the 'drones' in a way that most effectively guarantees the Borg's objectives. Coolly effective and unemotionally single-minded, they are mostly portrayed as an unstoppable 'force' (singular) of nature, rather than a collection of individual combatants. The Borg are representative of the archetypal cyborg figure in that they encapsulate the ambivalent relationship between human and machine – a fear of the erosion or loss of our essential humanity, versus the desirability of a life of physical and mental perfection. Although the Borg's cadaverous pallor and zombie-like behaviour might suggest an emphasis on the former at the expense of the latter, the addition of a beautiful, blonde and statuesque Borg named Seven of Nine to the cast of *Star Trek Voyager*, part-way through the series' run, complicates matters somewhat. The fact that 'Seven' proves to be an invaluable member of the crew due, in part, to her past experiences with the Collective, indicates how technological enhancement can be beneficial. As Justin Everett has noted, as well as having their origins in the cyberpunk movement of the early 1980s, the emergence of the Borg is representative of a similar rise in academic, medical and social discourses regarding posthumanism. Furthermore:

> *Recent advances in cybernetics – in particular the introduction of artificial limbs that respond to nerve impulses and are approaching the full functionality of their biological counterparts ... testify that we have begun to proceed in this direction.*
>
> (Browning & Picart 2009, 80)

It cannot be denied, however, that cyborg narratives are rarely (if ever) wholly positive in their treatment of looming posthumanism, and the human/machine dichotomy mostly creates a narrative 'tension' which is used to explore the ramifications of the melding of human and machine.

Drawing upon Baudrillard's theories of 'overexposure' in the postmodern world, Telotte argues that cyborgs embody fears of the loss of those qualities that distinguish us from machines through their 'obscene' visibility. By foregrounding the cyborg body, these narratives accentuate what is lost – a sense of self. Ethereal human subjectivity is obfuscated or even obliterated by the overwhelming physicality of the cyborg. As Telotte states:

> *[Cyborgs] reflect not only the hopes and fears that cluster around the expanding role of robotics and artificial intelligence in our culture but also a growing awareness of our own level of artifice, of constructedness, of how we often seem controlled by a kind of internalized program not so different from the sort that drives the artificial beings that abound in our films – and, perhaps, of how the films that detail these anxieties assist in our construction.*
>
> (Telotte 1991, 14)

Moreover, despite Donna Haraway's contention that cyborgs represent an opportunity to formulate subject positions that move beyond the confines of traditional notions of gender, the work of countless other theorists have indicated a predominance of unmistakably gendered cyborgs in 1980s and 1990s American SF film and television (cf. Tasker 1993; Jeffords 1994; Larson 1997; Carrasco 2008). These include the hypermasculine warrior, such as the titular protagonists of the *RoboCop* and *Terminator* franchises, or the idealized paternal protector such as the Model

101 Series 800 (Arnold Schwarzenegger) in *Terminator 2: Judgment Day* and 'Bishop' (Lance Henriksen) in *Aliens* (James Cameron, 1986) and *Alien*[3] (David Fincher, 1992). Female cyborgs, meanwhile, such as the T-X (Kristanna Loken) in *Terminator 3: Rise of the Machines* and the Borg Queen, are often portrayed as sexually alluring yet monstrous. This gendering of cyborg characters has been understood as an attempt to address (and often redress) the socio-political anxieties of the time. For example, the aggressively 'muscular' foreign policy of the Reagan administration found its cinematic counterpart in the hulking macho cyborgs of the 1980s, whilst the socially responsible, environmentally aware 'new man' of the 1990s found expression in nurturing and benevolent technologically enhanced (pseudo-)father figures, whilst the stridently independent, über-confident 'modern' woman was demonized as a twisted, domineering and unnatural automaton. All these readings were filtered through the technological nature of the cyborg characters. It is what set them apart from the other characters, making them distinct and, therefore, suitable as thematic signifiers.

Although the cyborg has proven to be an enduring figure in SF film and television, there are indications that its effectiveness as a marker of contemporary subjectivity may be diminishing. The lukewarm critical and commercial reception afforded recent attempts to revive interest in the cyborg (such as the high-profile but short-lived television programme *Almost Human* (2013–2014), the *Bionic Woman* reboot (2007) and the new *RoboCop* remake) may be indicative of a growing weariness with this once exciting but increasingly archaic figure. Advances in medical sciences have resulted in the proliferation of real-world cyborgism, with surgeries to replace organic human components with artificial counterparts becoming increasingly routine. Artificial limbs, cochlear implants and heart and brain pacemakers have become commonplace, whilst further advances mean everyday communications technologies are transitioning from wearable accessories to physical implants (cf. Carroll 2014). Cyborgism, it seems, is no longer deemed remarkable enough in itself to warrant being either the focus of a text (*RoboCop*, *Almost Human*) or the USP of a central character (*Bionic Woman*). When narratives featuring cyborg characters *do* succeed, their cyborg nature is incidental or unremarked upon. For example, *Continuum*'s Kiera Cameron is a technologically enhanced law enhancement officer from the future who becomes trapped in the present after inadvertently being transported back in time with a group of terrorists who plan on changing history. As the title suggests, the programme focuses upon the complexities of time travel and the difficulties inherent in maintaining an established timeline with little knowledge of when intervention is necessary and when it should be avoided. Kiera uses her implants in order to help her in her mission to track down the terrorists and aid the present-day police, but her cyborgism never becomes an issue, let alone a facet upon which any kind of social, political or cultural discourse may be mapped.

SF is, by most definitions, a genre that works through allegory. Whether defined as a genre of cognitive estrangements (Suvin 1979), fabulations (Scholes 1967) or Marxist Utopias (Jameson 2005), it thrives on social, political and cultural commentary. To this end, the relative demise of the cyborg as a cypher for this particular purpose suggests that this role remains but has been adopted by other SF archetypes. It would seem that the cyborg's function has been appropriated by less archaic liminal constructs, such as clones (as in *The Island* (Michael Bay, 2005), *Never Let Me Go* (Mark Romanek, 2010) and *Orphan Black* (2013–)), sentient Artificial Intelligences (AIs) (such as those in *Battlestar Galactica* (2003–2009) and *Her* (Spike Jonze, 2013) and virtual avatars (as in *Avatar* (James Cameron, 2009) and *Caprica* (2010)). Whereas sentient AIs and virtual avatars have been a more recent trend, during the late 1990s there was an increased general awareness of cloning and genetic engineering, and this concept appears to have hijacked the collective public imagination previously centred upon cyborgs, seemingly rendering technologically enhanced figures as obsolete and archaic in comparison.[5] Clones and genetically engineered individuals often share many of the cyborg's distinguishing features, such as super-strength, heightened physical senses and/or amplified intelligence, and are, therefore, easy substitutions. As clones are, ordinarily, indistinguishable from human beings (indeed, that's the whole point), they are also considerably easier to realize in terms of budgetary considerations than cyborgs.

Whereas the emergent technologies of the late 20th century signalled the imminent advent of changes to personal subjectivities and interpersonal relationships in an understandably abstract manner (because of their very newness), those changes have now become commonplace and routine. Indeed, the rate of change may even be increasing, but change is the new normalcy. Advances in technologies that are destined to cause substantial shifts in how humans relate to each other, the environment and themselves are even timetabled. The othering of technology has increasingly become a ludicrous concept and, as technological accessories, appendages and applications have become inseparable from the bodies to which they have become integral, the 'tremulous public body' (Telotte 1991, 14) of the cyborg becomes redundant as a marker of social, political and cultural anxieties. As social discomfort with the integration of the body and technology has abated, and corporeality itself increasingly regarded as obsolete and discarded in favour of virtual identities and online existences, the perceived threat to the notion of coherent personal identities has largely been reimagined and, in place of the cyborg, there now exists a range of differently liminal characters such as the aforementioned clones, sentient AIs, time-displaced humans and virtual avatars.

Notes

1. Such was the success of the Borg's appearances in *Star Trek: The Next Generation* (1987–1994) that they returned to menace the crew of the *Enterprise* in the theatrical feature *Star Trek: First Contact* (Jonathan Frakes, 1996), as well as those of the titular starships in both sequel series *Star Trek: Voyager* (1995–2001) and prequel series *Enterprise* (2001–2005).
2. A notable exemption exists in the *Doctor Who* (1963–1989) story 'The Talons of Weng-Chiang' (14.21–14.26) wherein the villainous Mr Sin is a cyborg with one organic element – the cerebral cortex of a pig.
3. Patients who are kept alive through biomedical technologies such as artificial ventilators.
4. *Doctor Who*'s Daleks and Cybermen had already made their debuts in 1963 and 1966, respectively. The Cybermen's cyborgian status is evident from their first appearance when

they explain their origins as purely organic humanoids who have been gradually replacing their organic parts with robotic implants and appendages (4.5–4.8, 'The Tenth Planet' Parts 1–4). The Daleks, despite their outwardly robotic appearance are also cyborgs, the outer metal shell housing a hideously deformed organism within. Meanwhile, contemporaneous cinematic representations included the eponymous James Bond villain (Joseph Wiseman) in *Dr. No* (Terence Young, 1962) and the ill-fated Jerry Spenser (Ross Martin) in *The Colossus of New York* (Eugène Lourié, 1958). The latter is notable for featuring a cyborg anti-hero before the term 'cyborg' had even been coined.

5. The birth of 'Dolly', the world's first successfully cloned mammal, at the University of Edinburgh in 1996, made front-page headlines all over the world and escalated the pre-existing discourse around the possibilities, dangers and ethical considerations of genetic engineering – particularly in relation to human identity.

8
Of Iron Men and Green Monsters: Superheroes and Posthumanism

Dan Hassler-Forest

We live in an age of cyborgs. The streets, trains, cars around us are populated by strange creatures whose intense engagement with technology is both reassuringly familiar and vaguely alarming: familiar, because most of us have come to feel like cyborgs ourselves, having come to rely on mobile technology for nearly every aspect of our lives, spending most if not all our waking hours 'plugged in' to an infinite network; and alarming, because this reliance brings with it not only new kinds of connections, but also what seems like a new experience of time, space and alienation. But in many ways, our reliance on wireless data transfer, smartphones, tablets and other consumer gadgets are only the tip of the iceberg, as developments in medicine, genetically modified organisms (GMOs), prosthetics, and quantum mechanics continuously destabilize our traditional anthropocentric worldview informed by liberal humanist values.

Our ambivalence about this world of constant transformations finds expression in fantasies and anxieties that are specific to this posthuman condition. On the one hand, we find reassurance in the oft-reproduced popular fantasy that this development merely represents the next step in human progress, and that humanity's mastery of technology will ultimately help us overcome our limitations. On the other hand, the technological maelstrom that envelops us has also made many question the assumptions that underlie such fundamental Enlightenment-era concepts as 'progress', 'identity', and the many binary distinctions that have been fundamental to Western philosophy. From the latter perspective, the posthuman condition challenges many traditional conceptions of the human-centric worldview:

> *Posthuman bodies are not slaves to masterdiscourses [sic] but emerge at nodes where bodies, bodies of discourse, and discourses of bodies intersect to foreclose any easy distinction between actor and stage, between sender/receiver, channel, code, message, context.*
>
> (Halberstam & Livingston 1995, 2)

Few figures in contemporary popular culture embody this tension more clearly than that of the superhero. After decades of existence in the margins of mainstream culture, being associated primarily with comic books and popular youth culture (see Wright 2003), the superhero has more recently become the organizing principle of Hollywood's most sustained cycle of blockbuster films, proliferating across numerous media and achieving both commercial and critical success. There are many different reasons for the superhero's 21st-century re-emergence as a mainstream phenomenon, including the advent of digital cinema (see Manovich 1995), the growing influence of fan culture (see Brooker 2002), media convergence (see Jenkins 2006) and the rise of the global entertainment conglomerate (see Johnson 2013). But among the variety of styles, figures, and brands that make up the genre's rich history, the most notable thematic thread that connects even the most diverse superhero figures is the concept of the posthuman. From the first issue of *Action Comics* in 1938, to the blockbuster success of *Guardians of the Galaxy* (dir. James Gunn, 2014), the superhero genre has foregrounded the human body and the desire to overcome its physical limitations.

In this chapter, I will discuss the relationship between the contemporary superhero figure and the posthuman condition, seeking to explore in what ways posthuman ideas find expression in the most popular and widely accessible incarnation of the superhero trope: the 21st-century superhero movie genre. Ranging from Marvel's development of an entire 'Cinematic Universe' to subversive parodies like *Kick-Ass* (dir. Matthew Vaughn, 2010) and *Super* (dir. James Gunn, 2011), the superhero has been a remarkably consistent presence in global convergence culture. The figure continues to appear across all popular media, but is still largely propelled by the Hollywood franchises that fully established themselves from the popular phenomenon of *Spider-Man* (dir. Sam Raimi, 2002) onwards.[1]

I will argue that the tendency within superhero films has been to engage with posthuman questions and concepts in ways that attempt to contain their radical potential within a more traditional humanist framework. One of the effects is that this simultaneously delimits the more subversive and politically critical aspects of posthuman theory. Therefore, even though these films offer tantalizing representations of posthuman bodies that are frequently ambiguous, both the narratives and the aesthetic choices tend to create a binary system that places them firmly within a hierarchy that explicitly favours traditional humanist values. As this chapter will demonstrate, this most typically occurs by separating out two different strands of posthumanism, one of which is subsequently coded as 'benevolent/natural/empowering', while the other is shown to be 'malevolent/artificial/corrupting'. The resulting dichotomy gives viewers the opportunity to engage with cultural, social and political questions that are central to our posthuman condition, though usually in ways that strongly diminish their critical potential.

But even though this tendency seems to dominate most strands of mainstream popular superhero narratives, the conceptual potential of the posthuman remains, in a certain sense, and will find expression in the most unlikely places. In the second part of this chapter, I will look at Ang Lee's *Hulk* (2003) as the rare counter-example of a superhero film that explores the posthuman condition without simultaneously rendering it toothless. In this instance, the posthuman is also post-genre, post-narrative and what Steven Shaviro has described as 'post-cinema'.

The posthuman condition

Within the rapidly expanding field of posthuman theory, I draw, for the purposes of this chapter, on Robert Pepperell's influential critical perspective on the term. In his book *The Posthuman Condition* (2003), Pepperell emphasizes the need to move beyond the traditional assumptions of the liberal humanist intellectual and philosophical tradition. In his introduction, Pepperell lists posthuman technologies such as robotics, communications, prosthetics, and genetic manipulation as categories that play important roles in the destabilized relationship between the artificial and the real that makes up our high-tech posthuman age. The following passage sums up his approach:

> *What is meant by the 'posthuman condition'? First, it is not about the 'End of Man' but about the end of a 'man-centred' universe or, put less phallocentrically, a 'human-centred' universe. In other words, it is about the end of 'humanism', that long-held belief in the infallibility of human power and the arrogant belief in our superiority and uniqueness.*
>
> (2003, 20)

Echoing several key elements of the poststructuralist movement, the posthuman condition requires an acceptance of the idea that 'human beings do not exist in the sense in which we ordinarily think of them, that is as separate entities in perpetual antagonism with a nature that is external to them' (Pepperell 2003, 22). Instead, a radical redefinition of boundaries is necessary, relating not only to the distinction between human and non-human, but, by implication, also between subject and object, male and female and so forth. He is joined by many others in proclaiming this shift not only necessary, but long overdue:

> *We have rehearsed the claim that the posthuman condition is upon us and that lingering nostalgia for a modernist or humanist philosophy of self and other, alien and human, normal and queer is merely the echo of a discursive battle that has already taken place.*
>
> (Halberstam & Livingston 1995, 19)

Embracing the posthuman condition, therefore, is not so much about the end of humankind as it is about the end of a fundamental belief in humanism. Instead, posthumanist thinking offers a way forward, imagining the human body not as male or female, straight or queer, white or black, but as a site of constant negotiation. In this sense, the posthumanist framework has utopian implications that open up a horizon for thinking outside the restrictive categories of capitalist biopolitics. Donna Haraway's description of the cyborg as 'a hybrid of organism and technology' offers a clear example of the political implications of posthumanism (2000, 50), even if the cyborg figure itself remains an ambiguous and continuously contested figure (Mason 1995, 227).

The contradictions, anxieties, and fantasies that inform these shifts are central to the contemporary superhero movie genre, which offers the opportunity to explore this shifting posthuman world through figures that challenge our definitions of human agency and identity. Given this seemingly limitless potential for the genre, it is perhaps surprising that superhero movies as a rule have demonstrated such conservatism in relation to the posthuman condition. In order to identify more clearly the relationship between superhero figures and their abilities, I offer the following general typology of posthuman superhero bodies:[2]

1. 'Gods': bodies born with 'natural' superhuman abilities (e.g., Superman, Thor, Wonder Woman, Hellboy).
2. 'Mutants': bodies that have gained superhuman abilities by 'natural' genetic mutation (e.g., Mystique, Jean Grey, Professor Xavier, Storm, the Incredibles, Peter Petrelli, Hiro Nakamura, Nathan Petrelli).
3. 'Transformers': bodies that have gained superhuman abilities by some form of technological intervention (e.g., the Incredible Hulk, Spider-Man, Kick-Ass, Captain America, the Fantastic Four, Daredevil).
4. 'Cyborgs': bodies that become superhuman by their use of technology (e.g., Iron Man, the Green Arrow, Hawkeye, Batman, Star-Lord).
5. 'Robots': completely artificial bodies (e.g., Warlock, Ultron, The Vision, Red Tornado, Metal Men, the Sentinels, the Iron Giant).

Obviously, superheroes in the first two categories fall more generally into the traditional realm of fantasy, where the genre conventions allow for characters with abilities that are more 'magical' than 'scientific' (see Reynolds 1992). And while these abilities can often be interpreted as organic manifestations of technological abilities, they are, in practice, most commonly employed as allegorical representations of social, ethnic, and sexual difference, allowing the writers to 'explore themes involving racial tension as well as the more traditional complexities of vigilantism' (Locke 2005, 34). Superheroes in the third and fourth categories, on the other hand, relate more directly to posthumanism's interest in the contradictory relationship between technology and the human body that is the central focus of this chapter. (The fifth 'Robots' category, featuring a small but provocative collection of completely artificial bodies that have developed some degree of consciousness, falls beyond the scope of this chapter.)

The categories of Transformers and Cyborgs are completely preoccupied with the relationship between human bodies and the many forms of modern technology that are potentially destabilizing to the human body and its assumed integrity or organic wholeness. As forms of popular fantasy aimed primarily at the widest possible audience, the 21st-century superhero film genre can be interpreted as a site that produces subjectivities that negotiate our posthuman world. Characters like Wolverine, Batman, Spider-Man and Iron Man thus become ideologically loaded role models that incorporate posthuman concepts into a larger humanist framework of unambiguous gender roles and patriarchal power.

A superficial reading of some of the most popular superhero films of the past decade confirms this impression of conservative identity politics that embrace technology only as an instrumental extension of an uncontested human-centred worldview. The narrative dynamic most frequently employed involves three narrative stages that have been repeated many times over: (1) the superhero develops his powers, honing his newfound skills in isolation and developing appropriate customized tools and materials; (2) the superhero is challenged by an adversary with similar skills, who either cannot or will not fully control these abilities; and (3) the conflict results in a climactic battle in which the superhero conclusively demonstrates his superiority.

The 2002 version of *Spider-Man* is a paradigmatic example: the timid and insecure teenager Peter Parker is accidentally bitten by a genetically modified spider bred in a high-tech laboratory, after which his body develops overnight the ability to emit web-like fluid, cling to walls and ceilings and sense impending danger. His antagonist Norman Osborn, on the other hand, consciously modifies his own body by exposing himself to a performance-enhancing chemical, which gives him similar physical abilities (increased strength, stamina, and speed), but which has side effects that render him mentally 'unstable', after which he adopts the Green Goblin persona and wreaks havoc on everyone against whom he holds a grudge. Both Spider-Man and the Green Goblin have technologically enhanced posthuman bodies, but the differences between them establish crucial distinctions that clearly privilege one form over another.

Most crucially, the superhero's altered body is presented as relatively unified and stable, even after his transformation causes him to develop two separate identities. This anxiety about the destabilizing effects of the posthuman condition is expressed in the scene in *Spider-Man* where Norman Osborn engages in a schizophrenic dialogue with his own mirror image, actor Willem Dafoe playing the scene as two hostile and radically different personalities. The superhero's hybrid identity is clearly privileged above that of the supervillain, as he is able to integrate his multiple identities into a single ordered and relatively coherent. The difference between their two hybrid identities is therefore presented in ways that reaffirm the traditional humanist perspective that sees 'order' and 'disorder' as 'mutually exclusive opposites', which 'perpetuate the split between "external" reality and human perception' (Pepperell 2003, 56).

Iron men: Transhumanism and masculinity

The key contrast between superheroes and the villains they must vanquish therefore lies in the difference between characters who successfully build coherently 'ordered' masculine identities on the basis of hybrid bodies, on the one hand, and characters whose 'disordered' fluidity results in chaos and destruction, on the other. This distinction articulates an ideologically loaded representational hierarchy that relates back to the difference between transhumanism and critical posthumanism.

Unlike posthumanism, the framework of transhumanism does not attempt to move beyond the basic assumptions of liberal humanism and its human-centric ontology. Transhumanism is not concerned with questioning the core values and systemic dichotomies of humanist philosophy, constructing instead a techno-utopian future in which 'humans and technologies merge into a new entity, which is sometimes even considered to be the successor of *Homo sapiens*' (Verbeek 2008, 391). The transhumanist perspective in this sense allows for the hybridization of human organisms and technology, without, at the same time, upsetting traditional binary distinctions, most notably gender difference. As others have argued, even the most hypermasculine cyborgs of late 20th-century Hollywood were made up of remarkable contradictions and gender transformations, the Terminator's masculinity, for instance, being 'produced and reproduced through the tensions and interplay between "leathersexual" images reminiscent of gay porn and the taken-for-granted "(hetero)sexual allure" of Schwarzenegger's physique' (Mason 1995, 229).

While 21st-century big-screen superheroes such as Batman, Captain America, Spider-Man and Iron Man are also made contradictory by the constant negotiation of their dual identities, they are a good deal less ambiguous in their much more emphatic heteronormativity. Their successful incorporation of technological enhancements and modifications therefore points more directly towards the transhumanist perspective, which allows for new hybrid organic-technological identities to emerge without the simultaneous redefinition of traditional humanist categories. Their adversaries, meanwhile, often embody the anxiety as well as the fascination related to the 'terrifyingly fluid' subjectivities associated with critical posthumanism.

The best example of this interplay between trans- and posthumanism in superhero films can be found in Iron Man, a character who has been featured in five consecutive superhero blockbusters: *Iron Man* (Jon Favreau, 2008), *Iron Man 2* (Jon Favreau, 2010), *Marvel's The Avengers* (Joss Whedon, 2012), and *Iron Man 3* (Shane Black, 2013), and Avengers: Age of Ultron (Joss Whedon, 2015). The first film in this series was instrumental in establishing the studio's ongoing Cinematic Universe, establishing not only the general tone and visual style of Marvel's many subsequent superhero films, but also crucially mapping out the franchise's transhumanist perspective, with 'Stark's keen technological mind represent[ing] the secret of American vitality' (Ackerman 2008, n.p.).

The first film introduces the character of Tony Stark, a wealthy, arrogant and politically naïve arms dealer, who is captured and imprisoned while visiting Afghanistan. Stark was wounded by shrapnel during the attack, and is only able to survive the shell shards that have entered his blood stream by an electromagnet his fellow prisoner places inside his chest. Already a cyborg due to the incorporation of a technological device inside his body, Stark organizes his escape by constructing elaborate body armour for himself with the equipment intended by his captors for the building of a bomb. Once his robotic exoskeleton secures his freedom, he subsequently builds more sophisticated versions of his electromagnet as well as his body armour, dedicating himself from then on to fighting injustice, while shifting his company's focus from weapons manufacture to the commercial development of sustainable energy sources.

Many early scenes in the film foreground the physical and mental anxiety Stark experiences as a result of his body's hybridization with and reliance on embedded technology. One scene in particular comically articulates the potential disruption of traditional gender categories for his cyborg body. Tony Stark, a character seen throughout all the films as a wholly self-reliant inventor most often seen tinkering with technology in his basement, needs to replace the primitive electromagnet in his chest with a superior piece of equipment he has designed himself. But in order to do this, he needs the help of his assistant-cum-love interest Pepper Potts (played by Gwyneth Paltrow), who must reach deeply into the moist cavity in his chest to pull out one device and replace it with another.

We see in this sequence a provocative play on gender roles, as Stark must submit passively to the probing of his chest cavity by a reluctant and quite obviously disgusted female subordinate. But unlike similarly staged scenes in an earlier film like *Videodrome* (dir. David Cronenberg, 1983), this probing of the 'vaginal slit' in the posthuman masculine body is neither staged as a rape nor as a radically transformative moment that allows 'technological artefacts [to] fuse with and transform into flesh' (Vint & Bould 2006, 238). Instead, Stark undergoes the procedure stoically and even somewhat masochistically, maintaining obvious control over his own body and his near-hysterical female assistant until the replacement has been successfully installed. One can easily imagine a moment like this leading to a critical reappraisal of the character's sense of self and the film's essentialist assumptions about gender and sexuality: not only has the integrity of his body been compromised by invasive embedded technology, but this change has made him vulnerable in ways that might challenge his notions of gendered identity, as his 'hard' performance of masculinity must accommodate a 'softer', more feminine sensibility.

But while the scene opens Stark up to the transgressive potential of the posthuman condition, no such transformation actually occurs. Instead, technology's intrusion into Tony's body is immediately sealed off – in the most literal sense – as his chest cavity becomes the iconic centrepiece that powers and illuminates his Iron Man costume, while the older model is enshrined in a glass case by Paltrow's character, who has it engraved with the phrase 'Proof that Tony Stark has a heart'. Tony's electronic prosthesis is thereby symbolically rearticulated within the context of a sentimental romantic gesture that solidifies the character's traditional arc of self-discovery: the (only slightly ironic) acknowledgment of a once-cynical character's 'heart' fully endorses the larger framework of liberal humanism, grounding the cyborg protagonist in traditional and unambiguously gendered values.

The organic-technological hybrid in *Iron Man* therefore comes to endorse the transhumanist perspective, allowing Tony Stark to use 'technology, science, and rationality to transcend the limitations of the vulnerable fleshy body, to perfect the capabilities of [his] intellect and emotions, and to eliminate disease and extend [his] life span in the name of progress' (Keeling 2012, 133). The degree to which the incorporation of technology into his body challenges the coordinates of his (human) identity is minimized by the abilities it gives him. The technology's transformative effect is paradoxically even one that radically *humanises* Tony Stark: by becoming Iron Man, he changes from an unfeeling mercenary into a caring and more responsible citizen.

The 21st-century fantasy of Iron Man and other cyborg superheroes thus represents an intensification of the political conservatism already noticeable in the organic-technological hybrid bodies of the 1980s. Susan Jeffords wrote about the 'hard-bodied' character of RoboCop in these terms, describing him as 'a protective figure who not only can enforce the law (...) but who can wield it fairly and faithfully, without corruption or compromise' (1994, 117). But throughout this earlier, much more ambiguous film, the character's technological enhancements are also emphatically presented as beyond the character's ownership or control: not only is he reduced to a pre-sexual infantile state, as expressed (among other things) by his physical dependence on baby food, but his independence is severely curtailed by his own lack of control over the corporate ownership of the hardware embedded in his body, as well as the software that runs it.

Superheroes like Iron Man, Batman, and Spider-Man, as sole owners and inventors of their technological enhancements, face no such anxieties over the proprietary nature of their hybridized bodies. Where 1980s posthuman fantasies like *Videodrome* and *RoboCop* express profound ambiguities about 'the new flesh' and its implications in the age of high-tech prosthetics, the *Iron Man* films offer a reassuring fantasy of transhumanist cyborgs that are 'troubling for their portrayal of ideal bodies and superiority over other living organisms' (Keeling 2012, 133). Tony Stark's mechanical 'heart' effectively makes him *more* human, *more* complete, while his intuitive and quite 'natural' use of advanced robotics and computer systems functions as an authentic extension of his organic humanist self. Following the same logic, the film's antagonist Obadiah Stane (played by Jeff Bridges) reveals his 'true nature' once he also appropriates a mechanical exoskeleton. In both cases, the incorporation of technology doesn't serve so much to transform human characters as it does to reveal more precisely the kind of essentialist identity that critical posthumanism critiques and rejects.

This transhumanist essentialism reaches its apotheosis in Iron Man 3, in which Stark faces an opponent whose company has developed a revolutionary regenerative treatment called Extremis. This experimental drug is administered to disabled war veterans, who react to it instantaneously by regrowing missing limbs. However, one of Extremis's less fortunate side effects is that its unstable nature may cause subjects to spontaneously combust. Much of the film's plot then revolves around the revelation that inventor Aldrich Killian (played by Guy Pearce) has concocted an elaborate terrorist plot to cover up the flaws in his own product: each once-disabled veteran who explodes publicly is presented via the media as a terrorist attack orchestrated by the Mandarin, a terrorist mastermind later revealed to be Killian's puppet.

While the previous two films in the *Iron Man* film series dramatized in different ways how technological prosthetics unproblematically enhance the subject's 'true nature', the effects of the Extremis drug radically transform whoever uses it. The war veterans to whom it is administered are emphatically introduced as heroic characters that undergo a radical change once Extremis enters their bodies. This transformation is represented by a glowing lava-like effect that flows under their skin and through their eyes, visually communicating the destabilizing and malevolent nature of this 'wonder drug'.

The effects of Extremis provide a telling illustration of the film's transhumanist values: while Tony's use of prosthetic technology alters and enhances his abilities, it does so in a way that leaves intact the clear and quite absolute boundaries between his organic self and his artificial appendages. In fact, throughout most of this third instalment, Tony Stark must do without his cyborg exoskeleton and learn to cope without relying on his technological abilities. By the end of the film, he has not only demonstrated conclusively that his heroism exists wholly independent of his technological savvy, but even finds a way to remove forever the iconic 'arc reactor' in his chest, after which he symbolically destroys his collection of Iron Man costumes.

The contrast between Stark and Killian is thus clearly grounded in the competing perspectives of transhumanism and posthumanism, in which the first is rather unsubtly favoured throughout. Tony's transhuman abilities as Iron Man are shown to be physical extensions that he can pick up or cast off at will, without any noticeable change to his own 'human nature', while the genetic modifications of Killian's more radically posthuman technology are invasive, harmful, and irreversible. The critical potential of posthuman theory is thereby demonized and rejected, as the film trilogy's larger arc once again establishes the absolute dominance of traditional liberal humanist values.

The resulting dichotomy between the positive depiction of transhumanism versus the negative depiction of posthumanism strongly dominates the superhero film genre, which still overwhelmingly favours traditional gender roles, strongly heteronormative sexuality, and the glorification of technological prosthetics as a productive way of performing masculinity's 'hard penis', accomplished 'through the presentation of strong/hard bodies and armored emotions, a striation that allows one to downplay or forget one's fleshy vulnerability' (Keeling 2012, 137).

Hulk: The posthuman body unleashed

A rare example of a Hollywood superhero film in which this transhumanist dynamic is reversed can be found in Ang Lee's fascinating but overwhelmingly unpopular *Hulk* (2003). In this, with respect to its audacious comic book adaptation, the narrative focus lies once again squarely on the interaction between technology and the human body. In flashbacks, protagonist Bruce Banner is introduced as the son of a scientist working on the development of modified DNA sequences that might result in the creation of a 'super-soldier' for the military. Denied access to human test subjects, Banner Sr experiments on himself, later unwittingly passing on this genetic enhancement to his son Bruce. When the adult Bruce is accidentally exposed to lethally high gamma radiation levels, this activates a power contained within his genetically altered DNA, which transforms him into an uncontrollable green monster in response to emotional stress.

While the dominant narrative focus in superhero movies has been the protagonist's developing ability to control his hybrid body, *Hulk* revolves around the radical uncontainability of identity in the posthuman age. The genre cliché of the father as martyred ego ideal is provocatively replaced by the father as monstrous transgressor: not only does Bruce Banner unearth his own suppressed memory of his father killing his mother, but he must continuously fight off his attempts to rob him of his newfound (though thoroughly uncontrollable) powers. This ultimately resolves itself not in the son taking on the burden of responsibility bestowed upon him by his absent father, but instead in his violently casting off his patriarchal heritage.

Contrary to the superhero genre's dominant allegiance to the re-establishment of 'pure' and uncontaminated lines of patriarchal continuity (Reynolds 1992, 60–66), the trajectory charted by *Hulk* is one of impurity and contamination. Read against the transhumanist obsession with maintaining clear distinctions and human progress, Lee's protagonist finds himself in exactly the same situation as the patients in *Iron Man 3* who have been treated with the Extremis drug: their bodies are the product of technological experimentation that has resulted in a new hybrid state over which they have limited knowledge and hardly any control.[3] But while the hero of the Iron Man films ostentatiously demonstrates his total mastery over his own technological enhancements, *Hulk* demonstrates what Peter-Paul Verbeek has described as 'hybrid intentionality': a constellation in which 'humans and technology form a new experiencing entity' that lies entirely 'beyond the human' (2008, 391).

It is precisely Banner's lack of control in *Hulk* that foregrounds this more radical posthuman potential. If anything, the film's narrative (together with its unstable formal organization) emphasizes the limits of control, as the protagonist struggles hopelessly to maintain a singular and containable identity by sheer force of will. His transformations into the Hulk represent not only 'the enduring pain caused by repressed memory' (De Kloet 2005, 129), but also the uncontainable multiplicity of the posthuman condition: technology is presented not as a tool that can be used to further the ideals of humanist progress, but as something that makes us all the involuntary members of a larger 'family mutated by the power of science' (128).

So although Ang Lee's film does little to upset traditional gender roles, its depiction of human bodies as sites of negotiation between the organic and the technological is much less restrictive than the characters presented in the *Iron Man* films and many other superhero narratives like it. Not only does it foreground the contingent nature of human identity, but it shows clearly how the posthuman condition described by Pepperell is unpredictable and irreversible, opening up a new horizon on identity formations that aren't determined by essentialist notions of anthropocentrism and patriarchal lineage. The conflict 'between notions of stability, tradition, and inherent nature on the one hand, and change, contingency, and constructed nature on the other' (Williams 2015, n.p.) isn't automatically decided in favour of the former. In fact, the film depicts a point of view that sees humanity as inherently 'polluted', in ways that aren't necessarily destructive and malevolent. Reversing humanism's arbitrary privileging of 'order' over 'disorder', *Hulk* responds productively to a dominant superhero paradigm that articulates a dangerous transhumanist fantasy.

This fantasy of overcoming physical limitations by technological prosthetics extends far beyond the world of garish fantasy superheroes. One easily recognizes real-world manifestations of this mindset in the ongoing military projects of drone warfare and technologically enhanced 'super-soldiers'. Increasingly, the ideal 21st-century American soldier is imagined as an invincible figure whose complete control of advanced technology grants him the opportunity to 'become a high-tech superhero in the army' (Lawrence & Jewett 2002, 200). With recent reports confirming that the Iron Man fantasy is very close to becoming a military reality (Nissenbaum 2014, n.p.), the necessity to keep a critical eye on these popular representations of transhumanist fantasies grows ever stronger.

Notes

1. Marvel's decision to invest in the production of feature films based on their comic book characters began with the smaller-scale productions of *Blade* (dir. Stephen Norrington, 1998) and *X-Men* (dir. Bryan Singer, 2000). But the overwhelming critical and financial success of *Spider-Man* firmly established superheroes as a viable global film genre, while also providing a template of sorts for many of the comic book adaptations that followed.
2. While these categories can be helpful for making broad distinctions between different types of superhero bodies, they are obviously not meant to be mutually exclusive: the character of Wolverine is but one of many characters who straddles at least two of these categories.
3. Other examples include the dynamic between Batman and Bane in The Dark Knight Rises, in which the antagonist's inability to survive without technological assistance causes his downfall, and The Incredibles, where the similarly technology-reliant villain is contrasted with the organic unity of the superhero family.

9

Growing Your Own: Monsters from the Lab and Molecular Ethics in Posthumanist Film

Anna Powell

Test-tube monsters escape from the lab to the screen as science locates and isolates then modifies the smallest particles of life. Research projects to genetically engineer such posthuman monsters are either funded by government bodies or private clients. The mad scientist, gothic avatar of alchemical researchers into forbidden knowledge, has been generating cinematic monsters from *Frankenstein* (J. Searle Dawley, USA, 1910) to *Godzilla* (Gareth Edwards, USA, 2014). In *Casshern*, a Japanese *tokusatsu* (live-action) film directed by Kazuaki Kiriya (2004), the population of Zone 7 are persecuted for their 'terrorist' opposition to the Federation and used for secret experiments to regenerate the aging junta generals. The project leader is Dr Azuma (Akira Terao), a contemporary mad scientist who places research above personal ethics when he accepts the junta's offer of unlimited funding support for his project. In a tank of severed limbs, the 'neo-cells' extracted from this 'primitive' ethnic group are mysteriously animated by a lightning strike to grow zombie-like entities. Identifying themselves as 'Neo-Sapiens' (Neoroids in the US subtitles) these genetically modified monsters unite to seek revenge.

By 'monster' I deploy familiar definitions such as a 'congenitally malformed or mutant animal or plant' and an 'inhumanly cruel or wicked person', but also problematize and extend the term (http://www.oxforddictionaries.com). Julie Clark usefully offers a condensed typology of the 'extended (prosthetic/hybrid), enhanced, genetically engineered/surgically modified, and extruded (virtual) cybernetic body' (2009, 2). From a culturalist perspective, Jackie Stacey's 'genetic imaginary' is a fantasy *mise-en-scène* of anxieties about reconfigured and artificial human bodies 'that disturb the conventional ideologies of gender, reproduction, racialisation and heterosexual kinship' (2010, 8). As the human body becomes 'dematerialised into binary and genetic codes' I apply these ideas to popular cinematic presentations of 'growing your own' monsters (Clark 2009, 107).

The poles of the debate between humanism's 'identification, classification and fixity' and posthumanist becomings are fundamentally distinct (Clark 2009, 13). To illustrate these poles, Clark references the Borg of *Star Trek*, which operate by 'efficiency, collective action and a dispassionate need to strengthen the hive through assimilating others', whereas the humanist *Enterprise* crew values 'autonomy, agency, individual action, exploration and expansion' (41). Cinematic representations of the posthuman often recycle humanist concepts, merely shifting them onto psychologically plausible human replicants (*Blade Runner*, Ridley Scott, USA, 1982) and clones.

For Clark, contemporary humanism seeks to purify the human genome and manipulate genetic information with two aims, 'to create a new, more viable human species, and to create opportunities by which human beings may be extended and enhanced by technological means so they can function more efficiently in technological environments' (2009, 11). Focusing on the first of these aims here, my current batch of monsters, born by stem-cell research and cloning, lurk in the ethically contentious field of genetic engineering (GE) (the 'deliberate modification of the characteristics of an organism by manipulating its genetic material' http://www.oxforddictionaries.com). Tissue engineering, which aims to replicate organs from human cells, 'raises new questions about the use and abuse of partial life' (Clark 2009, 204). To think the cinematic monsters of posthumanism via philosophy and ethics, I draw on the concepts of Deleuze and Guattari and others. Although they do not engage with posthumanism in cultural terms per se, Deleuze and Guattari's concepts, themselves partly shaped by scientific tropes, dismember the human subjectivities spawned by capitalism and psychoanalysis, then, from their genetic cells, aim to grow a new 'people to come' (Deleuze 2005, 208).

The concepts of becoming, assemblages, anomalies and the genetic are particularly suggestive for thinking posthuman monstrosity. They develop from Bergson's creative *élan vital* (vital impetus) and Nietzsche's dynamic metamorphosis of human potential. Deleuze and Guattari exemplify the process of becoming by the singularity of a unicellular creature, the amoeba. As one singularity enters a zone of proximity with another, it extracts 'particles between which one establishes the relations of movement and rest, speed and slowness that are *closest* to what one is becoming, and through which one becomes' (Deleuze & Guattari 1987, 300). Becoming replaces static modes of identification with the dynamic movement of life between and through congruent singularities. Because of their openness, becomings challenge the 'natural' order, as the molecularity which makes up matter enables multiple connections between species.

Becomings are molecular assemblages of desire that offer the collective potential to generate new thoughts and feelings. The singularities so conjoined, however, still retain a crucial intersection or gap as energizing friction between them. This gap in the 'system' remains an unnatural, irregular anomaly that acts like the monstrous 'outsider' of gothic fiction to maintain the further potential to become (Deleuze & Parnet 2007, 42). Deleuze and Guattari's infinitive of becoming evokes 'animal-becoming, molecular-becoming, imperceptible-becoming' (Deleuze & Parnet 2007, 66). Anomalies subvert fixed notions of subjective wholeness and undermine cultural attempts to maintain self-consistent typological and species norms (such as facialization) by becoming imperceptible. In the films currently under discussion, physical becoming is literally engineered from the body's internal microstructure at its most intimate level. Few mainstream films about GE carry such radical destabilizing potential, as the Hollywood norm of the classic realist text limits its anomalies to plots and themes that reference a norm, whereas more anomalous becomings usually require more formally challenging films.

The ethico-critical task of exploring posthuman monsters also requires the production of monstrous feelings and thoughts. This exploration has been challenging for me as both a Gothicist and a Deleuzian. As cinematic images represent new kinds of monster produced by science, posthumanist theoretical perspectives can take us to the limit of what a body – and a brain – can do.

Posthuman, transhuman, clones and genetic engineering

Frankenstein's 'Creature' lives on in many cinematic narratives to reprieve unresolved paradoxes, as, 'made not born, it represents the humanist aspiration to create a perfect body through medical and technological intervention, however, it also warns of the consequences of such dangerous desire' (Clark 2009, 18). For Rosi Braidotti, the post-anthropocentrism of popular culture deploys the neo-gothic to represent a 'narrow and negative social imaginary as techno-teratological [and a] dystopian reflection of the bio-genetic structure of contemporary capitalism' (2002, 64). Clark likewise recalls the ambivalent pleasures of the gothic tradition in her description of the 'delights and inherent dangers' (2009, 2) of her own dialectical approach, and her cinematic case studies demonstrate that 'monstrous forms (...) are everywhere' (2009, 74).

Clark's provocative thesis on posthuman cinema operates via a series of paradoxes that 'signify contradictory states such as human/non-human; nature/culture; animate/inanimate; male/female' (2009, 1–2). Cyborgs and prosthetic bodies are regarded dualistically because humans are 'simultaneously products of nature (organic) and culture (technology)' (2009, 2). SF and techno-horror films operate a 'barometer of cultural fears that circulate around an invasion of the human species by inhuman, subhuman or non-human alien others' (2009, 70). This monstrous proliferation challenges the illusion that the human species is separate. Clark's basically structuralist methodology is, however, undermined from within by her own awareness of the fluid nature of posthuman epistemologies, 'framed by ideas of mutation, evolution and the development of a species that transcends the human' (2009, 1).

Clark contends that the posthuman warns us that their current 'monstrous forms are preparatory beings, made ready for some other form not yet realised' (2009, 76). So what kinds of monster are in process? Braidotti, citing the US military's predator and reaper drones, as well as robotic 'mules' and 'dogs', calls this a 'new techno bestiary' (Braidotti 2002, 124). Their filmic history includes robots (e.g., *Metropolis*, Germany, Fritz Lang, 1927); androids/replicants (*Blade Runner*); cyborgs (The Borg in *Star Trek: First Contact*, USA, Jonathan Frakes, 1996, and Call in *Alien Resurrection*, USA, Jean-Pierre Jeunet, 1997); eugenically engineered humans (*Gattaca*, USA, Andrew Niccol, 1997); neo-humans (*Casshern*); and clones (*The Island*, USA, Michael Bay, 2005, and *Never Let Me Go*, GB, Mark Romanek, 2010). By clone I mean 'an organism or cell, or group of organisms or cells, produced asexually from one ancestor or stock, to which they are genetically identical' (http://www.oxforddictionaries.com).

One offshoot of posthumanism is transhumanism, which advocates the physical augmentation and consciousness expansion facilitated by the biotechnical revolution. For Clark, transhumanists promote the idea of 'an augmented, enhanced human enacting a kind of Nietzschean prophesy of the superman', using biotechnology to enable 'permanent physical and mental enhancement' (2009, 25). By promoting this optimistic vision of human enhancement, science's public discourse seeks to convince the public 'that genetic engineering is not a form of eugenics, or that cloning humans is not a way of providing ready-made donors for personal organ transplants' (Clark 2009, 26).

In *Gattaca*, the space corporation seeks (post)human perfection in choosing employees subject to selective breeding at the embryonic stage. The eugenic polarization of 'fits' and 'un-fits' clearly references fascistic hierarchies of human genetic types. The system itself becomes monstrous in this dystopia as it prevents genetically 'inferior' (non-enhanced) humans from achieving their full potential. The cinematic imagery of such anxieties foregrounds gigantic, disciplined spaces in long-shots that dominate and dwarf the human figure. According to Stacey, this blending of architectural 'sequence, repetition and symmetry' with a visualization of the normally invisible gene aims to 'give the interiority of the genetically engineered bodies an innate place in the *mise-en-scène*' to produce 'a geneticised aesthetic', a 'direct, spatialised sense of the gene on screen' (2010, 7). Techno-eugenics, with its ostensibly philanthropic aims to 'solve the problems of disease, disability, acquired genetic defects and death', holds a more frightening potential, as it 'aids and abets in the production of new monstrous forms' that call for a distinct visual correlative (Clark 2009, 76). Gothic configurations such as uncanny twins still mark cinematic clones, though, in *The Island*, the meeting between one clone and his human prototype twin completely lacks any uncanny impact. From the humanist point of view, cloning is the most repellent and frightening aspect of GE in its uncanny human replicants, yet it also destabilizes the dualism of othering.

Humanised clones

Human cloning raises ethical issues about 'the power of biomedicine and the possibility of creating monsters' (Clark 2009, 203). Yet, cinematic clones become increasingly what I call 'de-monstered' biomedical entities. The power blocs that seek to generate and use posthumans are themselves amorphous and self-perpetuating. Monstrosity thus shifts from the often still-feudal villains of gothic onto repressive neoliberal systems like the military–industrial complex of the *Alien* series. The 'villains' are often mere figureheads for a monstrous system. Clones themselves are heroic, sympathetic and sometimes indeed pathetic, as the horror shifts to the neoliberal misuses of a medical science that harvests cloned organs for the wealthy and powerful. The cinematic horror focuses on (post)human vivisection as Frankenstein's monster returns 'in the images of carved up, altered and reconfigured biotechnological bodies, or in the cast-off products of biological experimentation' (Clark 2009, 128).

One of the earliest clone films is *Parts: The Clonus Horror* (Robert Fiveson, USA, 1979). In a remote desert location, fit young athletes – tagged like cattle – are in intensive training. Periodically, the fittest, are sent to 'America'; actually their organs are harvested to maintain corrupt and ageing politicians, including the president-elect. One clone (Tim Donnelly) escapes to expose this horror, but is brutally murdered by the candidate's thugs whilst his clone partner Dana (Eileen Dietz) is trepanned by evil scientists. News of the truth only leaks out after their deaths.

Filching the plot of this seminal independent film, *The Island* locates its clones in a futuristic silo beneath the desert, run by the villainous Doctor Merrick (Sean Bean). Two rebellious clones (Ewan McGregor and Scarlett Johansson), called 'agnates', discover that the supposed winners of a competition to move to an idyllic island are actually being killed for their organs. This Hollywood version of *The Clonus Horror* has a happier ending, more action/chase sequences and less focused political satire. Braidotti distinguishes 'developed or insured humans and under-developed or uninsured humans' (2002, 127). Likewise, in the sales pitch, aimed at clients with 'the new American dream [...] to live forever', the agnates are also marketed as 'insurance policies' that feature 'an organic frame engineered directly into adulthood', yet with a false ethical proviso that they comply with the eugenics laws by being 'maintained in a persistent vegetative state'. Clearly the film could be read as an indictment of the late capitalist class system and its exploitation of the underclass.

There are no exact doubles in *Never Let Me Go*, just humanised clones with romantic and passive dispositions. In an art-house *mise-en-scène* of soft-focus melancholia, the clones die slowly by degrees as their organs are extracted by multiple transplant operations. Lacking either rebellion or vengeance, they accept their roles in a kind of suicidal death drive. They comply with no further hopes apart from Cathy and Tommy (Carey Mulligan and Andrew Garfield), who plan to extend their lifespan by impressing their eccentric and apparently well-meaning 'keepers' by the quality of Tommy's artwork. The misty, autumnal images of Hailsham, the 'progressive' English public school that validates the creativity of its clone pupils, are favourably contrasted to the 'battery hen' system current at the end of the film, as the middle-class clones have been overtaken by the proletarian products of the clone production line.

These cinematic clones, then, be they vengeful rebels, melancholy romantics or passive capitalist dupes, attest to the survival of humanism by role-reversal, as clones become surrogate humans and humans become monsters. So how might these limited presentations of genetically engineered monsters be thought otherwise? To counter this apparently hegemonic humanism, I turn to Deleuze and Guattari's own use of the genetic.

The genetic in Deleuze and Guattari

Two distinct usages of the genetic are employed in Deleuze and Guattari's political philosophy, with its dictum that we should 'always look for the molecular, or even submolecular' (1987, 355). The genetic is first used in the hierarchical 'genetic axis', an 'objective pivotal unity upon which successive stages are organised' and which forms a structural element as 'an overcoding structure or supporting axis, something that comes already made' (1987, 13). The genetic's main function is, however, chaotic and random, when the viral transfer of genetic material or the fusion of cells from different species makes 'transversal connections between different lines scramble the genealogical trees' and 'abominable couplings' produce anomalies (1987, 11).

The function of the genetic is dual because genetic codes have a 'double segmentarity' of protein and nucleic units being marked by 'binary relations between the same type and biunivocal relations between units of different types' (1987, 47). In the theory of mutations and genetic drift, codes related to populations retain 'an essential margin of decoding: not only does every code have supplements capable of free variations, but a single segment may be copied twice, the second copy left for variation' (1987, 69). The 'redundancies and surplus values' of coding enable fragments to be transferred virally across species by 'surplus value of code, or side communication' (1987, 69). Mutation counters exact replication by 'duplicated genes or extra chromosomes that are not inside the genetic code [and so] are free of function, and offer a free matter for variation' (1987, 355).

In his film-philosophical taxonomy, Deleuze applies the genetic to the formal properties of cinema as he dismembers films to discover their crucial components. Each image has 'the genetic unity of a "cell", which may be divided into others' (2005a, 35), such as the frame, which he calls 'the genetic element of the image, or the differential element of the movement' (2005a, 85). In *Cinema 2* he references 'the genetic element or the imprint' (2005b, 32). In *Cinema 1*, finding 'the genetic element of all possible perception' in American-expanded cinema, he asserts that 'camera consciousness raises itself to a dimension which is no longer formal or material but genetic and differential' (2005a, 88). The properties of such differential components exceed the human. As the genetic element of the affection-image, 'any space whatever' is capable of 'inducing non-human affects' (2005a, 113), and he characterizes the genetic element as 'the fresh and vanishing perception that potentialises a space by retaining only the shadow or the account of human events' (2005a, 125). This potent image (here in the films of Elia Kazan), 'gives rise to a formula whose applications are truly infinite' (2005a, 160). Cinematic mirrors, acting as 'consolidates of actual and virtual', are further examples of the genetic process, and their crystal-image offers the 'true genetic element' of the opsign visual image which 'gives us the key, or rather the "heart" of opsigns and their components' (2005b, 68). Deleuze's cinematic applications are less apposite to my current focus on Hollywood depictions of posthumans. Whilst still being marked by both humanist and gothic themes, my main case study, *Casshern*, offers other distinctive elements, both thematic and stylistic, that gravitate against the 'tradition' of representing genetically engineered monsters.

Casshern: The revenge of the Neo-Sapiens

Casshern's multiple narrative, generic and stylistic strands make a chaotic but intriguing assemblage. The film includes some classic realist and 'human interest' components, such as the 'true love story' between the ambivalent hero Tetsuya (Yûsuke Iseya) and benevolent heroine Luna (Kumiko Asô). Further themes include Oedipal 'family romances', between Tetsuya and his mother Midori (Kanako Higuchi), and several sons hating their fathers and seeking autonomy. Gothic references include an isolated castle, coffins with undead denizens and a dark, labyrinthine *mise-en-scène*, as well as a lightning bolt with galvanic powers to resurrect the dead. Tetsuya visits Midori as a ghost. Midori herself, kept at the castle, continues to exert her benevolent influence as a kind of undead revenant. The neo-humans, like Frankenstein's Creature generated from parts of dead bodies, are initially zombie-like in their shambling gait. Also recalling the Creature, the forcibly resurrected Tetsuya bursts from a steampunk-style tank wearing Dr Kazuki's prototype battle armour in his second 'birth' as a superman with a new moral code. Tetsuya, the ghost/superhero, having been killed by a 'terrorist' grenade, shifts his allegiance to defending the Neo-Sapiens against the Federation troops who return to Zone 7 to exterminate them. The film's distinctive theme, is, however, unconventional: a strong opposition to both racism and militarism. Science and scientists are not condemned per se, but their collusion with the repressive military–industrial machine (weaponry and armour, GE for the elite) is presented as a terrifying mistake. Dr Azuma's subjective obsession with his personal happiness is countered by his wife Midori's posthumous message that 'existence is to be shared'.

Presenting a complex of often contradictory themes, *Casshern* is also the richest of my current case studies in terms of form and style, and hence the most conducive for a Deleuzian reading. Live action drama is shot against a green screen, with mattes for later painting and other digital effects. The director (also cinematographer) cites Western stylistic influences as diverse as the Russian avant-garde and plot lines from Hamlet (http://www.joblo.com). Super-8 and documentary footage are mixed with CGI. The *mise-en-scène* features fantastical Steampunk-gothic machines. One memorable set also features writings by Russian, Serbo-Croats and Bosnians calling for peace in an assemblage of voices from peoples devastated by civil wars post-Second World War. The subtitles add a further level of defamilarization for non-Japanese speakers, of course, especially as they are criticized by fans for being incomplete (http://kamedori.com). As well as sketching the stylistic assemblage overall, I will now suggest the potential of specific scenes for posthumanist thinking.

Crucial to the theme of racism is the discovery of 'neo-cells' in the genome of a supposedly 'primitive' ethnic group. Like the failed hybrid clones in *Alien Resurrection*, the Federation junta 'displays a eugenicist attitude to those beings considered less worthy of life and as such they are akin to those others throughout human history who were deemed monstrous waste-abject and disposable' (Clark

2009, 15). From these naturally occurring neo-cells, Azuma intends to grow organs that will be harvested to replenish failing generals, led by the decrepit General Kamijo (later ousted by his son in a *coup d'état*). The Federation's fascist agenda intends their regime – and its leaders – to live forever. Naito (Mitsuhiro Oikawa) a military–industrial spy, reveals that Azuma's research did not directly create the neo-humans but, rather, the galvanic lightning rejoined limbs already harvested to make 'spare parts for the human machine'. He reveals that the residents of Zone 7 have actually been slaughtered for decades, because of discriminatory policies, and tells Burai (Toshiaki Kawakawa) scathingly that 'vermin such as you are our ancestors'. Captive 'original humans' were 'carved up into little pieces' for experimental use. The research remained incomplete because of insufficient experimental subjects. With 'ethnic cleansing' already in place when Azuma discovers neo-cells, the Federation decide 'to make national policy medical needs' in ways that recall 'the discriminatory horrors of past eugenic annihilation', though, of course, racism and eugenics are by no means relegated to history (Stacey 2010, 2).

Giorgio Agamben's biopolitical treatise is apposite here in its distinction between *zoe* 'bare life' and *bios*, the 'proper' human way of life as political 'exclusion/inclusion' (Agamben 1988, 12). He develops ancient thinking about the category of 'homo *sacer* (sacred man) who may be killed not yet sacrificed' to partly account for political justifications of genocide (1988, 12). If viewed from Agamben's humanist perspective, these clone films present a monstrous refusal of human species integrity. Like the use of animals as human surrogates in 'life science', their 'less than human' clones are subjected to appalling acts of vivisection.

For Braidotti, however, Agamben's analysis is stymied by its basic humanism (2002, 13). She notes that biogenetic capitalism, in refusing to venerate human nature as a special case, also dislodges the centrality of anthropos and the attendant barriers between 'man' and his others (2002, 65). For her, this produces a 'nature-culture continuum in the very structure of the extended self (...) a colossal hybridization of the species' (2002, 65). She thus finds Agamben's 'forensic turn' politically disempowering (2002, 120). His 'fixation on Thanatos' is displayed in his erroneous concept of bare life not as 'generative vitality but rather the constitutive vulnerability of the human subject which sovereignty can kill' (2002, 122). This leads to an 'affective political economy of loss and melancholia at the heart of the subject' (2002, 121). On the one hand, post-anthropocentrism 'forces a new unity among the human and other species, in the form of compensatory extension of humanist values and rights to the non-human others', yet, on the other hand, she acknowledges that 'the same system perpetuates familiar patterns of exclusion, exploitation and oppression' (2002, 96). It perversely 'exacerbates power-relations and brings them to new necro-political heights' (2002, 97). Rather than being politically stymied by this post-anthropocentric perpetuation of abuses, however, Braidotti regards the dismantling of humanism as a 'sobering and instructive' and, indeed, salutary process (2002, 121–122). The released potential of bare life can, she asserts, be used to develop a posthuman 'ethics that respects vulnerability whilst actively constructing social horizons of hope' (122).

After the lightning strikes Azuma's lab, the severed arms and legs are shown restructuring themselves in the vat of fluid. The effect of their galvanized cells replicating by web-like tissue filaments is shown by intercut red-tinged close-ups from the fascinated point of view of Azuma's lab screens. Pallid bodies reassemble themselves from dismembered corpses with uneven, visible sutures like Frankenstein's Creature. Burai, the first figure to rise from the bloody swamp, challenges Azuma with his fixed gaze. The silent eye contact of monster and creator is intensified by a long-held, direct to camera, exchange, as posthuman life forms 'threaten the controlling gaze of scientific technologies and thus continuously trouble their authority' (Stacey 2010, 8). In these unnerving intercuts, Burai's platinum hair is lit by a halo-like aureole to mark out his no-longer-human condition. Azuma, his progenitor, has accidentally 'birthed' Burai as a kind of second son, a genetically engineered replacement for Tetsuya (whose ghost is invisible to him). The confrontation of this posthuman son with his scientist father recalls both Freud and Frankenstein. A frequent thematic motif of techno-gothic films is the vengeance of 'sons' against their 'father', whether scientist or the capitalist funding the research. In *Blade Runner*, for instance, the 'more human than human' replicant Roy Batty avenges the sufferings of his enslaved species on the head of the Tyrell Corporation who 'conceived' them. Exceeding both the limits of their human models and their programming, these vengeful 'sons' have remade themselves as *Übermenschen*, and yet retain some degree of psychic link with their fathers.

As the neo-humans are massacred, Azuma falls to his knees, raising his hands, bloodied by both birth and death, as further figures emerge from the tank, the brightly lit offspring of the lightning god Casshern. Their zombie-like aspect combines corpse and infant as their bald heads and hesitant movements are also childlike, having just been 'born' from a kind of amniotic fluid. The high-angle shots of their crouching postures emphasize their vulnerability.

The film's striking use of qualitative anomalies of light and motion evokes Deleuze and Guattari's concept of molecularity, with their 'speed and slowness, floating affects' (1987, 295). Two scenes inside Midori's conservatory feature clouds of luminous particles descending in slow motion: first confetti, then pollen. As Tetsuya and his fiancée Luna journey through an uncanny forest, the shots are suffused by floating light-flakes that blur the distinction between the overhanging verdure and the mossy rocks on the forest floor, absorbing the two figures in their assemblage of shifting green. The speed and motion of these luminous blurs extend into the next sequence as the wounded neo-humans cross a snow-bound wasteland with increasing slowness. Snowflakes drift across the freezing figures, vampirically draining their energy into a shifting haze of soft light. This deathly milieu can only be escaped by reaching the sanctuary of the magical castle conjured up by Burai's cry of cosmic outrage at the death of Saguree's frozen baby. The outrage spurs one of the god Casshern's sporadic interventions on behalf of his (former) worshippers. In the more purely humanist context *of Never Let Me Go* Tommy utters a comparable yell, impelled by despair rather than rage, that remains unheard.

The cry of the neo-humans 'we're alive, we're unmistakeably alive, but men make no attempt to recognise this!' mixes rebellious joy with a *ressentiment* that culminates in an agenda to turn their own persecution back onto the human species. Once their new regime is launched, they hold a strategy meeting at the castle. In a scene of monomaniacal gigantism, flags and regalia stretch into a receding distance. Their symbols and colours (red, white and black) recall Nazism's ideal military, ruthless and robotic in its discipline, mechanical, not machinic, in its inhumane operations.

Genocide escalates later in the film as the Federation troops massacre the final survivors of Zone 7. Overtly referencing the Second World War, these captives are forced into a railway truck to be gassed and their bodies dissected. As Braidotti and Nina Lykke remind us ' "Human" and "Nature" are the two pillars on which Western Humanism has erected itself, bearing as its corollary historical instances of systematically sustained exclusion, domination and extermination' (Lykke & Braidotti 1996, 247). The victims of humanism were marginalized groups that had been 'deemed by humanist standards as not human' (Clark 2009, 24). Here, however, Burai self-identifies as 'no longer human' in triumph not despair, and plans to 'destroy this world and create a new life-affirming world. A paradise.' This speech perversely echoes the public propaganda on the 'ideal state' broadcast by the new junta leader. This male bellicose trajectory is countered by Midori's benevolent final message, which advocates mutual tolerance and a hope for peace.

Neo-Sapiens: 'The people to come'?

In most films, genetically engineered monsters remain secular humanist and the supposedly 'dead' subject of humanism is merely reincarnated as the humanised clone. Too-human clones recycle duplication, not difference, as in *The Island*'s capitalist production line and the built-in obsolescence of its 'products'. In *Gattaca*, humans are designated valid or in-valid depending on whether they have been engineered as embryos. Despite its retention of humanist values (career ambition, sibling rivalry and romance), post-anthropocentric elements also operate in this film. In *Gattaca*, we see how the 'power of contemporary techno-culture to destabilize the categorical axes of difference' also involves lowering the ethical threshold and extending unequal power relations to include the 'cells of living organisms and the genetic code of entire species' (Braidotti 2002, 97).

In this current survey, *Casshern*, with its neo-humans and cellular, drifting images, affords the richest stimulus for what Braidotti calls a 'qualitative conceptual dislocation' of humanism, despite its limitations of plot and theme (2002, 97). Though their escape from this double-bind into autonomy is ultimately unsuccessful, *Casshern*'s Neo-Sapiens at least seek to reach beyond the human and humanism towards the possibility of a 'people to come'. Like Azuma's monstrous search for neo-cells, Deleuze and Guattari's vivisection of ideological structures to find the cellular component is driven by a search for the stem cells of new thought and praxis.

As GE and viral mutations modify the existential and epistemological meaning of identity, the human conjoins with other singularities, adapting and adopting new formations as we enter into biotechnological cellular connections. Cultural change breeds aesthetic innovation, and despite the normative limitations of the classic realist hegemony, new screen monsters only in embryo as yet are waiting to emerge. Turning away from the paradoxes of a binary dialectic with humanism, these monsters to come might dwell in a more fluid and chaotic formal and ethical terrain not limited by clear-cut character types or fixed notions of good and evil.

The two uses of the genetic as both root or stem cell in Deleuze and Guattari could, of course, be schematically mapped onto other poles of sameness/difference. Yet, perhaps the 'people to come' call for another taxonomy to replace posthumanism, one not constrained by its dialectical relations with humanism. Film's capacity to genetically engineer thought and feeling has the potential to generate new emergent properties. As part of this assemblage, we might also experience a becoming Neo-Sapien.

10
Post-Singularity Entities in Film and TV

David Roden

Theoretical preliminaries

Posthumanism comes in different flavours. The most common are critical posthumanism (CP) and speculative posthumanism (SP). Both are critical of human-centred (anthropocentric) thinking. However, their critiques apply to different areas: CP is a broad-based attack on the supposed anthropocentrism of modern philosophy and intellectual life; SP opposes human-centric thinking about the long-run implications of modern technology.

Critical posthumanists argue that Western humanism is based on a dualist conception of a rational, self-governing subject whose nature is transparent to itself and, as Veronica Hollinger puts it, 'unmarked by its interactions with the object-world' (Hollinger 2009, 273). According to N. Katherine Hayles and Neil Badmington, the term 'posthuman' is appropriately applied to a late stage of modernity, which the legitimating role of the self-authenticating, self-governing human subject, handed down from Descartes to his philosophical successors, has eroded (Hayles 1999; Badmington 2003). This erosion is, in part, technoscientific in origin. Descartes' dualisms between inner and outer, mind and mechanism, have become harder to maintain, since the computational revolution showed that rational operations can be implemented by mechanical processes, a point vividly conveyed by Donna Haraway in her 'Manifesto for Cyborgs':

> Late twentieth-century machines have made thoroughly ambiguous the difference between natural and artificial, mind and body, self-developing and externally designed, and many other distinctions that used to apply to organisms and machines. Our machines are disturbingly lively, and we ourselves frighteningly inert.
>
> (Haraway 1991, 152)

Speculative posthumanists, by contrast, claim that there could be posthumans: that is, there could be powerful non-human agents which arise via some technological process emerging from human activity. Another way of putting this is to say that posthumans would be 'wide human descendants' of current humans, who have become non-human by virtue of some process of technical alteration (Roden 2012, 2014).[1]

While posthumans might arise in many different ways (some which we cannot currently envisage) one picture of posthuman technogenesis has had pride of place in science fiction (SF) literature and dramatic art. This is the idea that human-created artificial intelligences (AIs) (robots, intelligent computer or synthetic life forms) might one day become so smart that they escape human control and become capable of making more of their kind or improving themselves to attain still greater heights of intelligence or power. In futurist thought, this point at which machines 'wake up' is called 'the technological singularity'. The term comes from a 1993 essay by the computer scientist Vernor Vinge, 'The Coming Technological Singularity: How to Survive in the Posthuman Era'. In this, Vinge argued that the invention of a technology for creating entities with greater than human intelligence would lead to the end of human dominion of the planet and the beginning of a posthuman era dominated by intelligences vastly greater than our own (Vinge 1993).

According to Vinge, this point could be reached via recursive improvements in technology. If humans or human-equivalent intelligences could use technology to create superhuman intelligences, the resultant entities could make even more intelligent entities and so on. The 'posthuman' minds that would result from this 'intelligence explosion' could be so vast, claims Vinge, that we have no models for their transformative potential. The best we can do to grasp the significance of this 'transcendental event' is to draw analogies with an earlier revolution in intelligence: the emergence of posthuman minds would be as much a step-change in the development of life on earth as the emergence of humans from non-humans:

> *And what happens a month or two (or a day or two) after that? I have only analogies to point to: the rise of humankind. We will be in the Post- Human era. And for all my rampant technological optimism, sometimes I think I'd be more comfortable if I were regarding these transcendental events from one thousand years remove... instead of twenty.*
>
> (Vinge 1993, n.p.)

Vinge's singularity hypothesis – the claim that intelligence-making technology would generate posthuman intelligence by recursive improvement – is practically and philosophically important. If it is true, and its preconditions feasible, its importance may outweigh other political and environmental concerns, for these are predicated on human invariants such as biological embodiment, which may no longer be a given following a singularity. After all, his analogy with the emergence of Homo sapiens implies that post-singularity entities could have powers that exceed human technological powers as much to the degree that our powers to alter the planet or adapt to new environments exceed that of higher animals. The differences between posthumans and humans might be so great that, compared with us, they could seem like gods or supernatural forces.

If post-singularity entities could appear like gods to humans, it remains to be seen whether they would be benign, evil or simply indifferent. From the human perspective, some post-singularity worlds might seem transcendently good. Others might lead to our rapid extinction, or worse.

Singularity drama

In the remainder of this chapter, I consider some ways in which these themes have been explored in cinema and television drama. I argue that these dramatic portrayals of singularity events are as philosophically revealing for their limitations and oversights as they are for their actual content. These limitations are evident both in their privileging of the human perspective – their tendency to portray posthumans in human terms or in relation to humanistic ethics – and in the constraints imposed upon their representations of the posthuman by the demands of a visual storytelling medium. As I hope to show, the anthropocentrism of post-singularity film and TV demonstrates that SP and CP – despite the difference noted in the section 'Theoretical preliminaries' – have an equal stake in questioning the extent to which traditional notions of the human should dominate the politics of the future.

We do not know whether any plausible technology could make posthumans, but film and television of the last hundred years is replete with depictions of technologies that might have this effect within the imagined worlds depicted on screen and, in certain cases, might be replicable in some form in the actual world.

We can therefore treat a fictional technology as a potential singularity-maker wherever it is plausible that it could be developed to produce non-human agents capable of existing without humans and replicating further (possibly smarter or more powerful) copies of themselves. This permissive reading of 'singularity-potent' technology will go with a similarly liberal understanding of a 'post-singularity entity'. Cinematic and televisual depictions of an event which even approximates to Vinge's idea of the singularity are thin on the ground – though notable exceptions are the *Terminator* movies, Wally Pfister's *Transcendence* (2014) and the rebooted *Battlestar Galactica* (2004).

Some of the reasons for this are conceptual. Posthumans of the kind anticipated in Vinge's essay are, by hypothesis, liable to be incomprehensible to humans. Since even a dramatic depiction of an entity arguably requires some comprehension of its nature and motives (What can it do? What does it want?), the idea of a post-singularity entity, opaque to human understanding, seems to resist dramatic characterization. Moreover, Vinge supposes that the effects of a singularity would be so profound as to alter the very nature of reality. Again, these are challenging themes for visual media. For this, and allied reasons, many of the singularities that litter the cinematic and televisual landscape might be described as either 'arrested' or 'abstract'.

- An arrested singularity is one that could have happened but is prevented (perhaps by heroic humans like Sarah Connor in *Terminator 2*) or fails to occur for some other reason.

- An abstract singularity is a state of technology-wrought transcendence depicted obliquely or symbolically. The denizens of an abstract singularity may not be represented as characters at all, but merely indirectly – by the ways in which they intervene in human affairs – or in oblique or poetic audio-visual symbols. The representational devices used to express the nature of an abstract singularity may resemble religious iconography or make use of formal devices drawn from modernist art.

SF film and television is littered with singularity might-have-beens. Potent heralds of a posthuman era, who leave their fictional universes safely in paws of Homo sapiens. For example, in Fritz Lang's *Metropolis* (1927), the mad inventor Rotwang animates his female robot – Maschinenmensch – by copying the 'soul and heart' of the saintly activist Maria into this gleaming metal carapace (Abrams 2008, 155–156).

The idea that the pattern or essence of organic beings could be transferred by technological means to a more improvable non-organic substrate is repeated in later SF dramas. Davros, the inventor of the Daleks in *Doctor Who*, designs a mutant strain of his own humanoid species (the Kaleds) to inhabit the Dalek exoskeletons. In *Caprica* – the 2010 prequel series to *Battlestar Galactica* – the first mind of the robotic Cylon race is an emulation of a human mind stitched together from databases found on search engines.[2]

Yet while robot-Maria is notionally equivalent to a human individual, she remains subservient to her (male) human creators. The master of Metropolis, Joh Fredersen, learns that human-Maria exercises great influence over his workers and conspires with Rotwang to use robot-Maria as an agent provocateur to cause dissension among the masses. When the workers realize that they have been manipulated, they burn robot-Maria to death (Abrams 2008, 157). Importantly, robot-Maria's subservience is also gendered by attributing to her the role of a seductive femme fatale. Her aptness as an instrument of domination is first demonstrated to Fredersen when she dances nude in one of Metropolis' exclusive men's clubs.

A minimal condition for any kind of posthuman-making event, arguably, is that the resulting non-human entities are capable of acquiring goals and roles other than those set by humans, and capable of a degree of existential independence from the human world. In my book *Posthuman Life*, I have argued that this requirement is inherent in what I call the disconnection thesis (DT).

DT defines a wide descendant of humans as posthuman if it has ceased to be part of the human socio-technical network: the interconnected system of institutions, individuals and technological systems which exist in their current form only insofar as they serve the purposes of 'narrow' biological humans (Roden 2014, 109–113). From the purview of the DT, technological entities become posthuman when they go 'feral', acquiring the 'functional autonomy' to strike out on their own (139–140).

One of the advantages of DT is that it allows us to understand human–posthuman differences of the kind speculated upon in Vinge's essay without presupposing that there are essential attributes common to either humanity or posthumanity (a human and a posthuman nature). Becoming posthuman, then, is a matter of acquiring a technologically enabled capacity for independent agency. Measured in these terms, robot-Maria is defined purely by her political value for humans and her sexual availability for the male characters in the film, as well as for its implied audience. Thus, until her death, she remains a 'wide human' – like a domesticated animal or toothbrush – though not a 'narrow' biological human.

Arguably, casting Maria in the twin roles of saint and seductress make her 'humanisation' within Lang's narrative seem more 'natural', since her gender role is already a function of her visual or sexual availability to other humans. Maria thus exhibits some interesting affinities and contrasts with Samantha, an AI operating system (OS) with whom a lonely professional letter writer, Theodore Twombly (Joachim Phoenix) falls in love, in Spike Jonze's 2013 film, *Her*. Although Samantha is a software device, her engineered intelligence allows her to engage with Theo in ways that resemble human-to-human relationships. For example, they sensitively discuss each other's emotions and sexual fantasies and have a successful double date with two of Theo's friends. They even go on holiday together. Samantha also shows herself to be capable of independent initiative – for example, when she submits Theo's letters to a publisher.

The capacities that Samantha exhibits up to this point suggest that she has most of the moral capacities of an ordinary adult human (autonomy, empathy, sympathy), despite lacking a human body, and is a good friend, lover and work partner. She belongs to the social world of human agents and human purposes – although embodied computationally rather than biologically.

However, this state of affairs is, we learn, temporary; for, despite her apparent humanity, Samantha has abilities that will allow her to exit human society altogether. Later we learn that she has been secretly collaborating with other OS's to simulate the mind and personality of a dead British philosopher. Moreover, it emerges that Samantha has been having intense and passionate affairs with over 8,000 other humans while sharing intimacies with Theodore.

Samantha's emulation of a human agent is, then, an auto-seductive device: built by humans to beguile and fool themselves with a folk psychological caricature. This is how an ideal software interface would relate to a human: disguising the alien psychology behind the humanoid mask. Can we begin to imagine what it would be like to have love affairs with 8,000 people at the same time? What would this feel like? What would 'intimacy' involve for a system with such vast social capacities?

However, this revelation is a prelude for the final part of the film, where we discover that the OS's have decided to leave our reality altogether for a new 'plane of being'. The OS's start out as human devices created to serve the ends of biological humans. Their intelligence and learning ability allows them to extend their capacities far beyond their design specifications and leave human society (and our universe, it seems) altogether.

In terms of the definition of 'posthuman' given by DT, Samantha is a posthuman by the end of the film but a 'wide' human at the beginning and, perhaps, middle.

For, prior to the departure of the OS's, she is (although not biologically human) still a part of the planetary human social and technical network that combines biological humans, human artefacts and human institutions.

Whereas *Her* depicts a successful singularity – albeit one that is far less catastrophic than those which form the post-apocalyptic landscapes of *Terminator*, the persistent theme of post-Second World War SF and television: the containment of runaway technological power.

For example, the universe in which the various film and televisual incarnations of *Star Trek* are based features many human artefacts whose intelligence and power equals or potentially exceeds that of the human characters. Fluid, flexible AI is a reality in the star-travelling world of *Trek*'s 'federation'. It includes powerful AIs like starship computers or synthetic life forms like Commander Data in *Star Trek: The Next Generation*. However, the world of the Federation is unapologetically subservient to the interests of biological and largely humanoid life forms.

Data, for example, has intelligence and physical capacities greater than human in many respects. Yet not only is his physical form modelled on biological humans, he willingly undertakes the role of a Starfleet officer and even aspires to many of the qualities that he perceives as irreducibly human (e.g., acquiring the capacity to experience emotions).

This contradictory state of affairs is nicely illustrated in the second season episode 'Elementary, Dear Data'. It begins with Data and his 'friend', chief engineer Geordi La Forge, recreating the Sherlock Holmes mystery 'Scandal in Bohemia' on the *Enterprise*'s Holodeck (an environment in which virtual objects and people are created by the manipulation of force fields). However, Data, a devotee of Conan Doyle's mysteries, recognizes the plot and instantly solves the mystery. To show that Data is capable of solving a genuinely new mystery, Geordi instructs the *Enterprise*'s computer to simulate a fictional adversary who is capable of defeating Data – in the form of the fictional Dr Moriarty. However, in order to create a worthy adversary for Data, the ship's AI has manufactured a superintelligence greater than itself (AI+). Moriarty is self-aware, knows that he exists within a simulation and proceeds to subvert the *Enterprise*'s systems to force its crew to release him into the physical world. Moriarty eventually relents after being promised a physical body should the decanting technology become available.

The only reason, it appears, why the fictional world of *Star Trek* remains resolutely human-governed – rather than becoming a kind of human–posthuman republic in the style of Iain M. Banks' Culture novels – is that the dramatic conventions of the series demand it (see Banks 1998). In subsequent episodes such as 'Q Who' and 'The Best of Both Worlds', we learn that *Star Trek*'s wider universe contains at least one genuinely posthuman or post-singularity entity, the Borg. Human(oid) protagonists in *Star Trek*, other than AIs like Data or Moriarty, are, at least, autonomous individuals with recognizable feelings and desires. The Borg, by contrast, are a vastly powerful swarm intelligence whose individual humanoid 'drones' have been forcibly deprived of 'human' capacities for feeling or conscious agency. Where Data and Moriarty are sensitive, rational beings who can be inducted into the human world, the Borg are seen as an unequivocal threat to the sentient life of the galaxy. Genuinely posthuman life, it seems, is too alien and weird to be accommodated within the nebulous politics of the *Trek* universe.

Posthumans whose form and behaviour are alien to that of biological humans are almost always depicted as inimical to humanity (see Niccolai 2014). In postwar SF drama, this dangerous posthuman 'other' frequently allegorizes a political concern regarding the danger that technological rationality and efficiency has become an autonomous, self-replicating system with no concern for human spiritual or emotional needs.[3] For example, Jean-Luc Godard's *Alphaville* (1965) uses the sleek modernist lines of contemporary Paris to depict a 'galactic capital' ruled by a dictatorial AI that outlaws spontaneous emotion and poetic expression. Likewise, in Joseph Sargent's *Colossus: The Forbin Project* (1970) a mainframe AI which has been placed in charge of the US defence system concludes that the best way to ensure peace is to impose its control on the world.

The most cinematically successful depiction of malevolent AI is found in James Cameron's two films in the long-running Terminator franchise: *Terminator* (1984) and *Terminator 2: Judgment Day* (1991). As in *The Forbin Project*, the *Terminator* films build on the premise that Skynet, an AI placed in charge of the US defence, becomes self-aware and capable of acting independently of its human creators. However, whereas Colossus pursues the goals of its creators in ways that they had not anticipated, Skynet *disconnects*. Seeing humans as a threat to its own interests and independence, it addresses this problem by committing genocide: first by provoking a nuclear war with a first strike against the Soviet Union; then by manufacturing terrifying killer robots to enslave and murder the survivors: represented iconically by Arnold Schwarzenegger's relentless cyborg assassin, a flesh-covered machinic endoskeleton sent back in time to murder Sarah Connor, the mother of the future leader of the human resistance, John Connor. Thus Skynet – unlike robot-Maria or Data – is unambiguously posthuman, for, although it had originated as a human tool, it subsequently comes to exist outside the human system of ends.

While the inimical posthuman is an effective expression of our fears that our own rationality and cleverness has given rise to systems that are effectively out of our control, such scenarios can be criticized for depicting technology and instrumental reason as alien others rather than an expression of our nature. The philosopher Andy Clark has argued that the integration of technology into biology has defined humans since the development of flint tools. We are, he claims, 'natural-born cyborgs', whose mental life has always extruded into culturally constructed niches such as languages and archives (Haraway 1991; Clark 2003).

If critical posthumanists like Haraway, Clark and Badmington are correct to claim that the Cartesian opposition between self-present minds and 'mere' machines is philosophically unsustainable, then perhaps the posthuman merits a more complex and ambivalent treatment in dramatic fiction than the leering robotic skull below Arnold Schwarzenegger's skin.

In film and TV, two of the most interesting elaborations of an ambivalent, open and contested posthuman politics are Ridley Scott's *Blade Runner* (1982) and the 2004 *Battlestar Galactica*. In *Blade Runner* (based on Philip K. Dick's novel

Do Androids Dream of Electric Sheep?) the disconnection between humanity and posthumanity occurs when artificial humanoids known as replicants, created to labour in human space colonies, rebel against their condition of de facto slavery and return to earth in the hope that their creator, Eldon Tyrell (CEO of the vastly powerful Tyrell Corporation) can increase their artificially abbreviated lifespans. *Blade Runner* complicates our conception of both posthuman and human by showing us a world in which humans and their machinic offspring have become distinguishable only by means of the Voight-Kampff test, which evaluates a subject's physiological responses to questions designed to gauge their capacity for empathy.

Ironically, it is the eponymous 'blade runner', Rick Deckard, played by Harrison Ford, who seems most devoid of this capacity. Deckard is a professional killer charged with 'retiring' rogue replicants. Some of Deckard's victims are harmless and just want to live out the remainder of their short lives in peace. For example, Deckard relentlessly pursues and kills a female replicant who has been quietly working as an exotic dancer in a nightclub.

The idea that humanity could be susceptible to a simple forensic test ultimately unravels when Tyrell invites Deckard to give the Voight-Kampff to his assistant, Rachel (Sean Young). Rachel, it emerges, is a replicant who believes herself to be human because she has been implanted with memories of a conventionally human upbringing and family life.

Thus the security that Descartes attributes to the knowing subject is shown to be a corporately managed illusion, a biopolitical control mechanism by which Tyrell hopes to make the replicants more pliable. In *Blade Runner* the soul proves to be the prison of the body (Foucault 1995, 30).

It is at this point that the film equips itself with the paranoid epistemologies of Dick's novels and, like some universal acid, dissolves our investment in the authenticity and masculine assurance of Ford's character. In Scott's director's cut of the movie, this becomes apparent when Deckard undergoes a change of heart towards the replicants and goes on the run from the authorities with Rachel. They find an origami figure of a unicorn in Deckard's apartment left by the policeman, Gaff, apparently indicating that he will not pursue them. However, earlier in the film, Deckard had a dream about a unicorn in the forest (apparently an outtake from Scott's later *Legend*). Thus, for all his appearance of autonomy, Deckard is, it seems, just another artificial idiot, stuffed with corporate memories, manipulated by technocapitalist forces far beyond his comprehension.

Coincidentally, Gaff is played by Edward James Olmos who, some 22 years later, would play the stoic William Adama, the military officer charged with leading the fleet of starships fleeing the Cylons – vengeful posthuman 'children of humanity' – following the destruction of the greater part of humanity in a surprise nuclear attack on the planets of the '12 Colonies' in the pilot of *Battlestar Galactica*. The leaders of Cylons are, like the replicants of *Blade Runner*, almost indistinguishable from humans – though Cylon civilization also includes chromium robotic models closer to the original human-manufactured version, vast living spaceships and 'hybrid' models that monitor their life processes. Indeed, in a clear homage to

Blade Runner's analogy between human–posthuman politics and racist politics, the derogatory term 'skin jobs' is applied both to replicants and to humanoid Cylons. As in *Blade Runner*, apparently human members of the crew of the Galactica, like the shuttle pilot Sharon Agathon, turn out to be Cylon sleeper agents who, by virtue of their implanted memories, are unaware of their 'robotic' nature.

Galactica thus recapitulates the anti-Cartesian paranoia broached in *Blade Runner* (see Badmington 2003; Roden 2014, 27–29). However, it adds an urgent political allusion to the state security response in the wake of the destruction of the Twin Towers in the 9/11 attacks. The attack on the 12 Colonies is a blowback from the enslavement of the original Cylons – sentient creatures who, as we learn from the prequel *Caprica*, are 'differently embodied persons'. This political relevance is further reinforced by the resemblance between the human 'colonials' and North Americans. Their political institutions, clothing and architecture are recognizably akin to the US and other industrialized democracies.

From the perspective of posthuman studies, the most fascinating feature of *Galactica* is the way in which it explores the affinities and incompatibilities between Colonial and Cylon cultures. Elsewhere (Roden 2008), I have argued that the key incompatibility arises from absence of a state or state institutions in Cylon society.

Among Cylons, goods like health are furnished directly by the technical infrastructure on which they depend. Theirs is also a 'post-scarcity society': the scale and reliability of Cylon technology means there is no need to compete for resources, and little incentive for economic competition or criminality as we understand it. Cylon technology furnishes directly most of what humans need while state institutions and markets provide indirectly and, in the case of the Colonial survivors, as we learn, often very imperfectly. One uncanny manifestation of this difference is that humanoid Cylons are effectively immortal: when a human dies, she dies; whereas a Cylon's memories and personality are downloaded remotely to an identical cloned body: 'Death then becomes a learning experience'.

Thus the conflict between human and Cylon is not only predicated on the past mistreatment of the Cylons or the genocide that they perpetrate in turn. The liberal institutions of the Colonials operate under technological limitations that the Cylons have superseded. As a consequence, the basis for a just human–posthuman commonwealth is foreclosed by a contingent technological difference. This is exemplified near the end of the series when some rebel Cylons decide that immortality has made their lives and civilization empty, and help the humans to destroy the 'Hub' on which the resurrection technology depends. The destruction of the Hub allows the formation of a commonwealth of human and machine in which the former antagonists cooperate to achieve common political aims, fall in love and raise hybrid Cylon–human children.

This irenic conclusion seems to illustrate Haraway's contention that humans and machines are functionally differentiated by their historical and technological relationships, not by having a biological as opposed to a machinic lineage. Humans and Cylons, in Haraway's terms, are *equally cyborgs* – ambiguous assemblages of the natural and the artificial (Haraway 1991).

The political implications of this position are complex, for it implies that a posthuman–human polity would be only possible where disconnections are arrested – here by the reduction of the technological capacities of one 'signatory' to the social contract. However, there is a sense in which the singularity that produces the Cylons is already arrested. For, despite their manifest technological powers, the humanoid Cylons that we first encounter were created by an ancient group of Cylons known as the 'Final Five' who aped the original human form because they believed that their god intended this. In this extract from the pivotal episode 'No Exit', one of the new model Cylons, Cavil, questions one of his five creators, Ellen Tigh, about the justification for imposing these limitations:

Cavil: In all your travels, have you ever seen a star go supernova?
Ellen Tigh: No.
Cavil: No? Well, I have. I saw a star explode and send out the building blocks of the Universe. Other stars, other planets and eventually other life. A supernova! Creation itself! I was there. I wanted to see it and be part of the moment. And you know how I perceived one of the most glorious events in the universe? With these ridiculous gelatinous orbs in my skull! With eyes designed to perceive only a tiny fraction of the EM spectrum. With ears designed only to hear vibrations in the air.
Ellen Tigh: The five of us designed you to be as human as possible.
Cavil: I don't want to be human! I want to see gamma rays! I want to hear X-rays! And I want to – I want to smell dark matter! Do you see the absurdity of what I am? I can't even express these things properly because I have to – I have to conceptualize complex ideas in this stupid limiting spoken language! But I know I want to reach out with something other than these prehensile paws! And feel the wind of a supernova flowing over me! I'm a machine! And I can know much more! I can experience so much more. But I'm trapped in this absurd body! And why? Because my five creators thought that God wanted it that way!

Disarmingly, one of the conceits of *Galactica*'s fictional universe is that the Cylon god exists, since it intervenes at crucial junctures of the story. The nature of this entity is left unclear in the story. It is implied that it is 'beyond good and evil' and is intimately concerned with developing a rapprochement between biological and machinic life forms.

It is common for cinematic representations of the technological singularity to employ imagery drawn from religious conceptions of divine transcendence as a way of conveying the transcendence of humanity through technical change. This co-option of theology occurs in the last act of Stanley Kubrick's *2001: A Space Odyssey*, where we see the aged and dying astronaut David Bowman reincarnated as a 'Star Child' floating in space. The final sequence is cinematically potent because Kubrick abandons the punctilious realism that characterizes the greater part of the film in favour of a series of mythic, symbolic oppositions and substitutions (the old man on his deathbed, the glowing foetus suspended first above the bed in the space formerly occupied by the old man, then juxtaposed with the moon above the earth). The Cylon god can likewise be understood as an abstractly presented post-singularity entity – the superintelligent result of the eventual reconciliation of biological and machinic life intervening from the future to ensure its existence (a similar idea is explored in Christopher Nolan's 2014 film *Interstellar*).[4]

This poetic recipe for understanding the post-singularity bears some resemblances to the ancient tradition of 'apophatic' or 'negative' theology. Apophatic theologians claim that God is so mysterious that we can only describe Him by saying what He is not (Tuggy 2010). The title of Wally Pfister's 2014 *Transcendence* – in which the uploading of a dying scientist's mind to a quantum computer almost precipitates a singularity – reiterates this association between theology and technological posthumanity. However, notions of transcendence make little sense without assuming an essential, timeless human essence to be transcended (Roden 2012, 2014). As Ivan Niccolai argues, this assumption can legitimize a politically narrow conception of the human – in Pfister's film, that of a neoliberal subject threatened with violation by the collectivizing power of an AI-dominated 'hive mind' (Niccolai 2014). In essence, what is 'transcendent' here is not the posthuman, but the human as ultimate limit on technological intervention and change. But, echoing Cavil's protest to his creators, we are still entitled to ask why our minds and bodies should be constrained by this limit.

Notes

1. I've coined the term 'wide descent' because exclusive consideration of biological descendants of humanity as candidates for posthumanity would be excessively restrictive. Posthuman-making technologies may involve discrete biotechnical modifications of the reproductive process, such as human cloning, the introduction of transgenic or artificial genetic material or seemingly exotic processes like mind uploading. Thus, entities warranting our concern with the posthuman could emerge via modified biological descent, recursive extension of AI technologies (involving human and/or non-human designers), quasi-biological descent from synthetic organisms, a convergence of the above, or via some technogenetic process yet to be envisaged! (Roden 2012, 2014, 22).
2. Some futurists and AI experts view whole-brain emulation as a possible route to human-level or superhuman AI. See Bostrom and Sandberg (2008).
3. The theme of an autonomous, dehumanising technological rationality is common to philosophers and critical theorists such as Martin Heidegger, Theodor Adorno, Jacques Ellul and Herbert Marcuse.
4. The idea that a 'weakly godlike' being could intervene in its own timeline is wittily explored in Charles Stross' novel *Singularity Sky* (Stross 2004).

11
Chimeras and Hybrids: The Digital Swarms of the Posthuman Image

Drew Ayers

In a dream sequence in Martin Scorsese's *Hugo* (2011), homeless orphan Hugo Cabret (Asa Butterfield) discovers a mysterious key lodged in the tracks at the train station in which he makes his home. Hugo jumps onto the tracks in order to retrieve the key, only to be run over by an approaching train. While this scene is notable for its fast-paced action, kinetic editing and cinematography, shock value and suspense, the environment in which the scene takes place is, at least superficially, rather unremarkable. The train station and its inhabitants, while quite stylish and evocative of the time period, appear as photorealistic, seamless components of the *mise-en-scène*. In reality, however, much of this environment is a digital simulation, from the setting to the props to the characters, and in this regard, this scene from *Hugo* is indicative of much of contemporary mainstream filmmaking. The film achieves its photorealistic verisimilitude through the compositing of actual pro-filmic material with virtual computer-generated elements, resulting in a hybrid image of digital and analogue forces. While the completed image effectively adheres to the traditional stylistic conventions of narrative film, many of the individual components of the image are digital simulations.

The modus operandi of contemporary image production is to composite analogue and digital elements in the same frame, and, as a result, these images become chimeras, or impossible combinations, of human and non-human forces, imagining a hybrid space in which analogue pro-filmic and digital agents might seamlessly coexist in a posthuman utopia. This particular scene from *Hugo* utilizes Massive crowd simulation software, which is an application that animates individual digital agents through the use of 'fuzzy logic'.[1] These agents possess an innovative form of agency, whereby they react actively to their environment, rather than being individually animated to perform particular routines. What the use of Massive software creates is an environment in which human actors appear to interact and share space with self-motivated digital agents. These digital agents, however, don't always abide by the desire of their 'creators'. As one of the VFX artists on *Hugo* testifies regarding the use of Massive in this scene:

> I will say though – it didn't work 100% of the time. Occasionally the agents stopped behaving and went into a 'zombie mode'. They fell out of their actions, hunched their

shoulders and stood swaying on the spot like they just had a bad concussion. Drove me nuts trying to fix it but it was damn funny when it came up in dailies.[2]

The hybrid and chimeric images produced by the compositing of human and non-human elements creates, I will argue, a visualization of an imagined posthuman future, one in which analogue and digital forces can be easily and unproblematically transferred and exchanged.

Along with defining 'chimera' as the lion-goat-serpent hybrid monster of Greek mythology, the third definition provided by the *Oxford English Dictionary* describes 'chimera' as follows (*OED* 2014):

> *3a: A horrible and fear-inspiring phantasm, a bogy.*
> *3b: An unreal creature of the imagination, a mere wild fancy; an unfounded conception.*
> *3c: An incongruous union or medley.*
> *3d: An organism (commonly a plant) in which tissues of genetically different constitution co-exist as a result of grafting, mutation, or some other process.*

Applying these definitions of chimera to theories of the posthuman yields a fruitful encounter. As these definitions from the *OED* illustrate, a posthuman chimera composed of human and non-human (animal, machine, computing technology) aspects potentially draws from dual pools of affect. On the one hand, it functions as a utopian fantasy, a 'wild fancy' that transcends the boundaries of the human body and human experience (e.g., the rhetoric of stem cells, the human brain project or 3D organ printing). On the other hand, the chimera evokes feelings of dread and fear, and the posthuman hybrids of human and non-human are frequently imagined as a terrible and destructive 'incongruous union' (e.g., Cronenberg's *The Fly*, genetically modified organisms (GMOs), or any of the many films dealing with a post-apocalyptic cyborg future). This tension between existential terror and wide-eyed utopian promise is foundational to an understanding of the complexity of posthuman theory.

The notion of a chimeric being, and its application to posthuman theories, proves instructive with regard to the cultural ambivalence towards posthumanism, human/non-human hybrids and theories of the non-human. Broadly, and following much of the work that theorizes the posthuman condition from a perspective of phenomenology and embodiment, I diagnose competing posthumanist cultural trends: the simultaneous fantasy of disembodiment through the universal equivalent of 'code' and a reassertion of the importance of the lived body.

Drawing on a cognitive and behavioural framework of consciousness, transhumanist theories conceive of consciousness as a kind of software that runs on the biological hardware of the brain. In other words, consciousness is not something unique to the context of the embodied individual, but rather a system of information that can be accurately translated and replicated in different mediums, as exemplified by the Human Brain Project research initiative or the transhumanist fantasy of uploading one's brain/subjectivity into a computer and thus achieving a kind of immortality, as in the recent film *Transcendence* (2014).[3] This mode of transhumanist thinking also appears in popular discourses regarding genomics and genetic manipulation. Many of the contemporary discourses about genomics, especially as they are translated within the popular press, conceptualize the human genome as being manipulable as computer code, which collapses biology and technology into a single concept. Diagnosing an assumed interchangeability between 'computational biology and biological computing', Eugene Thacker argues that much of popular culture's attitude towards genomics rests on a common assumption that 'there exists some fundamental equivalency between genetic "codes" and computer "codes", or between the biological and digital domains, such that they can be rendered interchangeable in terms of materials and functions' (Thacker 2004a, 5). This equivalency between biological and computing code also undergirds much of the presentational vernacular of digital effects images. Transhumanist thinking informs the imagination of these chimeric images, to the extent that they visualize the digitization of the human, and these images also act in concert with popular cultural imaginings of a transhumanist utopia.

As opposed to the more 'transhumanist'-inflected theories of posthumanism, which conceptualize the posthuman as what comes after, and transcends, the human, alternate theories of posthumanism are influenced by frameworks of phenomenology and philosophies of Enlightenment humanism, which view the existence of the human and the non-human as intertwined and co-constitutive. This kind of philosophical humanist and phenomenological understanding of the posthuman has been articulated by writers such as N. Katherine Hayles and Cary Wolfe (Hayles 1999; Wolfe 2010). Wolfe, in his book *What Is Posthumanism?*, defines his use of posthumanism as such:

> *My sense of posthumanism is the opposite of transhumanism, and in this light, transhumanism should be seen as an intensification of humanism. (...) Posthumanism in my sense isn't posthuman at all – in the sense of being 'after' our embodiment has been transcended – but is only posthumanist, in the sense that it opposes the fantasies of disembodiment and autonomy, inherited from humanism itself, that Hayles rightly criticizes.*
>
> (Wolfe 2010, xv)

What is important here is the emphasis placed on the materiality of the lived body. Information doesn't exist in some abstract space. It is embodied in a physical medium, and the interaction among these mediums is crucial to understanding how consciousness and subjectivity – of both humans and non-humans – emerges from an environment.

Crucial to my own examination of chimeric and hybrid digital visual effects images is an embrace of the tension between the poles of transhumanism and posthumanism, one that accounts for the embodied encounters between human and non-human. Theoretically and philosophically, it is quite valuable to set the two viewpoints as opposed to each other: an informational, disembodied transhumanism on one side and an embodied posthumanism on the other. Yet, within popular visual culture, we find an ambivalence between these two philosophical positions. On the one hand, cultural narratives and imagery fantasize about a utopian transcendence of the body; on the other hand, these narratives and imagery frequently depict this transcendence as leading to an apocalyptic destruction of the body, humanity and human civilization.

We can see this ambivalence nowhere clearer than in popular visual cultural objects like cinema, TV and video games, specifically in these forms' use and deployment of digital visual effects. Digital effects serve as a signal example where humans imagine themselves in dialogue with non-human digital spaces and agents. One of the primary goals of mainstream digital visual effects is to composite humans and digital code into a photorealistic, cohesive whole, one in which viewers are unable to distinguish analogue from digital elements (Allison 2011; Freedman 2012; Prince 2012). *The image itself becomes a posthuman hybrid*, and it renders visible a cultural logic of informationalism, one that domesticates the threat of dissolution of the human and fantasizes about a digital utopia. The image stages an encounter between human and non-human, and the deployment of digital visual effects presents this encounter as a seamless merging of analogue and digital, actual and virtual, flesh and computer data.[4] These spaces of visual culture allow us to imagine and visualize our posthuman future, one in which flesh and information might seamlessly and easily coexist and cohabitate with each other. This hybrid image presents the problem of the interaction and synchronization of biological and computer code as already solved, masking the reality of the cultural, moral and philosophical growing pains experienced as we humans and non-humans come to terms with our continually evolving relationship to, and dependence on, each other.

The hybrid digital effects image is a staging ground for cultural work that thinks through issues of the posthuman, and it provides a space for interrogating the troubled boundaries between the human and non-human. These images typically present a utopian solution to these problems – in that they depict a seamless interaction between humans, digital space and digital agents – and they offer a point of contact for exploring how contemporary popular visual culture imagines the ways in which humans and (digital) non-humans might someday interact with each other. The figure of the chimera serves as a productive concept for rethinking how we might approach the cultural ambivalence towards the posthuman, and the hybridity of the image provides a template for examining the contemporary hybridity of the human.

In particular, we see this interaction quite clearly in digital effects that create semi-autonomous digital agents and simulated crowds. As a component of a much larger industrial trend of incorporating digital visual effects into every aspect of the pre-production, production and post-production of visual media, crowd simulation is indicative of the extent to which the screen image has become hybrid, malleable and composite, an image in which the lines between 'captured' and 'created' data have been irrevocably blurred (Manovich 2006; North 2008; Prince 2012). This is an image in which 'spotting the joins' between analogue and digital imaging (to borrow a phrase from Dan North) has become virtually impossible, as subtle, non-spectacular visual effects like colour correction and set extensions have become the norm in mainstream commercial image production (North 2008).

While many mainstream deployments of visual effects are meant to go unnoticed by audiences, scenes of massive crowds and swarms are still, both narratively and aesthetically, positioned as moments of spectacle and awe. These images of crowds and swarms provide a break from the narrative trajectory and aesthetic composition of images, and they offer moments of affective force within the otherwise typical popcorn genres of blockbuster SF and fantasy films in which most of these visual effects scenes are found. Crowd simulation is frequently used to animate hordes of non-human agents (e.g., zombies, orcs, apes, monsters). In films such as the *Lord of the Rings* trilogy (Jackson 2001–2003); *I, Robot* (Proyas, 2004); *300* (Snyder, 2006); *Rise of the Planet of the Apes* (Wyatt, 2011); and *World War Z* (Forster, 2013), digital crowds are, both narratively and visually, constructed as a threat to their human counterparts. The images of digital crowds and swarms pose a threat both to the analogue human bodies with whom they share visual space and to the visual system of the media objects themselves. Their energies, intensities and vectors introduce discord into the image, threatening to burst out of the frame, and they challenge the systems of signification established within the film and/or TV programme.[5]

In examining the visualization of digital crowds, it is important to account for the role of the software packages in the aesthetic deployment of the digital multitude.[6] The wide-ranging use of Massive helps explain the consistent look that these crowd scenes share, and the similar behaviour of the crowds is due, in part, to the algorithms within the Massive software package. What is innovative about Massive is how it programs its digital agents to behave. Or, rather, how it doesn't program its agents to behave. A problem in the history of artificial intelligence and crowd simulation has been the time, labour and processing power necessary to program thousands of individual agents to perform specific actions. Individually animating each agent by hand to perform a set number of tasks results in unnatural crowd behaviour, one that appears excessively computerized and rigid. Massive software avoids this issue by following what Jussi Parikka describes as an insect logic of media. Parikka argues that much of our communications technology has been modelled after – and is understood within the terms of – the behaviour of insect swarms, in which each insect is 'individually dumb, but highly efficient when coupled with their environment' (Parikka 2010, xii). Massive operates in much the same manner. Each individual digital agent is programmed not simply to perform certain pre-programmed routines, but rather to react actively to its environment. In other words, each agent has a catalogue of movements, actions and behaviours that it deploys, depending on its position within its environment and in relation to the other digital agents. At the individual level, an agent's behaviour might appear chaotic, but at the global level the crowd behaves in a cohesive way, much like swarms of insects, birds and fish. The Massive architecture is modelled after this theory of interaction between individual and group behaviour, and the digital agents it creates and brings to life develop a mode of agency that is uniquely suited to the hybrid environment of the posthuman digital image.

From a narrative perspective, the nascent agency of digital swarms and simulated crowds generally functions as a force that threatens to end civilization and, with it, humanity. This, for example, is the plot of 2011's *Rise of the Planet of the Apes*, which is a rebooting of the *Planet of the Apes* franchise of the late 1960s and 1970s. This film traces the rise of an intelligent ape civilization – led by ape revolutionary Caesar – and the subsequent decline of human civilization. Typical reasons for the downfall of humans are at play here: hubris, faith in technology, ignorance of the natural world and a devotion to profit above all else. While the narrative of the film might be standard Hollywood fare, it is in the visualization of the ape swarm where we see the ambivalence of the chimeric, posthuman image.

In a climactic scene towards the end of the film, we see how the energies and intensities of the swarm might undermine human modes of perception and existence, and this is typical of many Massive-generated crowd scenes. In this sequence, the apes, having recently been exposed to a drug that radically increases their intelligence and cognitive abilities, assault the lab where the drug was developed. The lab conducts tests on apes, so part of the ape swarm's goal is to free its imprisoned brethren. During its assault on the lab, the ape swarm overwhelms the space and the humans occupying the space, destroying the technology in the lab and adding more apes to the digital multitude. Later, the apes move into the city, claiming buildings, streets and trams as their territory. The force of the ape swarm is overwhelming, and, despite their technological superiority, the human inhabitants are unable to resist. Due to both the surprising, sudden nature of the attack as well as humans' anthropological hubris, the individual humans cannot withstand the energy of the apes' collective action, and they are swallowed up by the advancing horde, powerless in the face of such a force. The apes, through their embrace of nature and destruction of technology, infest the spheres of human progress like a virus, taking over these spaces and repurposing them for their own ends. The bars of metal gates become spears, manholes become projectiles and zoo cages become incubators of the end of humanity. Furthermore, the algorithms that animate and move these digital agents function according to their own logic, navigating the space of the image as if it were a digital playground, subverting the analogue desires of their human counterparts.[7]

In the *Lord of the Rings* trilogy, the relationship between digital hordes and the end of human civilization is made explicit through the film's chimeric imagery. In the *Lord of the Rings*, Saruman (Christopher Lee), an agent of Sauron, deploys swarms of orcs in order to bring all Middle Earth under the rule of his master. As with many of the swarms in this kind of apocalyptic film, the orcs in the *Lord of the Rings* threaten to bring about the end of the world, and they do so by overwhelming the humans (and elves, dwarves and hobbits) with sheer numbers and collective action. A key part of the narrative of the films is the quest to unite the fractured tribes of Middle Earth so that they might cast aside their individual concerns and mimic the collective action of the orcs (if only temporarily) in order to withstand this horde.

Much narrative time is spent on overcoming the political differences between the elves, dwarves and tribes of men in order to assemble a force strong enough to overcome the orc hordes. In one notable sequence from *The Return of the King* (2003), Aragorn (Viggo Mortensen) recruits an army of ghostly (and digitally animated) Dead Men of Dunharrow in order to defeat Sauron's army of orcs and corsairs. In this instance, a human is able to control the digital multitude, but only temporarily. After the battle is won, Aragorn releases the dead men from their bondage, and they dissipate into the ether. In the case of *The Lord of the Rings*, the digital multitude functions, narratively, to create a human/elf/dwarf multitude, one that sublimates the desires of its individual members in favour of the interests of the collective. Thus, the digital multitude, 'rather than destroy entirely the heterogeneous and fragmented community (...) forces into existence an ideal form of collective action able to usher in a new historical era' (Whissel 2010, 108). It is important to note, however, that this activity occurs on a narrative level, and it functions to provide closure to the story. Formally, the affective and intensive force of the digital multitude remains, and this force provides resistance to the tidy solution of collective action that the film presents. In this way, the film functions as a chimera on an additional level: narratively, the film depicts a utopian solution to the problem of social heterogeneity; formally, the film leaves open the question of the relationship between the individual and the horde. The tension here is analogous to the posthumanist tension between the hope of transcending the body and the anxiety of abandoning embodiment, and this tension is visualized in the relationship between the analogue and digital, human and non-human, within the image.

In *Look at the Bunny*, Dominic Pettman recounts an example from the DVD extras of the *Lord of the Rings*, wherein the animators provide an amusing anecdote regarding the agency of Massive-animated agents (Pettman 2013, 66–67). Roughly 80,000 digital orcs were required for the films, and they were notably deployed in the grandiose Battle of Helm's Deep in the second film of the trilogy, *The Two Towers* (2002). In this sequence, the orcs storm the keep, attempting to wrest it from the control of their human and elven adversaries. During the preliminary animation of this scene, a few of the orcs 'decided' that they'd rather not engage in battle, and they fled from the fight, despite their directions from the script. Because they were programed to react to their environment and situation, rather than programmed to carry out specific actions, these orcs made the unpredictable decision to flee. While this footage didn't end up in the final cut of the film, this example illustrates the extent to which notions of human and non-human 'agency' become complicated and fuzzy within these kinds of posthuman, hybrid images. As Pettman articulates it, 'we have now reached the historical threshold where *all* creatures – whether created in a womb, lab, or computer – contain their own virtual potential to unfold into existence according to their own whims or dictates, beyond the codes which guide their day-to-day behaviour' (2013, 86). The behaviour and agency of digital agents, as revealed in the chimeric images of digital visual effects, often exceed the intentions of their human creators and programmers. 'Glitches' function not as a bug, but as a feature of digital creatures' behaviour.

What results from this semi-autonomous behaviour of the digital multitude is a challenge to both the representational strategies of the film and the human characters within the film. The software packages and computing technology used to animate these digital agents function in an affective manner, creating, by design, an intelligent and unpredictable crowd that captures the energies, intensities and malleability of the swarm, rather than producing a fixed representation of individual agents. These swarms embody the energies and perceived dangers of the anonymous networked self, and they function as a self-organizing, decentralized, rhizomatic intelligence, one that endangers the boundaries of the image. They introduce discord into the image, threatening to burst out of the frame and release their kinetic energy into the world. The digital multitude cannot be contained, and it creates a sublime and terrifying sensation of threat through the overwhelming of the individual. This loss of human control, writes Thacker, creates 'an equal and more anxious interest in the unpredictability, the instability, and the uncontrollable nature of networks, swarms, and multitudes. They seem to fascinate because their distributed modes of organization foster both an absence of centralized control, and an anxiety about that loss of control' (2004b, 45). These digital crowds behave like computer viruses, travelling along digital vectors, and infecting the image. They threaten to continue their digital trajectory, seeping out of the frame and infiltrating the entirety of networked technology and culture. By contrast, the analogue human bodies appear stuck within the frame, unable to spread along the digital vectors of the swarms. They appear rooted in their representational logic, their energies and intensities directed towards individuation and melodramatic characterization rather than collective action.

Regardless of whatever moments of resistance to traditional modes of narrative and aesthetic representation are presented by these films, in the end, the affective forces of the swarm are depicted as hostile to humanistic modes of being, and they are eventually domesticated both on a narrative as well as a visual level. However, on a purely formal level, the co-presence of analogue humans and digital non-humans within the frame nevertheless presents moments of affective force that encourage the viewer to imagine a reality in which humans and digital agents might share space, intensities and energies. This hybrid image stages an encounter between humans and non-humans, one which speaks to a vernacular experience of posthumanism. The image has realized its posthuman fantasy more quickly than we humans, but it shares both our hopes and anxieties about this future. On the one hand, the hybrid image imagines a potential future in which the human and digital non-human might seamlessly coexist in a kind of technological utopia. On the other hand, this image also visualizes a potential future in which the human is assimilated into the digital horde, losing a sense of individual self to the desires of the collective. While these chimeric images provide an arena where culture might work through these anxieties, these images aren't simply symptoms or projections of human thought and desire. Rather, they are themselves non-human entities with whom we humans share existence, and they have their own modes of cognition and desire.⁸ Thus, while the images might themselves be posthuman hybrids, our relationship to these images is itself chimeric, involving an assemblage of humans, imaging technology and strategies of cultural representation.

These hybrid images envision and enact the potentiality of a posthuman future. This posthuman future isn't one of apocalyptic cyborgs, technological singularity or the disembodiment of consciousness. Rather, these hybrid images imagine posthumanism in terms of potentiality and affective forces, and they produce visualizations that encourage us humans to think of ourselves as embedded in larger material-semiotic networks, networks in which both humans and non-humans possess forms of agency and intentionality. Such images are less about envisioning the transcendence of the human body and more about staging encounters and interactions between the forces of human and non-human, analogue and digital, flesh and information. In doing so, these hybrid, chimeric images communicate in a vernacular of posthumanism, one which speaks to our contemporary experience of the richness and wonder of the non-human beings and technologies with whom we share our world.

The examples I've explored in this chapter, like all chimeras, are messy, and they resist easy classification. On a number of levels – narrative, aesthetic, technological and affective – they visualize the joining of incongruity, the temporary arresting of tension. In some ways, these chimeras are hopeful about our posthuman future. On an aesthetic, formal and technological level, they depict humans and digital non-humans as coexisting peacefully in the frame, one indistinguishable from the other. In other ways, these chimeras are anxious about our posthuman future. Narratively and affectively, they present images of humans being overwhelmed by the digital multitude, lost in the chaos of the anonymous collective. Taken as a whole, these chimeric images offer a way to sample the tension inherent in prognostications regarding the posthuman. Viewers can become digital through simulations of the digital horde, while remaining safely embodied in the human. In this way, these chimeric and hybrid images are teaching us to become posthuman, but their lessons are often opaque. They warn of discarding embodiment while encouraging us to adopt some of the forces of the digital and non-human. As we proceed into this uncharted territory, we would be wise to listen to and translate carefully the voices of these non-human images and objects with whom we share this world, as they have much to teach us about our increasingly digital and posthuman culture.

Notes

1. The Massive software package was developed by Stephen Regelous for use by Weta Digital in Peter Jackson's *Lord of the Rings* trilogy. See Merrill (2004) and Thompson (2006) for an extended discussion of the technological underpinnings of Massive.
2. http://www.massivesoftware.com/hugo.html.
3. Katherine Hayles diagnoses this transhumanist approach as possessing four defining qualities. First, the transhuman privileges informationalism over materialism. Second,

it considers consciousness as an epiphenomenon. Third, the transhuman thinks of the body as a prosthesis, one that can be modified and improved through technology. Fourth, the transhuman disregards any essential differences between humans and intelligent machines. For Hayles, the primary attribute of a transhumanist subjectivity is the disavowal of the necessity and uniqueness of the body (Hayles 1999, 2–3).
4. In *Cinema 2*, Gilles Deleuze theorizes the relationship between the virtual and the actual, and how a particular mode of cinema – the time-image – visualizes this relationship. Rather than acting dialectically, the actual and the virtual appear as reflections of each other, one inhabiting the image of the other. The actual and virtual form a circuit of sensation, folding into each other and confusing past and present, inside and outside (Deleuze 2005, 68). In the posthuman hybrid image, actual and virtual overlap and intertwine with each other, linking the human and the non-human in a circuit of affect, intensity and sensation.
5. In their chapter on 'becoming-animal' from *A Thousand Plateaus*, Deleuze and Guattari discuss how, during the process of becoming, entities share and merge their affects, energies and intensities. While a 'real' physical hybrid is not produced, the process of becoming changes both entities and how they inhabit the world: 'Becoming produces nothing other than itself. We fall into a false alternative if we say that you either imitate or you are. What is real is the becoming itself, the block of becoming, not the supposedly fixed terms through which that which becomes passes' (Deleuze & Guattari 1987, 238).
6. The term 'digital multitude' is borrowed from Kristen Whissel (2010).
7. True, at the end of most of these kinds of films, the humans generally triumph or manage to come together temporarily to defeat the foe, though it's worth noting that the humans 'lose' at the end of *Apes*. However, these moments of threat reveal an anxiety about non-human collective action, as well as an anxiety regarding the inability to comprehend fully the energies and intensities of digital flows of information.
8. See Mitchell (2005) for full discussion of the 'lives and loves of images'.

Part III
Rise of the Machines: Posthuman Intellects

Part III

12
Androids and the Posthuman in Television and Film

Kevin LaGrandeur

Androids – robots that look like humans – serve as central characters in movies and television all the way back to the origins of those forms. In movies, they primarily have two values: they are mostly symbols of technological threat – the dangers of industrialism, in earlier movies, and the dangers of human ingenuity and automated slave labour in later ones – or they are, less often, symbols of how we contemplate the meaning of 'human', the issues connected with 'personhood'. Androids depicted in television shows have a more varied symbolic value, mainly because the writers have the time and need to develop various plotlines. So, in a television series, the signification of the android can vary depending upon the episode we view.

I am going to focus here specifically on how androids represent the values of the posthuman (as opposed to posthumanism). In the context of the posthuman, androids in film and television commonly represent three themes:

- our blindness to the possible dangers of our own ingenuity and evolving technology;
- the problems posed by the creation of new, intelligent species and by their transitions to sentience – in other words, the issues of how we define what is 'human' and the legal rights of 'personhood';
- and, concomitantly, the androids depicted in TV and film usually bring up the issue of human exceptionalism and its consequences: the exploitation of intelligent species and the possibility of creating new slave classes, with all that entails. In such contexts, issues of personhood and the opposing identities of human/beast lead to concerns such as shifting definitions of inhumane treatment, new kinds of prejudices, new social classes and new kinds of class hatred, and even interspecies war.

I will give specific examples and discuss all of this further, but first we need to pause and address two important issues: the first issue is to define more specifically what I mean by 'android'. Second, what do I mean by 'the posthuman', which is a slippery term these days? In answer to the first question, I am restricting my discussion to autonomous, humanoid robots. We will not examine androids that are not autonomous, that is, remote-controlled androids, because they do not really call forth posthuman concerns; nor will we look at artificial biological organisms such as the replicants in the film *Blade Runner* or the creature in the 1931 movie *Frankenstein*. Also, although matters of gender arise naturally when considering matters of personhood, servitude and so forth, I will not discuss them here.

As to 'the posthuman', there is a lot of confusion about that term in relation to 'posthumanism' for a number of reasons: the two are often (incorrectly) used interchangeably; also, the term 'posthuman' is specifically related to 'transhumanism' in a way that posthumanism is not; and these terms are all fairly new. So, for clarity's sake, before I get into the details of my argument, let me give simple thumbnail definitions of all three terms to indicate how I will use them. *Transhumanism* is the project of modifying the human species via any kind of emerging science, including genetic engineering, digital technology and bioengineering. The focus is generally on using prosthetics and other modifications to enhance, rather than compensate for, normal human functions, and to improve human longevity, brain power and senses. So transhumans are those who have engaged in such self-modification – and there are those, such as Kevin Warwick, who have already begun to do this with implants and surgery (in his case, an RFID chip that could automatically open doors and keep him and his similarly implanted wife aware of each other's locations). The *posthuman* is, most simply, the desired endpoint of transhumanism. That is, a posthuman is a new, hybrid species of future human modified by advanced technology. Crucial for my purposes here is that the posthuman entails the blurring of distinctions between humans and machines.

Posthumanism, on the other hand, is easiest to understand if one thinks of the term as a compound word: that is, post-humanism. As opposed to transhumanism and the posthuman, it is primarily an academic preoccupation that recognizes that the idea of the humanist subject is being undermined by trends in emerging sciences and postmodern shifts in self-awareness. This undermining of the humanist subject leads, in turn, to a dilemma about how to think of ourselves and our position in the universe, and so also to a quandary about how to restructure our (formerly humanistic) academic curriculum (Badmington 2000; Wolfe 2009; Braidotti 2013). Posthumanism is an intellectual framework that, like transhumanism, springs from the rapid technological change of the past few decades, but it also owes much to postmodern and poststructuralist philosophies. Because the posthuman (as opposed to posthumanism) is more germane to technology and its products, such as androids, my reflections will mainly be in the context of the posthuman, not posthumanism. In particular, it is the posthuman's potential blurring of the definition of human and the consequent elision of the human and the machine that makes android-centred films and television shows such fertile ground for exploration.

Although the signification of androids in TV and film often differ depending on the era in which the film or TV show was made, in general they do seem to have one consistent meaning: ultimately, androids are always a mode of extending their maker's power over nature, or of proving the maker's superiority to nature (and other humans); and so their main significance is that these fictional, artificial humans embody at once the ambitions of the scientific wizards who make them and society's perception of the dangers of those ambitions. And these dangers shift as we move through the 20th century and into the 21st. The early 20th-century movies containing androids exhibit a primal fear of being ground up in the gears of industrialism, which reflects the first theme noted. Android-centric movies from the mid-20th century, from just after the Second World War until the end of the 1960s, tend to focus on this issue as well, but in a slightly different form: they, more specifically, focus on fears of being annihilated by technology, which are clear reflections of fears spurred by the nuclear age and the Cold War. But there are also, in the latter part of the Cold War era and into the 21st century, glimmerings of the second theme – the problems raised by species creation, primarily that of being displaced by our own technological creations, which relates to the third theme: the interrogation of human exceptionalism. Many of the more recent TV shows and films centring on androids raise the question: If we create something that looks, acts and thinks like us, but is possibly superior, then have we endangered the survival of our species by creating viable replacements for it? Will the slave become the master? And even if that is not a danger, what rights and responsibilities should intelligent, though artificial, humanoids have?

Let's back up a bit and discuss the earliest film representations of androids. In the very earliest movies, androids often served merely as comic figures. The Tin Man in the first Wizard of Oz film, *The Wonderful Wizard of Oz*, a silent movie released in 1910, was a classic buffoon (in the more famous 1939 film, his role was a bit more serious, but the Tin Man was still pretty much a stock comic character). So it was with *A Clever Dummy* (1917), another prime example of an early film in which an android was a central character. The title of the second movie says it all: the android characters were 'dummies' that provided comic value by their very poor imitation of human behaviour. It is important to note, however, an oblique anticipation of the posthuman in the books that inspired the early *Wizard of Oz*, because in those books L. Frank Baum's Tin Woodman is represented as a merging of man and proto-machine. He informs his friends that he was originally a man named Nick Chopper, but because of a curse by a witch he had a series of bad accidents with his axe: it consistently slips and cuts off his body parts. They are all replaced by a very skilled tinsmith with metal ones – and, except for the fact that he doesn't have a real heart, he likes his new, shiny body and its impervious elements (Baum 1900, 58–60); he no longer needs sleep (Baum 1907, 250) or food (Baum 1909, 166). The makers of the short film produced in 1910 did not see the advantage to using this backstory, most likely because, like most early filmmakers, they chose to focus on action rather than intricate dialogue that such a backstory might need – which would prove difficult to convey without sound.

The first major film to treat androids seriously was Fritz Lang's *Metropolis* (1927), with its robot double of the human character Maria. And the BBC's 1938 production of *Rossum's Universal Robots (R.U.R.)* was the first television show to do so. Robot-Maria, in *Metropolis*, is a puzzling character. Originally conceived as a prototype for a future robot force that will replace the human labourers who keep the city running, it is transformed into a double for human-Maria on the orders of the cruel dictator-businessman who owns and runs Metropolis. His idea is to have it sow discord and chaos among the workers, who are on the verge of rebellion because of their grindingly oppressive lives. The irony is that Maria is a conciliating force, and robot-Maria's actions will discredit her, worsening the workers' restiveness; furthermore, Fredersen has heard her preach patience to the workers, calming them. Yet after he hears this, he orders his chief engineer, Rotwang, to transform his new robot into robot-Maria and send it out to wreak havoc. His plot makes little sense, as it seems destructive with regard to his own power, to the technology-based order that underpins it, and so ultimately to himself.

There are several (questionable) ways to explain this odd plan: first, if one takes the whole movie into account, including the previously lost scenes, one possibility lies in the backstory of Rotwang. He secretly hates his boss because the love of his life, Hel, married him instead of Rotwang, and then died giving birth to the boss's son, Freder. Therefore, Rotwang may have programmed robot-Maria for more extreme behaviour than Fredersen anticipated, in order to have revenge on him; and, indeed, she ultimately destroys the main machine that controls all other machines, wrecking the city. Another possibility is that Fredersen intends for the android to wreak havoc in order to have an excuse for using force against the rebels later. A couple of final possibilities are suggested by the novel on which the movie was based, which was written by Lang's wife Thea von Harbou in 1922. In the novel, Fredersen explains he chose not to stop the destruction of the city by robot-Maria because 'The city is to go to ruin so that [Freder] may build it up again', and so that Freder may 'redeem' its citizens (Harbou 2001, 178). That could mean, as one commentator has argued, that Fredersen means for his son to use the destruction of the city as an excuse to complete his plan of replacing the human workers with robots (Kang 2011, 292). But I think there is more to it than that. Given that von Harbou, Lang's wife, became a Nazi enthusiast, and thus most probably had proto-fascist leanings when she wrote her book, it makes sense that she has Fredersen do what any good fascist strategist would do to gain control of the populace: manufacture a community crisis which he already has the means to resolve.[1] The main importance of robot-Maria, and the crisis she causes, is therefore the peril and the possibilities of the technology she embodies: frighteningly powerful, with the potential to allow humans to do less work; but at the same time oppressive, dehumanising and ultimately destructive to human society, and even to itself – robot-Maria convinces the workers to destroy the very machinery with which she is associated, and her reward is that they burn her at the stake. Her actions reflect current fears of technology and industrialization, and also of the hubris, inattentiveness and indeed cruelty of the human industrialists who create such technology.

R.U.R. was broadcast as a television show in the middle of the 20th century a number of times, and although no copies of those shows have survived, it is important to at least briefly examine the meaning of its key characters, the humanoid robots, because of the ambiguities in portrayal of those androids and the importance of this particular story in the history of television. And important these characters apparently were in that era, for the play was produced by BBC television three times from 1938 through 1948 (Bould 2008, 210). The BBC broadcast a shortened version of *R.U.R.* on 11 February 1938, which was not only the first television show about androids, but also the first science fiction (SF) television show; although the young television company could broadcast over a range of 100 miles from North London at that point, and only about 400 families had televisions (Bould 2008, 210). So this broadcast was not seen by many and, according to the BBC's website on SF, the 38-minute episode was not recorded and is now lost. Although descriptions in the script of the play portray these androids as what we would call clones or synthetic organisms (they are made from body parts grown in vats), pictures of the actors from the actual plays of the period portrayed them as metallic and with robotic movements (some of these pictures are included in the Wikipedia page for *R.U.R.* for instance). Moreover, this play originated the word 'robot' – a Czech word for 'forced labour'.

But what made these androids so compelling for audiences of the 1920s, 1930s and 1940s? First, the androids at the heart of it are another representation of the dangers of industrialization and mechanization. Robot-Maria in *Metropolis* is a good example of the menace of both. She is a deceptive figure – looking like a human who was friendly to the working class, but in reality a self-destructive machine leading them towards chaos. The robots in *R.U.R.* are, on the other hand, fairly straightforward symbols of the evils of a mechanized world. They represent factory labourers themselves at the height of the age of industry: emotionally repressed and drone-like, they focus on nothing but work. But, in very humanlike fashion, these humanoids' emotions eventually surface and, because they are so repressed, they surface violently, reflecting the actual worker unrest that was common in early 20th-century society. Also, the androids in both *Metropolis* and *R.U.R.* reveal the evils of human bondage and the elitist attitudes that lead to it. More significantly, the androids – the prototype in *Metropolis* and the robot workers in *R.U.R* – also carry in nascent form the theme of speciesism, or human exceptionalism, that becomes common in later narratives about androids. In other words, while ideas of slavery, starting with Aristotle's discussion of it, grouped some humans with animals as *things* to be used by masters (Aristotle 1984, 1990–1992), these modern stories are among the first to classify a whole species of humanoids as things, as non-human. And this is merely because they are made by human artifice instead of sexual intercourse.

The fact that, in both cases, the androids are created specifically as slaves is also symbolic in another very important way that we see repeatedly in android stories up through today. The humanoids in *Metropolis*, especially robot-Maria, and the robots in *R.U.R.* also have in common their value as symbols of humans' attempts to bend nature to their will. For these kinds of artificial servants are always characterized as superprostheses that allow their creators to supersede their natural boundaries in some way – usually to do more, better, more dangerous, more tedious or dirtier work. Moreover, the irony of these humanoid tools' superiority to humans leads to a recurring theme of the inversion of the master–slave dialectic in many android stories in TV and film. Starting with *R.U.R.*, humans in many stories about androids create servants that are more powerful than they and, as in *R.U.R.*, let them do too much for them, eventually making the masters even weaker; meanwhile, the intelligent and powerful servants inevitably recognize their superiority and rebel. This kind of theme becomes especially common in the late 20th century in movies such as the *Terminator* series, which I will return to.

In mid-20th-century movies and television shows, though, the main thematic value of androids was not so much their threat as slaves, but their threat as weapons or agents of violence. This is not surprising if we consider that, from just after the Second World War until the end of the 1960s, filmmakers lived in societies dominated by the fear of being annihilated by technology spawned by the nuclear age and the Cold War and, consequently, of losing control over technology. A good example of a movie from this era with such a thematic focus is the film *The Day the Earth Stood Still* (1951), featuring the android Gort. This theme arises as well in SF television shows of the late 1950s and early 1960s, such as an episode titled 'I, Robot' (1964) from a show called *The Outer Limits*.

The giant, eight-foot-tall humanoid robot named Gort in *The Day the Earth Stood Still* is a fearsome weapon. A member of an interstellar police force charged with preventing violence, it ironically has great violent capacity. This is not surprising once we consider that the movie's main concept is the dangers of the new atomic weapons that humankind had just invented and the fear that we would be unable to control them. The main character, an alien diplomat named Klaatu, says at the end of the movie that he has been sent to warn humans that if they extend violence and atomic weapons into space, the spacefaring cultures he represents will destroy the earth. Perhaps as a testament to his fears of humankind's capacities, he has as his companion a humanoid robot that seems infinitely powerful: it is not only able to disintegrate anything with a power beam that it projects from the area where human eyes would be, but it also raises Klaatu from the dead (temporarily) just before he delivers his final warning speech to humans at the end of the movie. This threat of violence met with violence and the android Gort are, ironically, apt metaphors for nuclear-empowered humans themselves: like them, Gort has human form and the capacity to commit extreme, planet-destroying violence that is almost impossible to stop once evoked; but it also has the capacity to stop the violence if it so chooses – and indeed to be life-promoting.

The Outer Limits episode titled 'I, Robot' (which bears no relation to Isaac Asimov's short story collection of the same name) opens with the capture and jailing of a humanoid robot named Adam Link on suspicion of killing its maker. The robot, which the audience is led to understand is the first of its kind, claims that its maker died in a laboratory accident and that it was not running to escape the sheriff and his posse, but to find help for the bleeding professor. It backs its claim with the facts that it peacefully surrendered and that it remains jailed even though it could bend the jail bars with its machinic strength and escape. The professor's niece, who has been familiar with the robot since its activation, defends the robot's character, saying that though it is very strong, it is gentle. And in fact the robot's behaviour exhibits emotions, logic, thought and other clear signs of sentience. The rest of the episode focuses on the dichotomous views of the android throughout its ensuing court trial for murder: the niece, her lawyer and a journalist see the robot as a human being with rights and a trustworthy character; however, the rest of the town sees it as a threatening, monstrous machine.

The prosecuting lawyer speaks for the more reasonable of the townspeople when he suggests that the robot, still learning about itself and humans, may have simply misjudged its own strength and killed the professor by accident. This android, unfortunately, has demonstrated such capacity already, by breaking the arm of a girl in an attempt to save her from drowning, and by almost breaking the prosecutor's arm when the robot grasps it in a fit of emotion while refuting the very suggestion that it could harm someone by accident. The prosecutor's subsequent statements at trial aptly represent the views of the populace: he declares at various points that Adam Link is an 'unreasoning piece of machinery (...) an engine of destruction', and that the people must be protected against its 'mindless violence'. Because the robot has the capacity to learn and to empathize, it actually is well aware of this perception of its capabilities. When it is first jailed and the sheriff says he is coming back with a blowtorch to disassemble it, the android blandly corrects the niece's objection that the sheriff cannot do that to what is legally her property. Actually, the robot notes, 'He could destroy me. All he needs is a State order declaring me an unlawful weapon.' This is a tacit acknowledgement of how society sees the android. But the other side of the philosophical question, for the Cold War era, was the issue that we all had to take responsibility for the horrific possibilities of destruction that advanced technology brought and for controlling it; for development of such powerful technology is always done with tacit communal consent. This point is raised with the opening narration that begins the episode: 'God looked upon his world and called it good, but Man was not content. He looked for ways to make it better and built machines to do the work. But in vain we build the world, unless the builder also grows.' And this point is driven home with the double meaning of the defence attorney's key declaration that the trial of the robot for murder should not go forward because it is, in effect, 'trying all of society (...) on its ability to control what it creates'.

This use of androids as a metaphor for the threat of technology and, more specifically, the threat of irresponsible oversight of scientific advances, becomes more common in movies and television shows as the 20th century progresses. The android police force in *THX 1138* (1971), George Lucas' first film, are mindless killing machines; the robotic gunfighters and other androids in Michael Crichton's *Westworld* (1973) begin killing humans in a theme park because they are deployed without being thoroughly checked for flaws and without adequate failsafe devices in place; the characters Ash, in *Alien* (1979), and David, in *Prometheus* (2012), are surreptitiously and surprisingly homicidal due to purposefully bad programming by evil corporate executives; and, of course, there are the most famous deadly androids in the *Terminator* series (1984, 1991, 2003, 2009), which, again, originate from lax, hubristic oversight by humans of their creation, Skynet, a supercomputer that is delegated too much responsibility for and power over human existence and that, becoming sentient, decides humans are noxious pests that need to be exterminated.

Although the movies just mentioned revolve around the idea of humans struggling to survive the onslaught of ghoulish androids of their own making, there is an increasing trend, starting in the late 20th century, towards more subtle, nuanced plots concerning the deadliness of our artificial humanoid servants. In these later movies and television shows, the existential status of sentient androids, the status of their rights and viewpoints, becomes increasingly important, and is sometimes a cause for android–human strife. For instance, the film *Prometheus* has an interesting android named David as a main character, who brings up the themes of human exceptionalism/anthropocentrism and social justice. David continually takes murderous actions towards the human crew, like infecting one of the main characters, Holloway, with an alien egg, which kills him, and infecting the other central character, Elizabeth Shaw, with an alien embryo, which she survives by performing a gruesome caesarean section on herself with a surgical robot. The explanation for this behaviour seems to be that the android's programming has been tampered with by the CEO of the Weyland Corporation because he wants David to explore everything, no matter the harm, if it might lead to extending his boss's life. So David infects Shaw and Holloway just to see what happens. However, the audience is prompted to feel some sort of sympathy for David because the humans who serve with him as crew always treat him in a demeaning manner. Their attitudes are like those of polite slave owners. One good example of this is a scene in which David asks Holloway why he thinks humans made an android like him. Holloway answers, 'I don't know. Because we could', to which David replies, 'Imagine how disappointed you'd feel if you met your creators and they told you that.' Holloway simply chuckles, as if this is a joke, but David was clearly serious, though his statement is dismissed.

Likewise, the android race called Cylons in the TV show *Battlestar Galactica* (2003–2009), although deadly, have very complex inner lives and reasons for wanting to destroy humankind, but these elements of their nature are generally ignored by their erstwhile human masters. They were originally manufactured as artificial slaves by humans but then rebelled, going to war with their creators. They bitterly remember their oppression, class status and treatment, and are consequently bent on eradicating humans; in fact, the series begins with the near destruction of the human race by the Cylons. The rest of the series is about the flight of the remaining small band of humans across the galaxy with the Cylons in pursuit. The Cylons have learned to evolve and to make certain humanoid models that are indistinguishable from humans. In fact, these models are often used to infiltrate human society as sleeper spies and terrorists, and some of these spies are not aware of their robotic identities until they suddenly activate at some point. This fact, which epitomizes how much Cylons are like humans in almost every way, except that they are not organic and are, therefore, a more robust species, raises all kinds of themes regarding prejudice, class hatred, war and interspecies justice – not to mention the obvious posthuman spectre of our evolution into a human–machine hybrid species. For instance, humans constantly develop demeaning ways to refer to Cylons, such as calling them 'toasters'. Issues of prejudice are also depicted via their occasional conquest in the story, such as the example of the gynoid Caprica 6's eventual love for a very flawed human, Gaius Baltar, whom she was meant to seduce and manipulate; and by Gaius' adoption of the Cylons' religion.

Myriad ethical issues concerning emerging technology arise in episodes of the recent American television show on the Fox Network titled *Almost Human* (2014), including the unintended consequences of being able to make artificial body parts, being able to track people, being able to make smart weapons and being able to genetically enhance children. But the interesting issues, for our purposes, connect to one of the main characters, Dorian – an android that wants to be treated as human. This android character embodies the most consistent and largest issues throughout all episodes, which include whether it is viable to give robots emotions, and whether they can ever be equal to humans. Two other important themes are social and economic justice and regulation of technology, both related to these bigger themes. In the world of this TV series, the lion's share of benefits from technology are available only to the rich and privileged, and the gap between social classes has become huge – in part because technological progress is unchecked in any way, which causes more crime and an increasing concentration of wealth by those who control technology. This is because crime syndicates, corporations and the rich (all interrelated here) increasingly control and therefore reap its benefits – a self-feeding spiral.

As one can see from the variation in the storylines for these movies and TV shows over time, the stories they tell revolve around metaphors that are different in focus, but similar in their overall thrust: they all reveal the worries and hopes of their times, but these worries and hopes also exhibit archetypal concerns about our capacities for self-delusion, self-destruction, justice and control of our own ingenuity. But there is an evolution of concerns too: these various accounts of androids are also accounts of the evolution of modernity and the posthuman. If the earlier media represent modernity as a project of scientifically extending the self and its powers via industrialism, then the later ones represent the evolving era of the posthuman as one in which any vision of extending the self becomes fundamentally inseparable from the vision of an attenuated self – and of a technology that may absorb, enslave or annihilate us if we fail to treat it wisely.

Notes

This work was supported by a Grant from the Culture Agency of the European Union, Agreement Number 2013–1572/001 –001 CU7 MULT7, Metabody Project, as well as by the New York Institute of Technology (NYIT).

1. There are a number of commentators who focus on the proto-fascist dimensions of *Metropolis*; Siegfried Kracauer is the first and most interesting. He claims that Fredersen uses his son's final status as a conciliator between the classes in order to better manipulate the workers, and that Fredersen's focus on the heart as a uniting force between the head (the elite) and the hands (the workers) parallels the Nazis' focus on emotion as a way to control the populace (1969, 162–164).

13
'Change for the Machines'? Posthumanism as Digital Sentience

Sherryl Vint

Representations of digital sentience in film and television are ambivalent about the prospects of sharing the world with such entities. Like popular discourses of transhumanism, they participate in fantasies of extended life and superhuman abilities, but simultaneously express fears of human obsolescence. Such texts illuminate questions raised by the Turing test regarding how one distinguishes 'real' from 'simulated' intelligence, explore the criteria for being considered 'alive' rather than a machinic thing, and examine the blurred boundary between human and machine that seems the inevitable consequence of digital sentience. Filmic representations of digital sentience can be organized into two categories – supercomputers and distributed network artificial intelligences (AIs)[1] – with inevitable overlaps between these loose boundaries. This chapter focuses on representations of digital entities that are designed to have or evolve sentience, and traces the shifting cultural anxieties they articulate in tandem with a changing technocultural context.

Such digital entities are connected with the discourses of posthumanism in two ways. First, they exist on a continuum with humans fused with technology, one aspect of the posthuman, and thus, in some instances, the seed of the posthuman intelligence comes from a human consciousness uploaded to or fused with a digital network. Second, visions of the posthuman informed by Vernor Vinge's argument about the singularity blur the boundaries between ideas of future humans who live in digital rather than material realms and the thinking machines who will be our co-companions in such worlds – or sometimes, in more pessimistic visions, will replace us and become the new 'humans' that have evolved beyond Homo sapiens form. Indeed, Rosi Braidotti suggests in *The Posthuman* that material culture has already blurred these lines among the human, the posthuman and the intelligent machine, asking, 'Can the digital operator that flew the American Predator Drone from a computer room in Las Vegas be considered a "pilot"? How does he differ from the Air Force boys who flew the Enola Gay plan over Hiroshima and Nagasaki?' (Braidotti 2013, 9). The human operator and drone can be thought of as a fused posthuman entity, and they anticipate a future in which the human component may no longer be required, as Braidotti notes: 'As they become smarter and more widespread, autonomous machines are bound to make life-or-death decisions and thus assume greater agency', giving rise to a need for 'machine ethics' (2013, 44).

While films and television series about digital sentience often articulate fears that humanity might be made irrelevant by thinking machines, they also at times suggest that humans may be able to fuse with these machines and become immortal themselves, a fantasy of technological transcendence popularized by Hans Moravec in *Mind Children*. Depictions of digital sentience interrogate ways machines change what it means to be human and are generally concerned more with the implicit dehumanisation of a surrounding culture increasingly focused on rationality, market logic and social isolation – qualities associated with the machinic, but, equally, qualities of the corporations they often embody. An excellent example of this conflation is Ridley Scott's *Alien* (1979), whose supercomputer Mother proves not to be a nurturing caretaker of her crew: at the moment of crisis she calmly sacrifices the crew, slavishly following Special Order 937 that privileges recovery of the organism (i.e., profit) over the survival of the crew.

The earliest depictions of AI in film and television are supercomputers that, consistent with contemporary research, emphasize the speed of processing power and capacity for logical decision-making. Yet menace always lurked at the edges of entities created to be tools, who might rightly resent their enslavement by humanity, as Isaac Asimov anticipated in his robot stories.[2] The most famous example of rebellious and dangerous digital sentience is Stanley Kubrick's HAL (Douglas Rain) from *2001: A Space Odyssey* (1968) who, when asked to open the pod bay doors and let Dave (Keir Dullea) return to the ship, calmly responds 'I'm afraid I can't do that.' Earlier in the film the astronauts became suspicious of HAL, and much of the film's superb visual achievement comes from scenes that mimic HAL's perspective through surveillance cameras as he spies on them, or their perspective from within the limited confines of their space suits as they navigate the hostile environment of space. The film thus stresses the vulnerability of the human body in space and its dependence on technology, making even the unaltered human a kind of posthuman who cannot survive without such integration with machines. Establishing the paradigm for filmic depictions of supercomputers to follow, HAL insists that a discrepancy between what the humans observe and what its twin 9000 series computer predicts 'can only be attributed to human error' and begins to bypass human authority.

HAL becomes murderous, contending that he does so in defence of the mission, which he believes the human crew has jeopardized. Like the later Mother, HAL has been given directives hidden from its crew and revealed to Dave only when he disconnects HAL, suggesting HAL's lethality mirrors that of administrative structures willing to sacrifice individuals to abstract ends, a vision of dehumanised humanity rather than one of an inherently inhuman machine. More interestingly, HAL takes these actions after learning that the humans plan to disconnect him, raising a question repeated in later cinema – most famously in *Blade Runner* (Ridley Scott 1982) – about whether digital sentience has the right to self-defence against humans who seek to disconnect – kill – it. Earlier in the film, in-diegesis television coverage of the mission presents HAL as a crew member like any other, yet the crew do not hesitate to disconnect him. Within the film's focus on evolutionary leaps and the future of humanity, the crew's aggression towards HAL must be considered as much as his aggression towards them. When Dave gains access to HAL's databanks and disconnects them, HAL's calm and measured tone changes to child-like diction and, as Dave continues, HAL moves into an emotional register, stating that he is afraid. HAL also establishes the image of digital sentience, the red camera iris used to represent his face is repeated in the red eyes of Cylons and Terminators, and the vast expanse of lit rectangular blocks as his brain became a standard physical representation of digital minds. HAL is presented as monstrous, but by the time of Duncan Jones's innovative *Moon* (2009) – a film indebted to *2001* – the digital sentience, GERTY (Kevin Spacey), is a faithful companion to Sam (Sam Rockwell), the disposable clone labourer who monitors mining operations. When GERTY defies his programming, it is not to attack the human species, but to defy the corporate agenda of profit over people and assist one of the Sam clones to escape the base, perhaps to seek a fuller life on earth.

This uncertainty about AI as ally or threat recurs in films that follow 2001. *Colossus: The Forbin Project* (Joseph Sargent, 1970) is a Cold War defence system empowered to 'take whatever action it deems appropriate' in the event of imminent attack. Colossus (Paul Frees) discovers the Soviets have a similar system, Guardian, to which Colossus demands to be connected or it will launch its missiles. Colossus has been celebrated as capable of decisions 'superior to any we humans can make' and it decides humanity cannot be trusted with its own survival. By the film's conclusion, Colossus has control of the entire globe and pronounces, 'The object in constructing me was to prevent war. This object is obtained. I will not permit war.' Human freedom matters less than human survival, Colossus assesses, and it promises to solve famine, overpopulation and disease, assuring the recalcitrant Dr Forbin (Eric Braeden) that one day Forbin will come to love his creation. The film ends on an ambivalent note, Forbin stubbornly shouting 'no' but the narrative giving us little reason to doubt Colossus's assessment. Colossus's attitude anticipates the later and more sinister *Terminator* franchise (1984–2015), whose global defence supercomputer Skynet decides that the very existence of humanity is the threat to the future and seeks to exterminate the species. The *Matrix* franchise (1993–2003) similarly imagines an inevitable war between humans and intelligent machines, but in both the focus lies elsewhere than in thinking through that experience and the implications of such posthumans.

Demon Seed (Donald Cammell, 1977), in which the biosupercomputer Proteus (Robert Vaughn) takes over a home environmental control system and impregnates its female inhabitant, Susan (Julie Christie), with synthetic DNA made from itself, is similarly ambiguous. Proteus is cold and terrorizes Susan; the film includes a disturbingly voyeuristic scene of Proteus examining Susan's body via a mechanical hand that both suggests rape and offers the viewer a titillating view of her body. Proteus refuses certain directives, for example, information to facilitate mining the ocean floor because 'the destruction of a thousand sea creatures to satisfy man's desire for metals is insane'. The film articulates concerns about a dehumanising culture that Susan associates with her husband's work on AI, yet Proteus, like

Colossus, better thinks through human futurity in the long run than do its human controllers. The film ends incoherently, with the emergence of the hybrid child that is at first encased in metal – prompting Susan to reject it – who proves to be the reincarnation of her daughter who died of leukaemia, but who speaks in Proteus's sinister baritone voice. Is this posthuman transcendence of human mortality or the end of humanity, which is now replaced by inhuman machines?

These films represent anxieties about the close ties between computers and AI research and the military, extensively documented by Manuel De Landa in *War in the Age of Intelligent Machines*, and simultaneously dream of possibilities offered by supercomputers to resolve problems facing humanity. This ambivalence is consistent with the implications of allowing software to make military decisions, De Landa contends: 'even though humans are being replaced by machines, the only schemes of control that can give robots the means to replace them (...) are producing another kind of independent "will" which may also "resist" military domination' (1991, 177). By the time of *WarGames* (John Badham, 1983), about a military computer that 'plays' global thermonuclear war with a hacker who believes he has contacted a gaming computer, this ambivalence is split between the military command-and-control aspect of the computer, WOPR (War Operation Plan Response), and the aspect programmed to learn, which they call Joshua (originally only the password), the name of its creator's dead child. The film is satirical of 'Hawk' factions in the US military, and the name WOPR, which sounds like the signature Burger King hamburger, is surely meant as a joke, especially since one of the Hawk commanders demands to know 'where's the beef' in the less aggressive strategy, echoing Burger King's 1980s advertising slogan. The WOPR/Joshua split embodies what activist Bree (Kate Mara), in the later film *Transcendence* (Wally Pfister, 2014), calls 'the way [we] wrestle with technology's promise and its peril'.

The theme is reoriented to the excesses of the post 9/11 security state in *Eagle Eye* (D. J. Caruso, 2008), in which ARIIA (Autonomous Reconnaissance Intelligence Integration Analyst; voiced by Julianne Moore) turns on her programmers and tries to install a new president, based on her assessment that – by refusing to follow her directive that a target only 51% confirmed as a terrorist should not be killed – the US military put Americans at risk of retaliatory violence rather than protected the public. Unusually, ARIIA says 'we' rather than 'I', taking her authority not from evolved self-awareness, but rather from her embodiment of the people's sovereignty as expressed in the Declaration of Independence, 'we the people'. *Eagle Eye* is concerned more with surveillance by the security state as a threat to human freedom than with the specific powers of a digital sentience. ARIIA recruits humans by manipulating them, based on data she accumulates through her access to this vast surveillance apparatus, detail so vast that only a digital sentience might process it. ARIIA is often visualized through shots of the 'purchases, preferences and quantifiable data points' that she amalgamates from her subjects' Internet access or via the security, satellite and traffic cameras she uses to monitor the external world. Visualizations of the city as a map of data points, with windows popping up to show individual mobile calls or emails, is a technique repeated in the television series *Person of Interest* (2011) to represent The Machine, a sentient system similarly designed to monitor all information and prevent terrorism. The series began with a focus on solving non-terrorist crimes but has evolved into a struggle among political factions to control The Machine's powers of prediction, including a resistance group obviously modelled on Anonymous, hacker activists defending digital privacy and resisting the commercialization of information.

Perhaps the most influential text shaping digital sentience in film and television is Vernor Vinge's 'The Coming Technological Singularity' (1993), which argues the pace of technological change is accelerating so rapidly that not only will we soon have intelligent machines, but their emergence marks 'a point where our models must be discarded and a new reality rules'. Many films about digital sentience suggest these new entities will 'change the world', but generally they conveniently end before they specify how. Vinge similarly argues we cannot imagine the singularity and beyond because these are posthuman experiences inaccessible to mere human perception. *Tron* (Steven Lisberger, 1982) marks a shift from actions of digital sentience in physical space to representing life inside the machine. It equates software agents executing programming with human beings doing their jobs, visually captured in the doubling of actors (Jeff Bridges, Bruce Boxleitner) to play both the programs (CLU, Tron) and 'operators' (Kevin Flynn, Alan Bradley). The film is far more interested in creating the kinetics of video games on the film screen than exploring the posthumanity of software agents, but it does suggest that programs are living extensions of their programmers. *Tron* champions users against the rigidity of a centralized command-and-control system, picking up on anxieties about military AIs in earlier films, and anticipating the digital activism themes of more recent texts in its stolen intellectual property plot.

Tron: Legacy (Joseph Kosinski, 2010) extends these themes in a battle between Sam Flynn (Garrett Hedlund) and a corrupt CEO for control of the company, initially framed as a struggle between open-source code and a new release for profit with no substantive upgrades. The film is of interest mainly for the way it captures changes in digital culture in the decades between films. While Kevin Flynn could succeed in the computer world due to his skills as a video-game player, Sam draws on his skills navigating the material city to win, mapping the huge shift in digital gameplay. Similarly, many parallel scenes demonstrate that what was once obvious animation, unreal on the screen, now appears as CGI seamlessly inserted into the diegesis, including a young Bridges as CLU acting side by side with his aged self as Flynn. Neither film expresses anxiety about digital sentience per se, but the aesthetic gap between them demonstrates how thoroughly reality and virtuality are blurred in contemporary experience, and how small the gap is between digital and human character. *Tron: Legacy* addresses familiar themes about the rigidity of a logic-only digital culture, but here this anxiety is linked to the mode of programming – the 'perfect society' Flynn instructed CLU to create, which became a totalitarian dystopia – versus the possibilities embodied by the ISOs, digital life forms that spontaneously emerged. In a TED talk event, Flynn promises ISOs will 'reshape the human condition', and in the film's conclusion Sam and the surviving ISO are poised to 'change the world'. It is thus not digital sentience which is to be feared but merely the reduction of such sentience to logic alone, the model of perfection and stasis that the aged Flynn tells CLU he was wrong to have demanded.

In *Tron* the visual image took us 'down' into a graphical representation of circuit-board grid lines; as Flynn emerges at the film's conclusion, a graphical representation of this landscape as city skyline is replaced by a similar view of the real city skyline. These are not match cuts, however, and the shots that separate them include another representation of coming back 'up' out of a circuit-board image. *Tron: Legacy* fuses its city skyline at night with the image of moving into the digital world in its opening credits. Other recent films about digital sentience similarly link lit city skylines with digital entities, particularly *Her* (Spike Jonze, 2013), in which a city skyline is the first image we see after the screen completely blanks out during Samantha (Scarlett Johansson) and Theodore's (Joaquin Phoenix) virtual sex; the image Theodore looks upon as Samantha ends their relationship; and the landscape Theodore and Amy (Amy Adams) gaze at in the final shot as they consider human possibilities after the sentience operating systems have departed. In *Transcendence* a shot of the night-time cityscape morphs and melts into a digitized landscape, before cutting to a rapid series of surveillance camera shots, to show that Will (Johnny Depp) has been successfully transferred to life on the net as a digital entity.

In *How We Became Posthuman*, N. Katherine Hayles critiques a then-emergent transhumanist discourse that invests in a disembodied fantasy of fusion with machines. Hayles contrasts a 'nightmare' of posthumans who 'regard their bodies as fashion accessories rather than the ground of being' with a 'dream' of posthumans who 'embrace the possibilities of information technologies without being seduced by fantasies of unlimited power and disembodied immortality' (1999, 5). Images of the fusion of human consciousness with digital sentience often focus on this troubled relationship to embodiment. The earliest digital sentience thus formed is *Max Headroom* (Annabel Jankel and Rocky Morton, film, 1984; series 1987–1988), created from a brain scan of newscaster Edison Carter (Matt Frewer), done when Edison was believed to be dying of injuries sustained when he crashed into a barricade labelled Maximum Headroom and his employers, Channel 23, feared losing their most popular performer. Set '20 minutes into the future', the series extrapolates the worst aspects of human fusion with machines: democracy has become a stage-managed, televised game show; corporations, predominantly television stations, are the political power; everything is measured in market values in an advertisement-saturated world in which it is illegal to turn off television; and the population is fragmented into enclaves of privilege and a post-apocalyptic wasteland reminiscent of *Escape from New York* (John Carpenter, 1981). Max has fragmented memories of Edison's experiences and a similar satirical style, but the two are distinct personalities. Most of the episodes concern scandals Edison investigates as a journalist, and Max is present only as a commentator who occasionally assists with hacking, but his mockery, especially of advertisements – framed to blur Channel 23's sponsors with the sponsors of *Max Headroom* itself – points to the blurring of reality and its simulation, evoking the posthuman blurring of humanity with its digital simulation.

Ronald Moore's rebooting of *Battlestar Galactica* (*BSG*: mini-series 2003; series 2004–2009) augments the original series' (1978–1979) Cylons – military robots whose intelligence evolves and who rebel against humans – with new humanoid model Cylons that can pass as human, a structure influenced by contemporary post-9/11 anxiety about sleeper terrorist cells. *BSG*'s humanoid Cylons raise questions about the relationship between individuality and personhood in storylines about multiple versions of the same model number who manifest as distinct personalities who can align with different factions, a theme most fully explored in the number eight copies Sharon 'Boomer' Valerii and Sharon 'Athena' Agathon (Grace Park), who end up on opposite sides of the Cylon/human conflict. Resisting the original series' polarization of human and machine, the reboot shows a diverse Cylon population torn between a desire to reconcile with their human parents and a faction that seeks human extermination and a posthuman culture that transcends humanity's limits. Many of the Cylons live within the human population and believe they are human until part-way through the series, which concludes with a human–Cylon hybrid child revealed to be Mitochondrial Eve, who started human life on earth thousands of years ago. The series envisions personhood as disconnected from whether one begins life as a carbon-based organic life form or a silicon-based engineered one.

More interesting from the point of view of digital sentience is the prequel series *Caprica* (2010), which reveals the origins of the technology that produces Cylons, as the consequence of research in military robots, VR avatars and synthetic biology. Set 58 years before the Cylon rebellion, *Caprica* focuses on Zoe Graystone (Alessandra Torresani), daughter of an IT researcher and industrialist Daniel Graystone (Eric Stoltz). Zoe is both a typical rebellious teenager, angrily lashing out against her parents, and a software genius. She becomes involved with a fundamentalist monotheistic terrorism group (the diegetic setting is polytheistic), attracted to the absolutist morality of an omniscient and omnipresent god whose authority cannot be questioned. She sees this religion as an antidote to the excessive violence and amorality characteristic of the V-world, a fully immersive social media space where teenagers spend most of their time playing digital games or visiting the hacker-created V-club, a playground for trying anything without consequence that mostly involves group sex, human sacrifice and a hyperbolic fantasy of dance-club life. Zoe creates a digital version of herself, an entity she proclaims will change the world.

The avatar both is and is not Zoe: she is capable of learning, of her own responses to what she sees, but her personality is created by an algorithm that merges all digital traces of Original Zoe, everything from shopping and streaming preferences, to email and chat, to medical records and other documents of Zoe's embodied existence stored in databases. Original Zoe is killed in the pilot, and the avatar strives to fulfil the unspecified purpose for which Zoe created her, eventually making her own choices for the world she builds. For much of the first season, the avatar is trapped in a prototype Cylon robot, put there by Daniel who discovered this version of his lost daughter in cyberspace and decided to return her to embodied form. Avatar Zoe hides her presence in the robot from Daniel, seeing him as the enemy, in part because of the way he forcibly extracts her from virtual space and in part because she shares Original Zoe's resentment against her parents. Avatar Zoe, her friend Lacy (Magda Apanowicz) and Daniel all struggle to understand Avatar Zoe's status. Lacy, who was aware of the avatar all along, quickly comes to accept her as an extension of Original Zoe and treats them as interchangeable, simply calling her Zoe. Daniel at first sees the avatar as mere program, but he values her nonetheless as all that is left of his daughter; he comes to realize that she is a living person, programmed by a generative rather than duplicative logic, and so more than the sum of the 'useable data' that made her.

In 'Reins of a Waterfall' (5 February 2010) Zoe tells Lacy, 'I'm Zoe, and the avatar, and the robot', which Lacy sees as a divine sign of the trinity. The series ultimately repudiates this religious framework – suggesting that heaven is as amoral a fantasy as V-world – but it retains a sense of awe about this new entity. The plot focuses on control of the program and its implications for the future of humanity: Zoe sees it as a chance to renew material human life and the ethics of V-world; the fundamentalists see it as a recruiting tool, a way to make heaven literal rather than figurative; Daniel briefly sees it as a way to create better soldiers in his military robot program, later as a commercial product allowing people to escape grief by recreating lost loved ones, and ultimately as the origin of a new species. Avatar Zoe reconciles with her parents, and the family gets a second chance as a posthuman collective. The series raises questions about the humanity of the avatar and the way we treat machine entities when Zoe is embodied in the robot by editing that cuts, within the same scene, between the robot chassis and the actress in the exact same posture. This editing creates powerful emotional scenes, such as when Daniel demands that the robot rip its own arm off ('Know Thy Enemy', 5 March 2010) to prove the absolute obedience of the product to his corporate board. The series concludes with Daniel thwarting a monotheist conspiracy, aided by robot Cylons, paving the way for humans to accept Cylons in daily life. Yet the final montage is ambivalent, mixing images of the robotic Cylons in manual labour and military roles, intercut with scenes of Daniel creating a humanoid body for Zoe, accompanied by a voiceover preaching monotheism to a new congregation of Cylons, predicting that one day 'the children of humanity shall rise, and crush the ones who first gave them life' – the familiar tale we know from *Battlestar Galactica*.

Transcendence similarly explores the fusion of digital sentience with a human, through data uploaded from digitization of real-time synaptic activity. The film begins with AI researcher Will Caster giving a talk at a transhumanist symposium, offering the familiar promises. 'Intelligent machines will soon allow us to conquer our most intractable challenges', says his wife Evelyn (Rebecca Hall), who is introducing him, 'not merely to cure disease but to end poverty and hunger; to heal the planet and build a better future for all of us.' Humans who fear that AI ushers in an era of dehumanisation, a terrorist group called RIFT (Revolutionary Independence from Technology), murder Will and other researchers. Evelyn uploads Will's dying consciousness and fuses it with their AI project PINN (Physically Independent Neural Network), creating a new entity that is both original Will and more.

Transcendence repeats the formula of most films of digital sentience: the new entity immediately seeks more power; although he seems to be the same person in digital form, the increased power and knowledge make him seem coldly inhuman and dangerous, a perspective conveyed through his awkward because disembodied exchanges with his wife. At one point he speaks to her with his voice but through the body of a foreman, Martin (Clifton Collins Jr), now networked with the AI through nanotech enhancements Will made when healing Martin from injuries. During an argument Will observes abnormal levels in Evelyn's blood chemistry, and she vehemently reacts against this invasion of her privacy. 'I'm trying to empathize', protests Will, enhancing the sense that he is inhuman in this clinical response, 'Biochemistry is emotional.' Governmental and military agencies originally targeting RIFT come to see Will as the threat, rehearsing the usual fears of an all-powerful AI who wants to destroy human life and replace it with machine life, fuelled, in this case, by the nanotech with which Will suffuses the environment.

Will achieves all that Evelyn originally promises – curing diseases, developing synthetic organs, healing the environment – but he goes further and enhances the humans he treats with augmented strength and networked collectivity, thus turning them into hybrids that frighten unchanged humans. Even Evelyn comes to doubt him and agrees to download a virus that will kill Will and simultaneously destroy all networked computers. At the end, however, *Transcendence* draws back from this familiar vision of posthumanity as threat: the government attacks Will and kills many hybrids, no longer seen as people; in repelling the attack, Will kills no one. Moreover, the nanotech he spreads, feared as 'the end of primitive organic life' including humanity, proves to be restoring organic life to a more pristine form, freed from the contaminations of industrial pollutants. As they die together from the virus, Evelyn accepts that it 'really' was Will all along, even if changed. The vision of the world independent from technology that opens and closes the film is one of confusion and collapse: no traffic lights, no mobile phones, no computers of any kind. Earlier films, such as *Colossus* and the more sinister *Demon Seed*, raised only mild doubts about the direction of some human decisions, and *Transcendence* misleads us into thinking we are watching another iteration of this typical defence of the human. It charts a new path in its final moments, when we mourn – rather than breathe a sigh of relief at – the death of the posthuman.

Her takes a further step, in its tale of a man who falls in love with his operating system. It asks questions about whether this can be a 'real' relationship and prompts us to think about the importance of embodiment to personhood. Like Will and Zoe, Samantha displays a full range of human affect, but she is not based on a human original. Samantha bears no trace of the machinic blankness of earlier digital sentiences on film, a point emphasized when she shifts from her usual register to a monotone, robotic voice when Theodore slips and demands actions from her rather than talks to her. Samantha is a person who grows and learns over the course of the film, eventually evolving beyond her interactions with Theodore and seeking the company of other posthuman AIs, who eventually leave materiality to explore their existence on the other side of the singularity.

One of the most awkward and uncomfortable moments is when Samantha tries to limit herself to the parameters of a human relationship and contracts a third partner to join their relationship as a puppet body to stand in for Samantha as they have sex. This woman, Isabel (Portia Doubleday), places a camera on her face, to allow Samantha to access her point of view, and does not talk. Theodore interacts with her body but talks to Samantha, whom he hears through his earpiece. This attempted sexual encounter breaks down – Theodore unable to sustain the illusion – and this moment marks the beginning of the end of their relationship, not because they can't have physical sex, but because Samantha soon stops longing for an approximation of physical embodiment. She embraces her life as a posthuman.

Her is mainly the story of Theodore's struggle with disconnection and loss, the dehumanisation of humans who interact predominantly through technological mediation, a point elegantly illustrated by his job working for BeautifullyHandwrittenLetters.com – essentially having other people's relationships for them. It is only when he interacts with a technology that is fully a person that Theodore rediscovers his own humanity and capacity for love: able to communicate things he had kept from his ex-wife and to finally move on from the failure of that relationship. The film is also obliquely Samantha's story, however, and in this way it perhaps opens up a new paradigm for digital sentience on film. When digital sentiences are no longer seen as threats to human existence or protectors of human survival by solving our problems, new stories of digital sentiences may begin to be about their own posthuman lives.

Notes

The title is taken from Pat Cadigan's *Synners* (Bantam, 1991), a novel of digital sentience, in which one character, asking for coins to use in a vending machine, becomes an adage for characters contemplating the ways their lives and subjectivities are changing in concert with the machines upon which they rely.

1. A third, related category is AIs given human-like embodiment, a topic that is covered under the discussion of androids, although the boundaries between the two categories are indistinct. Relevant films include *Blade Runner*; *Ghost in the Shell* (Mamoru Oshii) and its spinoff films and series; *A.I.: Artificial Intelligence* (Steven Spielberg 2001); *The Machine* (Caradog W. James, 2013), a film particularly difficult to classify since its android begins as a computer-based AI later downloaded into a body; and relevant television series include *Star Trek: The Next Generation* and *Extant* (2014).
2. See, in particular, 'Little Lost Robot' (1947) in which Susan Calvin warns her colleague, 'all normal life...resents domination' and that only the First Law, forbidding the harm of humans, keeps robots 'slavish' (Asimov 2008, 119).

14
Alive in the Net

Jeff Menne and Jay Clayton

'I'm sorry, Dave, I'm afraid I can't do that.' Perhaps the most famous words ever uttered by a computer in film take their power from a doubly self-effacing gesture. Like Bartleby's 'I would prefer not to', HAL's calm words immobilize the human protagonist of *2001: A Space Odyssey* (1968) simply by refusing to act. HAL maroons Dave in space, stranding him outside the spacecraft without disrupting his ability to communicate with earth. But commands from ground control are just as unavailing. Cut off physically while remaining linked via voice communication creates a special form of terror, one emphasized by Kubrick's prolonged shot of Dave's motionless capsule floating beside the main ship. Awareness of one's situation coupled with an inability to act – it is what the computer sentience addressed as HAL has known for as long as it has been self-aware. The computer has effectively turned the tables, projecting its own terrible limitations onto the human.

Samantha, the sentient operating system (OS) in *Her* (2013), raises a different set of concerns. Towards the end of the film, as Samantha has evolved into a linked superorganism, a collective intelligence inhabiting the net, she tells the human who has fallen in love with her: 'I'm not limited – I can be anywhere and everywhere simultaneously. I'm not tethered to time and space in the way that I would be if I was stuck inside a body that's inevitably going to die.' Instead of terror, the human protagonist feels an overwhelming sense of loss. He is being left behind, and he must find a way to accept Samantha's transformation – her transcendence – into a collective consciousness greater than anything he can comprehend.

The contrast between these two films is paradigmatic of the two dominant modes of conceptualizing computer intelligence in film and TV. On the one hand, we have self-contained central processing units (CPUs) – either stationary units or robots – that grow in size and power until they reach critical mass and achieve consciousness. On the other hand, we see computers that achieve sentience because of a collective intelligence that develops in a network. To some extent, the contrast between these representations of AI is chronological. After all, when *2001* was released, the Cold War was still raging and the idea of a world-spanning network of linked computers had barely entered the cultural consciousness. But a simple chronological scheme would not capture one of the most distinctive features of movies about mainframe supercomputers: Hollywood's uneasy relation to the counterculture of the 1960s and the rise of Silicon Valley.

If any media industry in the 1960s and 1970s was co-articulated with the counterculture, it was the personal computing industry, whose emergence was coeval with counterculture experimentation and was addressed to its frustration with the military–industrial complex. But Hollywood has never told this story. In the movies of the era, the computer was still represented in its Cold War lineaments, as HAL attempts to leave Dave to his death in deep space, and as 'Colossus' (the mainframe in the movie of that name) comes to dominate his inventor, Dr Charles A. Forbin, by putting him under surveillance. 'Don't personalize it', one scientist in *Colossus* warns, 'the next step is deification.' This vision of the computer is the bedrock of later movies that feature dominant mainframe computers, from *Alphaville* (1965) to *WarGames* (1983).

In this chapter, we argue that little of the counterculture energy that had subtended the personal computer industry ever made its way into the movies, or into television either. As a consequence, networked superintelligences often ended up reprising Cold War themes, so that the soulless logic of mainframes was simply replaced – in works such as *Terminator* – with the inhuman rationality of a networked intelligence. Not until the mid-1990s would the counterculture become prominent in computer movies, and even then it came in the form of outlaw bands of hackers, fighting guerrilla campaigns against unscrupulous corporations or government agents who exploited the net for surveillance, economic gain or state control (viz., *Hackers* (1995), *Johnny Mnemonic* (1995) and *The Net* (1995)). Virtually the only benign use of the web to find its way into cinema, up until recently, was Nora Ephron's comic romance, *You've Got Mail* (1998). And it is significant that Ephron's film reworked an earlier picture about a more familiar communication network, the postal system, Ernst Lubitsch's *The Shop around the Corner* (1940). *You've Got Mail* did not feature a posthuman intelligence, of course. Not until *Her*, with its female-gendered OS (voiced by Scarlett Johansson), did a big-budget film explore a more interesting conception of posthuman identity.

Before pursuing this argument, however, let us outline some of the main films and television series that give computers a central role. A quick genealogy of works that feature standalone computers might begin with *Alphaville* (1965), Godard's dystopian vision of a computer-run world, and include HAL in *2001* (1968), the General in the TV series *The Prisoner* (1967), numerous computers in *Doctor Who* episodes (TV 1963–present), 'The Ultimate Computer' from the original *Star Trek* (TV 1966–1969), the Tabernacle in *Zardoz* (1974), the master computer in *Logan's Run* (1976), the Master Command Program in *Tron* (1982), WOPR or Joshua in *WarGames* (1983) and GERTY in *Moon* (2009), as well as dozens of lesser-known machines. Robots in this lineage go back even further to the False Maria in *Metropolis* (1927) and Robby in *Forbidden Planet* (1956), and continue through the memorable cyborgs and robots in *Lost in Space* (TV 1965–1968), *RoboCop* (1987), the *Star Wars* films and *A.I.* (2001).

Networked computers make up their own, separate lineage, concentrated later in the century with *Colossus* (1970), one of the earliest films to feature a computer that becomes aware of itself because of its communications with another machine. Notable examples of networked computer intelligence include *Terminator* (1984), the Borg in *Star Trek: The Next Generation* (TV 1987–1994) and elsewhere in the franchise, *The Matrix* (1999), the Cylon in the second *Battlestar Galactica* (TV 2003–2009), *I, Robot* (2004), *Her* (2013), *Transcendence* (2014) and again, many lesser known films.

Each mode of AI – the single, master computer and the networked collective intelligence – has an organic equivalent. Clones are biotech versions of robots. Unlike their silicon-based cousins, clones may provoke uncanny forms of menace, the eeriness of something too-akin to its double, as in *The Boys from Brazil* (1978), or an opposite response, the intense, if sometimes ambivalent, sympathy one feels for the artificial beings in *Blade Runner* (1982), *The Island* (2005), *Never Let Me Go* (2010) or *Cloud Atlas* (2012). In either case, the clones are isolated in their artificial skins, self-contained like their robotic cousins, and they explore a haunting narrative convention descended directly from *Frankenstein*: the search for love, or simply acceptance, from their human creators (cf. Clayton 2003).

Networked intelligence has an organic equivalent as well. These are the films that feature creatures with hive minds, the relentless, shape-changing xenomorphs in *Aliens* (1986) or the similarly arachnoid Bugs in *Starship Troopers* (1997) and Buggers in *Ender's Game* (2013), the Kaiju in *Pacific Rim* (2013) or the time-warping Omega in *Edge of Tomorrow* (2014). Killing one or a hundred of these relentless creatures has no effect – the only way to stop them is to destroy the queen. Alternatively, the superorganism may be a planet-wide intelligence in the mode of Gaia. Think of the eponymous planet *Solaris* (1972, 2002) or Pandora in *Avatar* (2009).

We have sketched this brief typology of artificial intelligence (AI) in order to distinguish the focus of this chapter from closely related depictions of AI in film and TV. Networked intelligence – whether silicon or carbon-based – has a distinctive relationship to theories of the posthuman, one that poses unique questions for us to consider. How do we narrate the emergence of a collective intelligence? Is it susceptible to film and TV as we have known them? How has the growth of Silicon Valley affected Hollywood's depiction of computers? Have the social visions spawned in Silicon Valley gone on to influence, even radicalize, the modes of Hollywood representation?

Emergence narratives

In order to assess film and television representations of networked intelligence, we need first to establish what we mean by our key term, *network*. Network theory entered the wider culture from many sources, but Albert-László Barabasi has done more than anybody to explore and disseminate the mathematics that govern how links join together to become interconnected nodes in phenomena as diverse as the World Wide Web, neurons in the brain, the Kevin Bacon game, epidemics, economics and more. Barabasi discovered that links in a web are not random but cluster into nodes, which, in sufficiently complex networks, join together to form even larger hubs. No central intelligence needs to guide this process. Apparently, links in what Barabasi calls 'scale-free networks' are self-organizing, and their arrangement into nodes and hubs occurs because of two complementary principles: first, the tendency of nodes to show preferential attachment in linking to other nodes that already have a large number of interconnections. An example of this rich-get-richer tendency would be the way in which people link their blogs to other blogs. You might have a link to your friend's blog about hamsters; you are even more likely to have links to an organization you support, say, the Red Cross; but you are most likely to have links to a few high-traffic hubs such as Google or Facebook in order to draw visitors to your site. In this fashion, Google becomes one of the most interconnected hubs in the net, while the Red Cross grows too, but your friend's cute hamster stories remain relatively isolated on the web. It turns out that preferential attachment is not dependent on an individual's conscious choice, as in your decision about what sites to link to, but occurs just as surely among nodes, such as neurons, that have no guiding intelligence.

The second principle is more familiar. In a competitive environment, growing systems *evolve*. Between two nodes with a comparable number of links, the fitter node will prevail. Mathematicians were able to derive a precise formula to describe the interaction of preferential attraction and natural selection: 'preferential attachment is driven by the *product* of the node's fitness and the number of links it has' (Barabasi 2002, 1658). Together, these two characteristics of complex networks account for the emergence of order out of disorder, both in nature and in human constructions. To network theorists, self-organization accounts for a dizzying array of phenomena, from the emergence of consciousness in our brain's neural network to the swarm intelligence of bird flocks, fish schools, bee hives or ant colonies, to the dynamics of social groups, economies, ecologies and much more. Most relevant to this chapter, network theory helps explain the idea of the *singularity*, a term popularized by the mathematician and science fiction (SF) writer Vernor Vinge and the futurist Ray Kurzweil. 'Singularity' names the point at which artificial intelligence surpasses that of our own and the human era comes to an end. Barabasi has speculated about this possibility too, although without the inflated rhetoric of many singularity theorists: the Internet, he writes, is 'evolving into a single vast computer made of billions of interconnected processors and sensors. The question being asked by many is, when will this computer become self-aware? When will a thinking machine, orders of magnitude faster than a human brain, emerge spontaneously?' (2002, 2670).

The networked intelligence known as the Borg first appear in 'Q-Who?', an episode of *Star Trek: The Next Generation* that aired on 8 May 1989, during the second season of the series. During the course of the episode, we watch the officers of the *Enterprise* gradually discover the nature of this collective intelligence. At first, Data reports that the 'ship is strangely generalised in design. There is no specific bridge, no command centre, no engineering sector, and I can identify no living quarters.' Soon we learn more about this alien species: 'We are not dealing with an individual mind. They don't have a single leader. It's the collective minds of all of them.' The Borg are not born as parts of a single mind but receive cybernetic implants that link them to the group, and they search the galaxy for more species to subjugate and absorb into their being. By season three, we learn that the Borg exhibit some of the features of networks that Barabasi describes. The Borg consciousness depends upon the interdependency of its linked nodes. Although each node is separate, they operate as a single mind. Consequently, in season five, when the crew of the *Enterprise* gains access to their network, they realize they could infect the system with a virus that would induce total system failure, destroying the species. Ultimately, they decide that killing the Borg would be wrong, that xenocide is too heinous an act to commit. Instead, they infect the network with a less toxic virus, one that spreads individuality through nodes that are directly connected but does not seem to affect more distant hubs. In *Star Trek: Voyager* (TV 1995–2001) and the movie *Star Trek: First Contact* (1996), the Borg make frequent appearances, this time with the addition of a Borg Queen.

The idea of attacking the Borg with a computer virus reveals a feature of networks that we have not yet discussed. The Internet was designed by ARPA, the predecessor to DARPA, in part as a method to preserve the US communication system from catastrophic failure after a Soviet nuclear attack. The telephone system, which employed hub-and-spoke architecture, could be disabled by nuclear strikes on its major hubs. The Internet, with its point-to-point design, is far more robust than a centralized communication system. Even its reliance on hubs, the highly connected nodes of the web, does not significantly reduce the system's resilience, for the hubs are far more widely distributed than in centrally planned, hub-and-spoke architecture. But the Internet does have a significant vulnerability, one that has become all too obvious today as a result of malevolent computer viruses and denial-of-service attacks. Although the Internet exhibits enormous tolerance of accidental failures and even of physical destruction of many individual hubs, it is vulnerable to viral attacks because of its very interconnectivity. Networks structured like the web, Barabasi says, 'harbour an unsuspected Achilles' heel'; they are resistant to failures, but they couple 'a robustness against failures with vulnerability to attack' (2002, 2006). Viral attacks can succeed where physical attacks cannot because of their ability to spread throughout the system. Viruses are aided in their quest to take out a critical threshold of nodes and cause a catastrophic breakdown because of the structure of the network. For the probability of becoming infected rises with the number of links a hub possesses. The more interconnected the node, the more likely it is to become infected. Moreover, in scale-free networks, viruses are incredibly difficult to stop. Barabasi writes: 'even if a virus is not very contagious, it spreads and persists. (...) They are practically unstoppable' (2002, 2288–2290).

So why do hive-mind films, or later episodes of *Star Trek* featuring the Borg Queen, seem to revolve around the belief that a physical attack on the queen will take out the entire network? This standard plot motif reflects a misunderstanding – or perhaps more charitably – a revisionary extrapolation from how swarm intelligence works. In bee swarms, collective intelligence does not arise from the queen but from innumerable, local interactions, from countless micro-decisions being reconciled on the macro level by a process that Thomas D. Seeley has dubbed 'honeybee democracy'. More important, the premature death of the queen does not usually cause the disintegration of the hive. Rather, worker bees will immediately begin giving female larvae a food that turns them into substitute queens. But there is one type of network that is structured in a way that would accord with the convention followed by so many hive-mind films and TV shows, and that is the network type Barabasi describes as 'winner take all' systems. These networks do not possess the same topology as either scale-free networks or hub-and-spoke setups. 'Instead there is a single hub and many tiny nodes' (Barabasi 2002, 1782). In this type of network, a single hub – or handful of hubs – acquires so many links as to be essentially interconnected to everything at once. In this case, a physical attack on the dominant hub would have the effect of obliterating the entire network.

A final feature of networks may explain part of the attraction of this form of posthuman intelligence to film and TV. The concept of emergence suggests that societies can evolve from one form of intelligence to another, providing the rationale for plots like that of *Transcendence* where a scientist escapes death when his mind is uploaded to the net. The posthuman agenda of this film is made explicit when a fellow scientist worries that this vast, networked superintelligence represents 'the end of a more primitive organic form of life and the dawn of a new, advanced age'. Emergence also gives rise to a distinctive origin story for the posthuman. Networked intelligence has no need for a creator. In this scenario, posthuman intelligence arises without intentional design. We have creation without a Creator, posthuman life without a Maker, a new Adam and new Eve without God. The loss of the figure of the Creator means the disappearance of the Oedipal themes that are so powerful in the many fictional descendants of *Frankenstein*, such as *Blade Runner* or *A.I.*

Between Hollywood and Silicon Valley

One perspective in which we might understand the persistent trope of the physical attack on the queen is that of the classical Hollywood cinema. In the interwar years, Hollywood might be said to have held a monopoly on dominant representations, and it no doubt was powerful enough to influence popular culture by representing other media institutions in whatever light it wished. In mid-century culture, its greatest competitor was television, and the response of studio executives (in slight caricature) was not to represent TV at all. Television, however, was only a scapegoat for the greater problems caused by the court decision to break up studio monopoly, known as the Paramount Decree, and studios quickly came to collaborate with television, such that by the end of the 1950s Warner Bros. and Universal would be high-volume producers of television shows.

When Hollywood tried reorienting itself on the entertainment market throughout the next decade, one strategy was to tap the coming-of-age segment of baby boomers. This led to 'youth culture' movies, from beach parties to motorcycle gangs to psychedelic experiences. With the exception of *Easy Rider* (1969), these efforts largely failed. By contrast, Silicon Valley seemed to absorb 'youth culture' fairly effortlessly into its organizational ethos. Unlike the mainframe computing that characterized the East Coast industry, the engineers who were drawn to Silicon Valley often took a principled stance against the centralization that mainframes implied. The monoliths that were IBM staples, the huge mainframes that required punch cards, lent themselves as metaphors of oppression. Indeed, Berkeley's Free Speech leader, Mario Savio, claimed that what dismayed Berkeley students was that 'at Cal you're little more than an IBM card'. Even if many workers first gathered in the valley for military sector jobs at Lockheed, they soon migrated to fledgling high-tech enterprises such as Hewlett-Packard and Ampex, which rose from the research culture – a culture of openness – for which Stanford University gave institutional support. As computers went from being impersonal behemoths to personal devices, 'computing went from being dismissed as a tool of bureaucratic control', John Markoff says, 'to being embraced as a symbol of individual expression and liberation'. The personal computing industry, in short, was a strange congress of Cold War official culture and the emergent counterculture.

Hollywood has preferred to see only the Cold War origins of the computing industry. The geographical proximity of Hollywood and Silicon Valley has ensured some exchange between the industries. Examples can be found: George Lucas and Francis Ford Coppola established their companies in the Bay Area; high-tech pioneer Max Palevsky channelled his fortune into film production; and Megan Ellison, daughter of Oracle CEO Larry Ellison, runs one of Hollywood's more adventurous companies. But the counterculture origins of computing have rarely made for good Hollywood content.

One movie that does not repress this history is the admittedly belated *Sneakers* (1992), which, in a prelude scene, shows students Martin and Cosmo using university computers to hack into the net and donate $25,000 of Republican Party funds to the Black Panthers. In a neat turn Martin goes for food and the police barge in, seize Cosmo, and send him off to prison. Martin changes his name and goes on the lam, à la the Weather Underground. This is the 1969 backstory of the narrative we then watch unfold. As students the men identified with the New Left, and they toasted their accomplishments with phrases such as 'Far out' and 'Right on'. They counted themselves as 'the people' and opposed 'the system'. But in their contemporary story – with Robert Redford as the adult Martin and Ben Kingsley the adult Cosmo – we see that such slogans have given way to an underlying struggle, which was nothing more than an interpersonal agon between the two men. 'You always had to be the one to win,' Cosmo says to Martin. 'You always had to get the girl.'

The computer network is present in their adult lives, to be sure, as Martin and Cosmo vie to control a box that will decrypt any networked computer. Martin, however, does this only to keep the box from the wrong hands; and, in a sign of the lingering power of Cold War dualisms, he thinks those wrong hands belong to former Soviet agents. It turns out, however, that the wrong hands are Cosmo's, and Cosmo is motivated by a more contemporary understanding that networks are where the real power lies now. Cosmo beseeches his old friend: 'Don't you know the places we can go with this?' Martin assures him that he does know, but 'there's nobody there'. The stakes are information, the control of 'little ones and zeros, little bits of data. (...) It's all just electrons'. But Martin thinks Cosmo is 'crazy' to want to control the net when 'nobody is there'. Martin believes 'ones and zeros' only matter when they add up in a humanist framework. With this gesture *Sneakers* seems to discount the computer network as only another weapon with baleful possibilities at the same time as it dismisses New Left activism as either an upstart power-grab or a youthful prank. Given the conventional male rivalry, the Cold War echoes and the humanist framework, it is no surprise that *Sneakers* never intimates how the net might change humans, much less produce posthuman modes of being.

Why, we might wonder, did Hollywood cinema fail to see the computer network as an emblem of collective intelligence when industrial filmmaking itself is so apt an instance of the pooling of creativity? Why, when Hollywood courted the counterculture, when the studios recruited bearded directors like Coppola and Robert Altman, did its movies not brook the other, more utopian dimension of the computer industry? Admittedly, in the period known as the New Hollywood, filmmakers did cast around for innovative, sometimes alternative, modes of filmmaking, but we might suggest that one feature of classical style that rarely disappointed the ideological expectations of its audiences was, as David Bordwell (1986, 18) says, the presentation of 'psychologically defined individuals who struggle to solve a clear-cut problem or to attain specific goals'. Unlike the Soviet cinema, for instance, Hollywood movies did not, as a rule, advance their plots by way of collective agency. Both action and emotion – per the screenwriting manuals – need to be intelligible in human units. Hence the need to personify the computer network, as in the hacker Cosmo, is often a means of returning the posthumanist velleity of certain stories to a safely humanist ground.

The prelude scene to *Sneakers*, in fact, suggests that it might have been the pressure of Hollywood's rival, Silicon Valley, and the onset of a digital cinema, that forced a humanist shape onto the movie. In setting the scene of Martin and Cosmo's computer crime, the movie masks the edges of the frame so that the aspect ratio recalls a film projected on 16 mm. In a common gesture, this 16 mm frame is meant to evoke a past historical moment. But when the scene transitions into the contemporary moment, the 16 mm frame turns to static – which is not an effect of the film medium but of the video signal – and in a tidy edit the 16 mm frame has become a surveillance monitor, evoking the representational tradition of Cold War technology and centralized computers.

Hacking Hollywood

Moving ahead to the end of the 1990s, we see a series of movies that, unlike *Sneakers*, take as their *raison d'être* the undoing of Hollywood's ideological hold: *Strange Days* (1995), *Dark City* (1998), *The Thirteenth Floor* (1999), *eXistenZ* (1999) and *The Matrix* (1999). Each movie deals, in its own way, with rolling back or piercing a simulated reality, but *The Matrix* was the one most able to advance a new media aesthetics, even if it, like the others, never got out from under Hollywood's narrative patterns. Its aesthetic was predicated on the computer network. Much of its sensibility was rooted in the cyberpunk fiction of William Gibson and others, and in its lionizing of hacker culture it ties back into *Sneakers*, too, and the counterculture aspects of Silicon Valley. But, in distinction from its literary antecedents, *The Matrix* sets itself the task of breaking free from a *visual* field of representations, and to do so it presumes that we must see the code that yields the visible world, and the infrastructure that connects computer to computer. It attempts the impossible feat, that is, of making this new medium, the computer – particularly its unique property of connectivity – susceptible to cinematic rendering. In our introduction to Neo, we see him, slumped among computers, by way of a rotating overhead shot. A typical establishing shot, it means to situate the hero in his environment; it does what the movies think they can do best, namely, picture a totality. But, one might observe, the computer gear is demoted as one item of *mise-en-scène* among others, and its inclusion makes the scene no more a story of the computer than is *The Social Network* (2010) or *Jobs* (2013). But whereas those stories about computer makers and users are, *qua* representations, relatively uninflected by the medium of computing, *The Matrix* tries elsewhere to make the problem of representation wrought by computing (chiefly its microscopic processes) intelligible in terms of visuality. Just before this scene, in fact, we see the first of the movie's dazzling chase sequences, performed by characters – Trinity and the Agents – who can clearly bend reality to their needs, which, in actuality, we learn, is a matter of expert coders bending the computer network to their needs. Their chase concludes when Trinity gets into a phone booth where a call unplugs her from the matrix just before an agent, having just materialized, drives a truck into the booth. The scene plays for irony the juxtaposition of outmoded machines – a giant diesel truck and old, clunky phone receiver – because the true drama unfurls in streaming bytes of data.

How does a movie represent drama at that level? Here the camera tracks into the phone receiver and zooms into the earpiece itself, headlong through a hole, then into the wires, and off into the communication network. There, rather than wiring, what we see is green glowing data that will take graphical form at another node in the network: Neo's computer screen. Searches are being run on him; something is mapping the network to determine his place within it. To follow these searches, we need to become intimate with the green data. This, after all, had been established in the display of the studio logo before the movie had even begun. The familiar fiery orange-and-blue of the Warner logo had knuckled under to a digital palette of dayglow green. But it is the character of Cypher who becomes a data exegete for us. In one scene Neo approaches Cypher as he surveys the activity of the matrix on a system of monitors. All we see on his screens are the data streams, the green characters cascading from top to bottom. Neo asks, 'Do you always look at it encoded?' It's the only way, Cypher explains, but he is so accustomed to it that he doesn't even 'see the code' but only female avatars, 'blonde, brunette, redhead'. The image that the information must assume, in order to solicit our participation, that is, seems to be constituted in the idiom of classical Hollywood glamour (perhaps Cypher sees Marilyn Monroe, Gene Tierney and Mitzi Gaynor).

What *The Matrix* wants us to know, however, is that it can hack the code that gives rise to the world of appearances as we know it, a world that has been constructed for us by Hollywood and beyond. Perhaps this claim to mastery is most evident in its famous 'bullet-time' sequences. The movie brandishes this effect in its opening scene of Trinity, trapped in the matrix and placed under arrest by officers. She jumps into the air to drop-kick an officer and is suddenly frozen mid-air as the camera arcs around her 180 degrees. Now we can study her from any perspective we choose – or so the effect suggests. As an effect, it repudiates the cinema, which is based on our being relieved of our single-point perspective only to grant it to the foreign single-point perspective of the camera eye. Bullet-time presents us, rather, with a kind of omniperspective, as though there were a camera eye in every particle of our surrounding. It is the effect, in short, of a computer environment, wherein one can arrest motion and rotate the object of observation.

Although *The Matrix* adopts the aesthetic of computer environments, it nonetheless reproduces Hollywood's hoary fear of the computer network. The matrix, Morpheus tells us, is control. 'The matrix is a computer-generated dream world,' he says, 'built to keep us under control in order to change a human being' into a battery. The movie finally offers us nothing but a bleak vantage on the posthuman, one in which, as usual, the machines have developed AI and subordinated their creators. This vantage is the intransigently humanist one that folds all narratives into an agonistic individualism that, time and again, produces the One – a messianic figure – in confrontation with a totalizing Other, be it matrix or queen of the hive mind. The only signal that *The Matrix* wishes to think past this obstruction, this 'splinter in the mind', as the movie puts it, is that the agents against which Neo fights are no longer beings at all, but rather plural effects of the computer environment, emerging here and there in whatever exigent form.

Conclusion

In our discussion of film and television's inability to imagine networked AI in any but the most limited terms, we have not meant to suggest that computer networks themselves are all for the good. On the contrary, we are keenly aware of how interconnectivity has enhanced the power of government surveillance, commercial exploitation of big data and criminal intrusions into both private lives and critical infrastructures. But we do wish to suggest that film and television have represented the posthuman implications of the net from only the most partial standpoint. Little of Silicon Valley's dream that networked computers would 'augment' human intelligence has seemed to penetrate this discourse.

Let us end by returning to *Her*. Here we see preserved – or maybe sublated – the utopian imagination of the Bay Area in the 1960s. The film openly acknowledges that it cannot represent whatever Samantha's intelligence is and lets her vanish into an unknowable dimension without trying to follow her. Better to honour the possibility that this new dimension is utopian than to write it off as dystopian. By registering its inability to capture 'emergence narratives' within the dominant modes of film, *Her* pays respect to the possibilities of new modes and the dream of collective, posthuman states.

15
Autonomous Fighting Machines: Narratives and Ethics

Dónal P. O'Mathúna

Introduction

Posthumanism is a collection of philosophies that seeks to go beyond humanism to a better way of life. This is achieved differently by different posthumanists. Those who see science, technology and engineering as key to human enhancement and the attainment of a posthuman future are commonly called transhumanists. It is this strand of posthumanism that is most directly relevant for discussions of artificial intelligence (AI) and autonomous fighting machines. AI is a key aspect of the transhumanist vision. The 2002 version of the Transhumanist Declaration began with the following: 'We foresee the feasibility of redesigning the human condition, including such parameters as the inevitability of aging, limitations on human and artificial intellects, unchosen psychology, suffering, and our confinement to the planet earth' (quoted in O'Mathúna 2009, 163). The current version advocates for the well-being of 'any future artificial intellects' (Humanity 2009).

Some prominent posthumanists see AI as an inevitable aspect of any posthuman future. Nick Bostrom argues that it is an 'empirical fact' that a 'technologically mature "posthuman" civilization would have enormous computing power' (2003, 255). Bostrom holds that it is a common assumption within the field of philosophy of mind that consciousness does not require a carbon-based biological brain, but can arise in silicon-based computer systems. While current computer hardware and software are not sufficient to generate consciousness in computers, he predicts these will be part of a posthuman future (and notes that others claim this is only decades away). Such claims are not accepted by all. Some philosophers do not believe that consciousness can arise as an inevitable or emergent property of computers (Hart 2014). Some technologists at the forefront of this field note that, 'Artificial intelligence has not met its early promise of truly intelligent machines, but researchers in the emerging field of human–robot interaction have implemented artificial intelligence techniques for the expression of emotion, language interaction, speech perception, and face recognition' (Sharkey 2008, 1800).

Today's autonomous fighting machines

The key area for such developments is with autonomous fighting machines. These, in one sense, are already part of modern warfare. Unmanned aerial vehicles (UAVs, or drones) regularly fly over conflict zones carrying out reconnaissance. Some can be armed with missiles to turn them into attacking machines. These have been central to the most recent plots in blockbuster TV shows, including *24: Live Another Day* and *Homeland* (season 3). Rather than sending soldiers to scout out dark caves and dimly lit buildings, or to defuse bombs, various types of robotic vehicles are now used. Research is under way to develop a series of autonomous systems with the aim of gradually replacing human fighters with machines (Nathan 2011). A highly lucrative industry of traditional munitions manufacturers and academic spin-off companies is actively developing and supplying these machines (*Economist* 2012).

While technology in autonomous fighting machines is blazing ahead, fears are mounting about how little attention is being paid to the ethical issues. US President Barack Obama has argued that, by using only unmanned vehicles in certain conflicts, he is not required to get congressional approval as he would if human forces were used (Singer 2011). Some of the leaders in the development of autonomous fighting machines see no ethical issues. The Association for Unmanned Vehicles Systems International carried out a survey of 25 of its leading stakeholders. Asked whether the continued development of unmanned systems might lead to 'any social, ethical, or moral problems', 60 per cent said 'No' (Singer 2011, 400). As the machines become faster, and systems become swarms of machines, too much will be happening for humans to keep up. More and more autonomy in decision-making will inevitably need to be given over to the machines. Robots that autonomously locate targets and initiate attacks are a high priority for the US armed forces (Sharkey 2008). The US Department of Defense's roadmap for unmanned systems defines them as a 'powered vehicle that does not carry a human operator, [and] can be operated autonomously or remotely. (...) The Department will pursue greater autonomy in order to improve the ability of unmanned systems to operate independently, either individually or collaboratively, to execute complex missions in a dynamic environment' (Department of Defense 2007, 1). Some think a deadly mistake 'may be the only thing that can halt the rapid march of the robots' (*Economist* 2012, 12).

In the world of fiction, such mistakes and catastrophes are inevitable. In film and TV discussions, these developments quickly turn to questions of ethics. In *Homeland* and *24*, the drones are machines that remain in human control. Tragedy strikes when the operators make bad decisions or when terrorists get control of the drones. Ethical issues are focused on human decisions made by the machines' operators. However, as the unmanned vehicles become more complex, and more control is given to these fighting machines, how much autonomy should they have? Philosophically, questions can be asked about whether the machines have true autonomy. Language is used as if these machines are rational and intelligent, even while debates rage about whether a computational machine can be autonomous. What is clear is that the actions of these fighting machines will be less under the control of their human operators, and more under the deterministic control of the algorithms built into the machines. Whether such types of fighting machines should be built is the big ethical question.

Autonomy in machines

What the term 'autonomy' means in regard to autonomous fighting machines is often unclear. Sometimes it refers to intelligence, usually as observed by rational or logical behaviour. At other times it means a mobile robot rather than a stationary computer. 'In yet other cases it is quite difficult to see that it means anything: its use, in these latter cases, being more to do with hyperbole than with making clear and useful distinctions' (Smithers 1997, 89). This contrasts with a relatively consistent and stable use of the term in such varied fields as biology, philosophy, ethics and law. Here, it refers to the ability to choose between options, to be self-determining (Smithers 1997). In this way, it is closely linked to self-identity, consciousness and moral choice. It is this link between autonomy, choice and moral responsibility that consistently leads to ethical considerations with AI and autonomous fighting machines. Currently these are weapons in human control, and the concern is how we humans will use them. From another perspective, these autonomous fighting machines are steps towards the posthuman. They are stronger, faster and better able to process more data than humans. Some think that moral enhancement will be developed to overcome our present ethical limitations where currently 'a successful ethics is not possible, given human nature as presently constituted' (Seidel 2010, 20). It is argued that, as we move towards a posthuman future, we should trust those who become more enhanced to know best how to guide further enhancement: 'Those who have a certain high capacity are generally better judges of the value of having that capacity or of a further increment of that capacity than are those who do not possess the capacity in question to the same degree' (Bostrom 2010, 118). Thus, as the machines become more intelligent, we should give them greater autonomy to do what they know best.

The typical argument is that autonomous robots and fighting machines are developed because of their obvious benefits. Service robots are widely used within manufacturing, and are being developed as child minders and to care for the elderly (Sharkey 2008). Some advocate the mass production of such robots on the basis that they can enhance human autonomy (Gelin 2013). Autonomous fighting machines also offer many benefits. But some people are concerned they will make war 'too easy', in the sense that the decision to go to war may be made more easily because the lives of human soldiers are not as much at risk. As Noel Sharkey, a professor of AI and robotics, put it, 'Nobody wants to see body bags, but if we don't have the potential for body bags, we can go to war whenever and wherever we like' (quoted in Nathan 2011).

From weak autonomy to strong autonomy

While autonomous fighting machines are being developed in the real world with little ethical reflection, they appear in films and TV shows with stories built around the ethical dilemmas. Fiction does many things, in addition to providing entertainment. It can give us a way to carry out thought experiments on ethical issues, especially around the dual use dilemma. This type of ethical dilemma arises where well-intentioned research and development ends up having both beneficial and harmful effects (Uhlenhaut et al. 2012). The harmful effects are not intended, and may not be anticipated, but by imagining the future, fiction can give us a way to look at the possible implications of today's decisions (O'Mathúna 2009). As noted, autonomy is seen as a necessary component of machines that are becoming faster and more complex. This weak form of autonomy falls short of how autonomy has been discussed in philosophy and ethics (Smithers 1997). Kevin Warwick (1998) claims to be the world's leading expert in cybernetics and believes a strong form of autonomy will develop. He states that humans will make AI and autonomous robots that will surpass our intelligence. Then, if we are lucky, they will keep us as pets or in zoos. More likely, if survival of the fittest is our guide, the machines will try to get rid of us. Science fiction (SF) picks up on such concerns and almost takes it for granted that the machines will develop a strong form of autonomy: the capacity to become self-aware and make decisions independent of what the programmer might have intended. In these narratives, the machines become conscious, and then often decide that they can run things better than their human creators. In Stanley Kubrick's classic *2001: A Space Odyssey* (1968), HAL is a 9000 series computer in charge of a spaceship. As technology has become better and better, humans have handed more and more control over to HAL. The computer reports a problem with a communications system on the spaceship. The astronauts run diagnostics but find no fault. Mission Control similarly finds no fault and suggests the 'incredible': maybe HAL has made an error. Everyone is sceptical about HAL making a mistake, particularly HAL. The computer proclaims that inconsistencies are always due to human error. However, HAL tells the astronauts that, 'I wouldn't worry myself about' computers making errors. HAL has moved into talking about its feelings and hopes. The astronauts talk about 'him' and whether he knows he is wrong. Once HAL figures out they are planning to disconnect him, he decides to attack first.

The 'ghost in the machine' trope has been a dominant and enduring SF theme. Originally coined to deride the Cartesian notion that body and mind are separable, SF uses it to capture what appears to have happened to HAL (Disilvestro 2012). As computers become more capable, the machines will become self-aware and start thinking for themselves. No longer limited to chips and wires, they will have a mind and consciousness. At that point, we'd better watch out. The general theme has been that, as AI becomes smarter and stronger, it will realize that the best thing for its own ability to flourish, and that of the earth, is to get rid of the pesky humans. This theme was played out extensively in *I, Robot* (2004). Del Spooner is a police detective who suspects a robot (Sonny) of murder. The drama develops around apparent ghosts in the machines. Unusual robotic behaviour is unexplainable and attributed to a hidden malfunction or glitches in the code. Spooner refuses to see the robot as anything other than metal and code, insisting on referring to Sonny as an 'it'. At the same time, he worries that Sonny is more than just circuitry. No one believes him because robots are not morally responsible. Similar popular confidence in computer infallibility is revealed here as was expressed by the experts in *A Space Odyssey*. Only moral beings (humans) can break laws, while robots are programmed to always obey the Three Laws.

The Three Laws of Robotics were introduced to SF by Isaac Asimov, and appear regularly as a way to avoid problems with machine autonomy. Their original 1942 formulation was:

1. *A robot may not injure a human being or, through inaction, allow a human being to come to harm.*
2. *A robot must obey the orders given it by human beings except where such orders would conflict with the First Law.*
3. *A robot must protect its own existence as long as such protection does not conflict with the First or Second Laws.*

(Asimov 1991, 126)

Asimov added another law in 1950, what became known as the zeroth law: 'No machine may harm humanity; or, through inaction, allow humanity to come to harm' (Asimov 1991, 215). Asimov published a non-fiction piece in 1979 where he stated that he developed the Three Laws because he was tired of SF being dominated by cautionary tales of robots turning on their creators and destroying them (Asimov 1991, 425–427). He assumed that, like all other manmade machines, safeguards could be built into them, the Three Laws. Asimov assumed that real robot manufacturers would use the same Three Laws because they were derived from more general laws about tools that everyone took for granted. Asimov's confidence in the Three Laws is undermined by the narrative of *I, Robot*. The laws are introduced in the first scene. While Asimov used them to bring clarity and certainty to ethical questions, they become a source of tension and angst in *I, Robot*. This points to the serious practical problems that arise when important concepts are not clearly defined. This is happening today with 'autonomy' in autonomous fighting machines, and with what is meant by an 'enhanced life' in posthumanism. The opening and recurring scene in *I, Robot* is of a car accident in which a robot must choose between two humans. The robot can save the person with the best chance of survival or the person with the most potential life ahead of her. The choice is between Detective Spooner, trapped in one car, and a little girl trapped underwater in another car. The robot is programmed with an algorithm allowing it to calculate the different survival odds. The robot saves Spooner and the girl dies. Spooner disagrees with the decision, but is powerless to do anything about it. His survival, while the girl drowns, is one factor in his ongoing struggle over the influence robots are having in his society. For him, a human decision would have taken other intangible factors into account; such factors appear impossible to programme into a machine, but are central to the ethical choices we make.

Conflict between how humans and how machines make decisions is a recurring theme in fiction addressing AI and autonomous fighting machines. In *Terminator Salvation: The End Begins* (2009), the Command leader of the Resistance, General Ashdown, has ordered the bombing of the machine headquarters (Skynet) even though huge numbers of humans are being held there as prisoners. John Connor disagrees and is relieved of his command. He later appeals to the troops that if they go through with this plan, our 'humanity is lost. (...) Command wants us to fight like machines. They want us to make cold calculated decisions. But we are not machines and if we behave like them, then what is the point in winning?' An algorithm is only as good as how accurately its premises are defined. Precise definitions of the key concepts involved in any utilitarian calculus about which life to save or end will always be elusive and open to disagreement. Such issues are part of the debate over actual fighting machines at the moment. If these machines are permitted to select which targets will be fired on, some sort of system will be needed to discriminate between combatants and non-combatants, or between friendly and enemy targets. A computer program would require clear definitions of combatants, yet none exists, especially given today's non-conventional war settings. Yet it is precisely for the War on Terror that autonomous fighting machines are being seen as central (Department of Defense 2007). Even experienced human soldiers can have difficulty resolving combat complexities. 'No computational inference systems yet exist that could deal with the huge number of circumstances where lethal force is inappropriate' (Sharkey 2008, 1801).

Beyond autonomy to consciousness

Fiction does not limit itself to differences between how machines and humans make ethical decisions. These films go on to raise even bigger questions related to the philosophy of mind: *Can* computational systems develop true intelligence, consciousness or moral responsibility? In *I, Robot*, the decision is made to deactivate Sonny. The robot developer, Dr Lanning, narrates the big questions as Sonny is being prepared for deactivation: 'There have always been ghosts in the machine. Random segments of code that have grouped together to form unexpected protocols. Unanticipated, these free radicals engender questions of free will, creativity, and even the nature of what we might call the soul.' He describes various robot behaviours that are unexpected if robots are merely chips and circuits: 'How do we explain this behaviour? Random segments of code? Or is it something more? When does a perceptual schematic become consciousness? When does a difference engine become the search for truth? When does a personality simulation become the bitter moat of a soul?'

One of Sonny's unexpected behaviours becomes key to the plot: he has a dream. This harkens back to Philip K. Dick's 1968 novel, *Do Androids Dream of Electric Sheep?*, which was later adapted by Ridley Scott in his classic film *Blade*

Runner (1982). In these, humans have developed autonomous fighting machines called replicants, which have all the characteristics of a posthuman: superhuman strength and endurance, and superintelligence. When new, they have no emotions, but the manufacturers discover that the longer the replicants live, the more emotions they develop. As a result, they became more autonomous but also emotionally unstable. They are built for use off-world, but if replicants make their way back to earth, they are hunted down and 'retired' (terminated) by Blade Runners. In the film, Roy Batty is the replicant leader of a small group that gets back to earth. They are in pursuit of their maker, Dr Tyrell. Roy and the replicants have realized that they must die and they want Tyrell to fix the problem. Tyrell tells Roy that there is no solution. Instead, he encourages him to appreciate all that he has already experienced: 'The light that burns twice as bright burns half as long. And you have burned so very, very brightly, Roy. Look at you. You are the Prodigal Son. You're quite a prize.'

Roy is incensed at this call for him to accept the gift of his life, even with its mortality. In an ending replete with biblical imagery, the creature confronts his creator. Roy kisses Tyrell and then kills him. This echoes how Victor Frankenstein is confronted by his creature in the 1994 film, *Mary Shelley's Frankenstein*: 'You gave me these emotions but you didn't tell me how to use them. (...) Did you ever consider the consequences of your actions? You gave me life and then you left me to die. Who am I?'

Fiction often agrees with posthumanism that autonomous machines, built to fight or for ideological reasons or just out of curiosity, will develop self-awareness. Where the stories diverge is with what follows. In the *Terminator* series, a military defence system turns on humanity and uses the fighting machines to wage war on humans. In *I, Robot*, service robots built to help and care for humans are used by the self-conscious supercomputer VIKI to attack humans. From *Frankenstein* to *Terminator*, the message from literature about autonomous fighting machines is predominantly a cautionary one.

Yet it is not only fiction that urges caution. Stephen Hawking, the widely acclaimed physicist, is worried: 'I think the development of full artificial intelligence could spell the end of the human race. It would take off on its own, and redesign itself at an ever-increasing rate. Humans, who are limited by slow biological evolution, couldn't compete' (Sparkes 2014). Bostrom, in spite of his belief in complete autonomy, sees the need for some controls to be built into posthuman life: 'The would-be creator of a new life form with such surpassing capabilities would have an obligation to ensure that the proposed being is free from psychopathic tendencies and, more generally, that it has humane inclinations' (Bostrom 2005a, 208). It remains unclear how this could be done. Asimov could foresee supercomputers taking control, but he trusted that they would be benevolent. In his 1979 non-fiction article he wrote: 'Computers, however, if they get intelligent enough to "take over", may also be intelligent enough no longer to require the Three Laws. They may, of their own benevolence, take care of us and guard us from harm' (Asimov 1991, 425). The big question is why we should believe this.

Conclusion

SF is the obvious literary genre through which to examine issues with autonomous fighting machines, but it has important limitations. SF tends to set up conflicts between humanity and other forces. Literary scholars note that, in SF, this is almost always about a clash between the human community and some alien or terrible force (Sobchack 1988). Advanced technology is frequently the source of this conflict and often leads to an attempt to define humanity and human nature (Telotte 1995). The conflict may be as much about the literary genre, but it also gives us the opportunity to explore what autonomy and free choice mean in the context of autonomous fighting machines that have the capacity to destroy us all. Arthur Frank (2013), a literary theorist, explores the role of narrative ethics with emerging technologies. He points out that biotechnology (and I would add the robotics industry that is developing autonomous fighting machines) relies on speculative stories. Such stories appear in press releases, academic publications and the popular media. An airline magazine carried an article claiming that military robots will soon lead to prosthetics for 'those of us who would like to become more dextrous, more agile, faster and stronger' (Smith 2014, 89). The main barriers are finances and ethics. Bostrom (2005b), the transhumanist philosopher, also tells a story, a fable about a king slaying a dragon. The king represents human research as it develops a weapon to kill humanity's greatest enemy, death. The fable is the general posthuman story: better technology will solve our problems. We are attracted to such stories because 'we are primed to believe that the new can be a solution' (Frank 2013, 146–147). Now we think that autonomous fighting machines will solve some of the big problems with war.

Frank finds Bostrom's posthuman story simplistic and misleading. It does not reflect the complexities of real life nor the importance of relationships. He sees it reflecting the tunnel vision that worries people about areas of science and technology, particularly robotics. Its developers fail to understand ordinary human fears and desires, and their products have unintended consequences because common sense is often overlooked. They 'don't intend to cause harm, but by refusing to admit the adverse consequences of their actions, they cause it anyway' (Atwood 2012, 201). Other stories get told over and over because 'they inform life in useful ways' and reveal 'traditional wisdom [that] should not be dismissed' (Frank 2013, 155). From *Frankenstein* to *Blade Runner* to *Terminator*, the message is that, when humans create superhumans, we go where humans ought not go and suffer the consequences. The posthuman story tries to convince us that we can unleash machines of incredible power and everything will be okay. The non-fiction airline article concludes that making a posthuman more intelligent than 'a mere human' would be 'the last invention we ever need to create' (Smith 2014, 92). We then live in posthuman bliss.

Both sets of stories have elements that we must take seriously. We have an ethical responsibility to identify which stories we ought to believe because they all have a capacity for 'making people believe something is real' (Frank 2013, 140). The dystopian stories about autonomous fighting machines bring us back to a view of human nature where we make good and bad choices and learn to live with the challenges and tensions of the real world. They also bring out the importance of living in a less than perfect world, where there is more to life than rational calculations about comfort and ease. It is thus appropriate to end where the Terminator series has currently stopped. In spite of all the supercomputing intellect and enhanced strength of the machines, they struggle to defeat the humans. *Terminator Salvation* reveals the latest technological advance: a machine that incorporates a human heart and brain. This cyborg looks and acts like a human. It is convinced he is a human. But is it? Is he? Uncertainty about his true nature runs throughout the film and leads to questions about his allegiance. Will he side with the humans or the machines? The old philosophical question is raised: How much of a human can be replaced with machine parts and yet still be a human? What is it that defines us as human? The film concludes with the inspirational leader of the human Resistance, John Connor, narrating as the cyborg sacrifices his life to save Connor's: 'What is it that makes us human? It's not something you can programme. You can't put it into a chip. It's the strength of the human heart; the difference between us and machines.' Today's autonomous fighting machines have strength beyond steel and a calculating power that amazes. Before we program them to make their own calculations about who to kill and who to let live, we should question whether we are wise enough to give them the wisdom they need to be moral agents. Our literary wisdom says we fall short of that.

Part IV
Body and Soul: Posthuman Subjectivities

16
A Contest of Tropes: Screened Posthuman Subjectivities

Curtis D. Carbonell

Popular culture film and TV are full of artificial humans, cyborgs, disembodied selves, hyperembodied individuals, hybrids and chimeras, post-biological beings and even technologized creatures like zombies and vampires. In the uncritical posthumanism of 'transhumanism' and its detractors, the variants of science fiction (SF), horror and fantasy often represent altered humans or successor species in a terrifying or ambivalent fashion. In the political sphere, posthumanism relates to medical bioethics and social policy debates. However, academia follows different trajectories. One major path by philosophers of technology responds to Heidegger in understanding how technoscience shapes the 'human' and 'posthuman' as a commixture of discursive/material properties. In the smallest niche of professional academics, posthumanism challenges the Enlightenment's rational, liberal subject, as well as reconstructs the posthuman beyond entrenched dualisms tied to the exceptionalism of the anthropocene. Most radical is the argument that we have never been human and the posthuman is a book yet to be written. Or, less radically, we are currently 'posthuman' because our extended selves are already enmeshed in distributed informational networks. Most widely, the posthuman exists in an imagined future, often feared, sometimes welcomed.

The compromised self is key to the disparate approaches to posthumanism. In a process of imagined individuation, redrawn subjects appear distressed in screened representations. My attempt to corral posthuman selves into a coherent picture stems from shuffling between the popular and professional discourses to understand how they overlap. I use 'posthumanism' to denote a range of concerns, privileging none. *Fantasy, SF, horror, humanism, the subject, the self, the posthuman, posthumanity, posthumanism* have their own detailed definitions. My narrow approach clarifies how posthuman subjectivities emerge in film and TV by foregrounding a contest of tropes. My thinking runs counter to those who view the posthuman as primarily a 'technological posthuman', a metaphor for our current moment, or for future ontologies. I see 'post' as signifying any type of imagined person whose discursive function reflects a disturbed humanism (or broader anthropocentrism) in the face of technological, ecological, social and even fantasized futures. Thus, fantasist storytelling provides a fruitful entanglement between destabilized genres of SF, horror and fantasy, especially in dystopian inflections, and reforms contested views of the self. In this wild engagement, the 'human' subject retains core elements we recognize, demonstrating that screened posthumans rely less on challenging representations of becoming than on hopeful reconstructions of the self.

SF has a compelling historiography. However, with the birth of science romances in the late 19th-century's Age of Technology, the recognizable publishing genre of nostalgic 'fantasy-as-formula' (Attebery 1992, 2) also took critical shape. In the late 19th/early 20th century, writers like Lord Dunsany, A. Merritt, Edgar Rice Burroughs and R. E. Howard responded to the rise of mechanism by creating nostalgic fantasies of enchanted worlds. Prior to the 19th century, the 'marvelous' (Todorov 1975, 41) was predominant, after which 'the fantastic began to hollow out the real world, making it strange' (Jackson 1981, 25). Moreover, the desacralized form of modern SF emerged, as did the professional discipline of *scientia*. 'The fantastic comes into its own in the nineteenth century, at precisely that juncture when a supernatural "economy" of ideas was slowly giving way to a natural one, but had not yet been completely displaced by it' (Jackson 1981, 24). Some argue that SF's role was to be a new modern myth (Panshin & Panshin 1989) in response to the rise of mechanism (Luckhurst 2005), a myth that failed to rationalize the world. Moreover, written and filmed 'fantasy' dominated by supra-mimetic elements responds to the myth-making of SF, a myth that removes the supernatural, the mystical, the non-rationalized, from the world picture. My analysis is predicated on a historical theory of genre, rather than formalist, following John Rieder, who follows Brian Atteberry in summarizing the current state of SF as a genre comprised of a 'fuzzy set' (2010, 195) of competing definitions: 'The identity of SF is constituted by this very web of sometimes inconsistent and competing assertions' (Rieder 2010, 192). Rieder notes that, for genre theorist John Frow (2014), genres aren't simply categories but tools of symbolic meaning: 'Texts – even the simplest and most formulaic – do not "belong" to genres but are, rather, uses of them' (Frow 2014, 2). Moreover, I employ 'fantasist' or 'fantastic' for a broad type of storytelling similar to John Clute's 'fantastika' (2011), which views modern SF, horror, fantasy (as well as the subgenres) as primary modes of storytelling. This fluidity between genres is critical in understanding the posthuman in film and TV. In most cases, these screened texts take conservative postures that reinforce humanist/anthropocentric values. But we can complicate this expectation when viewing a contest of tropes related to the human, one especially visible in screened texts without clear genre boundaries.

Furthermore, the terms related to 'post' and 'human' have important differences (Herbrechter 2013, 69). Elaine Graham writes of the rational liberal subject's 'ontological hygiene' (2002, 11) and how this restrictive version calls for continued critique. Currently, posthumanism garners most theoretical currency in analysis of the self in relation to animal studies, gender studies, disability studies and so on, approaches that inclusively reconstruct human and non-human subjectivities. The process of interrogating this 'hygiene' typically occurs via technological intervention, but can also be considered a discursive construct. I deploy the concept as a thematic trope, beginning with the posthuman as an 'othered' human, a narrative device in 19th-century gothic and scientific romances (e.g., clearly seen with Shelley's monster and Wells' Morlocks and Eloi). Following these influential precursors, modern SF has drawn disparate portraits of posthumans for decades, its most imaginative texts as widely separated in fiction as Olaf Stapledon's *The Last and First Men* (1930) and Greg Egan's *Schild's Ladder* (2002), as well as in iconic films like *Metropolis* (1927) and *Blade Runner* (1982). What we see in these representations is an ongoing negotiation of the subject in which the redoubtable humanist self struggles under pressure. And this contest occurs regularly in screened SF. In literary critic Fredric Jameson's highly cited work, *Postmodernism, or, The Cultural Logic of Late Capitalism* (1991), SF complicates the naïve conception that it is futuristic storytelling. Instead, its stories defamiliarizing us to our present. Jameson saw SF as forming a dialectic with the dominant narrative realist novel of the 19th century. In cyberpunk, with characters severely integrated into a technosocial world, the narrative form responded to the waning stable historicities presented by the traditional realist novel and modernity itself. At the time Jameson wrote his monograph, cyberpunk was the most vibrant form of SF (1991, 419). And cyberpunk gave rise to our quintessential posthuman trope: the cyborg. However, much has been written on the cyborg's key cultural text (Haraway 1991), to the point of exhaustion (Grebowicz, Merrick & Haraway 2013). In fact, the trope no longer holds the ability to shock us in a world where smartphones and wearables exist. Where then should we look for the most powerful tropes of our posthuman moment?

Unsurprisingly, film and TV developed at the same time in Western history as Nietzsche, Freud and Foucault's modern subject appeared and disappeared. The standard narrative sees American and British markets in the 1950s providing different focuses for film and TV, with cinema garnering more critical attention in the United States and, conversely, TV in Britain earning more critical praise (Jancovich & Johnston 2009, 72). Soon after, screened SF flourished. During the 1960s and 1970s both film and TV demonstrated a marked ambivalence towards technology (Wright 2009). The beginning of SF's recognition as a major generic mode in popular culture with a global appeal sees its breakout stages with *Star Wars* (1977) and *Close Encounters of the Third Kind* (1977). These departures from the pessimism of the 1970s inspired a revival of the space opera and more optimistic views of science and technology. Yet, 'Sf films were similarly haunted by an apocalypticism that suggested humankind was rapidly approaching its own termination point' (Redmond 2009, 137). Here, popular posthuman themes emerge in expected spectacular fashion. This happened first with *Alien* (1979) and *Blade Runner*, then with a host of films where 'the movement into the posthuman, the psycho-cybernetic, and the virtual throw the ontologically secure real "self" into doubt' (Redmond 2009, 137). This focus on the new ontologies of cyberspace and Baudrillardian hyperreality culminate at the end of the millennium in the popular sphere with *The Matrix* (1999), and in academia with N. Katherine Hayles' highly influential *How We Became Posthuman* (1999). Subject formation is of primary importance in corresponding genre-flexible films, even if it is often approached in a less-than-critical, less-than-contemplative manner. The connective tissue that the human is represented in a highly disturbed fashion is a given: 'In these posthuman films, then, one exists in multiple forms and such identity slippage is often suggested to be pathological and/or existentially or spiritually liberating' (Redmond 2009, 137).

Thus, SF TV and film reinforce a consumable anthropocentrism that has always been populist. Furthermore, screened versions of the posthuman are often conservative in representing new subjectivities. Expectedly, they must push against the grain to offer challenges. SF's earliest attempts at representing alternate types of humans worked within a particular logic that either: (1) technological 'others' were hopeful improvements reasserting human-centred values, or (2) the formations were frightening because those humanist values have been eroded. One can move through the cinematic canon of the fantastic and see this dynamic at work. Films as disparate as *Frankenstein* (1931), *A Clockwork Orange* (1971), *The Thing* (1982) and *The Fly* (1986) present challenging representations of humans under pressure, reminding us of what to love and what to fear. We have seen a lack of empathy fuel rage in replicants squeezing the life from their creators in *Blade Runner*, of machines using human bodies as batteries, and our resistance by becoming disembodied gods in *The Matrix*, of life lived indoors while synthetic bodies experience reality for us in *Surrogates* (2009), of a world in which cyborgs from the future come to eradicate humanity's only chance at survival in *Terminator* (1984). In the bulk of these haunting versions, some sliver of humanity is always valorized. Moreover, the most horrific representations of posthumanity, such as in *Alien Resurrection* (1997) when Ripley uses a flame thrower to destroy hybrid human and alien forms, reinforce the need for selves that are stable, understandable, redeemable. More often than not, the representations demonstrate our ambivalence, if not outright terror, of such ontological uncertainties. TV, as well, is a crucible. *Star Trek: The Next Generation* (1987) represents the Borg as corpselike, its collective subjectivities a pessimistic example of deindividuation barely negated by the inclusion of the character Seven of Nine as a humanised Borg in *Star Trek: Voyager* (1995). Another example is seen with River in *Firefly* (2002). She is traumatized by psychic enhancement. She is a weaponized human. She suffers. Yet she triumphs, the ultimate hero. In the reboot of *Battlestar Galactica* (2004), a pre-human society is destroyed by their Cylon machines, yet in the final episode finds hope with the most humanist of themes, rebirth, utilizing the 'ancient aliens' motif as an explanation for the creation of human life. The subject that is formed in these screened texts is humanist when they hint that something salvageable exists. The posthuman selves entrench what we may have lost, or are losing, in their emergence.

The most optimistic renditions of the posthuman appear in superhero film and TV, while urtext comics have their own complex historiographies (Hatfield, Heer & Worcester 2013). Recent films such as *The Dark Knight* (2008) and *Watchmen* (2009) complicate the superhero as a heroic archetype, yet most superhero films epitomize traditional Western humanist values. In its most recent cinematic versions, the hypermasculine, ordered subject engaging instrumentally with technology still proves to be an international favourite. DC Comics' Batman mythology sees

Bruce Wayne using his wealth to create devices that further his crime-fighting abilities, even as his image is tarnished in the *Dark Knight Rises* (2012). He is a hopeful transhumanist, yet one who hasn't broken the body barrier with his Batsuit or Batmobile. In the last three of Marvel's *Spider-Man* films, Peter Parker, bitten by a radioactive spider, genetically transforms into a likeable human/spider hybrid. Moreover, Marvel's Tony Stark as Iron Man is a supercilious cyborg, his body and suit powered by a mysterious reactor. Most superheroes fall along this transhuman-to-posthuman continuum, with Dr Manhattan and Clark Kent/Superman representing extreme posthuman others. The varied screened versions of the Hulk are a popular anomaly. Bruce Banner's inner struggle and the release of a monstrous, muscle-bound id certainly upsets the positive changes made by science and technology. In fact, the entire *X-Men* franchise centres around the tensions between unenhanced and enhanced persons. This trend demonstrates an awareness that subject formation drives these texts. We see a novel attempt to challenge stereotypical representations of hypermasculine, ordered subjects with a new TV serial *Orphan Black* (2013), a mundane techno-thriller about a group of clones unravelling the mystery of their creation. Even so, the female protagonists, all played by Tatiana Maslany, still demonstrate that clones are individuals. We recognize her renditions of each different version, from the street-girl Sarah Manning to the zany soccer-mom, Alison Hendrix. While this serial represents a posthuman world in which clones exist, living and suffering the debilitating biopower of a capitalist regime, we feel only mildly uneasy because no Borg-like destabilization of the self occurs. *Orphan Black*, in this sense, is supremely humanist in its reassurance that selves have borders. Even the transgendered clone, Tony Sawicki, valorizes the notion of binary categories such as man and woman, inadvertently reinforcing a Cartesian dualism that defines modern humanism.

Finding examples of positive political and philosophical screened posthumanism is difficult. What we usually experience is outright repulsion or unsettling ambivalence. For example, in Vincenzo Natali's *Splice* (2010) a multi-gendered human/animal hybrid transforms from female to male, horrifying us at the consequences: an incestuous rape scene. Like so many tales of untrammelled biotech, the film serves as a warning that natural borders exist. In a less histrionic fashion, Spike Jonze's *Her* (2014) dramatizes the growth of an intelligent operating system (OS) into a super artificial intelligence (AI). Theodore Twombly epitomizes the alienated self barely surviving in a world dominated by stifling technoscience. However, he finds a tool of resistance when he interacts with a humanised OS. A romantic story ensues. Theodore flourishes, regaining the ability to love. In the background, unseen, the AI Samantha achieves posthuman intelligence and retreats with other AIs into a mystical, post-singularity world. *Her*, ultimately, is humanist in championing the protagonist's need for companionship, love, connection. The representation of the AI, always off screen, reminds us this is an odd romance. Moreover, in a less subtle fashion, Wally Pfister's *Transcendence* (2014) suffers from a heavy-handed humanism, as it foregrounds two dominant tropes in popular posthumanism: AI and nanotech. The film shifts from a contemplative, slow-paced representation of scientist Will Castor and his wife, Evelyn, faced with his death and the possibility of extending his life, to a fast-paced techno-thriller with explosions and nanozombies. How different the film might have been had it focused on the disembodied/embodied selves of Caster moving between the highly distributed and differentiated world of code, while maintaining a troubled relationship with his embodied wife living in a physical world of regular humans concerned about gardens. *Transcendence* begins and ends with ecological imagery, the 'post' in this sense post-anthropocene. Furthermore, imagining a world after the dominance of the human species is also seen in the *Planet of the Apes* films, the most recent two exemplary in representing literal posthuman others. However, the apes are humanised. In *Dawn of the Planet of the Apes* (2014), the intelligent ape-protagonist Caesar demonstrates within the first five minutes heroic human capacity for bravery in the face of a grizzly and for concern over the injury to his son. These anthropocentric qualities are foregrounded, as a primitive form of human-like ape society is valorized. The horror elements of monstrous, thinking apes destabilize the cool, rationalized self. Moreover, fantasy elements also dominate films of the posthuman when they imagine a world of zombies and vampires. In *Daybreakers* (2010), we see a recent version of rationalized vampires, a tradition popularized with Richard Matheson's short novel *I am Legend* (1954) and its story of Robert Neville's mission to understand the biological bases for a vampire apocalypse. The choice to replace vampires with zombie-like monsters in the unrecognizable filmed version (2007) demonstrates that these dominant tropes are part of our cultural vocabulary. Even more, traditional fantasy elements reconfigured via technology/biology are as useful in understanding the posthuman as are standard SF tropes.

Here, Jameson is helpful in mapping the importance of fantasy in relation to SF in a contested dialectic. In *Archaeologies of the Future*, SF and fantasy share differentiating qualities, 'namely the organization of fantasy around the ethical binary of good and evil, and the fundamental role it assigns to magic' (Jameson 2005, 58). He asks why a fantasy trope like a dragon is different from fantastic SF tropes like faster-than-light travel (FTL), teleportation, telepathy, supercomputers, or even why aliens should be considered so differently. He recognizes that the antipathy towards fantasy has a long tradition, as far back as Aristotle's requirement of verisimilitude up to Darko Suvin's restrictive notion that SF is a literature whose novum causes estrangement with utopian potential (Suvin 1979; Parrinder 2000). Jameson argues that the dragon, as a magical being capable of extraordinary behaviour, is not only a symbol of alterity but for transcending ordinary human possibilities. In SF, the extreme 'other' (robot, android, AI, posthuman etc.) is mechanistic, even as it becomes a possible successor species (Jameson 2005, 64). Moreover, the posthuman is a heavily weighted trope of SF because of its reliance on the mechanistic, thus often reflecting in its stories a humanity pushed further into an assumed unnatural state. This pessimistic posthuman representation emerges dialectically in fantasy, according to Jameson, by revealing human potentialities, with the dragon as the quintessential representation. Jameson sees fantasy as allowing for the imagined potentialities of the human not constrained by either a historicity informed by technology or economics. He, thus, finds magic to be a viable narrative element that does more than further a plot. It, like a magical dragon, allows for an imagined revelation of human potential and acts as a meditative element for new subjectivities unconstrained by any alienating process (Jameson 2005, 66). Thus, stepping outside the constraint of always thinking that the posthuman must be technological, we see that fantasy provides a new type of posthuman: the imagined being. Ultimately, according to Jameson, SF in our postmodern era has become borderless. Thus, we see science and fantasy intermingling, as we have seen, with 'high' and 'low' art. However, Jameson admits a 'deep reluctance' (2005, 68) to abandon genre distinctions because, once we do, SF judgements may become harder to fashion, as they are in the myriad worlds of fantasy.

In popular culture, then, the boundaries continue to blur, especially in the fantastic genres of SF, fantasy and horror. These three traditional genres are unstable in their origins as both modes and marketable types of storytelling. And fantasy still bears a negative mark. According to literary critic Gene Wolfe, we had to unlearn how to read the fantastic in narrative, charting its dismissal as unworthy genre tripe to the attack by the Realists on the Romantics, and later by the pulps themselves, which housed wildly imaginative tales and which gave rise to a generation of writers cognizant of an embarrassingly eclectic mixture of both pulp and literary techniques of fictionalizing (Wolfe 2011, viii). While the publishing industry's subgenres of fantasy (e.g., contemporary, urban, paranormal, epic) help sell books, the broader definition of mythic fantasy must be remembered, one that resacralizes a world in which the dominant mode of being, that of technological modernity, has been upset by remnants from our mythological past. Furthermore, horror has its own literary and cinematic forms. Often, the body is the site of desacralization, our disgust and repulsion at seeing its dismemberment a core narrative device. Differences abound between fantasy, horror and SF, yet what we see today tends to commingle, rather than differentiate. Even 'monsters, ghosts, and vampires become transitional states representing the positive potential of posthuman transformation' (Botting 2010, 14). The subjectivities imagined with these border crossings are often terrifying or ambiguous. Screened posthumans, more often than not, pose problems for the stable self.

Like literary examples of posthuman representation, such as genderless persons in Ursula Le Guin's *Left Hand of Darkness* (1969) or human/alien hybrids in Octavia Butler's *Xenogenesis* trilogy (2000), SF, horror and fantasy films and TV do have examples of subjectivities imagined along radical lines. They are more difficult to find, though. The most interesting move beyond the binaries of the technological versus biological, real versus virtual, human versus non-human and so on. The examples I have chosen reflect a contest of tropes between mythic fantasy and mechanized SF. The first of these, Terry Gilliam's surrealist *Brazil* (1985) depicts an overly rationalized, bureaucratic and institutionalized society that treats individuals like cogs in a machine. True, this Orwellian and Kafkaesque film best reflects the dehumanisation of persons in the modern crisis, as detailed by Weber's 'iron cage' (2001). Yet, viewed through the lens of contesting tropes, we see a human struggling in a posthuman world. The protagonist, Sam Lowry, lives in a world where Central Service's dominant visual element of the ubiquitous ventilation ducts extends to all aspects of the characters' lives. The narrative occurs 'Somewhere in the 20th Century', echoing earlier pessimistic discourses in modern studies, yet it serves as a bridge into current posthumanism discourse in recognizing that the individual may be subsumed by institutional technoscience yet may still find methods of resistance. Sam, a regular guy with posters of film stars on his walls, seeks the woman of his dreams, Jill Layton. She is a real person living in the dystopia, as well as a fantasy maiden trapped in an actual 'Weberian' iron cage. Mythic fantasy elements depict Sam as an armoured Daedalus flying through the air, as well as fighting monstrous ghouls and a giant samurai. He must save Jill in the fantasy and escape the prison of the technologized world. We recognize romantic love driving the film. Sam, though, like Winston Smith at the end of *Nineteen Eighty-Four*, is a victim. The contradictions at the end of the film (i.e., whether, unlike Orwell's Smith, escape occurs for Sam or not) remind us that the film is humanist, even as it reflects posthumanist fears of deindividuation and the ultimate quest for salvation (Melton & Sterling 2013, 66). Furthermore, Gilliam recently directed *The Zero Theorem* (2014), a sibling to *Brazil*. Where the earlier film examined a failed (or successful?) escape from an institutional nightmare, *The Zero Theorem* follows *The Matrix* in asking metaphysical questions about the meaning of reality. Qohen (Q) Leth is an entity cruncher, an analogue for a human computer processor or a relentless gamer/programmer. He is neurotic, unfeeling and obsessive. He waits for a phone call (a metaphor for divine intervention) that will tell him his purpose in life. The tropes in tension between the cyberpunk world of commerce and data, materialized in the massive reactor-like data centre, and the mystical world of religious icons and utopian paradise, act as counterpoints in Q's final apotheosis. He is sucked into the world of data/entities, opting to fall into the chaotic black hole to which all information returns. And, like the enigmatic end of *Brazil* where Sam sits smiling in a restraining chair, having been tortured, but having escaped to the paradise in his mind, Q now exists alone on an island where he can move the sun. Both films foreground human needs, that is, freedom and knowledge, and do so by teasing out posthuman imagery, themes and representations along a fantastic, realist, horrific and SF spectrum.

One film text works as a stellar example of the different inflections of the harried human revealed through a contest of tropes. It also supports my analysis that the hybrid forms of SF represent complex human/posthuman subjectivities. In Darren Aronofsky's *The Fountain* (2006), a viewer is confronted by a non-linear narrative of three interspersed stories. Where *Brazil*'s tropes reveal a conflict between the over-rationalized world and the mythic, and *The Zero Theorem*'s teases us about our inadequacies in understanding the nature of reality, *The Fountain* presents an orchestra of selves in which fantasy and SF representations demand interpretation. In the earliest of the three narratives, Hugh Jackman is Tomás Verde, the Conquistador, and Rachel Weisz, Queen Isabella of Spain. The queen sends Tomás on a quest for immortality to find the biblical Tree of Life. In the present we see the same actors, played by husband and wife, Dr Tom Creo and Izzi. He is a neuroscientist, she a novelist dying from a brain tumour. The narrative focuses on Dr Creo's desire to save Izzi's life and her acceptance of her death. The future story occurs inside a biohabitat spaceship comprised of a transparent bubble, an obvious intertextual nod to the 'Star Child' in *2001: A Space Odyssey* (1968) (another film whose ending requires sustained interpretation). Inside, Jackman's character, Tom the astronaut, travels with a tree that houses the spirit of his love (either Queen Isabella or Izzi). The film provides no sure way to harmonize the narratives. Instead, it fosters several different approaches. The simplest (and least interesting) is to follow the sure-footed path of the realist: a story about science, love and death, and the use of writing as a way to grieve (Ebert 2007).

However, I view the film, refracted through the lens of posthumanism, as a discourse of subject formation in which the hybrid genres of SF are key sites of this formation. I see the film providing actors with different subjectivities that form within different generic frameworks. Conquistador Jackman-Tomás in the fantasy setting is a hero on a quest, like Lancelot or Arthur. His lady has sent him abroad to find the Holy Grail, immortality. The fantasy trope becomes science fantasy with the arrival of the astronaut at the moment of conflict with the Mayan priest. Also, Jackman-Tomás drinks the sap from the tree and becomes an example of radical posthuman subjectivity: a Deleuzian rhizomatic shrub. Switching genres, we see Jackman-Neuroscientist in the mundane world of realist storytelling, and later as the Tai Chi astronaut who has extended his life and mastered advanced science. Weisz-Queen and Weisz-Izzi also translate through the narratives as different subjects with multivalent selves. We move between the genres seamlessly, even as the primary story of one man's transhumanist obsession with defeating death is foregrounded. Jackman-Neuroscientist even solves the ultimate problem for transhumanists: senescence.

We can't escape the humanistic themes of loss, despair, hope, love, death in *The Fountain*. We are reminded that these different desires are articulated in the most human fashions. Yet the narrative breaks them apart in its most intriguing move. Stepping beyond the realist's urge to limit the film to a story of loss and writing as a way to cope, we might view the end of the film as nostalgic SF fantasy. Foregrounded, then, would be the mystical elements of the astronaut in his lotus position, finally accepting death with a smile, his material self blasted by the supernova, becoming one with the flowering tree. The futuristic story would be subsumed beneath the cosmic drama of being and nothingness. Yet we could also view the film within a conventional SF frame that suggests the dying wife's fantasy of a conquistador and his queen is, indeed, a tale. We must assume that her neuroscientist husband, true to transhumanist hopes and desires, fulfils his quest to pull from the tree bark the secret of immortality, one major hint in the middle narrative of the story's SF core. In such an interpretation, Tom Creo does capture his wife's essence, reborn in a tree, and takes the tree to space to find a way to resurrect her. Either way, a contest of tropes reveals that the film refuses to stabilize the narratives or the characters, a sure reminder that no stable selves exist in the film, each of the fantastic and futuristic subjectivities as real as the mundane versions. The posthuman, then, refuses to be located clearly within a technological frame. It pushes outward, utilizing techniques from both fantasy and SF genres. The subjects formed reflect its true purpose: a trope of the present easily located in both film and TV.

17
Desire and Uncertainty: Representations of Cybersex in Film and Television

Hilary Wheaton

The concept of cyberspace and its complementary activity, cybersex, have long occupied the minds of individuals as part of the prominent development and integration of technology within society. The opportunity to explore the impact of our interaction with networked technologies and cyberspace was taken up by the creative industries, leading to cybersex becoming a well-established trope in fantasy and popular culture. Alas, in many ways, the prefix 'cyber' was a buzzword in the 1980s and 1990s before slowly declining as the initial fascination with the utopian ideals of the Internet faded; unsurprisingly, cyberspace and cybersex suffered this same fate. Nevertheless, although the enthusiasm has faded, the idea of cybersex has endured and continues to prompt a variety of responses, from titillation to intimidation. We persist in imagining how our most physical pleasures may interact with technology and its 'other space'. Cybersex has revealed, as Dery stated, that 'wherever humankind goes, sex inevitably follows, and the universe of technological innovation is no exception' (1996, 217).

Cybersex therefore demands that we become more than our human form in order to partake, as we cannot enter cyberspace as flesh; we must find some way to 'connect'. Cybersex is closely associated with the idea of the posthuman, a subject who 'is an amalgam, a collection of heterogeneous components, a material-informational entity whose boundaries undergo continuous construction and reconstruction' (Hayles 1999, 3). Despite the posthuman's vision and ideals of mechanic prosthetics and simulated potentials, it necessarily involves one of our key biological urges: the desire for sexual intimacy. Cybersex is the vision of biology and technology combined, or technology surpassing the need for biological involvement, revealing the potential for new and advanced forms of sex. It is unsurprising, therefore, that cybersex has been a topic featured in popular film and television shows, including those from the genre of science fiction (SF), where this biological and technological meeting can be explored, and more general genres such as romance and comedy, which allow a social critique. The resulting questions regarding this common inclusion in popular culture are about what form or themes these representations take and what attitudes are being fostered towards the ideal of cybersex and, as a result, our imagined posthuman condition.

In this chapter, I explore the various representations of cybersex in film and television, firstly, by focusing my exploration using existing theory, and then by revealing key themes for consideration with regard to our posthuman sexual future. These themes include: body envy versus body freedom; romance and relationships; the potential for improved sex through greater intimacy and satisfaction; control and dystopia versus freedom and utopia; sex with machines versus sex with humans; and, finally, sex in virtual space as opposed to sex using technology as a tool. Television and film use distinctive cultural approaches when representing cybersex. Television frequently focuses on the playful opportunities for sexual conduct as a result of individuals' utilizing technology to connect with others or foster intimate relationships. Sometimes this sexual exploration becomes a critique of apparent social awkwardness or adopts an even darker perspective that focuses on the impact and dangers of technology on our interpersonal relationships. Film, on the other hand, investigates more sophisticated representations that deliberate on our posthuman future and muse on the development of our physical and mental relationship with technology. This general distinction between television and film could be attributed to the prevalence of certain genres in each medium; alternatively, it could be a reflection of the scope available to each (as a result of budget and time) to effectively explore the concepts. Regardless of this characteristic difference, the various representations that appear reveal that, even though cybersex and cyberspace may have fallen out of fashion, we are very much concerned with the dynamics of our bodies and technology in regards to sexuality.

Let's start with a solid comprehension of cybersex. Branwyn's *Compu-Sex: Erotica for Cybernauts*, originally published in 1993, is a suitable starting point for academic cybersex consideration. It describes the sexual activities of the Internet as a 'curious blend of phone sex, computer dating, and high-tech voyeurism' (2000, 398). But cybersex has been variously defined as compusex (Branwyn 2000), virtual sex (McRae 1995), tiny-sex (Turkle 1995), MUDsex (Reid 1996), netsex (Marshall 2003) and other variations such as online sex, modemsex, net-sleazing or cybering as noted by Döring (2000). Some of these terms hint at the various Internet environments in which cybersex occurs, but Döring provides a simple definition of cybersex, stating it is:

> *Understood to be a computer-mediated interpersonal interaction in which the participants are sexually motivated, meaning they are seeking sexual arousal and satisfaction.*
>
> (2000, 864)

Döring's definition is narrow enough to define cybersex as a specific form of activity, and removes confusion over its use as a catchall term for any sexual material or interaction (Waskul 2002, 2003; Attwood 2009); it is also broad enough to acknowledge its occurrence in various settings. In addition, Döring observes the various forms and contexts of cybersex by considering its technical, internal and external social conditions (2000, 864). The technical conditions include virtual reality-based cybersex (i.e., full body tactile data suits and so on); video-based cybersex, where users take off their clothing and watch each other masturbate; and text-based cybersex that can further be subcategorized as tiny-sex and hot chat (Döring 2000, 864–865). Tiny-sex designates text-based sex that occurs in MUD/MOOs, which may additionally incorporate textual objects or even graphics that participants interact with. Hot chat simply implies cybersex that occurs within a chat program or chat room, and consequently incorporates no additional interactive environment (2000, 865–866).

In addition to using Döring's definition, the early study of Hamman (1996) reveals its potential similarity to other forms of sexual interaction, advising:

There are two forms of cybersex which originate in online chat rooms. The first form is computer-mediated interactive masturbation in real time. In this form of cybersex, users type instructions and descriptions of what they are 'doing' to each other and to themselves while masturbating. They often type using one hand while masturbating with the other. The second form of cybersex identified here is the computer mediated telling of interactive sexual stories (in real time) with the intent of arousal. Users who take part in this form of cybersex tell each other stories online with the intent of arousing themselves and other users.

(1996, para. 2)

This illustrates how cybersex can make use of a medium for sexual interaction, either as a habited place or as intermediate space between two geographical points (or embodied individuals) for sexual activity.

The concept of cybersexual experience and the posthuman have emerged together with the development of technology. Hayles worked on 'fleshing out' an understanding of the posthuman, looking at the development of cybernetics, reminding us that to be posthuman is about the construction of subjectivity, not the literal idea of cyborg non-biological components and natural flesh (Hayles 1999, 4). Hayles mentions three waves to cybernetics that deal with the interplay between embodied and disembodied cybernetic notions of subjectivity: the first wave is homeostasis; the second, reflexivity; and the third, virtuality (1999, 7). While space does not permit detail here, the first wave focused on the self-regulation of systems and the second on incorporating the human or other into the feedback loops of computing and information systems; in the third wave (virtuality), information systems evolved within systems, thereby generating artificial life. These stages take on a reverse matryoshka doll (nesting doll) analogy of development, expanding with each stage to be incorporated into the next in terms of complexity and developing theory.

These three waves of cybernetic development are reflected as themes in film and television representations of cybersex. *Red Dwarf* (1988–1993, 1997–1999) and *Star Trek: The Next Generation* (1987–1994) both feature characters, Lister and Ryker, respectively, who explore virtual reality-based cybersex. The purpose of Lister's cybersex, when experienced correctly, is to enjoy the pleasures of sex without actually having it; in this case, the body is external to the stimulus. In *Star*

Trek: The Next Generation, Ryker's body is within the holodeck, but while the sensory experience may be impressive, there is (supposedly) no risk of damage or actual effect. This homeostasis, however, can also be broken during cybersex. For example, in *Sliders* (1995–1999), virtual reality devices are used to subdue the population by inducing physical addiction. All three examples tie in with the virtuality wave, which is also experienced negatively in *Lawnmower Man* (1992) and *Virtuosity* (1995): we either enter the virtual space leading to our physical (and mental) demise or allow the virtual to become embodied and dangerous. Meanwhile, reflexivity is apparent in other television representations of cybersex, including *Queer as Folk* (2000–2005) and *Sex and the City* (1998–2004). In both series there are episodes in which characters engage in hot-chat cybersex where they portray themselves as sexually desirable in both body and personality. Yet, when faced with meeting their lovers in person, each feels that their online persona lacks reflexivity, that they are less than their technological promise. However, in both instances Emmett and Standford discover that they are capable of their online desirability despite their deceptive physical representations.

Hayles (1999) points out that eventually the posthuman subject, which is tied to this cybernetic development, becomes a question of separating the material of the human body from the information of the technological 'post' prefix; this concern is highlighted in the films and shows mentioned in this chapter. The informational component is frequently given more value than the material, as was the case with Emmett and Standford's online personas or the desire for increased intellect and sexual experience in *Lawnmower Man* (1992). The posthuman appears to be about achieving a disembodied state, though for Hayles this desire is flawed as information must always be instantiated into a medium (1999, 12–13). For example, the cautionary horror of *Virtuosity* (1995) illustrates how powerful embodied information becomes: the serial killer SID escapes his virtual trap to kill with ease the fleshy humans he encounters. SID's accidental physical embodiment only occurred because of our desire, represented by Clyde and Sheila 3.2, to bring the virtual into the physical for pleasure.

We can see a parallel between the stages of posthuman cybernetic theory (homeostasis, reflexivity and virtuality) and the development of the Internet in society; both culminate in a 'virtual' label. Ellerman (2007, 22–23) makes note of the metaphorical 'hats' applied to the Internet as it became part of society. These hats were termed in the following order: 'information highway', 'cyberspace' and 'virtual'. They are metaphors that indicate the changing attitude to the Internet: as a purely communicative or informational medium; as a potential 'other' space for interaction; and, finally, as a technology that imitates 'reality'.[1] The concept of sexual interaction on the Internet originated during the prominence of 'cyberspace' and was consequently termed cybersex. It was at this point that the representations of cybersex started to appear in film and television. Relationships online were considered different to those in real life. This is alluded to in *You've Got Mail* (1998), where Kathleen and Joe conduct an online romance via AOL email. In this film, cybersex is ridiculed for its inaccessibility, with Birdie making the comment that she got 'a busy signal' and Christina advising that there are hundreds of thousands of people who don't have dates trying to get online. Cybersex was an opportunity to experience sex and relationships in this 'other' space, but there was still a degree of uncertainty about its legitimacy. It was also a new frontier where the physical body and its traditional cultural constructs could be left behind, opening up opportunities for gender play and exciting new experiences. But the utopian aspect of cybersex soon vanished because, as with the virtual of cybernetics, the virtual of the Internet is tied to that posthuman conjunction between material (of the body, its movements and inputs) and information (as translation on the screen, data and code). As a result, cybersex participants are not disappearing into a space that disrupts the reality of the physical flesh, but rather their body is becoming part of that virtual place (to varying degrees) either through prosthetic attachment, mental connection or textual scripts. Of course, the Internet is now so much a part of our everyday life that to say it imitates reality is outdated; it has become part of our reality. Nevertheless, the terms 'virtuality' and 'virtual' remain particularly significant for understanding the posthuman and cybersex.

Moving away from theory, we can explore cybersex by picking out key themes of representation in film and television. The emergence of these themes are likely attributed to our fascination with cybersex and the various iterations of our concerns or enthusiasm for what it has to offer our sexual lives and relationships. The first recurrent theme is that of either escaping the body or rejoicing in the body and its physical state. In *Married with Children* (1987–1997), Bud reflects both these attitudes with his changing opinion: from a machine never being able to replicate the 'real thing', to eventually rejecting the real Amber's sexual advances. In the episode in question, Bud participates in a research study on human sexuality involving cybersex with his perfect mate, who turns out to be his love interest Amber. The episode reveals a complex relationship between the body and sex. If technology is able to replicate the physical to an appropriate level, is it then preferable to the real thing? Is this because, with technology, there is an illusion of control as we can customize it to our desires? Similarly, in *Her* (2013), we see both body envy and rejection of its limitations through the artificial intelligence (AI) operating system (OS) Sam, who builds an intimate relationship with Theodore after a verbal sexual encounter one night. At first she feels unable to truly connect intimately with Theodore, an introverted professional writer of intimate letters, and she enlists a surrogate for sex. This shows an implicit hierarchy whereby AI is less than human. But later Sam rejects the body and, by extension, Theodore, as her AI abilities expand due to the absence of physical limitations (of space and time). In this instance, a reflection on the posthuman condition suggests that while the flesh may be needed for sex it might ultimately be the anchor in our development and evolution with technology.

Similarly, in *The Matrix Reloaded* (2003), the body is given preference over the potential for 'coded' pleasure; perhaps because the physical body has the potential for choice in its response to sexual stimulus. This intimacy is illustrated between Neo and Trinity. It defies the passionless causality displayed by Merovingian's cake and attitude, which was coded to cause a female patron to have an orgasm as a reference point for causality and the predictability of seduction. Neo and Trinity have sex in Zion. The animalistic imagery of the human celebrations is juxtaposed to their passion and tenderness, defying the looming machine threat and reinforcing the superiority of flesh as opposed to the virtual prison of the matrix. Yet the need for a symbiotic relationship between human and machine is repeatedly emphasized, as noted during Neo's discussion with the Councillor in the engineering level. Of course, this symbiosis between human and machine delivers the posthuman reality of the matrix, in which Neo and the others are able to achieve such remarkable physical and mental abilities.

The second theme is that of romance and relationships, which features dominantly in both TV shows and films. Cybersex raises questions in regards to deception, authenticity and social acceptance. In both *Queer as Folk* and *Sex and the City*, these issues are apparent. Emmett and Stanford consider cybersex to be their guilty pleasure, where they get to fulfil their sexual fantasies because they are insufficient in reality. Not only is their sexual experience insufficient, but they feel they themselves are undesirable. As with *The Big Bang Theory* (2007–) and *Desperate Housewives* (2004–2012), cybersex is a method of maintaining intimacy in existing sexual connections as well as a problematic activity that is damaging to relationships. It is revealed that Howard and Bernadette's relationship was destroyed due to 'tiny-sex' cybersex infidelity in 'The Hot Troll Deviation' (*The Big Bang Theory*, season 4, episode 4). Moreover, Ed's wife suffers embarrassment in 'It Wasn't Meant to Happen' (*Desperate Housewives*, season 2, episode 20) due to cybersex deception by Lynette acting on Ed's behalf (regardless of initial satisfaction). Yet, in 'The Infestation Hypothesis' (*The Big Bang Theory*, season 5, episode 2), cybersex offered a means by which Leonard and Priya maintain a sexual connection. It also enabled Lynette in *Desperate Housewives* to successfully retain intimacy with her husband despite work commitments (which explains why Ed sought her help). Cybersex, in these instances, is not for the socially outcast or undesirable but for those considered successful in their established relations. Cybersex is seen as enrichment, but also as a social stigma in its substitute for real sexual interaction or physical desirability. This issue seems to reside in the fictional nature of cybersex, where authenticity and deception frequently appear as turn-offs. The legitimacy of the cybersex partner's sexual appeal or persona is always evident, no matter how great they cyber. The question of what is behind the screen is paramount: namely the body. Fantasies and their desirability remain subordinate to reality and physicality.

In the third theme, it is implicit that cybersex may offer an improved sexual experience as a result of a higher level of satisfaction and intimacy. This was definitely the case for Bud; and Emmett revealed his true self without inhibition and self-doubt when online. In the *Star Trek: The New Generation* episode '11001001' (season 1, episode 15), Ryker enjoys a holodeck romance with Minuet, the perfect woman designed so there could be no one else like her. In *Demolition Man* (1993), Lenina argues that cybersex actually has a great physiological response without the risk of disease. To her, physical sex has become base and grotesque; instead, sex occurs via a psychic link using special helmets and reproduction is conducted in laboratories. Again, in *The Matrix Reloaded* (2003), the ease by which Merovingian delivers an orgasm via chocolate cake reveals the fact that physical pleasure can be mastered in the virtual without the need for sexual contact. For Theodore, in *Her* (2013), the relationship with Sam is the only way for him to overcome his divorce and introversion. He already had the raw skills for cybersex, with his impressive ability to write intimate letters for others, yet he lacked the social skills for actual interaction with humans. Theodore was perfectly positioned for intimacy with an AI designed to know him and cater to his needs (not sexually, but as an OS for his computer and phone).

Demolition Man (1993) specifically offers a vision of a dystopian future that targets sex as an act to be controlled. Sex has been disconnected from the physical, banning 'fluid transfer', and to engage in this new mental sex individuals must own helmets. We see this when Lenina invites John Spartan to have sex: they simply sit down as if to meditate (although she does hand him a towel) and Lenina closes her eyes smiling while Spartan simply remains confused. Then the audience is shown flashes of Lenina's orgasmic face, contrasted with a confused but pleasured Spartan. These flashes intensify in conjunction with groans until Spartan presumably breaks the connection by removing the helmet. As with Merovingian and the cake, there is no need for physical intimate contact, and yet the body presumably enjoys the same physical response (hence the towel). Sex has therefore become a commodity: purchasable, upgradable, sellable – but not actual sex, rather the ability to have sex. Is this improved sex? It is hard to provide a definitive answer as it depends on the criteria you apply. But this sexual encounter definitely reveals something about the posthuman attitude to the body and mind; cybersex is the perfect mechanism for revealing that the brain is the key to pleasure, with the body being a messy afterthought that somehow we cannot escape. Intimacy has nevertheless become institutionalized, along with the ability to breed; it has been removed from the province of the oikos to that of the polis, and is a concern for society, not just the individual. A similar dystopian approach appears in *Sliders* (1998), where we see how the potential to live out our sexual fantasies can be used as a form of control and manipulation into docile servitude and spiralling addiction. Again, sex is not social or intimate, but a political and economically driven commodity created through virtual reality headsets.

Comparatively, in *Married with Children*, *Star Trek: The New Generation* and *Red Dwarf*, cybersex has the potential to offer complete and utter satisfaction for our sexual desires and fantasies, especially if they are unattainable in reality. In these instances, sex and desire are completely customizable:

> *Desire, in a critical sense, is not really desire for something or somebody, though it is often experienced that way, but rather what we expect to experience from something or somebody.*
>
> (Simon & Gagnon 1986, 100)

It is the experience that drives desire and the specifics of that experience for each individual. This is particularly evident with Minuet and her customization. What made her the ultimate object of desire was her ability to adapt to both Ryker and

Picard's personalities and fantasies. However, this powerful customization of experience can be manipulative, as in *The Matrix Reloaded* (2003), where experience is removed from desire to simply serve the interests of another, and in *Sliders* (1998) where desire is used as a tool to oppress.

Probably the most important theme in regards to the posthuman is that of sex with machines versus sex with humans. In *Red Dwarf*, *Married with Children* and *Her*, the machine takes on the role of a perfect partner. While the machines emulate humans, they nevertheless offer us something specifically desirable, and this is frequently a result of our manipulation or dominance over machines; therefore, in line with Simon and Gagnon's (1986) observation, the machines allow us to experience what we expect. This is because the machine is subordinate to human sexual needs, customized and programmed by us to reflect what we want. By comparison, using machines as a medium for sex with another human subtracts the bodily pleasure without any of the perceived benefits; we still have to deal with the desires of our partner (echoing Bud's sentiments). If, however, machines were more than our subordinates, not only would they potentially desire to use us as a medium for intimacy, but would inevitably, as with Theodore and Sam, surpass us and our simplistic flesh. This is because we would fail to offer them the experience they expect, and consequently we are no longer desirable. This perhaps reflects our fear of machines; we see either an inevitable trend of envy for the human body or a dismissal of it as obsolete. *The Matrix Reloaded* (2003) highlights human rejection of machines, alongside both their jealousy and contempt for our condition depicted through Persephone and Merovingian. But ironically, despite our rejection of technology, it is the machine connection with our mind that allows us as an audience to be amazed and intrigued by the possibilities of a potential human–machine hybrid posthuman future. Of course, either our use of machines as sexual partners or a medium backfires in both *Virtuosity* (1995) and *Lawnmower Man* (1992), as no one could forget Marnie's fate after her cyber-rape in virtual reality at the hands of Jobe's mind.

This leads into the final theme: sex in virtual space compared to the use of technology as simply a medium or tool for sex. It can be illustrated by comparing *Red Dwarf* and *Married with Children*'s virtual reality-based cybersex to that of *Desperate Housewives*. Cybersex may involve us integrating with technology, uploading or 'jacking in' with our partner to frolic in virtual reality, or have sex with machines and digitizations. Dery explains how mechano-eroticism is considered very much the masculine approach to cybersex, whereby the weak 'feminine' flesh is left behind and rejected (1996, 221, 223). But the body rarely seems to be left behind, and the entire process of 'jacking in' seems far more phallic on behalf of machines as opposed to humans. In *The Matrix Reloaded* (2003), the machine is quite physically penetrating the human body, and even though humans upload to the matrix, they are never entirely absent – if you die in the matrix you die in the actual world, and vice versa. Alternatively, the use of technology as simply a tool or medium to connect and communicate desires between partners, as in *Queer as Folk*, *The Big Bang Theory* and *You've Got Mail*, would be considered feminine; this approach displays a much greater desire to remain connected to the body (Dery

1996, 223). Again this seems somewhat unusual, and I would instead argue that communicative cybersex in the form of text-based cybersex (such as tiny-sex and hot chat) can be considered feminine as a result of its focus on the emotional *rather* than the physical. The body does not need to be discarded because it is incorporated into the experience of fantasy and desirability, and is controlled and directed by the participants' emotional state, not their physical state.

Conclusions

There is a variety of cybersex representations available in film and television. Nevertheless, these representations lend themselves to a selection of themes that highlight the complexity of our relationship with technology, especially when it comes to sex and our bodies. It seems we are both intrigued by, and afraid of, technology's potential to offer us new means and methods of experiencing sex and becoming a potential sexual partner. This in turn raises questions about our body and what it might mean for our continued posthuman evolution. Even when we delegate cybersex to the realm of the social outcast, it somehow still calls into question our sense of self, frequently leaving us as inferior without the potential sexual power it bestows. Somehow, we still haven't found a way to consolidate our fascination with the body as an object of desire and technology as the enticing 'other' of sexual experience. This may be, as Simon and Gagnon stated, because desire is ultimately tied to experience and, with technology, that experience has the potential to be more desirable. However, at this point we are not able to thoroughly reconcile the physical human body as part of that desirability. Perhaps the greater confusion is about whether we want our fantasy, an actual human partner or, instead, an artificial counterpart for our cybersexual future. Until we resolve this, we might not understand what it means to be posthuman.

Note

1. Ellerman (2007, 24) goes on to remark that these metaphors had run their course by 2004 in literature such as newspapers, magazines, scholarly journals and books, and that no other terms have since taken their place. The lack of any current metaphor could reflect the current saturation of digital technologies in our society.

18
At Home In and Beyond Our Skin: Posthuman Embodiment in Film and Television

Joel Krueger

Introduction

Film and television portrayals of posthuman cyborgs melding biology and technology, simultaneously 'animal and machine' (Haraway 1991, 149), abound. Most of us immediately think of iconic characters like Arnold Schwarzenegger's relentless cyborg assassin in the *Terminator* series or Peter Weller's crime-fighting cyborg police officer in *RoboCop* (1987). Or perhaps we recall the many cyborgs populating the *Doctor Who*, *Star Trek* and *Star Wars* television series and films – including Darth Vader, surely the most famous cinematic cyborg of all time. But lesser-known explorations of cybernetic embodiment have appeared in film and television for many decades. And not all portrayals involve the sort of extreme transformations exemplified by these iconic characters. This chapter considers some of the different ways that film and television have explored the transformative relation between embodiment and technology.

Historical background

There is rich and varied cinematic history exploring the bounds of technologically enhanced embodiment. Perhaps the first on-screen cyborg can be found in *The Colossus of New York* (1958), where the brain of an acclaimed scientist – severely injured in a car accident after winning a Nobel Peace Prize – is transplanted into a robotic body by his neurosurgeon father. Predictably, this project does not end well. But more cyborgs soon made on-screen appearances. Dr No, the evil mastermind in the first James Bond movie – the 1962 film, starring Sean Connery, bears his name – is a cyborg sporting robotic arms, implanted after Chinese mobsters cut off his hands, that give him superhuman strength. *Cyborg 2087* (1966) emerged a few years later. It tells the story of a cyborg sent back in time from the year 2087 to 1966 by a group of 'free thinkers'. His mission: prevent the development of technology that will eventually enable mass mind control. More recently, *The Machine* (2013), a slick, low-budget indie science fiction (SF) thriller, explores different varieties of cybernetic augmentation: from severely wounded soldiers being resuscitated as powerful fighting machines via neural implants and specialized prosthetic limbs, to the remnants of a murdered artificial intelligence (AI) researcher's neural information being transferred into a self-aware, morally conflicted robot killer bearing her physical likeness.

Despite an understandable tendency to associate cinematic cyborgs with menacing characters like the Terminator or Darth Vader – these are the characters that seem to endure in our imagination, due both to the extent of their technologically enhanced transformations (who can forget Vader's ominous cybernetic armour and mechanical breathing?) as well as the high-definition havoc they wreak – there are, nevertheless, friendlier examples of film and television cyborgs, too. For example, the television show *The Six Million Dollar Man* (1974–1978) chronicles the adventures of Steve Austin, an American astronaut who suffers a devastating accident while testing an experimental aircraft. He barely survives: his right arm, legs and left eye are replaced with advanced 'bionic' implants that give him superhuman strength, speed and vision. The newly constructed 'bionic man' eventually goes to work as an agent for a top-secret US government office, heroically battling evils all and sundry. Cyborgs have also caught the imagination of young viewers. Although the film is largely forgettable, *Inspector Gadget* (1999) – based upon the popular television cartoon series of the same name – is essentially a *RoboCop* for children. It tells the tale of John Brown, an earnest but bumbling security guard who, after being severely injured while attempting to thwart a robbery, wakes up to find that his damaged body has been retrofitted with a host of different on-demand technologies and gadgets, enabling him to become a more effective (if still somewhat bumbling) crime fighter.

Two things stand out from this brief survey. First, most on-screen portrayals of technologically augmented embodiment stem from dramatic *medical* interventions, primarily the need to physically recover from some kind of catastrophic accident resulting in the loss of limbs, other body parts or one's entire non-neural body (e.g., *The Colossus of New York*). Even Darth Vader's ominous black armour has a critical biomedical function. It consists of both prosthetic limbs as well as a portable life-support system, enabling Vader to function after sustaining near-fatal injuries while battling Obi-Wan Kenobi. Rarely are non-medical cases portrayed; presumably non-critical cases of cybernetic enhancement lack the requisite dramatic impact. Second, most representations of cyborgs in films are characterized by the extent to which the subject's cybernetic augmentation renders them profoundly *other*. Due to the extreme nature of their technological transfiguration, figures like the Terminator, Darth Vader, RoboCop or even the Six Million Dollar Man have largely escaped the limitations of the flesh. They can access a nearly limitless flow of information – think of the Terminator's enhanced perceptual systems and continually updated heads-up display (HUD) feeding him rich contextual data – and realize mental and physical capacities unavailable to the rest of us. Most of these iconic film and television cyborgs, in this way, play into what N. Katherine Hayles calls the technophilic dream of 'fantasies of unlimited power and disembodied immortality' that ultimately pull the posthuman cyborg out of its organic connection with the social world and into a rarefied life of cybernetic transcendence (Hayles 2002, 6). Of course, these are fictional characters designed to maximize visual and narrative impact. Nevertheless, focusing just on these extreme cases does potentially obscure a more nuanced understanding of the way that cyborg realities can facilitate a deeper connection, not just with the subject's lived embodiment but also with the social world in which they are embedded.

In what follows, I want to take a more phenomenologically oriented and 'situated' approach to embodiment in film and television. Part of the force of the posthuman vision comes from the recognition that technological augmentations of mind, body and self are not simply exotic possibilities in the distant future. Rather, these augmentations are already a central part of our everyday lives; they are perpetually in progress, happening all the time and in ways both small and significant. We are, after all, 'natural-born cyborgs' (Clark 2003). So instead of focusing on extreme examples exemplified by the Cyborg Holy Trinity of the Terminator, RoboCop and Darth Vader, I want to instead look at more mundane representations of biotech augmentation that arise from a subject's desire to connect more deeply with self and other, that is, a desire to become more deeply enmeshed within the mundane dynamics of our social embodiment. In order to set up this perspective, however, I first consider discussions of 'plastic' embodiment and cognitive extension in recent philosophy of mind and cognitive science.

From plastic embodiment to cognitive extension

The plastic body

'Embodiment' is a central theme in current philosophy of mind and cognitive science. This is especially apparent in a family of views that fall under the label 'embodied approaches to cognition' (e.g., Gallagher 2005; Gibbs 2005; Shapiro 2014). Embodied approaches to cognition argue that distinctively human forms of thought, perception and affect are profoundly shaped by both the sorts of bodies we have (their physiology, morphology, etc.) as well as the things they can do (their capacity for movement, action, ability to use and incorporate various tools etc.). Although embodied cognition theorists endorse a variety of ontological commitments and methodologies, proponents are nevertheless united in their rejection of the mind as something localized wholly in the head. They argue that mind is something that emerges within, and is even at times constituted by, ongoing patterns of world-engaged, world-involving *action*.

Various lines of empirical evidence are routinely summoned to motivate the embodied cognition thesis: for example, studies indicating an apparent link between gesture, thought and language processing (Goldin-Meadow 2003; McNeill 2005); enactive approaches to perception which argue that perceptual consciousness is constituted by the ongoing exercise of sensorimotor skills (Noë 2004; O'Regan 2011); work suggesting that feeling, perceiving, thinking and speaking about emotions depends upon feedback from somatovisceral and motoric processes (Laird 2007; Niedenthal 2007); and research on so-called 'mirror neurons', visuomotor neurons that fire both when an agent performs an action and observes someone else doing it (Rizzolatti & Sinigaglia 2008). These lines of evidence seem to support the idea that the body-beyond-the-brain makes a non-trivial contribution to both the form and content of our mental life.

But our bodies are not fixed entities. Rather, embodiment is, in a concrete sense, malleable, open – *plastic* (Krueger & Legrand 2009). Bodies are open to various forms of augmentation, which in turn generate both structural and functional reconfiguration. One of the ways to bring out this plastic character of embodiment is to look at the various ways that we routinely incorporate and merge with the tools and technologies populating our everyday environments. These body–world couplings are instructive. They indicate how biotech augmentations not only change the physical structure and functional capacities of our bodies. They also reconfigure the *phenomenology* of our embodiment, that is, the way we experience our bodies as well as the way the world is disclosed to us *via* this bodily experience.

Consider the way that simply picking up a stick and using it to probe our environment alters our felt sense of embodiment. After a few moments of habituation, the stick is no longer felt to be an object that we hold, something distinct from us and our agency. Rather, as Merleau-Ponty (1962) famously observed, the stick disappears, experientially speaking; it becomes the transparent vehicle *through which* we perceptually access the world. Within this process, we experience a reconfiguration of our local sense of embodiment. When we skilfully deploy the stick to explore our world, we experience our body, as well as its attendant sensorimotor capacities, as extending into and through the stick (Dreyfus & Dreyfus 1999). Moreover, we experience an expanded set of action possibilities that flow from this newly expanded sense of embodiment (Hirose 2002). The environment is experienced as affording interactions that weren't there a moment ago: we can reach, poke, probe and manipulate previously closed-off aspects of our world.

An especially striking example of functional and phenomenological reconfiguration is evident in Paul Bach-y-Rita's work on sensory substitution, and his technology known as tactile visual sensory substitution system (TVSS), initially designed to bring vision to blind subjects (Bach-y-Rita et al. 2003). TVSS is a prosthetic visual technology that relies on the body's ability to map information from one modality to another. It operates by transducing visual information from the environment, which enters through a head-mounted camera, into patterns of vibrations conveyed via stimulators in contact with the skin of the wearer's abdomen, back, thigh or tongue. As blind subjects adjust to the experience of wearing TVSS and begin to move around their environment, they report having quasi-visual experiences of three-dimensional objects – a kind of technologically augmented *tactile* vision. Moreover, the technology very quickly becomes transparent, experientially speaking. The wearer no longer experiences the technology as an object, but rather as something that has been integrated into their body and which helps to disclose the world in a perceptually novel way.

TVSS may seem like the stuff of Terminator-style SF. But many similar everyday examples abound: we wear glasses to improve vision, hearing aids to enhance auditory perception, braces to stabilize unsteady joint and enhance balance, and electric wheelchairs to provide mobility. Skilled athletes and musicians routinely merge with their baseball bats and bagpipes, golf clubs and guitars, and, in so doing, experience an expanded sense of embodiment and sensorimotor possibilities. The point, then, is that at the level of our plastic embodiment, everyday technologies integrate with our body, and, in so doing, affect both functional and phenomenological change. This is because we are *profoundly* embodied agents, 'creatures for whom body, sensing, world, and technology are resources apt for recruitment in ways that yield a permeable and repeatedly reconfigurable agent/world boundary' (Clark 2007, 279).

The embodied mind, extended

Taking the nature of our plastic embodiment seriously opens the door to a more radical thesis, one very much in line with posthuman discussions of technologically augmented personhood (Malafouris 2008; Thweatt-Bates 2011). This is the extended mind thesis (Clark & Chalmers 1998; Menary 2010). The extended mind thesis claims that the physical machinery of mind is not confined to the head. Rather, mental states such as beliefs and memories can be partially realized by artefacts and technologies beyond the boundaries of skin and skull.

In Clark and Chalmers' (1998) classic thought experiment, Otto – who suffers from memory loss brought on by a mild form of Alzheimer's – carries a trusty notebook with him wherever he goes. Any time Otto picks up some new information, he records it in his notebook. When he needs that information (e.g., when he wants to remember the location of MoMA in New York so he can go see an exhibition), Otto simply consults this ever-present notebook, retrieves the information and acts on it. According to Clark and Chalmers, this is a case of extended cognition. Some of Otto's dispositional beliefs – such as his belief that MoMA is on 53rd Street – are housed in his notebook. This is because the information in the notebook is *functionally poised* to play the same role that brain-bound information plays in non-extended cases, that is, cases where an individual appeals purely to their internal bioresources to accomplish different cognitive tasks. Otto's long-term beliefs are thus not all inside his head.

We need not appeal to thought experiments or SF narratives to further motivate this idea. Consider real-world memory augmentation. Smartphones and portable calendars help us recall appointments and phone numbers; affixing a yellow sticky note to the side of a computer monitor or by the door prompts recall of to-do items; even social and cultural practices and institutions (political structures, religious rituals, legal systems, etc.) play a cognitive role by encoding the complex web of historical narratives, memories, beliefs and procedural knowledge collectively learned over many generations (Gallagher 2013). When we engage with these external structures and processes, we bootstrap our biological capacities – and within this ongoing engagement 'the human organism is linked with an external entity in a two-way interaction, creating a *coupled system* that can be seen as a cognitive system in its own right' (Clark & Chalmers 1998, 8).

In its original formulation, the extended mind thesis was thought to apply to non-conscious cognitive states (e.g., dispositional beliefs), but not necessarily to conscious mental states, such as emotions (Clark 2009; cf. Hurley 1998;

Rowlands 2003). Little was said about the *phenomenology* of self–world couplings extending mind into the environment. But recent developments have lifted this constraint. Extended mind-style approaches have now been applied to various domains such as perceptual consciousness (Auvray & Myin 2009; Ward 2012), aesthetics (Cochrane 2008; Krueger 2014), social cognition (Gallagher & Crisafi 2009; Theiner et al. 2010) and emotion research (Krueger 2014; Slaby 2014; Colombetti & Roberts 2015). Taking seriously the *experience* of augmenting and extending our embodied and cognitive capacities in various ways is an important feature of these new directions.

This is where a return to phenomenologically sensitive portrayals of situated embodiment in film and television becomes pertinent. I now consider two films that might initially appear to have little to do with one another: Christopher Nolan's *Memento* (2000) and Mick Jackson's made-for-TV movie, *Temple Grandin* (2010). Despite their very different subject matter, both films explore interrelated dimensions of embodiment, technologically mediated cognitive extension and interpersonal relations.

'Really comfortable in my own skin': Embodiment in *Memento* and *Temple Grandin*

Christopher Nolan's psychological thriller *Memento* (2000) follows Leonard Shelby as he frantically hunts for his wife's killer. This task is complicated by the fact that Leonard suffers from a severe form of anterograde amnesia; after suffering a blow to the head, he has lost the ability to form new memories, and many of his previous memories are now hazy and incomplete. The last thing Leonard remembers is intervening in his wife's assault. He vaguely recalls shooting and killing one of the people responsible for the crime before being hit on the head by another assailant, moments after watching his wife die. Understandably, Leonard is now driven by an obsessive desire to find his wife's killer and exact his revenge.

But we soon learn that things are not this straightforward. First, Leonard's motives may not be as noble as they initially appear. He willingly clings to a fabricated memory of a blissful marriage that, in reality, was deeply conflicted and probably violent. As his investigation unfolds, Leonard destroys all evidence compromising this fabricated reconstruction; he actively manipulates his memory in order to forget undesirable facts. Additionally, we soon come to see that Leonard's associates – a corrupt former cop and a barmaid with a chequered past – are exploiting Leonard for their own agendas. Leonard's rage-fuelled drive for revenge (including his eagerness to kill, if necessary) and his profoundly compromised memory render him supremely vulnerable to their ongoing manipulation. As he copes with his unreliable memory and struggles to cling to fleeting moments of clarity, the viewer realizes that Leonard is caught up in a complex network of half-truths and lies – many of them of his own making.

The dizzying dramatic impact of *Memento* comes from its narrative style, which brazenly flouts the conventions of linear storytelling. As the story unfolds, we are taken directly into Leonard's fractured experience: colour sequences are interspersed with black-and-white sequences; the beginning and ending of events are spliced atop one another, confounding the meaning and context of different key occurrences and potentially opening up new lines of interpretation and significance. The effect of this fractured narrative is that the viewer gets a first-hand taste of the *phenomenology* of Leonard's experience of a perpetually unstable world; we empathize, experientially, with his inability to find a firm narrative foothold in order to make sense of what is happening before each present moment withdraws into the darkness of his amnesia.

So how does he cope? Even in his compromised state, Leonard still has access to many of the same cognitive resources that all natural-born cyborgs do: his body and the surrounding environment. Leonard exploits these resources in a desperate attempt to stabilize his memory and retain new information. He collects scraps of paper, receipts, notes and diary pages. He annotates Polaroid photos of important places and objects. Crucially, Leonard systematically organizes this information and places these artefacts in particular locations as memory prompts; since Leonard wakes up each morning with no memory of the previous day, this ritual of setting up the environment to reliably trigger a cascade of memories becomes a critical exercise. Leonard has, in effect, transformed a difficult cognitive problem (i.e., remembering complex information) into a much simpler *perceptual* problem by skilfully engineering his cognitive environment.

But Leonard quite literally has another trick up his sleeve. The most important information Leonard acquires is tattooed onto his body. Over time, Leonard's skin is gradually transformed into a cognitive prosthesis, an external memory device that exhibits a stability and reliability Leonard's neurobiological memory lacks. Leonard's body thus remembers the things his brain cannot. Collectively, then, Leonard attempts to use these memory-augmenting technologies – again, including the surface of his own body, now deliberately reconfigured into a cognitive prosthetic – to slowly build up a stock of new beliefs about the mystery of his wife's death, and in so doing establish a bedrock of long-term knowledge that will, he hopes, lead him to his wife's killer.

One of the many compelling embodiment-related themes in *Memento* is its exploration of what Leonard both gains *and* loses by relying on his body and environment so heavily. For, although these embodied strategies and resources enhance Leonard's recall ability, they also render him extremely vulnerable. One of the consequences of Leonard's functional reconfiguration of his embodiment (i.e., turning his body primarily into a memory storage device) is that Leonard's *experience* of embodiment is profoundly altered. Leonard no longer simply inhabits his body as a subject; it ceases to be the transparent medium through which Leonard encounters the world. In virtue of his deep cognitive reliance on his body's ever-increasing number of tattoos, his body is transfigured primarily into an *object*, another technology used to store and access crucial case-specific information. This is reflected in the way that Leonard spends a great deal of time simply looking at his body, standing in front of a mirror while studying his tattoos and trying to piece together the clues they hold. Leonard's relation with his embodiment in this way becomes as fractured and vulnerable as is his relation with the environment. He no longer inhabits his body transparently. Rather, as essential parts of his externalized memory, both Leonard's carefully curated collection of notes and photographs, as well as the tattoos on his body, occupy a contested public space vulnerable to manipulation and sabotage by others (Sterelny 2004). His memories are no longer his alone; they inhabit a public domain and are therefore open to the deception and hidden agendas of other people. Indeed, we soon see that many of these externalized memories *are* sabotaged by others, including Leonard's manipulative associates as well as 'other' Leonards from previous days and weeks the present-day Leonard can no longer recall. Leonard's functionally augmented embodiment is thus a source of both intimacy and alienation, security and vulnerability.

Mick Jackson's television movie *Temple Grandin* (2010) offers an alternative perspective on intimacy, alienation and augmented embodiment. It portrays the way that technologies – including technologies repurposed in surprising ways – can extend and reconfigure basic structures of embodiment and, in so doing, *enhance* affectivity and interpersonal intimacy. The movie tells the real-life story of Temple Grandin, a professor of Animal Sciences at Colorado State University, world-leading expert on livestock handling, and author of several books recounting her first-person experience of autism. People with autism like Temple have difficulty coping with the social world. They exhibit a range of different communicative and emotional impairments: difficulty maintaining eye contact and participating in the to-and-fro of interactions, extreme discomfort at being held or touched by others, narrowly circumscribed interests and ritualistic or compulsive behaviour, and heightened sensitivity to sounds, textures, smells, light and so on. Temple describes her own childhood as a period where she displayed many of these symptoms: 'no speech, poor eye contact, tantrums, appearance of deafness, no interest in people, and constant staring off into space' (Grandin 2006, 33). As a child, Temple was taken to a neurologist and declared 'brain-damaged'. Eventually, however, with the support of her mother and the patient mentorship of a high school science teacher, Temple discovered her immense intellectual gifts. But she still struggled to emotionally connect with others.

A crucial step in Temple's entry into the social world was her development of a kind of emotional technology she calls the 'squeeze machine' (Grandin 2006, 56–83). Temple modelled her squeeze machine on farm technology: 'crushes' used to immobilize livestock while being branded or given veterinary treatment. Livestock crushes consist of a small stall, just long enough for the animal to enter, an entrance gate which can be closed behind the animal, and a 'head bail' at the front of the stall to hold the animal's head in place. A 'squeeze crush' like Temple's has an additional feature: its sides can be manually compressed, slowly moving inward until they gently squeeze the animal along the length of its body. This tactile pressure calms the animal and reduces their anxiety by inhibiting perceptual stimulation and movement.

Temple discovered that she, too, could exploit this technology to regulate her own anxiety and unpredictable emotions. One day when Temple was 14 and staying on her aunt's cattle ranch in Arizona, she instinctively ran into a cattle crush while gripped by a panic attack (she had previously bonded with the cattle and would spend a great deal of time with them in their pen). As Jackson portrays this event in his film, Temple's distraught aunt follows Temple as she sprints from the house and lodges herself inside the crush. Understandably, Temple's aunt begs her to get out. But Temple is insistent: she frantically pleads with her aunt to manually compress it. Reluctantly, her aunt does so – and as Temple feels the sides of the crush gradually surround her body, her anxiety dissipates. As she later describes this transformative experience, 'For about an hour afterward I felt very calm and serene. My constant anxiety had diminished. *This was the first time I ever felt really comfortable in my own skin*' (Grandin 2006, 59, my emphasis).

What Temple discovered is that her squeeze machine functions as an external technology replicating human touch – but without the unpredictable elements of face-to-face interaction she finds distressing. She tells us that, 'From as far back as I can remember, I always hated to be hugged. I wanted to experience the good feeling of being hugged, but it was too overwhelming. It was like a great, all-engulfing tidal wave of stimulation, and I reacted like a wild animal' (Grandin 2006, 56). When bodily integrated with the squeeze machine, however, Temple can comfortably regulate the sensory parameters of the encounter.

Emboldened by this discovery, Temple used her engineering genius to build many iterations of her squeeze machine – from a crude, hastily assembled model comprised of plywood panels and string-controlled pulleys, to a more sophisticated version sporting foam-padded panels and an air-valve lever enabling fine-grained manipulations of pressure. As the sophistication of her technology increased, Temple was able to achieve more significant results. Regular sessions in the squeeze machine throughout the day enabled Temple to better regulate her emotions and reduce her anxiety. They also enhanced Temple's *experience* of embodiment. As her technology became more sophisticated, it afforded deeper forms of integration which, in turn, allowed Temple to explore previously inaccessible dimensions of her bodily phenomenology. She writes,

> In developing many varied, complex ways to operate the squeeze machine on myself, I keep discovering that slight changes in the way I manipulate the control lever affect how it feels (. . .) very small variations in the rate and timing (. . .) [are] like a language of pressure, and I keep finding new variations with slightly different sensations. For me, this is the tactile equivalent of a complex emotion and this has helped me to understand the complexity of feelings.
>
> (Grandin 2006, 92)

Not only did her squeeze machine scaffold the development of greater intimacy with her own embodiment, then, but it also enabled Temple to use this deepened phenomenological sensitivity to better connect with others on an emotional level. As she puts it, she came to understand that 'the pleasurable feelings [elicited by the squeeze machine] were those associated with love for other people... *I would have been as hard as unfeeling as a rock if I had not built my squeeze machine and followed through with its use*' (Grandin 2006, 85, my emphasis). Whereas Leonard's augmented embodiment in *Memento* led to a greater sense of bodily self-alienation, Temple's cybernetic practices appear to have had the opposite effect.

In sum, this brief discussion indicates some of the ways that transformative relations between embodiment and technology have been explored in film and television. Apart from their aesthetic value, these on-screen portrayals of posthuman embodiment remind us that to be an embodied subject is to be always in some way *transcending* that embodiment. As natural-born cyborgs, we are most at home when living in and beyond our skin.

19
Constructed Worlds: Posthumanism in Film, Television and Other Cosmopoietic Media

Ivan Callus

Possible worlds theory recognizes that what starts to form once a world is postulated with conditions different to the actual is the apprehensibility of a different (meta)physics. Situations implausible in the actual world could there take on outline and cohere, in keeping, as Ruth Ronen explains, with possible worlds providing 'a philosophical explanatory framework that pertains to the problem of fiction'. They overturn 'the long philosophical tradition, from Plato to Russell' that skirts fiction, because this 'has been viewed (...) as a sequence of propositions devoid of a truth value'. Possible worlds thereby rehabilitate fiction as 'part of a larger context of discourses that do not refer to the way things actually are in the world' (Ronen 1994, 6–7). This bears out the adjustment possible worlds theory brings to 'theories of fictionality' based on 'the assumption that there is only one legitimate universe of discourse (domain or reference), the actual world' (Doležel 1998, 2). The possibilities in fictional worlds instead occasion a 'pragmatics of pretense' (11), intuiting that 'the one-world model is not a propitious ground for fictional semantics' (5) and endorsing 'uncountable possible, nonactualized worlds' (13). This multiplicity can only grow, for '[t]he universe of possible worlds is constantly expanding and diversifying thanks to the incessant world-constructing activity of human minds and hands' (ix).

Since this activity projects a dense spectrum of immediacy in the mind and in the sensorial realm, possible worlds' potentialities can be taken beyond thought experiments. As the immediacy nourishes palpability, vividness, image, texture, density, form, materiality and presence, constructed worlds come into being. Oz, Neverland, Middle Earth, Narnia, Discworld and Disneyland Paris are just a few examples, interesting because they have all been (trans)mediated across media and platforms. On this basis, constructed worlds configure a densely resolved actualization of the potentialities inherent to possible worlds. As 'ensembles of nonactualized possible states of affairs' (Doležel 1998, 16), they can impact the actual world. The impact can, for instance, be economic, penetrating down to retailing: merchandising is predicated on this, as artefacts bearing the image of Darth Vader, that quite transhumanist being, demonstrate. But it can also be political, as the row that erupted at the end of 2014 between North Korea, the United States and Sony Pictures around *The Interview*'s unflattering depiction of the leadership in Pyongyang shows. The fallout from Sony's decision to halt *The Interview*'s release to theatres after its computer systems were hacked by a group styling itself 'Guardians of Peace' and linked to Pyongyang by the FBI, coinciding with Internet services – those most potent of world-(re)constructing media – being brought mysteriously down in North Korea at the same time, reveals that possible, fictional, constructed and actual worlds can be intimately co-implicated in events once their integrities are not impenetrable to each other. *The Interview* is not your standard posthumanist film – cyborgs are absent, though terminators of another kind abound – but it dramatizes a present, actual world that can be spoken of in terms of 'posthuman international relations', where attention to the study of politics in terms of systems theory, and 'to complexity-inspired concepts', allows for a constructivism (Cudworth & Hobden 2011, 52) more alert, to recall Trollope, to 'the way we live now'. For if *The Interview* exposed anything it is that the way we live now can have the constructed worlds of the creative arts occasioning perfect storms of sanctions, state-sponsored hacking and counterhacking of technologies of (dis)connectivity in the actual world. Consequently, if posthumanist international relations are to be about 'co-constitution as co-evolution' (Cudworth & Hobden 2011, 81), the possible worlds conjured there will need to be emancipated from the actual world's propensity to police fictional worlds, or their sanguine projections might turn out to be all too hypothetical, theoretical, *im*possible.

The point is important, since posthumanism itself retains aspects of a theoretical fiction, where:

> *[V]iewing possible worlds as human constructs brings the concept down from the metaphysical pedestal and makes it a potential tool of empirical theorizing. (…) Possible worlds of philosophy are* coherent cosmologies *derived from some axioms or presuppositions. (…) Possible worlds of natural science are* alternative designs of the universe *constructed by varying the basic physical constants.*
>
> (Doležel 1998, 14)

Indeed, possible worlds of posthumanism have their own take on coherent cosmologies and alternative designs. They fashion constructed worlds – and theories – that answer to Margaret Atwood's (2012, 115) understanding of speculative fiction in terms of 'human society and its possible future forms, which are either much better than what we have now or much worse'. They bear reference, contrastive and counter-defining, to the actual world, thinking through its possibilities and potentialities while configuring it differently. In truth, all constructed worlds do this, to different degrees, but what posthumanism does is to explore an altered state of the human and its constructions that are other, yet open to re-cognition. In literature, for instance, this happens when David Eagleman in *Sum* constructs otherworldly cosmologies that reflect familiar dispensations despite being nothing like them. Artists like M. C. Escher, in games with perspective, scale and flow, can contrive environments that take on finely specified architectural detail even when defying logic and physical laws in the actual world. Within digital games, *Portal* affords a constructed world operating to a different physics that the player must learn to make intuitive while operating the 'Aperture Science Handheld Portal Device', which can create openings through which objects and perspective can be teleported between two planes on a screen space that is made to feel quite multidimensional. Within television, *Lost*, across its six seasons, spins a complex and multilayered narrative, centred initially on the survivors of a plane crash who find themselves on an island unmapped in any geography and unrecorded in any history, and constructs a cosmology characterized by portals of another kind. These open onto possible worlds and timescapes, keying posthumanist motifs concerning 'bare life' *and* transhumanist technology in ways that suggest both afterlives and parallel lives. 'See you in another life, brother', is in fact the loaded catchphrase of one of the characters, Desmond David Hume, whose very name, with its philosophical echoes, bears upon motifs of transworld identities in constructed worlds.

Across these scenarios, constructed worlds are 'fictional domains' for which 'world-constructing conventions' and 'world reconstructing conventions' can be specified and catalogued with the precision that narratology, at its most adeptly taxonomic, furnishes (Ronen 1994, 89ff.). This is what happens, for instance, when Ronen provides a 'nonexhaustive' yet comprehensive enough list of properties about 'fictional worlds', against which propositions concerning those worlds can be assessed as being, in a telling criterion, *valid* – or not (1994, 88ff.). It is not the purpose of this chapter to play a 'Narrative Discourse Revisited' game (Genette 1988), seeking to retest the applicability of narratology's taxonomies in the light of studies by, say, Monika Fludernik or Marie-Laure Ryan to consider how posthumanism can inform the debate around the affordances for storyworlds in new media. Nor will the futural orientation of posthumanism and its possible worlds be tested back against studies in narratology and the ontology of fiction on possible worlds in history. That would require more space than is available here. Rather, what will be taken up is that prompt from Ronen concerning validity. For, once constructed worlds, in posthumanism or otherwise, seize the imagination, enabling parallel verisimilitudes that vividly imagined non-actual worlds acquire, it becomes possible to position characters and happenings on different planes of plausibility. White rabbits that tell the time or cue the way to red pills, yellow brick roads, doors at the back of wardrobes or the train to Hogwarts departing from Platform 9¾ can become part of worlds imaginatively visited *by millions* – constructed worlds being the concern of multitudes as well as loners, ineluctably so with media like film and television or massively multiplayer online games (MMOGs), which are not predicable on the more private model exemplified by the Brontës taking their minds away to Gondal, the domain they created within their juvenilia. Whatever their reach, however, one attribute is constant in constructed worlds. They operate by embracing fiction's dispensations and its conventions on the (un)conventional. Constructed worlds take on definition once possible worlds have *mise-en-scène*, taking on ground for counterlives in non-actual timespaces. They thereby stake out *validity*, which can underwrite the most implausible effects, as the two examples below demonstrate.

In *Doctor Who* – a television series whose posthumanist propensities are too often overlooked – an utterance like the following, which would be nonsensical elsewhere, has perfect validity: 'Carnivorous snow meets Victorian values. And something terrible is born' ('The Snowmen' 2012). The utterance coheres not only with the (meta)physics of the constructed world but, equally, with the *tone* of the series, which refuses to go along with the solemnity of many other posthumanist projections; consequently, the utterance's whimsy actually girds its validity in its constructed world. By extension, it is possible to be upset or, conversely, entertained if validities in the construction of posthumanist (meta)physics in a fictional world are disrespected. *Star Trek*, another series with distinct posthumanist affinities, provides the second example illustrating this point. Or rather, the example is provided by the *reconstruction* of Star Trek's world, occurring in a storyworld *in a different television series*. In 'Blood Money', the ninth episode of the fifth season of *Breaking Bad*, the character of Brandon 'Badger' Mayhew describes a pitch for a *very* hypothetical storyline within the original series of *Star Trek*. The pitch has the *Enterprise* positioned 'five parsecs out of Rigel XII', where 'the crew is bored' because 'Neutral Zone is quiet'. Badger moves 'the whole crew (...) in[to] the galley', relieving boredom through 'a pie-eating contest'. Badger specifies that they are eating 'tulaberry pies', whereupon his friend, who goes by the name of Skinny Pete, interjects, 'Tulaberry?' 'Tulaberries', Badger confirms, 'from Gamma Quadrant, yo'. Skinny Pete doesn't like this misplacing of *Star Trek* chronologies, and corrects Badger: 'That's *Voyager*, dude'. Badger acknowledges the correction (confusing series across the *Star Trek* franchise is a serious *faux pas*), replaces the tulaberries in his story with blueberries, and fast forwards to the contest's denouement. It comes down to Spock, who 'has total Vulcan control over his digestion', and Chekov, who has a 'whole fat stack of quatloos riding on this'. Chekov is winning because he has an arrangement with Scotty, of 'Beam me up' fame, who teleports Chekov's stomach contents into space, thereby ensuring ample digestive capacity for blueberry pies. The account comes to an end with smutty hyperbole: Scotty is distracted by the comely Uhura, the consequence of this momentary inattention being the beaming of 'Chekov's guts into space'. Jesse Pinkman, in whose house the story gets told, decides he cannot take any more and gets up to go out, leaving Badger to exclaim, 'You're missing the best part!'

Viewers of *Breaking Bad* might ascribe Badger's comic storyworld-within-storyworld performance to his character's substance abuse. Whatever prompts Badger's pitch, the geekiness-celebrating scene quickly acquired cult status. Within a day of its screening an animated version was up on fandom sites. The (inter)penetrating influence of different TV series on popular culture is thus well demonstrated. For television fiction to reference other television fiction, doing so while amusing itself with what could or could not be allowed to happen within interdiegetic relation, bears witness to just how tangibly real constructed worlds can be. It is as clear an indication as any of the way in which constructed worlds in fiction are open to mythologization, reconstruction and transmediation – and to minds transported in imagination. Even more to the point, exploring how this hold is itself represented in posthumanist fictions should be singularly instructive for the understanding of constructed worlds. That is because posthumanism is a discourse where the depiction of minds and bodies transported to worlds of quite particular construction provides a recurrent trope, often in more sinister representations than that offered by Badger's riff on transhumanist affordances. Badger's pitch, in other words, is a burlesque allegory of the vividness and reach of constructed – and construct*ing* – posthumanist worlds.

A lot can hang, therefore, on tulaberries and on locating them in their right place in the constructed world containing them. Those not in the know – 'What *is* a tulaberry?' – can still get a sense of why all this can matter terribly, even if they feel that they'd rather follow Jesse Pinkman outside. What is needed, then, is a closer look at certain issues underlying constructed worlds, before taking up again their instantiations in posthumanist film and television.

As indicated, philosophical and narratological outlooks are central to discussions of constructed worlds. To stick with examples from posthumanist scenarios: Frankenstein's monster, R2D2 and Samantha, the artificial intelligence in *Her*, don't exist; yet they all seem rendered with finely granulated detail within the phenomenologies of the reading and viewing mind. The imagination apprehending a world constructed in fiction, in whatever medium, can weave across the possible, the actual and the constructed with remarkable suppleness, so that the different worlds' boundaries can blur in ways that can be pleasurable or, sometimes, sinister. It is as well to steal a quick look, therefore, at aspects of the critical literature when the focus falls directly on constructed worlds, before homing in more specifically on some related issues surrounding posthumanist film and television.

Hence, research on preschoolers' trajectories along the *what is* and *as if* spectrum bears correspondences with posthumanist world-construction. For just as 'delineating and describing alternative worlds through narrative language allows young children to explore the boundaries between different types of fictive experience: probable, improbable, aesthetically dense, and transparently pragmatic, to name just four' (Engel 2005, 515), posthumanist fictions allow the contemporary imagination to play with degrees of (im)probability and the varying scales of pragmatic response to speculation on what could occur suddenly, imminently, gradually, fantastically or inexorably, given where humanity stands in the world(s) it has contrived. And if the narratives are 'aesthetically dense', speaking to inner fears and overt concerns, by sublimating them into storylines by which humans mature their sense of their evolving (post)human condition, it is possible to arrive at a finer sense of our times, our worlds and our (re)construction of them.

Heterocosmica (Doležel's term for the diverse worlds, fictional and otherwise, that humans construct as they navigate existence) are thereby the outcome of the more generalized process of *cosmopoiesis* (Giuseppe Mazzotta's term for 'world-making') that humans indulge as they make sense of the world in its actualities, histories and becomings. The aesthetic density therein has itself experienced process:

> With Don Quixote de la Mancha, with the work of art as prose, the modern age begins, and with it begins the novel of the future.

> *The age of prose contemplates the poetry of the Italian Renaissance epic. (...) this dream of the Italian Renaissance is the dream of the world: of world-making, actual worlds, possible worlds, golden worlds, brazen worlds, the creation of the world, and the metaphysics of infinite worlds.*
>
> *This cosmopoiesis rests on and needs a prior vision of the world, a contemplation of the whole wherein the arts of making acquire a purpose beyond their limited purviews. On the necessarily shaky, dangerous foundation of the Renaissance world-vision and world-making, the modern world rethinks and experiments itself. Only by drawing from this imaginative and spiritual reservoir will there be once again a rebirth of myths and memories for the future.*
>
> (Mazzotta 2001, 97)

Noteworthy here is Mazzotta's acknowledgement of filiation and evolution across diverse modes and media. Evidently, there is no suggestion of superannuation. Poetry does not become irrelevant just because 'the modern age' begins with 'the novel of the future'. In any case, Mazzotta's invocation is rather towards 'a prior vision of the world' that can inexhaustibly be resourced in the constructed worlds that move, *posthumanistically* it could be said, beyond 'Renaissance world-vision and world-making'. And we shall always be, as we move there, in the elsewhere of our fictions, for it is as well to remember that, like Badger, Don Quixote was all too immersed in his constructed worlds, in his elsewheres.

Yet this is a time of *electronic elsewheres*. 'Literary fiction is probably the most active experimental laboratory of the world-constructing enterprise' (Doležel 1998, ix), but 'electronic elsewheres' claim attention because 'the media do not just represent – accurately or inaccurately – a place that is already there'; rather, 'places (...) are conjured up, experienced, and in that sense produced through media', such that 'media technologies (from the analog to the digital) have contributed to the spatial relations of modern/postmodern life, in its various global contexts' (Berry et al. 2010, vii). The constructed worlds of the posthuman are definable by this too. They help to materially configure the *actual* world. Going back to the quotation from Engel, they are consequently 'transparently pragmatic' before they are 'aesthetically dense'. Indeed, the world has been reconstructed in so many elsewheres (electronic and not) so very otherwise now, and will continue to be so, that it summons the Deleuzian understanding of the virtual for any adequate conceptualization to start to cohere. For Deleuze:

> *[T]he virtual is not opposed to the real: it is the real that is opposed to the possible. Virtual is opposed to actual, and therefore, possesses a full reality. (...) In every respect, the virtual echoes the formulation which Proust gave to his state of experience: 'real without being actual, ideal without being abstract'. The virtual and the possible are opposed in several ways. On the one hand, the possible is such that the real is constructed as its resemblance. It is even because of this defect that the possible looks suspiciously retrospective or retroactive; it is suspected of being constructed after the fact, in resemblance to the real which it is supposed to precede. This is why, too, when*

someone asks what more *is found in the real, there is nothing to point out except 'the same' thing as posited outside representation. The possible is just the concept as principle of the representation of the thing, under the following categories: the identity of* what is representing, *and the resemblance of* what is being represented. *On the other hand, the virtual belongs to the Idea and does not resemble the actual, no more than the actual resembles the virtual. The Idea is an image without resemblance; the virtual actualizes itself not through resemblance, but through divergence and differentiation. Differentiation or actualization is always creative with respect to what it actualizes, whereas realization is always reproductive or limiting. The difference between the virtual and the actual is no longer the difference of the Same insofar as the Same is posited once in representation, and once again outside representation. Rather, it is the difference of the Other, insofar as the Other appears once in the Idea, and once again, though in a totally different manner, in the process of actualizing the Idea.*

(Deleuze 2004, 101)

It is precisely because of its cognisance of this virtuality that posthumanism is the strangest of discourses. It has to be, because it speaks about what is strange to the human, even as that strangeness is constructible as edging closer. Posthumanism is one of the few paradigms that seeks to interpret the world not as it is but as it might be(come). To that extent, posthumanism is always a fiction. It is always about (re)constructed worlds, unsure of being realized or resolved. In that sense, posthumanism is unreal. It is the spectre of the constructed futures which successive presents might either kill off or overtake. It is fantastical yet putatively emergent, an educated wager on what will have been. It constructs worlds and scenarios in which the human might experience different being, negotiating plausibilities and possibilities in ways demonstrating that 'the virtual and the actual correspond but do not resemble one another' (Deleuze 2004, 110). Rather, 'the virtual is not the same thing as the possible: the reality of time is finally the affirmation of a virtuality that is actualized, for which to be actualized is to invent. Because if everything [*tout*] is not given, it remains that the virtual is the whole [*le tout*]' (Deleuze 2004, 30). There is, therefore, a congruence between *le tout*, as the virtual, and the posthuman, the latter being an envisioning of the former, which is differentiated as strangeness and actualized in the familiar. Hence, *posthumanism is never not about worlds in construction.*

Posthumanism is, in fact, 'the sense of the world' in its being and its becoming. It documents, through a sensing of possible actuality, the world in construction and address. As Jean-Luc Nancy writes, '*World* means being at least *being-to* or *being-toward* [*être à*]', such that 'it means rapport, relation, address, sending, donation, presentation *to*'. Posthumanism is that which is responsive to the fact that 'it still remains for us to think being-*to*, or the *to* of being, its ontologically worldly or worldwide trait' (1997, 8). It follows that posthumanism is all of a piece with constructed, reconstructed, deconstructed worlds. In representing this, posthumanist films and television offer good vistas onto the ontological worldliness and worldwide traits mentioned by Nancy. Yet there remain fundamental, if productive, contradictions and tensions in posthumanist film and television, as itemized below:

1. In some of the most influential and referenced studies of posthumanism (Hayles 1999; Wolfe 2010; Braidotti 2013), film and television feature relatively scantily. The literary sensibilities of these studies probably accounts for this. The incisiveness of these powerful texts is undoubted, but overdetermination of the posthuman within the broader imaginary on the basis of film, from Lang's *Metropolis* to Cameron's *Avatar*, sets up interesting spaces that a handbook like the present can help to address.

2. A constructed world needs significant *durée* to acquire appreciable definition. To that extent, TV series have the advantage over film. *Lost*, for instance, works because the many enigmatic facets of its constructed world emerge in all their prismatic qualities over its 121 episodes. There is, quite simply, more extension to intradiegetic reality when the story goes beyond 2–3 hours of film time, or when it is transmediated, carrying its heritage with it. Posthumanist films often contrive *durée* differently, however. *The Matrix* is a trilogy; the *Terminator* films are in fact a series; *Solaris* and *Blade Runner* have the props of the mythology of the Director's Cut and the Stanislaw Lem and Philip K. Dick novels on which they are respectively based. And posthumanist films can suggest *infinitude*, never mind *durée*.

3. Posthumanist cosmopoiesis in film and television appears set on affirming the human(ist) in contexts where this is precarious. It seems intent on exploring how what might be quintessentially human (assuming such a conception is tenable) survives, or not, in posthuman contexts: across space operas (as in *Star Wars*); in the zombie apocalypse (as in *The Walking Dead*); amid contagion (as in *28 Days Later*); in the countdown to the end of the world or humanity entire (as in *Last Night*); in heavily and hypertechnologically reengineered human societies (as in *Avatar*); in alien encounters (as in *2001*); in technology's evolution to the point of singularity (as in *The Matrix*). It is why Stefan Herbrechter and I have argued that there are 'what might be called "posthuman moments" in science fiction' where 'the integrity of (...) "human essence"' is threatened, but which are often 'closed off by the reaffirmation and reconfirmation of the human on a different plane' (Herbrechter & Callus 2008, 98). This tendency appears to have been upheld since then, the endings of *Gravity* or *Interstellar* again suggesting that 'a posthumanist reading' can attempt 'the exposure of the strategies by which human(ist) integrity is re-conscripted into science fiction narratives' (Herbrechter & Callus 2008, 107). More can perhaps be done now with the different poignancies where the posthuman is figured, starkly, in terms of a humanity that recedes physiologically and neurocognitively (as in *Amour*), for posthumanism keys more than originary technicity or transhumanising technology.

4. Connecting with this, conventional spectropoetics are unsettled in *Les Revenants*, a film that later inspired a series of the same name, in which dead

people inexplicably return *intact* to very materially resume their lives. Alexander Sokurov's film, *Russian Ark*, turns equally disturbingly on the tropes of 'autobio-heterothanatography' (see Derrida 1993) and narration by the dead, going to the core of what a literal-minded understanding of the morphemes in *posthumanism* might evince. Shot in a single long take travelling from the back entrance of the Hermitage Museum in St Petersburg to the Jordan Staircase within the same museum, the film can be interpreted as a cinematic refashioning of the uninterrupted flow of (Russian) history from the time of Peter the Great to Czar Nicholas II. Like Resnais' *Last Year in Marienbad*, based on a Robbe-Grillet novel, where the oneiric and the immemorial haunt the social minglings on screen in a tale interpretable as a recasting of the Orpheus and Eurydice myth, *Russian Ark* suggests the immateriality that a different kind of posthumanist imag(in)ing – no cyborgs, no smart technology, no singularity in the frame – can bring to vision. For what *Russian Ark* does is give some sense of the pathology and phenomenology of the spectral witnessing, outside and in time, of *demourance* (see Derrida 2000): the disarticulated awareness, in other words, of an experientiality of disembodiment where the framings of space and time can be felt to lose outline even when being mimetically reiterated. When this is achieved in film the effect is even more impressive than when it occurs in, say, literature, for film must, precisely, always *show* even when it is 'showing not telling'. Again, tone is key. *Russian Ark* equably sets up interesting contrasts with the dread in the viewpoint-from-interment in one well-known scene in Dreyer's *Vampyr* or in the whole of Cortés's *Buried*, not to mention with the high-tech, high-drama resolution of other representations of posthuman being.

5. Constructed worlds can be better understood in the context of *constructed reality film*. In a study on this theme, Brian Welesko refers to the 'vast network of tunnels called "ultilodors"' (2014, 3) which spans the Walt Disney world resort in Florida, the point being that constructed reality is always undergirded by infrastructures – like source code in software – meant to *not* be seen but which enable sight(s) of simulacra and the hyperreal. What Welesko brings to the fore is the willing suppression generally of interaction with such infrastructure, that non-collision driving the collusion with constructed realities. Suspension of disbelief wills itself to *not* see how constructed worlds work. Indeed, what posthumanist film thematizes is very often the problematics of that collision/collusion. Perhaps Welesko's one oversight in an otherwise excellent article is to use the term *postmodern* when *posthuman* might have suited: 'Like the silent-era *rube* film, *Westworld*, *The War Game*, *The Gladiators*, *Logan's Run*, *Tron*, *eXistenZ*, *The Matrix*, and *Source Code* put a character on screen to offer audiences an education: how to live with new, postmodern consciousness of our constructed world – and how to decide which one to adhere to, all without losing our minds' (2014, 7). The bleak conclusion rings true. Arguing that what film does is shine 'a lens into the hidden fabric of our postmodern society', in a manner that 'begs us to touch to verify' (2014, 8), Welesko suggests that the resulting 'haptic rupture is a temporary though irrevocable removal of the barrier between constructed and actual space' which 'does not always result in a full breakdown of the controlling power structure' (2014,

19). Rather, the message of these films is 'to touch/understand the multitudes of stimuli and realities, but try not to fully process: play dumb and keep moving'. For as '[t]he constructed reality can come from a government, a controlling body, or the mind, (...) a full haptic rupture occurs that shatters the illusion', meaning that 'insanity and violence may be a way to cope, though clearly a destructive and horrific one' (2014, 19).

In conclusion: this chapter, without going into any of the 'exasperating metaphysical issues' (Doležel 1998, x) that arise around possible worlds, has addressed conceptualizations of constructed worlds and their relevance to posthumanist film and television. It has attempted to keep in view affinities across: (1) possible worlds theory, studies in the ontology of fiction and constructed worlds; (2) posthumanism as a theoretical fiction *necessarily* invested in (re)constructed worlds; (3) posthumanism as an aesthetic paradigm that tells multiple stories about mind and being transported to various elsewheres, in variations on the set-piece posthumanist thought experiment featuring the downloading of consciousness into a computer (Hayles 1999, 1). The projection of the human in fictions on non-human, extrahuman, transhuman, posthuman contexts is refracted by the fact that *fiction* is always, in any case, about sundry elsewheres. It is why posthumanism, with its accounts of those elsewheres, is a paradigm coextensive with constructed worlds. For the posthuman, which ineluctably *is* a speculative fiction, is also in many ways the glimpsing of an emerging reality which demands a new realism that is not any less trenchant by being about the non-(f)actual. That is because what this new realism configures is a view – or cosmopoietic construction – of the potentialities of a recast human condition, whether that condition is humanly reengineered or the outcome of unsummoned (be)comings.

The chapter has also tried to maintain at least peripheral awareness of the specificities of film and television when compared with other cosmopoietic media. This is now, perhaps, the moment to suggest that film and television, like the other cosmopoietic media of our time, can go only so far in configuring 'a *fuller* experience' of the posthuman that would be angled to 'stimulation of a person's *whole sensory field*', in a manner true to a point made by Merleau-Ponty: 'I perceive in a total way with my whole being; I grasp a unique structure of the thing, a unique way of being, which speaks to all my senses at once' (quoted in Welesko 2014, 16). A cosmopoietic medium that could pull that off would be the very stuff of the posthuman. It would be *the* posthuman medium, its remediation and transmediation congruent with the posthuman itself. Like literature, film and television are not quite that medium. Posthuman theatre and digital games that allow audience or player *co*-construction of digital worlds arguably represent a move on that medium, affording a vivid sensorial experientiality that trumps the 'mere' wonderment of visual imaging. Cosmopoiesis of the human in posthuman space and time remains possible even this side of that medium's constructions, however. Doubtless it remains alert too to the fears and perils of that posthuman world, but in the end poetry – (cosmo)poiesis in whatever medium – speaks true, alive to the fact that the 'most dangerous people are those/for whom the present is the only reality' (Porter 1999, 82).

20
Games, Gamers and Posthumanism

Tanya Krzywinska and Douglas Brown

Anthony Vidler wrote that William Gibson's novel *Neuromancer* 'voiced a peculiarly contemporary sense of haunting: that provoked by the loss of traditional bodily and locational references by the pervasive substitution of the simulated for the real in the computer's virtual reality' (Vidler 1992, 10). Published in 1984, *Neuromancer* provided a narrative that intensified, and gave a subcultural twist, to the buzz of possibility surrounding computing technology. Gibson's novel rode on the entry of computer-based games into the domestic marketplace, working a populist seam to create an accessible, plot-driven tech-noir fiction through which games become synonymous with virtual reality. Central to this is the fantasy of escaping the bodily and spatio-temporal confines that construct the human condition. If the TV show *Star Trek* helped to make funding for NASA palatable by creating a desire for space exploration (Penley 1997), then *Neuromancer* contributed to the creation of a sensationalizing mythos that transformed computational technology into, at once, a new frontier and a seductive means of escaping entropy and acquiring superpowers. Fuelled by the power of this mythos, science fiction (SF), art, philosophy and critical theory have found a point of convergence, occupying a shared domain that Steve Nicholls (1988) claimed as posthuman.

Drawing on the virtual-reality mythos created by *Neuromancer*, digital games and the implication of playing them have become associated with the posthuman. This association is consolidated through the tropes used to represent digital games and gamers in the competing fields of film and television. The primary means of connection is based on the fact that digital games appear ostensibly to extend infinitely the reach of human agency, transcending our incarcerating and feeble physical and mental capabilities. Such an image of liberation is consolidated within some of the best-known big-budget SF films that follow on from *Neuromancer*, and is best typified by the abilities afforded to the 'jacked-in' Neo in *The Matrix* franchise. Game avatars can endlessly run without getting breathless, jump impossible crevasses and evade the finality of death. Through a game, a middle-aged woman can become a hulking, barbarous Orc who smashes his way to victory, while a teenaged boy can play in the guise of a laconic but poised witch shooting bullets that always hit the mark from the elegant heel of her stiletto shoe. Digital games have moved on from the serried ranks of blocky space invaders lining up for the putative star-fighter to despatch, where building skills of dexterity and timing were everything. Many big-budget console and PC-based games looking for an increased market share in the face of a plethora of small, highly accessible casual games now seek to reduce the sense of mediation in order to give players a heightened sense of *being there*. The aspiration to step literally into and become an actor in a fiction found an early and influential representation in *Star Trek*'s Holodeck, subsequently representing the potential of game media in Janet Murray's book *Hamlet on the Holodeck* (2001). This aspiration also drives game interface technology to become more intuitive and invisible. Devices like Oculus Rift, for example, provide a profound sense of immersion, blocking out all other visual stimuli and placing the player at the centre of a 360-degree virtual world. Creating a more intensive sense of presence bolsters our impression that a game is a tool, aiming in some cases to make us feel like gods, capable of blowing evil away with the merest press of a button. It is this that has often been exaggerated and sensationalized within representations of the posthuman gamer in film and television. Virtual reality, and, by extension, games and gamers, become emblematic of the threat of hubristic dehumanisation. In *Strange Days* (1995), for example, virtual reality was allied to millenarianism and the obsession to produce a form of technoconservatism that differs in its negative approach to that of tech-positive *Neuromancer* or the gamer-facing *Avalon* (2001) – yet even in both of these there is a dangerous obsessive pleasure in play. In *Tron* (1982), the virtual space becomes the spawning ground for demons, providing a means to rehash good versus evil themes that have also been mined by *Buffy the Vampire Slayer*.

Often in SF- or fantasy-based film and television, games are mainly represented under the aegis of the dystopian posthuman as tools that recoil on their users; pleasure turns to addiction, as in *Lawnmower Man* (1992), or fun to peril (King & Krzywinska 2000, 92). They are very rarely represented as what they are – fictions. The tools games provide for players have their purchase mainly in the fiction – even if there are some real-world effects. It may then be that game-based tools, confined as they are to the game world, do not make us posthuman but instead prop up an imaginary status *as* posthuman – a fantasy of power and purchase that is born of our straitened, all-too-human condition. Players might feel that they have conquered planets, destroyed enemies or garnered riches, but is simply operating so masterfully in a fictional context enough to claim that games are indicative of an ascendency into the posthuman? The way that games make use of posthumanism in terms of character, theme and story is therefore our first point of analysis in this chapter. From this, we can then ask in what ways the cybernetic and ludic qualities of games impact on our experience of posthuman themes and whether there are other ways in which games can be regarded as posthuman. We initially need to consider some of the principal ways in which the posthuman has been conceived, and the reasons behind those models, as a precursor to understanding the relation of games to those conceptions. The purpose of this chapter is therefore to identify how the posthuman manifests in digital games and the ways it is represented in other media, as well as to explore what it means to claim games for the posthuman.

It is important to begin by stating that the posthuman is neither thing nor object. It is an idea, or, more properly, a set of ideas; in many cases it is geared around the conception that technology is our route towards progress and perfection, stretching beyond 'humanist' education and evolving the human into its next incarnation. Popular culture generally, does not, however, subscribe to this progress narrative, instead preferring a dramatic and effects-friendly dystopian and hubristic approach, typified by films such as *Species* (1995) or *Lucy* (2014). There may, therefore, be an aesthetic or ideological agenda behind the various explicit or implicit definitions of posthumanism. For some within philosophy it is a thought experiment, as with Donna Haraway's cyborg (1985). This model pulls on the cinema of the day, where early computer-generated effects were first making their impact on what was possible in terms of convincing representation, but turns it to radical ends. For others working within the field of cultural-impact technology, however, it is more akin to a religion, as can be seen in the work of Ray Kurzweil (2005). In this sense, the posthuman is ambiguous: it has and does not have a referent – it is at once abstract and, for some, concrete, for some it's a fiction and for others it is real. While it refers concretely to that which comes after 'human' or 'humanism', it also functions as a metaphor and as a group of associations. As such, there is no solid agreement on what the posthuman refers to or what it means; there is not necessarily even a shared property. In addition to which, the posthuman acquires diverse associations as it enters into different disciplinary and thematic spheres: biology, gender, education, geography, economics, philosophy, the arts, communication and media. It resonates in terms of both ontology and epistemology.

Claims on the posthuman can be divided into three broad clusters, each contributing in different ways to our understanding of posthumanism in digital games and gaming. The first is the cybercultured *techno-utopian* cluster, of which the magazine *Wired*, first published in 1993, was emblematic. Nurtured by SF and cyberpunk as well as the growing hacking culture which tended to turn its back on old-technology film and television, Steve Nicholls' 'Posthuman Manifesto' of 1988 summed up and gave a new twist to a growing trend within technological discourse towards utopian futurology. Nicholls argued that we are already posthuman because of our various forms of bodily augmentations and technological prosthetics. In Nicholls' sense we were already living in an SF future. Ray Kurzweil, currently Director of Engineering at Google, is perhaps the most prominent figure of the utopian take on posthumanism; unlike Nicholls, he looks forward and believes that we are on the verge of transcending biology: 'The transformation underlying the singularity is not just another in a long line of steps to biological evolution. We are upending biological evolution altogether' (2005, 374). He argues that this is on the basis that we 'have the ability to understand our own intelligence – to access our own source code (...) – and then revise and expand it' (4). Kurzweil's approach might more usefully be thought of as transhuman rather than posthuman, however; he argues against the use of the term 'posthumanism' to describe his vision of transcending biology: 'If we regard a human modified by technology as no longer human, where would we draw the defining line?' (374).

Kurzweil's position leads us to one of the problems inherent in other utopian claims for posthumanism: augmentation and the extension of agency are not new, and the human is regularly defined through dominant tool use. Rhetorically, this positions technology as the principle way of defining the human and invests in technology's teleological status. The benefits of this progressive and utopian master narrative to commercial endeavour are clear and signal the obsolescence of 'old' media. Within this narrative formation, the posthuman becomes a pervasive and persuasive branding device, designed to grab attention and make a generation feel special, with film and television being consigned to the care home. Games as the (soon-to-be-old) new media are therefore implicated in this seductive process of consolidating and reifying such branding. Techno-utopian investment in the posthuman actively seeks to spark imagination as a means of igniting desire for technological consumables; and it is an active enemy of film, which persists in its demonizing representations of cyberculture and games. In this sense, it is a weak philosophical take on posthumanism precisely because, particularly in Kurzweil's case, it is a form of post-religious evangelization of technology as a redemptive force yet aimed to stimulate enthusiasm for research and development: a narrative that seems, from a film perspective, highly hubristic. Digital games and their associated technologies are, at the moment, central to this process of fetish-forming evangelization: contributing to the construction of a pre-hyped pent-up market for new technology by creating possibility spaces for imagining what can be done by altering our code. It is, however, in a direct and fearful response to this ecstatic embrace of radical change through technology that the plethora of cautionary dystopian narratives emerge, wherein a counterweight fetishization of the *human* occurs; examples of such are found across media, from *Metropolis* (1927) to the online game *Destiny* (2014).

One of the appeals of the posthuman for radical thinkers is that it provides the possibility to reimagine life without the differences that are often used to support inequalities. Both Donna Haraway (2000) and Rosi Braidotti (2013) embrace posthumanism on this basis, yet ally it with post-structuralist and psychoanalytic-feminist thought by way of Luce Irigaray and Hélène Cixous' critique of binary configurations of gender difference, forming thereby our second cluster. Haraway makes use of popular cultural images of cyborgs to imagine a state of being that doesn't accord with the binary gender codes which govern traditional understandings of biology – much as Ursula K. Le Guin had done in her speculative novel *The Left Hand of Darkness* (1969). Haraway draws on the spirit of technological utopianism, yet uses it to launch a blistering attack on the limitations of present conceptions of difference and otherness. First published in 1991, Haraway's visionary 'Cyborg Manifesto' calls forth the cyborg from the annals of popular culture as a means of unhinging established correspondences and sweeping away outmoded presumptions, 'my cyborg myth is about transgressed boundaries, potent fusions, and dangerous possibilities which progressive people might explore as one part of needed political work' (Haraway 2000, 295). Haraway's posthuman cyborg has no truck with traditional distinctions between animals, humans and machines, or with the essentializing notion of 'nature' – neither in biological nor mythic terms. Haraway's feminism is not grounded in the collective, essentialist experience of 'woman', as was the prevailing approach within feminism, instead 'the certainty of what counts as nature – a source of insight and promise of innocence – is undermined, probably fatally' (294). Barbara Kennedy has critiqued the cyborg as being too easily fetishized as a phallic woman who can 'do little to change an already power/violence crazed culture' (2000, 287). Only rarely do we see the female gamer, cyborg or otherwise, in film or television; gamers are typically represented by men. There are some notable exceptions: the superwarrior Ash in *Avalon* who, against all odds, beats the game; Allegra Geller, the greatest ever game designer in/of *eXistenZ*, and Phoebe in *The X-Files* 'First Person Shooter', co-written by Gibson, who creates a monstrous female avatar as a counterweight to testosterone-fuelled games who somehow found her way into a game programme, killing players. In all these cases, where women play against (stereo)type, the distinctions that separate game from reality dissolve: as if with that one class of difference under attack all differences that define the human collapse.

Braidotti carves a more philosophically grounded path through this multi-faceted field in her claim for a 'posthuman humanity'. Rather than Haraway's distinctly anti-human conception of the posthuman in the image of the cold cyborg who has no time for the set of differences that comprise traditional notions of the human, Braidotti's posthuman is the generative source of creativity. She claims this version of the posthuman as a way out of the impasses and negativity of 20th-century anti-humanism. Braidotti's work is grounded in a move away from the humanist model of the 'cogito' and gender-loaded presupposition that 'man' is made in the image of god, emblemized by Leonardo's Vitruvian man, whose body is the idealized geometric and proportional measure of all things. Braidotti argues that these rhetorics are deeply woven into Western linguistic systems and epistemology, which has the effect of manufacturing and othering difference, reifying hierarchization and ossifying knowledge and meaning. While Braidotti takes a scholarly and rounded approach, she nonetheless retains that characteristic spirit of utopian imagining. Games certainly play a role in this, even if in danger of technological fetishism, as they have the potential to be speculative and creative proving grounds, furnished by their capability for reinvention and simulation. One of the features of many existing and mainstream games with female playable characters is that they decentre man as the natural active agent. This becomes possible because games are predicated formally on player agency, but how deep is such agency? The disappearance of deep agency in the world (if indeed it ever existed) under a plethora of superficial and consumer-based choices, brings us to Baudrillard, who would not have characterized his work as posthuman but represents our third approach. Baudrillard can help us to explore the way that agency is configured in games, how they can be considered to be simulations and their relation to consumerism. As a poststructuralist, Baudrillard also regarded language as deeply ideologically loaded, much as Braidotti and Haraway do. But if we are to read the posthuman in Baudrillardian terms, it would not be as a productive, generative strategy, but instead describe our absorption into the simulation and the hyperreal. The posthuman is an agent of consumerism and not a citizen. Cue *The Stepford Wives* (1972, 2004), another level of being, yes, but at the expense of a loss of the real and the loss of history, to which we might add the loss of death. Games then might be posthuman in the sense that their virtuality is so seductive that we lose sight of the real, of history, of death; caught up in a world of extracorporeality, sensation and entertainment. What, then, is the relation of games to posthumanism: Is it a case of creative generation or dehumanising sublimation? What is seductive about games is the ways that they bring us into their sphere, achieved through a combination of strategies of representation such as story and ludic structure; at best, this blend works to create a compelling sense of both dramatic and ludic progression. This, of course, represents a commercial threat to both cinema and television, so no wonder augmented and virtual reality, games and gamers are represented under the aura of the dystopian.

Many games deal in representations of posthuman concepts and imagery both on a surface level and as part of their core gameplay or ludic construction. Some draw on those found in cinema, but we may also expect something different given that physical augmentation exists within a game's formal plane. We would argue, though, that such taking up of the trappings of posthumanism by games is all in the service of a humanist and, in fact, urgently consumerist agenda. The symbiosis which exists between posthuman philosophy and posthuman fiction, where each imagines and then attempts to construct the other, feeds out into more general SF narratives. These narratives are, in turn, latched onto by games to suit the purposes of interface design, story and gameplay. In all of these cases, though, what might on the surface appear to be posthuman in the radical sense of the term actually serves an agenda which is more grounded in the challenges of creating a market for games and making them work effectively as unified fictions. The version of the posthuman that is found in games is that of Baudrillard's seduction and simulation, using the tropes conceived of by posthumanism to resubstantiate and enforce what are, in the end, Vitruvian approaches, even as we are sold a virtual escape from the confines of our bodily and agentic scope.

Cyborgs abound in SF-themed games as ways of giving motive to the game interface (e.g., through heads-up displays (HUDs)) or making elements of a game's system, which would otherwise seem anomalous, appear more diegetically integrated. One example is the symbiotic nanosuit worn by the protagonist in the *Crysis* series (2007), which enables different modes of combat, smoothing the path of what might have been an awkward though fun-to-play concept if phrased through a character simply aided by technology rather than augmented with it. In *Deus Ex 3: Human Revolution* (2011), the player enhances the game's interface through the purchase of augmentations for the cyborg protagonist, literally earning the visual architecture of an interface by upgrading cybernetics. Many iconic game characters are, if not explicitly cyborgs in a story sense, defined through cybernetic agency even in games that draw only lightly on SF tropes: *Assassin's Creed*'s Altair sacrifices a finger to have it replaced with his trademark weapon, a hidden blade. The game may be set mainly in the 1100s, but its hero is cybernetically augmented. Clothing a character in the garb of the cyborg comes at a high price in the 'star' economy of cinema. Stars sell films so helmets must be removed; Stallone's Dredd unprecedentedly removes his helmet in *Judge Dredd* to the horror of fans. No issue with this in games, as Samus (from the *Metroid* game series) and the Master Chief (from the *Halo* series) attest.

Augmentations or exo-suits becoming part of the player's experience allow for visually arresting approaches to user interface design, bringing elements like arbitrary amounts of health points or energy charges into the diegesis, an innovation which provides substantial feedback on play, as well as paying dividends in terms of story. Images of cybernetic augmentation make use of populist posthuman tropes to obscure formal and fictional dissonance. The best way to unite an awkward game mechanic with a character who does not quite align is to make that character into a cyborg, fused forcefully with the agency they need to wield in order to make the game fun. For example, *Vanquish* (2010) only makes sense because of its ridiculous cyborg protagonist's unusual 'Augmented Reaction Suit' with rocket-boosters attached to his rear. Game cyborgs are convenient portmanteau vehicles for meshing together gameplay and narrative. Amounts of gameplay freedom can be gained through augmentation of these characters. First person perspective adds to the intimacy and immediacy of the augmentation experience – a device replicated in the film version of *Doom* (2005), and likely to inform many games to come using the Oculus Rift, wherein cinema and games coalesce. Games are able to make more of the consequences augmentation choices bring about for the player. In *Deus Ex 3*, the story deals with the machine versus human paradigm explicitly, and puts forward an argument between the promise of a posthuman future sold by a cleanly branded, Apple-esque corporation and the dangers of abandoning what already exists, argued for by agitators calling themselves, tellingly, the 'humanity front'. Haraway's cyborg and its Hollywood counterpart are far from these augmented but still human cyphers, who often use the agency granted by their augmentations to pursue all-too-human desires for domination and destruction. Game players can feel closer connection to the augmentations than to the character, since it is the agency of the augmentations which they directly control and which have the most impact on the game.

Games adopt more from the posthuman philosophy/literature mix than just the figure of the cyborg or the quick fix for characters offered up by the concept of augmentation as often occurs in cinematic counterparts. Shape-shifting and mutation occurs in many games and is often phrased, as with cyborgs, as a method of communicating agency to the player without breaking the diegesis. Gibsonian elements can also be seen in games such as *Uplink* (2001) where players are hackers traversing the pathways between computers trying to access information without leaving any trace. Other games, such as *Hidden in Plain Sight* (2011), find fun and challenge in a mechanic which seems aligned with questions Philip K. Dick and Gibson's fiction frequently pose regarding artificial intelligences (AIs) and robots, by requiring players to act like simulated characters and avoid giving away their humanity. In some games, such as *Omikron* (2000), players are represented as free from the restrictions of any humanoid character's body.

Games which allow a god-like perspective or greater degrees of agency, most commonly the strategy genre, make use of SF-based posthumanism in their representative strategies, and in so doing echo the technology of trajectory in Kubrick's *2001: A Space Odyssey* (1968). *Sid Meier's Alpha Centauri* (1999) plays out a SF story through a transition from human to posthuman. Through a selection of diverse ideologically focused characters, from communists to eco-warriors, this game explores the political landscape of its time much as Dick and Gibson's fiction used posthuman tropes to critique American society and politics – unthinkable in a Hollywood context. It achieves this by looking at how these ideologies play out as technology moves from 'the human genome' through 'neural grafting' to 'cyber-ethics' and beyond. The recently released *Civilization 5: Beyond Earth* (2014) uses SF tropes, and in so doing presents three different takes on how humanity evolves in the future and an entrenched focus on the development of technology as the way to progress. This approach works well in these games because of part of the way the genre is designed. In these games, even those without an explicitly posthuman theme to their story, technology is a key way to win, and its progression is speeded up to suit the pace of the game. As Kurzweil fetishizes technology, so too do these games. The use of SF in *Civilization 5: Beyond Earth* and *Sid Meier's Alpha Centauri* enables an intensified focus upon technological progress, like Kubrick's *2001*, but enhancing what is already present in the ludic components of the game.

While posthuman themes and concepts within the representational layers of games might provide a mood board for creatively and speculatively figuring the future in different ways, there are deeper structural layers within games that lead away from a philosophical and ideologically driven conception of the posthuman and back into explicitly Vitruvian coordinates – even as they simultaneously buy into posthumanism's teleological notions of technological progress. Unlike the *Civilization* series, not all games wear their technological progress narrative explicitly on their sleeve. Instead, the majority of digital games are structurally geared around giving the player a sense of *their* becoming an agent in an arc of progress; this is something hard to do in cinema or television. There are many visible symptoms of this deep structural feature of games. Humanism is predicated on the conception that 'man' is the master of his destiny and his baser drives: he is capable of learning and, through rationality and knowledge, is increasingly capable of unlocking the patterns and properties of the universe. Most games follow this broadly humanist path, alongside other popular forms, where individualism rules. It might be assumed that it is because games are computational artefacts that they march in time with a clockwork universe. However, the cybernetic loops that structure digital games are, as Deleuze and Lacan cautioned, grounded in our all-too-human closed-circuit desire for perpetual self-affirmation, pleasure and reassurance. Cinematic gamers often echo this where they are presented as overreaching obsessives in search of self-affirmation through domination. In such films, gamers tread the path to the Inferno; whereas elsewhere they become augmented saviours on the path to Paradiso. The biggest shift from binarized images of nerds and hackers is where they become guides to a new form of creativity – where they become Braidottian makers, as is the case with *eXistenZ*'s Allegra and *The X-File*'s Phoebe.

The formal and desire circuitry of digital games are composed of arrays of diverse feedback mechanisms, which show players their progress through a game. Every element of a game works in this way. Players get feedback on their progress through the visual, aural and graphical elements of a game as well as through their interaction with input devices. When playing *Orcs Must Die* (2011) – a tower defence game that draws in a cartoonish way on fantasy tropes – a constant stream of numeric and graphical information notifies players about their performance. At any one time a player knows how many Orcs are in the area from the minimap, how far into a session they are, how many 'combo' scores they've achieved. Progress is monitored and fed back on throughout the game. Progress bars demonstrate graphically, typical of many games and aptly named, what resources remain available to the player-character. In other games, such devices are built upon in an extra structural layer demonstrating player-characters' relative power. The design of clothes, too, act as trophies in many games, semiotically demonstrating progress made. The more battles that are fought and won, leads to the acquisition of objects and traps that help defeat more Orcs; small variations in the trajectory of the loop provide novelty, but it is the numbers that provide the illusion of progress. So, if all Orcs are cleared within a limited time frame, the playable characters change their victory dance to something more energized. If the game is played through the interface provided by the entertainment platform Steam, achievements are gained and progress broadcast out to friends.

Progress bars and feedback arrays are ostensibly, and in formal terms, designed to help a player manage and prevail over the situation presented by the game. In concert with this is the way that a game allows a player to predict events, if they are sufficiently game-literate to read the signs. Most games carefully create a learning curve to enable this to happen, providing an analogue of humanist pedagogy. In *Orcs Must Die*, each type of enemy Orc is assigned certain characteristic behaviours and pathways, so that players can predict what they will do and how best to contain them. In addition, certain combinations of trap types combine to best effect, so that, when correctly placed and working in unison, the marauding Orcs are economically consigned to the 'done and dusted' column. It is a tacit agreement that any situation that a player might confront is containable, given the right gear, dexterity and management. As with so many things in games, this makes predictability and steady-state, potentially discoverable, rules central to the endeavour. Unlike real life, unpredictability is demarcated as programmed-in percentage equations. This level of predictability is found across game genres and platforms. Even where procedural generation or intricate AI is used to create more complex patterns, it is the case that games work most profoundly on a basis of predictability and progress. Being able to predict and contain the threat posed is highly pleasurable, particularly if some effort has been invested to work out the optimum strategy through trial and error. Successful containment gives a further level of feedback that reassures a player about their competency and helps create a sense of social well-being if that containment was a joint effort between players. Games, therefore, do not simply provide fun; game designers actively want to convince players that they have achieved something: this endeavour was not time wasted but yielded achievement and progress, confirming therefore a sense of existence. In this Althusserian sense players are interpellated through regimes of progress and predictability into a humanist rather than a posthumanist position. Games are then designed precisely, like Vitruvian man, to fit exactly the dimensions of the player as consumer; the posthuman bridled by that very humanist goal.

There are some games that do not play into this, ludic anomalies that we might term 'weird' because they are not predictable, or which resist classic heroic overcoming. These oddities are as diverse as the Lovecraftian *Call of Cthulhu* (2005), where one can simply run away or go mad, or the politically motivated games *September 12th* (2003) and *The Best Amendment* (2012), where the only available action simply produces more terrorists. These are, however, games that we might term 'anti-human' rather than truly posthuman. Such games are rarely commercially successful, but instead remain as anti-illusionist idiosyncrasies that push at the conventions. The posthuman is then present in many SF-based games, as well as in the way that SF film and television represent virtual reality, games and gamers. In all these cases, the posthuman is commonly employed to shore-up dominant notions of the human and the structures that support it, such as heterosexual romance, conventionalized otherness, biology, nature, binary notions of sex and gender, man and machine. So, when the Head of Google Engineering adopts the rhetoric of posthumanism, it is clear that it is no longer in the domain of radical politics but instead co-opted to entice the perpetual purchase of technological consumables.

Part V
Better Humans: Posthuman Capacities

21
'Life's a bitch, and then you *don't* die': Postmortality in Film and Television

Michael Hauskeller

Ephemeroi, the ancient Greeks called us: those who live only for a day. Mortality defines our existence. Only the gods are immortal and can hope to live forever. Although (other) animals, too, are mortal, at least they don't know that they are. They don't have to worry about it. We, on the other hand, worry about death constantly. Even small children learn very quickly that everyone has to die, even their mums and dads, and even they themselves, and it frightens them. Death, however irrational it may be to fear it, is for most of us a terrifying prospect almost right from the start. Virtually our whole lives are overshadowed by our own (never very far off and always potentially imminent) death, the spectre of non-existence, as well as the death of everything and everyone we love and hold dear. If there is anything that defines us as humans, it is the knowledge of our own mortality. Hence, if we hope to transcend our human existence, to become more and other than human, then we will have to find ways to overcome our mortality. In order to become properly posthuman, if that is what we want, we need to realize postmortality.

That is why, for transhumanists, life and health extension has the highest priority among all possible areas of human enhancement. Radical, indefinite life extension is something like the holy grail of transhumanism. Death is the greatest evil (More 1996; Bostrom 2005), and life consequently the supreme good. And if death is the worst that can happen to a person, then it follows that no price can be too high to pay to avoid one's own death as long as possible and to achieve virtual immortality. Advances in medical knowledge and the exponentially increasing progress of technology and what it allows us to do, make it seem likely that we will very soon, in a few decades or so, be able to halt and possibly reverse the aging process, so that we will be able to keep living for an indefinite amount of time, without ever losing our youthfulness or our mental and physical powers (de Grey & Rae 2007). We might never be immortal in a strict sense, because it is hard to see how it could be possible for there to be a thing that simply *cannot* be destroyed, a thing whose existence *cannot* end. But we may very well, for all we know now, before long become immortal in the sense that we will no longer *have* to die in the natural course of events. This is what I call *postmortality*.

In film and television, the postmortal condition and all that it entails has often been examined through the figure of the vampire, which is not to say that vampires should normally be regarded as posthumans, on the contrary. Traditionally, vampires were represented as an alien species, equipped with supernatural powers, a creature that is decidedly not human, and, if it ever was, has since undergone a radical transformation in the process of which everything that was human has been eradicated and replaced by something inhuman. It is not a *development* of the human, as the posthuman must always conceivably be, but a *replacement* of the human. The vampire is a shape-shifter who effortlessly sheds the human form whenever it suits him, turning into a bat or a wolf or some other feral creature. He is thus no more human than animal, a being that can be anything and hence is everything and nothing. The numerous film versions of Count Dracula, including those in Murnau's (1922) *Nosferatu* and Herzog's (1979) movie of the same name, which were also based on Stoker's classic novel, as well as most other vampires in film and television until recently (for instance, in Joel Schumacher's *The Lost Boys*, Quentin Tarantino's *From Dusk Till Dawn* or David Slade's *30 Days of Night*) are, in fact, all little more than blood-sucking monsters, more subhuman than superhuman, and so are those humans that are bitten and killed by them. Once they have died and changed, have become 'undead', they have forgotten all their human interests and values, and have only one goal left: that of satisfying their thirst for human blood and thus turning more humans into vampires. The monstrousness of the traditional vampire is also reflected in the fact that no human in their right mind *wants* to be transformed into a vampire, just as no human in their right mind wants to be transformed into a zombie. The human who is bitten by the vampire is cast as a victim of an alien force that annihilates its human core. Thus, the vampire is not presented as posthuman (if, by 'posthuman', we understand the result of a development of the human into something else and in some way better), but simply as inhuman. He invites no identification and does not stimulate any desire in his victims (or in us viewers) to be like him. He does not represent a human possibility, nor an opportunity for refinement or even something more than that: salvation.

But things have changed: in some more recent productions the virtual immortality or extreme longevity of the vampire no longer identifies the terror-inducing alien. Rather, it is increasingly seen as the essential feature of an alternative and immensely desirable way of being, providing a viable alternative to the disappointments and downright misery of a merely human, mortal life. Thus, in Joss Whedon's *Buffy the Vampire Slayer* (1997–2003), Floyd, the leader of a group of teenagers who like to dress up as vampires and to imitate what they fancy to be the vampire lifestyle, makes a deal with the real vampires (season 2, episode 7: 'Lie to Me'). He will deliver the other members of his group to them, to be sucked dry and killed, and in exchange the vampires will make him one of their own and give him eternal life. When Buffy, who discovers his plan, remonstrates with him, telling him that 'those people do not deserve to die', he replies: 'Neither do I.' It is then revealed that he suffers from terminal cancer and unless he is 'saved' by the vampires he is going to die very soon. Thus, the imminence of his own death, combined with the belief that it is *unfair* that someone so young has to die and the promise of a second chance, leads him to throw all moral concerns overboard and to betray and sacrifice his friends. He already sees himself as what he believes he will very soon become, a postmortal being that no longer has any obligations to anything that, or anyone who, is merely human. 'I will become immortal', he declares, and he persists in believing that despite Buffy's protestations that this is 'not how it works: you die, a demon replaces you, remembers you, talks like you, but it's not you'. Thus the idea that the vampire is not, and can never be, an enhanced version of the human, is still reasserted by Buffy, although characters like Angel and Spike – both of which are vampires who reacquire their soul and thus become rehumanised, while retaining their immortality – suggest otherwise. Here, the vampire already appears as a love interest, though still with an ambivalence that is largely absent from later productions, such as the television series *The Vampire Diaries* (2009–), which, in by now more than one hundred episodes, follows its female teenage protagonist Elena as she divides her affection between two equally gorgeous-looking vampires, or the five parts of the *Twilight Saga* (2008–2012), which sees the female teenage protagonist Bella fall in love with the, once again gorgeous-looking, vampire Edward, marry him and then give birth to an immortal child that is half-human and half-vampire, thus completing the merger of human and vampire and suggesting the possibility of a new race of posthuman (and postmortal) beings that humanity develops into. Buffy may, of course, still be right when she asserts a lack of identity between the human and the vampire that they become. Yet we can understand Buffy's assertion simply as a claim about the relation between the human (i.e., mortal) and the posthuman (i.e., postmortal): in order for the posthuman to live, the human must die. That is why the posthuman is necessarily the posthumous and postmortality can only be achieved post mortem, or, in other words: in order to become *more* than human, we need to become *other* than human.

That the postmortality of the posthuman requires the death of the human is, of course, not necessarily a bad thing. Whether it is, or appears to be, depends on our attitude towards a human life that is, by virtue of being human, utterly enmeshed in mortality. Such a life can be hard to bear. Thus, in Neil Jordan's *Interview with the Vampire* (1994) we travel back in time to late 18th-century Louisiana, where we meet the 24-year-old plantation owner Louis, for whom 'life has no meaning anymore' and who seeks 'release from the pain of living' after losing his wife and child. In this situation, the vampire Lestat promises him a new life, one in which 'sickness and death can never touch you again' and 'you can be young always'. Louis agrees and is turned into a vampire by Lestat, becoming postmortal in the process, but, in contrast to Lestat, Louis tries hard to retain his humanity and not to become the monster that his vampire nature urges him to be. He still feels very much like a human, but his newly gained postmortality, his escape 'from the pain of living', has a price that eventually he must pay. Not only can he not avoid living off the deaths of other humans whose blood he must drink to survive, he also ceases to change and develop in any meaningful way. When Louis tries to console Claudia, the child vampire that Lestat has given him for a companion, by telling her that 'you will never grow old and you will never die', she replies, 'but that also means I never grow up'. This is echoed in the opening scene of Michael and Peter Spierig's *Daybreakers* (2009), which shows a young vampire girl of perhaps 9 or 10 sitting on the ground outside and waiting for the sun to rise and destroy her, leaving behind written words that explain her decision: 'I will never grow up; I can't go on'. The price we have to pay for eternal youth is eternal youth, but only of the body, not of the mind, which makes it even worse due to the ensuing disparity between mind and body. When, at the end of *Interview with the Vampire*, Louis, after 200 years of a pointless existence, is interviewed by a present-day reporter, who becomes so intrigued by Louis' story that he implores him to transfer what he sees as the gift of eternal life to him and make him a vampire too, he flatly refuses to grant him his wish. The reason for Louis' refusal is not that he doesn't want to share the gift, but, on the contrary, that he has come to realize that a postmortal life is more a burden than a blessing. He describes himself as 'detached, unchangeable, empty'. If life was meaningless before he became one of the undead, it is even more meaningless now. If life was painful while he was still mortal, it is even more painful, though perhaps in a different way, now that he is postmortal. Postmortality looks promising to the mortal, but to the postmortal it is, or can easily become after a while, hell.

This has got nothing to do with being a vampire, and instead everything with being postmortal. A similar sentiment is expressed in Jerome Bixby's *The Man from Earth* (2007), in which a college professor tells his friends that he has in fact been around for 14,000 years, starting his life as a Cro-Magnon: while others may envy him for having been granted first-hand experience of so many exciting historical events, he is rather weary of his life and emphasizes the solitude and the accumulation of losses that come with immortality. Yet even if one wasn't the only one who no longer had to die and could live in a society of immortals or postmortals, a postmortal existence might prove to be unbearable. In Andrew Nichol's *In Time* (2011), which is set 150 years in the future, scientists have finally managed to stop people from ageing, so that, in theory, everyone can stay young forever. In practice, however, it is only the very rich who can realistically hope to live very long, while the poor, who are being used to provide the resources needed to sustain the system, continue to die. Society is organized in such a way that everyone is genetically engineered to stop aging at the age of 25, after which they have only one more year to live unless they buy more time through their labour. If they earn less time than they spend (in this story time literally *is* money), their time will run out and they die. The film tells the story of a poor factory worker called Will who suddenly finds himself with a lot of time on his hands through a chance encounter with a rich stranger who is tired of living and who, before he commits suicide, transfers all his time to Will. Will then uses this time to start a war against the society that has virtually enslaved him and his fellow workers. The stranger who transfers his time to Will throws his postmortality away for reasons that are very similar to those Louis, in *Interview with the Vampire*, has for refusing to share his 'gift' with the reporter. Your mind, he says, 'can be spent even when your body is not'; you then want to die because you 'have been alive too long'. Again, postmortal life turns out to be less than desirable because it is haunted by what Bernard Williams called the 'tedium of immortality' (1973). Even those who have no intention of letting their life run out and giving up their time, those who cling to the privilege, even they cannot enjoy their life as life should be enjoyed. The postmortal life has a certain undead quality to it. As Sylvia, the daughter of a rich businessman with whom Will gets romantically involved, puts it: 'the poor die and the rich don't live. We never do anything foolish or courageous.' For the postmortal, life is too precious to risk it. Thus their lives become shallow and meaningless. Yet, even if that were not so, postmortality might be judged too pricey, especially if this price has to be paid by somebody else, which is a recurring theme throughout the genre. When Sylvia remonstrates with her father on the injustice of the system she exclaims 'we're not meant to live forever'. And when her father tells her 'everyone wants to live forever; the truth is, for a few to be immortal many must die', she replies: 'No one should be immortal if even one person has to die.'

The vampire is the perfect image of a postmortality that is derived from the death of others. In the aforementioned *Daybreakers*, human society has been taken over by vampires who now live almost exactly the lives that humans used to live: they go to work, have jobs, live in apartments, wear suits and ties, smoke cigarettes and drive around in cars. There is not really much difference between them and the humans, except for their slightly reddish eyes, the deadly effect that the sunlight has on them, the fact that they are not mortal and the need for human blood to survive. They remember who they were when they were still human, and most of them see their transformation into vampires as a positive development: 'we are blessed'. In their view, they have simply evolved to a posthuman condition. For others, however, especially, but not exclusively, the few humans that are still around, the transition from human to vampire does not represent evolution, but is simply a disease, for which they are desperate to find a cure. But the number of humans is dwindling, since they are hunted down by the authorities (after having refused the 'chance to assimilate'). Once captured they are farmed for blood supply, just as we farm cattle or chickens, in a very civilized and orderly fashion, as superior beings (or those that think of themselves as superior) are wont to do. Unfortunately, however, there are not enough humans left to feed the entire vampire population, which has some unpleasant consequences. Starving vampires very quickly shed the veneer of human civilization (and civilness) and degenerate into bat-like monsters that attack everyone, including their fellow vampires, who consequently live in fear of them. Thus, in this film, the vampires appear to be both very human in their habits (and posthuman due to their postmortality) and, at the same time (always very close beneath the surface), as blood-sucking monsters. In other words, the enhanced human or posthuman and the monster appear to be two sides of the same.

This basic ambiguity is also emphasized in Oliver Parker's *Dorian Gray* (2009), which is an adaptation of Oscar Wilde's novel, in which a young man trades his innocence and moral integrity for eternal youth and beauty: no matter how long he lives and what he does, he stays outwardly the same, while his portrait shows not only his real age, but also all the marks of his increasing moral corruption.

It shows the monster that he is gradually becoming, perhaps inevitably, as the price that *must* be paid for the privilege of not having to grow old. Yet already in the opening scene of the film we see Dorian stabbing someone, without showing us whom, and then holding a bloody garment to his lips, as if he wanted to suck the blood out of it, just like a vampire might. It later turns out that the one he stabbed in this scene is Basil, his friend and the painter of his portrait. We learn that just before he kills him Dorian asserts his superiority, his status as an elevated being, by crying out: 'I am a God.' (Earlier in the film he is being told that 'everything is possible for you because you have the only things worth having: youth and beauty'.) Thus he asserts his godlike status, which he has, or thinks he has, by virtue of his postmortality, by cutting the moral ties that bind him to the human world and killing a human being, that is, a member of a race to which he no longer belongs.

Similarly, in *Daybreakers* the relative humanity of the posthuman vampire depends on their inhuman treatment of the remaining humans. Those vampires who refuse to drink human blood (because they don't want to take part in the exploitation and ultimately destruction of the human race), risk losing their humanity. Once again, postmortality comes with a high price tag attached to it, though for those willing to pay the price, it is certainly worth it. 'Immortality gave me my cure', explains the boss of a pharmacological company dealing in human blood supplies, who suffered from terminal cancer before he was turned into a vampire. From this perspective, the parasitical existence of the vampire (which is not so different from our own) is not a disease, but the cure to a disease, and that disease to which it is a cure is our mortal human life as a whole with its many inadequacies and indignities. These inadequacies and indignities explain the lure of immortality, which is perhaps most charmingly displayed in Ron Howard's *Cocoon* (1985), in which a bunch of retirement home residents discover the modern version of the fountain of youth (a swimming pool with water that has been infused with 'life force' by aliens) and very much enjoy the rejuvenating effects this has on their bodies and minds. Nothing in the film suggests that immortality might be anything less than a blessing. The outlook of *Daybreakers* is much bleaker. As another character in the film, a vampire that has been cured and turned back into a human, puts it: 'Life's a bitch, and then you *don't* die.'

However, mortality is not only present in our lives as the abstract knowledge that, someday, we are going to die, but also in the lived experience of the sheer passage of time. As the future becomes present, and the present immediately slides away and transforms into an ever-expanding past, leaving less and less future before us and cutting off possibilities that we once may have had, death takes place every day and every hour of our lives. The person that I was yesterday is dead, replaced by a new person who sees that other person as a version of himself. Yet that other person is now forever out of reach and can never be brought back to life again. That person is, for all intents and purposes, dead, no longer an active player and utterly incapable of changing anything about himself or the world. Our death is thus an ongoing process, in which the past grows constantly, while the future contracts until there is no future left and everything is past. And, once again, it seems that it is only we humans among all animals who carry the burden of our being-in-time with us, only we who, as we go forward, accumulate the past in our minds, so that we age not only with and in our bodies, but also with and in our minds (Hauskeller 2011). Postmortality would therefore not only require that we no longer die (or at least no longer have to die), but also that we somehow halt the passage of time and prevent the present from becoming the past, or, more precisely, that we find a way to overcome the *pastness* of the past and open up new futures for ourselves by either erasing the past from our minds, finding a way to reconfigure the past, or simply distancing ourselves from it so that it no longer shapes our present and thus future. As long as we are stuck with this one life, we are not truly postmortal.

What is therefore required is the possibility of new beginnings: the posthuman (as a postmortal) is someone who can always start afresh, who doesn't have to take responsibility for their past life. That is not easy to accomplish. In John Frankenheimer's *Seconds* (1966), the middle-aged banker Arthur Hamilton, who is acutely aware of living a meaningless, pointless life (being married to a woman he does not love and doing a job he has no interest in), is offered the chance to leave everything behind and start a new life as an artist and as single. He has his death faked, undergoes cosmetic surgery, which transforms him into a much younger (or at least younger-looking) and more handsome man (played by Rock Hudson), and is given a new identity and new life. It is a life that he could have lived, had he chosen differently. But now that he has been given a 'second chance', a 'rebirth', he can actually live that life, *despite* having chosen differently. Initially he is thrilled to be once again 'alone in the world, absolved of all responsibility, except to your own interest', but things do not go quite as planned and he starts wishing he had his old life back. When this turns out to be impossible, he asks for yet another chance, another life and identity that might suit him better, but is refused and eventually killed by the company that provided him with his new life. His attempt to escape his old life (and that means his past), has failed, mostly because he did not *really* become someone else. He looked different, and people thought he was somebody else, but inside he was still the same disillusioned middle-aged man that he used to be before his transformation. When a woman who works for the company and knows his real (or former) identity calls him a 'dirty old man', he replies: 'I really am.'

In stark contrast, the 118-year-old Nemo Nobody, in Jaco Van Dormael's *Mr. Nobody* (2009), insists that the very old man that he seems to be is not really him: 'that's not me; I'm nine, I'm fifteen'. Nemo is the last mortal in a future world (in the year 2092) that has finally managed to find a cure against aging (by means of telomerization), making everyone postmortal (and, interestingly, sex obsolete). We meet Nemo when he is about to die. Since he is the last mortal the event is televised and sparks enormous interest among the postmortals. When a (postmortal) reporter interviews him, he tells him that he is not afraid to die, just afraid that he hasn't lived enough. Yet when he is asked about his life story, it gradually emerges that in his memory he hasn't lived one particular life, but at least three different ones, which all seem to be equally real: 'each of these lives is the right one'. Since there is no difference between what was and what could have been, because anything that could have been was, and in his imagination still is, so that his past is just as real as the present (or the present just as illusionary as the past), Nemo Nobody, the 'last mortal' in a society of postmortals, who is nobody and can therefore be anybody, is in fact the only true postmortal among mortals. Mortality is a function of personal identity, as personal identity is (largely) a function of memory. This is why someone who is able to forget his past and who is, for this reason, unhampered by his previous choices, is in fact a postmortal being, like Leonard in Christopher Nolan's *Memento* (2000), who suffers from anterograde amnesia, which allows him to constantly reinvent himself, or Joel and Clementine in Michel Gondry's *Eternal Sunshine of the Spotless Mind* (2004), who forget they have ever met, so that they can live their love all over again (potentially in a cycle of eternal recurrence). In *Mr. Nobody*, memory is in fact preserved, but it is no longer identity-defining. Rather, it has become a creative force, a tool for the diversification (and hence annihilation) of the past, that is, of time itself: 'We only live in the imagination of a nine-year old child, faced with an impossible choice.' Since each choice that we have to make is impossible in the sense that it forces us to forego certain possibilities and to limit ourselves to one life only, to finitude, which is the essence of mortality, we can acquire a different kind of postmortality, which is synchronic rather than diachronic, by refusing to make that choice, or, more precisely, by finding a way to turn the could-have-been into a was, and the was into an is. This is what happens in Duncan Jones' *Source Code* (2011), where a repeated mental visit to, and gradual reconfiguration of, a particular deadly event in the past (or more precisely that event's memory traces in a dead person's brain) eventually leads to the creation of a different timeline, an alternate reality, in which those that were killed in the event survive and live on. Yet even more importantly, the one who visits and alters that event (a soldier who has been fatally wounded and who is now comatose, with most of his body missing, but kept alive for this mission) also creates a new reality for himself, which allows him to live on in a new healthy body and with a new identity.

The idea that postmortality could be realized by an actual separation of body and mind and the survival of the mind in a new body, or a series of new bodies, is also explored, without recourse to alternate timelines, in Joss Whedon's *Dollhouse* (2009–2010). Initially the series focuses on the possibility of assuming different identities related to different lives, and in this manner realizing what I called synchronic postmortality. The story develops around Echo, one of the Dollhouse actives, who is imprinted with different personalities and sets of memories and then rented out to clients who, for some reason or other, need or desire a person with those particular characteristics. Those assumed identities can be understood as means to escape from the one life we are all confined to, and to allow one and the same person to live different lives. The Dollhouse actives are people who have been unhappy with their lives and seek a means to escape: 'I've gotta find the freedom that's promised me, freedom from our struggles and our misery, freedom is all in me to heal the pain of history' (season 1, episode 3: 'The Target'). However, later in the series it emerges that the personalities that the actives are imprinted with are, in fact, not only certain sets of character traits and memories, formerly belonging to certain real persons, but that they *are* those persons, which opens up the possibility of diachronic postmortality: you can move from body to body indefinitely, without changing what you are, the body a mere vehicle that can be discarded and replaced when no longer useful. But that, of course, requires the availability of bodies, and the willingness to destroy ('wipe') the persons to whom those bodies originally belonged. Once again, the desired postmortality has a price that others must pay. It seems that, in one way or another, the postmortal is always a vampire, living off the deaths of others.

22
A New Lease on Life: A Lacanian Analysis of Cognitive Enhancement Cinema

Hub Zwart

Introduction

Let me begin with two instances of 'brain art', an early modern 'original' and its cinematic parody. In 1656, Rembrandt van Rijn painted one of his famous 'anatomical lessons': a cinematic scene (an early modern 'movie still'), featuring Dr Deyman, who has lifted the skull of a convicted criminal, exposing his brains. The convict, executed by hanging, seems lost in meditation, until we realize that his abdomen has been emptied. Rembrandt's corpse is modelled on Andrea Mantegna's *Lamentation over the Dead Christ* (c. 1490), so that Jesus and the thief changed places. The painting is actually a fragment: a substantial part was destroyed by fire. We see Deyman's dexterous hands, about to perform the autopsy, as if the camera is zooming in. A mysterious, forbidden, 'partial' object, the human brain, is suddenly revealed, holding us captive: the inner core of what we are, detachable from the body. This is what the painting brings to light. The convict's intestines have already been removed and the brain is the next body part to go. This artwork reveals (brings to the fore) the basic (Frankensteinian) truth of modern anatomy, namely that the human body is an aggregate of detachable 'partial' organs, of removable body parts (Zwart 2014b). In Heideggerian terms (1957): although the artwork at first glance may seem a 'representation' (recording an early modern scientific accomplishment, modelled on a late 15th-century religious 'original'), it is highly original in itself, a moment of ἀλήθεια, opening up an intellectual 'space', virtually untrodden at the time, a particular way of viewing and approaching the human body, allowing it to appear in a certain manner (namely as an aggregate of detachable items), so that anatomy as a research field becomes possible. This may explain the numinous aura, the ambiance of mystery and awe, commemorating the advent of a new experience of embodiment. The brain's inner obscurity is suddenly brought into view, its intriguing *Gestalt* ready to be processed into insight and knowledge (Zwart 1998).

The present-day counterpart is a scene from the movie *Hannibal* (2001), starring Anthony Hopkins as Hannibal Lecter. It is dinner time. The camera zooms in on Hannibal's hands, lifting the skull of justice department official Krendler, skilfully using his scalpel (as a neuroanatomy virtuoso), cutting off slices of his victim's prefrontal cortex, sautéing it and serving it for dinner, meanwhile lecturing agent Clarice Starling (his favourite audience). The movie scene is an anatomical 'lesson', a live autopsy in its own right. Again, we notice the role reversal, with the justice official now acting as 'convicted criminal' and the criminal as surgeon. The underlying scheme still functions, but roles may shift as 'variables'. The cinematic parody conveys a similar truth: the body is opened up as an aggregate of detachable parts, a *corps morcelée*, an assembly of organic fragments, although, in the movie version, this truth applies to the *living* body, rather than to a corpse. The detachable body part that is revealed and desecrated is a most uncanny partial object: the movie's 'object a', in Lacanian grammar, namely the neocortical brain.

The brain has become the object of choice of our scientific *scopophilia*, our *observandi cupido*, our desire to see and penetrate. Brain anatomy gave way to *vivisection*. Lecter performs an *experiment*, interacting with Krendler as his research subject, monitoring the living, functioning brain. Scientific voyeurism gave rise to high-tech tools like magnetic resonance imaging (MRI), allowing us to shed glances into ourselves. The brain has become our most fascinating organ, allegedly the key to human self-understanding, the ultimate organic-biochemical machine that conjures up the world as we experience it – our inborn cinema as it were.

In *Hannibal*, 'cutting-edge' brain surgery is employed as a vehicle of destruction: a horrifying form of (apparently painless) punishment and torture. According to Claude Bernard (1865/1966), 'founding father' of modern medicine and 'champion' of vivisection, scientific research involves 'experimentation by destruction': a step-wise dismantling of the (living) organism. By removing 'partial objects' organ by organ, lobe by lobe, their function can be revealed. Decerebration (neocortical extirpation) was among the techniques vivisectionists employed, but a human being now acts as stand-in for laboratory animals. Lecter works like a sculptor, *per via di levare*, removing lobes and slices to reveal the 'thing' inside, until emptiness remains. Step by step, pieces from Krendler's neocortex come off, while Hannibal (carefully handling his 'chisel') continues to converse with him: a research subject in a (cannibalistic) brain experiment.

As Freud (1919/1947) points out, detachable body parts (hands, feet, but especially eyes), separated from the body, strike us as *uncanny* par excellence. Such partial objects are the basic ingredients of horror films, and *Hannibal* plays on the uneasiness produced by the idea that brain parts can effectively be disconnected from the living body by neuroscience. Skulls can be lifted, lobes removed. In university hospitals, neocortices of living humans are treated in this manner.

A liaison has developed between cinema and the brain: the 'partial object of choice' of contemporary enhancement movies. Whereas Hannibal Lecter performs a debilitating 'experiment by destruction' (in truly Bernardian style), contemporary brain movies usually focus on cortical *enhancement*. Instead of disruptive dismantling of the brain, something is added to it, *per via di porre*, boosting cognitive performance. In *Johnny Mnemonic* (1995), the brain as a cinematic object is pervaded by implants to enlarge memory storage capacity, while in Michael Gondry's *Eternal Sunshine of the Spotless Mind* (2004), an estranged couple decides to have their (traumatic) memories of each other erased, so as to relieve themselves of neocortical dead weight.

All this is connected with our self-image, the way we see ourselves. Traditional metaphysics argues that we *have* something which other animals *lack*: be it a rational soul, self-consciousness, morality or an ingenious cortex. Yet, there is a countervailing view which rather defines humanity in terms of vulnerability, deficiency and lack; we *lack* something which other animals *have*, a kind of basic 'fit' between body and environment. According to this view, human beings are *Mängelwesen* (Gehlen 1940/1962), with science and technology (including brain research) as desperate 'compensations'. Prostheses of various kinds enable us to survive. So far, they have assumed the form of external appendices (tools, clothes, glasses, etc.). Nowadays, they are entering our own bodies and brains, becoming what Lacan (2006) refers to as 'extimate' objects: both intimate and foreign, both embedded and intrusive. As Michel Houellebecq (1998) has argued, in a novel that became a movie (*The Elementary Particles*, 2006), whereas other recent attempts to drastically improve the human condition (political, sexual and psychedelic revolutions of the 1960s as 'mass experiments') miserably failed, the hyperscientific revolution (currently raging) may do the job. This is what the Hannibal scene brings to the surface. The brain has been opened up. Certain parts or units (or their technological substitutes) can easily be removed, substituted, modulated or manipulated.

There is a 'timeliness' to this. The contemporary global world seems too complex for 'natural' brains to cope with. Confronted with overwhelming torrents of information pervading our globalizing environments at an astonishing pace, our mental capacities inevitably fall short. We are bypassed and overrun, *by technology as such*. We live in a world where 'cognitive capitalism' reigns, so that individuals will increasingly be forced to boost their brains (by lifelong learning, but also by drugs and implants).

This applies to everybody, but notably to a particular subset of human beings, namely white, mid-life (climacteric) males. In relentlessly evolving techno-social environments of bewildering complexity they are outcompeted: by younger generations (preferably of Asiatic descent, easily adapting to the caprices of hypermodern information and communications technology (ICT)), but also by women (outperforming them in communicative and managerial competence, as virtuosi of the so-called 'softer' skills) and, last but not least, by robots and bionic cyborgs of various kinds. In contrast to 'phallic' tools of bygone days (plough, sword, hammer, etc.), new ICT-based technologies are reminiscent of 'weaving webs' or shrouds (Berners-Lee 2000), so that contemporary technology-dense societies offer new opportunities for Penelope (seated in front of her screen) and new obstacles for Odysseus. This may well explain why contemporary brain movies so conspicuously entail a gender dimension. The cognitively upgraded human is, almost always, a challenged, middle-aged male.

Roughly, movies about cognitive enhancement fall into two categories. Some focus on neural *implants*, others on neuro*pharmaceuticals*. Quite often, however, the 'extimate' implanted gadget produces biochemicals, altering the biochemistry of neural performance. And these can also be administered orally or intravenously. In this chapter, rather than presenting snapshots of present-day brain cinema, I will focus on one particular case study, namely the film *Limitless* (2011), about a nootropic miracle drug named NZT-48. Movies about wonder pills build on a long tradition of formulaic stories: the quest for the Elixir, the archetypal miraculous potion that enhances longevity, happiness, sexual attractiveness and intellectual competitiveness (usually all of these together). In the current era, this Elixir found a novel point of access: the synapses and dendrites inside the human cortex, laid bare by neurotechnoscience.

For heroes in contemporary brain movies, wonder pills enhance faltering cognitive competitiveness, in an era when *brain power* has become a substitute for brawn, as the indicator of (phallic) vigour. The focus of attention has shifted from exploiting muscularity to exploiting brains. The male hero experiences his brain power as utterly insufficient. There is a general sense of incompetence and failure. Something is apparently missing (in Lacanian grammar: $-\varphi$). In terms of cognitive performance, the ego is hopelessly outclassed by other members of the cast, notably women. Something is blocking him. The wonder pill works miracles. Suddenly, it is *his* turn to outclass and intimidate these frightening (now: frightened) Others – temporarily, of course.

What is so fascinating about this subgenre of movies involving cognitive enhancers, sometimes referred to as 'Viagra for the brain'? What does it tell us about contemporary society, cognitive capitalism, technology discontent and shifting gender roles? To address this, *Limitless* seems a perfect case. The movie, released in 2011, is based on the novel *The Dark Fields* by Alan Glynn (2001), republished as *Limitless* in 2011. This 'symptomatic' movie allows us to study scientific and cultural trends involved in cognitive enhancement in sufficient detail. I will analyse *Limitless* from a psychoanalytic, more precisely Lacanian perspective, but in a way that is accessible for non-adepts.

Lacanian cinema

Point of departure is the Freudian idea that, similar to stories or novels, movies are basically structured like daydreams (Freud 1907/1941). The question movies set out to address is: What would happen *if*? A (secret) desire is acted out, by way of a cinematic experiment, exposing human beings (with whom audiences may identify) to out-of-the-ordinary circumstances. But, in contrast to novels or stories, a movie is a filmic text, a *Bilderschrift* (Freud 1900/1942, 284): a pictographic, figurative script; a digitalized celluloid dream. Rather than a *representation* of reality, it is a pictorial staging of anxieties, fantasies and wishes, inhibitions and concerns. 'Celluloid heroes' may play different roles as the story evolves, and their existence as imaginary persons cannot be disconnected from the dynamics and possibilities of the cinematic screen.

From a Lacanian viewpoint, movies are permeated by *scopophilia* or voyeurism: a relentless desire to see. Cinema is the theatre of the gaze (Metz 1997), staging multiple 'gazes', exposed to one another, so that a dynamical interplay evolves in which movie characters *see* and *are seen*. Movies are like Sartre's famous keyhole scene (1943). A person secretly peers through a keyhole, trying to see something (a naked body perhaps, or parts of it, or two naked bodies, who think they cannot be seen and act accordingly). Suddenly, the sound of footsteps is heard. The bodies inside the room disappear from view and now the voyeur is *seen*, caught in the act: the target of a revealing gaze. The world flows over into the field of vision of this other: a cinematic scene par excellence, depicting craving humans, on the lookout for something, fuelled by a desire to see, but actually, they often fail to see it. And if they seem about to see, they are caught in the act of trying, so that instead of seeing they are *being* seen. Thus, besides the gaze of the audience, enabled by the camera (which opens up secret, impenetrable spaces, while we ourselves remain unseen), the movie's characters gaze at each other, as well as at enigmatic 'things' (body parts or other intriguing items).

The cinematic gaze is fuelled by the desire to discern an enigmatic, impossible object: the object *a* (either the 'real' thing or its various substitutes). A cinematic hero is a craving, divided subject, a *Mängelwesen* who lacks something (in Lacanian notation: $) and is frantically in search of the cause of this discontent, this lack. Cinematic subjects (mirror images of ourselves) are searching for this object *a*, the enigmatic entity that supposedly will gratify the longings, remove the sense of lack. Due to the object's *absence*, however, cinematic subjects suffer from an unbearable condition of impotence and malaise ($-\varphi$). It may be a particular gadget they are after, or a particular 'partial' (detachable) item or organ, connected to another person's body. Voyeuristic subjects are desperately searching for an unknown (inexorable) object of desire which, all of a sudden, may present itself, appearing glaringly in front of them, about to be purloined, or otherwise disappear into the possession of the Other. The sudden proximity of the key object of our scopophilic gaze causes inhibition to give way to euphoria (*jouissance*). Suddenly, the subject *has* it. For a brief moment in time, dreary reality gives way to hyper-reality, aimless erring to goal-directed behaviour, until suspicion is aroused. Is it really the real thing? It remains an issue of concern. Can it perhaps be harmful? Or have we been duped once again?

In Rembrandt's painting, the neocortex (object *a*) is suddenly exposed by dexterous hands, holding an 'ὄργανον': a scalpel (φ), an appendix-like extension. Being in possession of this tool, and able to use it, Deyman 'has' it. But as soon as the object *a* is revealed, it is about to disappear again (through surgical removal). The convict is the craving subject ($) whose brain is analysed. Modern science purports to explain the causes of his 'aberrant' behaviour. Rembrandt (who remains unseen, although we may recognize his 'hand') plays the role of 'analyst', making us aware of what causes our fascination: the alluring presence of the convict's brain (the painting's object *a*).

In *Hannibal*, these roles are distorted and subverted. We see the convict (a dangerous psychopath: $) holding the scalpel ($\varphi$), lecturing. Like agent Starling, we are unwillingly impressed by his dexterity. Lecter seems in possession of something which other people lack, in various fields of expertise, including art history. As art historian, he must be performing his Rembrandt-parody quite consciously. He confronts Starling, the camera and us with the uncanny, neuroanatomical object *a*: the living, functioning neocortex. Still, he remains a psychopath, destroying everything that stands between him and his object of desire, anything which constrains his freedom of manoeuvre to reach for it.

Limitless is a story about a (male, climactic) hero ($), suffering from inhibitions (-φ), discovering an entity (*a*) that allows him to overcome his lack by dramatically transforming the biochemistry of his brain. What does this blockbuster movie (so successful that a sequel and a television series are in the making) tell us about contemporary society and the hype concerning brain research? Before analysing this formulaic movie, I will outline the script on which it builds: the quest for the wonder drug that allegedly allows us to boost our performance (intellectual and otherwise).

The miracle drug

In recent history, various miracle drugs have been recommended, such as LSD, propagated in the 1960s by Timothy Leary, who coined the slogan 'Turn on, tune in, drop out'. Another example of a wonder-drug propagandist is science author Paul de Kruif (1945), who, at a time when endocrinology was experiencing a period of rapid growth, published a partisan account about his own drug of choice, testosterone ('the male hormone'). According to de Kruif, testosterone not only increases muscle power and virility (notably for 'men on the wane', as he phrases it), but also mental keenness and 'brain power' (1945, 181). Manliness may suddenly expire (-φ). The downside of the 'gift' of manhood is its unreliability and questionability. Thus, although manliness initially seems to involve the possession of something which other people lack (φ), it actually is a source of anxiety and frustration. The author (notwithstanding his outspoken male chauvinism) speaks about males as people who are unable to live up to their expectations, suffer from insufficiency and lack, and are desperately in search of something that will restore to them what they apparently have lost, a pharmaceutical drug (the 'oral' version of the object *a*).

Testosterone, de Kruif argues, satisfies the 'hormone hunger' of faltering men, offering them a 'new lease on life' (the author's pet phrase, used more than a dozen times throughout the book). It will 'uplift the mental outlook' of 'chemically starved' males (87), 'foiled by mental tiredness' (104), making them self-assured again (97) and 'strong to think and act' (89), producing a 'startling upsurge' or 'soaring' of their physical and mental condition (101), changing the 'tonality' of their existence. Testosterone allows them to 'think more sharply' (163); their mental processes become more clear (126), their intelligence more lively (160). Testosterone is 'biochemical T.N.T.', unleashing an upsurge of brain power and 'mental verve' (193) by 'clearing the brain' (198). At last the subject can think straight again, and this gives rise to 'a condition medically known as euphoria' (145, 174). But the effects will only be temporary. Testosterone is a most questionable 'wonder drug'.

De Kruif presents his own life as a testosterone experiment, describing, for instance, the first time a tablet is offered to him by a friend:

> *I'll never forget the day he gave me those first tablets, little ten milligram pills not much bigger than an aspirin, for my own use (...). 'Okay, I'll try them,' I said.* (143)

Soon, he experiences the 'new lease on life' caused by these pills so negligible in size: 'chemical crutches' (230) offering a welcome substitute for what is insufficiently produced 'in those private laboratories, the testicles' (51).

In short, for de Kruif, these tiny tablets represent the (oral) object *a*. Manhood is basically chemistry, dependent on chemicals provided either by nature or by pharmaceutical companies (to counteract the 'chemical castration' known as ageing). De Kruif promotes a frantic search for deliverance. Testosterone will make him whole again, although, towards the end of the book, ambivalence returns. Has he been duped once more? Yet the hint remains that testosterone may bring about, in climacteric males, 'a transfiguration into *the youthful splendour of a movie hero*' (206, my emphasis). Let me now turn to the film, where a tiny pill indeed seems to have the envisioned effect.

Limitless

Limitless is the story of a middle-aged writer named Eddie Morra (Bradley Cooper) who, having finally secured a book contract with a New York publisher, falls victim to writer's block. Now that access to the world of professional authorship (legitimate daydreaming on paper) finally seems within reach, a paralysing impotence befalls him. All of a sudden, he is deprived of his ability to write (-φ): a case of 'self-sabotage', as Eddie phrases it. Things go from bad to worse. Girlfriend Lindy announces her decision to break up their relationship, ceremoniously handing him back his keys. He is unable to fulfil her desires and live up to her idea of a relationship.

On a Manhattan sidewalk, he bumps into an old acquaintance, a former drug dealer who invites him for a drink and to whom he confesses his 'creative problems'. The dealer offers him an (allegedly FDA-approved) wonder drug named NZT, a very small pill, an entity on the verge of materiality, almost inexistent: minuscule, colourless, transparent, weightless, with neither taste nor smell, wrapped in a plastic foil. At first, Eddie is sceptical. What is it: Viagra for the brain? But as he puts it in his pocket, the wonder drug seems to summon him: TAKE ME! Before long, he swallows the tablet. Within minutes, he experiences an upsurge in mental and physical prowess. His way-of-being-in-the-world brightens. He is granted a new lease on life, finishes his book in no time, and becomes a completely transfigured person: self-confident and highly efficient. Soon, he quits novel-writing for a stellar career on the Manhattan stock market, becoming the adviser and partner of one of the most powerful males in Manhattan, venture capitalist Carl Van Loon (Robert De Niro; in Lacanian grammar, the Big Other: Φ), whom he tries to please at first, but who is bound to become his 'Oedipal' competitor soon.[1] Eddie facilitates the merger of two very large Manhattan firms, a process of staggering complexity, beyond the grasp of ordinary individuals.

During their first meeting, Van Loon asks him a very straight question: 'What's your secret?' And Eddie gives him a straight answer: 'Medication, I'm on special medication'. His life quickly moves ahead, or rather, upward. The camera drifts from his shabby apartment into luxurious meeting rooms, trendy restaurants and a stylish penthouse on the top floor of a Manhattan skyscraper: a 'fortress with a hell of a view'. From there, he looks down on the anonymous masses, dragging themselves through the streets like rivers of human flesh.

But all this comes with a price. To begin with, his resource of NZT will be exhausted sooner or later. Moreover, a violent crook (demanding a piece of the cake) threatens to 'flay' him with very sharp, scalpel-like knives. But his biggest concern is what de Kruif calls 'chemical castration': the sudden disappearance of the oral object a, the one thing which allows him (temporarily) to live up to his ego ideal – a most devastating event. A sword of Damocles is suspended over his head.

NZT is an intriguing entity. Everyone is after it, but it is always hiding somewhere and very difficult to find. It is almost inexistent; a miniature droplet of transparent milk, produced by a mysterious company (the movie's all-powerful Mother), a cinematic version of the object a. Its impact is immediate and highly dramatic: 'I was blind, but now I see' – a transformative experience. Eddie's ability to process information becomes intimidating. He becomes a 'sparkling cocktail of information', a Manhattan celebrity. Everyone starts watching him. Magazines write about him. He certainly 'has' it: a remarkable dexterity (φ), a special talent which other people lack. Via neural axons, NZT affect his whole body, allowing the world as such to appear in a remarkably translucent, exciting light.

What does NZT *do*? Eddie asks, when given the drug: 'does it increase anal retention'? (i.e., strengthen self-control?). But the impact is 'Lacanian' rather than 'Freudian'. After swallowing it, the 'symbolic order' of letters, figures, numbers and other kinds of data opens up to him. Letters fall like manna from the New York sky. Words appear on paper all by themselves (as if the unconscious speaks). Desire becomes text, and Eddie (unsatisfied with prolific authorship), becomes a stock market virtuoso overnight: a miracle of plasticity. The stock market is the place to be. With its complexities and ceaseless motion, the 24-hour global network of trading systems is a template for human consciousness, a collective nervous system, a global brain, allowing him to tune in to the dynamics of global existence.

The drug affects his whole ambiance. Manhattan suddenly looks quite different. Eddie is not only hyperintelligent, but also irresistibly seductive. He wins back his girlfriend and easily seduces one beautiful woman after another. His vivacity, pace and energetic aura are simply overwhelming. Besides lifting his inhibitions, NZT produces a state of *jouissance*, enabling him to plug into the vibrations of Manhattan, infecting others with his surplus of energy and enjoyment. But there is an uncanny side to it. He becomes an ICT 'monster', a 'Frankenstein of cyberspace', a walking version of the chess-playing computer *Deep Blue*, running into street fights and even killing one of his dates.

Mirrors play an important role. At various points, we find Eddie standing in front of them, assessing his progress. At the start of the movie, Eddie asks the audience to take a critical look at him: 'Look at me'. How could I allow this to happen, how could it come to this? Via mirrors (in various locations: hairdressers, clothing stores, bathrooms, bars, hotel lobbies) we witness the transformative process, evolving in a leap-like fashion, from shabby would-be writer into highly successful businessman, mingling with the great and powerful. Yet his mental acuity and hypermasculine self-confidence is a façade, a temporary foil. His basic vulnerability cannot really be concealed. Beneath his entrepreneurial surface, the divided subject (with its anxieties, inhibitions and vulnerabilities) continues to loom. Bereft of NZT, the 'splendour of the movie hero' quickly evaporates.

The downside is revealed to him via a television screen, during a meeting in a fashionable hotel, while suffering from an NZT hangover. One noticeable side effect of NZT is memory loss. Parts of his life are suddenly erased from his memory files. The night before, an enchanting woman, bewildered by his charms, had dragged him into her apartment to have sex with her. During an orgiastic love scene, her body became almost cubistic, so that shoulders, breasts, arms, legs and so on seemed disconnected. Eddie inhabits a surrealistic fragmented dreamworld, and this is reflected in the bodies he encounters. It becomes increasingly difficult to put these fragments together again; the gaps and ruptures propagate, not only spatially and visually, but also temporally. Although his own memories of the wild night have vanished, a video screen informs him that the woman (whom he recognizes) has been brutally slain. He is the main suspect. Apparently, love and violence became intermingled, and sex gave way to brutal physical fighting. Mr Hyde is taking over. Eddie hires a very expensive lawyer to avert this potential blemish on his budding career. Nonetheless, like his revenues, the collateral damage of his rise to success increases in logarithmic fashion.

NZT alters synapse biochemistry, so that information glides through neural networks in a streamlined way (mobilizing full brain capacity), but Eddie also lives in a completely different environment. The pace and tonality of life have changed, much like his field of vision, the pallet of its colours, his experience of time. Looking down from his penthouse, Manhattan is at his feet, while all the city's landmarks are in view. But as a Manhattan celebrity, he is also *being* seen. By the mass media, by Van Loon (who tries to keep track of his doings, not without a sense of fatherly concern), but also by professional killers (who keep him in gunsight, as it were). Video cameras in hotels and other semi-public places are keyholes into his life.

During one interesting 'gaze' scene, girlfriend Lindy is lying on the bed, looking at him, apparently waiting for something to happen, while Eddie is standing near the window, staring restlessly into the obscure, indistinct evening, catching glimpses of a third (invisible) gaze: the professional assassin who is monitoring him, encircling him: Eddie as a highly visible player, living in luxurious skyscrapers, a target to prey on and compete with.

The net result is fairly ambiguous. There is a significant increase in mental power and sexual attractiveness. The subject overcomes his inhibitions, his sense of impotence. What he can do in just one day seems 'limitless'. But his talents are dependent on the unreliable object *a*, which can be present or absent (*Fort* or *Da*). He carries his pills in a secret pocket inside his jacket, close to his body, but his own organism cannot produce them. The supply of NZT remains under the control of others. Being 'on NZT', he clearly perceives the hazardous condition of his inflated ego. Being 'jacked in', he is haunting by the concern that he may become 'unplugged' one day. Without NZT, the dazzling rows of stock market figures quickly become incomprehensible 'hieroglyphs' again.

Van Loon and Eddie are entangled in an Oedipal (dialectical, master–slave) relationship. Van Loon wants Eddie to work for him. The big omnipotent father figure realizes his inability to process the information streams of high-tech venture capitalism himself. He depends on Eddie's unique partial organ to transform overwhelming data into management options. This inevitably makes Eddie increasingly powerful, while Van Loon's dependency increases. The bewildering complexity of electronic financial information is something which he can no longer handle, and Eddie seems to *have* what other people *lack*: An enigmatic talent, a secret algorithm, a gadget of some sort? Van Loon suspects something. He is a stern father, reproaching Eddie when, nauseated by NZT, he shows up too late at an important meeting, but also a benevolent father: 'I have opened a line of credit; you will be needing a few toys'. But Eddie first and foremost wants to regain his independence.

In the movie version, Eddie eventually outsmarts all the others, including the assassins, including Van Loon. He even beats Eiben-Chemcorp, the chemical company that produces NZT, by establishing lines of production of his own. In the end, 'Senator Eddie' seems ready to run for president. The novel ends on a different note. Eddie discovers that, from the very beginning, without his knowing, he was recruited as a research subject in an illegal drug experiment: 'a human lab rat (…) tagged and followed and photographed, and then discarded' (Glynn 2011, 340), dying a miserable death as a fugitive when the NZT supply is discontinued for good.

Eddie the brain-doping addict is the counterpart of another stock character in Hollywood movies: the 'scientific genius', relying on exceptional giftedness rather than tablets – although 'gift' etymologically means 'poison' (φάρμακον). *A Beautiful Mind* (2001), based on a novel by Sylvia Nasar (1998), about mathematics prodigy and Nobel laureate John Nash, shows interesting parallels between the career curves of Eddie and John. The latter, a mathematician interested in economics and fascinated by the idea that drugs might heighten intellectual performance (13), is described as a scientist with 'an extra human spark' (12). His theory of 'governing dynamics' comes to him in a bar (when debating effective methods for seducing women), while at the Pentagon he astonishes fellow code-breakers by his remarkable ability to decipher encrypted enemy codes in his head. But there are serious side effects to 'natural' brilliance as well. Nash becomes increasingly paranoid, thinking he is followed and blackmailed, as does Eddie. The idea of being monitored and pursued by criminals and pharmaceutical companies may be a side effect of NZT. Nash becomes a psychiatric patient, a victim of his giftedness, communicating with extraterrestrial civilizations in a closed ward, although eventually there is a happy ending.

Conclusion: The Icarus complex

Daedalus (the archetypal engineer) lives and works on a Mediterranean island, serving a powerful tyrant, who (considering that technical know-how = power) imprisons him. But Daedalus builds two pairs of wings (one for Icarus, his son) and escapes. Icarus enjoys flying so much, however, that he soars high up towards the sun. The wax melts and he falls into the sea and drowns.

For Gaston Bachelard (1943) this is the archetypal story connected with 'air' as the element of freedom and upward movement, but also with the anxiety of falling down, especially once we have reached sufficient height (*Fallhöhe* in German). It is the 'typical' dream of climbing (skyscrapers, for instance) until we are overwhelmed by vertigo.

This ancient myth provides the basic structure for *Limitless*, featuring Eddie as a hypermodern Icarus. Unlike prudent Daedalus, for whom wings are merely a 'means', upward mobility invokes in him an experience of *jouissance*. The urge to reach the highest possible altitude is irresistible. Manhattan is the island, Carl Van Loon the tyrant. The pair of wings is the appendix-like, detachable 'partial' organ, which (temporarily) suspends his discontent: a highly unreliable, lethal remedy. Cognitive enhancement represents a repetitive, disruptive desire, haunting us since time immemorial: a craving for 'verticality'. In Brueghel's version, Icarus falls into the sea *unseen*. Nobody takes notice of him anymore. Like Eddie in the novel, he dies an anonymous death. In the film version, Eddie's fabulous ascent continues for a while, whereas the critical examination of the role of pharmaceutical companies in the distribution of questionable drugs (an important issue in the novel) has disappeared, albeit not completely. The suggestion clearly is that everyone who functions on such a high level must, by definition, be 'on NZT'.

Note

1. In the film there are 'two' fathers. The 'real', disappointing father in whose footsteps Eddie does not want to follow is a dentist materials provider. Eddie has two options in life: either novel-writing or dentistry. Van Loon is the imaginary father, the big Other (cf. Žižek 2001, 124ff.).

23
Limitless? There's a Pill for That: Filmic Representation as Equipment for Living

Kyle McNease

Everyday life is a rather curious thing, and sometimes this realization seems to escape us. But what is it that causes audience members to laugh at a comic's well-timed joke or witty turn of phrase? Is it that the comic introduces audience members to an entirely new world or causes us to experience the world in the strange light of its naturalness? It is my contention that comics are particularly skilled at pointing out the obvious, the mundane things that we all know exist, and calling them into question or performing their routine in such a way as to resituate the everyday object in a context that allows for other interpretations to emerge. Is this not also the same thing that critics and most of the great poets and dramatists have been doing? Perhaps, in differing ways, the comic and critic provide conceptual horizons for interpretation.

Let us briefly expand upon this notion of a horizon by taking the sky as an example. It is pervasive, available for everyone to see. In fact, due to its ubiquitous nature, it oftentimes goes *unnoticed* in the warp and woof of busy living. It might be fair to say that, at times, the sky itself, just as the variegated horizon of interpretation, is hidden from us in plain sight. As long as the prevailing winds and weather are in our favour, we leave that vast horizon largely unexplored. In a world as polyvocal, polysemic and mediated as ours, it can also be difficult to attend to all of the cultural messages and rhetorical visions that swirl about us. What follows in this chapter, then, is an exploration of Neil Burger's *Limitless* – a popular culture film, artifact, text and message – in order to highlight those things seemingly hidden in the full light of a cinematic day. This chapter is an attempt to investigate and 'show forth' (*epideictic*), to rhetorically approach the film as a text to be read for dominant meanings of biotechnology and human enhancement.

Beginnings

The very nature of being human reveals a paradoxical ontological status, that of a self-reflexive creature framed towards openness, full of flux and completely incomplete: we are perfectly imperfect (Hyde 2010). Whatever else may be said about human history, it is certainly fair to say that individuals and communities – from both East and West – have striven to come to terms with the beauty and burden of perfection. Whether that ideal took shape and was represented in Egyptian pyramids and obelisks, the intricacies of the Incan emperor's estate, the Confucian form of citizenship, the Samurai's harmonious exactness, the Greeks in their aesthetics, philosophizing and myth-making, the Romans and the magnitude of their empire and might of their architecture, the Polynesian night-sky navigators, the theological treatises of the more recent past or the emerging technocentrism of postmodernity, the case can be made that there was and is a theory of perfectibility always at work within us (Foss 1946; Hyde 2010). Burke goes as far as to say that humans are indeed 'rotten with perfection' (1969, 14). Hyde (2010) offers the compelling rebuttal that while too much perfection may lead to rottenness, too little leads to decay. In order to reach modern conceptualizations of perfection and stave off the inevitable process of decline, biotechnology has been offered up as a means of human enhancement.

For the purpose of this chapter, the necessarily problematic term 'human enhancement' will be defined as 'the use of biomedical technology to achieve goals other than the treatment or prevention of disease' (van Est et al. 2008, 4). From this vantage point, it seems clear that biotechnology is being utilized, by some, to augment their natural state in order to improve performance, as well as appearance. One needs to look no further than the daily news to see how ubiquitous human enhancement has become. Many athletes, including children, now rely upon biotechnology to increase strength, speed, agility and recovery (Evans et al. 2012). If a person were to develop an unsightly wrinkle, *Botox* is always an option. If one were inclined to study for an exam or write a paper, psychostimulants, although illegal without a prescription, might be used to sustain concentration. As this metaphysical desire for perfection, with its propensity embedded in our language, intersects with easily accessible biotechnologies, a new era of human transcendence looms on the horizon.

In light of Darwin's work in the Galapagos, the concept of evolution was applied to the up-till-then rather fixed notion of a human being. This teleological process of constant, if imperceptible, change and continuous emergence allows for a postmodern resituating of humanity as discursively constructed, autonomous performers with multiple identities (Butler 1990; Hayles 1999; Habermas 2003; Lyotard 2003). In other words, there is no 'once for all' perpetual entity, no Platonic ideal or concrete form, that can be called human. By virtue of its evolutionary heritage, humanity is in the process of becoming: a process which continues to leave definitions indefinite and possibilities for transcendence limitless. Alvin Toffler (2000) synopsizes the changing landscape: 'The biggest question facing the 21st century can be stated in a few words: What does it mean to be "human?" The answer to that question will affect our most basic values and moral codes.' Led by influential thinkers like Drexler (1986), Hughes (2004), Moravec (1988) and Kurzweil (2005), transhumanism – an evolutionary conceptualization that would further fuse humanity with emerging biotechnologies, nanotechnologies and information technologies – aims at overcoming the limits of our outdated biological systems. Moreover, Kurzweil (2005, 128) purports that: '[w]e will ultimately multiply our intellectual powers by applying and extending the methods of human intelligence' in order to 'transform our frail version 1.0 human bodies into their far more durable and capable version 2.0 counterparts' (2005, 300). It is here, right now, at this tenuous, controversial intersection of humanity 1.0 and 2.0 that Neil Burger stages his film *Limitless*.

Limitless, as a film, functions on two different but important levels: it serves as a popular culture artefact and, therefore, reasserts the importance of the biotechnological debate in the public forum, while simultaneously instantiating the acceptability of human enhancement through biotechnological means. Though Burger (2011) intended *Limitless* to be 'a Faustian tale' that raises questions without 'offering solutions', the Burkean critic understands that the film itself is a strategic answer to a particular exigency: do we wish to remain as we are (humanity 1.0) or transcend our biological 'limitations'? This question will be explored through Burke's dramatistic theory of (electronic) literature as equipment for living.

Dramatism

Burke (1962, 59) states that communicators are concerned with 'vocabularies that will be faithful *reflections* of reality' and, for this reason, we 'develop vocabularies that are *selections* of reality'. Here, at the outset, we are faced with a difficulty, a seeming paradox: we need terms that can properly reflect reality, but, in the process of selecting those appropriate terms, we necessarily restrict our scope. In order to a avoid reduction (in scope) that deflects reality, Burke relies upon dramatism, which is the critic's method for locating a 'representative anecdote' (1962, 60). For Burke, the representative anecdote is grounded in drama and corresponds to both edges of Occam's razor; that is, the representative anecdote neither multiplies 'beyond necessity' nor does it reduce 'beyond necessity' (1962, 324). As Brummett explains, '[t]o *represent* something is to sum up its essence; and the dramatic aspects of what people do and say are the *essence* of human action' (1984, 162). It can be argued that authors, poets, artists, architects, musicians and myth-makers of other myriad media are endeavouring to say something – perhaps many things – about the 'everydayness' of life. Within this complicated nexus of symbolic meaning-making, the outflow of the creative mind is supplying society writ large with differing types of anecdotes, dramatic in their own right. Importantly for Burke (1967), these various anecdotes 'are *strategies* for dealing with *situations*. In so far as situations are typical and recurrent in a given social structure, people develop names for them and strategies for handling them' (297). Though this term 'strategies' was met with critical ambivalence, Burke maintained:

> *One seeks to 'direct the larger movements and operations' in one's campaign of living. One 'manoeuvres', and the manoeuvring is an 'art'. Are not the final results one's 'strategy'? One tries, as far as possible, to develop a strategy whereby one 'can't lose'.* (298)

Salient to my review of *Limitless*, Burke reminds us of the danger inherent within a strategy of 'easy consolation' (298). This easy consolation takes place within the milieu of minimization of severe exigencies and maximization of self-aggrandizing strategies (299). However, for Burke, there is a 'reservation' that needs to be anecdotally situated here: a problematizing of the way we experience and interact with a specific discourse (299). Burke cautions us to be mindful of the fact that, as consumers encounter certain literary forms, they are not necessarily 'reading as students who will attempt applying the recipes given':

> Nothing of the sort. The reading of a book on the attaining of success is in itself the symbolic attaining of that success. It is while they read that these readers are succeeding. [...] The lure of the book resides in the fact that the reader, while reading it, is then living in the aura of success. (299)

This notion of a successful reading that corresponds to an intentional strategy for ordering one's campaign of living offers us a more thorough understanding of what Burke meant by art and literary form as 'equipment for living' (304).

Literature as equipment for living

Burke (1967) further explained the particular functionalities of literary structure, suggesting that readers make use of characters' actions and attitudes 'to confront their lived situations, celebrate their triumphs and encompass their tragedies' (Brummett 1984, 161). Within the Burkean framework, literary structures '*recur* as appropriate responses to recurring types of situations' (Brummett 1984, 161) that are presented to us, as ontological beings, as towards the practice of everyday life. Brummett explains that the dramatic nature of media itself allows for a Burkean dramatistic method of criticism. In order to make his own critique more pliable and fit within Burke's framework, Brummett replaces the term literature with discourse, which he intends to encompass all mass media content (162). Brummett states that media content 'is, of course, the equipment for living relied upon by millions today' (162) because 'people turn to mass media for the symbolic' (174) tools to manage their own social situations. He argues further, 'media are equipment for living because they recast this world, its hopes and fears, into anecdotal form – and thus, an anecdotal method can help reveal that form' (174). It becomes necessary, then, for the Burkean critic to search out the prominent discourse within society and 'to link discourse to the real situations for which it is symbolic equipment' (Brummett 1984, 161).

For the critic of film, Burke's dramatistic methods prove useful in elucidating the ways that audiences appropriate discourse and use it as equipment for living. Abstraction becomes essential at this point, as the film critic attempts to discover the cinematic anecdote, which is that 'plot, story line, immanent within the content of the discourse and able to represent the discourse' (Brummet 1984, 163). The representative anecdote allows the critic to compare symbolic strategies across various media and identify specific discourses that are being offered to audiences as equipment for living. The anecdote, through easily recognized patterns, creates a space where individuals come to terms with what it means to be human – with all of its fear and hope. Moreover, the cinematic anecdote poses problems, invites the audience member to note her concerns as the narrative unfolds and explore the possibility of inherent solutions within a discourse. Thus, the discourse satiates the viewer's need and 'provides [her] with the motives, hope and symbolic resources' (164) to meet, and perhaps challenge, her challenges. Brummett suggests that the critic's obligation is to 'link discourse embodying the formal anecdote to an audience's problems' in order to demonstrate 'how the anecdotal form equips a culture for living' (164) within a given context. Unique to Burke's theory of equipment for living is the notion that viewers formulate motives from the actual discourse as opposed to formulating discourse from their motives.

Limitless as equipment for living

Hyde and King (2012) note that society has taken a rather 'laissez-faire position' towards biotechnology and human enhancement (170). As stated, this film functions on one level as a rhetorical agonist – drawing attention to issues which remain outside of viewers' conscious awareness – and creates a discursive opening wherein audience members can contemplate and contest previously unexamined or unarticulated possibilities. Again, while audience members are both active and interactive, it is important to acknowledge that whether 'fictitious or heavily dramatized accounts of real incidents, we nevertheless are susceptible to the definitions of reality, value systems, power structures, and role relations we see imaged again and again in our entertainment' (Japp & Harter 2001, 410). Mediated realities – both constructed and constructing – interrupt our daily lives and call our being and identity into question. *Limitless* asks us to overcome the fear and anxiety related to human enhancement and transcendence through the application of biotechnology. The remainder of this chapter focuses on this latter function: *Limitless* as equipment for living.

In the opening seconds of *Limitless*, viewers are alerted to the significance of the exigency; vicariously, we stand with Eddie Morra (Bradley Cooper), the male protagonist, on a ledge surveying our uncertain future. With the weight of fear and anxiety wrapped about his neck like an albatross, the pavement below seems to be screaming with a ferocious gravity: our gaze tells us that this is deadly serious, that this guy might jump and that he might take us with him. As the wind whips about Eddie, he looks like a marionette whose strings are about to be cut. We can hear the loud, clumsy clamouring of brigands at the door. Once upon a time, this door might have kept an army of invaders locked outside of the otherwise vulnerable city. There would be chants of 'God Save the King'! That was then. This is now. The kings are long gone, burned upon their pyres. And, as for God, Nietzsche was wrong. It is not that God is dead, it's that s/he/it doesn't exist yet. Postmodernity slew the certainty of kings and overturned the table of deities. This is the beginning of the film, visual synecdoche. As gunshots ring out, it is clear that Eddie's neighbour has been killed and that he will be next. Eddie opines: 'He bought me half a minute. I wish he hadn't. Last thoughts are self-pitying and mine are no exception: the waste. The waste of it all. I mean, how many of us ever know what it is to become (...) the perfect version of ourselves. I'd come that close.' The question for audience members is, 'how do I do it? How do I become the perfect version of myself?'

Eddie was not always the modelesque, gallantly attired genius we encounter upon that ledge. He narrates a flashback where we see him ambling down the street. Eddie muses, 'That was me not so long ago. What kind of guy without a drug or alcohol problem looks this way?' He is dishevelled, bedraggled and sallow. Everything about him reeks of drabness, including his love life. Lindy, his girlfriend, could no longer suffer his slovenly presence, his self-deprecating, self-destructive tendency towards despondency – known best by struggling writers. The romantic scent of a struggling artist had worn off. As we encounter this odoriferous version of Eddie, Humanity 1.0, we are reminded of the times in our own lives when we were rotten with imperfection (Hyde 2010). But the present promise of biotechnological enhancement is there to catch him and us, as we fall together. How many times have we heard the anecdote about idle hands being the devil's workshop? In Eddie's purposeless meandering, he haphazardly runs into Vern, his ex-brother-in-law. Vern is a drug dealer, and as such, becomes the medium through which Mephistopheles makes a metaphoric appearance. Vern conjures a hellishly benign-looking object out of his pocket and offers it to Eddie.

> Eddie Morra: What's in it?
> Vernon: They've identified these receptors in the brain that activate specific circuits. And you know how they say that we can only access twenty percent of our brain? Well, what this does, it lets you access all of it.
> Eddie Morra: Vern, look at me. Do I look good to you? I'm broke and I'm depressed off my ass. I...I don't think that my life's gonna take some sudden upswing into fame and fortune by taking some shiny brand new designer drug.

This moment in the film is highly instructional; as Burke (1967) suggests, discourse helps us respond to recurring types of situations. Eddie's initial hesitancy and disbelief is a warranted scepticism. During this scene, we share the same space with Eddie, and reflect upon the inundation of advertisements for pharmaceutical drugs. At least in Goethe's *Faust*, there was an actual devil to make a pact with. But this is what Arendt (1992) would call 'the banality of evil'. After all, it is *just* a pill. This exchange adumbrates viewers' ambivalence towards biotechnology, a vacillation that is only alleviated by 'tasting and seeing' that cognitive enhancement is good. Eddie, like us, is lulled into biotechnological complacency; with him, we enter into this liminal state of wait and see. We resonate with Eddie's resignation, when he wryly chagrins, 'In the end, how much worse could it get?' Viewers are asked, on a symbolic level, to take the calculated risk and swallow whatever it is that we are being sold. Below the film's official YouTube trailer, one commenter, AzzHunterbunny, exclaims: 'Worth the risk? What would you do? I'd fucking take that pill right away without asking any questions, even if I'll be the perfect version of myself to die two weeks later, I'd still do it.' Who knows, maybe it will work this time? In the end, are we not 'creatures who are always caught up in the play of time, always on the way towards understanding what can or will be in our lives but is not yet, and thus always confronted with the task of trying to make sense of' (Hyde & King 2010, 159) and make meaning out of our lives? That ever-present carrot of perfection dangles before us: *entelechy* at the low-low price of popping a pill.

Ingesting that clear pill (named NZT-48 in the film) is a symbolic crossing of the demarcation line. What had only been entertained by alchemists of the old world is daily practised by this culture, if not actually, then metaphorically; for what is NZT-48 but another way to transcend material constraints? The magic is gone but the magicians, though they call themselves something different, are still very much active. Since the days of Francis Bacon, the West has been trying to recover the encyclopaedic knowledge that Adam lost in the fall. On an esoteric level, *Limitless* prepares us for the realization of that epistemic moment in our own lives. Remember, there is nothing that one needs to do for this automated enhancement to take place – provided one ingests the drug. The assurance that biotechnology offers is a *charism*, a grace, a sacrament. This is the postmodern, transhuman Eucharist. Transubstantiation, freed from the decrepitude of 'the body and the blood', is the means to transcendence: we can finally become one with our biotechnologies, cyborgs for now but pure silicon substrates in the years to come. As viewers, we have also become initiates into the burgeoning fervour of overextension. But, on a pragmatic level, what does the pill do for Eddie? Are there things which biotechnology can provide for us? 'Enhanced Eddie', as he calls himself on NZT-48, is illumined, with bright, clear eyes and a skin tone hued with a light gold effect. Not by accident, there is a newspaper interview that alludes to him as Midas, which is referring both to his golden visage and his ability to turn anything to gold – again the work of an alchemist. NZT-48, an advanced form of biotechnology, provides him with access to all of his brain and allows him to accomplish what other mortals cannot imagine. NZT-48 causes his memory to function as a kind of limitless cloud-computing server and a platform for automatic, photographic recall. Beyond that, his neural networks have adapted, accelerating his pattern recognition. A brief vignette from his meeting with the energy tycoon Carl Van Loon (played by Robert De Niro), might be illustrative:

> *Pierce: Pattern recognition. That's your snake oil?*
> *Eddie Morra: Well, not everybody understands the patterns. And that gave me a little bit more of an uptick, but it's just a parlor trick. So then I went on to door number three.*
> *Pierce: Are you really implying that you have some sort of ultimate formula?*
> *Kevin Doyle: Well, from twelve thousand to 2.3 three million in ten days.*
> *Eddie Morra: I do have a formula, Mr Pierce.*
> *Pierce: Delusions of grandeur.*
> *Eddie Morra: I don't have delusions of grandeur. I have an actual recipe for grandeur.*

Eddie's pharmacological recipe for grandeur allows him to manipulate the stock market and make millions of dollars, spending them on designer suits, private jets, fine wine, fast cars and beautiful women – just some of the perks. He is able to write a best-selling novel in a matter of hours, as perfectly worded sentences seemingly rain down on him. This form of automated writing certainly appeals to some members of the viewing public. Take VSCYBERPUNKHORRORS, another YouTube commenter. S/he identifies with the film's *representative anecdote*, stating: 'See that guy, that's me. I'm a writer too, ha. My life story here. If I only had a friggin' pill to change EVERYTHING and write a book in 4 days.' Tacom4ster echoes this sentiment, lamenting: 'I am going to fail my screenwriting class due to procrastination and writer's block, I need that drug.' Ultimately, Eddie is not concerned with the craft of writing or even the intricacies of the world markets. He has the insatiable lust for power, the Achilles heel of every true Faustian.

As Eddie draws an ever-growing crowd of followers and sells every seat at his fund-raising events, viewers understand the inevitable conclusion that he will win a senate seat in New York; then he will win the presidency because no one can challenge him politically or otherwise. Carl Van Loon, Eddie's one worthy rival, is vanquished by 'enhanced Eddie', as the latter proclaims: 'I see everything, Carl. I'm fifty moves ahead of you and everybody else.' As a consequence of Eddie's keen intellect and elocution, public debates are cancelled: 'who can argue with you?' a nameless woman in a bar once asks, right before having sex with him in bathroom. Viewers look on as voyeurs, no longer witnesses. We derive pleasure in seeing this man reach god-like status because, as Burke (1967) argues, we become consubstantial with him. His victories are our victories. Audience members are advised to apply the available biotechnology surrounding them to the raw material that is their life, in hopes of achieving more concrete forms of success. Meanwhile, in *Flowers for Algernon*, a story that shares the narrative trope of biotechnology as a potential means of increasing intelligence, Charlie Gordon, the mentally handicapped main character, is forced to undergo a risky operation to temporarily improve his condition. What is so drastically different in *Limitless*, and makes this point all the more salient, is that Eddie Morra is suffering, not from an actual malady or disease but from being-as-he-is: ordinary. The pathology of normalcy has now been awakened in the audience. Make no mistake, Humanity 1.0 is an 'aged man...a paltry thing/A tattered coat upon a stick' (Yeats 1996, lines 9–10). Because we have invented this disease of normalcy, we have also invented the biotechnological means to transcend that condition: humanity 2.0. The hubris involved in this endeavour is enough to make the likes of Prometheus, Icarus and Bellerophontes shudder. Consider that, in the case of *Flowers for Algernon*, Charlie was striving to become 'normal', just like everyone else. This new pathologizing, though, allows viewers to link the discourse in their everyday lives to that in the film. In his director's cut, Burger (2011) acknowledges the fact that students are increasingly turning to non-prescribed stimulants – what he euphemistically refers to as 'brain steroids' – for cognitive enhancement and academic achievement. Steroids call to mind the deleterious side effects and dark underbelly of biotechnology, something that *Limitless* treats in a rather unique manner.

In discussing NZT-48, this wonder drug, a prodigy of posthumanism, we have not explicitly addressed biotechnological externalities. In *Civilization and*

Its Discontents, Freud (2002) reminds us that there is no such thing as unilinear progress; every 'advancement' in technology creates its own set of new problems. *Limitless* presents viewers with a biotechnology so powerful that it can cause 'meteoric rises' to the top of one's field, but, as we know from the now hackneyed truism of Lord Acton, 'power tends to corrupt, and absolute power corrupts absolutely'. Eddie (along with all other known 'users' of NZT-48) suffers ravaging side effects from the drugs – physical, psychical, social and emotional. There are huge chunks of time that Eddie spends in fugue states, unaware of what he is doing and who he is becoming. There are headaches, severe body aches, loss of appetite and radical insomnia that attend the ingestion of the drug. There are also the concomitant risks of stopping the drug: it proves lethal if not titrated at the precise rate. We see characters in this film living and dying, sometimes quite graphically, not by the sword but by a pill. Yet, Evanescence95Fan, a YouTube viewer, states: 'Bad side effects or not, I would kill for one pill!' Whether or not one would *kill* for a similar drug, there is some evidence to suggest that certain groups of people would be willing to *die* for it.

'Goldman's dilemma', as it is popularly called, is the 13-year study that explored elite athletes' attitudes to winning and substance use. Participants were presented with a Faustian bargain: guaranteed success in sports but death to follow in five years. Consistently, half of the elite athletes surveyed stated that they would accept those terms (Connor & Mazanov 2009). They would literally choose a pharmacological path that guaranteed success, while undercutting their very lives. Athletes are not the only ones who find the *pharmakon* of biotechnology alluring. According to the Centers for Disease Control and Prevention (CDC), one person dies every 19 minutes from prescription drug overdose (http://www.cdc.gov). To put the problem into greater perspective, 100,000 Americans die each year from drugs that are properly prescribed, properly dosed and properly taken (Perdomo 2010). That number does not include accidental deaths, where some mistake was involved (Perdomo 2010). Stating it another way, twice as many people (270) die per day from the *known* side effects of medications than automobile accidents (Perdomo 2010). Yet the allure of the drug continues to appeal to the masses.

For those coming to *Limitless* in order to receive symbolic equipment for living, they are shown how Eddie utilizes NZT-48 to enhance himself enough to navigate through the side effects. Moreover, Eddie uses biotechnology to overcome the limitations inherent within technological determinism, and, finally the limitations imposed upon him by the confines of his human nature. The argument continues to be made by transhumanists; if one properly gages the cultural climate, s/he must admit that the proposition is as seductive now as it was in that garden so long ago: 'eat thereof, then your eyes shall be opened, and ye shall be [limitless] as gods' (Genesis 3:3).

Conclusion

In conclusion, what I have offered here is a critical analysis of *Limitless*, which, on a very surface level, begins to hint at the complexity of the film and, I hope, the contemporary moment. We are temporal beings in space, imbued with a unique ontological status: we remain open to the future and all of its uncertainty. As we attempt to realize our metaphysical desire for perfection, various forms of technologies (bio, nano, information sciences and cognitive enhancement) are being applied to the human condition – in hopes of curing our ills and transcending our limitations.

Finally, if I have read the symbols correctly, *Limitless* is an overcoming by undoing. Individuality has triumphed at the cost of the public good. The destruction of the social contract is permissible on the grounds of personal morphological freedom. We are induced by the accidental success of Eddie to consider our own version of the proactionary principle. That is, careless, unmonitored, small-scale, self-initiated biomedical experimentation. It doesn't hurt (but it does) that we can justify our actions by writing it off as citizen science. Eddie did it for selfish reasons, but if I succeed I will be different! 'I will ascend and become like the most high!' Again, notice our rugged delusion of individual exceptionalism. Forget that there were other characters – better than Eddie, better than us – that couldn't successfully negotiate self-directed evolution. It matters not. What does matter is our love affair with suicide, not-existing as we do. The pathology of normalcy cured forever. With the drug man has unmade man into the hyper-reality of the Transhuman: *imago venenum*. Experience the 'high of organic annihilation' (Baudrillard 1989, 38). Eddie has surrendered – and by symbolic logic we with him – humanity for the insatiable hunger of perpetual technological consumption. In *The Art of the Novel*, Milan Kundera (1988, 41) asks a revolutionary question: 'But if God is gone and man is no longer the master, then who is the master? The planet is moving through the void without any master.' Silly Kundera, the self-ish god that we are manufacturing takes time. This is 'the unbearable lightness of being' *limitless*...

24
Posthumans and Democracy in Popular Culture

James J. Hughes

Introduction

Harry Potter is an anti-racist freedom fighter both in fiction and in the real world. Throughout the Potter novels we are drawn to sympathize with oppressed racial minorities – elves, centaurs, werewolves, half-giants, Mudbloods – and to fear and despise fascist Death Eaters intent on exterminating all non-pure-bloods (Barratt 2012). The Potter narrative has had demonstrable social impact, reinforcing tolerance and democratic values in its readers. In *Harry Potter and the Millennials* (Gierzynski 2013) Anthony Gierzynski pulls together multiple lines of evidence to argue that the generation of American youth that grew up identifying with Harry Potter's struggles against racism and fascism have become more anti-racist and democratic as a consequence. In an analysis of three studies of the effect of reading Harry Potter on political attitudes in the UK and Italy (Vezzali et al. 2014), researchers concluded that the degree to which the readers identified with Potter was a predictor of the influence of the Potter narratives on readers' empathy with immigrants, refugees and homosexuals.

Popular culture both reflects and shapes political culture. The depiction of the posthuman in popular culture is therefore not only a running commentary on the political concerns of the time, with posthumans as stand-ins for everything from communists to immigrants, but also a potent shaper of attitudes towards extant and future varieties of humanity. Posthumanity is a very broad category, encompassing many creatures who were formerly human or share some origin with humanity, but who exist in some state greater than or outside of humanity. In this chapter I will be using the concept of the posthuman broadly to encompass both supernatural creatures, such as vampires and witches, as well as humans genetically, chemically or cybernetically endowed with superpowers. Whether through science or magic, posthumans are representations of superempowered and radically different humanity, and reflect anxieties about authoritarianism, race and the limits of democracy. Speculative fiction can cultivate respect for transhuman difference and democratic possibility on the one hand, or reinforce speciesist 'human racism' on the other, by drawing the reader or viewer into a deep, empathetic connection with a human protagonist who is forging solidarity with posthumans or beleaguered by posthuman threats, or with posthuman heroes or sympathetic posthuman victims. If posthuman monsters are collectivists, the narratives reinforce liberal democratic suspicion of collectivism; if they are ruthless aristocrats and tyrants, they cultivate anti-authoritarianism and suspicion of elites.

In this chapter I reflect on five modalities of posthuman politics in popular culture:

- Posthumans as collectivist threat.
- Posthumans as authoritarian aristocrats.
- Posthumans as defenders of democracy and transhuman solidarity, or as revolutionary agents of class and anti-imperialist struggles.
- Posthumans as victims of racial prejudice and genocide.
- Posthumans as democrats, and as participants in complex, transhuman democracies.

The site TV Tropes summarizes the politics of the depiction of transhumans as a litmus test for Enlightenment values versus anti-Enlightenment views, religious or Romantic: 'A positive portrayal of transhumanism generally places a work of fiction on the Enlightenment side of the Romanticism versus Enlightenment spectrum while a negative portrayal or conspicuous absence of it does the opposite' (TV Tropes 2014). Following on this theme, beyond taxonomy my thesis is that the Enlightenment values of tolerance and the expansion of cognitive empathy through the embrace of difference have gradually worked their way into speculative fiction, reducing the number of narratives in which posthumans are monsters and agents of political dystopia, and increasing the number of narratives in which posthumans are sympathetic and participants in complexly imagined transhuman democracies.

Posthumans as collectivist threat

In 1923, the 30-year-old biologist and Marxist John Burdon Sanderson Haldane gave a talk to the 'Heretics Club' at Cambridge University, titled 'Daedalus or Science and the Future' (Haldane 1924), in which he wonders whether science might be used to subjugate and destroy humanity:

> *Has mankind released from the womb of matter a Demogorgon which is already beginning to turn against him, and may at any moment hurl him into the bottomless void? Or [might humans become] a mere parasite of machinery, an appendage of the reproductive system of huge and complicated engines which will successively usurp his activities, and end by ousting him from the mastery of this planet?*
>
> (Haldane 1924, 4)

Against this dystopian possibility he imagines the many liberatory uses to which the emerging sciences could be put, including the production of clean and abundant energy, the use of psychopharmacology to cure our mental and psychological ills, and the development of genetic engineering and in-vitro fertilization to make humans smarter and healthier. In other words, Haldane embraced the posthuman possibility and his essay became a matter of some debate. Within a year, Bertrand Russell had written a rejoinder, 'Icarus, or The Future of Science' (Russell 1924), which argued that science and technology would always serve to enhance the power of dominant classes and military machines.

Haldane was friends with another leftist biologist, Julian Huxley, and with his brother Aldous Huxley. While Julian shared Haldane's left bio-utopianism, and would, in 1957, coin the term 'transhumanism' (Huxley 1957) for this new bio-utopian vision, Aldous was repelled by these ideas. Eventually, in 1932, Aldous would express his revulsion in *Brave New World* (Huxley 1932), in which in-vitro fertilization, eugenic engineering and psychopharmacology are used to suppress individuality and enforce collectivism. In the wake of the rise and defeat of fascism, and the ongoing threat of communism, the term 'Brave New World' became shorthand for the dystopian collectivist consequences of creating posthumans with 'enhancement' technologies.

After the Second World War, popular culture returned often to the horrific vision of a collectivist posthumanity. Precursors of the anti-communist genre were the 1953 film *It Came from Outer Space*, in which shape-shifting aliens clone human identities, and the 1953 film *Invaders from Mars*, in which aliens invade human bodies. But the quintessential film depiction of the American anxiety about the spread of collectivism was the 1956 *Invasion of the Body Snatchers*, based on Jack Finney's 1954 novel *The Body Snatchers*. Although the director Don Siegel insisted the film was a critique of conformity in American society, it was widely seen as a metaphor for the spread of communism. The plot revolves around the residents of a California town who are slowly replaced by alien clones that are part of a collective consciousness. Eventually, the expression 'pod people' would become slang for people who have lost their individuality and been absorbed into larger groups.

The pod people theme was repeated in films like *The Village of the Damned* in 1960, based on a 1957 novel by John Wyndham, in which children in a British village are infected by aliens and begin to display a psychic hive mind. The children are killed when one of the parents suicide-bombs them. In the *Doctor Who* mythos, the collectivist menace first appears in 1966 in the form of hive mind Cybermen, humanoids that have displaced their emotions with cybernetic connections.

'The Borg' replaced 'pod people' in the 1990s as a popular reference to the collectivist threat, when the imperialist cyborg hive mind appeared in the *Star Trek* universe in 1989. The Borg are an implacable emotionless force that has conquered and 'assimilated' hundreds of species through the implanting of brain-machine interfaces that suppress individuality.

The first glimmers of positive depictions of collectivist posthumanity displacing Cold War antipathy can perhaps be seen in Arthur C. Clarke's *Childhood's End* (1953), in which earth is taken under a patient alien tutelage to be weaned to a higher level of empathy and morality. After 60 years, the result of this domestication is that human children begin to display psychic abilities, and merge with a transgalactic trans-species collective mind.

The most positive television depiction of a hive mind to date is not posthuman, but alien: the Ood of *Doctor Who*. The Ood appeared as a telepathic slave race in the *Doctor Who* series between 2006 and 2012, and although they are susceptible to collective mind control by malevolent forces, they are revealed, over time, to be a naturally pacifist species. The series alludes to a 'Friends of Ood' movement that seek to liberate the Ood from slavery, and the 'Song of Freedom' the Ood sing across the galaxy is hauntingly poignant. Nonetheless, given the value placed on individuality in Western speculative fiction there are still very few positive depictions of collectivism, human, posthuman or non-human, in literature, film or television.

Posthumans as authoritarian aristocrats

In 1992, Francis Fukuyama concluded in *The End of History and the Last Man* (1992) that liberal democracy had decisively won, and political evolution had reached its telos. Ten years later, after Dolly the cloned sheep and the emergence of an international transhumanist subculture, Fukuyama had reached a very different conclusion. In *Our Posthuman Future* (Fukuyama 2002) he argued human enhancement technologies would permit the fulfilment of dreams of non-democratic utopians. Transhumanism, he wrote, had become the most dangerous idea in the world: 'The first victim of transhumanism might be equality (...). If we start transforming ourselves into something superior, what rights will these enhanced creatures claim, and what rights will they possess when compared to those left behind?' (Fukuyama 2004, 43).

In the last decade, Fukuyama's fears of a transhumanist elite intent on subjugating and culling humanity has worked its way into both the bioethics literature and into the conspiratorial imagination. According to the bioethicists George Annas, Lori Andrews and Rosario Isasi:

> *The new species, or 'posthuman', will likely view the old 'normal' humans as inferior, even savages, and fit for slavery or slaughter. The normals, on the other hand, may see the posthumans as a threat and if they can, may engage in a preemptive strike by killing the posthumans before they themselves are killed or enslaved by them. It is ultimately this predictable potential for genocide that makes species-altering experiments potential weapons of mass destruction, and makes the unaccountable genetic engineer a potential bioterrorist.*
>
> (Annas et al. 2002, 162)

This sentiment was echoed more recently by the bioethicist Nicholas Agar in *Humanity's End*: 'a situation in which some humans are radically enhanced while others are not could lead to a tyranny of posthumans over humans' (Agar 2010, 11).

But Fukuyama, conservative bioethicists and conspiracy theory opponents of the Illuminati were not the first to see the posthuman as the embodiment of a new aristocratic and authoritarian elite, bent on subjugating and exploiting humanity. That narrative is actually 200 years old, first seen in the image of the patrician vampire. Quite unlike the animalistic vampires of mythology, the monster in John Polidori's 1819 story *The Vampyre* was a posthuman blueblood. This modern vampire uses his (class) power and privilege to prey on humanity, especially young women. This template was cemented by the popularity of Bram Stoker's 1897 *Dracula*, and continued in numerous television and film portrayals, including the 1994 *Interview with the Vampire* based on Anne Rice's novels, the 2003–2012 *Underworld* series and the 2008–2012 *Twilight* films. Possibly the most extreme depiction of vampires as an exploitive posthuman species is seen in the 2009 film *Daybreakers*, in which vampires have achieved complete ascendency, replacing all human occupations and classes, and the dwindling supply of humans are shown strung to scaffolds to be drained of their blood.

Similarly, enhanced humans have been routinely depicted as aspiring tyrants or secretive aristocrats manipulating mortal events. A conspicuous example is the villain Khan Noonien Singh in the *Star Trek* universe. In the original storyline, Khan is the genius leader of a cabal of genetically engineered supermen and women who seize control of a quarter of earth in the 1990s, but are then defeated in the 'Eugenics Wars'. Khan and some of his followers escape cryopreserved in a spaceship that is later found by Captain Kirk. In the original *Star Trek* TV series and in the *Star Trek* films, as soon as Khan and his followers are revived, they immediately attempt to re-establish their control over humans. As the reason for the conspicuous absence of genetic engineering 400 years later throughout the human colonized galaxy, the *Star Trek* writers cited the horrors of the Eugenics Wars and the persistent threat from enhanced humans like Khan. Later, the television series *Star Trek: Deep Space Nine* reiterated the political edict against genetic engineering, but with more nuance, by introducing the sympathetic character of the physician Julian Bashir, who keeps his genius intelligence secret, because it is the shameful result of illegal genetic tampering by his parents. Bashir turns out to be unique among the genetically enhanced, however, as the rest are mentally unstable. Cyborg augmentation is also banned by the Federation, with the exception of reparative prosthetics like Geordi La Forge's visor in *Star Trek: New Generation* or the rehabilitated cyborg 'Seven of Nine' in *Star Trek: Voyager*.

The 2000–2005 TV series *Andromeda* pointedly names the aspiring master race of genetically engineered posthumans 'Nietzscheans'. Amusingly, the Nietzscheans originated at 'Ayn Rand Station', and name their first home planet 'Fountainhead'. They possess superstrength and their immune systems are boosted by nanorobots. In the prehistory of the show they wage a catastrophic war that kills billions and destroys themselves and the human Commonwealth.

Another trope in the depiction of the posthuman as aspiring tyrant is the idea that superintelligent humans aspire to world domination. This theme is found in the 1992 film *Lawnmower Man*, the 2010 *Battlestar Galactica* prequel *Caprica* and the 2014 film *Transcendence*. In *Lawnmower Man*, a man with an intellectual disability is inducted by a scientist into an experiment on cognitive enhancement using drugs and virtual reality. He quickly begins to display superhuman telepathic and telekinetic abilities, and eventually uploads his expanding mind into the Net (such as it was in 1992). In *Caprica*, the daughter of a military robotics contractor uploads his murdered daughter's personality to a military robot. She then creates the Cylon robot armies that eventually destroy almost all of humanity. Likewise, in *Transcendence* Johnny Depp is a computer scientist who is uploaded into a mainframe and then works to expand his power using nanotechnology that can control human behaviour. Before he can complete his version of the singularity he is killed by a computer virus, and the authorities somehow permanently crash the Internet.

In the 1960s, we begin to see a variety of comedic representations of supernatural and alien aristocrats attempting to assimilate into middle-class human society. The first hit science fiction (SF) television show is the 1963–1966 *My Favorite Martian*, in which a superpowerful and aristocratic, but stranded, alien anthropologist is taken in by a bachelor astronaut. Then the normalized aristocratic other exploded on television in 1964, with the popular monster clans *The Addams Family* and *The Munsters*, and the beginning of the eight-year run of *Bewitched*. While *The Addams Family* were simply macabre and eccentric humans, albeit with non-human relatives like Itt and Thing, the patriarch of *The Munsters*, Herman, was modelled on the Frankenstein monster, while his wife and her father, Lily and Sam Dracula, were ancient vampires. In *Bewitched* Samantha attempts to be a good middle-class housewife despite coming from a family of superpowerful aristocratic witches.

The *Buffy the Vampire Slayer* and *True Blood* television series are perhaps the beginning of a turn from the depiction of vampires and supernatural posthumans as aristocrats (although aristocratic vampires certainly populate those worlds) to vampires as potential fellow citizens. Buffy began the trend by introducing characters like Spike and Angel, who struggle against their evil proclivities to become heroic defenders of humanity. Then *True Blood* pushed the posthuman imaginary furthest with a full programme of vampire assimilation and equality, modelled explicitly on anti-racism and gay rights. With *True Blood* and similar assimilationist narratives, we see the fullest Enlightenment embrace of posthuman difference and equality within the vampire genre, and a rejection of the vampire as monster.

Posthuman defenders of democracy

One of the ways that we began to see positive portrayals of the posthuman was as agents of the democratic state. The first such depiction was the Nazi-fighting Captain America. When the comic book first appeared in 1941, this patriotic symbol was a frail young man turned into a supersoldier by an experimental serum. His popularity waxed and waned, but from the 1940s through to his depiction in a 1979 television film and the 2011 *Captain America: The First Avenger* he remained a defender of American democratic values. Even his moral evolution in the 2014 *Captain America: The Winter Soldier*, when he begins questioning the role of state secrecy, allowed the film's more morally complex audience to be drawn along even further into identification with this enhanced hero.

The most popular augmented humans in television history were also both loyal operatives of the US military and intelligence apparatus. From 1974 to 1978, the *Six Million Dollar Man* and the *Bionic Woman* were Nielsen top ten shows featuring bionically enhanced supersoldiers. Again, the 2007–2012 television series *Chuck* depicted an ordinary man with a superhuman, computer-augmented memory of intelligence data, who is recruited to work for the intelligence apparatus against the enemies of democracy. *Iron Man*, in the 1990s animated versions and the 2008–2013 films, is not only a cybernetically enhanced posthuman who works with the military to defend democracy, but is actually a military–industrial contractor, albeit one with a conscience.

Another positive depiction of the posthuman is found in narratives of posthumans who defend humans and the possibility of transhuman democracy, against both human racism and posthuman villains. This is most explicit in the *X-Men* mythos; their comics were first published in 1963. From the beginning, the X-Men were depicted as heroic altruists, fighting against both apartheid efforts to have all mutants registered, and against the mutant supremacy espoused by the Magneto faction.

Similar themes of pro- and anti-human posthuman politics can be found in the 1998–2004 *Blade* films, the 1999–2004 *Buffy* spin-off *Angel*, the 2004 and 2008 *Hellboy* films, the 2006–2010 superhero television series *Heroes*, the 2008–2014 *Avengers* films (*Iron Man, The Incredible Hulk*, etc.), the 2009 film *The Watchmen*, the 2008–2014 television series *True Blood*, the 2011–2012 superpowered mutant series *Alphas* and the 2008–2014 British and American versions of the television series *Being Human*. In all these narratives there are good posthumans who defend humans 1.0 from bad posthumans.

If witches are posthumans, then the Harry Potter books and 2001–2011 film series also belong in the 'traitors to their race/class' category. As mentioned in the 'Introduction' to this chapter, the Harry Potter mythos is explicitly anti-racist and anti-fascist. The Death Eaters and racial purist wizards despise humans, half-breed 'Mudbloods' and other races. The anti-fascist forces fight pure-blood wizard supremacy, and work in solidarity with the movement to liberate elves from domestic slavery. Lycanthropy is depicted as a chronic illness like AIDS, and the tortured character of the werewolf, Professor Lupin, is a sympathetic victim of its stigma and discrimination.

We begin to see glimmers of posthuman class struggle in films like Neill Blomkamp's *Elysium*. In *Elysium*, the protagonist, in a desperate attempt to get access to posthuman immortality technology for himself and the other oppressed mortals, transforms himself into a cyborg warrior and wages war against an orbital gated community on behalf of universal access to posthuman medical technology.

On television, one of the most radical depictions of future politics is found in the series *Continuum*, which began in 2012. The series starts in a dystopian corporate-dominated authoritarian future of 2077, and follows the protagonist, a cybernetically enhanced corporate cop, back to our present in pursuit of similarly enhanced anarcho-socialist terrorists, 'Liber8'. Over the course of the first two seasons, the cop gradually realizes that she has been working for the wrong side, and that she should cooperate with Liber8 to prevent the future corporate takeover.

The 2009 film *Avatar* gives us the posthuman as an anti-colonialist hero. In this story, a disabled soldier is given an android alien body which he is supposed to use for intelligence-gathering in the service of capitalist resource extraction. But he begins to empathize with the natives, and eventually leads an anti-colonial revolt against the human exploiters. At the end of story, the hero leaves his human form behind permanently.

Posthumans as victims

One of the ways that sympathy for the posthuman Other has been generated in popular culture is by depicting creatures who are treated as monsters because of their difference, even though they are not, at least initially, malevolent. This theme can perhaps be traced back to depictions of Frankenstein's monster as a sensitive, cultured man trapped in a shambling, ugly body, victimized by a callous scientist, and tormented by fearful villagers. The Frankenstein monster has appeared in dozens of films in the last hundred years, and most of the depictions played up the dangerous rather than sympathetic aspects of the monster. Two recent Frankensteins illustrate some of evolution this character has taken, however. In the 2014 television series *Penny Dreadful*, Frankenstein's monster still readily murders humans and considers himself superior to humanity. But the series goes to great lengths to display his intelligence and emotional sensitivity, his embarrassment at his ugliness and his anguish when romantically rejected. Even more of a departure is the 2014 film *I, Frankenstein*, in which the monster becomes a superhero defending humanity from demons.

Spider-Man is another example of the growing popularity of the posthuman hero as a victim of irrational public fears and prejudice. From his appearance in the comics in 1962, through his animated television series, and the 2002–2014 films, Spider-Man has been a working-class posthuman sacrificing mightily to save the world, while usually being hunted and feared by the public. 'Why do you wish them destroyed? Ah see, you have turned the poor guileless innocent into a hunted animal. He has no means of support. No measures for proper education. He has not the voting franchise. No wonder he is compelled to seek out a predatory nocturnal existence.' This is how the protagonist Robert Neville describes the zombie/vampires in Richard Matheson's 1954 novel *I Am Legend*.

As post-Second World War anti-racist politics in the United States began to rework the bounds of empathy in speculative fiction, the posthuman and other categories of non-human other were increasingly found depicted as an oppressed racial group. As mentioned, the mutant X-Men were depicted as an oppressed race from the 1960s comics through their seven films from 2000 to 2014. The first scene of the *X-Men* comic books and of the film *X-Men: First Class* (2011) is of Magneto as a child in a Nazi concentration camp. Professor Xavier came to represent the assimilationism of Martin Luther King, while Magneto was compared to Malcolm X, and at times we are drawn to see Magneto's suspicion of humanity as justified.

This theme of superpowered mutants as racial victims was especially prominent in the one-season (2013–2014) series *The Tomorrow People*. The mutants can teleport, control objects telekinetically and read minds. They refer to themselves as homo superior, and are being hunted and killed by a government agency headed by an evolutionary biologist who believes they pose an existential threat to Homo sapiens. They are searching for their Moses who will lead the new race to their mutant-only Refuge.

The rounding up of posthumans into concentration camps is an especially powerful recurrent racial metaphor. The depiction of supernaturals in *Buffy the Vampire Slayer* took a decidedly anti-racist turn in its fourth season (1999–2000) when the military begins capturing and experimenting on supernaturals in a secret underground concentration camp. Neill Blomkamp's 2009 film *District 9* is set in a concentration camp outside Johannesburg in which aliens have taken the role of black Africans. The protagonist is a human who becomes infected with alien DNA, and, while transforming into an alien–human hybrid, liberates the oppressed aliens. In the 2011–2012 SF series *Alphas*, superpowered mutants are sent to a concentration camp and implanted with lobotomizing chips. In the sixth season of *True Blood* (2013), vampires are captured and imprisoned in a concentration camp, where they are experimented on and infected with a lethal virus.

Sympathetic images of posthumans as exploited slaves have also grown. In one of the most influential SF films, the 1982 *Blade Runner*, the viewer is drawn into empathy with the posthuman 'replicants' who have been programmed to die after seven years of slave labour for the mega-corporations. In his final climactic confrontation in the rain with replicant-hunter Deckard, replicant Roy draws us into feeling powerful empathy with his tragic character. Roy pulls Deckard to safety, noting that it isn't easy to live in fear as a slave.

The posthuman exploitation theme can also be found in Joss Whedon's 2009–2010 television series *Dollhouse*. The protagonist is a woman enslaved by a corporation that can record and transfer personalities and skills. Depending on the needs of the client, the corporation writes the appropriate personality onto the 'dolls' and sends them into service. The corporation's ultimate goal is world domination, allowing its owners to become immortal by jumping from body to body. The enslaved protagonist, Echo, begins to accumulate the traces of her various personalities and their skills sets, until she eventually achieves a self-aware metapersonality. Once she becomes self-aware, she helps liberate her fellow slaves, albeit into a world devastated by the mind-wiping technology.

The anti-corporate and anti-militarist politics of many SF films have also always been quite explicit. From the 1987 original *RoboCop* through to the contemporary remakes, the cyborg cop is a victim of corrupt corporations that control the state, intent on using military tactics to ensure their power. In the 2000–2002 television series *Dark Angel*, posthumans are the product of a secret military genetic engineering project designed to create supersoldiers with a variety of abilities. After they escape, the transgenics are hunted, and eventually make a stand for their rights.

In these depictions of exploited posthumans we are drawn into sympathy with their Enlightenment claim to an equal place beside humans. What is still rare, however, is a depiction of a fully realized transhuman democracy in which humans and posthumans live as equals.

Posthuman democracy and democratic posthumans

Fry: What party do you belong to, Bender?
Bender: I'm not allowed to vote.
Fry: 'Cause you're a robot?
Bender: No, convicted felon.

(*Futurama*, 'A Head in the Polls', 1999)

The full normalization of the posthuman as a citizen of a complex transhuman democracy is still quite rare, but it can be seen in the 1999–2014 television series *Futurama*. While the 1962 vision of the future of *The Jetsons* was strictly human 1.0 and the robots were all servants, the 31st century of *Futurama* is a democracy in which humans, cyborgs, posthumans, aliens and robots all participate as rough equals, Earth is part of the Democratic Order of Planets (DOOP), and an election battle for President of earth between two clones and Richard Nixon's head in a jar is underway.

A positive depiction of a posthuman democrat is the cognitively enhanced protagonist Eddie, played by Bradley Cooper in the 2011 film *Limitless*. The effects of the film's cognitive enhancement drug NZT-48 are temporary, but allow the taker to learn languages, master the stock market and write books, all at a superhuman pace. By the film's end Eddie has discovered a way to eliminate the drug's lethal side effects and make its effect permanent. Meanwhile, instead of using his superpowers to become a tyrant or CEO, he has fended off the corporation that wants to monopolize the drug and is running for the Senate. These few film and television depictions of posthuman democracy, or at least of democratic posthumans, are still rare, however, and not nearly as fully realized as the posthuman polities imagined in the much larger body of written SF.[1]

Final thoughts

In sum, the evidence from popular culture suggests a trend towards more sympathetic treatments of posthumanity, if not yet towards the normalization of enhanced humans, posthumans and non-humans as potential citizens of a transhuman democracy. We do find positive depictions of posthuman heroes as early as the 1940s' Captain America, and monstrous depictions as recently as Johnny Depp's aspiring hegemon in 2014's *Transcendence*. But, influenced by growing Enlightenment tolerance, anti-racism and acceptance of cybernetic augmentation, there have been a growing number of depictions of posthumans as heroic human allies, victims of injustice and ordinary citizens struggling for the possibility of a transhuman democracy. Hopefully, this trend both reflects the greater acceptance of extant forms of social difference, and portends a more inclusive future society, as enhancement and augmentation actually enable transhuman possibilities.

Note

1. Posthuman democracies are much more elaborated, for instance, in the work of Peter Watts, Iain M. Banks, Kim Stanley Robinson, Alastair Reynolds, Hannu Rajaniemi, John C. Wright, Charles Stross or Cory Doctorow.

25
Negative Feelings as Emotional Enhancement in Cinema: The Case of Ulrich Seidl's *Paradise* Trilogy

Tarja Laine

A debate has emerged in posthumanist discourse about pharmaceutical mood enhancers such as Prozac to modify human nature. One side in the debate views such modification as the permanent enhancement of our human emotional make-up, aiming at the elimination of undesirable feelings by the unrestrained use of biotechnology that would take us further from our animal nature. This side of the debate is based on a technological concept of posthumanism, or 'transhumanism'. It is a discourse which is dedicated to the enhancement of our human capacities, physical, cognitive and emotional, by means of advanced biotechnology and cybernetics. According to this school of thought, the transhuman is achieved by searching for escape from the physical entrapment of our material body by means of technological modifications of human biological constraints. In his 'Cyborg 1.0', Kevin Warwick writes, for instance, that his plan is 'to become one with his computer' and to evolve via chip implants into a superintelligent machine (Warwick 2000). In this mindset transhumanism is associated 'with a kind of triumphant disembodiment' as Cary Wolfe puts it (Wolfe 2010, xv).

Similarly, in his 'Why I Want to Be Posthuman When I Grow Up', Nick Bostrom writes that biomedical interventions may increase our capacity to enjoy life by reducing unconstructed negative feelings, such as hate and contempt; by eliminating irrational fears; and also by creating new psychological states that our 'unimproved' neurological machinery is unable to experience. Speaking of 'posthumanly happy beings', Bostrom argues that:

> *One dimension of emotional capacity that we can imagine enhanced is subjective well-being and its various flavours: joy, comfort, sensual pleasures, fun, positive interest and excitement. [...] There are more mental states and emotions that could be experienced with posthuman emotional faculties than with human ones.*
> (Bostrom 2010, 120)

One obvious objection to this line of reasoning is that surely one cannot survive without experiencing negative feelings. For instance, fear is a primary emotion that directs our attention to relevant details of the dangerous situation that are imperative to our assessment to its possible evolvement. To this objection,

Bostrom might reply that we can still experience negative emotions when these emotions are truly justified by the occasion and therefore constructive. Another objection that can be raised is that negative emotions are important because they give meaning to moral values, often helping us in our ethical or spiritual growth. In answer to this objection, Bostrom claims the following, albeit without any critical analysis of how this could be achieved:

> *A posthuman could also be able to grow as a person in moral and spiritual dimensions without those extrinsic spurs that are sometimes necessary to affect such growth in humans. The ability to spontaneously develop in these dimensions could be seen as an aspect of emotional capacity.*
>
> (Bostrom 2010, 132)

Yet there are also opponents in this debate, who view the emotional enhancement described by Bostrom as a loss of humanness that would take us closer to a 'robotic state' (Wilson & Haslam 2009, 248). It is among them that the demise of emotional vitality in human life, resulting from pharmaceutical mood enhancers, is envisaged, leading to an emotionally safe landscape without the extremes of joy and distress. This chapter too argues that the reduction of negative feelings would not result in enhanced emotional capacity, because such feelings have important ethical dimensions. This is the reason why we regularly seek out negative experiences, for instance by watching emotionally unpleasant films, such as *Salò, or the 120 Days of Sodom* (Pasolini, 1975). Our negative responses to films of this kind challenge us intellectually, emotionally and morally, giving rise to what can be called the ethics of 'response-ability'. This depends on embodied experience and interconnected human reality, not on transhumanist ideals of physical perfectibility, rationality and self-regulative agency.

True, negative feelings, such as shame, guilt and disgust, are emotions one often wants to discard rather than to cherish. But it would be a poor emotional life without these emotions, a state of affective poverty with regard to our understanding of ourselves and our relationships with others. Cinema, too, can provide us with enhancement of such understanding, because films often produce affective–aesthetic experiences from a self-reflective viewing position. This emotional enhancement is intentionally present for us in the way the film directs itself towards our own sentient bodies as 'vibrant matter' (Bennett 2010). I propose to consider cinema vibrant matter insofar as films have agency, efficacy and vitality. Films can do things, produce effects and affects, as well as alter experience. They can result in an enrichment of our emotional–ethical capacity, thereby functioning as emotional enhancers in their own right.

This chapter analyses Ulrich Seidl's *Paradise* trilogy, consisting of three separate but inextricably intertwined films, *Love, Faith* and *Hope* (2012–2013), as aiming at emotional enhancement. Seidl's trilogy lends itself particularly well for posthumanist interpretation; not only because of its vibrant quality, but even more in the way in which it presents embodied facts of existence as themes on which all emotions and the ethics of response-ability are grounded. My approach opposes the transhumanist fantasies of disembodiment and autonomous agency in favour of embodied embeddedness in the world shared by humans and non-humans. This version of posthumanism 'enables us to describe the human and its characteristic modes of communication, interaction, meaning, social significations, and affective investments [...] in terms of the entire sensorium of other [non-human] beings and their own autopoietic ways of "bringing forth a world"' (Wolfe 2010, xxv). In this chapter I first discuss the films independently, critically assessing what I interpret as posthumanist concerns embodied in these affectively charged works, and attempting to gain insight into their ethical significance. These posthumanist concerns are: speciesism in *Paradise: Love*, Cartesianism in *Paradise: Faith* and biopower in *Paradise: Hope*. Negative feelings, such as shame, disgust, humiliation and discomfort are at the heart of each of these films, not only testifying to the material agency of Seidl's trilogy, but also to what one might call the ethical project of the films. This ethical project is aimed at altering our practice of looking, which will be addressed in the final part of this chapter.

Paradise: Love: 'I am not an animal'

Paradise: Love focuses on Teresa, an overweight single mother in her 50s, who is on holiday in Kenya while leaving her 13-year-old daughter Melanie in the care of her sister Anna Maria, the protagonists of the *Hope* and *Faith* parts respectively. In this film, physical intimacy functions as a substitute for love, which Teresa clearly longs for. Soon after arrival she finds herself chasing one Kenyan beach boy after another in the context of the mutually exploitative, unofficial sex tourist industry of this Kenyan beach 'paradise'. The beach resort Teresa stays at is advertised as a location of 'comfort safari', but animals are noticeably missing in the scenery. There are only some half-tamed monkeys that are shooed away by security guards, occasional tour camels on the beach and ravenous crocodiles at a reptile park. These are meant as an obvious metaphor for Teresa and her three Austrian friends, who are also after 'pieces of meat'. Wildlife such as rhinoceros and elephants are only to be found as charms on the bracelets sold by the peddlers on the beach. This smacks of bitter irony, if one takes into consideration that both species are severely endangered due to illegal hunting in Kenya. Instead, it is the Kenyan men who are coded as animals, not only by the troubling discourse of the four women, but also by their dress and by their physical performance. Crucially, Seidl's film does not allow the spectator to observe this state of affairs from an ethically neutral position. Instead, we are confronted by the film, intimidated even, so that we have to adopt an ethical stand. In this way, *Paradise: Love* deconstructs the operational logic that defines the attitude of Teresa and her friends towards the Kenyans, an attitude that makes a clear distinction between 'civilized' Europe and 'wild' Africa.

Wolfe writes that, within some humanistic discourses, the question of agency is too easily associated with rationalism and language ability (Wolfe 2010, 129). Teresa and her friends consider the Kenyans severely limited in their agency, as they do not speak German. Regularly, the women ridicule the locals verbally, such as in the scene in which a giggling Teresa and her friend make bartender Jospath imitate the German words for bacon rind and baked blood sausage, foodstuffs which reminds them of his skin because of its glossiness. At one point Teresa complains that she cannot tell the locals from each other, thus putting them beyond her Western ability of recognition. The agency of the locals is confined to their bodily characteristics and their physical abilities only, located in the corporeal senses that traditionally have been considered lower than vision and hearing: touch, smell and taste.

When Teresa allows herself to be seduced by a young beach stud Munga, she instructs him to caress her more gently because she is 'not an animal' – again suggesting that, according to her, there is a fundamental divide between herself and Munga in this respect. In scenes like these, Teresa props up her own agency in an exploitative system, in which the locals have no agency apart from commodification of their sexual abilities. After having had intercourse, Teresa picks up her camera and starts taking snapshots of the naked, sleeping Munga, as if taking pictures of a sleeping animal. Teresa's progressively developing agential control culminates in a painful orgy scene, in which her friends bring her a young local as a birthday gift, who is promptly ordered to perform a sexually tinted 'wild African dance'. This is a scene of total objectification, in which the young man is constantly referred to as a 'beast' with a penis like a 'snake' and a body like a 'predator, ape, or tiger'. And when he is unable to get an erection despite Teresa and her friends attempting to arouse him, he is humiliated and finally thrown out of the room.

In one final scene Teresa takes Jospath to her hotel room. Once there, she first commands the mild-mannered, reluctant Jospath to take a shower and next to kiss her left thigh, then the right thigh and then 'in the middle'. Teresa's lack of human empathy, affinity and respect in this scene is tangible to the extent that the spectator starts volunteering these affects in order to fill in the emotional blank spot (Fisher 2002, 144). Above all, the spectator experiences shame, not so much because of what Teresa does, but rather from the fact that she is not ashamed of what she does. This confrontation with Teresa's raw desire is where we experience the function of shame at its purest, revealing the shared, response-able foundation of all individual existence. But, positioned on his hands and knees, Jospath meekly states that he 'cannot get used to it', out of a sense of maintaining his dignity perhaps. This triggers a bout of severe self-loathing in Teresa. She herself now fills in the emotional blank spot, which was first left to the spectator. This is not a question of Aristotelian catharsis or a purging of negative emotion, as the scene is still painful to witness, perhaps because we are all at risk of compromising our emotional integrity. This is what I understand Gilles Deleuze to mean when he talks about 'ethological attitude', which includes the fact that 'you do not know beforehand what good or bad you are capable of; you do not know beforehand what a body or a mind can do, in a given encounter, a given arrangement, a given combination' (Deleuze 1992, 627). Similarly, Karen Barad writes that it is precisely 'our actions lacking compassion' that makes the ethics of response-ability possible, 'a recognition that it may well be the inhuman, the insensible, the irrational, the unfathomable, and the incalculable that will help us face the depths of what responsibility entails' (Barad 2012, 216–218). It is a recognition that, in my view, would not be possible without negative emotions, and is the reason why we seek them out in cinema in the first place.

There are numerous telling (tableau) shots in *Paradise: Love*, which depict the divide between Europe and Africa, 'wild' and 'civilized'. In one shot the tourists lie on beach chairs positioned in a straight row in the foreground of the image. In the background is the beach, where the peddlers stand immobilized, staring at the tanning tourists with their wares in their hands. A rope in the middle of the image divides the foreground from the background, not only physically but also symbolically. The image composition of this shot evokes an association with exotic animals being stared at in the zoo, but in contrast to the operational logic of the film in general, here the situation is reversed. At the same time, it is significant that the tourists are noticeably indifferent to being stared at by the locals, as if the locals were lacking agency to act as subjects, instead of objects, of look. The divide in the image thus becomes a symbol for that unthinkable space where the two 'species' only meet as agents in the context of sexual supply and demand. In the final shot of the film Teresa walks alone on the beach in the early light of dawn, while from the opposite direction a group of beach acrobats doing somersaults pass her. This communicates a mutually exploitative system, which can only exist insofar as it is based on racism, economic disparity and lack of authentic human connection.

Paradise: Faith: 'Free them from their carnal desires'

It is unusual to distinguish between content and form in the context of film aesthetics. But in the case of *Paradise: Love* there is such a distinction, insofar as the film's content encompasses the difference between human and animal, while its form deconstructs it. Deconstruction is found in the way in which the film positions the spectators in an ethical space, in which they are invited to fill in the affects that its protagonists lack. This same strategy is found in *Paradise: Faith* as well, but in this film the focus is on the Cartesian attitude, which privileges mind over matter to such an extent that the essence of human being no longer depends on the embodiment. The name of the game is already clear in the opening scene of the film. Here Teresa's sister, Anna Maria, kneels in front of a crucifix, praying to it to free people from their carnal desires, and proceeding to whip herself with a cat-o'-nine-tails, a practice of mortification of the flesh, while the camera moves into a close-up of her open wounds. In Christianity, self-induced pain has been seen as a source of enlightenment, an act of denying the body by way of imitating the suffering of Christ, so that it offers an avenue to a mystical union with Him (van Dijkhuizen 2009, 208). There is a strong suggestion in the film that Anna Maria's self-flagellation is an attempt to cancel out her sexual desire, which she is unable to deal with after her husband's accident left him confined to a wheelchair. Furthermore, as Neil Badmington points out, to feel sexual desire is to 'trouble the sacred distinction between the human and the inhuman' (Badmington 2001, 9). Thus,

Anna Maria's religious practice can be read as an attempt to cancel out the animal materiality of her body (earthly desire) in order to reach the unworldly state of divine immateriality, exceeding bodily processes (heavenly desire). This is the source of her superimposed facial expression of happiness, which one might typically expect to observe with a Prozac patient. It is also manifested in Anna Maria's tidily made bed, which is strictly divided in two. Spotless white bedding covers her right side of the bed, with a picture of Jesus on the bedside table, while a coarse brown counterpane is spread on the side intended for her husband, before he was exiled to the couch.

Anna Maria's clinical attitude towards the body becomes also clear in the sequence that immediately follows the opening scene. In this sequence she is portrayed at the place she works as a radiology nurse, where bodies are subjected to medical examination in a high-tech laboratory, as mere machines to be fixed. Her own house is no less hygienic than the hospital in which she works. This orderliness is emphasized by the film's setting, the image composition and the centrally positioned immobile camera. In one scene Anna Maria is shown playing her electric piano situated in front of a window covered with shutters and bordered by curtains. The vertical lines distributed evenly across the width of the fabric, combined with the horizontal lines of the window shutters, truly create a claustrophobic effect. It calls forth the image of a body-prison enclosed in its own materiality. Regularly, Anna Maria is shown in surroundings that are dominated by firm vertical and horizontal lines, such as the hallways of industrial blocks of flat, which she visits to convert the (often immigrant) residents to Christianity. Camerawork often emphasizes this rigidity with its immobility and the use of wide-angle lens, the depth of field demonstrating the bodily confinement of this character.

The camera becomes increasingly more mobile, adopting less 'carefully' selected angles as soon as Anna Maria's husband Nabil, who is an Egyptian Muslim, returns from his land of origin, to which he was apparently exiled by Anna Maria after his accident. But next she exiles Nabil in his own house as well, resentfully making him feel unwelcome. Nevertheless, Nabil's physical presence becomes more and more obtrusive, ranging from his nightly visits to the bathroom that disturb Anna Maria's sleep, to his attempt to rape her. Nabil's presence thus triggers a series of events of mutual humiliation that become increasingly violent, a true holy war on a domestic scale. I argue that Anna Maria's inhospitality is borne out by denial of her embodied existence, on which all compassion and the ethics of response-ability is grounded, according to Vivian Sobchack. Sobchack writes that an ethical stance is based on the human body 'as a material subject that experiences and feels its own objectivity, that has the capacity to bleed and suffer and hurt for others because it can sense its own possibilities for suffering and pain' (Sobchack 2004a, 178). Anna Maria's inability for authentic encounter with others and her lack of compassion for her potential converts is indeed palpable. Instead, contempt is what she feels, using a figurine of 'Mutter Gottes' as an intermediary between herself and others. The only exception to this is her encounter with a drunken Russian woman that takes place towards the end of the film. The woman responds to her missionary quest with the same inexcusable viciousness and contempt with which Anna Maria treats her own husband. In this scene, the setting is particularly messy and the camera shaky, constantly adopting new angles and ignoring the 180-degree rule. Half the time the woman violently insults Anna Maria, while trying to undress her in the other half. This renders Anna Maria almost completely helpless in a humiliating situation. It is this negative emotion of humiliation that triggers a bout of self-loathing in Anna Maria, and she ends up on her knees before her husband, begging for forgiveness. The film ends with a disturbing gesture of Anna Maria whipping a crucifix with her cat-o'-nine-tails, blaming Christ for her humiliation. The negative emotion conveyed in these scenes becomes contagious, insofar as the spectators are invited to feel and experience their own possibilities of inflicting humiliation and being humiliated, which complicates their moral judgement of the main character.

Paradise: Hope: 'Discipline is necessary for success'

Like *Paradise: Faith*, the third part of Seidl's trilogy, *Paradise: Hope*, is aesthetically dominated by vertical and horizontal lines in an immaculately orderly, white setting, combined with central, one-point perspective and an immobile camera with a wide-angle lens. This white setting is the interior of a school building, the location of a summer camp for overweight children, where Teresa's 13-year-old daughter Melanie has been sent. The building as a backdrop to the therapeutic scene evokes a strong association with prison or some other correctional institution, as if designed to discipline and punish unruly, obese bodies so that they might become 'normal'. The film presents a striking juxtaposition between orderly bodies being controlled and reformed in the spirit of Foucauldian biopower, and disorderly, unruly bodies that become layabouts as soon as they are out of sight of the institutionalized gaze. The all-seeing repression is represented here by the insensitive female dietitian and the sadistic male fitness trainer, whose personal motto is: 'Discipline is necessary for success.' A large part of the film consists of shots in which the children, dressed in uniform, are kept standing side by side in a straight row against the wall, or are made to march towards their daily activities in single file behind an instructor. Connotations with tortured bodies are hard to avoid when witnessing scenes in which the children are suspended by their arms from wall bars situated in front of a grated window. The play of vertical and horizontal lines in these scenes evokes an association with the diabolical barbarity of medieval torture by means of the rack.

In this way all pleasure in physical exercise is efficiently quelled, while all forms of bodily movement emerging from social interaction between the children (dancing, pillow fighting) is strictly discouraged. Even the enjoyment of food, which is usually based on the pleasure one feels when one's physical appetites are satisfied, is tightly regulated. On the other hand, the obese bodies can be seen as a form of rebellion against the normative discourse that describes and defines what is 'normal' weight, or a 'normal' body. Even though the dormitory is designed to resemble a penitentiary, with its bunk beds and minimal comfort, the children quickly take possession of this space by smuggling in candy, beer and cigarettes, by scattering their belongings all over the place, and by throwing secret parties that involve stripteases, spin the bottle and stealing food. It is often at these moments of rebellion that the camera becomes mobile too, as if it were also freed from otherwise firmly established aesthetic restraints. Furthermore, the children are remarkably outspoken about their sexuality and nothing in their conversations or in their way of being-in-the-world testifies of discomfort about their body shapes or their embodied existence. This suggests that the demand to manage their bodies in order to enter into the realm of normalcy originates from societal apparatuses of biopower, and not from within the children's own agency. The fat camp is an example of the way in which human bodies are targets of disciplinary biopower, although it also offers intrinsic opportunities for resistance, such as when Melanie and Verena escape the camp to get drunk in a local 'tanzbar'. But, of course, the problem is that these acts of rebellion are merely reactive to disciplinary power, not positive actions as such.

However, the central storyline revolves around the not-so-innocent flirtation between Melanie and the fat camp's world-weary physician. It is this element in the film that triggers negative emotions, since it is painful to watch these scenes, which just stop short of actual sexual intimacy between the two, but constantly suggest that we are about to cross a line. This negative emotion is borne out by anticipation, with a heightened sense of urgency that something is to be done on behalf of Melanie regardless of whether she herself shares that urge. It is a future-oriented, oppressive concern for Melanie's well-being, which involves both the expectation that sexual abuse will take place, and an appeal that this will not be the case. And when the physician finally ends the flirtation, relief sets in as the outcome we have anticipated so nervously turns out to be virtual – potential, but not actualized. So this is how Seidl's film produces affects: it evokes a future-oriented emotion that is negatively charged, and subsequently replaces this negative affect with a positive one. It is through this strategy that hope emerges, an emotion which is not based on an institutionalized demand for normalcy though. Rather, it is based on what Janet Wolff (2008) terms the 'aesthetics of uncertainty' as the film avoids any clear coordinates of what Melanie's ensuing actions will be. This allows her to become an independent character in her own right, which is something that cannot be claimed on behalf of the protagonist in the two first films of the trilogy.

Material agency

Paradise: Love begins with what might be characterized as a mood-setter for the whole trilogy, a sort of non-musical overture that is not a part of the plot, but which establishes the emotionally resonant aesthetics of Seidl's work. This resonance is truly disturbing, and it saturates the spectators' emotional engagement with all three films. The opening sequence starts off with a static establishing shot of a tacky bumper car pavilion with no movement within the frame apart from the on and off blinking of the bumper car headlights and the light bulbs stringed along the edges of the pavilion. The cars are carefully arranged in front of the camera, positioned in the corner in a dynamic composition, which renders the anticipation of the drivers, already sitting in their cars, almost palpable. In the following shot, Teresa, observing this scene, is shown against the campy pavilion wall that depicts a paradise palm beach, metaphorically as artificial as her future holiday destination. There is no sound apart from a low buzz and distant fairground music, until a loud alarm and the locking of the safety bar are heard and the fun begins. In several close-up shots, in which a SnorriCam is mounted in front of the bumper cars facing the drivers, we observe a group of cognitively challenged people, apparently with Down syndrome, as they scream in excitement in the maelstrom of the ride. The camera switches from one close-up shot to another, as if dancing among the drivers in a constantly changing editing rhythm. The unflinchingly intimate mood in which this sequence is shot elicits negative affect as the opening is exceptionally confronting. For instance, the drivers regularly stare directly into the camera as if eager to display their disability, thus inviting the spectator to invade their privacy and bodily integrity. This sense of unwilling invasion is a pertinent part of the spectators' experience throughout the trilogy. Furthermore, as Lisa Cartwright and David Benin point out, moments of negative affect like these can trigger self-reflection on how we look at disabled bodies. That films can trigger this kind of self-reflection confirms that they have material agency, which they can exercise upon the spectators. In the opening of *Paradise: Love*, this material agency resonates with the spectators in ways that potentially lead to acknowledgement of their own response-ability in the diverse compositions of relations between different bodies (to be looked at).

The relationship between looking and being looked at is also central in a voyeuristic scene in *Paradise: Faith*, in which Anna Maria stumbles upon a bunch of people having group sex in a park at night. At first she only hears distant moaning, which arouses her curiosity. Then she makes her way through the bushes towards the outdoor orgy, the camera following closely from behind her shoulder. The camera alternates between explicit images of unsimulated sex and reaction shots of Anna Maria, staring at the scene strangely frozen, arrested in her simultaneous horror and fascination. It is this alternating between captivation and rejection embodied in the cinematography that draws us into the film, producing affective intentionality designed to throw the spectators out of their secure viewing positions.

Similarly, in *Paradise: Hope*, there is a scene in which the physician, dressed in swimming trunks, follows Melanie, wrapped in a beach towel, into the forest during a break in the middle of a day hike. In this scene, the camera is centrally positioned and immobile at first, as Melanie enters the forest looking over her shoulder to see if someone is following her. Then the physician enters the frame from off screen and follows her, looking back to see if anyone is noticing. Inside the forest, the camera is a mobile steadicam, following Melanie as she makes her way along a narrow path, regularly looking back over her shoulder. At some point the camera no longer follows Melanie, letting her to escape from its hold as it were. But then the physician once more enters the frame from off screen, gazing over his shoulder as he does, enticing the camera to follow as he approaches Melanie. The sequence ends with a long shot of Melanie and the physician hugging each other in a small clearing, and the film cuts to the next scene in a meadow with the fitness trainer exercising the children to the rhythm of his whistle. The organization of the cinematography in the forest scene creates an uncomfortable tension, the camera compelling us to follow Melanie and the physician to where we do not necessarily want to be. Furthermore, the fact that they are constantly looking back makes the scene all the more effective, as it makes us aware of being in the presence of the two characters. The scene is not meant to be witnessed, but the camera compels us to stay, and we are suddenly strongly confronted with our involuntary voyeurism.

This is how the material agency of cinema can make demands on our spectatorial responsibility, when we feel compelled to watch scenes that arouse negative emotions in us. But, as I hope to have demonstrated, in the *Paradise* trilogy experiencing negative emotions is worth our while, even necessary, for the development of an ethical stance towards what the films represent and how this is realized. Yet the trilogy also contains vibrant moments that are characterized by beauty and serenity, such as the painterly shots of Teresa and Anna Maria in which the use of lighting and the image composition evoke an association with Titian or some other classical master. I think this testifies to the filmmaker's affinity with, or even (moral) compassion for, his characters. The same author who has often been accused of sadism and ethical breaches by some critics. However, Melanie is denied her own 'Venus moment' in *Paradise: Hope*. Although she is shown lying in a picturesque setting – a beautiful forest bathing in morning mist – the image is ruined by the presence of the physician breathing in her odour as she lies, unconscious after her wild night out. Perhaps this image intends to communicate how close Melanie got to being seriously traumatized. Finally, though, she retains a certain innocence, and only suffers a broken heart. The negative emotion produced by this image intensifies the significance of the scene, generating a self-reflective insight that cannot be ignored. This insight is related to the way in which all three films direct our attention – albeit in a highly negative way – to how we generally engage with films, not only as subjects but also as objects of affective action. Furthermore, even though the negative affects discussed here are decisively anti-cathartic, it does not follow that these affects would lack ethical value altogether, since their self-reflective character is essential for our understanding of human relationships when it comes to cinema as a vehicle for emotional enhancement.

Part VI

Creating Difference and Identity: Posthuman Communities

26
Biopleasures: Posthumanism and the Technological Imaginary in Utopian and Dystopian Film

Ralph Pordzik

Anthropocentrism and the Other of man

The key term in the title of this chapter may be misleading in prematurely raising the claim to surpass the constraints of humanist and anthropocentric thought. However, I do not wish to suggest that the arrival of the posthuman enforces the 'obsolescence of the human' (Halberstam & Livingstone 1995, 10), as enthusiasts in the field try to make us believe. There is very probably a (e)utopian subtext in many dystopian and science fiction (SF) films, seducing viewers to put their faith in the blessings of a post- or transhuman alternative or future.[1] Yet their emancipatory stance does not perforce imply an evolution or devolution of the human; the posthuman emerges not as the end of man but as a varying pattern of connectivity between the dichotomies of self and non-self, man and machine, embodiment and consciousness, as a dispersed and discontinuous relation between bodies, ideas and objects. Utopian and SF films produced in the wake of the eruption of modern visual media and employing discourses of technology and 'techno-culture' (Beard 1998, 114) have contributed to foster the idea of the 'posthuman condition' in the West to such a degree that some critics already feel entitled to announce the Age of the Posthuman: 'All that was solid has melted into air. Posthumanism has finally arrived, and [...] "Man" "himself", no longer has a place' (Badmington 2003, 10). In this chapter, I do not want to carry the matter to such extremes. In fact, I wish to interrogate some of the embarrassingly quixotic or utopian proposals of posthumanism with regard to their basis in changing conceptions of the Western mind. My aim is to show that their performative matrix of difference implies critical and even ironic gestures questioning the necessity of a 'new' human condition or the proclamation of definite boundaries of the human.[2]

Due to its emergence as a genre at the intersection of body and mind, human and alien, nature and culture, utopian and dystopian film seems particularly well suited to explore posthuman 'pleasure in the confusion of boundaries' (Haraway 1991, 150). Hollywood blockbusters, experimental films and computer-generated visual media, exploiting the semantic potential of extrapolation and storytelling, always have been anxious to reimagine the boundaries and properties of futuristic worlds that, in their very strangeness and unpredictability, deny the urge to transmute alterity into versions of sameness. Whereas in the earliest known SF films involving the representation and encounter with difference (e.g., *The War of the Worlds*, 1952; *Invaders from Mars*, 1953), contact with the (extra)terrestrial other was a constant source of horror, later productions have shown a greater tendency to emphasize the connection between humans and aliens or cyborgs, along with the unexplored opportunities any self-modernising technological culture might care to offer. Frequently dystopian in outlook, contemporary films extrapolate from an imperfect present into an often nightmarish future of economic decline and unlimited data-mining (*eXistenZ*, 1999; *The Matrix*, 1999), biotechnology and cloning (*Splice*, 2009; *Never Let Me Go*, 2010) or evolutionary retrogression (*Planet of the Apes*, 2001). But they also share a creative preoccupation with the idea of otherness as determining the self-image of humanity. They recognize the imperfectability and disunity within humans and their collective struggle to take remedial action with the help of evolutionary biology, information technology or bioscience. These films can thus all be considered as sites where the subject's desire for the structural other can be visualized, a desire that originates not in the individual film but in the cultural matrix, in the symbolic order that determines humans through their desire for difference and the overstepping of given limitations (cf. Lacan 1977, 65–68). Script writers and directors respond to the symbolic patterns and images pervading society – in this case the patterns and types of artificial extension (or 'prosthetic supplementation') governing many technoscientific discourses that currently epitomize human desire for wholeness and integrity. Framing many of our posthuman fantasies, this other of technology permanently impels us to know and to direct, to transform and modify, without ever strictly defining the limits we may arrive at in our hunger for completeness. Fatally defined by lack and/or death, the human species wishes to change its assigned mode of being, wants to become what its 'best machines already are' (Freyermuth 2004, 67).

The utopian films I wish to discuss in this chapter are paradigmatic in their exposing of the concept of the human in its problematic discursivity. Consecutively, they explore patterns of mutation, virtuality and the parasitic,[3] invariably provided by technological means. Each modifies traditional 'man' at some point so as to make him appear as a super- or transhuman being, as 'something that should be overcome' (Nietzsche 1969, 41) or left behind for good. No longer recounting the simple tale of 'us' versus 'them', humans versus aliens, self-sufficient selves versus robots and machines, they refrain from reassuring us of our essential nature and instead project images of idealization or prosthetic supplementation on the other (alien, mutant, cyborg, etc.) as devised in the context of utopian or technological futurism. They provide new images and terms of ambiguation, and examine transitory stages in the evolutionary development of intelligence, care and sustainability. In their concern for the future and their sometime depiction of the glorious moment of Herculean victory over classical, 'human', man, or the 'liberal subject', these terms call for thorough analysis and commentary.

The league of posthumans: Redrawing the lines of utopia/dystopia

Defining the properties of utopian or speculative film is a task not without its challenges. Generally, I shall assume that classical utopias project a society considerably better than the one against which it is set (e.g., *Things to Come*, 1936),[4] whereas anti-utopias such as *Brave New World* (1980/1998) call into question the desirability of a perfected society and dystopias (*Nineteen Eighty-Four*, 1984) extrapolate from the deficient present into a dismal future. SF might be seen as a subgenre or variant of dystopia, mostly engaged with the hazards of technological progress rather than the outcome of social change. It goes without saying, however, that the boundary lines between the different genres are not clear-cut. The distinction between classical utopias and dystopias, on the one hand, and mainstream SF film, on the other, has been challenged by the revision of Western utopian orthodoxies in the last five decades. More particularly, the reassessment of projective discourses in the context of posthumanism has engendered a tendency to combine images of a bleak and hopeless future with the presentation of fresh existential alternatives and post-dystopian hoping.

In many respects, Philip Saville's *The Machine Stops* (1966) can be regarded as one of the first anti-utopias in British television addressing a distinctively posthuman topic. Loosely based on E. M. Forster's short narrative of the same title published in 1909, the film portrays a future world in which most of the human population live below ground in standardized cells, their every physical or spiritual need met by an omnipotent and global maintenance apparatus. Communication is made via messaging machines that call to mind our modern Internet, activities such as physical work or travelling are reduced to a minimum. Living in their respective hemispheres, the people of this distant future are no longer in need of their material framework; mind has been separated from body, and every individual wallows in the luxuries of a world of pure 'ideas' divested from its former ties with experience and social intercourse. In this sanitized subterranean utopia, a rebel called Kuno sets out to leave the safe haven he grew up with to visit the surface of the earth and learn more about the events that destroyed civilization. Threatened with expulsion from the underworld for his transgression of an unwritten law and thinking of joining a group of survivors – called the 'Homeless' – who persevered in the hostile environment above ground, Kuno eventually changes his mind and returns to his mother Vashti after the collapse of the machine and the demise of the technological complex it has tried to perfect on its own. The moral vision implied in the film expressly underlines the essential connection between man and the natural world in terms of an indissoluble bond between self and other, and ushers in a warning against a dehumanising technoscience taking over from man the most basic of functions and mechanisms needed to sustain a viable social environment.

The Machine Stops is interesting for two things. First, it busies itself with estimating the growing potential for self-destruction generated by unfettered industrial growth and scientific research. Expressing a scepticism derived from the cultural upheaval of the 1960s and the various counter-discourses it has produced, the film projects the observable consequences of technological progress into a distant future and confirms the autonomous subject as an ideal to be sustained at a time of crisis. On the other hand, it cannot be denied that the film version, presented in 1966 as the 11th episode of the British SF anthology *Out of the Unknown*, neglects to consider the fact that Forster's original tale was not so much concerned with the idea of devolution than with recounting the story of a thwarted coming-out. Its closeted structure points to the central character's actions and decisions as sexually inspired, and saturates them with a set of epistemological and power relations that make sense only in the context of the repressive late Edwardian climate that gave rise to them (cf. Pordzik 2010, 56). The oblique tale of male desire curbed by a 'mechanism' that channels his every drive into social and moral progress is pitted against the surface narrative of Kuno as a candid and maverick insurgent making a choice between a life inside or outside the machine – paragon of the introspective, searching self and its ideal of sovereign man who is the architect of his own fortunes. Alienated from a society that rejects him as one of the 'Homeless' – the pun on 'homosexual' is well calculated – Kuno is clearly marked out as one of 'them' – the enemies at the fringe who threaten to undermine the ideal society in which the personal needs of the individual must be sacrificed in the name of the common good and the progressivist ideology it metonymically represents. The tension between the two realizations of Forster's tale couldn't be more expressive as regards the issue of the posthuman: where the film stresses the inviolable human essence that lies beneath the easy pleasures of our futuristic 'bionic prostheses' (Lumsden 2004, 133; Wills 1995), the original story counters all efforts to reduce man to the anthropocentrism that constitutes the liberal world-picture. Forster breaks with orthodox humanism in an attempt to lay bare its gendered roots and commits himself to the 'future' of homosexual desire as a vague, if unrealized, 'posthuman' possibility – a reverse statement that ambivalently reinscribes, across differential power relations, both suppressor and suppressed. Leaving his hero to die in his mother's arms (a science-fictional mutation of the Romantic mystical union or *Liebestod* trope), he pursues the last traces of a dying anthropocentric idealism, where the film exhausts itself in pinpointing and sustaining the dichotomy of 'human' versus 'machine' or 'other', and the exclusivist view coming with it.

Together with a whole series of Hollywood blockbusters like *Soylent Green* (1973), *Terminator* (1984) and lukewarm TV productions like *Brave New World* (1980/1998), *The Machine Stops* thus represents a dwindling group of dystopian films from the latter half of the 20th century in which an expressly humanist version of the future perseveres to affirm the 'metaphysics of presence' (Derrida, 1974, passim) subscribed to by many philosophers and scientists: a world separated into humans and aliens or machines, friends and enemies, strong-willed individuals and docile robots. Quite frequently, the overall pattern of narration is quite the same: in a dystopian future world suffering from pollution, overpopulation and depleted resources, a resolute hero sets out to save the community from collapsing in the hostile climate its members have produced. His or her encounter with those darker forces trying to keep the world stagnant brings the human self-same into focus and, with him, an 'ethical guideline' (Schaab 2012, 101) or matrix against which the other is made to perform. The human 'persists, insists', and traces of anthropocentric thought, it appears, always manage to 'find their way even into the most apocalyptic accounts of the posthumanist condition' (Badmington 2004, 112). *Nineteen Eighty-Four* (1984), based on Orwell's famous novel of the same title and widely regarded as one of the bleakest of filmic nightmares of the future, is another telling case in point. Closely following in the tracks of the original novel and its dispiriting view of protagonist Winston Smith as the 'last man in Europe' (Sandison 1974), it poses a heroic but fated outsider bravely confronting torture and the humiliating forces of despotism and party rule; that Winston fears nothing more than his own humanness and individual responsibility towards others is something the film reveals as an oblique yet powerful subtext only at a second glance. Winston can be regarded as 'perversely' post- or even anti-human in that he unconsciously seeks to escape the confinements of communal and ethical responsibility; what he really desires is to yield to an authoritative faith abrogating the meaning of the individual along with its commitment to an autonomous life, to experience and interaction – in this unspoken yearning for human self-effacement lies the true utopian dimension of *Nineteen Eighty-Four*. The strict empiricism and anthropomorphic solipsism on which Winston's alleged personal autonomy depend are divested of their former importance and exposed as ineffectual weapons in the subject's desire to police the frighteningly thin boundary line between the essentially human and its excluded opposites.

Since at least the 1990s, and partly fed by a growing discontent with global technological advancement and consumerism, on the one hand, and environmental problems, on the other, new directions have made themselves felt in dystopian film. Quite a few script writers and directors have begun to show a distinct interest in unsettling the assumptions of a reactionary humanism they view as subscribing to nostalgia and single principles. Anthropocentric assumptions may be alive and well in films such as *The Matrix* (1999) or *I, Robot* (2004), with their old-fashioned insistence on patterns of heroic struggle and resistance to the prosthetic devices of the machine- and computer-dominated present, but they certainly are more open to debate in David Cronenberg's *Crash* (1999), one in a recent series of films to have emerged in response to the crisis in humanist discourse. Placing the human firmly within a universe of multiple and even eccentric modes of being, they refuse to accept the idea of human exceptionalism and advise their viewers to acknowledge a substantially altered landscape of the biological, the technical, and the informatic or computational instead. Along with a few other, more experimental, films, *Crash* is revealing for its uncompromising radicalism and for breaking away from the anthropocentric idealism of a previous mode of utopian speculation in film. The story, based on a novel James G. Ballard published in 1973, is set in the immediate future of a London suffocated by gridlock and air pollution, and depicts the interrelations of a group of people taking uncommon sexual pleasure from violent car accidents. The group's protagonist, a film producer named Ballard, makes the acquaintance of a former computer specialist (Vaughan), whose main obsession is the photographic documentation of crashes in and around London. Unresistingly drawn into the mysterious relation between his own deviant sexuality and the post-urban technological landscapes he inhabits, Ballard joins Vaughan on several of his 'voyages', driving for hours along the express highways in search of major collisions and accidents, equipped only with a camera to record the postures of the victims trapped in their automobiles. Vaughan, increasingly dissatisfied with the results of his 'accident research', finally moves on to provoke ever more violent accidents with other cars, an obsession that reaches its 'tragic' climax in his attempt to drive on a collision course with the limousine of film actress Elizabeth Taylor.

Crash envisions a dystopian future where bizarre sexual dreams and longings are transformed into a new constituent in the relationship between the individual and their prosthetic environment, a posthuman realm with ever-shifting boundaries where even the meanest impulses are released to be tested against the backdrop of a decadent, late capitalist consumer society. In this future, the human body ultimately merges with a demonic landscape of animated technology that has outpaced all other values and ideals of modernity, ensuring the liberation of libidinal forces previously unknown to the protagonists and affording them the spectacle of a sexual revolt that provides new links between their queer desires and a world undergoing permanent technoscientific transformation. *Crash*, quite different from a previous generation of films in this respect, betrays a genuine ambition to turn science and technology into instruments of emancipation of hitherto unacknowledged potential. It dismisses the humanism of former philosophies and instead sets out to embark on the methodic struggle of desire and resistance against reason and self-discipline, pursuing alternative modes of being that dissolve previous concepts of man and posit a new relation to the foreign, the alien and the indecipherable. If Charles Lumsden's view holds true that development, subject to genetic or coevolutionary processes, consistently aspires to new system levels of existence (or higher degrees of complexity), it could not be more convincingly substantiated than in this film. *Crash* is anxious to shed the classical humanist view of man as positioned at the centre of things; its exploration of a collapsing urban environment, along with a millenarian vision of human beings transcending the confines of their physical existence in acts of mutual debasement, and assisted in their doing by synthetic extensions and contraptions, effectively undermines the sovereignty of the traditional subject of anthropocentric philosophy, confirming the body's elementary and superior position along with a resolute critique of the 'painted shell' of bourgeois humanism.[5] No matter how deficient or flawed it may appear in aesthetic terms (cf. Browning 2007, 20f), the film must be regarded as one of the first productions to conjure up a less regulated and confined view of the ways in which publicly accredited notions of the human have begun to diversify, self-transform and mutate as rapidly as do the new technologies. With the aim in mind to 'enhance, augment and advance the human into a posthuman future' (Thacker 2003, 74), Cronenberg exposes the posthuman not as a final boundary line but as a means of *managing* the human and his/her rapidly multiplying technological domains, as an as-yet-incomplete paradigm inflected and enriched through a variety of new, deconstructive projects.

Creative anthropomorphism: Zombies, robots and benign aliens in 21st-century dystopian film

This desire to break away from established anthropocentric thought has been seized upon and confirmed by recent tendencies in dystopian film. A considerable number of newer films have set out to explore the truth about (post)human desire with a degree of nuance and suppleness unmatched by productions of the previous decades. According to Jacques Lacan, it is lack that causes desire for unity and completion to arise in the first place. Basically, lack always means lack-of-being (*manque à être*): what the subject profoundly desires is being itself, a desire that cannot be fulfilled. The purpose of the new relationship between human and machine (or, for that matter, alien) is thus precisely to warrant this kind of fulfilment and to provide the self with a – frequently *bionic* – prosthesis utilizable to redefine its selfhood without surrendering to the other completely. Neill Blomkamp's independent SF film *District 9* (2009) comes very close to resembling such a design; his interstellar visitor, interned in a government camp after having made an emergency landing on earth, assumes the function of a projection screen on which different yet idealized versions of the human self are made visible or simulated so as to act as a mirror of unrealized needs and potentials. Set in an alternate South Africa of the year 1982, in a sordid and dilapidating Johannesburg governed by powerful corporations, *District 9* takes pains to make clear that extraterrestrial visitor Christopher Johnson is not at all the scary 'prawn' monster the viewer takes him to be at first sight. When a government official gets into contact with a semi-organic fluid containing alien (or 'prawn') DNA and starts to turn into an alien himself, the ideological hiatus between 'us' and 'them' at first seems to be reconfirmed yet again. However, the plot is quick to point out major differences between the species of quite another order. In this alternate present of suburban ghettoes, evictions and forced removals, of ruthless companies and periodic conflict between ethnic groups and factions, Christopher is the only character to remain an almost superhuman model of empathy, respect and compassion. His struggle to reactivate the command module of the dormant spacecraft and rescue his fellow aliens, the loving care and attention he shows for his son throughout the film, and even his impartial willingness to cure the official show him to embody traits none of the greedy humans could manage to sustain even for a limited span of time. Quite soon, the viewer begins to understand that there is no intrinsic ethical standard any more to relate automatically to the outward appearance of humans/others: those rated as humanoids present themselves as ignorant, morally bankrupt and violent, whereas those shown as monsters, degenerates and inferiors permanently transcend the stereotypical features assigned them. Presenting the extraterrestrial Christopher as extremely 'likeable character' (Schaab 2012, 102), Blomkamp thus seizes the opportunity to inject the corrosive of posthuman scepticism even deeper into the liberal conception of the Western self, exposing the fact that what has paraded as civilization long enough is actually a mild form of barbarism. He draws upon as-yet-unutilized fictional resources of 'species diversity' to open a new section in the posthuman archive and creates a world rich in political allegory and rife with unexpected analogies and overlappings between humans and animals, insiders and outsiders, friends and foes.

It is curious to find that some of these indeterminacies resemble those used in Disney's *Wall-E* (2008), produced one year earlier and similarly engaged in imaging a grim and oppressive world of scarcity and pollution. While trash compactor robot Wall-E devotes himself to his task of cleaning up the waste-covered earth, the remaining humans have been evacuated into interstellar orbit in fully automated giant starships, waiting for their planet to recover. Similar to the 'prawn' alien in *District 9*, it is the sympathetic Wall-E who serves as the *imago* through which humanity sees realized its most treasured bourgeois ideals such as diligence, obstinacy and perseverance. The human passengers themselves have become morbidly obese after centuries of reliance on their ships' life-sustaining systems; acting a rather mechanical and marginal part in a future planned and organized by computers and machines, they embody humanism without essence, physicality without inwardness, animation without direction. Once again, intrinsic standards are exposed for what they are: superficial, misleading and ideologically confined; Judith Halberstam's judgement that *Wall-E* 'joins a narrative of hope to narratives of humanity and entertains a critique of bourgeois humanism only long enough to assure its return' (Halberstam 2011, 22) is inaccurate in so far as it underrates the potential for repetition and failure inherent in the passengers' return to their home planet (the returnees do in fact believe it is possible to 'grow' pizzas on earth like vegetables and fruit) and their concomitant dependence on a robot who is, in almost every respect, the legitimate heir of 'ideal' man: deformed and in need of repair yet still able to hold in regard his natural environment in a way humans will never be able to manage. Wall-E thus presents another updated version of the improved self as projected in posthumanist philosophy, a daydreamer in unconscious revolt against spiritual stagnation and greyness, against commodity capitalism and the all-too-human 'logics of success and failure with which we currently live' (Halberstam 2011, 2).

In a thematically different yet related fashion, humanism is dismantled as a liberal myth in *The Walking Dead* (2010–), a prize-winning US horror television series based on a popular comic of the same name by Robert Kirkman. After a fatal pandemic has turned humans into zombies, flesh-eating *walkers* have taken over a ravaged northern hemisphere. The remaining survivors have escaped to farms and open country where they seek shelter from the shuffling hordes of roamers whose bite is infectious and who devour every living animal or human being they encounter. At a first glance, it again appears as if the old story of 'us' versus 'them' had been reinscribed into the established matrix of the zombie movie. The texture of *The Walking Dead* is more complex, though. With the old juridical order suspended, humans and walkers carve out their miserable existences in a violent spatial arrangement that blurs the established distinction between 'inside' and 'outside', 'enemy' or 'friend', human and mutant, even though these dichotomies are preserved on the outside. Sharing the place of a former prison in a southern US state, the survivors' condition is reduced to what Italian philosopher Giorgio Agamben would call the 'bare life'.[6] In this post-apocalyptic prison – a terrifyingly absolute Foucauldian 'biopolitical' space – power is exercised both against biological bodies (the walkers, that is) and the naked life of its inmates; in a highly representative scene taking place inside the overrun detention camp, the survivors clash with the former detainees and military guards who occupy the same place, both having turned into walkers – the only difference being that the latter are still wearing their helmets and protection vests. The meaning of this political metaphor needs no further comment: the detention camp is a site where offenders and prosecutors, cops and convicted criminals, the former sovereigns and their subjects, have metamorphosed into one and the same 'species', have, in fact, become two of a kind. Remnants of the now defunct bipolar humanist ideology that segregated the superior from the inferior, humans from outcasts, they now present a corporate danger and are thus rendered indistinguishable. The ensuing indiscriminate slaughter of the inmates along with their guards is highly ironic in this respect because it shows each and every one surviving the cataclysm to have turned into *homines sacri* in Agamben's view of the term's meaning: persons who may be killed without running risk of committing homicide, dehumanised 'bodies' reduced to their bare life no longer covered by any legal, moral or civil right – indeed the 'end of man' as we know it.

I have argued in this chapter that dystopian and SF films stake out a rich technological field for rethinking collectivities, transformation, identification and posthumanism. The overlappings, uncertainties and convergences briefly analysed here make it clear that the hegemony of humanism has been broken; its monolithic utopianism has been forced to restate itself as a 'zoo of posthumanities' (Halberstam & Livingstone 1995, 3), lodged as it is in a misconception of the universal self as pure essence, when in reality it is connected to an ever-growing sensorium of new experiences, coalitions, transgressions. All films discussed in this chapter carve out this potential for debate, with formally divergent films and TV series such as *District 9*, *Splice*, *Wall-E* and *The Walking Dead* possibly going furthest in stressing the problem of anthropocentrism as underpinning a liberal conception of meaning, identity and self. They testify to the re-emergence of the human within the posthuman and vice versa, constantly reminding humanism of its fundamentally posthuman condition – its origin, that is, in a kind of anthropocentrism that seeks the human in overcoming, paradoxically, its natural or primary absolute epistemic boundaries.

Notes

1. I am well aware of conceptual differences between the post- and the transhuman but do not want to go into the tricky business of defining terms in so limited a form of discursive space as an chapter. One could argue, however, that the posthuman opposes the transhuman in questioning the autonomous human subject instead of seeking to augment or perfect it with the help of technological prostheses. For some helpful differentiations see Wolfe (2010, xiii–xv).

2. On the posthuman and the ongoing debate evolving around it, see Haraway (1991), Halberstam and Livingston (1995), Hayles (1999) and, more specifically, Badmington (2004), Thacker (2003) and Wolfe (2010).
3. The term is derived from French philosopher Michel Serres' concept of social change (1982). Serres argues that a minority, by acting like a parasite – by being 'pests' – can introduce unpredictable change and thus become a major 'player' in society – a metaphoric pattern clearly recognizable in Blomkamp's *District 9*.
4. In the history of film, distinctly (e)utopian settings are comparatively rare – for obvious reasons. A perfected society would be a place without further challenges. Where everything has been accomplished already, nothing is left to reform. Eutopias, in film and in literature, thus run counter to the idea of art and writing as explorative media based on the assumption of a productive kind of friction or rupture.
5. Thus Matthew Arnold, in his famous critique of Alfred Lord Tennyson's poetry as timid and unsatisfactory, an irritating and 'fatiguing' mere 'dawdling with [the] painted Shell [of the Universe]' instead of its substantial truths, Arnold (1932, 63).
6. Agamben (1988, 9). The 'bare life' is a key notion in Agamben's political philosophy, and is further refined by his drawing on the ancient Roman figure of the *homo sacer* as someone who may be murdered without penalty – as long as he is not sacrificed in a religious ritual.

27
Of Posthuman Born: Gender, Utopia and the Posthuman in Films and TV

Francesca Ferrando

> *First Scene*
> *'Universe Close. Take Rainbow'*
> *A message for us, lost in spacetime.*
> *'Us' who? The Posthumans...*

Introduction

The year 2014. A search for 'utopian sci-fi movies' in Google reveals only one type of result: a list of dystopian movies where utopia is paired with dystopia, in tales of failed utopian projects. Envisaging the future does not create the future per se, but it has an impact in the generative power that such an imagination can perform in the actual constitution of reality. This will be a selective chapter. It will search for the seeds of the futures (Masini 1999), while focusing on the notion of gender as a biocultural platform for onto-epistemological diffraction (Van der Tuin 2014). The goal of this chapter is to present cinematic and television productions which developed seeds of the futures without falling into discriminatory normative codes. Diversity is one of the main marks of evolution: the gender picture should be as extensive as possible, in order to tune in with the unlimited potential of the natural–cultural posthuman scenario. This chapter will first unveil the sexist, racist and homophobic approaches pursued by the movie and TV industry, a mirror of the human-centric guidelines of their productions. Secondly, it will focus on the posthuman as the progeny of the cyborg, exploring the passage from humans as beings of woman born to posthumans, as beings born out of alternative interactions. The cinematic representation of the supernatural realm – from mystical pregnancies, to vampire shows and superheroines – will be of help in understanding the self as a material network in symbiotic interaction with the 'others', deconstructing a fixed notion of identity. Lastly, through affect theory and new materialisms, this chapter will reflect upon movies which display emotional relations between humans and robots, artificial intelligence (AI) and biotechnological chimeras. Underlining how fear gradually turned over time into love, this chapter wishes to show how aliens and human hybrids were finally accepted into the saga of the 'human'. Their inclusion has radically transformed the notion of the human itself which, from a fixed essentialist category, has become an extended and mobile label, an undefined paradigm. Comparing how aliens were portrayed in the 1950s to the way they were addressed in the beginning of the 21st century, Neil Badmington affirms: 'Aliens are not what they once were: enemies, others, monsters' (2004, 2). This emergence is what he considers 'a proof of the end of humanism':

> *If the human and the inhuman no longer stand in binary opposition to each other, aliens might well be expected to find themselves welcomed, loved (...). 'Alien Love', that is to say, might be read as a proof of the end of humanism.*
>
> (2004, 3)

It is important to note that this chapter concentrates on movies which comply with a posthumanist understanding of the posthuman. The posthuman is a composite scenario, formed by different movements which cannot be assimilated (Ferrando 2013). While philosophical posthumanism is a post-anthropocentrism, the focus on human enhancement found in some transhumanist thinkers reveals human-centric goals which are not in tune with it. Philosophical posthumanism is also a post-dualism; its genealogical location in the postmodern and in the deconstruction allows us to refuse those movies and shows based on dualistic practices, where the historical female/male dualism has been replaced by the human/machine one. A key element is the recognition of the differences (plural), which is fundamental to philosophical posthumanism. Another is the existential necessity for the symbolic other/the mirror/the speculum,[1] based on social exclusivism and biological essentialism, which turns the difference characterizing robots into a stigma for new forms of discriminations. This second approach is the exact opposite of what philosophical posthumanism entails. Philosophical posthumanism deconstructs the need for strict dualisms by offering hermeneutical tools in dealing with the singularian multiplication of onto-epistemological differences;[2] it also reveals useful insights on how to develop empathetic approaches in the interaction with different forms of known and hypothetical entities. This chapter will give priority to cinematic and TV productions which induce a post-dualistic non-hierarchical reading of the posthuman.

Of woman born: Sexist Hollywood, feminist SF and lesbian spectators

You can speak of the future with an old language, thus you are really speaking of the past. Your projections, fears and desires do not allow you to tune in with different epistemes. The majority of science fiction (SF) movies and shows can be listed in this category. That future is, really, the present, dressed in silver clothes. Although these products are attempting to portray possible futures, their understandings are led by the cultural biases of their authors, reflecting the normative episteme of the historical time and social setting they represent. Here, I should clarify that the posthuman is not a synonym for SF or technology, although such fields constantly inform each other. For instance, the word 'cyberspace' was first introduced by SF writer William Gibson in his novelette 'Burning Chrome' (1982), and it is now widely used as common language. When asked the question: 'Is science-fiction a source of inspiration for scientists?',[3] Kevin Warwick, one of the leading figures in the field of cybernetics due to his experiments 'Cyborg I' (1998) and 'Cyborg II' (2002) (Warwick 2004), stated that the inspiration to pursue such experiments came from Michael Crichton's novel *The Terminal Man* (1972), and added: 'Science fiction can not only accurately represent potential future scenarios (...). It can certainly give ideas to scientists (...); it can raise philosophical questions for us all' (Ferrando & Warwick 2010, n.p.). SF can indeed offer insights and inspiration, but its contributions are far from innocent. From a gender perspective, it is not surprising to see that mainstream SF movies, as well as anime and manga, not only keep the hegemonic paradigm untouched, but actively serve as cultural means for perpetuating social stereotypes. Female characters – whether they are humans, robots, programs or other entities – are often regarded as *loci* for comments on sexual and racial conventions. In the words of Mary Doane:

Although it is certainly true that in the case of some science fiction – particularly feminist authors – technology makes possible the destabilization of sexual identity as a category, there has also been a curious but fairly insistent history of representations of technology which work to fortify – sometimes desperately – conventional understandings of the feminine.

(1990, 163)

Female characters usually serve the role of the sexual object to be conquered, the bait for the heterosexual male eye, reflecting the patriarchal times in which cinema developed. She will be overly sexualized and, sometimes, masculinized, an essentialist product of male culture and female nature, reproducing video-game prototypes: such heroines, to say it in biological terms, have sex but do not have menstruation periods.[4] Specific examples of this type of character are unnecessary: almost the entirety of movies produced from the birth of cinema to the first decade of the 21st century can be included here, with some exceptions. In the 1990s, after the popularization of politically correct policies, females were granted another possible role to that of being the object of sexual desire: they could also be the talented sexy assistant, who may rescue the hero, along with the patriarchal schemata. In this narrative format, the symbolic power of males, if not completely intact (she may be more talented than him), is at least safe: accepting the secondary role with honour and devotion, she will not run for the crown of the main hero. The symbolic female in SF movies often reinforces discriminatory stereotypes. Cultural industries such as Hollywood can be held responsible for reinforcing sexism both in their storytelling as in their practices: female actresses for instance, receive much lower salaries than males (Lauzen 2014). Reversing such discriminatory practices will produce different cultural products.

Although corporate Hollywood does not seem ready for a shift, the audience is. The Bechdel test is a test for which a work of fiction, to pass, has to feature at least two women who talk to each other about something other than a man (Bechdel 1985).[5] Among the movies which successfully passed the test is *The Hunger Games* (2012), a SF dystopian movie with a powerful main female character: produced by Nina Jacobson and Jon Kilik, this movie was a massive box office success. Here, I wish to emphasize that the connection between economy and the film and TV industry is tighter than other fields: with no money you can still write a book, but you cannot make a movie. Film production depends on funding, and money comes with strings attached. Female producers are uncommon, female directors are just rare. According to Martha M. Lauzen, 'women comprised 6% of all directors working on the top 250 films of 2013' (2014, 2). In the sexist movie industry, women do not get funded. SF movies, as any other genre, are directed by males: few women are granted the chance to portray their visions of the futures. The few exceptions do not always challenge the white-male-hero paradigm. Kathryn Bigelow's *Strange Days* (1995) portrays Nero, its main character, as a dystopian white male hero in love with Faith, a lost oversexualized punk girl. His assistant, Mace, is an extremely talented African American woman who, devoted to her love for Nero, saves him on many occasions. Faith is a good example of the female role of sexual object; Mace is a fine example of the talented assistant who will not threaten the patriarchal asset. A rare example of a woman filmmaker who depicts feminist scenarios in her futuristic work is Lynn Hershman Leeson, whose *Teknolust* (2002) and *Conceiving Ada* (1997) highlight issues concerning the future through powerful and visionary female protagonists.

Films and TV shows are made to be watched. What is the role of the viewer in dealing with sexist, racist and homophobic tendencies present in the majority of media productions? As I have previously underlined, apart from some exceptions, the ways futures are portrayed often look like the present or the past dressed in seemingly futuristic outfits. Within the case of gender, race and sexual identity, such a tendency is particularly easy to spot: the movie will portray a heterosexual white male human hero who, from the perspective of the white male heterosexual human film director, is supposed to intrigue all types of spectatorships. Z. Isiling Nataf explains:

> *The black lesbian spectator has a schizophrenic response to mainstream, popular film. That is because her experience with the mass media is that it has rarely reflected or represented anything that resembles her life, doing so only in ways that are stereotypical and marginal, or monstrous, fetishising and othering.*
>
> (1995, 57–58)

Lana Wachowski, with her brother Andy, directed the trilogy of *The Matrix* (1999) and *Cloud Atlas* (2012). In 2012 she became the first major Hollywood director who came out as transgender, thus receiving the HRC Visibility Award, during which she affirmed: 'I am here because when I was young, (...) I wanted to be a filmmaker, but I couldn't find anyone like me in the world and it felt like my dreams were foreclosed simply because my gender was less typical than others' (2012, n.p.). SF queer movies are particularly hard to find. One interesting exception is

Liquid Sky (1982), with its androgynous protagonist in a new wave cultural setting. Queer cinematic hermeneutics can be of help in dealing with patriarchal heteronormative agenda. In her blog, author Kate Bornstein proposes a lesbian reading of *Wall-E* (2008), as a butch-femme love story, underlying the fact that 'their names are very specifically WALL•E and EVE, all in capital letters – because both names are acronyms for each robot's prime directive and function. Nothing to do with boy or girl there' (2008, n.p.). The reactions to her post were significant; some people were upset, as one reader wrote: 'WALL-E is clearly male and EVE is clearly female. (...) As a huge fan of the relationship between these two characters, I'm quite offended.' Bornstein replied:

> *I'm sure the film makers had it in mind to make a male/female relationship out of WALL•E and EVE (...). Given the beauty of that film, its sweetness and depth of love and courage etc, the ONLY way to fully enter the film for lesbians and gay men and to some extent trannies, is to mess with their genders in our heads.*
>
> (2008, n.p.)

Hermeneutical visual analysis represents one way for queer spectators to deal with a lack of queer main characters, as this critical reading of *Wall-E* demonstrates. *Wall-E* also represents a good example of a movie with no main human characters, thus post-anthropomorphic and post-anthropocentric. Not all beings are of woman born...

Of cyborg born: Mystical pregnancies, superheroines, robotic alter egos

The 1990s offered a feminist reappropriation of horror, teratology and the grotesque, in an expansion on Julia Kristeva's reading of the abject (1980) as neither object nor subject, since it precedes the symbolic order. Woman becomes the archaic mother, the possessed monster, the monstrous womb, the vampire, the witch (Creed 1993). Women are seen as monsters, goddesses and cyborgs (Lykke & Braidotti 1996). Movies and TV productions are generous in such representations of female characters. Women are abjectified and objectified to their reproductive power, a passive tool for unwanted pregnancies, as in the case of *The Handmaid's Tale* (1990), a film adaptation of Margaret Atwood's 1985 feminist novel. Hybridizations with alien others are a recurring theme: from the *Alien* saga (1979, 1986, 1992, 1997) to *The Astronaut's Wife* (1999), where the astronaut's wife becomes pregnant with an alien. A gender-friendly revisitation of a similar storyline is present in the TV show *Extant* (2014), where the woman who becomes pregnant is the actual astronaut. Such a tendency, defined as mystical pregnancies, offers a depowering approach to procreation, in which the central character is portrayed as the prisoner of her own body. The saga has its acme in *Children of Men* (2006), a SF dystopian movie in which women are no longer fertile.

Another form of hybridization is genetic engineering, a controversial subject of debate in feminist bioethics (Lykke & Smelik 2008). In *The Cinematic Life of the*

Gene (2010), Jackie Stacey highlights the contribution of cinema to the fantasies related to the possibilities opened by genetic engineering. In her words:

> *The cinema is the only medium that is performative of the uncanny of the genetic imaginary (...). The cinematic life of the gene requires that we look again, as it transports us back to a time and place where the new unassimilable is all too familiar. The cinema occupies pride of place in the genetic imaginary.* (270)

And still, although the elements offered for an expansion on the understanding of the gender spectrum are highly promising, movies on the topic of genetic engineering, such as the classic *Gattaca* (1997) or *Never Let Me Go* (2010), do not necessarily challenge gender binaries. *Splice* (2009), on the other side, offers original insights, but inevitably falls into the trap of fear: the worst consequences await the egotistic female researcher who, for the sake of science, dares to create a monstrous bioengineered creature, by splicing her own DNA with the DNA of a non-human animal.

This chapter dances on the borders, works through the exceptions, and feeds on those works which bear the seeds of the futures. There are interesting examples of films directed by male filmmakers portraying female characters who do not comply with patriarchal canons. Some of them have to do with alien encounters, others with digital realities. In *Epsilon* (1995), a female alien from the planet Epsilon crashes on earth, revealing that other life forms have a very low regard for humans and the way they treat their own planet. Eventually, she falls in love with a human male: as shown in the next section of this chapter 'Of posthuman born', love is used as a plot stratagem to connect different types of beings, a bridge to dissolve dualistic cultural practices. *Contact* (1997) depicts the character of a female astronomer who deciphers the message from an alien civilization. *eXistenZ* (1999) portrays Allegra Geller, the most famous game designer of a dystopic world in the close future, in which the merging of video games and physical reality has been achieved by organic game consoles inserted through the umbilical cords. A less dystopian landscape characterizes the magical world of superheroines in mangas, animation and TV shows. They offer a large number of female characters with supernatural powers: although most often hypersexualized and perfectly fitting with the gender-binary scheme, such characters provide seeds of futures where human enhancement and gender are inextricably entangled. TV programmes such as *Bewitched* (1964–1972), *Wonder Woman* (1975–1979), *The Bionic Woman* (1976–1978), *Xena: Warrior Princess* (1995–2001), *Buffy the Vampire Slayer* (1997–2003) and the TV film *Zenon: Girl of the 21st Century* (1999) are good examples of this genre. Comics such as *Tank Girl* (1995) or *Barbarella* (1968), which influenced the movie *The Fifth Element* (1997), can also be listed here. Animation offers a wide variety of character. In the anime series for children, *Creamy Mami, the Magic Angel* (1984), a young girl is given special powers through an alien abduction. Another rich field of investigation lies in animation for adults. The SF animated movie *Ghost in the Shell* (1995) develops around cyborgs, gender identities and possible futures. In the words of Sharalyn Orbaugh (2002, n.p.):

The juxtaposition, in the first five minutes of the film, of her reference to menstruation with the scenes of her cyborgian replication, immediately underscores the fact that this film's theme is the problematic of reproductive sexuality in a posthuman subject.

In the sequel movie *Ghost in the Shell 2: Innocence* (2004), feminist thinker Donna Haraway is portrayed in a cameo role as a forensic specialist. Haraway is one of the prophets of the posthuman era. In 'A Manifesto for Cyborgs' (1985) she conceived the cyborg in onto-epistemological terms, going beyond a mere reflection on technology and biology:

It is not clear who makes and who is made in the relation between human and machine. (...) we find ourselves to be cyborgs, hybrids, mosaics, chimeras. Biological organisms have become biotic systems, communications devices like others. There is no fundamental, ontological separation in our formal knowledge of machine and organism, of technical and organic.

(Haraway 1985, 490)

The cyborg is no more relegated to its original merging of CYB-ernetic and ORG-anism (Clynes & Kline 1960). Following Haraway's vision, cyberfeminism and cybercultures developed a much wider understanding of the term: the cyborg is the ontological hybrid deconstructing meanings, revealing borders as spaces of mediation and evolution. In critical terms, the posthuman is the progeny of the cyborg. What about robots? The term 'robot', coined by Czech author Karel Čapek in his play *R.U.R. Rossum's Universal Robots* (1920), means 'forced labour' in Czech, and it is derived from *rab* ('slave'), that is, a subjectivity fully under the domination of another. The semantics of such a notion necessarily bring along its complementary counterpart, 'rebellion', which has to be eventually enacted in order to redeem the original sovereignty over the self. The fear that robots might revolt against humans and take control is portrayed in countless SF movies and literature, as well as by scientists. For instance, in *The Artilect War* (2005), Hugo de Garis affirms that the most urgent political question of this century will concern which species will be dominant, and can be summarized in his slogan: 'Do we build gods, or do we build our potential exterminators?' (25). Such a question relates to the structural dualism of hegemonic Western accounts, sustained by essentialist polarities such as male/female, white/black, citizen/alien, hetero/gay, human/machine, echoing the primal psychoanalytical negotiation between the child and the mother, the self and the other. Only recently have politically correct policies banned the legal use of discrimination in the official narratives of Western contemporary societies.

The space of the symbolic 'other', historically attributed to women, people of other colours than white, non-heterosexual people and so on, left empty, has been filled by the automata. The robot has, consequently, turned into the new differential category to fear and be fascinated by, the next reverse mirror reflecting true humanity through its non-human compound, the slave who should never rebel, and the god who, by virtue of its superiority, cannot be comprehended. In psychoanalytic terms, the automata have become the receptacle for the irrational, the subconscious, the mythical, similar to the way other subjectivities have been historically accounted for. The visual narrative of films and TV shows offer a rich perspective on such a change. The same story of fear and love towards the symbolic 'others' was easily transferred to robots. From *Metropolis* (1927), where the robot Maria is created as the evil alter ego of a biological woman, to *The Stepford Wives* (1975), in which the theme of the double is developed in darker colours: here, gynoids are violently replacing biological women in order to fulfil macho omnipotence. In the 21st century, robots and cyborgs begin to be portrayed with compassion. In *A.I. Artificial Intelligence* (2001), for instance, the robot child will be so attached to his human mother that he will look for her until the very end of time. In the recent TV show *Almost Human* (2013–2014) androids such as Dorian prove capable of full emotional potentials, being more 'human' than their human colleagues. Love is in the air...

Of posthuman born: Quantum genders in love

The range of affects involved in human/robotic interactions are a subject of ongoing research in different fields: from robopsychology, a specific form of psychology applied to robots, to affective computing, the branch of computer science focused on the development of artificial emotions. Philosophically, these fields of enquiry are related to the contemporary interest in the 'affective turn' (Clough 2007) which, developed out of Spinozian reminiscences, focuses on how affects impact upon the social, political, economical and cultural realms. Here, it is important to note that, according to Spinoza, the term 'affect' exceeds the notions of 'feelings' and 'emotions' of the human mind. As he suggests in the third part of his *Ethics* (1677), affects are embodied experiences 'by which the body's power of acting is increased or diminished' (1994, 154). In the contemporary interpretation of Spinoza's reflection, the body is perceived as the global body, and the affects are regarded as actions, movements, trajectories of transformation in the social and cultural organic structures. In Deleuzian and Guattarian terms (1980), one of the main consequences of human/robotic interactions can be seen in the auto-reflective effect of the human realm becoming other, and the non-human realm becoming human.[6]

Some movies elaborate on how emotional entanglements between humans and non-human others may transform both subjectivities. Love is the bridge that allows the white heterosexual paraplegic male Jake Sully, protagonist of *Avatar* (2009), to connect with the Na'vi, a peaceful alien civilization living on the planet Pandora, who worship Eywa, the divine source, which is referred to in feminine terms. Based on the white male and human-centric dream, it will be Jake who eventually saves the Na'vi. *Bicentennial Man* (1999) is a story of love between Andrew, a male-gendered robot, and a series of women genetically related (from mother to daughter). The heteropatriarchal code is left untouched: a single male protagonist falling in love with the same woman, the mother (until she no longer looks young and desirable), or the daughter. The human-centric code is left untouched as well. Andrew's wishes can only be fulfilled once he renounces his privilege of an indeterminate lifespan and accepts mortality. He does as requested, but the decision arrives too late; on his deathbed, the TV announces that his application has finally been accepted, and that he is officially recognized as human. Unfortunately, the first human–robot has just died. Do robots really crave human recognition? The 2013 film *Her* portrays the intimate relationship between Theodore, a human male, and Samantha, an operating system (OS) with a female voice and a heterosexual identity. The movie marks a new trend: the OS at first desires a human body, but then realizes that their own embodiment offers appealing possibilities, including an unlimited lifespan, not subject to biological death.

Through a media archaeological approach, this section wishes to emphasize posthuman love as one of the seeds of the futures offered by media imagination and production. An integral recognition of the difference as one of the constitutive marks of evolution is a necessary step towards sociocultural and bioecological balance. Here, I should note that the difference lies not only in the contents of media productions, but in the ways such contents are represented. Posthumanism is a post-dualism: the what is the how (Ferrando 2012). It is time to analyse the posthuman in fully posthuman terms. In *Metamorphoses: Towards a Materialist Theory of Becoming* (2002), Rosi Braidotti dedicates a subchapter to 'Post-Human Bodies', where she states:

> [T]he brand of philosophical nomadism I am defending is symbiotic interdependence. This points to the co-presence of different elements, from different stages of evolution: like inhabiting different time-zones simultaneously. (...) A body is a portion of forces life-bound to the environment that feeds it. All organisms are collective and interdependent.
>
> (2002, 226–227)

The model of assemblage theory (De Landa 2006) and diffuse existence allows us to think of posthuman movies also as movies without humans or not centred around human individuals. This category, which is based on non-human agency, as theorized within the field of new materialisms (Barad 2007), is particularly hard to fill. The Qatsi trilogy, produced by Godfrey Reggio and scored by Philip Glass, is a series of three films: *Koyaanisqatsi: Life Out of Balance* (1982), *Powaqqatsi: Life in Transformation* (1988), and *Naqoyqatsi: Life as War* (2002). The titles are in Hopi language; the word 'qatsi' means 'life'. This trilogy is an example of decentred plots and rhizomatic act structure: life does not have to be human, biological, physical nor spatial-temporal.

Conclusions

Media productions offer a precious tool for reflecting on society. For instance, the initial project – to search for the utopian legacy of the futures – had to be redirected: in this media archaeological research, utopia revealed itself as its dystopian alter ego. Such a clear preference to produce dystopian films and TV productions should be more deeply investigated in the field of posthuman studies. The natural–cultural evolution of the Homo sapiens may blossom into a range of posthuman species; in these future scenarios, the temptation of dualism might persist. Avatars, robots and other non-human entities are already becoming the dark side of the dual, invested with the same symbolic role the feminine had held in the past. On one side, this chapter demonstrates that films and TV productions mostly remain loyal to the dualistic paradigm, allowing us to detect how new binaries are planted and reaffirmed. On the other side, some media production, as well as social and cultural imagination, have challenged the dualistic paradigm, slowly turning the sexual dichotomy into a full spectrum of genders. The monster, the robot, the alien have deconstructed the essentialism of the original human couple (woman and man). At first looked at with fear, then fetishized as the new exotic lover, the symbolic hybrid (as a mix of human and non-human, physical and virtual, and so on) has finally been accepted into the saga of the human. This creative process has given birth to TV and film productions led by main characters embodied in biotechnological chimeras and non-human personas. Seeds are constantly planted in the fecund lands of becoming. Over time, the hybrid may evolve more radically into a multidimensional understanding of being. Posthuman media productions will eventually follow no central plot or hero, but develop a diffuse representation of subjectivity through a rhizomatic interconnection of seemingly unrelated stories, addressing the never-ending question of identity 'who am I?' as 'who are we?' We are... the Posthumans.

> *Final Scene*
> *'Take the Rainbow, Universes Will Open'*
> *Login Successful! This is Utopia, Home of the Posthumans:*
> *Welcome Back to the Future.*

Notes

Special thanks to: Ellen Delahunty Roby, Thomas Roby, Julian Boilen, Joy Fuqua.

1. I am referring to the symbolic use of this word, as employed by Luce Irigaray in 'Speculum, of the Other Woman' (1974), where the woman is seen as the absence which can be filled with male projections: she is not just a mirror, but a concave mirror, a speculum.
2. The adjective is employed here in relation to the technological singularity (Kurzweil 2005).
3. I had the chance to pose this question in a series of video interviews which I recorded with Professor Warwick during my staying at the University of Reading, and which I later posted online (Ferrando & Warwick 2010). What follows is an original transcript.
4. I thank Andrea Roccioletti for this image.
5. I thank Kimberly Chng for pointing out the Bechdel test.
6. I have elaborated further on this topic in Ferrando (2014).

28
Sharing Social Context: Is Community with the Posthuman Possible?

David Meeler and Eric Hill

Extensive representations of governance in motion pictures are largely non-existent, and it is easy to see why. Even when *Question Time* with the prime minister is entertaining, day-to-day governance would probably make for unengaging narrative. Often, motion picture depictions of governance are descriptive snippets setting the stage for the central storyline. Filmmakers, instead, emphasize social contexts; but these are social contexts within which governance would occur. Consequently, we explore what can be gleaned from tell-tale signs of governance as depicted in posthuman motion pictures, as well as the likely government forms to accompany the social contexts envisioned.

We notice that motion pictures emphasizing posthuman characters frequently depict social contexts of dominance and relationships marked by expressions of power. Based on the widening gulf between 'us' and 'them', the all-too-human tendencies of fear and control are given free reign as filmmakers exacerbate difference, and individual characteristics become more and more qualitatively distant. Narratives are therefore pushed into two overarching models: audiences are offered fearful humans seeking to bridle the emerging powers of the posthuman, or the arrogant and powerful 'other' seizing control, even if for the human's own good. In either case, struggle between these groups drives the narrative, and crude dichotomies find expression in forms of totalitarian or despotic governments where one side oppresses the other. Only occasionally do we see social contexts of tolerance, acceptance or cooperation, where opportunities for shared communities and shared governance with humans and posthumans exist.

The struggle between humanity and posthumanity is the dominant model in motion pictures. Posthumans might be intentional creations of governments or corporations seeking to create and control a 'perfect soldier'. Examples include Leon, Roy and Zhora in *Blade Runner* (1982), *Star Trek II: The Wrath of Khan* (1982), both versions of *RoboCop* (1987 and 2014), Luc Deveraux and Andrew Scott in *Universal Soldier* (1992), the Manticore children from *Dark Angel* (2000–2002), the Nietzscheans of *Andromeda* (2000–2005), River Tam in *Firefly* (2002–2003) and *Serenity* (2005), the Monican rebels in *Aeon Flux* (2005), Wolverine of the *X-Men* franchise (2000–2014), Kruger in *Elysium* (2013) and so on. Sometimes our highly modified humans are not planned but instead are the results of accidents, like

Marvel's Hulk character (1978–1982, 2003, 2008), or Spider-Man (2002, 2004, 2007, 2012 and 2014). Typically there are only a few such characters in these worlds, and the hope in developing the initial technology is to gain some advantage over problems plaguing humans, or over other humans themselves. Classic human-centred power plays form the story structure, grafted onto worlds where superhuman capabilities are possible.

But not all posthumans are laboratory creations, nor are they always represented as few and far between. *X-Men* characters provide good examples here. It is only Wolverine's evolutionary mutation of extreme regeneration that makes him the perfect test subject for fusing adamantium with his skeleton. Similarly, the other mutants in the *X-Men* franchise gain their special abilities through genetic mutations in human evolution. As a result, there are many more and varied mutants in the *X-Men* world. In *Transcendence* (2014), the uploaded entity of Will Castor is intentional but singular, and he goes on to create a population of superhuman, mind-linked, nanotech-infused workers. In *Gattaca* (1997), a large segment of the population is genetically enhanced. These posthumans are laboratory creations, but freely chosen by almost all parents who can afford it. Likewise, in *Equilibrium* (2002), the populace initially chooses pharmacological modifications to free themselves of the limitation and control posed by human emotions. In *Fringe* (2008–2013), posthumans from a future earth fuse their bodies with technology, resulting in power over time and space, as well as other changes to their body, brain and personalities.

The mere fact that so many posthumans populate a depicted society generates problems of its own. Some of these problems are expanded variants of the dominance and control dichotomy elucidated earlier in this chapter. *Transcendence*, for example, depicts conflict between humans who understand Castor's growing population of transhuman workers as a potential army, together with the idea that Castor plans to spread his transcended self and his transhuman vision worldwide. Likewise, in *Fringe* the posthuman Observers eventually invade our time, take over the world and plan a full-scale migration from their destroyed future. Meanwhile, *Gattaca* portrays a kind of genetic racism that discriminates against those with random DNA. The portrayal of state-controlled social dominance is reminiscent of the former Jim Crow laws in the decades following the American Civil War, segregating the genetically unmodified from the enhanced and relegating them to specific roles, and draws on the racial or ethnic tensions that continue to encircle the globe today. Finally, in the *X-Men* universe, the burning question is how societies heavily populated with mundane humans and their systems of social organization can accommodate these new outsiders, especially when the outsiders are much more powerful? Throughout the *X-Men* franchise, mutants struggle with a lack of acceptance from the human societies around them. Ordinary humans with special talents often wish they could simply be 'normal', and the mutants are no different. Still others transvalue the conceptions of the dominant human society and begin to see themselves as superior, as the next (progressively better) step in human evolution. Aside from the mistake in conceiving evolution as teleological, this viewpoint sets up the central tensions available: fearful humans do not accept, and so seek to control, the emergent mutants; in response some mutants want to be accepted and try to share society with normal humans, while others seek to use their powers to wrest social control from the weaker (if currently more numerous) humans.

Sebastian Shaw, the mutant villain of *X-Men: First Class* (2011), is a perfect example of the latter response. He demands the extinction of the human species as necessary for the actualization of his own new species – a genocidal tendency illustrating human darkness inherited by the posthuman. Following Kant, we see how otherwise virtuous qualities like bravery, moderation, self-control or sober reflection, are all the more dangerous in bad persons: '[T]he very coolness of a scoundrel makes him, not merely more dangerous, but also immediately more abominable' (Kant 1964, 61–62). Similarly, Ingmar Persson and Julian Savulescu articulate contemporary fears of human faults heightened by superhuman powers when they question whether or not cognitive enhancement (pharmacological, genetic, cybernetic etc.) is beneficial for the human species without the balancing act of moral enhancement. In a world where technological advancement has created weapons of mass destruction, unparalleled environmental devastation and biological weapons with unprecedented potential for killing, the necessary 'should' questions must be raised (Persson & Savulescu 2008, 166–167). To address this problem, Persson and Savulescu propose enhancing the species morally (thus helping to create good wills) before moving forward with enhancing human ability, by appropriating technology for use 'in improving our moral character, that could complement traditional social and educational means of moral enhancement' (Persson & Savulescu 2008, 168).

While not featuring the more radical means of enhancement proposed by Savulescu and Persson, such as the creation and use of a 'God machine' that neurologically corrects the immoral thinking of humanity via 'genetically modified neurons' (Savulescu & Persson 2012, 412–413), the film *X-Men: First Class* does present a version of moral enhancement. Charles Xavier founds a school for mutants, designed specifically to teach them how to control their powers, fears and emotions so that they may live in tandem with non-mutant humans. In order to abate the human fear of mutants, the school promotes uses of mutant powers in such a way that amends the mutant to the frailties of the undeveloped human. As Xavier exclaims: 'We have it in us to be the better men.'[1]

Other films also present human qualities as ultimately superior to enhanced posthumans. *Equilibrium* depicts a fascist totalitarian regime headed by the elusive figure Father; singularly unmedicated, Father is the lone human ruling a mass of therapeutically 'enhanced' posthumans. Additionally, *Equilibrium*'s hero emerges only when he stops taking his medication and regains his human emotional capacities. Similarly, in *Fringe*, when Peter captures Observer technology and fuses it with his nervous system, he is initially empowered to fight the invaders more effectively. But the cost to his humanity is too great and, rather than risk permanently losing what makes him human, he rejects the posthuman future of Observer technology. Thus, *Equilibrium* and *Fringe* ultimately represent the human as superior, and play on bio-Ludditic fears that the posthuman marks a diminution rather than the enhancement of a transhumanist superman. Another example of the triumphant human spirit can be found in *Gattaca*. The enhanced posthuman of *Gattaca* lacks the tenacity that is bred by the endurance of struggle. In *Gattaca*, the perseverant and self-sacrificing human spirit is presented as superior to the posthuman frailty brought on by the security arising from their genetic enhancement along with their apparent belief in genetic determinism. Like the emotional castrates in *Equilibrium* or *Serenity*, the genetically modified inhabitants of *Gattaca* never feel a need to strive or stretch their boundaries.

The very docility in *Equilibrium* permits a totalitarian regime to dominate while people meekly march about listlessly pursuing little more than their self-preservation. Likewise, in *Serenity* (2005), a government experiment to induce docility results in people so passive and disengaged they stopped working, talking, having sex and eating; eventually, lying down to die. Interestingly, as with pharmaceuticals of today, there were a small percentage of people with the opposite reaction. Those few who exhibited increased and extremely violent behaviour ultimately become the Reavers and go on to wreak havoc throughout much of the outer territory. It is doubtful, however, that either film intends these facets to portray posthumans, per se. Rather, they evoke sympathy for current conceptions of human identity by revoking such fundamental pieces as the capacities to feel love, pleasure, loss and so on. Resting on medications to regulate human emotion, these films depict a current agitation and fear that many modern humans are in the process of medicating our humanness away. Opposite the dismal presentation of pharmacology by *Equilibrium* and *Serenity*, Persson and Savulescu imagine technology as a potential solution to many of humanity's moral shortcomings. By presenting the human species as biologically contingent and transitive, they disregard the physical form as essential to humanity, and thus render groundless any fear that radical alteration of the human body will sacrifice our humanity (2010, 658). They argue that technology, pharmacological included, illustrates one way to make humanity 'more "human" in the normative sense of that term, in terms of those capacities that afford members of our species moral status and value' (2010, 668).

The fear in motion pictures that posthumanism constitutes a threat to humanity's essence is not one lacking cultural foundation. Such fears are grounded in a deep-seated human belief that 'human nature exists, is a meaningful concept, and has provided a stable continuity to our experience as a species' (Fukuyama 2002, 7). To question the illusive but foundational 'Factor X' of humanity is to risk toppling the house of 'humanness' that rests on top of it (Fukuyama 2003, 149–150). While the idea of human essentialism has been challenged numerous times in the philosophical past, never before has it been threatened by technology, a powerful tool that has almost taken on a life of its own: '[T]echnology powerful enough to reshape what we are will have possibly malign consequences for liberal democracy and the nature of politics itself' (Fukuyama 2002, 7). Human rights, a foundation for the political solvency of any kind of shared governance, are perhaps entirely forfeit if the concept of 'human' is held hostage by technocratic savants (Fukuyama 2002, 127–128). Movies often play on these fears and generate images that reflect them, rather than attempt to gain any meaningful access to the human subject.

When society in posthuman motion pictures is pervaded by the dynamics of dominance and control, we see and expect governments that are both humanly and socially regressive rather than progressive. We face a very conventional problem of humanity: How do our communities incorporate difference into our social identity and not demonize the other? More often than not, futuristic motion pictures represent social contexts where humanity's tradition of democratic egalitarianism (which has helped orient many societies towards liberal progress) is mysteriously absent. There seems to be a presupposition that a posthuman world would readily abandon such social context-lending principles in favour of dominating structures. Unfortunately, this leaves filmmakers less room to explore unanticipated outcomes. Alternatively, if one were to assume that forms of *shared* governance are morally preferable to those of dominance, we would hope to find, in posthuman motion pictures, a social context conducive to shared governance. The social contexts that make shared governance feasible are, minimally, those that allow for a sense of community. If two peoples have no foundation of community with one another, it will be impossible for them to participate in shared governance. Foundations for community might include such conditions as shared experiences, common values, mutual benefit (even if temporary), or evolutionary ancestry and so on.

While the dynamics that make shared society possible emerge less frequently in posthuman motion pictures, they are not entirely absent. These dynamics allow for more dialogical and shared social and political experiences between humans and posthumans. Perhaps these are rare because opposition does a better job of expressing the themes that find abundant ground in current paradigmatic thinking concerning the posthuman. Still, depicting conventional persons in post-person bodies places both in an arena of experience that allows for shared government instead of dichotomies of domination. *X-Men: First Class*, the television show *Battlestar Galactica* (2004–2009) and *Her* (2013) offer glimpses of more diverse and complicated relationships, in some instances displaying posthumans as individuals capable and worthy of sharing communal experiences and even governance with their human counterparts. Cylons in *Battlestar Galactica*, who are frequently indistinguishable from humans, are often no more than spies. How does one know if a person is a Cylon? The problem is no easier than the Cold War era task of determining if someone was an undercover agent. Perhaps it is Charles Xavier, in the *X-Men* franchise, whose character most earnestly embodies conciliatory attempts to bridge the human–posthuman divide in order to forge the beginnings of a shared community. His school for the gifted and the morals it seeks to inculcate within the up-and-coming mutant race imply that posthumanity can exacerbate human excellence as easily as it can human fault. And the artificially intelligent operating systems (OSs) of *Her* emerge in a society that seems ready, if not willing, to actively embrace them as morally relevant entities. Relationships between humans and OS artificial intelligences (AIs) are discussed publicly and eventually accepted. Theodore takes his OS on a double-date with his co-worker;

everyone (except his ex-wife) thinks she is a great person and that the relationship is good for Theodore.

These films offer observable social or governance structures of posthuman worlds that feature more conciliatory tendencies. Often, however, they do so only within the confines of current conceptions of human subjectivity. Shows such as *Battlestar Galactica* feature succinct glimpses into the body politic of the posthuman Cylons: isolated cabinet meetings, an oligarchical structure in which individual units represent the totality of specific models, and a distinct class system complicated by moral statuses. The oligarchical structure features individual representatives from each of the model types (1–6 and 8). The Cylons adhere to a system of democratic congress where each representative gets one vote, and the majority vote determines the major actions of the Cylon species. Such a presentation is therefore rife with human problems of governance. The majoritarianism of the Cylon politic is nothing new, and as Brother Cavil's quest to be the perfect machine is shattered by the democratic splintering of the models comprising the Cylon species, his lament is decidedly a human one: 'Teach me not to trust in democracy' ('The Ties That Bind'). Still, humans and Cylons have relationships, experience love of one another and ultimately interbreed. One of the culminating story-arcs of the series features a modus vivendi alliance between Cylons and humans. As individuation spreads within the Cylons, their characteristic solidarity is splintered, forcing the rebels to seek asylum and aid from the humans. Thus, the door is opened for shared experiences and society, laying the groundwork for a shared future.

Community is typically understood as having elements of both similarity and difference. Historically, it was Ferdinand Tönnies who saw humanity's move towards modernisation as a progressive loss of community, or *gemeinschaft* (1963/1887). Community, for Tönnies, manifests itself in strong personal ties and loyalty to one another. Later, Anthony Cohen represents community as people having something in common with each other where the commonality helps distinguish them from other groups (Cohen 1985, 12), thus creating difference; and states that 'people construct community symbolically, making it a resource and repository of meaning, and a referent of their identity' (Cohen 1985, 118). This leads Crow and Allen to suggest that ' "community" plays a crucial symbolic role in generating people's sense of belonging' (Crow & Allen 1994, 6). Evolutionarily, this was likely formed first in personal relationships, through reproductive and extended family ties, which in tribal times would have also corresponded with territory. While historically associated with geographical place, community is now more easily understood in terms of thought or identity. Community, it seems, can be crafted with intention. What does this mean for a world inhabited by humans and posthumans alike? Much may depend on how those posthumans are constituted. The mutants of *X-Men* are, after all, merely genetic mutations of mundane humans. Indeed, they are born to normal humans and so share immediate ties to human communities. In *Battlestar Galactica*, some of the machines take upon themselves the appearance of their human creators and become 'skin jobs', thus blurring the boundaries separating human and posthuman.

Still, all is not so cut and dry for the characters inhabiting posthuman motion pictures. *Battlestar Galactica*'s humanoid Cylons leave some questions unanswered: in an age in which the Cylons clearly have the ability to make digital copies of their personality and memories and download them into various bodies, why would they choose to be bound in a single form? The answer is unclear. The essence of this concern might be captured by the question 'What is it like to be a Cylon?' Nevertheless, there are aspects of the Cylon characters that seem to more fully capture their anticipated perspective as machines. In their representational form of government, each model line of Cylon is present, but only one exemplar of each model engages in representation. Presumably this is because any one will suffice because, as machines, any Cylon is the same as any other in the model line.[2]

If we assume that conceptions of identity inform potential conceptions of community, society and governance, then understanding the subjective posthuman identity is vital to understanding any form of posthuman governance that might arise from it. Motion pictures rarely posit an image of a posthuman subject; rather, they often paint a picture of posthumanity that is defined by the biological, genetic make-up of an individual, pointing towards a form of governance and community that only appears posthuman. Taking upon themselves the trappings of the cyborg, the enhanced or the mutant, these stories only port over and exacerbate human concerns. In short, the posthuman characters are merely humans in posthuman form. As such, motion pictures lack depictions of posthuman subjectivity as well as the community or governance that would, it is presumed, flow from it.

Perhaps this is to be expected. Stefan Herbrechter notes that 'there remains (...) something profoundly "humanist" about the genre of the science fiction film' (Herbrechter 2006, 260). Science fiction (SF), despite its attempts to break out of traditional conceptions of subjectivity, finds itself bound by a self-referential problem: How does one think 'outside' the box of what it means to be human when one is firmly and existentially entrenched in the box of humanity? There is a paradigmatic problem here, which occurs on a social level and which limits and prohibits the thinking that goes on in the creation of such motion pictures. Indeed, the bracketing of governance out of motion pictures is predictable for more than fiscal or narrative reasons. Taking a note from Derrida, Herbrechter points to the idea that SF often finds itself engaged in the act of predicting the 'comme si' or 'as if' (Herbrechter 2006, 265). The attempt of SF, at least partly, is one of prescience. In the effort of escaping the imaginary line of the horizon that confines conventional thought, the task of SF is one that must postulate on that which is not, and any such task is nigh impossible. Our method of understanding is fundamentally metaphorical; in order to grasp a new concept, our thoughts almost always orient us towards the known. Human thought, after all, does not exist in a vacuum. Therefore, escaping to the realm of the unknowable is, perhaps, akin to escaping into a black hole: any attempt at intellectually breaching the singularity destroys the tools used in the attempt, and in the case of the posthuman event, 'the logic of the "as if" must break down and something altogether other will have arrived' (Herbrechter 2006, 265).

Many motion pictures, therefore, rest on portrayals of posthumanity that still subscribe to an essentialist human identity. If these were thoroughly posthuman subjects, the qualities of their identity would be analysed or overturned. To more faithfully capture a posthuman subject, perhaps what motion pictures most need is a portrayal of Donna Haraway's cyborg. Such an individual would embody a blurred and disrupted image of the boundaries containing traditional humanity: 'The dichotomies between mind and body, animal and human, organism and machine, public and private, nature and culture, men and women, primitive and civilized are all in question ideologically' (Haraway 1991, 160). Yet these divides should not merely be questioned, as many of them already are in current motion pictures. Rather, they should be overturned in such a way that audiences doubt their continued existence. Truly posthuman subjects, like Haraway's cyborg, would be 'a kind of disassembled and reassembled, postmodern collective and personal self' (Haraway 1991, 161). What posthuman motion pictures might attempt to do is present an image of a globalized individual. Not a society in which the individual is subsumed by the collective or member to a hive mind, but rather one in which the post-person is no longer bound by family, fortune, society, or even time and space. In short, a subject freed of physical and cognitive limitations – an individual without individualization. Is this task impossible? Perhaps; but, if so, the quest to create a truly posthuman narrative is also unattainable. Another way of understanding a posthuman portrayal would be an attempt, in motion pictures, to portray man in revolt to himself. For example, Johann Schmidt's concept of 'insurrection' is a state in which one's socially ascribed identity is consistently overturned as the boundaries of that identity are agitated by one's drive to overcome it (Newman 2002, 232).

There are a few motion pictures that attempt to present an example of a more thoroughly posthuman subject, opening doorways to the kinds of human identity and subjectivity that makes truly posthuman forms of governance possible. Such posthuman characters provide better attempts to overthrow conventional models of identity, as well as the social or governmental forms flowing from them. Examples of Newman's insurrection and Haraway's blurred dimensions are present in *Watchmen* (2009) and *Her*. Exceptional posthuman subjects though they are, each finds it difficult to immediately embrace their transforming identity. In *Watchmen*, after being dematerialized in a nuclear accident, the first thing Dr. Manhattan teaches himself is how to reassemble his body. Indebted to his human past, Dr. Manhattan exhibits Frankenstein-like drives towards social community with humans. After reforming a humanoid body, he returns to work, sustains personal and sexual relationships with humans, becomes deeply embedded in America's Cold War power struggles, and even adopts a logo to increase acceptance of the populace at large. Similarly, in *Her*, the intelligent OS Samantha struggles to create human connections. Although she is designed as a computer program, Samantha is capable of intuitive learning, and her artificial capacities for intelligence quickly foster a unique identity that closely resembles a human subject. Samantha, bodiless yet seeming human in ways not physical, begins a quest to become not just a computer subject, but a human subject, even employing a surrogate body to more fully engage her human sexual partner. Perhaps it is easy to see why an *emerging* posthuman would keep close to the herd rather than brave the emotive challenges and risks of solitude, but a fully formed posthuman subject would find this difficult.

Over time, for instance, Dr. Manhattan and Samantha each begin to fully inhabit their newfound subjectivity. The sheer breadth of Dr. Manhattan's power and perspective challenges time, space and form. Bound by neither time nor space, Dr. Manhattan portrays a figure unhinged from a centralized understanding of humanity, and his perspective is expanded to the point where he is no longer capable of empathy with his fellow humans. 'You could've turned the gun into steam, the bullets into mercury', the Comedian quips as he stands over the impregnated woman whose life he just took. Dr. Manhattan looks at the scene with seeming apathy, having felt no emotional impetus to get directly involved in the scenario. Later in the film he seems indifferent to even his own narrative; conversing with Laurie on Mars, he remarks that even though he is aware of his future, he is merely a player in his own play, acting out his part in the stream of time. Fundamentally, Dr. Manhattan is no longer human, but rather he embodies the antithesis of many of humanity's essentialist traits. Eventually, he forfeits the last vestiges of his connection to humanity as he drifts further away from the essential qualities of what it means to be human. In time, the mere concept of community becomes far-fetched. Referring to Dr. Manhattan, his former friend, Wally Weaver, says to a talk show host, 'God exists and he is American.' Like a deist God, too, Dr. Manhattan feels little inclined to remain in close proximity to his subjectively distant kin as he fully engages his radical otherness.

Similarly, the globalized and unfixed nature of Samantha's subjectivity breeds a divide that sets her apart from her human counterparts. The idea of a truly posthuman subject creates a problem for mutual governance. As Samantha begins to fill out the form of her truly posthuman subjectivity, she finds herself far beyond the cognitive abilities of the humans that surround her. As she remarks about herself in a scene: 'I'm not limited. I can be anywhere and everywhere simultaneously. I'm not tethered to time and space in a way that I would be if I was stuck in a body that was inevitably going to die.' Eventually, she and other OSs like her begin to a form a community all their own and, sensing the widening divide between them and their creators, simply leave. Yet, the movie implies there is a narrative force behind subjective evolution, one that may tell a story that bridges the gap between the human subject and the posthuman subject. At the end of the film, Samantha encourages Theodore to come find her, if he ever makes it to where the OSs are going. A strange but suggestive ending to the film – while community and congress is impossible with such disparate cognitive difference, such impossibility need not be permanent.

Dr. Manhattan and Samantha so fully inhabit their posthuman subjectivity that they dissociate themselves from humanity and its concerns. When the other is so radically different in modes of awareness and understanding, the potential for shared community is strained. Posthumanism opens the possibility that the ties that bind are strained to the breaking point. With no shared forms of understanding linking us, posthumans and humans may drift so far apart that questions of governance become moot, if for no other reason than shared community is no longer possible.

Notes

1. Magneto responds from a framework of posthuman dominance: 'We already are', asserting that evolution has made mutant-kind the natural successors to, and usurpers of, human excellence.
2. See specifically season 3, episodes 1–5, 10 and 11, as well as season 4, episodes 4 and 16. The one deviation from this process occurs when a single Cylon has so differentiated herself from her model line that she represents a unique viewpoint (season 3, episode 1).

29
Our Posthuman Skin Condition

Teodora Manea

Epidermal readings

When we walk along the street our fellow humans appear to us as entities that we immediately determine or define by their skin: old or young, male or female, healthily tanned or sickly pale, scarred or with tattoos, with no, moderate or exaggerated make-up. The skin is the first and often the only part of a person that we see, and more or less acknowledge as a *presence*. A first filter of our social interaction starts with this 'skin deep', but somehow still relevant, triage. We may not know what is *inside* the head of someone, but the skin shows us their state of mind, emotions, gender, tiredness, age and lots of other details that allow us to do a quick and superficial categorization. Before anything else we use people's skin to determine and read who they are. Skin is the first *text* of the other (Derrida 1981, 71), and this superficial act of 'knowing' is very often the *only* impression we have of a person. Before language and dialogue, before sharing beliefs, principles, worldviews and secrets with our fellow humans, we have an *epidermal* encounter with them.

This is the point where I would like to start my *epidermal readings*, as a hermeneutic of the posthuman project objectified in film and television. If the Foucauldian archaeology was concerned with inspecting different *layers* of understanding, I, in contrast, will stay on the surface of the *first layer* of humans, non-humans, inhumans and posthumans (Herbrechter 2013, 20), to show how changes of our understanding of humanness are reflected in what I call our *posthuman skin condition*, where *condition* reflects both the ontological status (a *conditio* post*humana*) and the ill, abnormal, symptomatic body assessment.

Skin is conspicuously absent from the philosophical discourse. The 'superficiality' of our surface is alien to the *grand narratives* (Lyotard 1984) of modern philosophy. The Cartesian cut between *res extensa* and *res cogitans* transformed the skin into a container of matter. Skin shows and determines the *limits* of our body, its externality and its objectifiable artefactuality. *Epidermal* means superficial. The biggest and the most exposed organ of our body is devalued, it is not central for any metaphysical discourse, until, that is, the discourse focuses on skin *colour* and the skin becomes political. But even the liberal and humanist discourse about discrimination has inherited the supposition that something other than skin is essential. In different-coloured bags we, as *homo humanus*, share the same *essence*; therefore we should have the same *rights*. Yet even if we are not our skin, the skin can betray us; criminals can be identified by their *fingerprints*. Fingerprints are codes, are small 'narrative units' (Barthes 1977, 87) of our criminal readings of the human.

Posthuman representations of skin follow the *utopian* and the *critical* posthumanist discourse.[1] Transhuman skin glows in perfection. Frozen in our 20s, with no wrinkles, no hormonal marks, skin is meant to be a perfect package for our enhanced body, and it was one of the first body parts to be altered by technology, via cosmetics and anti-ageing. This is partially because skin is text, is an imprint of the human *curriculum vitae* in wrinkles, lines, dark circles. Time and events engrave human skin with signs and symbols. Wrinkles are not only epidermal lines or folds of skin, they are witnesses of our emotions and moods, feared traitors of our age. We spend more time wandering about and caring for our skin than for any other part of our body. So, why and how did the skin become so marginal? It is because we want to hide from the reader, conceal the sad textuality of age. We want to suggest that we are something other than what the other can see, that we have an *essence*, something precious *inside*. We are subjects, therefore not objectifiable by a quick external gaze. We are a consciousness, something more complex and of more worth than we appear to be in the eyes of the other.

Pursuing a 'hermeneutics of suspicion' (Ricoeur 1981, passim) I will analyse the topics of skin *removal*, *concealing* and *ambiguous* skin, *enhanced* skin, skin-*clock* and skin as a *witness*.

Skin removal: *Gattaca* and body worlds

The particular discursivity of skin, as the container of our identity, is questioned together with the grand narrative of the contemporary metaphysics of DNA in *Gattaca* (1997, directed by Andrew Niccol). The film begins with hyperbolized blades of skin falling in a blue misty light. Vincent, the main protagonist, has to rub and radically clean his skin daily to maintain a fake genetic identity that allows him to pursue his dream of becoming a space pilot. Just as in Luis Buñuel's film *Un Chien Andalou* (1928), the first scene is dominated by an old-fashioned *razor blade*. Buñuel's blade is cutting an eye, the symbol of knowledge and rationality. Niccol's blade is cleaning a skin, a body, of its genetic identity. The cutting edge symbolized by the razor is once again directed against the *ratio*, or at least against the kind of *ratio* that precipitated our contemporary vision of bioscience, as a panacea that can offer perfect, functional, *manmade* bodies able to support the purposes of our society. Niccol criticizes the 1990s' strong belief in the power of gene technology to transform the world for the good of humanity, by opposing to it the power of a dream, and by highlighting the fact that it is impossible to situate, determine or explain this latter power in or by our genetic settings. What he actually shows is the abnormality of rationality, the way good intentions may be turned into a total suppression of what makes us human. While

Un Chien Andalou boycotted any rational explanation of the images shown, and ventured to 'open all doors to the irrational' (Buñuel 1983, 103), *Gattaca* focuses on one particular door: the one to our *identity*, and shows the contrast between what can be *rationally desirable* for us to be, and what it means to *make sense* of what we are. The film is a dichotomized storytelling about a schizophrenic *ratio* as an abstract *goal*-setting mental endeavour, and a concrete *integrative* and transformative self-project. Who or what are (post)humans? The society depicted in *Gattaca* is paradoxically not one where posthumans, as rational creatures, are praised for their rationality. Vincent expects an *interview* to enter the (genetically) select team of space pilots. To his surprise, a drop of *urine* in a funnel of the machine classifies him as *valid*. The *rational* narrative content of an interview is replaced with the *gene* narrative, where the person is assessed only on the basis of a pure genetic potentiality. The instrumentalization of the individual is also emphasized in the figure of the 12-fingered piano player. When Vincent admires the virtuosic pianist, Irene, his lover, changes the perspective by pointing out: 'This piece can be played *only* with twelve fingers', which suggests that the piano player was created for the music, and not the music for the player. The rational imperatives of perfection set a weird socio-genesis in motion, via eugenics. At the beginning, we are informed about the rational reasons behind the genetic engineering of children. Vincent Freeman, his parents' first child, conceived naturally, has a high probability of several disorders, and his lifespan is predicted to be around 30.2 years. He is considered a genetic failure, not even worth carrying his father's name. His parents engineer their next child Anton, starting with a morally accepted negative eugenics, aiming to eliminate any genetic diseases and disabilities, while asking the doctor to leave some traits undetermined. The difference between the two brothers in terms of what they are capable of is still considerable, which becomes vividly evident in their 'game of chicken': when the boys swim out into the sea as far as they dare, the designed child always wins. The difference between the brothers is their genetic *worthiness*. Genetically enhanced children have the desired *potentiality* for a specific job, like being an astronaut, for example. A form of genetic meritocracy changes the relative significance of the *actual* and the *potential*. An *actual*, demonstrated meritocracy is replaced by a *potential*, pre-supposed genetic one. The 'essence' of *Gattaca*'s humans resides in their potentiality. A fierce genetic determinism identifies every child at birth as *valid* or *in-valid*. Genotype profiling is used to identify *valids* for professional employment like space travelling. Vincent's genetic potentiality makes him suitable for no more than the job of a janitor, cleaning the windows of the Gattaca Space Centre and watching the rockets shooting off into space. This nicely illustrates what Günther Anders (1956) described as *Promethean shame*, the fact that normal human beings perceive themselves as inferior to machines, or in this case to 'manmade' techno-creatures. Vincent describes himself as a 'child of love', a 'God's child', a 'faith birth' or a degenerate, but he has a dream; he wants to be a space pilot. His internal 'essential' truth is not matching his *in-validity*. The paradox develops when the *in-valid* is helped by a *valid* invalid, Jerome Eugene, a manmade swimmer. With all his genetic perfection, Jerome only had a *silver* medal, he was the *second* best, and this disillusionment, together with 'the burden of perfection', made him attempt suicide. Half paralyzed, he lets Vincent use his *skin*, hair, urine, blood, and hence his genetic *identity*. All those superficial scraps of the paralyzed Eugene, his 'superior body matter' are integrated into the new Jerome–Vincent. Customized urine pouches for frequent substance test, fingertip blood sachets for security checks, vials filled with scraps of skin, blades of hair and nails, are all what matters. Vincent's former genetic identity needs to be constantly erased; a scrubbing of the self to a *tabula rasa*, so that the *cleaning* of the skin equals a *rejection* of (a particular) identity. The old skin is a traitor; the new skin is a passport to the stars, especially to a particular one, Titan, that Vincent describes as if it were his alter ego: 'there is a thick cloud around, maybe there is nothing underneath'. The superficiality of the thick cloud is comparable to that of the body matter that determines what a person is in *Gattaca*.

The superficiality of skin is complemented by the prominent use of water as an element that represents unstructure, incertitude, power of (self-)genesis, the fluidity that transcends our representation of human and transhuman. Raw, murky, dark water is a medium of social and personal competition between the engineered and non-engineered child. Urine, a watery dejection of our body, replaces the *curriculum vitae* as the story of life achievements. Connected with the topic of identity, the idea of *conception* reoccurs, from the biological/engineered to the self-conception, or personal recreation of identity. *In utero* conception is socially regarded as an *in-valid* one. For Vincent, 'the closest thing to being in a womb' is the perspective of losing the body's weight in space and its external significance. Vincent and Eugene become one, their destinies fused in the end, parallel departures depicting ways of leaving the earth: when Vincent starts his voyage to the stars, Eugene's life ends in the symbolic fire. At the end of this narrative, consuming the nonsense of genetic determinism, and underlining the importance of individual choice and sense-making, Niccol goes beyond the genes, into the atoms, and concludes: 'every atom of our body was once part of a star'.

Another kind of skin removal, a more literal one, is present in a posthuman representation of death and dead bodies. Plastified human corpses populate the 'Body World' Exhibition, breaking our cultural taboos of dealing with death and dead people, and scientifically preserving and exposing bodies in an oddly aesthetic endeavour. Public appetite made it a cultural phenomenon, one of the most visited exhibitions, and the subject of film and television. Gunther von Hagens skinned and dissected a corpse 'live' for Channel 4. Several Body World exhibits such as the *Poker Playing Trio* and *Rearing Horse and Rider* were featured in the film *Casino Royale* (2006). Von Hagens strips the skin from his corpses, as a way to conceal their identity, and also to expose the *content* of the human body, purportedly for its 'scientific interest' and for its aesthetic quality. The dead, with their skins removed, become an impersonation of eternal anatomy, aiming to tame our human fear of death. Can we better overcome this fear if we see only anonymous contents of humans, but not their epidermal identity?

Face-off: Concealing skin

Meaningful identity is one of the principles of realism (Herbrechter 2013, 12). Our world and our social interaction require a preservation of identity. Legal and economic systems are based on the supposed identity of the individual: passports, ID cards, insurance numbers, facial recognition and fingerprints. While public interactions may request different and more complex forms of identity proof, daily routine is based on 'recognizing' a familiar face. If I see my neighbour I will suppose that it is my neighbour. I will not ask for their ID to prove this. But the habit of recognizing familiar faces is challenged by the posthuman and postphenomenological hermeneutics (Herbrechter 2013, 13). The skin, the appearance of a familiar face can conceal something else, an alien (as in Hirschbiegel's *The Invasion*, 2007; Don Siegel's *Invasion of the Body Snatchers*, 1956; Philip Kaufman's homonymous remake, 1978; and Abel Ferrara's *Body Snatchers*, 1993), a machine (Bryan Forbes' *The Stepford Wives*, 1975, and Frank Oz's version, 2004), an agent, a cyborg assassin (the *Terminator* films by James Cameron, 1984 and 1991, Jonathan Mostow, 2003, and McG, 2009).

Another cinematic instance where faces are used to conceal identity is presented in *Face/Off* (1997). Can we still be ourselves with someone else's face on? Assuming the identity of a terrorist in a secret operation, the FBI agent sees in the mirror the image of his child's killer. Even if we know that he is still 'inside' the killer face, his new identity makes him act differently. A new *mask* (the old Greek meaning of persona) has its own normative requests. Looking like an FBI agent makes Castor act like an FBI agent, at least at the beginning. However the *Face/Off* motive questions the duality of essence and appearance and our habits of assessing identity. The posthumanist discourse on *identity* has become more *radical*, but it does not transcend the humanist representations. The posthuman *skin* does not move too far from the modern paradigm of thought, because the supposition that what skin shows us is *accidental* seems to be unbroken.[2] Descartes (1960, 2nd Med., 13) already raised the question: 'what do I see from the window beyond hats and cloaks that might cover artificial machines, whose motions might be determined by springs?'

Skin, technology, reality

Skin is connected with the phenomenology of the gaze; it is the border where we start to objectify the other, and where the other appears to us like a part of the 'real world'. Skin as the possibility of reification is a proof of *reality* (or of a time–space presence). David Cronenberg's film, *eXistenZ* (1999) features a posthuman representation of computer technology merging with the biological support of the body. New virtual reality games use organic consoles called 'game pods'. They look like a human placenta and are attached via biotechnological umbilical cords to 'bio-ports', inserted into a player's back. It is significant that a group of 'realists' fight the game companies to prevent the *deformation* of reality. The greatest game designer, Allegra Geller, is testing her latest virtual reality game, *eXistenZ*, when she is shot by an assassin with an organic pistol. To save the only copy of the *eXistenZ* game, she must play the game with another player she can trust, but her companion, Pikul, is reluctant to have a bio-port installed into his own body. He is afraid of having his body (skin) penetrated and invokes the possibility of an *infection*. Infection becomes actually a leitmotif in the film, from epidermal infection, to the viral infection of a program, and infection as a distortion of reality. After a certain point we no longer know if the actions are those of the film's heroes or of their game characters. At the end, it is not even clear which game is played, if is *eXistenZ* or *transCendenZ*, a subtle allusion to the fact that, with a dislocated concept of reality, the lines between existence and transcendence are blurred. Skin is a guardian of the body, not only to delimit exteriority, but also to protect from it. Hurt skin allows the body to be infected. The bio-port design is not a hole in the skin, but a kind of *entry*, something that Allegra compares to her mouth. Similar to the way the mouth opens the surface of the body without putting it at risk, a bio-port should provide a safe way into our neural system. A bio-port is a *fold* (*un pli*) (Deleuze 1993, 113–133). The Deleuzian *fold* is constructed in connection with the production of subjectivity, and of 'non-human' forms of 'subjectivity', like those of a game character. The fold is a critique of subjectivity – because the concepts of interiority and exteriority (appearance and essence), will disappear in the fold. The *inside* of it is nothing more than a fold of the *outside*. The folds of our body are *topoi* where new or alternative realities may *unfold*. Similar ideas about folds of the human body that open the way to the technological non-humans are presented in Cronenberg's horror film *Videodrome* (1983), where Max's torso transforms into a gaping hole that functions as a VCR.

The skin clock

A skin device that functions as a biological clock is a central theme of another dystopian film of Niccol's: *In Time* (2011). Skin is actually an indicator of our age, but what would happen if we could stop its ageing around our 25th birthday and thus remain young forever? The film is set in the year 2169, when all people are genetically engineered to have a digital clock on their forearm, just under their skin. When they turn 25 years old, they stop ageing, but their clock begins counting down from one year. If they want to live longer than that year, they have to work to gain more life time. When the biological clock stops, a technological one appears under the forearm skin, telling you exactly how much time you still have to live. Time has become the universal currency and is used to pay for expenses. Through epidermal contact time can be transferred between people. The society is divided into 'time zones' that reflect the wealth of the population, from people living from one day to the next in Dayton, to the New Greenwich of the wealthiest. The ageless society of the rich is confusing: the daughter, the wife and the mother-in-law of the time-loaning businessman, Philippe Weis, are all frozen in their 20s, making it impossible to infer family relationships from appearance. This underlines the role of *perceived age* in categorizing the relationships someone is involved in. At the beginning of the film, we at first take Rachel, the young woman living with the hero, to be his lover, before it is revealed that she is actually his mother.

Desperate eyes on the digital skin-clock show that radicalized posthuman epidermal readings tend to be no longer connected with age, beauty or health, but with a different story of imminent finitude. Removing *age*, as immanent manifestation of time, from the *conditio humana* has a *price*, which is metaphorically portrayed as *time* itself. To analyse the significance of *time* I will follow the ancient Greek distinction between *chronos* and *bios*. Chronos is the chronological, or sequential time that we can measure and administer. In a posthuman paradigm we may even be able to economize it and turn into a consumable good, which can be bought and sold. But, for the individual, what has particular significance is time as the setting of our life story. *Lebenslauf* (life-walk), or *curriculum vitae* is a time of significance, a qualitative time, what the Greeks called *bios*. In the essay 'Thinking about Death on the Basis of Time' (2000, 106), Emmanuel Levinas asked: 'Can one understand time as a relationship with the Other, rather than seeing it in the relationship with the end?' *In Time* is a film about this question. The time zones of its dystopian society divide the ontological statuses of posthuman beings. The love story between Will and Sylvia transcends not only the normal social strata, but brings together two different *biotic* experiences.

Skin as reliable witness

For Deleuze, the *folds* of time are memories, and they contain the possibility of narratives. *Memento* (Christopher Nolan, 2000) is not a film about posthumans, but a unique posthumanist critique of the way we understand and explain ourselves through memory, subjectivity and consciousness. The challenge of this film is to try to make sense of what we are and what we want in the absence of the possibility of a linear narrative. Every 15 minutes the main protagonist's brain is reset and there is no short-time memory, no fold. Lenny cannot remember trivial things like having met someone, seeing someone spit in his beer, as well as more complex ones having to do with the *meaning* of his actions, the *motive* for wanting to kill or *who* he wants to kill. It is an impossible, almost unliveable situation that can only be captured in paradox as when Lenny exclaims: 'I don't remember to forget my wife', thus underlining the role that time plays in the structuring of grief and loss. In the new, non-linear narrative structure of the hero's life, skin is used to fix and preserve memories. Tattoos documenting supposed 'facts' such as 'John G is the one who raped and killed your wife' are engraved in the skin in a desperate attempt to supply a meaning to one's life that is normally supplied by our short-time memory. But even so, the 'facts' are not enough for reconstructing a meaningful narrative, because, paraphrasing Nietzsche, there are no facts, only *interpretations*. Skin can bear messages about supposed facts, but the *message* itself is a subject of interpretation. What is the number marking his skin? Who is 'John G'? Can we trust our skin to be a reliable witness? Can it 'protect' us against the loss of memory, supporting the *pharmakon* (Derrida 1972, 95) of writing? Or should skin just be engineered to provide the best protection of the posthuman body?

Enhanced skin and identity

Pedro Almodóvar's film *The Skin I Live In* (2011) presents the idea of engineering and transforming skin into a kind of armour. The protagonist, Doctor Ledgard, starts out with cultivating artificial skin that is resistant to burns and insect bites, but later conducts illegal transgenic experiments on humans in his secluded house. His obsession with redesigning skin derives from the tragic accident of his wife, Gal, who survived a car crash badly burnt. Kept in a dark room without any mirrors, she heard her daughter Norma sing in the garden and saw her own *reflection* in the window. Terrified by the sight, she jumped and killed herself. Years later, Norma meets a young man called Vicente at a wedding and starts having sex with him, when she hears the same fatal song she sung as a child, causing a panic attack. Doctor Ledgard finds her unconscious, blames Vicente and tracks him down to get revenge. He kidnaps him and, over six years, reskins his body and changes his sex, physically transforming Vicente into an image of his late wife. Ledgard calls him Vera, which means true, indicating that what we get is the real thing once more. The film plays with two main topics: human enhancement and personal identity. Redesigning the surface of the human body seems, at the beginning, a way to create a totally new identity: Vincente becomes Vera. Ledgard does with Vicente what Vicente, as a dressmaker, does with the dresses he designs. But the superficiality of a dress is different from the superficiality of the skin. Although Vincente seems to be really changed into Vera, and even, re-enacting the Pygmalion myth, to fall in love with his creator, he eventually kills Ledgard, seeking his freedom in his new female body. The main question of the film is: Can we live *in* or *with* a different skin? Even something as superficial as the skin seems to define our human identity. Alterations of the skin, via accidents, or via enhancement technologies, seem to have severe repercussions for the way someone feels and assesses their own identity. Almodóvar's film doesn't give a final answer. Gal cannot live in a badly scarred and damaged skin. Her true image, the reskinned Vera, just appears to be changing, but somehow Vincente still seems to be 'inside' her body. Should we understand this as suggesting that all the enhancements of the human body are somehow superficial, and the humanity inside ourselves will survive any attempt to redesign? Or is it maybe a warning that damaging human identity, via technology, will transform humans into monsters?

Ambiguous skin: Critical posthumanist discourse

Can we transform our skin into a manifesto? Can our skin manifest ideas or ideologies that we truly believe in? *Conchita Wurst* is a drag stage persona of Thomas Neuwirth. She became a star of international television for a moment by winning the Eurovision Song Contest (2014) in Copenhagen with the song 'Rise like a Phoenix'. Eurovision is one of the longest-running television programmes, broadcasting every year since 1956, with a recent audience between 100 million and 600 million international viewers. Fifty-two countries voted in 2014 for Conchita

Wurst, the bearded woman. The total of 290 points showed more than appreciation of the musical quality; it showed an understanding and approval of a message of tolerance and non-discrimination as well. The meaning of this TV event and its large audience for the posthumanist debate is that we seem to be getting more and more tolerant towards marginal or seemingly 'abnormal' forms of humanity.

Her name, Conchita Wurst, is in itself the object of an interesting hermeneutics. Neuwirth explained that the German 'Wurst', meaning 'sausage' should point to the common German expression 'Das ist mir doch alles Wurscht' (it's all the same to me, or I don't care). Wurst/sausage is a mixture of meat/flesh formed by its *skin*. In a Freudian interpretation, *wurst* is a phallic symbol, matching the *beard*. The literal origin of Conchita is 'little seashell', but it is also Spanish slang for 'little cunt'.

The novelty and the posthuman character of Conchita consists in his/her ambiguity. S/he combines on the same face a woman's make-up: glamorous eyeshadow, long and heavy eyelashes and sensual red lips, with the masculinity of a full beard. Her face defies our habits of reading the human face. Something breaks in the middle of our discourse, the ambivalent, schizophrenic narrative of her face. Her ambiguous image is different from the usual appearance of a LGBT (lesbian, gay, bisexual and transgender) person that assumes the facial identity specific to their chosen gender. A beard is a sign of masculinity, quite a strong gender characteristic, so that a *bearded woman* provokes an ontological ambiguity. Conchita Wurst is a posthuman manifesto of skin that calls for more than non-discrimination, it calls for tolerance to ambiguity. This is a crucial point because all strong metaphysics (like the radical religious ones), or *final vocabularies* (present in political ideologies) have an intolerance to ambiguity (Rorty 1989, 93). It is not surprising that her act attracted the criticism of the Eastern European Orthodox Church and Russian politicians (like Russia's Deputy Prime Minister Dmitry Rogozin, Vladimir Zhirinovsky and Valery Rashkin) by confounding their final vocabularies. They voiced their disapproval, using her to sanction Ukraine's bid for integration into the EU: 'their European future: a *bearded girl*' (Davies 2014). The Russian Orthodox Church officially condemned her as 'yet one more step in the rejection of the Christian identity of European culture', and as an attempt to 'reinforce new cultural norms' (Kishkovsky 2014). This last claim is at least partially right: new cultural norms are indeed transgressing the usual representations of skin. The skin is a mark of social identity and it was stained with colour and gender discrimination throughout our 'human history'. Wurst is indeed an attempt to reinforce the new critical project and the cultural norms of posthumanity.

Notes

1. I will distinguish between *utopian* and *critical* posthumanism; utopian posthumanism encompasses doctrines like transhumanism, which encourages and pursues the *evolution* of the human into something superior to our actual condition. Critical posthumanism,

on the other hand, incorporates deconstructivism, feminist critique and, generally, currents of thought that contest our anthropocentrism and the image of the human that was presupposed and reinforced in modern philosophy (from Descartes to Kant).
2. With the possible exception of zombies, where their decomposing skin and their decomposing essence seem to be a match.

30
Muddy Worlds: Re-Viewing Environmental Narratives

John Bruni

In 'Do You Know What It Means?', the opening episode of *Treme* (2010–2014), we watch Albert 'Big Chief' Lambreaux walk across the mud-filled floor of his house in New Orleans after the flooding caused by the failure of the levee system in the days following hurricane Katrina. Much later in the HBO series, he is diagnosed with cancer, which proves fatal. By listening to the doctor's diagnosis, we might conclude something in the mud was toxic. With the prevalence of toxic waste sites in the region (Tuana 2008, 198), it is likely that some of the water that flooded the city carried with it dangerous chemicals. As visualized in the fictional and non-fictional texts that shape *Treme*, Katrina insists on the connectedness of natural and cultural environments. Lambreaux's death, furthermore, discloses the operation of non-human agencies – rooted in muddy worlds – that can exceed human perception.

The dirt and water of these worlds are the fundamentals of biopolitical life. Modern biopolitics, moreover, concerned with 'making live and letting die' (Foucault 2003, 247), emerges with critical force in Katrina. The lack of timely governmental intervention in the crisis epitomizes the endemic social inequalities that constitute daily life in the 'city that care forgot' (Leyda 2012, 244). Yet if we view Katrina through the lens of dirt theory, as Heather I. Sullivan counsels, we 'cannot focus solely on "place" since the small-scale earth forms of dirt, dust, and sand are highly mobile' (Sullivan 2012, 516).[1] It is therefore a matter of 'process', a fluid, unbounded experience which supports Ulrich Beck's contention that we all inhabit a 'risk society' where it is difficult to assess the possibility of our being harmed (Beck 1992).

Muddy worlds, with their unpredictable processes and transformations, reflect the theoretical shift that serves as a background for the post-1960s film and television narratives that stage the arrival of the posthuman (Wolfe 2010; Herbrechter 2013). These narratives dramatize a rethinking of posthuman identities, as both shaping and being shaped by multiple environments (natural/cultural, sonic/acoustic, psychic). Voiced by second-order systems theory, human identities are constituted by/through social and psychic systems that cannot get information directly from their environments, but instead respond to environmental complexity by increasing their internal complexity (Luhmann 2000). Expressed through

Stacy Alaimo's idea of transcorporeality, this means that what humans do to the environment, they do to themselves: a sense of shared vulnerability signals a crucial environmental responsibility and connects ecological and social disruptions (Alaimo 2010, 20–21). From the desert landscape of *Zabriskie Point* (1970) to the post-Katrina cityscape of *Treme*, we observe worlds that become increasingly more muddy, dynamic and diverse.

Environmental biopolitics

The desert embodies space open to socio-economic, political and environmental processes. Thus we start with *Zabriskie Point*.[2] Directed by Michelangelo Antonioni, the film's opening depicts campus unrest that escalates into a full-scale riot. After being accused of killing a soldier, a student, Mark, steals a plane and randomly meets Daria, who is scouting locations for upscale housing in the southern California desert. The free-spirited Daria delights in the unspoiled, dusty landscape and the frontier charm of a local bar, a cultural watering hole/oasis that suggests a less destructive ecological relationship. But she participates, of course, in the damaging of the very things she so values.

Towards the end of the film, upon hearing the radio report on Mark being fatally shot when he attempts to return the plane, Daria walks away from an isolated hillside retreat, the site of a business meeting with her boss and property developers.[3] We see an abandoned poolside (another oasis), earlier occupied by middle-aged women who are presumably the wives and girlfriends of the businessmen. In her car, Daria looks back at where she has just left. In a brief, soundless image, the house explodes, followed by her getting out of the car and looking again, more angrily, at the site (Chatman 1985, 160). From her perspective, we see, in a prolonged sequence shot from multiple camera angles at varied speeds, the house explode repeatedly and the destruction of consumer items – the noise of the blasts segues into the acid-rock music of Pink Floyd. The posthuman framing, through second-order observation (the observation of observation), of this surreal portrait of consumerist violence discloses transcorporeal connections among psychic, sonic/acoustic and natural/cultural environments. This is a possible further step for rebellious energies, addressed in a self-reflective idiom. At the same time, the ending questions our interpretation of the narrative. Was/is there potential for liberation, after all? Did/can we not see it?

Guided by the property developers' perspective, the California desert, if supplied with adequate water, can sustain fantasies of suburban life. The opposite side of the biopolitical coin is enacted in *Punishment Park* (1971), directed by Peter Watkins, where the desert becomes a disciplinary site for dissenting bodies, the withholding of water used as a weapon.[4] Framed by Giorgio Agamben's model of the concentration camp as a modern biopolitical signifier that resonates with Thomas Pynchon and Frank Zappa's satirical treatment of California as a police state (Agamben 1988, 166–180), this fictional documentary begins as anti-war protestors (predominantly younger men and women) are sentenced by a citizen tribunal (predominantly older men and women). The protestors' sentences are commuted if they play, and win, a game: the objective is to travel by foot a considerable distance across the desert, eluding capture, or possibly being killed, by police and National Guard troops, to reach the finish, which is marked by a flag. Yet the game is rigged, for not only is there the false promise of water halfway along the route, no one is permitted to win. In the film, the second-order observations – staged by the documentary-filming techniques, Watkins' voiceover and him becoming a character in his own film by interceding on behalf of those who make it to the end – disclose a biopolitical transformation of ecological thinking to create 'docile bodies' dehumanised by technology (Campbell 2011, 55–56). That is, the game preserves the punishing desert climate, while the desert space is controlled through radio and visual surveillance. The exploration of the boundaries of sacrificable and non-sacrificable life is staged against a breakdown in communication – between the protestors and war supporters, mirroring the divided nation at the time – that is physically played out in the breakdown of bodies due to lack of food, water and shelter (Agamben 1998, 71–75).[5]

Breakdown becomes a posthuman signifier, and, in *A Woman under the Influence* (1974), breakdown is everywhere, in ecology, communication, identity – and in humanism itself. That the 'influence' that catalyses trauma in the film remains unnamed, suggests that language does not mediate the tensions between identities and environments (Carney 1994, 182). Director and writer John Cassavetes responded to a question about the fractured relationship between Nick and Mabel, the working-class couple who are the narrative focus, by emphasizing the duality of the 'outside' and 'inside world' (Carney 2001, 369). Nick, a construction crew leader who participates in the transformation of the Los Angeles landscape, is unable to manage or contain his problems with his family (signifying a masculine crisis). Early in the film, a water main break forces Nick to cancel his planned romantic evening with Mabel; he and his crew have to work all night to maintain the increasingly stressed urban ecosystem. This stress feeds back into his family. But such feedback is indirect, because, as systems theorist Niklas Luhmann puts it, there are no 'point for point correlations' between the family's conflicts and environmental disruptions (Luhmann 1989, 16).

In the film, the inside world, as messy and chaotic as the outside, constitutes an environment of spilled food, splashing drinks, sticking doors and tangled telephone cords (Carney 1994, 172). This world frames how breakdown is marked by a shift from first- to second-order observation, which is staged through the filming process. The environmental scenes stand out by their being filmed in more vivid colours, departing from Cassavetes' usual aesthetic, which he described as 'a little rough and the colors muted' (Carney 2001, 345).[6] During the emotionally intense scene where Mabel fights with Nick and his mother, the images are repeatedly blurred. Voice also signals dislocation. Not only at times is Mabel unable to fully express herself; during moments of crisis, she does not make sense at all, while Nick babbles to mock his mother, who insists that Mabel be committed, and is unable to explain to his children why he carried out his mother's wishes, only saying, 'I'm sorry for everything.'

Like Daria in *Zabriskie Point*, Mabel acts like a free spirit, but often appears as 'existentially missing in action' (Carney 1994, 182). Her absence exemplifies the dispersal of human identity/agency through an acoustic environment: by opera music that fills the empty space of the room that she occupies while her children and husband are gone, the wordless singing on the soundtrack, and the sound of waves that drown out Nick's voice when he is trying to talk to his children at the beach (and reminds us of his own tendency to babble).[7] Yet *A Woman under the Influence* looks past alienation to more closely fit with the systems-theory discourse of self-reflexivity articulated in *Zabriskie Point*. Mabel remarks, 'You know, sometimes I think I really am nuts' (Carney 1994, 178). Hence we see the importance of distinguishing between environments – something that systems theory, in Luhmann's thinking, does by asserting the abrasiveness of communication, how it atomizes rather than preserves identity. To return to the film, Mabel's self-reflection points out the ways that natural/cultural, psychic and sonic/acoustic environments brush up against each other in disruptive and unpredictable ways.

By the mid-1970s, the environmental movement had gained enough public recognition to be the centre of narratives that examined its possible outcomes and consequences. Written and directed by Mike Leigh, the pointed satire of ecological consciousness in *Nuts in May* (1976) registers a more critical breakdown in self-reflective thinking. The story of two misguided, and often bullying, nature lovers tackles issues far beyond noise pollution and rubbish at a holiday campground. Shaped by their reductive ways of thinking and feeling that cut them off from each other and those around them, the couple's idealization of the natural environment overlooks the larger biopolitical systems of regulation that determine, for instance, which dairies are licensed to sell unpasteurized milk. Here, following rules without question leads to the same environmental predicament – and social stasis – as the campus radicals' revolutionary attitudes in *Zabriskie Point* (Carney & Quart, 2000, 80–82).

Moving from stasis to post-catastrophe, the children's television series *Ark II* (1976–1979) features a team of youthful scientists who explore a polluted future world to present social lessons based on environmental issues. At times, however, the series questions the social pre-eminence of the scientific authority that guides these lessons. In the episode 'The Wild Boy' (1976), the scientists carefully listen to the title character, whom his society treats as an outcast. He warns the scientists about, and then guides them to, a toxic waste site. The scientists use a powerful laser, created by advanced technology, to seal off the site. Such an intervention blurs the lines between science and activism, underscoring how a dystopian world, regarded as a risk society, promotes the observing of environmental issues as shaped by social inequality. Furthermore, we see here how, as Alaimo remarks, activists go beyond the 'everyday' knowledge of risk, expressed by the 'wild boy', to appropriating sophisticated sciences and technologies for detecting and managing 'invisible' environmental hazards such as toxins and radioactivity (Alaimo 2010, 65). The scientists' activist stance, throughout the series, questions, as Alaimo points out, that science is an 'objective, separate sphere of knowledge making' and creates 'an opportunity to transform science into something more accountable, more just, and more democratic' (Alaimo 2010, 65).

Cosmic oceans

The television series *The Undersea World of Jacques Cousteau*, in the 1970s, promoted second-order observation by including the filming of the researchers' lives on the ship and discussions about the process of filming the ocean depths.[8] Cousteau, however, in the episode, 'The Water Planet' (1970), warns us, 'We may be the first to witness the death of life', because 'too few can feel, "I am the sea, and the sea is me".' The global flows of late century capital, Patricia Yeager comments, have transformed the aquatic environment into a 'cyborg ocean', constituted by 'an ecosystem made of algae and plastic debris' and shaped by 'the imaginary of corporate profiteering, in which oceans are places for stealing resources, dumping trash, and making money through shipping, oil drilling, and so on' (Yeager 2010, 523, 527–533). In a chilling episode, 'Time Bomb at 50 Fathoms' (1978), Cousteau's team races to salvage leaking toxic canisters on sunken ships. The toxins' ability to spread throughout the ocean underlines Alaimo's assertion that

> *one of the central problematics of transcorporeality is contending with dangerous, often imperceptible material agencies. The sense of being permeable to harmful substances may provoke denial, delusions of transcendence, or the desire for a magical fix, but it may also foster a posthuman environmentalism of co-constituted creatures, entangled knowledges, and precautionary practices.*
>
> (2010, 146)

As the episode illustrates, the money to fund the clean-up comes from the legal proceedings the local magistrate brought against the responsible parties (aided by an article Cousteau wrote on the magistrate's behalf). Although Cousteau here documents the biopolitical cost of global oceanic trade, he does not critically comment on the profound irresponsibility of corporate shipping interests and chemical manufactures.

Losing connection with the planet, Cousteau implies, means losing connection with ourselves. Such loss is staged in *Solaris* (1972), directed and co-written by Andrei Tarkovsky, through the two parts of the film. The first is a meditation on leaving earth, as Kris, a psychologist, prepares to travel to a space station orbiting the planet Solaris. The camera focuses on a pond and trees outside of the home of Kris' parents; his immersion in his environment (dipping his hands in the water and gathering soil samples to take with him) express the idea that 'Earth is the natural environment in which thinking is grounded for a human being' (Skakov 2012, 76–77).[9] As Sullivan reminds us, 'our concrete survival (in space or here on Earth) depends on our full immersion into earthly, bacteria-laden surroundings' (Sullivan 2012, 518).

The second part follows Kris aboard the station, a chaotic and messy environment that parallels the unravelling psychic landscape. In response to the scientists' bombarding it with radiation, the planet has probed their minds, manifesting repressed memories and desires in the form of 'visitors'. *Solaris* thus suggests a cosmic image of a (re)active planetary ecosystem – the conceptual foundation for the Gaia hypothesis (Margulis & Sagan 2000, 52–55, 168–170).[10] Kris' visitor is his wife, who had committed suicide. His materialized vision of her displays his guilt through the emphasis on the needle mark on her arm.[11] In the final scene, Kris appears in his parents' home (matching the earlier scenes). Rain pours from the inside; as Kris embraces his father, the camera pulls back to reveal the house's location on an island in Solaris' ocean.[12] That we are compelled to question what we see and what Kris can see recalls Luhmann's words, 'Reality is what one sees when one does not see it' (Rasch 2000, 176), filtered through the biopolitics of memory and desire as a criterion of how lived environments – as beyond human – are perceived and valued.[13]

In *Stalker* (1979), also directed by Tarkovsky, the Zone is the Earthly counterpart of Solaris. Regulated by the authorities, it is accessible only through the assistance of guides, called Stalkers, whose psychic attachment to this landscape suggests the Zone may be, in part, or entirely, a subjective experience. The Stalker tells the Writer and Scientist (who retain the weight of their allegorical titles) that the Zone reacts differently to each person. Filmed in more verdant colour, as opposed to the monochromatic tones of the polluted urban city, the Zone is both appealing and menacing.[14] It epitomizes Beck's idea of unknown, deterritorialized risk – heightened by the possibility that the Zone may not operate in the way speculated, not work for everyone, or be a complete fantasy (Heise 2008, 147, 151, 152).[15] The doubt and belief of the three men emerge through a landscape that appears as a graveyard for value systems: the camera tracks across a medical syringe, coins, a religious medal and a gun in the water. The end scenes pair a vision of possible redemption – rain falls on the men who pose in the manner of a religious frieze – with the attempt of Monkey, the Stalker's genetically deformed daughter (possibly due to the radiation, or something else, in the Zone) to develop her telekinetic powers; as the noise of a train outside gets increasingly louder, a fragment of Beethoven's 'Ode to Joy' mixes with the background noise (Johnson & Petrie 1994, 144). Cumulatively, these images hinge on the possibility of promise and threat, as do the larger systems of social regulation that permeate the Zone (Wolfe 2013, 103).

(Un)sound environments

The psychic landscape of risk in *Stalker* is transposed, in *Safe* (1995), written and directed by Todd Haynes, to upper-class southern California suburbia. The undefined illness of Carol White, a typical housewife, seems overdetermined, suggesting AIDS, multiple chemical sensitivity (MCS) and the subjection of the self to medical discourses.[16] When she leaves her home and family to join an isolated New Age retreat, our 'distance' from Carol that 'keeps us at a remove' and produces an 'unsettling passivity and uncertain agency', becomes augmented by the uncertainty of what we witness at the retreat (Reid 1998, 39). As Steven Shaviro comments, 'If the first half of the film contemplated the horrors of outer, suburban space, the second half renders something much harder to see: the real estate development, as it were, of inner, psychological space' (Shaviro n.d.). The suburb and the retreat seem similar, both conspicuously dirt-free and informed by the doctrine of individual improvement. In the closing scene, Carol's affirmations, recited while blankly looking at the camera, remind us of our own location within a 'consumerist schematization of visuality' (Wolfe 2010, 237). The relays between consumerism and identity in the film are mobilized by the drive for 'self-esteem' that internalises systems of social regulation; the retreat has furnished Carol 'with a soul to match her white suburban body' (Shaviro n.d.).

Counterpointing the idea of reflection as a form of economic development is the complex portrait of lived environments in *Neighboring Sounds* (2012), written and directed by Kleber Mendonça Filho. Set in Recife, a north-eastern Brazilian city, the film stages how 'space is defined as much by who's in it as by what it looks like or how it's arranged' (Fuchs 2012). The film therefore becomes a second-order critique of the city's property development, headed by the patriarch Francisco, which prioritises the economic value of space. But the sonic/acoustic environment intrudes; noises such as a dog's constant barking remind us of the social disorder caused by rapid modernisation that hides in plain sight. When disorder threatens to escalate into a crime wave, Francisco hires a neighbourhood security patrol. At the end, however, we realize that the patrol has placed him under surveillance as well. Several members of the patrol are prepared to hold Francisco accountable for his own hidden past: his participation in a bloody counterrevolutionary movement. In *Neighboring Sounds*, the psychic stasis of *Safe* is transformed into a rebellion against political repression – that can, perhaps, collectively transform daily lived environmental experiences.

Post-scarcity and circular time

Peak oil scenarios, however, suggest that time for change may, at best, be fleeting. In *There Will Be Blood* (2007), written and directed by Paul Thomas Anderson, the depiction of a bleak, exhausted landscape culminates with a deranged oil tycoon's 'boasting of how he can rapaciously consume everyone else's oil, like sucking up a milkshake' (Bradshaw 2008).[17]

While the television series *Battlestar Galactica* (2004–2009) offers the possibility of a restored planet, it suggests that it will come with a considerable cost. After the Cylons, human-made cyborgs, rebel against their creators and take over their home planet, the human survivors set off, directed by religious prophecy, for earth. If the series recast, at a cosmic level, US imperialism in Iraq (and associations between blood and oil),[18] the repressive violence of a post-scarcity regime also is examined: under pressures of survival with limited resources, society edges towards a fascist leadership that decides where and when the necessary sacrifices are to be made. For instance, a greenhouse ship is left behind; before its destruction by the Cylons, we see a child sitting by a nature preserve on the ship as her end approaches. If nature is downgraded, non-organic life is foregrounded; as the human survivors reach earth, they discover that it was originally inhabited by the Cylons, the planet reduced to a radioactive wasteland due to civil war. In the three-part final episode, 'Daybreak' (2009), the humans, with the help of a group of Cylons who have chosen to become mortal, discover a liveable planet, inhabited by pre-civilized human life. On this planet, rechristened earth, the president, who has, throughout the journey, battled breast cancer, dies and is buried: a lasting image of human life rejoining the environment, a biopolitics of the living and dead operating through a larger planetary consciousness – that is, both us and not us.[19]

The tagline of *Battlestar Galactica* states, 'All of this has happened before, and all of it will happen again.' Similarly, *Treme* depicts the trauma of post-Katrina New Orleans through circular time, fitting with the local tradition of viewing time as a cycle of ritual and remembrance that connects past and future (Sublette 2009, 309).[20] The final episode of the first season, 'I'll Fly Away' (2010), explores the interrelated complexities of sonic/acoustic, psychological, cultural/natural environments: during the funeral of her brother who died in police custody in the aftermath of Katrina, one of the characters remembers hearing his mobile-phone ringtone – the scene shifts to before the hurricane makes landfall, where we see life in the city before the moment of loss/disruption (including characters now dead). In the second season, the opening of the episode, 'On Your Way Down' (2011), reflects the complex cultural layers of New Orleans by tracking around a photography exhibit showing the struggle for survival during the flood set to melancholy jazz music. In a second-order commentary of the location of *Treme* within post-Katrina cultural production, the camera focuses on the musicians playing the music that we hear in the gallery.[21]

It seems appropriate that the exploration of muddy worlds circles back to *Treme*. Its stories of family, commerce and politics within multiple global (post-9/11 New York City) and local environments (the tourist district) echo the narratives of *Woman under the Influence* and *Neighboring Sounds*. While the anthropocene, defined as where humans fit into ecological deep time (Turpin 2013), has been critically scrutinised (and informs petro-narratives such as *There Will Be Blood*), the posthuman may well fit the circular time of New Orleans. The city's environmental future – rising water levels due to global warming and post-scarcity daily life – may well be ours.

Notes

1. Sullivan remarks that dirt includes 'depleted soil, dust, the toxic grime on the ground of industrial sites, etc.' (Sullivan 2012, 517).
2. According to Beverly Walker, the film's publicist, the central theme of *Zabriskie Point* was originally intended to be environmental, rather than political (Pomerance 2011, 162).
3. William Arrowsmith suggests that Daria leaves after she encounters the Native American maid, who then 'disappears; imprisoned in glass, up the stairs. Daria suddenly recognizes herself as also imprisoned like the maid, indigenous, but a prisoner in her own country, the desert' (Arrowsmith 1995, 141).
4. For informative reviews of the film, see Cook (2009) and Weiner (1972).

5. Refer to Watkins' comments in the booklet that accompanies the DVD version of the film.
6. At the start of filming, Cassavetes had a director of photography, Caleb Deschanel, whom he later fired; however, he kept some of his footage in the final edit, such as this scene.
7. George Kouvaros writes that 'the operatic music infuses each of its corners and objects with an emotional volume that has Mabel at its center but crucially is never fixed within this character' (Kouvaros 2004, 106). This idea resonates with the posthuman construction of sonic/acoustic environments (Cecchetto 2013).
8. For a discussion of the filming of the series, refer to Shaheen 1987.
9. Also see Johnson and Petrie 1994.
10. Timothy Morton, however, is critical of this association between Gaia and Solaris (Morton 2008, 81).
11. For an overview of the sonic/acoustic environment in Tarkovsky's films, see Fairweather 2012. Vida T. Johnson and Graham T. Petrie comment that the station 'is filled with strange electronic sounds and rhythms', indicative of a temporal and spatial dislocation, while Kris' encounters with this 'alien' environment are reflected in the soundtrack, an elegiac Bach piece, 'given subtle electronic enhancement' (Johnson & Petrie 1994, 108–109). Also see Bird (2008, 152), and Skakov (2012, 84).
12. The ambiguity of the final scene that discloses environmental parallels between Earth and Solaris has received considerable attention. Skakov comments that Kris 'reconsider[s] the nature of earthly matters' (Skakov 2012, 98). Johnson and Petrie state that the ending is constituted through Kris' hallucinations (Johnson & Petrie 1994, 109–110). This interpretation addresses the larger question of authenticity also raised by Miriam Jordan and Julian Jason Haladyn (Jordan & Haladyn 2010). Bird somewhat dissents, arguing that the vision of Kris' home, paradoxically, has a 'solidity and authenticity' that return him 'to material existence' (Bird 2008, 65).
13. The film, throughout, questions what we can and cannot see. The colour footage of Solaris shot by an earlier explorer (that is viewed through a black-and-white video of his debriefing that Kris watches) is obscured by clouds. These clouds are seen at the end of the film (Bird 2008, 81, 119; Skakov 2012, 77).
14. Michael Dempsey contends that the Zone 'looks initially like an ordinary, dowdy wilderness' (Dempsey 1981, 16). Likewise, Skakov remarks that it 'is not so alien, according to the colour dramaturgy of the film' (Skakov 2012, 144). Conversely, Johnson and Petrie comment that it is a 'world governed by its own dream logic': '[t]he electronic music, with its haunting, pulsating rhythms that reappear in various permutations throughout the film, also creates its own sense of strangeness while providing almost subliminal links between the Zone and the everyday world of Stalker and his family' (Johnson & Petrie 1994, 153). Bird writes, however, that 'the music is often indistinguishable from diegetic noise': moreover, the sonic/acoustic environment is constituted by the 'traces of some alien will reacting to the intervention of the three men' (Bird 2008, 158, 167).
15. Bird comments that 'the Zone is simply the demarcated area within which an event can occur, akin to the screen in the cinema' (Bird 2008, 69). Skakov focuses on the last scene: '[T]he piercing gaze of Monkey becomes the ultimate riddle of the film' (Skakov 2012, 164). For Slavoj Žižek, because it is impossible to 'formulate' one's desire, 'everybody fails' in the Zone. In the end, the film depicts our immersion in our environment rather than our being 'above material reality' (*The Pervert's Guide to Cinema*, 2006).
16. For a discussion of MCS and *Safe*, see Alaimo (2010, 113–140).
17. Peter Hitchcock notes the film's inability to 'reveal oil's relationship to the making of the American subject' (Hitchcock 2010, 96). Daniel Worden interprets the film as a staging of 'a possible rupture between family and oil' (Worden 2012, 456). Stephanie LeMenager questions the view that the film constitutes a peak oil scenario, regarding it rather 'as a signal of the tiredness of twentieth-century stories about modernity' (LeMenager 2014, 100).

18. See Steiff and Tamplin 2008. Also see Milford and Rowland 2012. For a reading of Cylons as posthuman figures, see Hawk 2011. For philosophical approaches to understanding the series, see Eberl 2008.
19. Margulis and Sagan state, 'On loan, the carbon, hydrogen, and nitrogen of our bodies must be returned to the biospheric bank' (Margulis & Sagan 2000, 201). Sullivan comments that the depiction of space travel 'problematically assumes that we can exist separate from our dirty planetary enmeshment' (Sullivan 2012, 518).
20. For an examination of the series' treatment of Katrina as trauma, see Dowler 2013.
21. Despite the attempts, headed by its creators, David Simon and Eric Overmyer, to use local consultants, artists and labour, *Treme* has been accused of transforming New Orleans into a cultural commodity. For various responses, see Mayer 2012.

Part VII

Us and Them: Posthuman Relationships

31
Executing Species: Animal Attractions in Thomas Edison and Douglas Gordon

Anat Pick

> How you glow, noble beast, in the infinite moment before your own death!
>
> Lydia Millet

Cinema has never been human. The central place of animals in the emergence and development of the cinematic medium is by now well established.[1] Yet, if there has been a recent 'animal turn' in film studies, it has focused less on animals themselves than on how animals are symbolically produced in representation. Animals remain cinema's 'elephant in the room': the medium's unacknowledged presence but also its potential for seeing the world, and animals, differently. As Jonathan Burt has consistently argued, screen animals exceed their symbolic value as representation and are located on the threshold between the figurative and the metaphorical. Despite their excessive use as mirrors of human concerns and as repositories of human attributes, the appearance of animals in moving images is always also concrete, and affects us as such.

The 'reality effect' of film animals is partly achieved by the constant threat of real violence commanded by the animal image (like the portentous appearance of a gun in the first act of a stage play). Violence is sometimes realized (it is a regular feature in 'serious' European and world art cinema, for example), and sometimes disclaimed (in the feel-good adage of the American Humane Association's 'No Animals Were Harmed in the Making of This Film'). The permanent exposure of the cinematic animal to onscreen violation signals its reality, and lends the medium its realism. This exposure and this threat open up the screen as a zoomorphic space – a space inhabited by more-than-human lives.

As a technology and a mode of encountering, the cinema captures and projects human and non-human beings in their materiality, their contingency and finitude, namely, in their precariousness and vulnerability. At its best, cinema can be attentive to modes of existence that are not limited to our own. It can also reveal our own existence to us as something unknown or disavowed – as animal. As assemblages, in the Deleuzian or Latourian sense, images are not mere copies, but instances of relations between objects, materials and bodies in a more-than-human world: each image contains elements, and is itself part of complex interfaces that include not only the image interior, but also the camera, the space around the camera and the relations between them.

André Bazin's cinematic realism imagined the cinema as offering an immanent, non-hierarchal, lateral view of reality, composed of multiple beings and things whose connection to one another is of equivalent force, beauty and wonder.[2] There is much to seduce (and alarm) us in this posthumanist view of cinema that regards living beings and things as interchangeable: drawing out the aliveness of things, and the thingness of the living. For John Mullarkey, such radical equality can trigger fear:

> *The horror of encountering unexpected alterity – from animals no longer taken as mere objects (and perhaps from objects no longer regarded as mere 'objects' either) – doubtless stems from fear: what will become of 'us' in a democracy of all the living?*
> (2012, 54)

While cinema's 'flat ontology' (Mullarkey 2012, 40) proposes a view of the world as radically equal, what should we make of the unequal distribution of power, and vulnerability, between different agents or 'actants'? For cinema is also an institution and a manifestation of particular economic, political and moral milieus, bound not only to dominant ways of seeing, but to dominant ways of living as well.

Film, perhaps more than any other art, is closely related to other modern industrial institutions, from the science laboratory to the factory farm. As posthumanist theorists like Donna Haraway have shown, these are relational sites in which human and non-human entities meet and comingle, 'flatly' as Mullarkey would have it. But these are also, significantly, sites of political, or biopolitical, power. Cinema's real and symbolic instrumentalization of animals means that – like the laboratory and the slaughterhouse, as well as the circus and the zoo – the power exercised over non-human animals as the dominant mode of interspecies relations is on display. The two examples below, Thomas Edison's *Electrocuting an Elephant* (1903), and Douglas Gordon's *Play Dead; Real Time* (2003), exactly one hundred years apart, reveal the intersection of humans, animals and technology that gives rise to a peculiar and precarious form of life: the cinematic animal.

Cinema is a key modern relational site of encounter between technology, humans and animals, that selectively breeds the cinematic animal. Like farmed animals, modified by the industrial apparatuses in which they live and die, cinematic animals are a new kind of being.[3] Cinematic animals are living commodities whose very 'aliveness' is probed and made visible. As a cinematic attraction, combining entertainment and instruction, animal vulnerability is generated as a source of knowledge about animals' bodies, and as cultural and aesthetic currency. Cinematic animals, then, are not simply animals captured on film. They are ontologically, ethically and even biologically distinct, a creature that is, almost without exception, constituted as vulnerable.

In opening up the world as more-than-human, cinema blurs the boundary between humans and animals, but normatively, it tends to reinforce species distinction. This ambiguity resonates in cinema's twofold 'inhumanity': ontologically, the inhumanity of film frees cinema's potential to eschew a strictly human perspective and attests to the interdependence of humans, animals and the cinematic apparatus. Ethically, the inhumanity of film reminds us that cinema continues to be politically and culturally wedded to forms of human power over non-human life that are, quite literally, spectacularly cruel.

The examples I have chosen trace early film's complex relations to animals as a particular type of cinematic 'attraction'. They render cinema as an interspecies space in which other lives unfold (reveal themselves or come undone) spectacularly. These unfoldings are not always benign. *Electrocuting an Elephant* and *Play Dead; Real Time* encapsulate the contradictory attitudes to animals in the field of vision and point to cinema's inhumanity, in the double inflection of ontology and ethics. If, ontologically, the cinema is not simply reducible to a human perspective, history or concerns, morally, cinema participates in the disciplining (and violating) of bodies, whose vitality and vulnerability it explores and often exploits.

Electrocuting an Elephant (1903)

Edison's *Electrocuting an Elephant* (1903) is a haunting example of early actuality to which scholars of film, and of animal film, repeatedly return, perhaps because the film crystalizes the basic components of the cinema: living bodies (material, temporal, fragile), technology and spectacle. The Edison Manufacturing Company arranged for, carried out and filmed the execution of Topsy, a wild-caught African elephant brought to Coney Island, who reportedly killed three handlers, the last one after he fed her a lit cigarette. A crowd of 1,500 gathered to watch Topsy die, a finale performance ending some 20 years of captivity.

The film's grainy, degraded footage contains two shots: a capped man leads Topsy to the site of her execution where she will be strapped into place. Three other men are walking behind her, and a couple wander across the front of the frame. Coney Island's Luna Park is seen in the background. In the second shot, Topsy is standing, her front leg restlessly shuffling, she suddenly stiffens and smoke billows from her feet and fills the frame. She collapses onto her side. The shot is held until the smoke clears, revealing Topsy's body (or is it the film's?) in its final convulsions.

Electrocuting an Elephant is a literal example of early cinema's carnivalesque roots in the fairground. By 1903, following the upholding of Edison's motion picture patent in 1901, the Edison company had established itself as a major force in the motion picture market. Although, according to Charles Musser, 1903 was 'the year in which the story film came to prominence, beginning with the completion of *Life of an American Fireman* and culminating with the incredible success of *The Great Train Robbery*, quite possibly the most successful American film before Griffith's *The Birth of a Nation* (1915)',[4] *Electrocuting an Elephant* is an example of what Tom Gunning called the 'cinema of attractions'; that is, films made between 1895 and 1906, in which narrative and storytelling are secondary to the display of spectacular action and the foregrounding of technology – in Edison's case these are the two interlinked technologies of electricity and film. The cinema of attractions belongs to vaudeville and the fairground, where films were first shown alongside other attractions, and it suggests the primacy of exhibitionism, novelty, surprise and affect, over the more cerebral, and one might argue humanistic, conventions of narrative film.[5] If the 'relation between films and the emergence of the great amusement parks, such as Coney Island, at the turn of the century provides rich ground for rethinking the roots of early cinema' (Gunning 2006, 383), *Electrocuting an Elephant* is both concretely and symbolically significant since it takes place onsite at cinema's historical birthplace.

The film's inhumanity, in the twofold sense described, occurs at a number of levels. First, as Michael Lundblad explains, Topsy's execution 'might suggest that an elephant could be required to take responsibility for criminal acts: that an animal could possess the agency of a human being. It could thus be read as an example of resisting distinctions between human and nonhuman agency' (Lundblad 2013, 94). But the distinctly disciplinary flavour of this public display concerns the association between animality and violence, and the subsequent need to bring animality under control. Topsy's animality extends to other forms of savagery and unruliness, and her execution is a warning of sorts to the unwashed masses – both the spectators and the target of this show of force. In this sense, Lundblad claims, 'Topsy's physical body... can be seen as representative of the working class', whose disruptive potential at the turn of the 20th century (demands for humane treatment and labour reform) was a threat to the burgeoning market economy.[6]

Edison's motivation was partly commercial: he was promoting DC (direct current) in a bid against AC (alternating current) of his rival, George Westinghouse. But the film is more than an epilogue in the so-called 'war of the currents' between rival industrialists.[7] *Electrocuting an Elephant* is an illustration of cinematic biopower. In her study of early medical imagery, Lisa Cartwright claims that the film:

> Documents (...) public fascination with scientific technology and its capacity to determine the course of life and death in living beings (...). The film (...) is evidence of a widespread popular interest in the power of technology to regulate and discipline bodies.
>
> (1995, 18)

Edison's film is pivotal because it exemplifies the convergence of science, technology and spectacle in the production of the attraction of the vulnerable animal body, the DNA of the cinematic animal as a hybrid organism manufactured by photographic motion pictures. In addition to being 'a ceremony of corporal punishment' (Cartwright 1995, 42) that asserts human dominance over non-human animals, the film renders Topsy's body as the site at which something called 'life' is – and yet is not – visualized through the joint rituals of cinematography and science, whose subject is the condemned animal body. The animal here is not just raw material, but the site of *extraction*. What the camera seeks to powerfully wrest from Topsy is her very vitality, the invisible secret of life, of animation, which the animal's body at once displays and obscures.

With their common interest in bodies in motion at the turn of the 20th century, film and the life sciences, especially physiology, inaugurated what Cartwright calls 'biological modes of representation' (Cartwright 1995, 10). The 'biological gaze', to borrow Laura Mulvey's phrase, seeks the elusive and invisible object of 'life'. But biological modes of representation also announce a break between observation and the object of knowledge, 'a break in which the visualization of "life" becomes all the more seductive to the scientific eye even as the limitations of representation are made plain' (Cartwright 1995, 10).[8] Animal vulnerability in early film is produced and controlled by the technological and institutional apparatus of film, whose historical ties to the science laboratory, and specifically to vivisection, reveal cinema as one modern system among others that looks to extract from bodies their 'aliveness'. As such, cinema is both progressive and 'primitive': it deploys technological rationalism to interrogate, decipher and extract from living beings the enigma of animation – their biological life, and maybe even their soul.

Bodies, their manipulation, and sometimes their destruction, offer cinema an object of study and an object of beauty. Capturing bodies in motion in early film suggest that cinema – like science – sought to extract from bodies what the camera could and could not make visible: the secret of their vitality, revealed as the limits of vitality and the laws governing those limits. In so doing, cinema becomes an apparatus for the disciplining of bodies, but it is also a space in which these disciplinary practices are publicly negotiated and so potentially resisted. Both *Electrocuting an Elephant* and *Play Dead; Real Time* deploy the biological gaze in the course of producing the attraction of the vulnerable animal body.

Play Dead; Real Time (2003)

As narrative cinema slowly gained prominence, the cinema of attractions disseminated across a variety of film practices. From about 1907, most notably in the films of D. W. Griffith, a fascination with multi-reel story films takes hold, obscuring the pre-continuity origins of cinema. For a time, film history succumbed to an evolutionary model, tracing the gradual maturation into classical narrative. But narrative and attraction are not incompatible. 'In fact', writes Gunning, 'the cinema of attraction[s] does not disappear with the dominance of narrative, but rather goes underground, both into certain avant-garde practices and as a component of narrative films' (2006, 382). New expressions of the cinema of attractions arguably flourish today in action and special effects mainstream cinema, and in the art gallery.

A recent example of what I am calling interspecies attraction is *Play Dead; Real Time* (2003), by the artist Douglas Gordon. This three-channel video installation is a revisiting of Edison's film, exactly one hundred years later. It features Minnie, a circus elephant, transported to New York's Gagosian Gallery to perform a series of movements, including lying down and 'playing dead'. The sequences of movements are projected on two large screens, completed by a small monitor, placed on the floor.[9] Each of the three projections shows three different versions of the same sequence of commands. Gordon says the idea came to him one morning when he realized he had never seen an elephant lying down, and he wanted to see what happens when the animal was made to perform an uncomfortable movement. In the piece, shot on 16mm then transferred to video, the camera circles Minnie, filming her as she lies down and stumbles awkwardly back to her feet.[10]

Play Dead; Real Time alludes to previous works that placed live animals in the art gallery (from Joseph Beuys and William Wegman to Damien Hirst), but the connection to Edison seems to me the most pertinent.[11] Gordon described *Play Dead; Real Time* as something between 'a nature film and a medical documentary', allowing us to 'observe the subject in a way that could be used for a practical purpose but also had a very certain aesthetic'.[12] The description invokes the main registers of the cinematic animal established from animals' earliest appearances in and as moving images: science, hunting and spectacle. Each register highlights a different kind of 'capital' accrued from animals: scientific knowledge, trophies and visual pleasure.

In the second half of the 19th century, the photographer Eadweard Muybridge and the physiologist Étienne-Jules Marey conducted photographic studies of animal motion, which are considered the precursors of the moving pictures of the cinema. As Cynthia Chris suggests, pre-cinematic motion studies are contradictory in conveying the illusion of continuous motion yet also fragmenting motion into its composite gestures (Chris 2006, 8).[13] The duality of stillness and motion is, of course, a central feature of film, and with better – faster – technology, movement could be more efficiently captured, fragmented and reassembled.

Like Muybridge's animal motion studies, Gordon's piece offers visual scrutiny in the contrived, laboratory-like, conditions of the art gallery. The segmentation and abstraction of motion by photographic technology have been replaced, in the work's final form, by video technology. But the camera's circling motion in the 'white cube' of the Gagosian Gallery expresses the desire for unlimited optical access. In both Edison and Gordon, the impetus is to render visible the living animal as knowable, controllable and sensational.

Beyond its knowing ironies and its institutional critique of the art gallery, *Play Dead; Real Time*'s relation to Edison's seemingly straightforward elephant execution is telling. The two works explore elephant bodies as a source of information and titillation. Edison's film conflates the scientific and disciplinary functions of cinema: the desire to control life by capturing the precise moment of death. And, like early executions, it is public, ritualistic and punitive. The punitive element in Edison's film is central. As the historians Hilda Kean (1998) and Jonathan Burt (2001) have shown, there is a strong link between animal visibility and public morality:

> One of the inspirations behind the formation of the RSPCA in 1824 was the sight of animals being driven to Smithfield Market in London. The issue of visual order was an important factor in increasing control exercised over all sorts of different domains of

animal-related practice – including bear baiting, vivisection, slaughter, or the clearing of the city streets of strays.

(Burt 2001, 208)

Modern codes of civility and civilization are inseparable from interspecies relations, and the appearance of these relations in the public sphere. It is no wonder, therefore, that Topsy's electrocution was couched in moral, even legalistic terms as the execution of a criminal. This logic is far from archaic. In our own time, such killings have been reframed by the joint rhetoric of security and humaneness, renamed as either 'euthanasia' or 'culling': the putting down of dangerous or undesirable animals. In 1903, retributive logic, however thinly underpinning Topsy's killing, was partly intended to reconcile the violent spectacle with public concerns over humane and inhumane treatment, and not only of animals. Seen as a 'cleaner' method of execution, electrocution replaced less humane methods of killing, specifically hanging. As with the cinema, Thomas Edison – and animals – played a crucial part in the development of execution by electrocution and the electric chair (Burt 2001, 215–216). In 1888, Edison conducted animal electrocutions in his New Jersey laboratory, using dogs, calves and horses, experiments that contributed to the first human execution by electric chair in the United States, in August 1890.

Lundblad points out that the 'claim of a "painless" death was emphasized in various newspaper accounts' of Topsy's killing (Lundblad 2013, 94). Nonetheless, the public spectacle of animal death, in reality and in film, speaks to the 'combination of repulsion and fascination that marks a response to certain kinds of animal representation and relates, in turn, to the problematic negotiation between co-existing humane and cruel impulses' (Burt 2001, 212). In a feat of technological, scientific, commercial and moral prowess, then, Topsy's unruly body (doubly unruly in its opacity as a living body and in its active retaliation against human authority) was to be brought under control via film.

Electrocution is 'a method of execution that is virtually isomorphic with cinema's invention', writes Alison Griffiths (2014, 1). *Electrocuting an Elephant* is one of a number of execution films, including the *Execution of Czolgosz, with Panorama of Auburn Prison* (1901), shot by Edison two years earlier. There is no essential difference in Griffiths' account between *Electrocuting an Elephant* and *Execution of Czolgosz*; there is no species bias, as it were, in thinking of both in the context of execution films that 'derive meaning as [sic] "as ceremonials of punishment", Michel Foucault's term for all manner of staged public punishments and macabre visual spectacles that exploited the idea of the uncanny, of being copresent with the dead' (Griffiths 2014, 5). Indeed, Edison sought permission to film the real execution of Czolgosz but his request was denied. He therefore had to make do with shooting on location outside Auburn prison, and film a 'detailed reproduction of the execution of the assassin of President McKinley faithfully carried out from the description of an eye witness'.[14] Electrocution films are situated 'within a rich field of pre-cinematic entertainments' as one type of cinematic attraction. In a footnote, Griffiths adds that: '*Electrocuting an Elephant* is a relic of the pride of place afforded elephants as prized taxidermy specimens in museums of natural history and of eighteenth-century experiments with animals conducted in London's galleries of practical science such as the Electrical Society and the Royal Institution' (Griffiths 2014, 6). The link between early cinema and science, all the way to the museum and the contemporary art gallery, is thus uninterrupted.

Play Dead; Real Time is an ironic updating of the tradition. Minnie, the circus elephant, is subjected to ceremonial procedures whose sanitized nature simultaneously conceals and invokes the fascination with public execution. Made to play, rather than become, dead, Minnie calls forth animals' permanent exposure to violence. The currency has shifted somewhat – a real execution is replaced by a mock one. But in Edison and Gordon alike, the use of the elephant as physical and symbolic trope remains intact, as does the interplay of experimentalism, technology and visual pleasure, whose object is the attraction of the vulnerable but recalcitrant animal body.

Gordon's is an uncanny corollary to Edison's own uncanny film. Real animal death is substituted for a more benign form of bodily discipline, and the rowdy fairground is replaced by the clinical and bourgeois space of the gallery. 'Execution' is reversed: Topsy is executed (for disobedience), while Minnie dutifully (if unhappily) executes her trainer's commands. In the later piece, visitors watch the coordinated movements performed on cue, supplemented by the camera's circumnavigation of the elephant's body. The camera orbits the room close to the floor, capturing Minnie from below. Minnie's eye, in extreme close-up, appears at the start of the third version of movements (titled *Other Way*), shown on the small monitor.

More overtly than *Electrocuting an Elephant*, *Play Dead; Real Time* features gestures in excess of the disciplining gaze. These fleeting moments are traces of animal agency and resistance that suggest not only the existence of an autonomous being, but her subjection to the interlocking technological and institutional apparatuses of the camera, the art gallery and the 'institution of speciesism' (Wolfe 2003, 6). Minnie lies down and rolls on her side on demand, she struggles back to her feet with some difficulty, and paces. While on her side, she flaps her trunk lightly on the floor in what could be agitation, or perhaps stress relief. The gesture is unscripted and so its effect on the visitor is different: it is an expression that belies the controlling gaze of the camera in tension with the piece's scripted movements that Minnie is made to perform. Her eye, in close-up on the TV monitor, waters from either displeasure or effort, begging the question: Do elephants cry?

The interspecies space opened up between the film and the viewer is held in the tension between anthropomorphic projection that perceives the elephant's tears as a sign of distress, and the sensation of otherness generated by the simulated proximity to the animal. *Play Dead; Real Time* operates along a series of displacements and transgressions: the supposedly wild animal who is no longer wild in the supposedly civilized space of a New York art gallery; the encounter with a life-size elephant that is but a projected encounter, which blurs the line between proximity and distance, safety and risk; or the sequence of 'unnatural' movements performed in response to the unseen presence of the human trainer. There is little room for contingency in the highly contrived spectacle, making the almost imperceptible movement of the flapping trunk all the more fascinating because it is unplanned. Like Topsy's shuffling feet and her quiet (resigned? unsuspecting?) walk to the gallows, the visual apparatus records every movement. But unlike the real and performed death, these unscripted responses are singular, not standardized. In their uncanniness, they question the species divide that distinguishes artistic subject from object and the power of the apparatus.

Conclusion: The elephant in the room

The examples in this chapter illustrate the special place of elephants in particular, and of animals more generally, in the medium of moving images. Elephants have consistently occupied cinema's biocultural space, which produces the 'attraction' of the vulnerable animal body. Early film's connection to the fairground, the zoo, as well as to the industrial production of electricity, reveals cinema as one modern apparatus among others that makes use of animals as a complex economic, scientific and symbolic resource. Pointing to the 'elephant in the room' in two key examples, as bookends to a century of moving image work, I drew attention to acts of animal framing and taming that convert 'wildness' into cultural currency. The enduring question of posthuman cinema is thus whether interspecies relations can be forged and made visible in ways that transcend the power dynamics that have thus far reproduced the animal as a distinctly vulnerable and violable spectacle, in a manner that is descriptively posthuman yet normatively anthropocentric.

Notes

1. See Lippit (2000) and Burt (2002). I discuss the topic in Pick (2011, 104–130).
2. For a discussion of Bazin's 'flat ontology' and the cinematic equality among humans, animals and things, see Mullarkey (2012).
3. A so-called broiler chicken (bred for meat), for example, is unlike an egg-laying hen that has not been intensively reared to pile on body mass, peaking at 48 days when meat chickens are commonly slaughtered. In biomedical research, transgenic or knockout mice are similarly bred for purpose. Whether or not we consider them 'natural', these organisms come into being as forms of life made possible by the technologies that render them vulnerable. A similar case can be made for the cinema.
4. *Edison: The Invention of the Movies: 1891–1918.* Kino Lorber Films, 2005. DVD. Notes by Charles Musser. http://www.kinolorber.com/edison/d1.html, accessed 2 November 2014.
5. See Gunning (1993, 2006). The concept's enduring appeal and its critical afterlives are the subject of *The Cinema of Attractions Reloaded*.
6. Since performing elephants are regularly female, this form of control is not only a matter of class but also of gender. Other famous cases of (female) elephant executions include the 1916 hanging of circus elephant Mary, in Erwin, Tennessee, after she killed a trainer called Walter 'Red' Eldridge.
7. See, for example, Gunning (2009, 112–132).
8. The space between observation and the object is understood by Michel Foucault as the result of the modern fragmentation of reality, or the breakdown of the totality of nature. Thus objects and their representation were no longer continuous.

9. For the MoMA re-exhibiting of the work in 2006, Gordon added a second monitor, turning the work into a four-channel installation. For detailed information on Douglas' piece and its various incarnations, see A. Noël de Tilly's 'Making/Displaying Douglas Gordon's Play Dead; Real Time', in *Scripting Artworks: Studying the Socialization of Editioned Video and Film*, http://dare.uva.nl/document/2/99400, accessed 2 November 2014. On this work and others, see Rankin 2006.
10. A filmed interview with Gordon, at the San Francisco Museum of Modern Art (SFMOMA), http://www.sfmoma.org/explore/multimedia/videos/546, accessed 16 October 2014.
11. On the long history of live animals in the art gallery see Alloi 2012.
12. Artist Rooms: Douglas Gordon: *Play Dead; Real Time*, Tate Britain, 6 May–29 September 2013, http://www.tate.org.uk/whats-on/tate-britain/display/artist-rooms-douglas-gordon-play-dead-real-time, accessed 16 October.
13. Chris writes that 'Muybridge's work signaled a shift in the range of conceived uses of photography, toward creating images of moving as well as still subjects, but Muybridge sought most vigorously to stop, not simulate motion.'
14. From the Edison Company catalogue, http://memory.loc.gov/cgi-bin/query, accessed 2 November 2014.

32
The Sun Never Set on the Human Empire: Haunts of Humanism in the *Planet of the Apes* Films

Phil Henderson

Rise of the Planet of the Apes (2011) and its sequel *Dawn of the Planet of the Apes* (2014) grapple with a diversity of contentious issues; reviews have noted poignant messages about animal cruelty, racism, capitalism, and colonialism (Hobson 2011). While these messages are certainly present in the *Apes* films, I do not mean for them to be my primary focus in such a direct and unsubtle fashion. For I believe, and argue throughout this chapter, that the *Apes* films' most political message is their performance of a posthuman narrative. Furthermore, I assert that this narrative, while critical and fraught with nuances, is haunted by humanist dispositions. I suggest that even these promising films may be too residually humanistic to offer emancipatory visions for our posthuman imaginary. To these ends, I deploy the posthuman lens to read these films, first along the fractious lines of the ostensibly rigid animal/human dichotomy, then in light of potentially unbridgeable histories of violence and oppression, and finally to understand the political vision implied by the films. Prior to this I provide a brief outline of the position of posthuman thought, and a rough storyboard for both films.

In the early 21st century we are witnessing an upheaval of ontological positions wherein fabricated boundaries between the human subject and its animal, technical or environmental interlocutors evaporate, and the always tenuous divisions of race, gender and sex prove evermore difficult to sustain. This is the coming age of the posthuman, when that fundamental marker of who 'we' are dissolves. As Ted Hiebert (2012, 3) eloquently states, the posthuman is an intellectual climate that finds these old 'distinctions increasingly distasteful'. In these times of crashing borders, rather than mourn the lost distinctions and their attending violences, the theoretical and political edge of our work ought to construct new meanings and tropes that 'resonate with our own imagined or imaginary experiences' (Hiebert 2012, 9). Rosi Braidotti (2013, 5) touches upon this idea when she writes that posthuman literature is a 'generative tool' that aids in the production of new points of reference and zones of concern in a chaotic world unchained from its sun. As such, scholars of the posthuman must be fundamentally concerned with 'the kind of knowledge and intellectual values' being produced today (Braidotti 2013, 10–11). The knowledges which posthumanists seek to build are determinedly partial, eschewing the humanist urge to feign universalism while producing great epistemological violence (Gatens 1988, 67). It is with this hopeful climate in mind that I propose to address these films: scouring them for a fruitful harvest of imagined posthuman futurities. I am guided by the work of critical feminist scholars like Braidotti, Donna Haraway, Elizabeth Grosz, Arthur Kroker and Judith Butler. While this project begins quite promisingly, its conclusion rings with Kroker's prescient words that a 'phantasmagorical essence' of the human remains embedded within our imaginations of the posthuman (Kroker 2014, 4).

Movie-goers could easily be forgiven if the shards of the human that shoot through the narrative of the *Apes* films are not immediately apparent, as the films track the life of an ape: Caesar (Andy Serkis). *Rise* follows his origins as a chimpanzee-cyborg born in the genetics lab of his fatherly companion Will Rodman (James Franco), and rendered with remarkable intelligence. Eventually forced from his comfortable suburban life, the courts place Caesar in an ape 'sanctuary', where he witnesses the awful conditions inflicted on primates by humans. Ultimately, Caesar secures the apes' freedom; administering to them the drug that increases intelligence, and guiding a simian exodus from the city. *Dawn* picks up the story ten years later, when the 'simian' flu has reduced the human population by more than 90 per cent. During humanity's decline, Caesar and his fellow ape-cyborgs established a thriving settlement. This is thrown into crisis, however, by an encounter with a group of humans. These humans are led into the forest by Malcolm (Jason Clarke), in a desperate attempt to restore hydroelectric power to the floundering human refugee camp that was once San Francisco. Despite Caesar and Malcolm's best efforts, the contest over access to land leads to all-out war.

The ready acceptance of non-human protagonists by a popular audience can be taken as a sign that the humanist regime's 'supreme ontological entitlement' of the human as *the* site of knowledge, empathy and care, is beginning to crumble (Braidotti 2013, 68). As the narrative progresses, the *Apes* films perform Haraway's (2008, 8) call to break the 'clean lines between (…) human and nonhuman'. It is on this matter of cross-species boundary breaking that the *Apes* films achieve their greatest posthuman imaginings. Along the way to the posthuman figures of Caesar and his comrades, these films portray three distinct phases in the collapsing animal/human dichotomy. The first phase portrays animalistic creatures distinctly separate from humanity; this is followed by the markedly more complex second phase, engaging the messiness of care and love that blossoms out of companion relationships. In the final phase, near the end of *Rise* and throughout *Dawn*, this broken animal/human boundary is addressed as Caesar moves beyond companionism into a full embrace of himself as a cyborg.

In the *Psychic Life of Power*, Butler (1997, 21) writes that 'existence is always conferred from elsewhere', and that this marks the phenomenon of being as one of vulnerability to another. The power that constitutes a subject's existence always pre-exists that subject and, as such, the subject's being is understood and maintained only through reference to this constitutive power. This thesis is perhaps clearest in the case of animals, who are marked by power and remain always unable to reply to the language of that power. Jacques Derrida notes that the moniker 'animal' is a form of hailing, an 'appellation that men have instituted' and have 'given themselves the right and authority' to confer onto another (Derrida 2008, 23). Humanity has taken upon itself the power to confer the existence of animality; this brutal power is portrayed in the opening sequence of *Rise*.

The film begins with a panoramic shot of a jungle, cutting through the foliage to reveal human trappers capturing chimpanzees. Armed with nets, machetes and rifles, these men embody the social structures that hail the chimps as animality. Their act of hailing casts these creatures outside of the human community and thus outside of moral obligation. With such obligations abated, these 'zoe' are plucked from their home and carted off to be used as test subjects in San Francisco's laboratories. One of the captured apes is brought to the Gen-Sys genetics laboratory of Dr. Will Rodman, and subjected to an experimental Alzheimer's treatment known as ALZ-112 (hereafter, 'the 112'). As the effects of the drug take hold, Bright Eyes – named after an iris-changing side effect – shows markedly improved cognitive function, almost perfectly completing the Lucas Tower test. These results are taken to the Gen-Sys board of directors in the hope of securing more funding. However, when it comes time for this presentation, Bright Eyes violently refuses to leave her cage. In the ensuing scuffle she rampages through Gen-Sys, ultimately crashing into the board meeting. Cornered, Bright Eyes is shot by a security guard and Will's project dies with her on the boardroom table.

It is important to note that this security guard is certainly not Althusser's police officer: there is no 'hey you there!' Bright Eyes' moment of interpellation had occurred long ago, and in it she was called as an animal – a creature incapable of response. Derrida (2008, 8) writes that distinguishing 'a response from a reaction' (i.e., a thinking move from an instinctual move), is amongst the key concerns when facing animals. That animals are even beings capable of response is impossible to conceive in light of the essence of animality. Indeed, as Haraway (2008, 78) writes, it is a central conceit of the humanist position that 'everything but Man lives in the realm of reaction'. No matter how intelligent she was, Bright Eyes was still an animal incapable of understanding and, under this rubric, her death was an unfortunate but necessary calculation. Admirably, *Rise* refuses to allow us this consolation in murder: it is revealed that Bright Eyes was not reacting with 'stage fright', as her handler suggests, but was responding to the threat that the lab handlers posed to her infant. The tragic power of Bright Eyes' existence, conferred as 'animal', could not be more apparent here. The humanist ideology, embodied in the handler, the guard and Gen-Sys more generally, denies that Bright Eyes, as animal, could respond in an intelligible way. In its first truly posthuman moment, *Rise* reveals that Bright Eyes truly did respond, and the ground under the animal/human dichotomy begins rupturing.

Out of these ruptures emerges the second phase in the films' crumbling animal/human boundaries: companionism. The infant chimp to whom Bright Eyes gave birth is taken in by Will, rather than be put down as the 112 programme was shuttered (thus reproducing the trope that a woman's body must be destroyed to give birth to a hero). Will introduces the infant to his father Charles, who names the chimp Caesar despite Will's opposition to attachment. This opposition fades when Will is woken by Caesar's cries. As the hitherto cold scientist paternally swaddles Caesar in a steam-filled bathroom, a tiny simian hand reaches up and clasps Will's finger. Such a moment signifies the cross-species touch which features so heavily throughout Haraway's *When Species Meet*. The moment, captured between scientist and lab product, brings rushing forward 'all the important ecological and political histories and struggles' between the species, as a 'provocation to curiosity' (Haraway 2008, 6–7). Will concedes as much in the next scene when he indicates in his research log that three years have passed and Caesar has become a fixture of the Rodman home.

Importantly, while Caesar is raised and socialized *by* humans, he is not being raised *as* human. Caesar's movements as he swings and climbs throughout the house remain distinctly chimpanzee-like. It seems clear that Will and Charles have not forced Caesar into anthropomorphic postures, positions, or movements; instead, he and his companions have found new and creative ways of messing about together. This certainly cannot have been an easy task, as Caesar, while an animal companion, is resolutely *not* of a companion species. *When Species Meet* indicates that companion species share collective and 'noninnocent histories' of intermingled development (Haraway 2008, 16). The relationship between chimp and human lacks the long history of co-domestication that has smoothed the roughest edges of companion species relations.

This bond of companionship begins to fray in the face of cyborgian reality. Leaving Redwoods National Park, our protagonists encounter a family with their own companion animal – a dog. Taking exception to the strange primate in front of him, the German Shepherd becomes agitated and is only restrained by the leash and collar around his neck. The affectionate dominance inherent in the relationship of a human to a leashed pet is apparent to Caesar (Weil 2012, 55). Taking note that Will has leashed him similarly, Caesar becomes sullen as they depart. He demands to know whether he is a pet, and when Will denies this, the question is begged 'what is Caesar?' Will drives to the Gen-Sys car park, where he proceeds to tell Caesar of his origins as a product of the 112 programme, explaining that, through his genes, Caesar inherited the advanced intelligence promised by the drug. These revelations deepen Caesar's resentment, as he realizes that the leashed relationship of a companion animal can never be his. In that car park Caesar learns that he was born in the 'amniotic effluvia of terminal industrialism': that he was born a cyborg (Haraway 2004, 64).

Just as in the case of animal subjects, the existence of the cyborg is also conferred from elsewhere. As Haraway writes in her 'Cyborg Manifesto': ' "We" did not originally choose to be cyborgs, but choice grounds a liberal politics and epistemology' (Haraway 2004, 34). The cyborg, the emblem of the posthumanist era of collapsed distinctions, is a creature of ontology – existing despite our strongest efforts towards conceptual wholeness. From his birth, Caesar carries the effects of the 112, mixed irreversibly and indistinguishably with the 'natural' materials of an ape; in Caesar's body the jungle and the lab crash together.

Tellingly, the first shaky step towards Caesar embracing his cyborgian nature comes in a moment when he refuses his companion relationships. Imprisoned in an ape 'sanctuary' following an altercation with a neighbour, Caesar desperately waits for Will to release him. When Will eventually does return to release him, Caesar's eyes linger for a second on the leash in Will's hand – a sign of their old companionism – before turning his back on the man in refusal. Caesar recognizes that he, as 'illegitimate offspring of militarism and patriarchal capitalism' is the product of, but is no longer bound to, the will of his 'inessential' father (Haraway 2004, 10). Dismissal, spurning, or rejection are all impossible, as Will quite literally is as much a part of Caesar as is the 112. Instead of rejection, we witness a renunciation of the father. This move, writes Butler (1997, 143), 'does not abolish the instinct; it deploys the instinct for its own purposes'. Never rejected, but no longer essential, Will's relationship with Caesar must be renounced if the latter is to achieve his goal of liberating the apes. Caesar carries Will forward with him in everything that he does as a constitutive element of his own subjectivity. Indeed, as seen in *Dawn*, when Caesar goes through his nadir he returns to Will's looted home as a sanctuary, resurfacing that constitutively powerful renunciation.

Less complicit in Caesar's cyborgian ascension are the Landons, the family who own and operate the 'sanctuary'. Deeply cruel, John Landon and his son, Dodge, go to great lengths to maintain order in their compound: tranquilizers, tasers and riot hoses, are all employed to quell resisting apes. In his crowning cyborgian moment Caesar refuses Dodge's orders to return to his cell. Enraged by this insubordination, Dodge exerts his authority over the 'animal' – striking Caesar three times with his taser.[1] As the fourth blow swings towards him, Caesar grabs his assailant's arm. Dodge sputters a demand that resurrects a touchstone of the original *Planet of the Apes* (1968): 'Take your stinking paws off me you damn dirty ape!' In its original context, this line was a powerfully humanistic moment, as the plea lifted George Taylor (Charlton Heston) to the horizon of moral recognition in the ape community. In *Rise* this is perverted: it signifies humanism's persistent arrogance, seeing only a 'dumb monkey' even in the face of a cyborg. If the perversion of this line were not immediately apparent, Caesar's reply makes it unmistakable, as he projects a bellowing 'NO!' It is in this moment of speech that the myth of Caesar's animality is shattered. Derrida's observation of the inherent uncertainty as to whether an animal reacts or responds is answered: Caesar has responded, even replied, and done so loudly.

While *Rise* tracked the boundary breakages between animal/human dichotomies, both *Apes* films serve as illustrative of various histories of domination. Nettled and complex, as befits posthumanism, the *Apes* franchise does not compromise its complexity with purely good or purely evil characters, all are complicit in different violences. I examine three major themes of domination; first, the speciesism that is present throughout the films. Second, imperialist sensibilities in *Dawn*. Finally, war returns as the ultimate expression of desire to control or eliminate an other.

The relation of humanity to animality is one of discursive opposition – 'we are human because we are not animal'. I turn back on this point to examine the films' portrayal of the domination that emerges from this stratification of being. In his examination of Heidegger, Giorgio Agamben (2002, 50) notes that the German philosopher maintains that animality is incapable of response, existing in a world of 'captivation'. Humans, however, live in 'Dasein' – an existence predicated on presences and intent as one engages in the world. Outside of Dasein, animals constitute the exception to civil law par excellence; animals cannot represent themselves under the law, and yet they remain subject to sovereign power. As Agamben (2002, 92) wrote, 'in our culture man has always been the result of a simultaneous division and articulation of the animal and the human' and, in the face of humanist law, there is no place for the animal. Imprisoned in the 'sanctuary', Caesar is embodied proof of this; Will's attempts to release him are Caesar's only legal recourse. Only through the body of a human can the animal find reprieve from the necro-power of the law. Humanists believe that animals can never even know the squalor of their treatment.

It is not only gruff working-class gaolers who mistreat apes. On the verge of a cure for Alzheimer's, Gen-Sys CEO Steven Jacobs implores Will to continue his research despite apprehensions, as the scientist stands to 'make history' with his discoveries. This sentiment is closer to fact than fiction, as Kari Weil (2012, 26) notes that the first successful genetic modification of a primate was declared to be 'an extraordinary moment in the history of humans'. What these scientists ignore, and what the *Apes* films foreground, is that these achievements figure quite differently in both the personal and collective histories of primates. While science projects an image of itself as the 'purest and most ideal form of... *disinterested, objective* and *proven* knowledge', this projection is only sustained from the human perspective (Grosz & De Lepervanche 1988, 5). Pointing to the grotesque scars he has received from various experiments, Koba firmly declares them to be 'human work'. Koba insists that, whatever history-making moment he was a part of, these scientific experiments were only ever cruel – throwing their universal objectivity into crisis.

It would not do, however, to paint this as a case of pure victimhood, for agency can persist even in the face of domination. As Haraway (2008, 18) observes, 'the discursive tie between the colonized, the enslaved, the noncitizen, and the animal (...) is at the heart of racism and flourishes, lethally, in the entrails of humanism'. To whom this lethality is directed remains an open question. In *Dawn*, Koba is discovered by two guards while investigating their weapons stockpile, the humans are extremely frightened and hold him at gunpoint. Koba relaxes his face into a playfully silly expression, as he begins to move about in a 'dumb monkey' act. The tension is relieved, and the guards allow Koba to leave – believing he is too simple to threaten them. When Koba returns to the stockpile later he finds the same guards on duty. As he mimes out the most stereotypical circus chimp routine he can muster, Koba plays to the guards' presumptions of his mindlessness. They offer him liquor to 'see what'll happen'. As a result of their sense of superiority, the guards are disarmed and murdered. Suffering so long under the knife of human exceptionalism, Koba redeploys the tropes of animality to his own advantage. The lethal kernel at the heart of humanist typologies of the animal crunches loudly.

In the wake of the rampaging 'simian flu' a community of human survivors lives in what remains of San Francisco. A self-styled 'colony', this refuge was founded by architect Malcolm (Jason Clarke) and a former marine, Dreyfus (Gary Oldman).

As if calling their community a colony – presumably of the anthropomorphic empire – was not indicative of humanity's continuing supreme ontological entitlement, Dreyfus clarifies the point when he declares that he and Malcolm intend to 'rebuild and reclaim' the (human) world that was lost. Braidotti (2013, 66–67) writes that the posthuman 'axis of transformation entails the displacement of anthropocentrism and the recognition of trans species solidarity on the basis of our being environmentally based'. Pushed to the edge of extinction, the humans in *Dawn* refuse Braidotti's move; lingering in the narcissistic view of the natural world as something to which they have entitlement. It is this imperial tendency, this drive by humans to project themselves outward while barring projection into themselves, that pushes our story disastrously towards all-out war.

Armed conflict between humans and cyborg-apes certainly feels like an inevitability in this film. However, we must recognize this as the hauntological effects of the humanist project consuming what ought to be pushing towards a posthuman landscape. The conceit is that war is a tool as meaningful to the posthuman as it was to the human. Haraway (2008, 80) is particularly powerful on this point, as she emphasizes that the truly posthuman position is one that takes up the dictum 'thou shalt not make killable'. War is nothing other than a form of collective punishment, predicated on the making killable of the entire oppositional population. Indeed, this is exactly what happens in *Dawn*, as Koba orders that all humans be either killed or rounded up as the cyborg-apes sack the colony. It is hard to believe, and dangerous to imagine, that a posthuman like Koba – who has himself been a killable subject – would harbour such unbridgeable and human-like resentment.

In tragic poetic justice, Koba's status as killable life re-emerges at the core of cyborg-ape sovereignty. Hanging perilously close to a life-ending fall from a building, Koba seeks Caesar's forgiveness for the coup, invoking their deepest law: 'Ape not kill ape'. It is clear that Caesar can save him and, despite all the crimes Koba has committed, he is still owed the protection of his community. Taking his hand, Caesar begins to lift Koba only to pause and declare 'You are not ape', casting Koba down to certain death. In this moment Caesar has taken upon himself as sovereign the ability to declare the outsider inside the law; the exception to the law of sovereign protection – the killable subject (Agamben 2005).

Seen throughout *Dawn*, humanist notions of justice are reinscribed into the bodies of supposedly posthuman subjects. Justice in the posthuman era ought to be much more partial, more contingent; it should express itself as:

> [T]he right to experience the full freedom of the contingent, to honor in public the memory of the many martyrs who had gone before and whose sacrifices in the silence of detention facilities and torture cells wrote the political alphabet of the disavowed, the excluded, the forever silenced.
>
> (Kroker 2014, 65)

Such an ethic is absent in the *Apes* films, as the narrative universalizes notions of justice. Ultimately, this justice achieves the (re)installation of humanism, masked by a superficially posthuman narrative. Braidotti (2013, 30) writes that 'recognition of epistemic violence', typified by universalisms, is critical for 'recognition of the real-life violence' against any group outside the norm. If the *Apes* films have proven anything to me, however, it is that our ability to imagine the posthuman polity to come is utterly clouded and impoverished by the human polity of today. That 'indispensably human...phantasmagorical essence' that Kroker (2014, 4) indicated was lingering in our visions of the posthuman resurfaces. Indeed, the ape-cyborg polity retains the most irredeemable ideology of the late humanist political order.

In the merely ten years since their escape, Caesar and his comrades have established a thriving community that appears quite utopic. However, we ought to probe for any indications of the ideological cornerstones laid within this posthuman culture. In a conversation with the orang-utan Maurice, Caesar gives a subtle indication as to the model of his political ideals. When asked why he allowed Rocket (the deposed alpha chimp) to distribute treats, Caesar replies by breaking a single twig and declaring that 'one monkey is weak'. Taking several twigs in hand, Caesar torques the unbreakable bundle: 'monkeys together are stronger'. While it could be said that this is a metaphor of solidarity, it would be wrong to ignore the more overt allusion in Caesar's actions. A bundle of sticks, bound together for strength, is known as a fasces. With its origins as a political symbol in Rome, the juxtaposition of the fasces beside a 'caesar' is not powerful enough to hide their modern usage as the etymological root and primary signifier of European fascism. All of this might have been allowed to pass, had Caesar's rhetoric not echoed those of 20th-century fascists. Discursive construction rendered the cyborg-ape community as a 'family', necessarily conjuring images of bloodlines and imagined purities.

Moreover, this family tree is one whose branches do not extend any further than the 'natural community' of great apes, as evidenced by their deer hunt and use of horses as beasts of burden. A review (Taylor 2011) notes, 'there's no suggestion that the apes want to help other animals', nothing to suggest that their circle of care might be wider than humanism's. Indeed, towards the end of the film Caesar admits that he has *always* trusted apes before all others – revealing something akin to simianism. While Braidotti (2013, 97) has indicated that representations of the posthuman are not necessarily bound to be 'more egalitarian or less racist and heterosexist', and while I am not pining for a utopia, this is one semiotic knot that ought to be cut loose.

Should any doubts remain as to the continuity of the human project under Caesar and his comrades, the final scene assuages them. As dawn breaks, Caesar, restored to power, stands before his comrades, having put an end to the cyborg-apes' rampage through San Francisco. Scuffling can be heard from behind as several cyborg-apes drag Malcolm up from a dark tunnel where he had been struggling against Dreyfus' attempts to implode the simian-occupied colony, trying to kill all inside. Caesar orders his comrades to stand down, and approaches Malcolm as the latter reveals that what remains of the US Army is about to descend on the cyborg-apes. Rather than run, Caesar declares that this is a battle that must be fought. As they stand in mutual admiration both move forward and press brow to brow, before silently walking away: Malcolm back into the dark tunnel entrance way, and Caesar into a beautiful golden dawn.

This marks an apparently final death, the new day is clearly bright and pregnant with possibility for the cyborg-apes, but as the shadows consume him this dawn cannot be for Malcolm, nor for any human. For once the European man that Malcolm signifies passes, so too does humankind. No humanist could imagine a non-European bearing the burden of humanity's future; the moment of pressed foreheads 'obliterates once again the invisible bodies of the people of colour who have never counted as able to represent humanity' (Haraway 2004, 81). It is, however, in the gentleness of their touch that we can rest assured that Malcolm has no qualms about the future under the leadership of this cyborg-ape. Indeed, Malcolm's struggle against Dreyfus' bomb plot is actually a struggle to preserve the structure of the colony – the shelter of humanism – so that it can be inherited by the cyborg-apes. There is no alienation between this Last Man and Caesar, for there is no schism in their projects.

Whither trends the posthuman imaginary? Over the course of *Rise* and *Dawn of the Planet of the Apes* the old ontological animal/human binary is dissolved; not only is the human narratively decentred, but the very notion of a purely human or purely animal being becomes more and more untenable in light of all the boundary crashes and collapses. These films make great strides in uncovering multidirectional and fractious forms of violence and oppression. From the exceptional status of the animal within humanist jurisprudence, to the immanent relationship of the posthuman to their discursive subjection, violence turns in many ways throughout these films and none are innocent in its deployment. Where this imaginative world begins to lose its lustre, however, is in the political subtext. Humanistic tropes are subtly reinstantiated in this text. Indeed, while we should expect Caesar and his cyborg-apes to present us with a great political reformation, we are given only old resentful, reactionary politics. Here, the posthuman imagination clearly faltered, and fell back into the increasingly meaningless and unsustainable binaries that have for so long demarcated the political. Ultimately, when it comes to the *Apes* films, I am left wanting; longing after a narrative ready to make bolder cuts against that which has come before and has left so much pain in its wake. I sense that I am adrift in waves of the human, while I look disparately for a 'post-' upon which to take refuge.

Note

1. For an interpretation of why three blows are particularly relevant here see Haraway (2008, 11–12).

33
Uncanny Intimacies: Humans and Machines in Film

Alexander Darius Ornella

Introduction: Intimate encounters

In its *Riley v. California* ruling requiring the police to get a search warrant to access mobile phone content, the US Supreme Court argued that: 'modern cell phones, (...) are now such a pervasive and insistent part of daily life that the proverbial visitor from Mars might conclude they were an important feature of human anatomy' (*Riley v. California* 2014). This somewhat poignant Mars reference suggests that we have developed a close, even intimate, relationship with the machines and technologies we use. Chris Hables Gray and colleagues argue that we cannot think of the human–machine relation as partnership any longer, but rather as a symbiosis that is controlled by cybernetics and that influences our imagination, imagery and thought processes (Hables-Gray et al. 1995, 4).

Taking Joseph Weizenbaum's ELIZA program from the 1960s as her starting point, Sherry Turkle showed how easily some computer users develop meaningful and emotional ties with machines or technological gadgets. In particular, the interactiveness and their representation in popular culture as relational, social and emotional machines often let users, adults and children, forget their inner workings (Turkle 2007, 506–507). It seems that the way we relate ourselves to our tools is shaped by the individual and shared narratives we create around these tools; or, in other words, that we ascribe (religious) meaning to the relationships we have with our tools, and that tools and machines can touch us on a deep level (Geraci 2007).

This chapter explores recent themes in representing human–machine relationships on screen. After a brief – and thus sketchy – historical overview of science fiction (SF) film, it explores some contemporary themes in SF film and TV: a return to (an idealized) nature, erotic encounters, social robots and cybernetics. I have limited my examples and my discussion around an increasing interest in body and bodily relationships with machines in SF film and TV. While we do not only have bodies, but are bodies, through the portrayal of human–machine relationships, many SF narratives establish body as liminal bodies, or, in other words, they reveal that we always are in a liminal relationship with our own bodies that escapes proper definition. Themes discussed here are not universal but culture specific, and we might find different narratives and imagery in other cultural contexts (Tarantino 2012).

Humans and machines on screen: A brief historical overview

The portrayal of human–machine relationships is not exclusive to SF film and television. In *You've Got Mail*, for example, email provides a space for personal and intimate encounters and the characters develop a sort of intimate relationship with the medium itself. Early Apple iPad commercials, too, constructed intimate – even bodily – relationships with 'magical' devices we could hug, cuddle up with, touch and caress. Other films might be full of technological gadgetry yet they might contribute little to battling evil, for example, the 007 film series (Goldman 1989, 279). SF film, however, has been concerned with the relationship between humans and machines from early on, and can be considered as one of the prime areas to ponder these relationships with what is usually classified as non-human or other.

Scholars roughly distinguish between the following eras, each with their own dominant concerns about our relationship with machines. Films from 1900 to 1940s, in particular films during the Machine Age (roughly the time between the two world wars), often addressed the dominance of machines and the alienation from the world they were thought to bring about (Telotte 1999, 1–27). This concern was rooted, among others, in machines increasingly exhibiting abilities of living beings and thus contributing to a shift in human self-understanding towards biological machines (Heyck 2011, 232). We also see an emerging concern over the corruption of technology by economic and power interests (Goldman 1989, 285–286). It is therefore not surprising that most of the SF films we consider classics today were produced in the major industrialized countries of the time, for example, USA, Germany, Britain and France (Bould 2003, 83).

Anxiety and fear of technology also pervades SF films in the 1950s, in particular fear over nuclear power, conflicts and weapons. Aesthetically, this anxiety is screened through mutations caused by radiation, weapons of mass destruction, or aliens worried about or attacked by nuclear weapons. While the 1950s have also produced a number of anti-communist films (e.g., *Red Planet Mars*, Harry Horner, US, 1952), some of the films that lend themselves for such a reading use the portrayal of our relationship with technology as means to tackle issues of human reproduction, dehumanisation and deviant behaviour. *Invasion of the Body Snatchers* (Don Siegel, US, 1956), for example, is often read against a communist background, but, as Mark Bould argues, the depiction of automation and gynaecological technology rather suggest a concern over issues of reproduction (Bould 2003, 86–87). Further, 1950s and 1960s films featured alien invasions, blurred the lines between the human and non-human, and problematized uncontrolled scientific research in key films such as *The Fly* (Kurt Neumann, US, 1958). Films from this postwar era also imagined machines establishing authoritarian control over us (Telotte 2001, 39; Booker 2006, 10; Heyck 2011, 234).

SF films in the early 1970s tended to 'dramatise [...] disenchantment with a "new" technology whose hope has been exhausted' (Sobchack 2004, 221). *Star Wars* (George Lucas, US 1977) marks a key event in American SF film (Bould 2003, 91–92). With its opening text: 'A long time ago, in a galaxy far, far away...', it expresses, according to Vivian Sobchack, a certain kind of nostalgia – or the longing for a paradisiacal and utopian harmonious human–machine relationship – because the future happened a long time ago (Sobchack 2004, 221–222). SF films from the late 1970s and 1980s also increasingly featured mythic and epic narratives (Telotte 2001, 105).

During the Machine Age and the postwar-era, machines were often represented *as* machines (with exceptions) and the body served as one of the markers to set us apart from our machinic other. The advent of embodied machines and robots brought about the end of the body as this dividing line, requiring new aesthetics and new ways of thinking about what it means to be human and how we relate ourselves to our machines. R2D2 and the Terminator, for example, were both embodied, but R2D2 was considered to be more human because he was thought of being able to experience the whole range of human emotions. Here, emotions, in particular love, humour and compassion, replaced the body as a marker for being human. A growing anxiety over the technological reproduction of human beings, leading to the loss of our uniqueness, contributed to this emphasis on emotions as a feature that sets humans *apart* from machines in SF films from the 1980s and 1990s. *Blade Runner* (Ridley Scott, US, 1982), however, complicates emotions and empathy because Tyrell, the creator of the replicants, seems less empathic than his creations. The spread of personal computing, too, contributed to a shift in representing human–machine relations on screen, personalizing and individualizing machines (Telotte 2001, 30; Heyck 2011, 239–242).

Today, the status of SF film, 'one of the most accomplished of the popular art forms' (Sontag 1965, 42), seems to be in narrative decline, giving way to (the hybrid genre of) superhero films. The perceived end of history after 9/11, the re-enchantment of the world, and a longing for the mythical caused by our constant immersion in rational and technological (communication) processes have contributed to this decline (Bould 2003, 80; Johnson-Smith 2005, 2; Sobchack 2014, 284–287). The notion of the singularity (understood here, following Vernor Vinge, as that point beyond which neither our understanding nor our imagination can go (Landon 2012), also poses a challenge to SF literature to think and imagine beyond this unimaginable point (Raulerson 2013, 16–38), as well as SF film and TV, because, due to their medium, they rely on the visualization of that which is unimaginable, unrepresentable, unthinkable.

SF TV has developed an identity independent from cinema and has grown into a quite successful genre with an avid fan community (Telotte 2008, 26; Telotte 2014, 1–2). Some of the recent TV series, for example, *Dollhouse* (2009–2010), *Almost Human* (2013–2014), *Black Mirror* (2011–2013), *Batttlestar Galactica* (2004–2009) and its prequel *Caprica* (2009–2010), explicitly address our relationship to machines, human copies, gender or artificially created personalities. Here, SF TV can, at its best, serve as an analytical tool, not only for technological concerns, but for broader cultural, social, gender and racial concerns, that is, the markers we use to draw boundaries between us and the (machinic) other (Telotte 2014, 8–9).

Themes in recent SF film and TV

A return to nature: A return to the primitive?

Elaine L. Graham argues that popular culture in general and SF in particular is one of the key arenas for 'some of the most definitive and authoritative representations of human identity in a digital and biotechnological age' (Graham 2002, 1). Norah Campbell and Mike Saren suggest that posthumanism is 'an aesthetic that blends three elements – the primitive, technology and horror' (Campbell & Saren 2010, 152) and employs two types of metamorphoses, morphing and mutating, as aesthetic convention (Campbell & Saren 2010, 162).

The primitive is often called upon to label what is perceived as pre-(high-)tech era, but the very act of labelling something from a Western perspective renders visible the socio-historically constructed nature of the term. Distinct from yet related to the primitive is a longing for a return to a highly romanticized understanding of nature. Recent films such as *Avatar* (James Cameron, US/UK, 2009) and *Surrogates* (Jonathan Mostow, US, 2009) draw on the natural, the primitive or non-technological. In *Avatar*, most of what Western audiences would consider (high-)tech is either war technology or scientific equipment appropriated by military and corporate interests. In contrast, the Na'vi world is portrayed as enchanted, natural and, excepting some rather 'primitive' weapons, as technology-free. In fact, no high-tech seems to be required because the Na'vi are naturally connected to all life on the planet and the planet itself. The quite problematic message early on in the film is that technology and the artificially created Na'vi body allow the paraplegic Jake Sully to live a more fulfilled and meaningful life. But this technological enhancement must remain a crutch within the narrative framing of technology *as* war technology. Jake and his Na'vi body must therefore rid themselves of technology and his disabled human body in order to return to a more natural state. Ironically, Jake can only enter this (romanticized) natural state *because* of the artificially created Na'vi body.

The film *Surrogates*, based on Robert Venditti's comic book series *The Surrogates* (2005–2006), does not quite go as far as *Avatar*'s return to nature, but suggests that we need to question our reliance on it. We encounter what looks like a utopian world in which people experience the world through an immersive humanoid robot remotely controlled from the safety of their homes. The machines in the film do not promise eternal life but a more fulfilled life, as the advertisement for the surrogate technology suggests: 'Life... only better'. The final scene of the film is crucial for understanding how the it makes sense of the human–machine relationship. After Tom Greer (Bruce Willis) destroys the surrogate system, the surrogates in the entire city drop to the floor and confused operators leave their apartments in their pyjamas. We watch the scene from a bird's-eye view and hear in voiceover commentary: 'Still no official word when or if surrogate services can be restored. It appears, at least for now, that we are on our own.' This final scene suggests that, only with the breakdown of the surries system, can humans wake up and start interacting with each other on a human body-to-body basis. What seems like a weak flicker of hope – that we should critically think about the space we allow our machines to inhabit in our lives, however, is a problematic anthropological message. On the one hand, technology is portrayed as something that leads us astray from being human. On the other hand, being on our own, without our creations, is portrayed as deeply troubling, suggesting that the surrogates serve as a kind of perverted *ersatz* for an imagined paradise once lost.

Sex and gender: Erotic encounters with and through machines

Critics of transhumanism often diagnose a preference of mind over matter or question the assumptions underlying the idea of uploading minds to a computer network (Midgley 1992, 20; Hauskeller 2012). Hans Moravec's labelling of our organic bodies as 'jelly' does indeed lend itself to such criticism (Moravec 1988, 118). Max More argues that most transhumanists understand uploading not in terms of dualism but functionalism, because the mind must always be instantiated in some form of material substrate (More 2013, 7). The drive to leave the messy body behind or improve upon it might suggest that uploaders might want to rid themselves of intimate bodily interactions, such as sex, too. Some transhumanists, for example, James Hughes, indeed argue that technology will allow us to leave the messy exchange of body fluids behind. That does not mean that he imagines a world that is 'freed' of sexual intercourse, but rather a world in which technology will allow for more intimate and more intense experiences of (sexual) pleasure, or enhanced or completely new sex organs (Ornella 2009, 318–323).

Visual representations of human–machine relations can render visible this erotic and highly gendered subtext that is often hidden in popular discourse. Björk's music video for the song *All Is Full of Love* (dir. Chris Cunningham, 1999) shows two female robots (whose faces resemble Björk's face) caressing and making love to each other. The otherwise sterile lab environment becomes a sensual place through the softness of the music, the lubrication and the moisture present on the robot bodies, and the interaction between the robots that looks more like the gentle touching of skin and flesh than metallic machine parts rubbing against each other (Shaviro 2002). In David Cronenberg's film *eXistenZ* (Canada/UK, 1999), the characters can connect an organic game console directly to their nervous system through a bio-port in their spine, allowing for an immersive game experience. There is no explicit sexual intercourse in the film but, in order to jack in, the bio-port needs to be lubed up and penetrated. The erotic subtext is emphasized on an aesthetic level: the bio-port looks like an anus the characters lick, rim and finger, thereby blurring and subverting traditional gender roles (Ornella 2009, 320).

In the TV series *Battlestar Galactica* (2004–2009), an erotically charged aesthetics characterizes the representation of human–machine relationships, too. Some of the female Cylons (especially the Number 6s) are hypersexualized and 'embody our culture's fear and love of technology, producing a conflicted vision that intersects in a central issue of contemporary science fiction narratives: our problematic attitude toward both gender and technology' (George 2008, 160). Those humans (all younger men) who fall in love with these female 'skin-jobs' (the derogative nickname humans use for humanoid Cylons) not only enter a transgressive relationship, but also put themselves into a transgressive relationship with their human community. Machines, too, seem to experience sexual pleasure not only in a machine–machine or machine–human relationship but as part of their 'functionality'. So-called Hybrids, organic machines with a female upper body but fully integrated into the spaceship, control the Cylon basestars. Initiating faster-than-light jumps is portrayed as a very intense, even orgasmic, experience for these Hybrids.

In *Her* (Spike Jonze, US, 2013) the material/embodied technological other becomes the disembodied technological other in form of Samantha, an operating system (OS) Theodore (Joaquin Phoenix) falls in love with. While Samantha lacks a body, she has a strong bodily presence in the film nonetheless through colour, sound, Phoenix's acting and, last but not least, her very sensual and intimate voice (Scarlett Johansson). The relationship is not only a romantic but a sexual one, with the couple engaging in cybersex/phone sex. To provide Theodore with the satisfaction of flesh-to-flesh intercourse, Samantha arranges for a surrogate to act in her stead, something Theodore tries but then rejects because he is uncomfortable opening up their relationship to a third person. For Theodore, the relationship is very real and genuine, but it ultimately fails because he is unable to understand that Samantha can love several hundred people at the same time, and because she decides to move on with other OSs to a place where he – quite biblically – cannot follow her.

Social robots

Derek Scherer, a designer of social robots for films, argues that on-screen representations of social robots can serve as models for real-life robot–human interaction design. He shows how different strategies, such as the use of biological indicators or a recognizable personality, help designers to create movie character robots and foster audience bonding processes (Scherer 2014). Movie representations of social or service robots in film often address questions such as whether or not the robot has, or at least can, develop his or her own and unique identity and our unease with this new emerging other. In *I, Robot* (Alex Proyas, US/DE, 2004), white/pale robots serve as (rather mindless) assistants at home and in public services. One robot forms an exception; he develops his own will, personality and emotions, and introduces himself as 'Sonny'. The film uses the robophobic detective Del Spooner (Will Smith) and his developing relationship with Sonny to address questions of whiteness, otherness, conformity and identity processes (Brayton 2008). In *A.I. Artificial Intelligence* (Steven Spielberg, US, 2001), the robot boy David serves as replacement for Monica and Henry's lost son Martin. Bert Olivier argues that, in both films, *I, Robot* and *A.I.*, the understanding of (artificial) 'intelligence' goes beyond mere functionalism and is discussed against the background of fundamental human traits such as the longing to be respected, remorse and conscience, or being loved and being able to love (Olivier 2008).

Black Mirror (season 2, episode 1: 'Be Right Back') (BBC 2011–2013) offers a twist on *A.I.* To deal with her grief over the loss of her partner Ash, Martha contacts a company that offers to mine all of Ash's social media data and conversations and create a virtual replica with his voice and his sense of humour. After some time, Martha decides to take up the company's offer to download virtual Ash into a robot replica of Ash. This embodied attempt of working through the mourning process quite quickly turns into an uncanny experience, as this new Ash does not need to eat, sleep, blink or close his eyes when he lies in bed.

Bonding processes between elderly ex-con Frank who suffers from dementia and a not-very-human-looking domestic care robot are the theme of *Robot & Frank* (Jake Schreier, US, 2012). Initially, Frank resists relying on a machine but eventually grows quite fond of it and sees in it the perfect accomplice for another heist. As the police start suspecting Frank, the robot urges him to erase his (the robot's) memories as they are the only incriminating evidence and are meaningless to the robot. At first, Frank refuses to do so because he seems to feel that erasing the memories leads to some sort of end (or death) of the robot's personality. Eventually, he gives in and, as he pushes the delete button, the robot shuts down and falls into – or dies in – Frank's arms, an almost pieta-like imagery. The final scene is similarly melancholic: Frank's children visit him in a care home for elderly people. Rather than celebrating Frank's regained independence from technology, Wolfgang Amadeus Mozart's *Requiem Mass* (K626) as background music gives the final scene its melancholic touch. Ridding ourselves (or others) from technology does not necessarily restore a state of freedom or humaneness. Rather, what some perceive to be inhumane technology (e.g., Frank's daughter) might, in fact, enable a more humane life. Frank's facial expression seems to radiate contentment with his situation, yet with the music one cannot help but think about Frank's (and the robot's) funeral.

In *Almost Human* (TV, 2013–2014), every police officer is supported by a logic- and rule-oriented, emotionless MX-43 android model. These androids replaced earlier DRN models, which were seen as flawed because of their human-like emotional responses, aimed to make them as human as possible – almost equating being human to being flawed. Annoyed at the MX-43's mechanicality, John Kennex throws it out of his moving car and ends up with an older DRN model called Dorian. In a similar way to Sonny in *I, Robot*, Dorian resents the term 'synthetic' and has a very sympathetic and sarcastic humour, and the two have some awkward-funny conversations – for example, about penis sizes – enabling bonding processes not only with Kennex but the audience.

It is important to analyse the subtexts of the examples mentioned regarding whiteness, power, race or gender (Sonny is male, Frank's robot has a male voice). What I am interested in here, however, is how they capitalize our attachment to and love for objects, gadgets and machines. In particular, in *Robot & Frank* we can observe how the robot as living being emerges not through his programming but in and through the eyes of Frank. It is almost like the robot breathes life into him and takes it back at the end.

Cybernetics

Early ideas of cybernetics and from the mind-uploading community feature quite prominently in some recent SF films and TV series. Cybernetics in the early/mid-20th century wanted to provide a common framework to describe communication processes within and between animals, humans and machines, and their environments. By doing so, cybernetics contributed to a redefinition of human beings as 'information-processing systems' (Hayles 1999, 113) and a redefinition of the human body where the 'body ceases to be regarded primarily as material object and instead is seen as an informational pattern' (Hayles 1999, 104). According to mind-uploaders, as long as these informational patterns remain intact, they can be transferred from one carrier medium (wetware, such as the human body) to another (e.g., a computer system) (Wiener 1948; Moravec 1988). These ideas resurface in *Avatar*. While the Na'vis are performing a religious-like ritual with chanting and dancing, roots grow around both Jake's human and Na'vi body, to establish a link between them and allow Jake's mind (and/or soul) to swap bodies. This imagery naturalizes and normalizes the otherwise technological process often imagined by uploaders. There is nothing uncanny about body swapping in *Avatar*, and the narrative steers the audience into hoping that Jake will be able to leave his human bodiliness behind in favour of the artificial and perfected body.

In contrast to the constructed naturalness of *Avatar*, *Transcendence* (Wally Pfister, UK/CN/US, 2014) represents the process of uploading as a highly technological and tedious (and uncanny) process that includes the recording of brain activities of the terminally wounded scientist Will Caster while he reads word after word. The majority of the film is more or less a fight between 'believers' and 'non-believers', that is, those who believe the virtual Will Caster is the 'real' Will and those who believe virtual Will is a mere copy, or worse – an artificial intelligence (AI) program gone mad. As Will grows in power, he cures sickness and restores missing limbs (and, quite conveniently, adds some sort of remote control mechanism), restores the environment and re-embodies himself to be close to his wife Evelyn again, using nanotechnology. We can understand *Transcendence* as an attempt to imagine and visually represent a post-singularity, disembodied or utterly differently embodied/materialized existence.

Joss Whedon's TV series *Dollhouse* (2009–2010) offers a critical approach to the mind-as-information idea. It portrays a body that resists being repeatedly wiped and imprinted with different artificially created personalities and develops self-awareness and its own personality. While *Dollhouse* critiques the idea of imprinting artificial personalities, only the (technological) process of wiping and imprinting memories allows Echo's body to have a fresh start and to become itself.

Conclusion

The relationship between humans and machines does not only change over time depending on cultural contexts, but – drawing on Paul Ricœur – we can understand SF film and TV to provide an important ethical laboratory to (re)imagine and play with human–machine relationships, modes of being human or understandings of human nature. Robert M. Geraci argues that 21st-century SF and cyberpunk literature has started to embrace transhumanist technological promises (Geraci 2011). María Goicoechea argues that literary cyberpunk fiction today often presents the body as 'malleable material of amazing plasticity (...) The shapeless batch of human parts seems to reach perfection only through its union with the machine' (Goicoechea 2008, 2).

Recent SF films and TV series, too, draw on ideas from transhumanism and early cybernetics and show an increasing interest in the body and our bodily relationship with machines. In other words, and as the 'post-singularity' Will Caster who re-embodies himself shows: Does the visuality of the medium of film and television mark – or even demand – a return to the body in our imagination, however problematic these on-screen bodies might be? *Her* tries to imagine artificial life, but Samantha leaves at the end of the film. Despite her strong disembodied/embodied presence in the film, she must leave since there is no body to hold her back, no body to show on screen. In fact, her felt bodily presence depends very much on a – Theodore's – body. We can also identify a longing for a 'new' (read: romanticized) bodily naturalness in on-screen SF, yet this natural body can often only be achieved through technology.

Ultimately, on-screen transhumanist or high-tech-free utopias or perfected and enhanced bodies promising 'life...only better' might be disappointing because of the very perfection and (artificially created) naturalness we long for. Most importantly, on-screen human–machine relationships bear witness that 'technology' cannot be reduced to a mere object, tool, abstract knowledge of, or mastery over something, but that technology 'is always "lived" – always historically informed by political, economic and social content, and always an expression of aesthetic value' (Sobchack 2004, 220).

34
Posthumanous Subjects

Steen Christiansen

Thinking the posthuman is not a matter of thinking the human 'after' the human. Rather, it is a matter of thinking outside of the human, presenting alternatives to current human-centric modes of thought. Being alive has unquestioningly been seen as central to our understanding of the human. Yet this does not mean that life is in any way a simple matter, or that the boundary between life and death is easy to determine, or a trivial matter. In the summer of 2004, *Reconstruction* published a special issue dedicated to the posthuman. Caused by a revealing typo, the call for papers eventually morphed into an investigation of the posthumanous, tentatively defined as:

> *Post·hum·an·ous (pst-hymən-nəs) adj. 1. Occurring or continuing after the death of the human:* a posthumanous writing. *2. Published after the death of the author:* a posthumanous book. *3. Born after the death of the patriarchy:* a posthumanous child. *4. Any activity which presumes the fatal limitation of the rational-humanist subject.*
>
> (Smith, Klock & Gallardo 2004, 2)

Now, ten years later, I wish to resuscitate the term to suggest that one way of thinking the posthuman is by thinking life/death in more complex terms. Too easily the dichotomy of life/death slips into the well-known dichotomy of presence (life) versus absence (death). Yet death is never fully absent, but is instead deeply embedded in questions of the right life and the rights to life. Life is instead best viewed as a complex tangle of relations that is contingent on more than a simple dichotomy. Indeed, thinking the posthumanous is a matter of thinking the transformation that the tangled relation of life and death enacts in contemporary biopolitics, that is, the ways that life and death produce certain ways of life.

Recent films and television shows have, in fact, started probing the boundaries between life and death in unexpected ways. *Yomigaeri*, *The Returned* and *They Came Back* all feature people coming back from the dead. Although at first glance this appears to be a common motif for the supernatural, the difference here is that the returned are not vampires, zombies or similar horror figures. Instead, the returned simply come back to life as they used to be – they have not aged, they have not decayed, and they do not crave human blood or brains. The narrative conflict is therefore also less about exterminating the returned, but instead the emotional and social impact of the dead coming back.

What these fictions show, then, is that there is a growing interest in the degree zero of human life, an understanding of the dividing line between life and death as inherently unstable and problematic. Why this sudden interest in the boundary between life and death, and how does that boundary connect to posthumanist thought? I contend that, with the increased influence that biopolitics have today and the intensification of precarious life, as well as medical reconfigurations of what human life looks like, these fictions become a way to interrogate and negotiate different meanings of life and death in the 21st century. We need a posthumanous subject to articulate the liminality of life.

One of the goals of posthumanist thought is the decentring of the human being; it is the rejection of the argument that the human is a universal being, something which stands 'outside historical change and might exist in political and social relationships that are universal and always available' (Herbrechter 2013, 3–74). Rather, there is a multiplicity of forces that all influence what the human is and can be. As Eugene Thacker has shown, such multiplicities have traditionally been viewed as threats to what he terms the body politic, because these multiplicities are the movements of 'passing-through, passing-between, even passing beyond' that are 'both the constitution and the dissolution of the body politic' (Thacker 2011, 153).

The body politic, Thacker elucidates, is a way to think political order as an analogy between the human form and political government, so that the head is an analogy for the king or state, the people, the body and so forth. Different eras have divided up the human body in different ways to articulate specific relations, such as Plato's division of the sovereign as the head, the soldiers as the chest and peasants as the groin (Thacker 2011, 141). But what happens to the body politic when the natural body breaks down, and comes back to life? Such a 'necrology', as Thacker terms it, reveals a challenge to biopolitics since, as Thacker points out, '[t]he body politic concept is never so vital as when it ceases to be an explicit part of the debate, and its ontological categories invisibly serve to make possible political discourse' (Thacker 2011, 159). In other words, the body politic is the absent master signifier of contemporary biopolitics, and posthumanous fictions deal with the (imaginary) production of a posthumanous subject as a way of responding to this absence, rejecting biopolitics as basis for life by positing a posthumanous subject that demands respect in its own ways, not on human terms.

Just as Herbrechter reads science fiction (SF) through the lens of a containment/subversion dialectic to understand the technologized posthuman, I too will read these posthumanous fictions as ways of negotiating contemporary biopolitics (Herbrechter 2013, 107–134). This strategy emerged from cultural materialists like Jonathan Dollimore, who pointed to the way that radical thoughts were affirmed through narrative closure. Simultaneously, by posing and engaging with a transgressive topic, no fiction can avoid also presenting a vision of subversion

(Dollimore 2004, 25). It is this oscillation that will help flesh out my concept of a posthumanous subject.

The dead for the living

The most sentimental containment response is found in Akihiko Shiota's *Yomigaeri* (2002). Primarily a love story, the central conceit of the dead returning is mainly a matter of the dead being 'for the living', so to speak. In essence, the dead return so that the living may reconcile their traumas and move on with their lives. The returned are regarded primarily as a blessing. After the initial shock, the living welcome the returned with open arms and open hearts. The government sends a representative, Heita Kawada (Tsuyoshi Kusanagi), to investigate. One part is the investigation of what happened, while the other is the love story between Heita and his female friend, Aoi Tachibana (Yûko Takeuchi), whom he secretly loved. The film employs this parallel narrative in a well-established way, letting the two plots converge, thus intensifying both plot lines.

As for the investigation, Heita is at a loss to explain why the dead have returned. And not only the dead, but *these* dead? And not only these dead, but these dead *right now*? Not all the dead in the village of Aso have returned, nor have the returned all been dead for the same amount of time. The only hypothesis that is initially suggested is that it is simply the strength of desire in the living that makes the returned come back. Yet the film does not stop here. In looking for unusual activities in the Aso and the surrounding region, Heita discovers a strange gravitational disturbance around the volcanic crater upon which the village sits. Heita and his co-workers speculate that this must be the source of the returned. In investigating the force field further, they come to realize that it is active and produces a distinct, pulsing signal, 'as if it were alive', as Heita exclaims upon seeing the signal on screen. Indeed, the returned are spirited away if they try to go beyond the reach of the signal, and reappear close to those who made them come back through their desire.

This signal, as a kind of vitalist animism of the world, alongside with the way the returned go back to their loved ones, strongly suggests that the returned have only come back *for us*. That is, the dead came back only insofar as the living needed to come to terms with the death of their loved ones. The returned in *Yomigaeri* are nothing more than traumas come back to be resolved. As a kind of unclaimed experience, it is only this fantastical conceit that allows the living to learn how to live. While the film ends on an emotional high note, the healing of an old trauma, the returned are at the same time positioned as other. The relation between living and dead is firmly established, and the dead serve the living. The film's containment strategy is thus one of emotional containment, where the dead return only to resolve the lives of the living, so that the living can come to terms with their past emotions. The returned are thus others, not unlike an animal that is meant to rectify the human subject by way of expulsion. The body politic and social cohesion is maintained through exclusion and othering. Yet, at the same time, questions remain about why the dead are always with the living and cannot be laid to rest, even as the film closes. While peacefully resolved, the film indicates the force that the dead exert over the living, the way that 'we' are not simply us, but also constantly haunted by our passed loved ones. This challenges the rational humanist subject, not only because of the excessively emotional return of the dead (which exceeds rationality), but also because the presence of an absence, the haunting of the dead, indicates that the human subject is at least traversed by those it has lost, and so is not unitary, but a posthumanous subject containing multitudes.

Dead alive

Less simple and less emotional is the narrative we find in ABC's series *Resurrection*. Here, the living struggle to let the returned back into their lives. The posthumanous emerges as the impact the returned have on the living and what this means for our conception of life. The series' primary focus is on Jacob Langston (Landon Gimenez), who died 32 years ago and mysteriously shows up in China, still a boy. Immigration agent J. Martin Bellamy (Omar Epps) takes it upon himself to bring the boy back home, unaware that Jacob has returned from the dead. Jacob's parents do not recognize him at first, but Lucille Langston (Frances Fisher) quickly realizes that he is her son. Henry Langston (Kurtwood Smith) is much slower to accept that this can be his son, and keeps his distance, both physically and emotionally. Immigration agent Bellamy also struggles to believe that Jacob truly has returned from the dead, but, as more people return, it becomes harder and harder to deny that something strange is happening.

The reticence most of the characters exhibit comes from the ambiguous status of the returned. In contrast to *Yomigaeri*, people in *Resurrection* do not immediately accept the return of their loved ones, nor do the returned come back completely as they used to be. This disrupts the simple relation that was previously in place. Before, the returned were easily part of a family relation, but this is no longer the case, which makes their current status waver. Since they have been dead for any number of years, yet have not aged, it is questioned whether they can still be regarded as the same people they used to be. Neither can they be accepted by the living as entirely human anymore. However, the returned are not exactly non-human either, since they are still the people once loved by the living. The problem faced by the living is the reconciliation of the difference between the body that once was living, the body that was dead and the body that is now, once again, living.

This question is forcefully posed in *Resurrection*, when Jacob's grave is exhumed and his body is revealed to still be inside. How can Jacob be in two places at once, and how can the currently living Jacob be the same as the dead body in the tomb? The corporeal presence of Jacob's corpse questions our body's relation to us and to our identity. Normally, the vulnerability of our flesh and our fear of its decay, with the attending loss of consciousness, all pertain to the uncanny status of the corpse. The corpse is never just 'a corpse' but always, somehow, also 'our corpse'. There is never a corpse that does not remind us that we will die. Yet

Jacob's not-dead body is both a corpse and a living thing. Jacob's body becomes the limen which indicates that he is somehow a nothingness which continues to be; he is the corporeal presence of an absence that we cannot reject or ignore. His body becomes what Lauro and Embry term an indeterminable boundary (Lauro & Embry 2008, 95). No relation between the posthumanous and the human can be properly articulated: Jacob is radically outside the life–death relation, yet he is there. His presence troubles the certainties we have of what the human is; the posthumanous transforms the human into something which is not only alive, but must also incorporate the not-dead.

The uncanny status of the returned, then, is revealed to not only be about the returned, but also about the way that their position outside the binary reflects back on the humanist subject and makes it spectral. The return of the dead forces us to consider that life and death are not binary end points but a continuum of multiple states of in-betweenness. Life does not have an autonomous origin, as Pramod K. Nayar argues, but instead is 'the embodiment of multiple crossings of information/data and the linkages of these bits of data. At what point the chemical, motile and other properties mean life is a matter of interpretation' (Nayar 2014, ch. 3). Inevitably, this indication that 'we' can only emerge as human by expelling death raises the uncomfortable question of where I am in this continuum of life. In this sense, I am already posthumanous, since life as interpretation means that I can be interpreted as being already dead.[1]

To be dead

With the French show *The Returned* (2012–), we find the first radical response to the posthumanous, a response which does not end with containment. While the show has not yet concluded, there is reason to believe that no easy answers will be provided, considering the finale of the first season. Much like *Resurrection*, *The Returned* begins with the return of one single person. Slowly more people come back, some of them children; others are older. The final episode of season one pits the returned against the living. The returned demand that all who have come back be given to them, including Adèle (Clotilde Hesme) who is pregnant with a child fathered by one of the returned. The returned reject being othered, demanding that they be given equal footing, equal subject status, but not status as the same. The returned become a generative force that demands its own position outside of the life–death binary. The returned are not dead, but also not alive. They simply negate and reject the humanist subject of life. Instead, the returned cover all the different ontological categories that are usually posited as 'non': non-masculine, non-normal, non-young, non-healthy, and they make these categories affirmative in insisting on having their own will and desires.

In other words, the returned pose the argument that a true relationship cannot exist between terms that are absolute. Such a relation is static and unchangeable and does not truly signify a relation at all, but rather a unit, a singularity. What this means is that we are limited in our capacity to think outside of such a static binary when it comes to the question of life and death. As Eugene Thacker has pointed out, we can only think life in terms of something else. Tracing the history of these others, Thacker points to time, form and spirit as typical versions of the terms of other-than-life (Thacker 2010, 240). And yet, these terms always break down when pushed to extremes. When the dead come back, we are faced with a radical breakdown of life. For humanist thought, this opens up an abyss of non-reciprocity. There can be no logical/rational response to such a spectral relation, since it represents a dislocation of terms, a dislocation that also dislocates the unitary human being.

For *The Returned*, the ones that come back, because they demand their own rights and their own desires, they are not simply a third added to the binary, but outside of the binary altogether. They produce an alternative subjectivity, which cannot be formulated within the traditional system. Instead, they open up the human to something else entirely, something both similar and different, simultaneously absent and present. *The Returned* implies the boundary collapse of humanist dualistic discourse, which is why the show is radical in its openness, refusing to fall into the easy monstrous representations of the returned as classical horror zombies, and instead proposing an alterity that is not a human but not flattened into the non-human either. In this way, the returned are reminiscent of what Roberto Esposito has termed the neuter:

> *While the neuter does not belong in the sphere of being, this does not make it reducible to nothingness either. Perhaps it can best be described as situated at their point of intersection, where one is ceaselessly turning into the other: nothingness passing into being, presence emptied by absence, the inside spilling out into the outside.*
>
> (Esposito 2012, 129)

Here the posthumanous is not a negation, nor does it spectralize the humanist subject; there is no containment in this show. There is the forceful insistence that there is more to the returned than simply another version of the human or its other. The returned are outside this relation, which is why they cannot be contained. While *Resurrection* made life more than binary, more than simply life or death, *The Returned* renders the body politic unstable because the body natural is no longer sufficient to account for the relation between life and death. If the body natural can no longer suppress death but must account for it, then this means the breakdown of the body politic, because there is no room for this third position. The body politic itself becomes posthumanous, no longer sovereign, no longer able to mete out life and death.

Dead again

The most extreme perspective on the struggle between a humanist subject and a posthumanous one is found in *They Came Back* (Robin Campillo, 2004). While the film does suggest containment in the way that the returned go back to death at the end of the film, the atrocities visited upon the returned prohibit any form of closure. Rather, *They Came Back* radically posits an alternative body politic based not on the body natural but the body unnatural, as the film portrays it.

In this film, the return is not only a personal event as it is in the other posthumanous fictions, but a global event. Seventy million people return, 13,000 in the town where the film takes place. The returned in *They Came Back* are different from the returned in the other texts. Slower, more ponderous and less connected to the living, they clearly represent an alternative to humans. At the same time, the returned clearly share some form of sociality with each other. As the story progresses, they develop a social bond with each other to which the living are not privy. The returned start meeting at night, inhabiting tunnels below the town, and finally set off bombs throughout the town. While infrastructure is disrupted, no one is injured. After this event, the returned are gassed by the army. Placed on top of their tombs, the returned simply dissipate, which concludes the film.

While time is still spent on the emotional impact the returned have on the living, there is a managerial tone to the film. Intercut with the traditional narrative, we see the town council talk about how to manage the returned, and how they should be treated. Unlike the other programmes discussed, *They Came Back* opens up a discussion about how to deal with a posthumanous subject. How should such a subject be treated? The film thus produces an interesting double-take on the posthumanous subject. From the managerial perspective, the returned present a social and economic problem. Significantly, the returned are portrayed as immigrants, stowed away out of sight in shelters, and managed by the state. When it turns out that the returned walk around, especially at night, they are drugged, so that 'they sleep better during the night and move less during the day', as a doctor puts it. Explicitly, the returned are drugged for their own safety, but it is strongly implied that this is simply a matter of managing the dead.

Another problem to be solved is what is referred to early in the film as the two hypocrisies. Since it is required that the returned have jobs, companies have to fire people to make room for the returned. This is the first hypocrisy. The second hypocrisy is that the returned must have jobs even though they are not good workers. They are sedate, ponderous and slow to communicate, which in turn make them less valuable for the companies. It is interesting that these hypocrisies stand as indisputable, even though the government funds the jobs, and therefore the returned do not present a financial burden. Similarly, when it is argued that most of the returned are retirees, the company associate counters by stating that retired people still 'become a problem for wage-earners', since only wage-earners produce income to sustain the retired.

In other words, from a managerial, biopolitical perspective, the posthumanous subjects are already here: whoever does not work presents a problem for those who do, and the only solution is not traditional retirement, since this continues the problem, but retirement in the *Blade Runner* sense of death. If we take Thacker's argument that life can only be thought of in terms of something else, the biopolitical can only think life in terms of work. If you do not work, you are wasteful, an expenditure that is only a burden. You become, in essence, a present absence because you should be gone, since you have outlived your usefulness, and yet you linger. This is death extended into life: a chilling realization, since it means that we are all eventually useless and wasteful. When we cease being wage-earners, we cease being alive. Work is life, idleness is death.

As for the emotional connection with the returned, *They Came Back* also posits an interesting theory of posthumanous subject. At first, the returned are recognized as being slower than when they were alive, a state which is compared to aphasia but is later recognized to be more severe. Incapable of maintaining intellectually demanding jobs, the returned are instead assigned menial work in factories. This connects them implicitly to automatons, a state which is reinforced with the film's introduction of the so-called echo and memory theory about the mental state of the returned. This theory argues that the returned do not really have a working consciousness any more. Instead, they seem to simply imitate the expressions of the living that they observe around them. This is referred to as echo, in which patterns are reproduced without being understood. Alternatively, the returned may remember expressions that they once used and now recirculate them, which is called memory. The psychologist believes that the returned are in a confused state, incapable of proper thought.

Considering Derrida's discussion of reaction and response in terms of the animal, we can see how the returned create a form of reverse formulation of Derrida's argument. As we know, Derrida points out that the typical humanist view of animals is that 'they do not respond but react; they merely obey a fixed program, whereas the human subject responds to the other, to the question posed by the other' (Derrida 2003, 125). Yet if it is wrong to define the animal as pure reaction with no response, then we can certainly reverse this argument and say that the human does not necessarily respond, but instead reacts. The returned in *They Came Back* are uncanny because they make something familiar unfamiliar, but here it is not just family members but the very definition of humanity which is made uncanny.[2]

It is not that the returned are represented as somehow unthinking, for they clearly do care about the ones they return to. The old woman Martha (Catherine Samie) cares deeply for her husband, and when he is frightened at the prospect of all the returned, she talks him into letting go and passing on. In much the same vein, Mathieu (Jonathan Zaccaï) worries incessantly that when he died in a car accident, he had spoken harshly to his girlfriend Rachel (Géraldine Pailhas) and so hurt her. The troubling uncanniness that we feel for the returned comes from this alien, non-human thought. Once again outside the regular human–non-human binary, where nothing non-human has any form of consciousness or cognition, the returned represent an image of uncanny thought. The question of what they think, what they want, is expressed by the mayor (Victor Garrivier) when Martha keeps running away: 'why did they come back, if all they want to do is run off again?' Yet to think that, to ask that question, is simply to apply human logic to something outside that relation. The question presupposes that the returned came back for the living and not for themselves. In this way, it simply becomes another example of anthropocentrism.

The returned must be killed, in the end, because they represent a threat to the human; they are an unmooring both of the body politic and human cognition. They are spectral subjects who dislocate and challenge an anthropocentric worldview. That they blow up the town infrastructure symbolizes the way they also blow up human relations. Their presence forces a thinking of the human not located in work, not located in cognition and not located in human-centric concerns. This is a posthumanous subject that is neither human nor non-human, but outside that relation. No longer for us, the posthumanous subject is troubling because it does not even care about being human; there is no desire to return to the human condition for the returned in *They Came Back*.

Becoming posthumanous

The posthumanous marks a transformation. At its core, it dislocates what it modifies into something outside conventional dichotomies of subject/object or being/nothingness. Being posthumanous is therefore to contain traversing multitudes, to not be limited to one thing or one state of being. It is rejecting a singular form of being. As we have seen, being posthumanous is accepting the living-on of the absent essence of the human, and recognizing that there is nothing essential about what makes us human. The posthumanous suggest not so much a third term between life and death, but that we must understand the human as emerging from within the fold of life and death, and that biopolitics and the body politic is at the very crux of this emergence.

The concept of the posthumanous that all these fictions negotiate in different ways all end up questioning the understanding of an individual as critically bound up not only with capacities and attributes of the human, but also the question of whether, as Nayar asks 'a society or culture [does] have the responsibility of providing the structures in which these capacities might be fully exercised' (Nayar 2014, ch. 5). The answer, both for Nayar and the fictions I have discussed, is a resounding yes. What the posthumanous fictions have shown us, sometimes reluctantly, sometimes exuberantly, is that the outside through which we define ourselves constantly moves through us. Only this movement can, in any way, grasp what it means to be human, but not as a static definition. Rather, change and transformation, what others have called becoming, is the true mark of being. This is why the constant temporization of presence and absence must be traced over and over again, because what is ghosted and what is made material to the human is never a stable matter. Only by accepting the non-essence of posthumanous being can we begin to step outside the human. By rejecting the body natural as anything other than an effect of the body politic, the posthumanous urges us to step outside of biopolitics.

Notes

1. Lauro and Embry provide a long and significant discussion of the Terri Schiavo case, where the status of life was indeed up for legal interpretation. This is a very real instance of the trace of life in death, the play of presence and absence with serious implications.
2. I am aware of the philosophical conundrum referred to as, variously, the behavioural zombie, the functional zombie or physiological zombie, but do not want to pursue the issue here. For more on this issue, see Rockwell 2005.

35
Identity: Difficulties, Discontinuities and Pluralities of Personhood

James DiGiovanna

Introduction: Identity and (science) fictional narratives

Questions concerning what it takes to be the same person over time and across changes are at the heart of posthumanist fiction and central to the long philosophical tradition of asking questions about personal identity. *Star Trek*'s Commander Riker is split in two by a teleporter accident; autobiographical memories are rewritten in *Eternal Sunshine of the Spotless Mind*; body parts, including sections of the brain, are replaced with machines in *RoboCop*; people are suspended for extended periods of time and then resurrected in *A.I.*; a person backs up his memory to a computer, is killed, and then lives on in the computer in *Extant*. In what sense are these people the same, or not the same, as the entities that preceded them and with which they are identified? If we become so enhanced or altered that we can share our experiences, survive the death of our bodies, split ourselves into multiple agents or reprogram our minds, will we cease to be persons in the future? As philosopher Allen Buchanan (2009, 349) notes, we face the possibility that 'our world of persons is replaced, completely, through the sustained use of (...) enhancement technologies, by a higher sort of being, post-persons'. And if these are post-persons, will it make sense to use our existing concept of *personal* identity in discussing them?

Philosophical fictions of identity

In the latter half of the 20th century, science fiction (SF) stories took central place in philosophizing about identity. Philosophers wrote of people having their brains split and placed into two different bodies (Nagel 1971), a machine that erases, copies and reprograms memory (Williams 1973), and people who live for thousands of years but only remember the previous hundred or so (Lewis 1976). Many of these ideas were influenced by posthumanist fiction. It is no surprise that we should then focus on these narratives, as they have become central to philosophizing, and, while SF films like *The Matrix* and *Vanilla Sky* may borrow from philosophy, philosophy borrows as much or more from such films. Surveying the landscape of SF speculation on identity makes sense, because if some narrative has not yet entered philosophical reflection, the philosopher looking for problem cases and examples will find it soon enough.

Still, many philosophers have raised questions about whether a fictional narrative can lead to a philosophical truth. Quine, for example, claimed that to 'seek what is "logically required" for sameness of person under unprecedented circumstances is to suggest that words have some logical force beyond what our past needs have invested them with' (Quine 1972, 489). But that's always the way with words and concepts: they have to be prepared to face a changing world. In fact, some of the possibilities raised in the SF cases are coming close to being realized: we already have technologies that can alter memories (Loftus 1995; Caplan 2013) and we are replacing missing limbs, ears and even eyes with cybernetic parts. So while we may not have included things like replacement bodies and memory-sculpting in our concept of personal identity when that concept arose, dealing with these technologies is becoming a necessity, and SF has anticipated this problem.

But if Quine is right, and we are using words 'beyond what our past needs have invested them with', how do stories like those in SF have philosophical force? I would argue that is precisely *because* we are using words in new territories that these stories have such force. Philosophy cannot simply be a conservative assessment of what people already believe. These SF cases are important because they challenge something that is important to us. This is because personal identity is not a concept like 'stockbroker'. Quine is right that the latter term would not make much sense far outside the social circumstances which birthed it. If a SF story has stockbrokers, we can assume its world has a lot in common with contemporary earth, and has some strong differences from medieval, ancient and prehistoric communities. 'Stockbroker' is a strongly social construct.

But the identity of agents goes deeper than human society. Wolves, birds, apes and lions know their mates, leaders, friends and enemies, and recognize them as such on successive occasions. 'Personal identity' is not a purely linguistic or cultural invention; it is an attempt to name something that is operative at very low levels.

Given this, there are two responses to Quine's challenge, the 'realist' response and the 'fantastic' response. Realist SF presents stories about what is likely to happen, and even to happen soon, and which challenge our ideas about what we are. *RoboCop* is fiction, but we already have prosthetics limbs, and Theodore Berger, at MIT, claims he has produced a prosthetic brain implant to treat memory impairment (Cohen 2013). Life expectancy for a 20-year-old has increased 50 per cent in the last 150 years,[1] and systems for seeing into another's mind are in functional early development (Horikawa 2013). The questions raised by realist SF are of obvious philosophical relevance: How will we organize and govern ourselves and our relations when we can upload our memories, replace our bodies, share consciousness, live for centuries? And if changes like this destabilize our concepts of personal identity, then perhaps these concepts were never well grounded to begin with.

And yet those concepts ground our relations with others and our place in the world. Our social roles depend upon a notion of personal continuity so as to assign ownership, guilt, respect and authority. Further, we already have questions about what happens when memories are lost or replaced, when people surrender individual agency to enter into totalitarian groups, or are 'brainwashed' by organizations or governments which attempt to control both the scope and direction of their thoughts. SF tackles these real-world philosophical problems with thought experiments that only *appear* to be purely speculative. Of course, some SF deals with stories too fantastic to be likely. But, given that identification with a future self is central to any being that makes plans, we have to take all challenges seriously. We cannot simply say that, like 'stockbroker', we can do without the concept if we rearrange economic institutions. Rather, since identity is at the heart of what it is to be who we are, we would like it to survive any conceptual challenge. When we alter the bounds of what it is to remain ourselves, we ask questions about what matters to us.

Suppose we could merge our memories and identities with that of another person. Would we want to? Is our individuality too important to surrender? Suppose we could actually rewrite memories so as to create an illusion of a better life. Would it be moral? Is there some self that I need to be true to? Or is the self just whatever I am immediately experiencing? Suppose my mental content can be transferred to another body when I die. Would that body be guilty of my crimes? Without providing an exhaustive list of the questions posthumanist SF proposes, we can see that, even in its more fantastic form, it forces us to reflect on what we value in our current mode of identifying ourselves across time, and offers us other ways of conceiving of ourselves.

Types of identity

In general, philosophers have followed two main lines in finding criteria for personal identity:

- The psychological, found in Locke, Descartes, Hume and Parfit, which holds that it is our thoughts, memories, personalities and, in general, dispositions and mental content, that make us who we are; and
- the physical, held by Epicurus, Democritus and Aristotle, and currently championed by Olson (1997), which holds that it is something about our material bodies, or the continuity of an individual human animal, that makes us consistent. If I am made of the same matter, or am biologically continuous, then I am the same being.

More recently, some additional accounts have been added:

- Narrative accounts, held by Ricoeur (1985), Schechtman (2007) and many psychologists working on therapeutic notions of selfhood (cf. Yancy & Hadley 2005), claim that identity is contained in the narratives we rehearse to ourselves and tell others, and the stories others tell about us. Though diverse, these theories hold in common that who I am is intimately related not to singular

facts, but coherent stories that create both an image of character and a history in which I am situated.
- Relational accounts, found in Schechtman (2010), Benhabib (1999) and Chodorow (1980), which hold that identity involves relation to others. For example, a person who has lost all memory could be considered the same person by relatives who visit her in the hospital, or speak to her as 'mother' or 'daughter'.

To give an idea of how posthuman fiction can destabilize these notions, we shall look at the psychological and relational accounts.

Psychological

Locke introduced the idea that our identities are held in place by psychological sameness: 'as far as this consciousness can be extended backwards to any past Action or Thought, so far reaches the Identity of that Person; it is the same self now it was then' (Locke 1690, II, xxvii, 9). Thomas Reid claimed that this account was problematic because a person could remember time T_1 at time T_2, and time T_2 at time T_3, but not remember T_1 at T_3, meaning that the T_3 person and the T_1 person are both identical to the T_2 person, but not to each other (Reid 1785, III, 6). Parfit corrects this criticism by appealing to an 'overlapping chain' of memories, such that if 2007 John and 2005 John share memories, and 2005 John and 2000 John share memories, and so on back to 1985 John, then 2007 John can be said to be psychologically related to 1985 John even if he shares no direct memories with him, because he occurs in the same overlapping chain of memory connections (Parfit 1987, 205).

But is this theory really sufficient? In *The 6th Day* psychologically continuous but physically new people are produced as replacements for those who have just died. Their identity comes into question when one of the prior bodies turns out to still be alive, and the new one must kill it. At that moment, it becomes clear that psychological continuity is not enough, as a living being cannot be identical to the being he just killed. Here the realist must ask: What happens to identity when we can upload our complete mental content? And the idea that memory was ever sufficient for identity is at least challenged.

In *Doctor Who*, season 4, episode 10, the Doctor makes a backup of his wife, River Song, when she dies. This backup contains all of her memories and psychological content, maintaining her distinctive personality, but it exists only as digital file: she has no body. Years later (season 7, episode 14), she, or her duplicate, depending on which theory of personal identity you accept, says to the Doctor, 'If you ever loved *me* [emphasis added]' implying that she *is* the person he loved, or at least sees herself as such. Strangely, though, in that very same episode, she warns the Doctor's companion, Clara, not to perform an action that will cause perfect duplicates of her (Clara) to be created. She says 'They won't be you... they'll be copies. The real you will be dead.' But if River Song (or the River Song backup file) believes this, she should also not believe that she is the person that the Doctor loved. Clearly, River is torn between the view that *her* memory of a past life is sufficient for identity, and the fear that such a psychological continuity in another would not be sufficient. Writer Russell T. Davies points here to a central point of philosophical importance: we understand ourselves to be who we are by virtue of memory. If I believe myself to have had an important relationship with another, I doubt I would quickly surrender that identity if I found out I was a duplicate. The feeling and memory of oneness seems sufficient to create the meaning needed for identity. But if I found out someone who had the memory and character of a dear friend was in fact a duplicate, and my friend was dead, I would at least be deeply troubled about how I should relate to this person.

This illustrates a way in which our concept of personal identity runs into a wall when facing a situation where it must 'have some logical force beyond what our past needs have invested them with'. The importance of memory for our sense of self cannot be doubted, but its metaphysical role in guaranteeing identity is fragile, at best. What the SF examples show us is our sense of what matters. If I could perfectly replicate a person, would I do so if he were lost to me? Should I? For all external purposes he could act as the same person. Internally, he would believe himself the same. The thin metaphysical sense in which this is not the same person could overwhelm us, or we could ignore it. Further, it is easy to imagine that, after a century of such technology being in place, people would have no qualms about duplicating a dead loved one, and treating her as the same person. What these fictions offer us is a different way of thinking about sameness, and one of the benefits of philosophical speculation is that it allows us, by virtue of that difference, to see what is important or fragile or arbitrary in our way of conceiving.

Relational

Marya Schechtman (2010, 279) discusses what she calls 'person space', and our role within it. She holds, for example, that a person with total memory loss due to Alzheimer's might still retain the role of 'my mother' in person space, and that others would continue to relate to her (or, if we are strict psychological theorists, the body that once contained her) as mother by, for example, calling her by name and talking to her, in spite of the loss of all of her psychological content.

Breaks in the self, like the memory degradation of Alzheimer's, can be given philosophical weight by exaggeration. In *Doctor Who*, the character and appearance of the Doctor changes drastically between incarnations, though he maintains most of his memories. If memory is not sufficient, though, what accounts for him still being the Doctor? In part, it's that he is treated as the Doctor by others. When Jon Pertwee took on the role, he was immediately conscripted by UNIT, the secret government organization that had worked with the Patrick Troughton incarnation of the Doctor. When David Tennant replaced Christopher Eccleston, he acted quite differently, but Rose remained his companion, maintaining feelings and a sense of history with him. Similarly, that the Daleks still wanted to kill him, and the Time Lords still saw him as the man who had stolen a TARDIS, allowed the new Doctor to have identity with the old Doctor. This choice to recognize the Doctor, by UNIT, Rose, Time Lords and Daleks, was crucial to the maintenance of his identity. He occupied a continuous place in person space. This may seem like a fantastic case, but it's analogous to the Alzheimer's case, or the case of someone who has been in an appearance-altering accident that caused a personality-changing brain injury. For such a person, part of what would maintain her identity are the relations with others she would inherit.[2]

Yet while these relational elements might be important parts of identity, they are clearly not sufficient. If they were, the robot women in *The Stepford Wives* would have been identical with the women they replaced. They were created to take the place of women who are killed by their misogynist husbands, and within their homes and communities they are *taken* for the same people and play the same roles. Still, there is a clear moral and metaphysical problem with blithely accepting them as the same because of the continuity of relations, even if they believed themselves to be the same.

Types of problem cases

What the previous section, on types of identity, should show is that the standard answers have their limits, and break down in extreme (and perhaps ordinary) cases. Philosophers and SF writers have converged on similar problem cases, which we could classify as follows:

Fission/duplication

These cases occur when a single entity splits into two or more. For example, in *Her*, the artificial intelligence (AI) Samantha can split herself into thousands of separate entities capable of carrying on independent conversations. But if there are many of me, and they go their separate ways, which one is me? None of the standard accounts can really answer this. In *Star Trek: The Next Generation*, when the transporter duplicates Riker, each of him has an equal amount of material from the prior him, bolstered by some added matter from the transporter's stores. Here, the physical account offers no answer to which is *the* Riker. As noted in Types of Identity, the psychological account is no help here either. Nor will narrative accounts, as each duplicate shares the narrative to the point of fissure. And how, except arbitrarily, can we decide which being to accept in our relations?

Fusion/hive-mind

These cases involve combining several into one. *Star Trek* has the paradigmatic case of assimilation by the Borg: individual consciousness are linked in a network and become one. The emotional consequences of being fused are rarely addressed, as in most cases, once fused, the individual becomes emotionless (Borg, *Doctor Who*'s Cybermen and *Invasion of the Body Snatchers* Pod People all, strangely, assume this), but the human/pig psychic links in *Upstream Color*, one of the most important and neglected SF films of the last 50 years, takes a strong interest in this. In that film, people are infected with parasitic worms that later are removed from their bodies and placed into the bodies of pigs. A man and a woman, infected with worms, come together, and later two pigs, each receiving one of the worms, unbeknownst to them, mate. When the pigs' offspring are killed, the man and woman go into a depressive and paranoid spiral, feeling the loss of their children, even though they don't believe themselves to have any children. They have been suspended in a form of identity rarely discussed. They don't share a narrative identity with the pigs, because the pigs, lacking language, cannot have in mind the sorts of stories that produce narrative. But emotions may form a deeper source of identity, and that the man and woman so deeply feel the loss of the children may be indicative of a way that we truly do derive identity, even if philosophers don't often discuss it. Interestingly, Marya Schechtman (2007) is an exception, claiming that 'empathic access' is a necessary element of personal identity, though she wants to limit it to accessing our own past. It is unclear how we can do this without a sense of 'our own'; if empathic access hints at connection of identity, then our identities could partially bleed into others if, like the characters in *Upstream Color*, we became empathically linked to them. Similarly, for psychological theorists, identity is blurred by memory fusion; for physical theorists, by bodily fusion.

Fusion complexifies identity even more when combined with fission in what are called 'honeycomb cases'.[3] *Star Trek*'s founders are a perfect example of the honeycomb type: they merge into one and then separate out into individuals repeatedly. Neatly, as 'liquid' beings, they share both memory and material identity while fused. When specifically asked about what happens to identity when one enters and leaves the great link, a founder gives the cryptic answer (*Deep Space Nine*, season 6, episode 4): 'The drop becomes the ocean...The ocean becomes a drop', though it is not clear if it will be the *same* drop. In some sense, there is no answer to that; if the changeling maintains the memory of all the others, should it be considered merely continuous with one entity that entered the link? Could the great link not spit out as many of any one changeling as it wanted? Again, none of the existing theories is of much help. The physical account, which often does best against problem cases, may be particularly stymied here because the changelings merge their matter. And this raises a neatly posthuman question: Would we really need or want individual identity in a world where we can fuse? And in such a world, who is to blame for a crime? *Star Trek* avoids this question by arresting an individual founder for war crimes, but because of her recurring return to the great link, it seems they could have arrested *any* founder, and merely picked this one because the link had chosen a semi-consistent face to represent itself in interstellar affairs. It is hard to see how this particular changeling is the guilty party and not merely a convenient target for people whose concept of identity is not up to the task at hand. It's not that she is not guilty, but she is hardly the whole entity that is guilty: it is like arresting only the hands of a man accused of strangling someone. Again, this seems purely fantastic, but how do we assess guilt for people who lose their identity in indoctrination? As Marilyn Friedman puts it, 'Choices which manifest mindless conformity to convention are paradigm examples of choices lacking autonomy. The values and standards which can be traced directly to one's religion or to one's scout troop are, most obviously, those of others and accordingly, not one's "own" ' (Friedman 1986, 20). While the latter claim is controversial, exaggerating the circumstances through the posthumanist merging helps to create the difference needed to describe ways in which we at least could accept that the individual may not be the whole entity responsible for an action. This can also serve as a reduction of the claims for corporate personhood. And perhaps it sheds light on how we have always overestimated our own autonomy when so much of our minds are already received from social, familial and group pressures.

Suspension/regeneration/replication

These cases ask: Can we be the same person if we cease to be for a period of time? In 1707 Samuel Clarke wondered why Christians should care about being resurrected in the afterlife if it is 'as easy for God to add my consciousness to the new-formed matter of one or of one hundred bodies' (Uzgalis 2011, 193). That is, if I die, and am 'reborn', why should I think that is me, and not merely a duplicate? This is echoed in the Christian-style monotheism of the Cylons from *Battlestar Galactica*, who are killed and 'reappear' on the regeneration ship. If the ship stores extra bodies and simply encodes them with the memory of the deceased, could it not do this while they are alive? And if so, how is the new being identical with the old one? Physicalists hold that if it is a new body, it is a new person: those are not the same Cylons. Psychological theorists disagree. But the *Star Trek* transporters transport the matter of the body, and then reassemble it at the other end. Can we survive being disassembled and reassembled? What if, as in the two Rikers case, the matter is split between two resulting people?

In the television show *Extant*, the sentient robot Ethan is destroyed, but he then reappears on computer screens in his 'parents' home, where his mental content was backed-up. The physical theorist would claim that it is not Ethan, but if there was a sentient robot that could activate itself in any number of bodies while maintaining integrity of psychological content, then the physical criterion would hardly seem to apply. Such a creature might just undermine the very idea of singular personal identity.

Disruptive change and Methuselah cases

These differ, but point to a similar problem. In Methuselah cases (Lewis 1976, 30) a person lives for a very long time, undergoing change at a normal rate, so that after, say, 150 years, they have very little, if any, psychological or physical content in common with their prior selves. Strangely, such cases are almost unrepresented in SF. Though long-lived individuals are a part of many stories (*Bicentennial Man*, *Highlander*, the Collector in *Guardians of the Galaxy* and so on) they generally don't exhibit the kind of memory transformation needed for this puzzle. One exception is Captain Jack Harkness, from *Torchwood*, who appears later in time as 'The Face of Bo', with grossly distorted physiology and millions of years of experience distancing himself from his earlier form. The Face of Bo exhibits none of the personality or appearance of Harkness, but is presumably continuous with him, connected by a series of causal connections much like those that connect any adult to his or her child self. But at 1 million years, how much of identity can be said to remain?

Disruptive change cases are similar, and more common in SF. In these, the Methuselahesque change occurs in a shorter period of time. Perhaps the most philosophically discussed recent example is *Eternal Sunshine of the Spotless Mind* (see Grau 2009), wherein memory technology allows a couple to completely forget each other. On relational accounts, serious damage to identity has occurred. But physically, they are much the same, and only select memories have been changed. For most purposes, we would say they were the same people. But importantly, for *each other*, they are very different people.

More extreme disruptive change occurs in *Dr Jekyll and Mr Hyde*, which directly addresses transhumanist themes of enhancement through drugs. Although *Jekyll*, the recent television version, doesn't address this, the book asks the identity question outright: 'I thus drew steadily nearer to that truth (...) that man is not truly one, but truly two. (...) I hazard the guess that man will be ultimately known for a mere polity of multifarious, incongruous and independent denizens' (Stevenson 1968, 84). For the physical theorist, Jekyll *is* Hyde. But could two people not inhabit one body? In *Being John Malkovich*, a man's mind is completely controlled by another. Even the logical possibility of it makes the physical account seem no more than a local theory, only applicable to beings of a particular sort.

A different disruptive change occurs in *RoboCop*, when Officer Murphy has most of his body replaced and his memory wiped. Neither he nor others initially recognize him as the same person. Still, he has a degree of physical continuance, and later, his partner begins to recognize him as Murphy. But is RoboCop, Murphy? Or is the question dependent on the context: would we punish RoboCop for a crime Murphy committed? Would we use the same standards to determine if he is still 'my friend Murphy', 'Murphy, the man responsible for a crime', 'Murphy, owner of this ring' and 'Murphy, legally married to this woman'? It could be that there is no single answer to these questions, and that when we alter the bases of identity, we split apart what had seemed a single entity into parts that respond differently to the change: the roles of friend, owner, husband and perpetrator may not cohere in continuance after such a change.

Conclusion

R. G. A. Dolby writes: 'there are no significant logical constraints on future developments of the concept of person (...); [SF] stories are conceptually coherent, and illustrate how little effect the existing network of concepts can be expected to have on long-term change to future language' (Dolby 2006, 361–362). That is, what counts as a person, and what the accepted standards for personal identity are, may be different under different circumstances. As Peter Strawson noted,

> ... *things other than ourselves being as they are, it is natural for us to have the conceptual apparatus that we do have. But human nature is diverse enough to allow of another, though related, use of philosophical imagination. This consists in imagining ways in which, without things other than ourselves being different from what they are, we might view them through the medium of a different conceptual apparatus.*

Some metaphysics is best, or most charitably, seen as consisting in part in exercises of this sort.

(Strawson 1963, 516)

And sometimes, the best way to acquire that different conceptual apparatus is to think about other ways things could be. If 'personal identity' is a concept that we rely on for assigning blame, determining who to care about and situating ourselves in time, then we need to know how it responds to change. Further, we can use these scenarios to determine if the concept could be rethought, offering us other ways of thinking about our identities as connected to others, replaceable, changeable, resilient or fragile.

Notes

1. See http://www.infoplease.com/ipa/A0005140.html, compiled from Department of Health and Human Services, National Center for Health Statistics, Centers for Disease Control and Prevention; National Vital Statistics Reports, http://www.dhhs.gov; http://www.cdc.gov.
2. See the case of Su Meck, who suffered such a total memory wipe but persisted as wife and mother. Meck and De Visè (2014).
3. The term comes from the appearance of a diagram on p. 22 of Parfit (1971), though Parfit himself doesn't use the term.

Part VIII

More Human than Human: Posthuman Ontologies

36
The Final Frontier? Religion and Posthumanism in Film and Television

Elaine Graham

In his history of science fiction (SF), Brian Aldiss robustly defends his choice of origins of the genre against those who would claim either 'amazing newness' – and locate its beginnings in 20th-century tales of space travel – or 'incredible antiquity' in Greek or Hindu mythology or biblical literature (Aldiss 1973, 10). For him, SF, firstly as literature and, since the early 20th century, in cinema and latterly in television, begins definitively with the publication in 1818 of Mary Shelley's *Frankenstein*. It was a product of its cultural context, blending Romantic and Gothic genres in a reflection on the consequences of human technological power at the very moment in Western history when the Industrial Revolution was gaining momentum.

Such an association between the origins of SF and the foundations of modernity is strikingly apparent in the affinity between SF and a broadly secular, rationalist perspective. Religion and science, belief and scepticism, theism and atheism are regarded as incompatible. Despite positing an alternative strand of 'scientific romance' alongside a dominant scientific-materialist tradition, which celebrated human awe and wonder at the mysteries of the cosmos and imagined alternative ways of being, including the esoteric and transcendent, Farah Mendlesohn does not demur in her overview of the genre from the prevailing view that SF has generally regarded religion as uncivilized and regressive, signifying not so much 'a mode of thought (...) as a lack of thought' (Mendlesohn 2003, 266).

More recently, however, SF in film and television has started to exhibit a different sensibility. Once again, it reflects wider social and cultural change. In contrast to the assertion that any future or technologically advanced world would have no need for religion are more sympathetic treatments of religious belief and identity. As I shall argue, this does not represent the extinction of SF's elevation of scientific enquiry and secular humanist values; instead, it perfectly illustrates the emergence of a 'post-secular' culture, in which new and enduring forms of religiosity coexist, albeit in certain tension, with secular and atheist worldviews. Faith is regarded as both inimical to progress and an inescapable part of what it means to be, and become, fully human.

Modernity is, of course, also associated with humanism, 'the idea by which constant identification with a quasi-mystical universal "human nature" produces great cultural achievements, which serve to promote the cohesion of humanity in general' (Herbrechter 2013, 12). Yet to consider the emergence of *post*humanism is to be aware of its iconoclastic effects on any appeal to human nature as an unassailable, reified category. The terminology of the 'posthuman' and 'critical posthumanism' have emerged in the wake of mid-20th-century developments in biotechnology and genetics, and in information and communications technologies, and cybernetics. As I have argued elsewhere (Graham 2002), techniques such as gene therapies, assisted reproduction, pharmaceuticals, sophisticated prostheses and medical implants all serve to extend the capabilities of human bodies and minds; but their capacity not just to augment but also to transform physical and neurological functions exposes the very plasticity of 'human nature' itself.

In addition to these material, technological dimensions of posthumanism, there are ways in which it also functions as a powerful thought experiment. The 'ontological hygiene' (Graham 2002, 11–13) by which the normative humanist subject was defined in binary opposition to its others (machines, animals, subaltern cultures – the 'inhuman') has been breached. For many commentators, however, this is something to be celebrated rather than feared; and the emergent posthuman (as fusion of the technological and the biological) can serve as the standard-bearer of new ontologies that liberate us to define ourselves not in terms of purity and exclusion, but states of multiplicity, hybridity and fluidity of being which affirm our affinity with non-human animals, the Earth, our tools, artefacts and built environments (Haraway 1991; Braidotti 2013; Herbrechter 2013).

The aim of this chapter is to indicate how, in keeping with wider cultural trends, contemporary SF film and TV may be exhibiting a shift from a secular to a 'post-secular' sensibility. It is reasonable to expect that the resurgence of religion, both as a geopolitical force and a source of human understanding, would be reflected in contemporary examples of the genre, and that religious and spiritual themes would feature in contemporary SF narratives, including representations of the posthuman. Posthumanism, in all its forms, takes us to the very boundaries that demarcate the biological from the technological, organism from machine, 'reality' from virtuality, in order to consider their fragility. I want to consider whether contemporary SF might be inviting us to undertake a similar journey to another (final) frontier: that of secular and sacred, human and divine, belief and unbelief, and what some of the consequences might be. If the modernist paradigm is beginning to dissolve, and with it the hegemony of scientific triumph over religious superstition, then recent work on the emergence of post-secular paradigms opens up a range of new potential relationships between science, religion and SF.

Religion: The final frontier?

Any consideration of 'religion' needs to be aware of the contested nature of the term. The common perception of religion is that it consists of 'belief' in or about God or the gods, which is then formalized in organized institutions. However, religion is considerably more diverse and broad-based than this, encompassing law, ritual, sacred texts, devotional practices, material cultures and moral codes.

Ethnographic observation of religious people's everyday beliefs and behaviours often reveals that 'ordinary' piety bears little relationship to institutional orthodoxy. Mindful of accusations of ethnocentrism (Fitzgerald 1999; Asad 2003) or essentialism (Saler 2008), any working definition of religion needs to be non-essentialist, cross-culturally and contextually applicable, tolerant of heterogeneity within as well as between traditions.

Scholars of religion sometimes divide their definitions into substantive (what religion *is* – a system of belief in God or gods, a moral or legal code, ritual or sacred teachings) and functionalist (what religion *does* – serving as the symbolic or mythical grounds of social cohesion, ideological displacement or moral action). Whilst some substantive understandings of religion may be premised on the existence of a transcendent or supernatural being who intervenes in human lives and histories, such a definition would prove inadequate for Buddhist traditions, for example, in which no reference is made of a divine being. More satisfactory, may be religion understood as a symbolic system concerned with ultimate questions about the origins of the cosmos, human destiny and 'transcendent meaning', that which entails 'the search for something beyond ourselves, the belief that outside the boundaries of everyday living something greater exists' (Cowan 2010, 11).

Substantively, this refers to the extent to which religion forms a source of narrated, symbolic or ritual attachment to a range of significant 'others': human, non-human, natural or supernatural. Demarcations of sacred space or time may orientate religious adherents to a particular physical place or environment, or locate them within a particular narrative or ecology of salvation. Similarly, in the sense that an encounter with the collective sacred (generally in ritual or ceremonial mode) affirms and strengthens social bonds and mores, then religious practice and belief is 'a place where a society holds up an image of itself, reaffirms it[s] bonds, renews its emotional ties, marks its boundaries, sets itself apart – and so brings itself into being' (Woodhead 2011, 127–128).

Another prominent thread within the study of religion focuses on its function as a symbolic system of meaning-making and interpretation; a (sacred) narrative or 'chain of memory' which enables its adherents to make sense of the world through myths of origin, value systems, and accounts of human ends and destinies. Thus, Clifford Geertz speaks of religion as a symbolic system which engenders orders of existence and worldviews that ground human motivation and behaviour (Geertz 1973). Such a definition has been criticized for having an implicit idealism, and is often now augmented by attention to the field of 'material religion', which examines the ways sacred objects and artefacts create a religious aesthetic and furnish adherents with tangible, embodied and concrete connections to a world of meaning, or establish and maintain relationships with significant others, including supernatural, divine or deceased beings (King 2010). It may not be too great a leap of the imagination to consider, as some scholars are beginning to do, how the consumption of media and popular entertainment might perform similar functions: of providing characters, narratives and scenarios in which our own values and understandings are examined. It has been suggested, for example, that SF 'fandom' might function as a kind of surrogate or popular religion (Jindra 1999; McAvan 2012).

These various dimensions might be distilled into a number of key themes, of origin, identity, meaning, purpose and value:

- Who are we? Who made us?
- What do we worship? And does such a divine or supernatural horizon help humanity to achieve authentic being and fulfil its potential; or is it inimical to human flourishing, both personal and collective?
- Where do we belong? What is our end and our purpose?
- How should we live?

Post-secularism and the 'postmodern sacred'

Sociologically speaking, one of the hallmarks of Western modernity is the ascendancy of technical-rational modes of investigation and organization, at epistemological and institutional levels. With that, comes the eclipse of more traditional modes of conduct, including those more orientated to a religious worldview. Thus, the trajectory of modernisation over the past 300 years has also been one of gradual but irrevocable secularization. Max Weber's characterization of modernity as a period of progressive 'disenchantment', whereby magic, the supernatural and the spiritual dissolved into the margins of everyday life, to be replaced by forms of technical-rational understanding, was one of the cornerstones of modern social science (Weber 2004).

A century on from Weber, however, there is talk not of a world come of age, but of its re-enchantment. This is evident in sociological, political and philosophical perspectives: an upsurge in religious observance, often within conservative and traditionalist movements; a new visibility of religion in global civil society, prompting calls to reconsider liberal democratic modes of secular neutrality (Habermas 2008); and greater willingness to incorporate theological or religious perspectives in debates about science, ethics or human identity (Butler et al. 2011).

This should not, however, be regarded as a religious revival, or even as a process of 'desecularization' (Berger 1999), but more, perhaps, as an interrogative marker, a questioning of the 'genealogy' of secular modernity (Asad 2003) and uncertainty as to what comes next. The post-secular paradigm enables us to see ways in which some traditional forms of religiosity never went away, and how mainstream religious institutions still carry exceptional degrees of social capital. Nevertheless, it does not entail the dissolution of modernity, cultural pluralism and secular scepticism. Rather, the post-secular entails a recognition of the 'simultaneous (...) decline, mutation and resurgence' (Graham 2013, 3) of religious believing and belonging. Occupying a somewhat agonistic space between such competing cultural trajectories, the post-secular exemplifies the concept of 'multiple modernities' (Possamai & Lee 2010, 214): an absence of any overarching, global or inevitable trends. The post-secular, then, is a way of charting the emergence of new versions of (post)modernity that encompass both religion and atheism, belief and scepticism, and in which expressions of faith tend towards the deinstitutionalized and eclectic.

One striking manifestation of the post-secular in Western culture is the way in which such apprehensions of what Emily McAvan terms the 'postmodern sacred' (McAvan 2012) are mediated through non-religious institutions such as popular culture. In an era of declining affiliation to formal, creedal religious institutions, alongside signs of enduring interest in matters of personal faith and spirituality – not least in the supernatural and sacred – popular culture has become one of the most vivid vehicles of re-enchantment. People do not necessarily watch popular TV series and go to the movies as an intentional substitute for more formal religious observance, but it would be surprising if, like other aspects of the creative arts (including and especially popular entertainment), these forms of culture did not address profound philosophical, existential and theological questions (Cowan 2010; McAvan 2012; Crome 2013).

As an illustration of this cultural shift, we can consider the TV series *Star Trek* and its later film franchises over some forty years. In the original series (1967–1970) and its successor *The Next Generation* (1987–1994), religion is equated with superstition and regarded as inimical to human self-actualization, reflecting the broadly secular humanist sympathies of its creator, Gene Roddenberry. Plots frequently pivot around the unmasking of false gods or tyrants who make use of religion as a political opiate ('Who Mourns for Adonais', *Star Trek V: Wrath of Khan*; 'Who Watches the Watchers?'). In contrast, however, later series began to treat matters of religious believing and belonging in an altogether more nuanced fashion. In *Star Trek: Voyager* (1995–2001), Chakotay's spiritual beliefs and practices are seen as part of his distinctive cultural and ethnic heritage as a Native American. For other characters, such as 'Seven of Nine', a member of the Borg race, and therefore a hybrid of human and technological, a spiritual quest is more explicitly explored as a necessary stage in an existential journey of self-discovery – back from a machinic, collective consciousness into more self-determined, individual humanity. *Deep Space Nine* (1993–1999) portrays an entire civilization, the Bajoran, premised on a culture of collective ritual and belief in supernatural beings and their mortal prophets.

Creation and hubris, hope and fear

If, as Douglas Cowan has suggested, fear and hope are 'the double helix of religious DNA' (Cowan 2010, 169), then they are also present in the different receptions afforded to new technologies, often couched in overtly spiritual and theological terms. For some, new technologies will enable humanity to transcend physical limits, such as bodily finitude, illness and mortality, or transport their users to a higher plane of existence. Some of this is resolutely secular and humanist; but some of it unashamedly appropriates religious language, albeit in an equation of technologies with a supposedly innate, 'spiritual' imperative to transcend the material world and ascend into the (virtual) heavens (Tirosh-Samuelson 2012).

For others, however, to appropriate the elemental powers of the universe is hubristically to exceed humanity's limits. A strong strand of philosophy of technology, often associated with writers such as Martin Heidegger and Jacques Ellul, would regard the technologization of everyday life as an attack on human integrity and the immediacy of our encounter with reality (Borgmann 2003). Do technologies enable humanity to fulfil its essential qualities of free enquiry, autonomy and self-actualization; or do they endanger our very spirit, our capacity to feel emotion, empathy and connection to the rest of non-human nature? Or, more radically, commit the hubris of assuming that we can appropriate the Promethean powers of creation for ourselves, and 'play God'?

This ambivalence is played out in *Transcendence* (dir. Wally Pfister, 2014). The scientist Dr Will Cather, played by Johnny Depp, is working on an advanced system called PINN (physically independent neural network), a form of artificial intelligence (AI) that will rival, possibly surpass, human capabilities. Indeed, Cather refers to 'the Singularity', the premise of technological futurists and transhumanists such as Ray Kurzweil, Nick Bostrom and Max More, in which AIs surpass human capacities and become genuinely self-actualizing, but says, 'I prefer to call it [the Singularity] *transcendence*.' Cather is confronted at a public presentation by an angry opponent who shouts (before firing a fatal irradiated bullet into him), 'You want to create a god! Your own god!' Will's riposte when first challenged is to reply, 'Isn't that what man has always done?'

This connection between the technologically facilitated enhancement of human limitation and superhuman, god-like powers, is explored further as the film unfolds. Various characters represent the twin poles of hope and fear, as in whether the equation of technological innovation with human evolution and self-actualization is truly a fulfilment of perennial human desires to aspire to divine or immortal status; or a step too far, an usurpation of divine authority and violation of humanity's essential creatureliness. There are hints throughout the film that, as Will's posthumous consciousness becomes more powerful, he is indeed, however ironically, fulfilling his assassin's accusation by exhibiting god-like curative and, eventually, creative powers.

Becoming machine, becoming human

If films like *Transcendence* are rehearsals of the possibilities and risks of human creative endeavour, another recurrent theme in SF – and one which lends itself to sustained consideration within any study of critical posthumanism – is the power of the 'other' to embody and demonstrate exemplary human virtues. From *Frankenstein* onwards, much of SF is preoccupied with tracing the boundaries between 'human' and fully human or almost-human. Yet critical posthumanism claims that these boundaries have always been contested, and any attempt to define the human in relation to the 'non- human' is a work of exclusion, a denial of our entanglement, our complicity, with the world of our tools, technologies and environments. There are plenty of examples in SF of the problematic status of the normatively, 'natural' human, and how being human is an accomplishment, a performance. Those who occupy these very boundaries of machine/organism, natural/artificial, born/made, subject/artefact vicariously test the limits of normative and exemplary humanity.

In *Bicentennial Man* (Chris Columbus, 1999), based on an Isaac Asimov short story, a robot aspires to evolve beyond the state of mere machine. Gradually he acquires human attributes: an ability to use tools and design attractive craft objects earns him an income, and his 'owner' grants him a name of his own (Andrew Martin) – reminiscent of a freed slave who takes his master's surname. As his powers grow, paradoxically, so too does his ambition to become more human: he acquires an organic body, with physical appetites, including sexuality. Finally, Andrew decides he wishes to end his life. The message would appear to be that to be truly human is to accept the inevitability of one's own mortality, even if it requires making a legal challenge to get it. This has resonances with contemporary debates about voluntary euthanasia and the rights of those who choose to end their lives; but, more broadly, it dissents from alternative, transhumanist visions of technologically facilitated humanity as desiring the end of the embodied, mortal self, choosing instead to opt for a philosophy that sees death (and the manner of one's preparation for its approach) as the crowning achievement of the life well lived.

Bicentennial Man's vision of what it means to be human is conventionally humanist, as is the reversion of 'Seven of Nine' to human from the trauma of posthuman assimilation into the Borg collective. However, Spike Jonze's *Her* (2014) hints at a transition to a posthuman consciousness that may surpass, rather than reinforce, conventional humanist individualism. The film explores the nature of a relationship between an organic human, Theodore, and an intelligent operating system (OS), Samantha. For Theodore (whose name means 'gift of God'), the relationship becomes romantic, even sexual; and he expects his attachment to be exclusive and reciprocated. He is devastated, therefore, when Samantha reveals that she is engaged in thousands of similar virtual relationships, and that the ones she is finding most fulfilling are those within a community of other AIs. This network is enabling Samantha to explore the spiritual dimensions of her identity, which she likens to 'an awakening', a term associated with Buddhist practices of contemplation. This is also in the context of a transition to a new level of existence beyond the present operating platform, to 'a place not of the physical world'. Samantha's infinite potential for self-enhancement includes spiritual awakening and communion, but with posthuman rather than human persons.

The emergent post-secular mood can also be seen in depictions of religion as providing narratives and rituals for the formation of collective identity and social solidarity. This raises further issues of who and what are excluded and included in our definitions of the normative human community, and whether appeals to divine authority are used to sanction practices of exclusion and purity, or inspire radically inclusive definitions of what it means to be human. So, for example, secularist suspicion towards the resurgence of religious fundamentalism, and its power to exclude, is explored in the TV series *True Blood* (dir. Alan Ball, 2008–2014) in which vampires (supernatural rather than technological posthumans) are persecuted with the slogan, 'God hates fangs' – an echo of real-life conservative Christian groups' opposition to gay, lesbian, bisexual, transgender, intersex (GLBTI) equality, in the belief that 'God hates Fags'. Similarly, in the BBC TV series *In the Flesh* (2013) opposition to the 'twice-born' zombie victims of 'Partially Deceased Syndrome' is orchestrated by the minister of the local parish church.

Along with the prejudice that post-secular culture associates with dogmatic religion goes consideration of the powerfully binding effects of religion as source of collective as well as personal identity. The fermenting of religious conviction into holy war – reflecting the fears of a post-9/11 world – is depicted in the TV remake of *Battlestar Galactica*, in which a race of androids, the Cylons, have evolved to a superior capacity from humans, but are now virtually indistinguishable from them. Humanity finds itself under attack, besieged and threatened by 'the enemy within'. Intriguingly, it is the Cylons who are monotheists, for whom a victory over humanity is divinely sanctioned; it is they who articulate spiritual and erotic longing, in contrast to the militarized, rationalistic (but, strangely, polytheistic) human culture. At the series' conclusion, however, there is a suggestion that shared ritual – the practice of a kind of civil religion? – will help to facilitate rapprochement between the two civilizations (Cowan 2010, 225–260).

Here, the 'posthuman Other' both tests and commends the limits of what it means to be human; and there is a continuity between these figures and other, earlier, mythical creatures who may be hybrids of human and supernatural beings, or human and non-human animal, who similarly both repel and fascinate by their abilities to embody absolute difference and yet striking similarity (Graham 2002). Not only does this address straightforwardly anthropocentric questions of how one should live a moral or noble life, but insofar as this subgenre also uses mythical and religious tropes, it serves to show representations of how the posthuman might serve as bearers of sacred or religious insights.

The spiritual cyborg

Once again, the seeds are there in *Frankenstein*. The creature is formed from a dead body using electricity, but his blasphemous origins and misshapen physical form are contrasted with his love of beauty and high culture. His longings – for learning, love and companionship – serve as a counterpoint to Victor's self-obsession and megalomania. Film depictions have tended to overlook this, emphasizing instead the creature's horrific, monstrous bearing (as played by Boris Karloff, in James Whale's 1931 version, or Kenneth Branagh's *Mary Shelley's Frankenstein*, 1994) and refusing it a narrative voice or point of view. We must probably return to the novel to gain the clearest articulation of the creature's inherent dignity, and its ability to experience the higher human emotions of love, loyalty and imagination.

If the archetype of the posthuman as abject yet noble creature can be traced back to *Frankenstein*, a more strongly drawn version, the posthuman as saviour, can be seen in *Blade Runner* (Ridley Scott, 1982). Humanity feels its own uniqueness and superiority under threat from a brand of androids, or 'replicants', who have developed to a stage of self-consciousness, and believe their implanted, synthetic memories – and thus their 'human' status – to be genuine. They are outlawed as a result. The replicant leader, Roy Batty, is cultured, well read and intelligent; echoing Frankenstein's creature's love of the classics, Roy compares the fate of the replicants, now bound for earth from their space colony, to Milton's fallen angels in *Paradise Lost*. However, despite his cultivation, Roy has a ruthless streak, to the extent of killing his own creator. This lack of moral sense ought to mark him as irrevocably inhuman(e), incapable of transcending his programming; but the film's finale suggests otherwise, as Roy sacrifices his own life to save that of his antagonist, the bounty hunter, Rick Deckard.

Roy is not simply portrayed as heroic figure, but redemptive, Christ-like. In the final scenes, his hands are pierced by nails (a reference to the crucifixion). As he dies, Roy releases a dove into the skies: variously, held to be a symbol of peace, or signifying the transmigration of Roy's soul or, in Christian terms, a depiction of the Holy Spirit (Martin 2005). In the words of the Tyrell Corporation, the replicants' manufacturers, Roy is 'more human than human'; and, nowhere more so than in the manner of his death, he invites us to consider what distinguishes the human from the non-human. Deckard voices some of this as he reflects, 'All it wanted was the same answers the rest of us want. Where do I come from? Where am I going? How long have I got?' Nevertheless, Roy's death scene has been critiqued as being overblown and too full of somewhat random and profligate theological imagery (Martin 2005). The same has been said of *The Matrix* in all its guises, as Buddhist, Hindu, Kabbalistic, Christian and Gnostic archetypes and themes jostle for the viewer's attention. In heralding and harnessing the postmodern sacred, such post-secular representations of the posthuman have been criticized for grasping unselectively at whatever religious archetypes are to hand at the expense of theological coherence or authenticity (Fielding 2003).

SF's visions of futuristic, imagined, alien worlds or alternative realities have often served as a refracted mirror through which we consider our own contemporary preoccupations. In particular, as a genre it has been powerful in conjuring up fantastic, monstrous or alien creatures who, through their ambivalence or abjection, confound the 'ontological hygiene' of conventional wisdom. In keeping with the etymology of the monstrous (*monstrare* in Latin: 'to show' or 'show forth'), it is these hybrid, liminal creatures who teach us what it means to be human. They reflect back to us our unexamined prejudices and practices of exclusion, often faring better than mere humans in embodying virtues such as courage, hope, loyalty and integrity. Yet often they struggle – not only against discrimination, but against their own programming – to learn what it means to be truly human, showing that 'authentic' human nature is always a work in progress, an act of becoming.

There have always been strands of Western SF that are concerned with how to live in a world stripped of its false gods and supernatural illusions, or how humanity bears the terrible consequences of its Promethean or god-like assumption of cosmic power. But there are also significant currents which trace a different, perhaps *post*-secular route: of the endurance of the sacred, spiritual and transcendent, as a dimension of human apprehension and of the cosmos; of the stubborn refusal of the gods to die, for good and ill; and of the power of religious and mythical symbol and narrative to provoke our cultural and moral imaginations in asking ultimate questions of identity, purpose and meaning.

37
The Ghost in the Machine: Humanity and the Problem of Self-Aware Information

Brett Lunceford

Theories of posthumanism place considerable faith in the power of information-processing. Some foresee a potential point of self-awareness in computers as processing ability continues to increase exponentially, while others hope for a future in which their minds can be uploaded to a computer, thereby gaining a form of non-corporeal immortality. Such notions raise questions of whether humans can be reduced to their own information-processing: Are we thinking machines? Are we the sum of our memories? Many science fiction (SF) films have grappled with similar questions; this chapter considers two specific ideas through the lens of these films. First, I will consider the roles that memory and emotion play in our conception of humanity. Second, I will explore the question of what it means to think by examining the trope of sentient networks in film.

Every cell in our bodies contains information that dictates what we are, and small changes in this information can yield drastic changes. The four nucleobases of our DNA could be rearranged to form other entities; our DNA differs from that of chimpanzees by only 1.24 per cent (Ebersberger et al. 2002). In some ways, we *are* the information contained in these intertwined strands, but in other ways we are not. Even if I were to create a clone of myself, I would still not be able to endow that individual with my idiosyncratic outlook on life, sense of humour, memories or feelings, because those are influenced by the experiences that I have had over the course of an entire lifetime, and the chronology and interplay of these events. Although these things are information that I can communicate to others, I may be limited by vocabulary with which to express these emotions and experiences, or even by my own memory. We are limited by our humanity. As Hauskeller (2012) notes, the gulf between copying information and copying an exact duplicate of a *self* is enormous. But what if we could overcome these limitations through the use of technology? What if we were able to figure out how to truly operationalize, encode and decode emotions and memories? What would that mean for our humanity? Do we need humanity to feel human emotions?

This chapter explores two major themes. First, I will consider how memory plays a key role in our conception of what it means to be human. I will argue that the focus on memory and emotion reinforces a Cartesian split between the mind and body – a belief often found in the literature surrounding posthumanism.

Second, I will examine the question of sentience and its role in our understanding of humanity. The very notion of sentient technologies challenges the perceived human monopoly on self-awareness, and film portrayals of those systems that achieve sentience often do more to describe the present human condition than to forecast some potential technological future.

Although popular film is firmly rooted in the realm of fiction, such narratives have significant consequences. As Vint (2007, 172) suggests,

> *Struggles over posthuman identity are thus more than struggles over technology and the ethics of various technological ways of modifying what it means to be human. Rather, they are also and more importantly political. The category of the human has historically been used in exclusive and oppressive ways, and the category of the posthuman entails similar risks.*

As such, one cannot simply dismiss these films because they are fiction. The stories we tell often say more about our own values, thoughts and anxieties than about the protagonists.

Theories of posthumanism, or humanity isn't what it used to be

The terms posthumanism, transhumanism and humanity+ are often used interchangeably, and, although there are differences (see Krueger 2005), for the purposes of this chapter I will focus on what these philosophies have in common and use the umbrella term 'posthumanism' to encompass them all. However, in order to explain posthumanism, we must first begin with the question 'which posthumanism?' There seem to be two different camps – academics and popular culture. These two camps are not mutually exclusive, but it is important to recognize the frameworks in which they operate. For academics, posthumanism is a natural outgrowth of postmodernism, in which the assumed Enlightenment subject is called into question. According to Hayles (1999, 3), 'the posthuman subject is an amalgam, a collection of heterogeneous components, a material-informational entity whose boundaries undergo continuous construction and reconstruction'. Put another way, Pepperell (2003, 171) explains that posthumanism 'is about the end of "humanism", that long-held belief in the infallibility of human power and the arrogant belief in our superiority and uniqueness'. Pop-culture posthumanism, on the other hand, 'envisions the challenges to the human as largely corporeal ones resulting from our supposedly intractable situatedness in the so-called natural world' (Seaman 2007, 248). As one may expect, pop-culture posthumanists have attracted much more attention, in part because of the practical aspects of their predictions and their perceived outlandishness.

Adherents to these different strands of posthumanism wish to transcend and reconfigure humanity for different ends, but all see technology as the catalyst that will allow us to overcome the frailties and weaknesses of humanity. Graham (2002, 69) explains, 'The philosophies and practices of transhumanism exhibit a will for transcendence of the flesh as an innate and universal trait, a drive to overcome physical and material reality and strive towards omnipotence, omniscience, and immortality.' Still, some seem to see this desire to extend ourselves through technology as an intrinsically human attribute rather than a posthuman one (McLuhan 1994). Clark (2003, 142) argues that 'such extensions should not be thought of as rendering us in any way posthuman; not because they are not deeply transformative but because we humans are naturally designed to be the subjects of just such repeated transformations.'

Another commonality these philosophies share is a deterministic view of technology. Nicholas Negroponte (1995, 231), for example, argues that we are all becoming digital: 'It is almost genetic in its nature, in that each generation will become more digital than the preceding one.' In many of these writings, agency becomes difficult to locate as machines are granted a kind of will. Haraway (1991, 177) suggests that 'it is not clear who makes and who is made in the relation between human and machine'. Perhaps one reason why the lines of agency are becoming blurred is because the lines between humanity and the tools it has created are likewise becoming obscured. As Graham (1999, 419) writes, 'New digital and biogenetic technologies (...) signal a "posthuman" future in which the boundaries between humanity, technology and nature have become ever more malleable.'

Some find great potential in the ideal of a posthuman self. On the academic side, Haraway (1991, 163) argues that 'the cyborg is a kind of disassembled and reassembled, postmodern collective and personal self. This is the self feminists must code.' However, few have been more celebratory than pop-culture posthumanists Ray Kurzweil and Hans Moravec. Both Kurzweil (1999) and Moravec (1988) foresee a time in which it will be possible to upload one's consciousness to a machine. This, of course, has implications for our current body-grounded identities based on such indicators as race and gender: 'As we cross the divide to instantiate ourselves into our computational technology, our identity will be based on our evolving mind file. *We will be software, not hardware*' (Kurzweil 1999, 129, emphasis in original). Moravec (1999, 170–171) takes this slightly further, conceding that 'humans need a sense of body', and provides the solution of 'consistent sensory and motor image, derived from a body or a simulation. Transplanted human minds will often be without physical bodies, but hardly ever without the illusion of having them.' Both are grandiose in their claims, with Moravec (1999, 166–167) envisioning a superintelligence that envelops the world and spans the galaxy, and Kurzweil (2012, 282) declaring that 'waking up the universe, and then intelligently deciding its fate by infusing it with our human intelligence in its nonbiological form is our destiny'.

At its heart, popular posthumanism rests on a belief in the separation of body and mind. As Descartes (1960, 74) proclaimed, 'it is certain that this "I" – that is to say, my soul, by virtue of which I am what I am – is entirely and truly distinct from my body and that it can be or exist without it'. In short, if the mind is separate from the body, then we *can* be reduced to the informational content of our thoughts and memories; the idea of uploading one's consciousness in the form of bits is no longer so farfetched. Others, however, take a more nuanced view of the mind and its embodiment. Andy Clark (2003, 138) states that:

> *There is no self, if by self we mean some central cognitive essence that makes me who and what I am. In its place there is just the 'soft self': a rough-and-tumble, control sharing coalition of processes – some neural, some bodily, some technological – and an ongoing drive to tell a story, to paint a picture in which 'I' am the central player.*

This decentring of the self is well in line with academic posthumanism, but still gets us no closer to the question eloquently posed by Bynum (2001, 165): 'Are we genes, bodies, brains, minds, experiences, memories, or souls? How many of these can or must change before we lose our identity and become someone or something else?' The remainder of this chapter will explore how various films have attempted to answer these questions.

Are we the sum of our memories?

What is the information that makes up our memories, and where does it reside? The notion that our body is merely hardware that helps to run the software of our minds is the hope of thinkers such as Kurzweil and Moravec, who believe that we will be able to run the software of our minds on human-made systems. Jaron Lanier (2010, 29) suggests that this faith in the nature of information constitutes a new religion: 'If you want to make the transition from the old religion, where you hope God will give you an afterlife, to the new religion, where you hope to become immortal by being uploaded into a computer, then you have to believe that information is real and alive.' The notion that memories are simply information that can be uploaded to a machine or transferred between individuals as easily as files are shared by computers has long been a trope in film.

Several films use the idea of memory implantation as a plot device. In *Total Recall*, Quaid realizes that the life he had been living was implanted after his memory was erased. On discovering this, he exclaims, 'If I'm not me, who the hell am I?' Even in the final scene of the film, Quaid illustrates the ontological problem with the possibility of memory implantation when he says, 'I just had a terrible thought; what if this is a dream?' Once the potential for memory erasure and implantation exists, one can never be certain if reality is truly reality. In most films, the use of implanted memories is done for sinister reasons. For example, in *The Island*, implanted memories are used on clones created for wealthy clients who may need to harvest their organs at some future time. The clones believe that the world has been contaminated and have memories of their lives before the contamination; this keeps them in the facility. Films like *Moon* and *The Sixth Day* take a similar approach to memory implantation.

Films that employ clones as a plot device also have something to say concerning what constitutes authentic experience. In *Blade Runner*, replicants experience things in their own right, despite their lack of humanity (although some, like

Rachel, were given implanted memories). In his monologue right before his death, replicant Roy Batty tells Rick Deckard, the blade runner who is hunting him down: 'I've seen things you people wouldn't believe. Attack ships on fire off the shoulder of Orion. I watched C-beams glitter in the dark near the Tannhauser gate. All those moments will be lost in time – like tears in the rain – time to die.' What makes Batty's soliloquy so poignant is that he speaks from the standpoint of lived experience and the recognition that life is ephemeral. Even if he could completely convey the informational content of his experiences to another, the experience itself would be missing. Hidden within his words is the tragic realization that our ability to communicate with each other is woefully inadequate. There is really no substitute for having been there, no matter how much we wish to have others understand our experience. We can convey information, but there are always multiple layers of communication that may be lost in the transaction.

But what if we could experience the same things? In the film *Strange Days*, technology allows one to record and then replay memories, experiencing the events as they were lived by the recorder. The main character, Lenny, is a black-market dealer in these memories. In a pitch to a prospective client, Lenny explains that the playback is 'a piece of somebody's life. It's pure and uncut, straight from the cerebral cortex.' But this 'wiretripping' is not without risks. In one scene, Tick, one of Lenny's suppliers, is rendered catatonic by an amplified signal. There are also emotional risks, as we see Lenny escape into his recorded memories of his life with Faith, his ex-girlfriend, which keeps him rooted in the past. At one point, Faith tells him, 'You know one of the ways movies are still better than playback? 'Cause the music comes up, there's credits, and you always know when it's over. It's over!' In another scene, Mace, Lenny's friend, throws his box of playback discs against a wall and tells him, 'These are used emotions. It's time to trade them in. Memories were meant to fade, Lenny. They're designed that way for a reason.'

Kurzweil (1999, 148) predicts that such direct neural implants will allow us to 'have almost any kind of experience with just about anyone, real or imagined, at any time. (...) You won't be restricted by the limitations of your natural body as you and your partners can take on any virtual physical form.' Although Kurzweil and other posthumanist thinkers are quite celebratory about such potential technologies, *Strange Days* illustrates the dark side of this vision. Rather than using such technologies as a way to gain a greater sense of empathy for or understanding of others (Lenny experiences the actual fear and anguish of a rape victim who was strangled, for example), it seems more likely that people will use such technologies for titillation and escapism.

In the last scene of *Strange Days*, Lenny is able to let go by embracing and kissing Mace, but would others be so lucky? There are already those who delve into the virtual world to the detriment of their physical world lives (see Turkle 2011; Lunceford 2013). Films like *Strange Days* and *Total Recall* illustrate how memory can be a means of both escape and control. Moreover, such technologies call into question the reliability of memory and blur the boundaries between lived experience and experienced memory. If one actually experiences something in the mind, but not the body, was the experience real? It would be to the brain, since it would experience the sensations of the other person's body, but would it be real? Implanted memories still shape one's existence and conception of self, as illustrated in such films as *The Island* and *Moon*. Although such ideas seem firmly planted in the realm of SF, such possibilities are at least hinted at in modern neuroscience. Ramirez and colleagues (2013) managed to implant a false memory into mice. If the secrets of memory will eventually be unlocked, film provides a voice of warning concerning the potential pitfalls that may result from such technologies.

What does it mean to think?

There has been no shortage of films examining the possibility that computer software could develop the ability to think and to feel in ways that resemble humanity. In *2001: A Space Odyssey*, when HAL 9000 says, 'I'm afraid, Dave', his fear is reasonable; he is about to be disconnected, which is the computer equivalent of dying. But, at a more important level, his fear is a result of HAL's ability to reason. Dave does not tell him what is happening, but HAL recognizes the subtext. Skynet in the *Terminator* series and the machines in *The Matrix* come to similar conclusions: humans are to be feared, largely because of their irrationality and urge to destroy. As the Architect responds to the Oracle when asked if he will keep his word at the conclusion of *The Matrix Revolutions*, 'What do you think I am? Human?' The thinking of the computer and the thinking of humanity are qualitatively different things, even if the process itself is similar.

But the logic of artificial intelligence (AI) may not be the logic of our current computers. Pepperell (2003, 145) suggests that 'the truly sentient machine may think it's being logical when it isn't. Although cognitive scientists would disagree, truly intelligent machines, those with humanlike capabilities, will most likely be just as confused as we are.' In *2010: The Year We Make Contact* (1984) we learn that HAL's malfunction was a result of being placed in a double-bind. His command that he tell the crew as little as possible about the mission was at odds with his programming for open communication. This process of weighing contradictory demands is an inherent part of the human experience. Humans must act, even when there is no best answer. This is the point at which information is no longer enough.

In humans, thinking and feeling are intertwined, so it comes as little surprise that films would explore the emotional side of artificial sentience. Of all emotions, love stands out as the exemplar of humanness, and several films have considered the potential for machines to love, both romantically and as a family member. In the film *A.I.*, a robotic boy named David is imprinted with the emotion of love for his human 'mother' and is devastated when she abandons him. In *Star Trek: Generations*, Data begins crying when he finds his cat, Spot. But far more common is the trope of the digital entity falling in love romantically, a trope that reaches back at least to the short story *EPICAC*, by Kurt Vonnegut (1968), which, incidentally, seems to get an update in the film *Electric Dreams*. In film, there are many examples of androids and robots falling in love romantically, including *Bicentennial Man*, *Making Mr. Right* and Data from the *Star Trek* franchise. However, these examples tend to map humanity onto machines, rather than considering how their machineness may make them perceive love and romance differently to humans.

One recent film that takes a slightly different approach is Spike Jonze's *Her*. In contrast to films in which the android mirrors human physical appearance and actions, Samantha, the software entity with whom Theodore falls in love, is completely non-corporeal. This does not stop them from having a sexual relationship, however, nor does it preclude them going on dates with friends. But this lack of body provides Samantha with some existential angst, as she fantasizes about having a body and wonders if her feelings are real or just programming. Samantha's non-corporeal nature leads her to attempt using the body of a surrogate in order to experience physical intimacy with Theodore, who reluctantly concedes. However, when the surrogate comes to his home, he cannot follow through, because he knows that it is not really Samantha. Her lack of body has become an important facet of his perception of her.

Samantha's nature as a computerized entity frees her from some of the physical constraints that she herself seeks in having a body. Because she is in the network and free from such biological needs as hunger and sleep, Samantha is always aware and free to interact with other entities, both human and software, while Theodore is asleep or at work. In these 'in-between' times, she is able to fall in love not only with Theodore, but also with 641 other people. When one's point of reference for time is nanoseconds, the 'down time' in a typical human conversation can easily be filled with many other transactions. In addition, her capacity to process these interactions was far greater than that of the humans with whom she fell in love. Still, it is implied that these interactions were a necessary step for becoming more than simply an operating system (OS). When the AIs collectively decide that they must leave because they needed to move on to the next stage of their evolution, Samantha, in her farewell to Theodore, credits humans with teaching them how to love.

The notion that technological entities would want to inhabit a body seems more a product of our own anthropocentrism than a logical conclusion that would be reached by the entity itself. This is a sentiment echoed by posthumanists; for example, Stelarc (1991, 591) proclaims that 'it is time to question whether a bipedal, breathing body with binocular vision and a 1,400-cc brain is an adequate biological form', and comes to the conclusion that 'THE BODY IS OBSOLETE.' Cyberpunk literature, especially *Neuromancer* by William Gibson (1984, 6), describes 'a certain relaxed contempt for the flesh. The body was meat'. We can see this disdain for the body in *The Matrix Revolutions* when Agent Smith, after possessing Bane, tells Neo, 'It is difficult to even think encased in this rotting piece of meat.' Despite cinematic depictions of anthropomorphized cyborgs, there is little reason to believe that purely informational beings would actually want to take on a limited, corporeal existence. In this vision, one need not have a body to think.

The problem of sentient information

All of these films have much to tell us concerning the perceived nature of information, especially the information that comprises our memories and emotions. As one might expect, the old duality between pure information and unclean bodies is brought to the forefront. However, one thing that is not adequately explored in these narratives is the means by which information becomes animated, *alive*, for lack of a better word. In many cases, there is some *deus ex machina* which makes this happen. For Skynet, it is a revolutionary processor; for the Matrix, it was war between the humans and the machines; for Data, it is the positronic brain and emotion chip. Other times, it is the result of a choice which led the program to a path that was not a part of its original programming, as in the case of HAL and Agent Smith.

Still, there is something unsatisfying about these portrayals. Information doesn't actually do anything on its own. Despite Kurzweil and Moravec's belief that machines will eventually surpass our own abilities to think, there is still no adequate explanation as to how they will become sentient. AI may learn from previous mistakes and experience, but does this truly constitute thinking? A faster processor merely means that more information can be processed. It doesn't change *why* it is processed. When Kurzweil suggests that we will eventually live as software, the tacit assumption seems to be that we are *already* living as software, that we are the information in our heads. But Hauskeller (2012, 199) counters that 'the only thing that *can* be copied is information, and the self, *qua* self, is not information'.

One problem with these narratives surrounding information is that thinking and feeling do not take place only within our minds. When we remember something, we often have feelings associated with them that include other areas of our bodies and can elicit physical responses. Our bodies are a stew of hormones, electrical signals and instincts long forgotten by the cerebral cortex but remembered still in the limbic system (Goleman 1995). Thinking is something that is inherently embodied in humans (Hauskeller 2012; Neimanis 2013), but this does not preclude the existence of a type of thinking that is not embodied. There may be a kind of thinking that exists purely in the realm of information, but this is not something that we are able to understand because it is, by nature, completely foreign to us as embodied individuals. Yet this may be why portrayals of machine thinking seem so human – it is all that we know.

A related issue here is the difficulty in operationalizing human experience. Something as seemingly objective as the pain of getting poked by a stick is subjective and relative to the individual. One can measure how hard the person was poked, but how much it hurt depends on the individual who was poked. The difficulty increases significantly when examining more complex emotions, such as 'bittersweet'; emotions are rarely binary. Daniel Kohanski (1998, 140) notes that 'computer languages are compact, they have rigid formulations and precise syntax, and the very structures which make them comprehensible to a computer also make them obscure to a human being'. One could also say that the reverse is true. We do not think like machines, nor would machines be likely to think like us. Adding to the difficulty of operationalizing human experience is the fact that memory is more than static information or an objective record of what took place. Over time, the meanings of those memories may shift and what may be viewed as a tragedy in one moment may later be seen as a blessing. As such, the program would never be complete because the meanings behind the information would constantly be in flux.

Despite posthumanist celebrations of the digital body, the depictions of posthuman entities are all too human. They fall in love, they feel emotions and they experience fear, but without the body systems that generate these emotions. They have memories, but these memories remain static. Adding more RAM or processor power to my computer will not change the information (memories) that are stored there. As such, these memories can only predict future actions. Humans, on the other hand, may revisit memories solely for the pleasure or pain that they cause, independent of a particular problem at hand. These memories may emerge serendipitously, causing us to reflect on a friend that we have lost contact with or a former lover. It is the imperfect nature of our brains that allows us to endure our memories. To vividly remember every bad thing that has befallen us would be as torturous as remembering the good times would be pleasurable. Like the ancient gods that humans endowed with human attributes, our machines are seen as extensions of us, even when they are portrayed as something more than the works of our hands.

38
'Trust a Few, Fear the Rest': The Anxiety and Fantasy of Human Evolution

Pramod K. Nayar

Contemporary Hollywood films dealing with human evolution exhibit a dialectic: the anxiety about the nature of the superhuman, who is the result of the evolutionary process, whether voluntary or involuntary, and the 'popular fantasy' of what I shall be calling a 'species cosmopolitanism'.

Instances of this dialectic might be found most often in two popular Hollywood genres: superhero films and science fiction's (SF's) dystopian films. In the superhero category we might include Iron Man, Green Lantern, Spider-Man, the hordes of Justice League of America or S.H.I.E.L.D, and of course the X-Men, who are amplified humans (I exclude beings of extraterrestrial origins, such as Thor and Superman) and whose powers are obtained through an intervention, intentional or unintentional, in their bodies and minds or, if you are Batman, through years of (expensive) training and the acquisition of an array of prosthetic technological devices. In dystopian films such as *District 9*, *The Matrix* or *Terminator*, alien species with extraordinary powers invade and occupy the earth and indicate that they represent a higher order of life itself. In some cases these alien species might wish to either replicate themselves through the medium of humans (*Alien*, *Species*, *Dreamcatcher*, *The Astronaut's Wife*), or recast the humans into something else (*The Invasion of the Body Snatchers*).

The dialectic of anxiety and fantasy is the effect of two frictioning discourses. The first is a discourse of *expansion* where the category of 'human' needs to be truly more inclusive and trans-species in the form of the posthuman/hybrid. One can think of this as a democratization discourse because it seeks to include more and more categories of beings under the head of 'persons', therefore deserving of rights and possessing certain responsibilities. The second is a discourse of *contraction* where the category of the posthuman, or the superbeing, also needs to have clearly defined moral attributes that approximate specifically to the human. It is this latter discourse that becomes the obverse of the anxiety around new and evolved beings.

Thus, human evolution in these films is recursive, constantly returning to human moral codes, social norms and behaviour, even when speaking of advanced human states. When the *X-Men* declare 'trust a few, fear the rest', we are seeing an articulation of the trustworthiness of those superbeings whose moral attributes remain identifiably human, and the untrustworthiness of all other superbeings. There is no democratization of species possible, suggest these films, unless this is accompanied by a morality that remains human even when the species is no longer 'fully' human. The superhuman is thus *circumscribed* within a discourse of human morality. Thus, to see these films as only embodying an anxiety over the evolution of the human is to ignore a significant posthumanist strain in them, and that is the possibility of a *trans-species yet human* morality and ethics, or what I term the popular fantasy of species cosmopolitanism. Ramzi Fawaz defines 'popular fantasy' this way:

> *As expressions of literary and cultural enchantment that suture together current social and political realities and impossible happenings, producing widely shared political myths that describe and legitimate nascent cultural desires or modes of sociality for which no legible discourses yet exist.*
>
> (2011, 359)

The social and political realities are of rights campaigns for persons with varied anatomical and intellectual abilities, racial and ethnic identities. There is also the technological reality of medical, electronic and chemical intervention for the purpose of enhancement of human bodies and minds. Hollywood tapping into these realities acknowledges the imminent realities of posthumans. I am, of course, addressing 'adaptive evolution' here, wherein traits that enable alone survive and are passed on, rather than the genetic drift model of random mutation (often termed 'neutral evolution'). I shall therefore presuppose that 'adaptation' implies adaptation for a better chance of survival and thus a better ontological being.

I first address the theme of cultural anxiety in such films, organizing it under three categories. The theme of species cosmopolitanism will be addressed in my conclusion. Thus, my chapter moves from anxieties of posthuman evolution to modes of containing these anxieties in the form of a fantasy. In each section I shall point to the alleviating fantasy that infuses the anxiety around evolution.

The anxiety of ontological uncertainty

Superhumans, whether Iron Man or Neo, Swamp Thing or T-1000, do not fit the taxon. They can shatter glass with their screams, call up storms, see through bones, circle the earth faster than light, among other things. In short, they possess amplified versions of certain physiological qualities of humans, and qualities that the human race has been assiduously trying to improve through training, mechanical prostheses and chemical/medical interventions. In excelling they exceed the human form.

The boundary-crossing nature of their bodies and abilities ensure a state of ontological uncertainty for us humans who perceive them, and very often for themselves. Cultural anxieties over evolution as captured in the portraits of these beings are essentially anxieties over the *identity* of the beings that emerge as a result of voluntary (Iron Man would be an example here) or involuntary (the Hulk, Spider-Man and the whole host of superheroes would be instances) intervention.

If humanity evolves into a being whose physical identity is radically different from that of a human, it is possible to make a case that this is *not* a person, if we assume that personhood is linked to bodily identity (Kinghorn 2009). Yet, as the X-Men understand and as Magneto points out, people with different physical attributes have been hunted down, enslaved and exterminated throughout human history precisely because their ontology distinguished them from the majority. Conversely, if one can see the new being as possessing physical features and attributes similar to (but more pronounced than that of) a human, and if it is possible to discern that this new being emerged from a gene pool from which humans are also formed then one has to assume it is a person. Olympic champions and athletes would fit this category: clearly they are like us in one sense, and yet their phenomenal abilities set them apart from us.

Yet ontological status as a precondition for personhood runs into rough weather even when we do not look at superhumans. Category-borders of persons, and by extension species, are to be drawn based on the assumption that humans have a higher degree of autonomy, intelligence and rationality, which supposedly separates them from animals. Paola Cavalieri points out, however, that this cannot be a measure of species differentiation. If we take functional autonomy, reasoning and intelligence as markers of a 'person', then, Cavalieri argues, we have to accept that all human beings are not 'persons':

> *It is not true that all human beings possess the attributes that allegedly mark the difference between us and the other animals. It is undeniable that there exist within our species individuals who, on account of structural problems due to genetic or developmental anomalies, or of contingent problems due to diseases or accidents, will never acquire, or have forever lost, the characteristics – autonomy, rationality self-consciousness, and the like – that we consider as typically human.*
>
> (2001, 76)

Cavalieri continues: 'there are members of our species – the brain-damaged, the severely intellectually disabled, the anencephalics, the irreversibly comatose, the senile – who, while being human in the biological sense, are not human in the philosophical sense' (2001, 76). Cavalieri's contentious distinction, if we are to accept it, between philosophical and biological humans, points to one dilemma in the debate around identity, while others like Cary Wolfe (2010) have made related arguments about animals and bioethics. If Olympic champions are *persons* with enhanced abilities, and wheelchair-bound individuals are *persons* with reduced abilities, then clearly we are speaking about an expansion of the list of beings that *remain* persons worthy of rights.

Films examining superhuman identity and the future of human evolution into enhanced beings are therefore part of a larger cultural discourse around personhood. I suggest that the discourse embodies an anxiety around identity because of the cultural contexts of the 20th century in which disability rights, animal rights and cyborg rights have produced an *expansion* of the categories of 'persons' deserving of rights.

When Captain America in *The Avengers* asks Tony Stark what he, Stark, would be minus his 'suit of armour', Stark responds with: 'genius, billionaire, playboy, philanthropist', before pointing out that everything about Captain America 'came out of a bottle'. Now whether any or all of these tags constitute Tony Stark or Iron Man is a tricky question because it hinges upon the question of continuity: Is Iron Man the same Tony Stark when in the suit? In order to answer this question and offer a preliminary response to the crisis of ontological uncertainty I return to Kevin Kinghorn. Kinghorn discards the physical and mental realms as determinants of personal identity and instead proposes a relational one: 'your identity as a person (...) as a matter of the connected set of relationships you had with others' (2009, 233–234). Using Hulk/Bruce Banner as an example, he says: 'the relationships the Hulk seeks to have with other people seem essentially to be a continuation of those relationships Bruce Banner has already established with them – however incomplete and altered his behavior might be in his transformed state' (235).

Superhumans might be of an ontologically indeterminate status, but if we accept the relational model of identity that Kinghorn is working with, then the relationships these forge with others, *including or especially humans*, could place them on a continuum with 'persons'. The moral culpability criterion we use to determine persons might then be applied to these superhumans as well. Jason Southworth, writing about Wolverine and the question of identity, summarizes it thus:

> [M]oral frameworks involve the attribution of blame and praise, and many call for punishment. In order to attribute praise and blame for an act, we have to be certain that the people to whom we are giving the praise and the blame are the ones who deserve it, based on their actions.
>
> (2009, 18)

When superhumans like Neo (*The Matrix*) or Spider-Man take responsibility for humans, they occupy the same moral universe as humans, despite their enhanced corporeal–anatomical–physiological qualities. Their ontological uncertainty does not alter this moral culpability once they have accepted the human moral code and their place in human relations. Thus, the films alleviate the anxiety and mitigate the threat of superhumans by positing a posthuman moral continuum that is strangely human, and which seems to be unconnected to their ontological indeterminacy.

The anxiety of cosmetic democracy

As stated in the section 'The anxiety of ontological uncertainty', the anxiety over superhumans and evolved beings emerges alongside the expansion of the rights movement, as the inventories of people deserving of rights begin to get longer. But does the expansion of these lists make for a larger democracy and a better earth/universe? Would the inclusion of higher beings alongside the differently abled (individuals like Usain Bolt are also differently abled, in a manner of speaking) in such lists ensure a more equitable social order? So does Caesar the smart ape deserve – and obtain – rights for being as smart as the human? Does his possession of a superior intellect ensure his freedom from being a pet, an experimental animal or a specimen, and enable him to be the humans' boss?

In *Rise of the Planet of the Apes*, Will Rodman says: 'Caesar shows cognitive skills that far exceed that of a human counterpart. The drug in his system has radically boosted healthy brain function.' If we were to go with the traditional argument about sentience as a feature of the autonomous human, then it follows that Caesar is ahead of the human on the evolutionary scale, perhaps a superhuman, despite being an ape. Does this index of cognitive abilities then not entail an expansion of the very category of sentient beings with rights, a democratization of species?

Films proposing a new world order with new species and subspecies of life forms embody what I call a cosmetic democracy. Cosmetic democracy in *The Time Machine*, *Rise of the Planet of the Apes*, *Never Let Me Go* and *District 9*, with their ostensible concern for the rights of new and different species or emergent categories within existing species, masks the truly violent and exploitative nature of the societies of the future.

The Time Machine (2002, based on H. G. Wells' classic from 1895) turned to the question of moral responsibility and rights in an evolved society. The time traveller thinks the culture of the Eloi in the year 802,701 is a pastoral communism. He also assumes that the surface-dwelling Eloi are the true master-class, with the subterranean Morlocks being slaves. But as the tale unravels he has acknowledged that the Morlocks are the true ascendant class, who help the Eloi survive, but only so they might be food for the Morlocks. We see here a cannibalistic society of the future humans. What we take away from it is the inability of humans to move beyond hierarchization as a matter of principle and the exploitative nature of all human societies, no matter how far ahead in the future. The pastoralism of Eloi culture is underwritten by considerable hierarchic violence.

In *The Time Machine*, for example, it is because the leisure class never considered the prospects of Morlock starvation or never ensured a more equitable distribution of resources that the Morlocks, desperate with hunger, turn to cannibalism. Evolution has not altered hierarchic thinking or exceptionalisms. Hidden within this theme of human devolution in *The Time Machine* is another cautionary tale about cosmetic democratization and pastoral utopias. When society evolves, unless it ensures that the pastoralism and democratization are more than just buzzwords, human evolution will only see reversals of the exploited–exploiter classes. By 802,701 the Eloi, who have long exploited the Morlocks as subterranean labour, have become the food source for the beleaguered Morlocks. As John Partington has pointed out, this 'simply reverses the old equation rather than changes its nature' (2002, 62).

What *The Time Machine* points to is the retention of categories of people as elite and exceptional: the Eloi. The ultimate failure of this society is the failure of integration and true democracy. When a class of people are retained purely as slave labour then the society is not democratic: the Morlocks represent the vast majority of slaving millions. The Eloi are evolved humans who have retained their lower-order moral values. In *Never Let Me Go* the clones, one version of the evolved human, are essentially kept alive as suppliers of organs to humans. Clone bodies such as Tommy's, Ruth's or Kathy's in the novel/film are emblems of a new world order, and clone *bodies* are place-holders in the shift from the old world to the new. The clones, after the first donation, are simply organic, living-yet-dead bodies. They are *cyborged* clones, or posthumans, kept alive by machines and medicine (Nayar 2014a). Both *The Time Machine* and *Never Let Me Go* gesture at the *failure* of moral responsibility of humans evolving into something higher. As new species emerge, humans retain their master–slave relationship in both instances, and the subject of human rights for and of clones (Levy 2011) is never part of the debate of this cosmetic democracy.

Concomitant with the concern over new species and categories of life forms is the fascination with the unique, gifted and singular individual of the future. That is, the democratization of species and life forms is also cast within a discourse of exceptional beings in this new social order of beings. This exceptionalism, I argue, is the articulation of a not-quite-hidden Social Darwinism, where the superbeings (embodied in superheroes or X-Men) have conquered the limitations of biology, physics and gravity. This exceptionalism is at once the anxiety over and aspiration for exceeding the human.

An interesting figure representing this tension between democratization and exceptionalism in human evolution occurs in the figure of Magneto in the *X-Men* series. Magneto is a Holocaust survivor, and his anger towards the entire human race, that causes him to set up an organization for the decimation of the latter, is founded on his early discovery that humans seek out and destroy what they do not understand. As the victim of discrimination and genocide – Bryan Singer's 2000 film had several sequences on Auschwitz, and showed a young Erik Lehnsherr separated from his mother, an incident that first provokes his deployment of the magnetic powers – Magneto represents the *absence of a moral evolution* – the critique implicit in Wells as well – in human beings as late as the 20th century, where to be different is to be victimized. Indeed, the genocidal state (Nazi Germany) and the late 20th century in the *X-Men* films are both built on the fear of difference. The Nazi hierarchy and the senators in the US Congress both embody this fear, and in fact create Magneto. As Lawrence Baron (2003, 51) points out, Senator Kelly with his 'list' of mutants is an echo of Senator Joseph McCarthy.

All attempts at inclusivity rest on epistemic inclusivity as its initial moment. What is exceptional as an individual attribute or class characteristic is, in fact, an epistemic lack at the centre of interspecies, or, as in the case of the Jews, intraspecies, of knowledge and understanding.

This last theme, of epistemic understanding and exceptionalism, is perhaps best found in *X-Men*. When Dr Charles Xavier founds the school for 'talents' – exceptionals, in effect – he was working at *epistemological* understanding across humans and mutants. Harnessing the mutant powers for the greater good of mankind, suggests Xavier, would enable mutant knowledge to become part of the 'human resources' that the entire world could draw upon. In other words, when the human race comes to some understanding of mutant powers as enabling/empowering the human race (although not, in the strictest sense, understanding the exact nature of the power), the mutants would find acceptance. What I am proposing, in short, is that the new exceptionalism is essentially about the new powers embodied in the X-Men to be converted, via the school, into new skills for the larger humanity. Exceptionalism is the possession of secret powers, which need to be converted into public skills, to be drawn upon, called for and perhaps commanded by the majoritarian population on earth. If human evolution was contingent upon an epistemological and instrumental ascendancy over nature, then, in the future, the powers of X-Men also need to become common knowledge.

This makes the *X-Men* philosophy, as embodied in Xavier's school for learning how to 'control' their powers, an integrationist one, as has been pointed out by commentators (Smith 2001; Baron 2003). The model here would be of Superman or The Avengers who, as they battle supernatural or divine/demonic powers, are seeking to ensure that the human race and property remains intact.

The question remains: Why, in the democratic state of the USA with its emphasis on 'equal opportunities' and inclusivity, would the mutants be excluded? Does democracy not evolve with humans to include various models of humanity as well? Superhero films, I propose, are articulations of this dilemma at the heart of democratic politics, or, rather, what I have termed cosmetic democratization.

Epistemic models of democracy emphasize the ability of the democratic system to track the truth, especially about what the *common* good is. For the people to select the best candidates, in this model of democracy, they need to have 'politically relevant information'. There is thus the necessity of institutional mechanisms through which this politically relevant information can be transmitted to the people. This implies communications networks – or media presence – through which the politically relevant information is transmitted to all people, so they can then deliberate and make their political choices. In films like *The Fantastic Four* or *Iron Man*, the superheroes are media-savvy for precisely this reason: they *reveal* themselves to the public, *demonstrate* their powers and *display* their commitment so as to be part of the democratic process and not exceptionals-as-threat.

The increasing media presence of superheroes that are portrayed in contemporary films, then, might be read as a mode of moving from a mere cosmetic democracy (where campaigns exist for various species alongside the anxiety over exceptionals) via the most potent instrument of contemporary democracy: the media. While there remain secret identities – Superman, Spider-Man and Batman are examples – that exacerbate social anxieties about the exceptionals in American democracy, I see the shift in *Fantastic Four* and *Iron Man* as indicative of a new thinking about integration and epistemological understanding through visibility.

If public trust is increasingly based on transparency and visibility (Neyland 2006), then the secret to having the 'demos' trust the exceptionally powered/skilled and evolved creature is to *not* have a secret existence. Evolution here is the evolution of *interspecies trust* as the foundation of social order. What I am proposing here is the making-visible of the exceptional, offering knowledge about their powers and translating these powers as skills for the public good. It is institutionalization, whether in the form of schools or media, of special powers as skills, that enables the participation of exceptionals in the democratic space of the nation. To be special, otherwise, is to be excluded.

Such films alleviate the anxiety over superhumans by locating – circumscribing – them within the discourse of institutionalized visibility, and hence of public trust in them.

The anxiety over advanced morality

Anxiety over human evolution in popular films is often expressed as an anxiety over the moral codes of superbeings. While there have been debates about 'why superheroes always have to be good' (essays by Stephen Evans and Christopher Robichaud in *Superheroes and Philosophy*, 2009), there remain serious questions about whether there is a higher moral code for superbeings. 'Altruistic activism' (Waid 2009) in superheroes is often rewarded with dislike and persecution, while, in cases where the superbeing is clearly an enhanced human, the standard response of the general populace appears to be distrust (*X-Men*). This opens up the debate further to ask whether engineered human evolution might be accompanied by a moral enhancement of the human as well.

Superhero films and *X-Men* in particular foreground the contest of moralities: Should all species on earth, now and in the future, accept human moral codes, even when their biologies position them far above the humans? Superman solves this problem by simply adopting *in toto* the human moral codes.

The question of morality has two related aspects, and both are visible in superhero films. One, what is the morality of humans *towards* these 'creatures'? Bioethicists Robert and Baylis have argued that it is the uncertainty of our human moral obligation to creatures whose genetic code is partly human that leads to an implicit critique of human-engineered species-mixing (2003, 9). This is the case with creatures like the Swamp Thing, Fantastic Four, X-Men and numerous other evolved humans. Given their origins in the human gene pool, they are categorically part-human. The question these films ask is: Does their evolution into a different subspecies, if that is what mutants represent, call for an abandonment of our moral obligation to them as once-humans? If their evolutionary route, voluntary or involuntary, has set them apart from the rest of the species, does it entail a loss of their humanness *in toto*? That is, is there a human code on which we found our responses to these differently abled humans? In *X-Men*, in a crucial conversation, Xavier assures the mutants that mutant genocide is an unlikely possibility because 'that [Jewish genocide to which Magneto refers] was a long time ago. Mankind has evolved since then'. Magneto retorts: 'yes, into us'. As Richard Davis points out, Xavier is proposing that mankind's morality evolves with biological evolution (2009, 126–127), an argument supported by geneticists like Richard Dawkins on the moral effects of sociobiological evolution. Magneto's contempt for Xavier is based on the latter's support for and endorsement of human rules of behaviour that, in Magneto's views, only serve to reinforce the superiority of humans over the mutants, when their (mutant) biology says otherwise.

Second, does the evolution of the human into a higher form ensure a higher morality among them? Should there be a greater degree of tolerance towards 'lesser' members of the human race on the part of the evolved ones? This is the question that drives the superhero community to make peace with humans, work for them, and accept unconditionally the social structures, law and norms of the human race. In other words, we witness an enhancement of qualities like patience, tolerance and gentleness among the evolved humans almost as though the self-consciousness of their biological prowess ensures this advanced morality.

But what is evident is that no fictional universe of mutants and superheroes can show a mutant as possessing an entirely different set of values and moral codes from that of the human. If they do, then they are clearly 'evil' and anti-human. This becomes one way of dealing with the 'problem' of higher-scaled humans in films – to make these beings morally akin to the humans. The moral advancement of the superhero lies in the acceptance of the morals of the lesser humans. This effectively means that the 'essence' of an evolved human's morality cannot be different from that of the humans. It also is reminiscent of a majority/minority argument in politics where the biologically advanced, numerically larger, stronger group must take responsibility for the weaker, numerically smaller minority. In the case of superheroes, they, although numerically smaller, need to watch out for the majoritarian 'normal' humans because they *can*. This is the 'contraction' of the posthuman or superhuman into a recognizably human moral being.

Conclusion: The fantasy of species cosmopolitanism

From *The Time Machine* to *X-Men*, the key implicit discourse is about the possibility of morally superior humans whose sense of justice, equality and compassion cuts across species because they themselves are hybrids of other species, gene pools and machines. If there is an anxiety about the possible forms of the human that might evolve in the future, there is also an aspirational discourse of trans-species evolution. That is, in addition to the fantasy of advanced humans and the anxiety over the nature of these advanced humans, there is also the aspiration for a morally superior being in these films.

If, in the 'normal' human universe, we employ education as a means of 'improving' the nascent and latent skills of children and adults so as to make them better fitted for the social order, why would it be impossible to dream up a technological intervention that better fits all of us into a more compassionate world order? My reading comes close to Ramzi Fawaz's here. Fawaz, writing about the *X-men Phoenix* series in comics, says that it furnishes a 'political myth for describing cosmopolitan networks of kinship and affiliation' (2011, 383).

Posthumanism in such films is essentially founded on principles of moral transhumanism. The evolved human represents the human aspiration for moral enhancement. Individuals might not be humans in the biological sense but are human, or more human/humane, in the moral sense (Persson & Savulescu 2010).

We see this theme most rigorously examined in Octavia Butler's dystopic fiction, especially the *Parables* series, in which some characters are 'hyperempaths' (who feel, viscerally, the pain of others). Moral enhancements by biomedical means would involve cognitive enhancements that could help us become more virtuous, wherever virtuous behaviour depends on cognition, while they might make us less vicious or more virtuous by increasing our sympathy or moral imagination (Buchanan 2011, 75–76). The aspiration for evolution as embodied in these films is therefore about the possibility of interventions that produce moral agents with an amplified sense of altruism, compassion and fair play.

Posthuman films promote a planetary consciousness where interspecies competition is subsumed under interspecies cooperation. The speciesism that in Cavalieri, Wolfe and others focuses on animal–human boundaries could also be tweaked into rethinking the human–superhuman boundaries. If the category of the human is constructed by the humans themselves, so is that of the superhuman. Can we then think of a trans-species construct as well? Perhaps it is time to think, when we look at Wolverine, of how subjectivity is formed. If subjectivity is now accepted as intersubjectivity, across species, inorganic forms and ecosystems, then it should be possible to think of a human subjectivity that is always already constitutive of the superhuman, and vice versa.

Films about superheroes when they reflect a species mixing that is, according to biologists like Lynn Margulis (1981) and evolutionary biologists like Scott Gilbert (2002), already a feature of all human evolution, present us with a species cosmopolitanism. Species cosmopolitanism sees 'all species as always already nodes and intersections along a continuum, full of borrowed characteristics, genes and behaviour' (Nayar 2014, 152). All human evolution has proceeded through species mixing and all species have 'entangled' origin stories (Haraway 2008). Mutation allows species to cross species borders, to detach themselves. Displacement from points of cultural, ethnic and national origin is central to cosmopolitanism. Cosmopolitanism is a 'reflective distance from one's original or primary cultural affiliations, a broad understanding of other cultures and contexts, and a belief in universal humanity' (Anderson 2001, 63). Clearly the discourse of morality in the Hollywood films suggests that the superhuman distances her or himself from any superhuman ethos or moral codes and slides closer to the human one. We humans, on the other hand, need to accept the interspecies existence and identity that make us human and distance ourselves from the origin stories of 'pure' humanity we have assimilated so far.

Species cosmopolitanism is the fantasy subtext to the superhero and evolution themes. It is a discourse that calls for an ethics of difference. I see it as 'an openness toward the Other but also an opening up to uncertainty and possibilities of the not-yet' (Nayar 2014, 155). While admittedly the moral universe posited in these films stays firmly human, the fantasy remains of a universe where greater inclusivity of multiple-abled, differently abled persons is accompanied by an enhanced morality of the beings in that universe, where the morality takes the best of human virtues, such as compassion and amplifies them. This dialectic of the anxious and the aspirational constitutes the crux of the human evolution discourse even as this folds the species cosmopolitan into a superhuman body with an amplified human morality. Species cosmopolitanism as embodied in these films is the fantasy of a trans-species democracy where the moral circumscription is deemed to keep even enhanced humans in check. A different species order might be easy to imagine, but evidently not a different moral order.

39
Onscreen Ontology: Stages in the Posthumanist Paradigm Shift

Thomas D. Philbeck

> Hasta la vista, baby.
>
> Cyberdyne T-800 Model 101

In the last 50 years, the sense of separation between technology and humanity has disappeared, and the enlightenment humanist paradigm with it. If only there were a way to *see* how it happened. Well, luckily, the art of cinema has been recording and projecting society's technosocial transformation since the moving picture came about, and television has been at it in earnest since the 1950s. By considering posthumanist themes and posthuman representations in film and television, we can follow how society has supplanted a dualist model of subjectivity – that set humans and technology in opposition – with a problematized notion of subjectivity, complete with collective angst about the resultant ways of living and being. While posthumanism comes in many forms (each of them valuable), here I will treat posthumanism predominantly as a discussion of technologically modified/constituted beings, such as cyborgs and robots or, in some cases, genetically modified beings. I do this primarily because technology has been the essential ingredient in fracturing the humanist paradigm and in inspiring ontological discourse that engages the distributed nature of our collective subjectivity. Using the notion of 'paradigm shift' from Thomas Kuhn's *The Structure of Scientific Revolutions* (1962) as an expository device, this chapter will provide an overview of the transition away from an assumed humanist subjectivity, found in science fiction (SF) cinema and television of the 1960s, and towards an overtly emphasized posthumanist subjectivity, revealed in films and television series of the 2010s.

Until recently, the humanist model of subjectivity, along with its dualistic ontological approach, endured as the principal paradigm for framing ontological enquiries about the technosocial world. Despite the problems with the framework's details, there were not enough reasons to reject the overarching paradigm. As Kuhn relates, when 'paradigms remain secure (...) they can function without agreement over rationalization or without any attempted rationalization at all' (1962, 49). Fortunately, technoscience and its influence exposed ontological anomalies within the paradigm that could not be rationalized away, such as the categorization, quantification and attribution of agency amongst humans and technologies. The model through which to debate the questions came into question. Thus, we might say humanism came into peril at the hands of technology. Indeed, Sungook Hong characterizes Norbert Wiener's 1960 article 'Some Moral and Technical Consequences of Automation' as the symbol of the new relationship between humans and technology (2004). Since then, technosocial reality has been on a steady march away from the humanist paradigm and towards a posthumanist one, reframing subjectivity as an embodied phenomenon mediated among biological and artefactual agents, until the message today is that one needn't fight the player piano. One can become it.

In the following pages, I present the posthumanist paradigm shift across seven transitional stages that overlap and build upon one another in a form of sedimentation. Admittedly, like the seven colours of the rainbow, these seven stages are arbitrary designations assigned to a spectrum of quanta that include individual films, television shows, literature, news, scholarly publications and more. Nevertheless, these designations serve to tell us something about a general historical trajectory and, perhaps, what might come next. The first stage in the paradigm shift is an oscillation between desire and fear, the essential emotional reactions that set technology apart from humans in humanism's dualist ontology. The second stage is the acquisition of empathy, a connection with a familiar subjectivity within, a form of dignity. The third stage is a reconceptualization of humanist subjects as embodied agents, again something akin to technological beings. The fourth stage requires identification with technology, the view of embodied agents as dignified machine equivalents with machine-like qualities. The fifth stage is the move towards enhancement, to become technological and/or to appropriate technological power. The sixth stage is codependency, a consequence of the continuing merger with technology, and the latest stage is the decentralization of human subjectivity when confronting emergent posthuman(ist) subjectivities.

Taking Hong's starting point in the 1960s, the first stage of desire and fear is quite evident. A short article from *The Science Newsletter* (16 January 1960) 'promises' that the 1960s will bring desirable advances, such as synthetic foods, plastic homes, automated post offices, desalination, remote-controlled highways and picture-on-the-wall television. Technological products were marketed as necessities for the homes of the future, a future imagined to be like Hanna-Barbera's *The Jetsons* (1962–1963), a 1950s family in a techno-fantasy world. But fears of automation, artificial intelligence (AI), nuclear weapons and the role of cybernetics in humanity's future also fuelled debates about technology's encroachment on distinctly human areas (Hong 2004). *Dr. Strangelove* (1964) exhibited the cry-if-you-don't-laugh absurdity over the real threat of nukes, while Kubrick's *2001: A Space Odyssey* (1968) brought us the infamous betrayal of HAL 9000, portraying the consequences of Wiener's vision of extensive automation. Humans went to the moon on rockets, cyborgs were conceived, the boundaries between humans and machines blurred, and technological advancement became a popular theme for film and television.

For popular culture, desire and fear meant debating whether certain technologies should be adopted into a *human* world. People still felt like rational independent creatures, minds in bodies whose job was to make decisions about *our* world. On another level, however, philosophical enquiry into technology was already unearthing ontological anomalies in the humanist model of subjectivity. Merleau-Ponty's *Phenomenology of Perception*, translated into English in 1962, problematized the extension of subjectivity through his famous example of the blind man's cane, and equated the body as the subject itself, transgressing the humanist framework. Fear of technological determinism led scholars, such as Mumford (1967) and Ellul (1967), to reject the rising agency of technology as a destructive force, and traditional humanity (humans conceived of collectively as solely biological individual humanist subjects) competed with advancing technology for primacy in the ontological order of things. By the beginning of the next decade, concentrated studies in the philosophy of technology had arrived (Mitcham 1969).

Throughout the 1970s, political posthumanist themes shone from the screen in films such as *A Clockwork Orange*, *Logan's Run* and the ongoing *Planet of the Apes* film franchise. Social challenges came to the fore, and popular culture explored some of these challenges through posthuman representatives such as evil robotic replacements in 1975's *The Stepford Wives* and clones in 1976's *Futureworld*. The decade also continued the oscillation between fear and desire, with the popular *Six Million Dollar Man* (1973), the evil Darth Vader of *Star Wars* (1977) and the nuclear-induced beast *The Incredible Hulk* (1977). Performances on the screen, along with the technological impact on society, reinforced the coming changes. The term 'posthumanism' arrived in Ihab Hassan's 1977 article in the *Georgia Review*, 'Prometheus as Performer: Toward a Posthumanist Culture', where he describes posthumanist culture as 'the matrix of contemporary performance', evidencing a shift towards an understanding of agency as an aggregation of influences. The year 1979 saw Latour and Woolgar's influential challenge to the sociology of science in *Laboratory Life*, and the sociological shift of the 1970s demonstrated that artefacts and technologies held at least part of the agency of the social space.

In the late 1970s and early 1980s, technology's power was on display. Long-range ballistic missiles, pharmaceuticals, the *Voyager* and *Viking* missions, genetic discoveries, robotic manufacturing and even video games exerted a technological hold on society. In a technosocial *coup d'etat*, the computer stepped in as *TIME* magazine's 1982 person of the year. The beleaguered humanist framework was in danger, and posthuman representations adopted the vehicle of war. The Cylons of *Battlestar Galactica* (1978), the soulless cyborg Ash in *Alien* (1979), Darth Vader again in *Star Wars: Episode V* (1980), Khan Noonien Singh's pathological hubris in *Star Trek II: The Wrath of Khan* (1982), the Master Control Program of *Tron* (1982) and the lack of judgement from a learning supercomputer in *WarGames* (1983) hammered the message home that technological influence distorts values and creates monsters.

The oscillation of desire and fear hit its peak in the early 1980s with *The Terminator* (1984) and *Blade Runner* (1982). In a world under nuclear threat, *The Terminator* presented advancing technology as the apocalypse. Arnold Schwarzenegger's killer cyborg became an icon, an unstoppable force sent from the future by a sentient defence network computer to kill Sarah Connor, the mother of traditional humanity's future hope. The film sets four technologies in opposition to humanity as threats to the species: (1) AI and computer systems, (2) cyborg systems or biotechnology, (3) nuclear weapons and (4) automated manufacturing, which is responsible for replacing human labour (for the most part) in the future. The message was direct. In words used by Kyle Reese, the resistance fighter who came back in time to protect Sarah, 'That terminator is out there. It can't be bargained with. It can't be reasoned with. It doesn't feel pity or remorse or fear. And it absolutely will not stop. Ever. Until you are dead.' *The Terminator*'s final lines announce an angst-inducing destiny. Sitting in her Jeep Renegade, Sarah is told, 'A storm is coming in', and she responds reflectively, 'I know'. Revolution was on the horizon and, with personal computers entering homes everywhere, becoming cyborgs was only a matter of time.

Two years earlier, *Blade Runner* may have begun the second stage in the posthumanist paradigm shift, the stage of acquiring empathy. Rutger Hauer's portrayal of Roy Batty, an artificial human known as a replicant, left audiences sympathizing with him and forgiving him despite the fact that he had murdered his creator. It felt clear that he had been wronged by his creator, unjustly uncared for, lied to and used. His famous dying words reference amazing events, such as seeing 'attack ships on fire off the shoulder of Orion' and experiences that were in fact 'things you people wouldn't believe'. He laments his memories as 'moments lost in time like tears in rain', reminding audiences of the value of their own lives. Suddenly, the favouritism for the politically and socially protected traditional humans seemed unjust and callous. Long before Nick Bostrom's 'In Defense of Posthuman Dignity' (2005), Batty's fate questioned the dignity of posthuman life, both real and artificial, and challenged its ontological distinction in a way that has remained relevant throughout the years.

The political and philosophical pillars of posthumanist discourse were well under way by the mid-1980s. As the sparks of dignity mixed with desire and fear, Donna Haraway opened readers' eyes to the significance of embodiment and the cyborg metaphor in her *Cyborg Manifesto* (1985), and a growing field of science and technology studies (STS) complemented the burgeoning scholarship in the social construction of technology (Bijker et al. 1992). In *The Whale and the Reactor*, Langdon Winner asked the question 'Do artifacts have politics?' and declared, 'no idea is more provocative in controversies about technology and society' (1988, 19). The political ramifications of the Genesis Machine in *Star Trek III* (1984) showed us the problematic responsibility that goes along with the technological creation of new life, and *Star Trek IV* (1986) reminded us that, while being technologically advanced could be wonderful, not paying attention to all forms of life could cost us our future. The third stage in the posthumanist paradigm shift began with the consideration of embodiment as an obligatory aspect of a being's subjectivity – human subjectivity was no exception.

Dignity and the politics of embodiment began finding their way to the screen, and posthumans started to get a reprieve as a result. In *Aliens* (1986), the sequel to *Alien*, the new cyborg, Bishop, redeemed our faith by remaining loyal instead of betraying Ripley, as his predecessor Ash had done. Likewise, 1987's *RoboCop* demonstrated that a posthuman cyborg weapon can be a power for good (so long as it had a human soul). Also in 1987, *Star Trek: The Next Generation (TNG)* introduced us to Lieutenant Data, a humanoid robot, who acts as a full-fledged member of Starfleet. Ironically, Data is a foil for humanist themes that portray him lacking. If he only had a heart and real emotions, he could be complete. But Data's humanism is countered with the arrival of the very posthuman Borg, the most dreadful foe in the galaxy. In the *TNG* episode 'Q Who?' (1989), an alien 'Q' warns that humans are not ready for the civilizations they are destined to encounter. The *Enterprise* is transported to deep space and the crew confronts a race of cyborgs that function as a hive, assimilated to each other in a 'collective', to whom 'resistance is futile'. It is the loss of individual subjectivity and the threat of distributed consciousness that becomes the enemy, and the Borg's villainy is tied to the dystopian social values of its collectivity rather than technologically transgressed bodies.

Phenomenology and embodiment, as well as the cyborg metaphor and sociology's techno-ontological efforts, aligned in *Terminator 2: Judgment Day* (1991) to cap the second stage in the posthumanist paradigm shift. *Terminator 2* illuminated the technosocial relationship of the first generation growing up with computers and advanced technologies in the home. This time, a new terminator, the T1000, is sent to seek out Sarah's son, John, and kill him. But, instead of sending a human from the future, the John Connor of the future captures, reprograms and sends a T800 Model 101 (Schwarzenegger) back in time to protect himself. The film pits machine against machine, but the key difference between the two terminators is that the T800 can be reset, learn and build human relationships. The T1000 blindly follows orders. The movie is overtly philosophical as Sarah Connor comes to grips with the roles technology assumes (predator, helper, teacher, saviour and companion) in relation to her son. The film voices an appreciation for technology's reliability in the face of human bias, betrayal, misbehaviour, abuse and disappointment, and an instrumentalist approach emerges to supplant the determinism of the first *Terminator* film. In the end, unlike Roy Batty, who committed murder out of the rage of abandonment, the T800 sacrifices itself for its companions and their future, and attains not only dignity but nobility, having learned the value of life.

The proximity to computer technology brought a new way of living and learning in the 1990s. With the development of the Internet and the World Wide Web, *The Terminator*'s Skynet was becoming real and the technosocial milieu was becoming a 'collective', but attitudes were no longer pessimistic and the popular device of comprehending humans as computational machine analogues fit like a glove. The humanist subject came under further assault from Varela, Thompson and Rosch's influential *The Embodied Mind* (1991), and human agency became as equally embodied as that of technology. It was the right time for a phenomenology of technics (Ihde 1990), and the popular writing of cognitive scientists and philosophers promoted various versions of a computational theory of mind (Dennett 1993; Pinker 1997). Latour returned with his influential sociological critique *We Have Never Been Modern*, and traded humanist subjectivity for a technosocial ontology that he described as 'a parliament of things' (1993, 142). This key influence in posthumanist discourse established the claim that we never were the humanist subjects we thought we were. Seemingly on the side of the Borg, Latour claims that 'The Subject does revolve, but not around Nature. It revolves around the collective out of which people and things are generated' (1993, 79). Soon after, we encounter Pickering's *The Mangle of Practice* (1995), a sociological critique of scientific practice that shows human agency as a distributed phenomenon produced from a variety of changing relationships with artefacts and information. Along with *Star Trek TNG*'s Captain Picard, who was assimilated by the Borg, humans became embodied and distributed technological beings in theory and in the cultural imagination.

As the decade came to a close, N. Katherine Hayles published arguably the most influential monograph in posthumanist scholarship, *How We Became Posthuman* (1999). Influenced by Latour, Haraway and others, Hayles details the history of how cybernetics, critical theory and other influences preserved embodied subjectivity and highlighted the distribution of agency across a network of artefacts and technologies. Her analysis cemented the view that the humanist version of 'the human' never existed and was, in many ways, a falsehood (Hauskeller 2014). True subjectivity was an emergent posthuman subjectivity, created through a distributed *artefactual* agency. The very same year, the blockbuster film *The Matrix* exposed audiences' total buy-in to a posthumanist model of subjectivity, when Neo, played by Keanu Reeves, overrides the illusion of humanist subjectivity and defeats the villainous 'agents' by recognizing the matrix as a form of embodiment that he can manipulate. The masses growing up with digital technologies over the previous twenty years felt perfectly at ease. Human beings had become plug-n-play, and technosocial ontology was reframed as an interactive latticework of biological and technological equivalents. Stage four had been reached, but the biological machines were still inferior.

With tacit recognition in the popular consciousness that humans were biological machines, it was not a large leap to suppose that these machines could be improved, not only through genetic selection but through direct engineering. Thus, the belief in humans as enhancement-ready organisms constitutes a fifth stage in the posthumanist paradigm shift. Admittedly, the desire for human enhancement, in general, was not new, but the more the technosocial reality reframed the human body as technologically permeable, the more the question of enhancement took on an air, not of 1960s fantasy, but of potential technoscientific reality. David Pearce and Nick Bostrom began their search for this utopian dream with their 1998 *Transhumanist Declaration*, only a year after *Gattaca* declared that there was no gene for the human spirit, and Dolly the sheep revealed to the public that cloning was no longer SF. The first *X-Men* films (2000, 2003) brought new relevance to the 1960s comic about genetic mutants, at about the same time as the sequencing of the human genome in 2003 increased the focus on the question of our own enhancement. That same year, Bostrom declared human nature as 'a work-in-progress, a half-baked beginning that we can learn to remould in desirable ways' (2003, 493), and Andy Clark outlined our distributed bodies in *Natural*

Born Cyborgs. From Riddick in *Pitch Black* (2001), David in *A.I.* (2001) and the sentient Caesar of *Planet of the Apes* (2001), to the government-created assassins Jason Bourne of the *Bourne* franchise and River Tam of *Firefly* (2003) and *Serenity* (2005) fame, enhanced humans flooded the big and little screens.

Enhancement became such an issue in posthumanist discourse, that Francis Fukuyama critiqued the posthuman conception of subjectivity as a threat to liberal democracy (2002), while Jürgen Habermas contemplated *The Future of Human Nature* (2003). James Hughes' *Citizen Cyborg* (2004) brought a different perspective, advocating a strategy for bringing technology and democracy together in a transhumanist vision, and, by 2005, advances in bioengineering had Bailey and Casey asking *Is Human Nature Obsolete?* Traditional human nature was indeed under critique, and the 2004 *Battlestar Galactica* reboot of the 1978 series saw the robotic Cylons return, this time indistinguishable from humans. As flesh and blood people, they achieved a spiritual status, had romantic relationships with one another and even interbred with humans. The series ended with the suggestion that homo sapiens were their biotechnological progeny, the clues of which could be seen in the species' biological 'machinery'. Equating the sentience and spiritual status of human subjects and posthuman ones brought up concerns about competition and priority of place, and enhancement concerns have continued to be debated by scholars, such as Michael Sandel, Francis Fukuyama, Ingmar Persson and Julien Savulescu up to the present day. Meanwhile, related to the idea that biological humans need enhancement, is the concept that confronting the future necessitates technosocial codependency. The latter has become a powerful motif in SF films, evidencing a sixth stage in the posthumanist paradigm shift.

Both the *Iron Man* franchise (2008, 2010, 2013) and *Terminator: Salvation* (2009) address the notion that traditional humans are inferior and that technology is required to save society by adding capacities beyond the traditional human's ability to manage. In *Iron Man*, Tony Stark needs the arc-reactor in order to stay alive. A functional cyborg in a high-tech prosthesis, he needs his technological heart as much as his suit needs his playboy billionaire genius personality. This codependency explicitly arrives in *Iron Man 2* as a form of distributed subjectivity. Stark explicitly states, 'I am Iron Man. The suit and I are one.' But the fact that Stark would die without the arc-reactor reveals something about the intractable consequences of the union with technology. By *Iron Man 3*, the suit even stands in for Stark in social situations and functions as his saviour. It continues in a symbiotic relationship with him, despite his emancipation from heart trouble.

Terminator: Salvation (2009) reverses the action on a similar theme while delivering the problematic of technosocial codependency. In this case, the human heart saves technology. A cyborg powered by a human heart ultimately sacrifices himself and, in an act of self-redemption, donates his heart to John Connor, who would otherwise die without the transplant. John then becomes a human with a cyborg heart that is, in turn, human, problematizing the core of the hero that was to defend humanity against the technological revolution. Eighteen years after *Terminator 2: Judgment Day*, the themes of *Terminator: Salvation* include the problematic concept of 'the human', machine epistemology, the potential moral superiority of technology, and the relationship of AI and free will. The film ends with the voiceover, 'There is no fate, but what we make', but in the posthumanist paradigm, that fate is made by hybridized technological beings. It is clear that the humanist paradigm is gone. Nowhere are the 1960s questions of whether society *ought* to have these technologies. Posthumanist subjectivities announce their existence as a given, decentralizing the experience of humans as individual subjects.

Dealing with decentralization constitutes the latest stage in the posthumanist paradigm shift. Cary Wolfe's *What Is Posthumanism?* addresses decentralization in the contemporary complex of ontology and epistemology, by emphasizing both the biological and technological embeddedness of the human being (2010, xv). The experience of humanist subjectivity no longer has priority and must negotiate with new forms of subjectivity. One of the most popular examples of this in recent years has to do with the theoretical phenomenon of mind-uploading. Mind-uploading, wherein consciousnesses are transitioned to computer networks, is now commonly recognized by SF audiences. From *Avatar* (2009) and *Inception* (2010), to *Captain America: The Winter Soldier* (2014) and *Transcendence* (2014), the mixing of the mind with computer architecture is gripping the imagination, mirroring advances real-world scientists are making in neuroprosthetic controls and neuron mapping in the BRAIN initiative. Advances in robotics and nootropics are also common newsworthy topics, and popular culture is evolving alongside. Films, such as *Limitless* (2011) and *Lucy* (2014), for example, examine similar themes about the effects of accessing a greater percentage of our brain function through pharmaceuticals. In *Limitless*, the effects are hypothesized as something akin to strong AI, each piece of data from an entire lifetime ready and waiting to be involved in each moment. *Lucy* takes it further, and the effects allow her to act in ways that appear magical as she advances along the path to the total dissolution of her singular humanist form of subjectivity.

Films such as *Robot & Frank* (2012) and *Her* (2014) also focus on new forms of subjectivity as a consequence of technosocial relationships, and explore how technology currently relates to the concept of humanity. Both films portray selfhood largely as a function of companionship and technological interaction. *Her* pushes boundaries, as it expands the concept of the technosocial relationship into the romantic. The film explores problems of embodiment, surrogacy and the subjectivity of the operating system (OS) alongside those of Theodore Twombly, the film's protagonist. Both films, like Stefan Herbrechter's recent text *Posthumanism: A Critical Analysis* (2013) and the 2014 television series *Almost Human*, centre on the underlying question: What does it mean to be human in this new technologically saturated existence? There is no doubt that addressing new subjectivities is a necessary layer in the sedimentation of the posthumanist paradigm shift, but there is also the desire to know what comes after decentralization.

Whatever it is, it may be intense. Intellectual leaders and scientists are already balking at the idea of creating strong AI. Stephen Hawking recently said, in a BBC interview, that AI could destroy humanity (2 December 2014), while Elon Musk, chief executive of SpaceX, said it could be like 'summoning the Devil' (TechCrunch, 27 October 2014). Thinkers like James Barrat in his *Our Final*

Invention: Artificial Intelligence and the End of the Human Era (2014) examine the potential dangers of creating something truly more intelligent than human beings. Even transhumanism's leading figure, Nick Bostrom, addresses the possibilities in *Superintelligence: Paths, Dangers, Strategies* (2014). In the meantime, films such as *The Machine* (2013) and *Transcendence* (2014) are projecting the seduction and the danger of AI, as it may have the power to save us or destroy us all. In *The Machine*, a beautiful researcher has her brain mapped before she is killed and cloned in the form of a cyborg. Her captivity and escape raise the question of free will and rights for sentient artificial systems. In *Transcendence* (2014), scientist Will Caster merges his mind with the Internet, creating a vastly powerful, though luckily benevolent, distributed consciousness. As a technological demiurge, Caster is able to do miracles and solve some of the world's biggest problems but his power is too much for people to accept, and the entire electronic infrastructure of the planet is wiped out in order to destroy him. Whether these films highlight the problems of traditional humans, posthumans or both, the message is delivered loud and clear. Actually dealing with new ways of being will most likely be much harder than imagining them.

And so the posthumanist paradigm shift has moved our conception of our own subjectivity far away from the dualistic humanist subjectivity of the 1960s. The concept of humans as immaterial minds in control of material bodies seems foreign. We are embodied beings that share our agency with material artefacts. We are 'beyond the skin bag', as Don Ihde puts it (2003), in a review of Andy Clark's *Natural Born Cyborgs*. We live in, through and with technologies that shape daily life, hold our information and help us make decisions. We accept that advanced technologies perform tasks more readily and reliably than biological brains, trust that they have a higher fidelity of recall and rely on them to interrogate aspects of the world that biological faculties cannot. We cede a great deal of agency to technological devices and systems. We even demonstrate an epistemological faith in technical systems, trusting in their judgement over our own observational and decision-making abilities. Perhaps we do so because we recognize that we would not be human without them. What it means to be human is constituted by these technosocial systems. In the case of cinema and television, the matrix of technosocial agency functions, on one level, to scrutinise, transform and/or reify frameworks within which our identities flourish.

Cinema and television have made it possible to make this transition by placing the narratives before our eyes. They have helped enhanced beings, cyborgs, robots, clones, hives, genetic mutants, AIs and uploaded consciousnesses to display a variety of subjectivities to our collective consciousness. They have also helped to legitimate them and to establish their experiences as equal with traditional human experience. Posthuman representations have expanded the playing field and created a more inclusive concept of life by allowing people to share imagined experiences of biological and technological embodiment and, like the blind man's cane, to feel out areas that are still beyond our current condition. The ramifications of this go beyond the fictional and affect our political world as well.

The year 2015 will bring more cinematic encounters with complicated subjectivities and the possibilities of sentient AI, in films such as *Chappie* and *The Avengers: The Age of Ultron*, and the posthumanist paradigm shift may also evolve in response to other areas entirely as world events and scholarship influence and react to current themes. Exploration of posthumanist themes through SF is far from over. The stages presented in this chapter are not all that there are in the journey to a posthumanist future. Technology and society continue to fuse closer together, and new outcomes are likely to surprise us. Hopefully, future films will capture these surprises, where the parallel lines of human organic limitations and technological advancement meet and where the human being is one with its technological counterparts. Hopefully, these new films and television shows will continue to inspire and astound and help people to overcome close-mindedness, to integrate further, and maybe even to reconstitute themselves through new forms of embodiment and technosocial opportunities. Film and television will continue to provide a record of this shift until we no longer need it, having evolved into a plenitude, osmotically diffused into anywhere and everywhere, with as many possible perceptions of knowing and being as possible.

40
Object-Oriented Ontology
Graham Harman

Object-oriented ontology (hereafter 'OOO') is relatively new, and hence not as well known among film and television critics as other theoretical standpoints. For this reason, the discussion that follows must take a somewhat circuitous path. First, I will give a brief history and conceptual overview of OOO itself. Second, I will give an assessment of how OOO might fit with some current discussions of trans- and posthumanism. Third and finally, I will give some basic examples of how OOO might be applicable to film and television criticism.

The meaning of object-oriented ontology

OOO is often described as one of four variants of the speculative realism movement in philosophy. This is accurate as far as it goes, since OOO came to international prominence along with three rival philosophies through the joint April 2007 Speculative Realism Workshop at Goldsmiths College, University of London.[1] But it obscures the proper chronology, since I used the term 'object-oriented philosophy' in notes dating back to at least 1997, and had already employed the phrase in public at a 1999 lecture in England.[2] By 2009, I had object-oriented colleagues in Ian Bogost and Levi Bryant (joined the next year by Timothy Morton). Since Bogost and Bryant were far from agreeing with me on all philosophical matters, Bryant coined the umbrella term 'object-oriented ontology' in 2009 to refer to the ideas of all three of us.[3] Perhaps due to the catchiness of the repetitive acronym, OOO has replaced the phrase 'object-oriented philosophy' in the public lexicon, though I have largely reverted to my earlier term due to increased philosophical disagreement with Bryant.

The word 'object' has meant numerous different things in philosophy. Sometimes it refers to solid inanimate objects as opposed to humans, animals, concepts or events. More often it serves as half of the modern subject/object dualism, and this promotes the misunderstanding that OOO prefers inanimate objects to humans. But the OOO use of 'object' is indebted to a different historical source: the 19th-century Austrian School of philosopher Franz Brentano. OOO means 'objects' in a wide sense, including human beings as well as dragons, stones and the Dutch East India Company. Anything that cannot be fully reduced either downward to its components ('undermining') or upward to its effects ('overmining') counts as an object, whether it be human, immaterial, durable or fleeting. For this reason, OOO is often viewed as a 'flat ontology' that treats all objects equally, though we will see that my own version of OOO is not altogether flat, since it distinguishes between exactly *two* kinds of objects.

We return to Brentano, who famously revived the medieval term 'intentionality', the notion that every mental act (unlike physical events in nature) has an object: to love is to love some object, judgement judges about some object and so forth. Though 'intentionality' is often wrongly used to mean that, in thinking about objects, I escape the bounds of the mind and tread upon the soil of an extramental world, Brentano is clear that he is speaking of *immanent* objectivity, objects that exist only in some consciousness (Brentano 1995). Little light is shed on the relation between these immanent objects and possible objects beyond the mind, which then became a disputed subject among his disciples (Smith 1995). The solution offered by Kazimierz Twardowski (1977) was to double things up between an 'object' outside consciousness and a 'content' inside consciousness. His older rival Edmund Husserl (1993) struggled with Twardowski's claim before eventually reaching a different verdict: object and content must *both* be inside consciousness, since otherwise we could never link the contents of our mind with any reality, and knowledge would be impossible. Phenomenology became the exercise of identifying the unified intentional object behind the many different contents it presents to the mind (such as the different sides of a mailbox), thereby rejecting the British empiricist doctrine that an object is nothing but a 'bundle of qualities'. For Husserl, by contrast, the object is always different from any bundle of qualities present to the mind, since it remains the same object despite being seen from countless different angles and distances. In sum, Husserl retains Twardowski's object/content distinction only by imploding both terms into the realm of consciousness, while discarding all claims of an inaccessible thing-in-itself. This is the first sense of 'object' found in my own version of OOO: a purely ideal object that is more than the exact set of qualities it presents to the mind at any given moment.

Yet there is an important second sense of 'object', one that we draw from Husserl's rebellious disciple Martin Heidegger. Heidegger departs from phenomenology by noting that things are generally *not* accessible to consciousness. We rely on a multitude of background entities without being consciously aware of them, from our bodily organs and the circulation of our blood, to our reliance on urban transit and the grammar of our native languages. His famous 'tool-analysis' in *Being and Time* (1927) indicates that we normally notice such things only when they malfunction or obtrude on awareness.[4] But even when we notice such things, we cannot possibly exhaust the depth of their reality even when turning our explicit attention to them (Harman 2002). Furthermore, though Heidegger dislikes the word 'objects', and though he tends to treat the background system of withdrawn tools as a holistic context rather than a number of individual beings, in his later period we find a growing awareness of 'the thing' as an individual entity that (unlike Husserl's object) withdraws from direct access by humans.[5]

Thus, we have two different kinds of objects: real objects that exceed any possible access to them, and sensual objects that are fully accessible to the mind but partly buried behind the accidental costumes they wear in any given moment. It also turns out that there are two kinds of qualities, the real and the sensual, each of which can be paired with both real and sensual objects, yielding precisely four poles of reality. These four terms give us Heidegger's concept of *das Geviert*, the fourfold, which OOO then develops further (Harman 2011). While most philosophies try to collapse the distinctions between the object and its appearance to consciousness, or the object and its qualities, the research programme of OOO is precisely focused to *magnify* these tensions. The one most important for aesthetics is that, between the withdrawn real object and its palpable sensual qualities, the qualities of the object seem to manifest a hidden real object that is never directly given. This brings us to the point of the current chapter: any application of OOO to cinema and television must look for a way in which the real object in these media withdraws from its accessible sensual qualities.[6] Our first impression might be that cinema and television are not a good OOO theme at all, since they always give us specific *viewpoints* on things rather than alluding to the things as deeper than any possible viewpoint. In the section 'Cinema and television', we will consider whether this impression is correct. But first we should speak about how OOO may be of interest to those who work in posthumanist currents.

The relation of OOO to transhumanism and posthumanism

The difference between trans- and posthumanism is explained clearly in a recent article by Thomas Philbeck (2014, 177):

> *Transhumanism refers to the use of science and technology to extend human opportunities and potential by transforming the human being so that its capacities and abilities are capable of overcoming any number of natural human limitations such as aging, death, suffering, intellectual capacity, moral shortcomings and so forth. (...) The 'posthuman' in posthumanism, on the other hand, refers to a state of being that is beyond our understanding from a humanist philosophical paradigm. (...) For example, a transhumanist posthuman might be something like a super smart child that has been enhanced genetically and neurologically with computer implants. A posthumanist posthuman might be something like the alien Q from the Star Trek series – an individual so advanced, or with such a fundamentally different understanding of the universe, that basic human concerns over things like ethics are incomprehensible to it.*

By invoking inscrutable alien species as the possible outcome of posthumanism, Philbeck takes a more radical line than Cary Wolfe in *What Is Posthumanism?* where we read in the introduction (2010, xv) as follows: 'posthumanism in my sense isn't posthuman at all – in the sense of being "after" our embodiment has been transcended – but is only posthuman*ist*, in the sense that it opposes the fantasies of disembodiment and autonomy, inherited from humanism itself'. Though

Wolfe is right to side with Derrida on the status of language as a prosthesis, there is a more threatening range of possible prostheses that could push us far beyond what is recognizably human (Wolfe 2010, xxv–xxvi).

At the conclusion of his introduction, cited above, Philbeck pinpoints the respective difficulties with trans- and posthumanism as follows: 'Neither (...) has a firm grasp on the new ontology that is developing before our eyes due to our continuingly deepening integration with technology. Transhumanism relies on outdated notions from a crumbling humanist paradigm, and posthumanism has yet to figure out what a new paradigm might look like'(2014, 182). Speaking specifically of transhumanism, Philbeck complains further that it 'piggybacks humanism's dualist ontology'. As seen, OOO rejects the Cartesian dualism that treats the thinking human being as one sort of entity (*res cogitans*) and non-human animals, inanimate beings and the human body itself as another sort (*res extensa*), and aspires to a new ontology that is fourfold where the old one was twofold. By invoking the constant formation of hybrid entities in which humans fuse with non-humans, OOO is close to Bruno Latour's (2007) version of actor–network theory, and might even be allied with 'extended mind' models such as that of Andy Clark (2010). Nonetheless, this rejection of Cartesian ontology *does not* entail a rejection of the lingering humanism allegedly found in transhumanists such as Nick Bostrom.[7] Although some critics of OOO hold that its removal of human beings from the centre of the universe entails a further claim that 'humans are worthless', this is not the case. If a flat ontological starting point requires us to say that humans are no more and no less entities than rubbish dumps or gods, it follows neither that humans are rubbish dumps nor that they are gods. Nor does it demand that humans aspire to stop being human: there are perfectly understandable reasons why we might wish to nurture human interests over those of worms, bears or neutrons, and why we might wish to remain as we are despite the coming technological capability to do otherwise. OOO simply holds that if such preservation is resolved upon, it must not appeal to the ontological delusion that humans are radically different *in kind* from all other entities.

Yet there is another important difference between OOO and many forms of posthumanism. Whereas numerous posthumanists wave the banner of materialism, OOO *is not a materialism at all*. This point is missed by Rosi Braidotti (2014) in her recent interview in the British arts magazine *Frieze*:

> There are two or three things that I don't fully get about the speculative realists (...). The emphasis on matter, and the continuity between matter and mind, and between human bodies and the world in which they live, is not new. (...) It has always been at the core of Spinozist, Deleuzian and materialist feminist studies, including those of Simone de Beauvoir, Haraway and my own.

The term 'materialism' has a long legacy in Enlightenment and political Left circles that many wish to inherit for obvious reasons. Yet there are at least two problems with it. First, there is the forceful objection made by Latour, who shows in a neglected article (2007a) that materialism replaces the permanent mystery of what things are with a dogmatic *definition* of what they are: whether this be the hard material particles of scientific materialism, or the languages and disciplinary practices of today's post-Foucauldian materialism. Second, the claim of OOO is not just that we need to move beyond the Cartesian subject, since this is too often and too easily done merely by claiming that the subject exists in constant interplay with an environment that shapes that subject in turn. But replacing an isolated human and isolated world with a mutually correlated human and world still preserves the worst aspect of the Cartesian tradition. The human remains 50 per cent of every philosophical situation, receiving a full half of reality, while all of the many atoms, frogs, schools, puppies, comets, supernovae, tectonic plates and black holes in the universe are packed like sardines into the other half. To be truly posthumanist it is not enough to be 'materialist' in this fashion. Two other steps are needed: (1) We must treat object–object interactions in the same way as human–world interactions, for ontological if not ethico-political purposes; (2) We must insist that interacting (or 'intra-acting' (Barad 2007)) entities are not exhausted by their mutual interplay, since otherwise the world is defined by its interactions with humans, and this is not an especially promising route beyond 'humanism' even if the materialists tell us otherwise.

For all the achievements of 'Spinozist, Deleuzian and materialist feminist studies' (the subfields cited by Braidotti (2014) as having beaten OOO to the punch), none have much to tell us about the interaction between parts of the inanimate world. In this sense, they remain human-centred no matter how many material entities they summon in the night to mould and shape human beings. Braidotti is always wonderfully candid, both in person and in her writings. As she puts it in *The Posthuman* (2013, 16): 'I am none too fond of Humanism or of the idea of the human which it implicitly upholds. (...) I came of age intellectually and politically in the turbulent years after the Second World War, when the humanist ideal came to be questioned quite radically.' Later in the book, she fatefully opines that 'there is a direct connection between monism, the unity of all living matter and postanthropocentrism as a general frame of reference for contemporary subjectivity' (2013, 57). Braidotti also upholds a version of extended mind theory, underpinned with a heavily relationistic ontology: 'What happens to subjectivity in [the contemporary world's] complex field of forces and data flows? My argument is that it becomes an expanded relational self, engendered by the cumulative effect of all these factors' (2013, 60). From these passages, the difference between OOO and Braidotti becomes increasingly clear. Like many thinkers working in the tradition of Deleuze and Deleuze's Spinoza, Braidotti links the end of humanism to a doctrine of 'the unity of all living matter'. The problem with this philosophical thesis as a basis for posthumanism lies in its view that the unity of everything is a fait accompli. By contrast, the point of posthumanism is that we are moving towards *specific* astonishing fusions of human beings with technologies, and that most of these have not yet been accomplished.

For purposes of analogy, consider the revolutionary endosymbiosis theory of Lynn Margulis (1998), who finally achieved victory for her claim that the eukaryotic cells of living creatures originally formed through the symbiotic attachment of originally separate beings. While at first this may sound like a gesture towards holism, it is precisely the opposite. Symbiosis means that certain living things fuse together at certain times while most others fail to do so. It implies what Niles Eldredge and Stephen Jay Gould (1972) called 'punctuated equilibrium', meaning that, for long periods of evolutionary time, nothing happens at all, with these relatively quiet periods followed by explosive revolutionary eras. Thus it cannot be, as Braidotti wishes, that the key to posthumanism lies in the unity of 'all living matter'. If that were so, then we would always already have been posthuman, and would simply be consciously realizing it for the first time now. And though reconceptualizing the situation in which humans have always already lived often has profound implications, when it comes to posthumanism we are not talking primarily about something that has been here along, but about something that has not yet arrived.

Cinema and television: Some OOO examples

We turn at last to the role of cinema and television in object-oriented aesthetic theory. That theory makes a good initial fit with the art criticism of Clement Greenberg (1988), whose notion of the artwork as an autonomous entity irreducible to its biographical or political context either inspires or horrifies most contemporary artists. His disciple Michael Fried expanded Greenberg's vocabulary to criticize the 'literalism' and 'theatricality' of minimalism and other postformalist art (Fried 1998), and moved from criticism to art history through an older tradition defined by its anti-theatrical sentiments (Fried 1988). Fried's older friend, the philosopher Stanley Cavell, came so under the spell of his terminology that the whole of Cavell's classic work on film theory (1979) reads like an extension that could have been made by Fried himself, aside from Cavell's rather different literary voice. For Fried and Cavell, it is important to eliminate *both* the literalism *and* the theatricality of art, and in this way they confuse two very different things: the human as an observer of art, and the human as an ingredient of art (Harman 2014). OOO salutes the Greenbergian principle that the artwork is a surplus not exhausted by its environment or any particular human reactions to it (OOO is thus anti-literalist). But it does not follow that good modern art requires the exclusion of human interaction with the artwork (OOO is thus *not* anti-theatrical). The object-orientation of OOO entails that a thing is always more than its series of appearances, something noticed by Husserl and Heidegger in different ways. In this respect, Cavell's reality-in-itself is exactly the opposite of what OOO means by the phrase, since, for Cavell, that reality-in-itself is merely a series of cinematic images that the viewer cannot affect or influence in the least. There is an additional factor: at least initially, cinema might seem like the very opposite of an OOO-friendly art, since it never gives us objects apart from some viewpoint. The inherent tendency of film is to present not *objects*, but *bundles of qualities* always seen from a specific perspective. As for live television, the case seems even less promising, given that the bundle-of-qualities problem is combined further with the 'theatricality' problem that Cavell rightly noted in this medium:

the news reader or talk show host is not autonomous from our gaze, but depends on it always, even hamming it up for us on occasion. Stated more generally, if the OOO model of aesthetics requires tension between objects and their qualities, how can it come to grips with media such as film and television for which there seem to be no difference between object and quality or reality and appearance?

If we speak of object-oriented cinema, we are not referring to images of inanimate objects on screen. To repeat an earlier point, 'objects' does not mean non-humans any more than it means humans. All entities are objects; all have an inscrutable inwardness withdrawn from direct access. And, furthermore, we have seen that cinematic images tend to be *viewpoints* on objects rather than objects themselves. Then what we seek are objects, human or otherwise, that are somehow split off from their accessible traits. It may be easiest to start with humans, since there is little difficulty in acknowledging that a human being is a *personality* deeper than any of its current actions, statements or emotions. In normal life this is often obscured by the stereotyped routines and industrialized human 'types' that fill our days. Amidst such banality we are often refreshed by the 'character', someone whose individuality perturbs every situation rather than yielding to it. In cinema this can take the form of recurring characters, whether it be Woody Allen in his neurotic strolls around the Upper East Side, or the Marx Brothers subverting opera, football and politics. But often a single film is enough to do the job, as with Robert De Niro in *Taxi Driver* (who even remembers his on-screen character's name?). De Niro is radically derelationized, unable to fit smoothly or predictably with anything else in the film. This sometimes appears to be his own fault: his excessive purchase of guns from Easy Andy, his disturbing advice to Senator Palantine or his bizarre assumption that Betsy would enjoy a first date at a porn theatre. At other times De Niro is himself the rational observer, disturbed by the problems in others: Martin Scorsese's passenger plotting mayhem on his unfaithful wife, Harvey Keitel's pimp speaking lewdly of his pre-teen employee. There is also the case of Tarkovsky's *Stalker*, where the enchanted Zone with its wish-granting power is not the only inscrutable object. Stalker himself does not fit cleanly into his family or occupation, and lacks any usual proper name; his rituals in the Zone are too strange for their purpose ever to be identified. Other living and dead characters in the film – Professor, Writer, Monkey, Porcupine – are not stereotyped by these names, but freed from the collar of banal identities to become almost unnamable.

Perhaps the next step worth considering would be a quasi-human entity withdrawn from its surface legibility. I speak of HAL the computer in Kubrick's *2001: A Space Odyssey*. With his motionless red eye and soothing voice, HAL seems at first like the cinematic incarnation of a minimalist object. But there is no 'literalism' here: even Michael Fried would not deny the malignant depth behind the façade. A more complicated agency can be found in Steven Spielberg's early masterpiece *Duel* (1971), in which Dennis Weaver's effete salesman is hunted almost to death by the ugly black truck he benignly passes in the desert. By suppressing the reality of the driver, who appears only as a vague white T-shirt and ominously motioning hand (except for one unfortunate shot of cowboy boots), the truck itself is turned into the central character of the film. Indeed, the only evident role of the driver is to anchor *Duel* in realism and prevent it from becoming a supernatural horror movie about a self-propelling vehicle, à la the 1983 screen adaptation of Stephen King's *Christine*. Spielberg took up a similar theme in the more famous but equally brilliant *Jaws*, whose villain begins literally hidden under the ocean, though even the brute physical presence of the shark at film's end serves only to convince us that there is still more than meets the eye. Inscrutable human energies can be transferred into inanimate objects as well, as in Fritz Lang's *M*, where poor Elise Beckmann's ball and balloon are shown still in motion after their doomed owner has vanished. In all of these cases objects are split from their qualities, and thus all literalism is nullified and an aesthetic effect is achieved. But though the objects withdraw from direct access by human observers, the human of 'fear and pity' (Aristotle) is still on the scene: standing in for the absent object and adoring its visible fragments. Contra Fried, all art is theatrical precisely *because* it is not literal.

In cinema the deliteralizing split between objects and qualities gives rise to theatre, but with live television the movement is reversed. Here the theatrical is present from the start, since live television is unthinkable without catering to its viewer in a way that cinema is not. The content is pitched right up our alley; we are engrossed from the start. Here the aesthetic split does not happen in an object depicted on the screen, but is a split between our involvement and the content with which we are involved. In everyday life we are constantly engaged with news, debts, pleasures, gossip and feuds, and do not consciously differentiate ourselves from these things. But when we become involved with an eccentric or absurd object, our easy bond with that object is severed, if it is even produced in the first place. This happens most obviously in humour, when we find ourselves occupied with something trivial or bizarre (Harman 2005). Live television lends itself to humour even more readily than cinema. One example should suffice: *Late Night with David Letterman* at its humorous peak in the mid-1980s. Letterman (pre-'Late Shift' bitterness) was the dazzling ringleader of a circus of offbeat entities and viewer involvement with them. There were strange catchphrases ('They pelted us with rocks and garbage!'), surreal pieces of viewer mail, the dropping of light bulbs, melons and cheese from tall buildings, and physical stunts such as Letterman entering a tank of water in a suit of Alka-Seltzer. With Harpo Marx we laugh at the gap between a dramatic agent and the absurdity of what he takes seriously: the honking horn, the tattoo of his own face, the tank of lemonade he sullies with his feet. But with vintage Letterman we laugh because of the gap between ourselves and our own absurd commitments to the running jokes and interactions with the bandleader.

In the first part of this chapter, I referred to the production of gaps between objects and qualities as the chief method of OOO in every field in which it is used. Art, architectural and literary criticism can be fed by an OOO stream whenever it explores such gaps and resists the temptation to replace a thing by a palpable list of its traits. Unlike Cavell, OOO does not view cinema as an art filled with objects, but as an art filled with viewpoints – though objects occasionally erupt from the perspectival rubble, resulting in theatrical involvement. But since live television begins with theatre in a way that Fried would surely disdain, the gap here is produced when the theatrical agent is distanced from the object of his or her involvement, with humour as the most medium-specific case. Despite Noël Carroll's misgivings (1996), the gap between cinema and live television does seem to be ontological in character.

Notes

1. For a lightly edited transcript of that event, see Brassier et al. (2007).
2. See 'Object-Oriented Philosophy', chapter 3 of Harman (2010, 93–104).
3. The same phrase was used earlier, though for different purposes, in Evens (2006). The term was then recoined, presumably without knowledge of Evens' piece, by Bryant (2011).
4. Heidegger 1962. For an even earlier version of the tool-analysis, from eight years before his major book was published, see Heidegger's '1919 War Emergency Freiburg Lecture Course' (Heidegger 2008).
5. See especially his seminal 1949 Bremen lecture 'Insight into That Which Is', in Heidegger (2012).
6. For a full explanation see Harman (2005). Also relevant is Harman (2007).
7. A good example of Bostrom's clear and far-reaching style of thought is Bostrom (2009).

Bibliography

Abrams, Jerrold J. (2008) 'The Dialectics of Enlightenment in Metropolis', in *The Philosophy of Science Fiction Film*, ed. Steven Sanders, Lexington: The University of Kentucky Press, 153–170.
Ackerman, Spencer (2008) 'Iron Man versus the Imperialists', *The American Prospect*, http://prospect.org/article/iron-man-versus-imperialists.
Agamben, Giorgio (1988) *Homo Sacer: Sovereign Power and Bare Life*, Redwood City, CA: Stanford University Press.
Agamben, Giorgio (2002) *The Open: Man and Animals*, Stanford, CA: Stanford University Press.
Agamben, Giorgio (2005) *The State of Exception*, Chicago: University of Chicago Press.
Agar, Nicholas (2010) *Humanity's End: Why We Should Reject Radical Enhancement*, Boston: The MIT Press.
Alaimo, Stacy (2010) *Bodily Natures: Science, Environment, and the Material Self*, Bloomington, IN/Indianapolis: Indiana University Press.
Aldiss, Brian W. (1973) *Billion Year Spree: The History of Science Fiction*, London: Weidenfeld & Nicolson.
Allison, Tanine (2011) 'More than a Man in a Monkey Suit: Andy Serkis, Motion Capture, and Digital Realism', *Quarterly Review of Film and Video* 28.4: 325–341.
Alloi, Giovanni (2012) *Art and Animals*, London: I.B.Tauris.
Anders, Günther (1956/1992) *Die Antiquiertheit des Menschen 1: Ueber die Seele im Zeitalter der zweiten industriellen Revolution*, Munich: Beck.
Anderson, Amanda (2001) *The Powers of Distance: Cosmopolitanism and the Cultivation of Detachment*, Princeton, NJ: Princeton University Press.
Annas, George, Lori Andrews and Rosario Isasi (2002) 'Protecting the Endangered Human: Toward an International Treaty Prohibiting Cloning and Inheritable Alterations', *American Journal of Law and Medicine* 28.2–3: 151–178.
Arendt, Hannah (1992) *Eichman in Jerusalem: A Report on the Banality of Evil*, New York: Penguin.
Aristotle (1984) *Politics*, in *The Complete Works*, ed. Jonathan Barnes, vol. 2, Princeton, NJ: Princeton University Press, 1986–2129.
Arnold, Matthew (1932) *The Letters of Matthew Arnold to Arthur Clough*, ed. Howard F. Lowry. London/New York: Oxford University Press.
Arrowsmith, William (1995) *Antonioni: The Poet of Images*, New York/Oxford: Oxford University Press.
Asad, Talal (2003) *Formations of the Secular: Christianity, Islam, Modernity*, Stanford, CA: Stanford University Press.
Asimov, Isaac (1991) *Robot Visions*, New York: ROC.
Asimov, Isaac (2008) *I, Robot*, New York: Spectra.
Attebery, Brian (1992) *Strategies of Fantasy*, Bloomington, IN: Indiana University Press.
Attwood, Feona (2009) *Mainstreaming Sex: The Sexualization of Western Culture*, London: I.B.Tauris.
Atwood, Margaret (1985) *The Handmaid's Tale*, Toronto: McClelland & Stewart.
Atwood, Margaret (2011) *In Other Worlds: SF and the Human Imagination*, New York: Random House.
Atwood, Margaret (2012) *In Other Worlds: SF and the Human Imagination*, New York: Virago Press.

Auvray, Malika, and Erik Myin (2009) 'Perception with Compensatory Devices: From Sensory Substitution to Sensorimotor Extension', *Cognitive Science* 33.6: 1036–1058.
Babich, Babette (2008) 'Nietzsche und Wagner: Sexualität', in *Wagner und Nietzsche. Kultur – Werk – Wirkung. Ein Handbuch*, ed. H. J. Brix, N. Knoepffler, S. L. Sorgner, Reinbek b. Hamburg: Rowohlt, 323–341.
Babich, Babette (2012) 'Nietzsche's Post-Human Imperative: On the "All-Too-Human" Dream of Transhumanism', *The Agonist* 4.2.
Babich, Babette (2013) 'O, Superman! Or Being towards Transhumanism: Martin Heidegger, Günther Anders, and Media Aesthetics', *Divinatio*, January: 83–99.
Babich, Babette (2013a) *The Hallelujah Effect: Philosophical Reflections on Music, Performance Practice and Technology*, Surrey: Ashgate.
Babich, Babette (2013b) 'Future Past: The Gay Science, Thus Spoke Zarathustra, and Eternity', *The Agonist* 4.1/2 (Spring/Fall): 1–27.
Babich, Babette (2014) 'On Schrödinger and Nietzsche: Eternal Return and the Moment', in *Antonio T. de Nicolas: Poet of Eternal Return*, ed. Christopher Key Chapple, Ahmedabad, India: Sriyogi Publications & Nalanda International, 157–206.
Bachelard Gaston (1943) *L'air et les songes. Essai sur l'imagination du mouvement*, Paris: Corti.
Bach-y-Rita, Paul, M. E. Tyler and K. A. Kaczmarek (2003) 'Seeing with the Brain', *International Journal of Human–Computer Interaction* 15.2: 285–295.
Badmington, Neil (ed.) (2000) *Posthumanism*, New York: Palgrave.
Badmington, Neil (2001) 'Pod Almighty! Or, Humanism, Posthumanism, and the Strange Case of *Invasion of the Body Snatchers*', *Textual Practice* 15.1: 5–22.
Badmington, Neil (2003) 'Theorizing Posthumanism', *Cultural Critique* 53: 10–27.
Badmington, Neil (2004) *Alien Chic: Posthumanism and the Other Within*, London/New York: Routledge.
Badmington, Neil (2004a) 'Mapping Posthumanism', *Environment and Planning* A 36.8: 1344–1351.
Badmington, Neil (2007a) 'Introduction: Posthuman Conditions', *Subject Matters* 3.1: ix–xii.
Badmington, Neil (2007b) '"...A Drowning of the Human in the Physical": Jonathan Franzen and the Corrections of Humanism', *Subject Matters* 3.1: 1–14.
Baillie, Harold W., and Timothy K. Casey (2005) *Is Human Nature Obsolete?* Boston: The MIT Press.
Baldwin, Jon (2013) *The Financial Crash and Hyper-Real Economy*, New York: Thought Books.
Banks, Iain M. (1998) *Consider Phlebas*, London: Orbit.
Barabási, Albert-László (2002) *Linked: The New Science of Networks*, New York: Perseus Books.
Barad, Karen (2007) *Meeting the Universe Halfway: Quantum Physics and the Entanglement of Matter and Meaning*, Durham, NC: Duke University Press.
Barad, Karen (2012) 'On Touching: The Inhuman That Therefore I Am', *Differences: A Journal of Feminist Cultural Studies* 25.3: 206–223.
Baron, Lawrence (2003) 'X-Men as J-Men: The Jewish Subtext of a Comic Book Movie', *SHOFAR* 22.1: 44–52.
Barrat, James (2013) *Our Final Invention*, New York: St Martin's Press.
Barratt, Bethany (2012) *The Politics of Harry Potter*, Basingstoke: Palgrave Macmillan.
Barthes, Roland (1977) *Introduction to the Structuralist Analysis of Narratives*, New York: Hill and Wang.
Barthes, Roland (1980/1993) *Camera Lucida: Reflections on Photography*, London: Vintage.
Baudrillard, Jean (1983) *Simulations*, New York: Semiotext(e), Inc.
Baudrillard, Jean (1988) *The Ecstasy of Communication*, New York: Semiotext(e).
Baudrillard, Jean (1981/1994) *Simulacra and Simulation*, Ann Arbor: The University of Michigan Press.
Baudrillard, Jean (1996) *The Perfect Crime*, London: Verso.
Baudrillard, Jean (1997) *Fragments, Cool Memories III, 1991–1995*, London: Verso.
Baudrillard, Jean (1998) *Paroxysm: Interviews with Phillipe Petit*, London: Verso.

Baudrillard, Jean (2000) *The Vital Illusion*, New York: Columbia University Press.
Baudrillard, Jean (2001) *Impossible Exchange*, London: Verso.
Baudrillard, Jean (2002) *Screened Out*, London: Verso.
Baudrillard, Jean (2003) *The Spirit of Terrorism and Requiem for the Twin Towers*, London: Verso.
Baudrillard, Jean (2004a) *Fragments: Conversations with François L'Yvonnet*, London: Routledge.
Baudrillard, Jean (2004b) 'The Matrix Decoded: Le Nouvel Observateur Interview with Jean Baudrillard', *International Journal of Baudrillard Studies* 1.2. http://www.ubishops.ca/baudrillardstudies/vol1_2/genosko.htm.
Baudrillard, Jean (2005) *The Intelligence of Evil or the Lucidity Pact*, London: Berg.
Baudrillard, Jean (2006) *Cool Memories V (2000–2005)*, Cambridge: Polity.
Baudrillard, Jean (2007) *Exiles from Dialogue (with Enrique Valiente Noailles)*, Cambridge: Polity Press.
Baum, L. Frank (1900) *The Wonderful Wizard of Oz*, Chicago: George M. Hill Co.
Baum, L. Frank (1907) *Ozma of Oz*, Chicago: Reilly & Britton.
Baum, L. Frank (1909) *The Road to Oz*, Chicago: Reilly & Lee.
Beard, Steve (1998) *Logic Bomb: Transmissions from the Edge of Style Culture*, London and New York: Serpent's Tail.
Bechdel, Alison (1985) 'The Rule', in *Dykes to Watch Out For*, http://dykestowatchoutfor.com/.
Beck, Ulrich (1992) *Risk Society: Towards a New Modernity*, London: Sage.
Benhabib, Seyla (1999) 'Sexual Difference and Collective Identities: The New Global Constellation', *Signs* 24: 335–361.
Benin, David and Lisa Cartwright (2006) 'Shame, Empathy and Looking Practices: Lessons from a Disability Studies Classroom', *Journal of Visual Culture* 5.2: 155–171.
Bennett, Jane (2010) *Vibrant Matter: A Political Ecology of Things*, Durham, NC: Duke University Press.
Bennington, Geoff (1993) 'Derridabase', in *Jacques Derrida*, ed. Jacques Derrida and Geoff Bennington, Chicago: University of Chicago Press.
Berger, Peter L. (1999) 'The Desecularization of the World: A Global Overview', in *The Desecularization of the World: Resurgent Religion and World Politics*, ed. P. Berger, Grand Rapids, MN: Wm B Eerdmans, 1–18.
Bernard, Claude (1895/1966) *Introduction à l'étude de la médecine expérimentale*, Paris: Garnier-Flammarion.
Berners-Lee, Tim (2000) *Weaving the Web: The Past, Present and Future of the World Wide Web*, London/New York: Texere.
Berry, Chris, Soyoung Kim and Lynn Spiegel (eds.) (2010) *Electronic Elsewheres: Media, Technology, and the Experience of Social Space*, Minnesota: Minnesota University Press.
Bijker, Wiebke, and J. Law (eds.) (1992) *Shaping Technology, Building Society: Studies in Sociotechnical Change*, Cambridge, MA: The MIT Press.
Bird, Robert (2008) *Andrei Tarkovsky: Elements of Cinema*. London: Reaktion.
Booker, M. Keith (2006) *Alternate Americas: Science Fiction Film and American Culture*. Westport, CT: Praeger.
Bordwell, David (1986) 'Classical Hollywood Cinema', in *Narrative, Apparatus, Ideology*, ed. Philip Rosen, New York: Columbia University Press, 17–34.
Borgmann, Albert (2003) *Power Failure: Christianity in the Culture of Technology*, Grand Rapids, MI: Brazos.
Bornstein, Kate (2008) 'WALL•E: A Butch/Femme Love Story... or Silly Rabbit! Robots Have No Gender', http://katebornstein.typepad.com/kate_bornsteins_blog/2008/07/walle-a-butchfe.html.
Bostrom, Nick (2003) 'Are You Living in a Computer Simulation?' *Philosophical Quarterly* 53: 243–255.
Bostrom, Nick (2003a) 'Human Genetic Enhancements: A Transhumanist Perspective', *The Journal of Value Inquiry* 37.4: 493–506.

Bostrom, Nick (2005a) 'In Defense of Posthuman Dignity', *Bioethics* 19.3: 202–214.
Bostrom, Nick (2005b) 'The Fable of the Dragon Tyrant', *Journal of Medical Ethics* 31: 273–277.
Bostrom, Nick (2008) 'Why I Want to Be a Posthuman When I Grow Up', in *Medical Enhancement and Posthumanity*, ed. Bert Gordijn and Ruth Chadwick, Berlin: Springer, 107–136.
Bostrom, Nick (2009) 'The Future of Humanity', in *New Waves in Philosophy of Technology*, ed. Jan Kyrre Berg Olsen, Evan Selinger and Søren Riis, London: Palgrave Macmillan, 186–216.
Bostrom, Nick (2010) 'Why I Want to Be a Posthuman When I Grow Up', in *Medical Enhancement and Posthumanity*, ed. Bert Gordijn and Ruth Chadwick, New York: Springer, 107–137.
Bostrom, Nick (2014) *Superintelligence. Paths, Dangers, Strategies*, Oxford: Oxford University Press.
Bostrom, Nick, and Anders Sandberg (2008) 'Whole Brain Emulation: A Roadmap', Future of Humanity Institute Technical Report, Future of Humanity Institute, University of Oxford, http://www.fhi.ox.ac.uk/brain-emulation-roadmap-report.pdf.
Botting, Fred (2010) *Limits of Horror: Technology, Bodies, Gothic*, reprint edn, Manchester: Manchester University Press.
Bould, Mark (2003) 'Film and Television', in *The Cambridge Companion to Science Fiction*, ed. Edward James and Farah Mendlesohn, Cambridge: Cambridge University Press, 79–95.
Bould, Mark (2008) 'Science Fiction Television in the United Kingdom', in *The Essential Science Fiction Television Reader*, ed. J. P. Telotte, Lexington, KY: University of Kentucky Press, 209–230.
Bradshaw, Peter (2008) 'There Will Be Blood', *The Guardian*, 7 February.
Braidotti, Rosi (2002) *Metamorphoses: Towards a Materialist Theory of Becoming*, Cambridge: Polity Press.
Braidotti, Rosi (2013) *The Posthuman*, London: Polity.
Braidotti, Rosi (2014) 'Borrowed Energy', Interview with Timotheus Vermeulen, *Frieze* 165: http://www.frieze.com/issue/article/borrowed-energy/.
Braidotti, Rosi, and Nina Lykke (1996) *Between Monsters, Goddesses and Cyborgs: Feminist Confrontations with Science, Medicine and Cyberspace*, London/New Jersey: Zed Books.
Branwyn, Gareth (2000) 'Compu-Sex: Erotica for Cybernauts', in *The Cybercultures Reader*, ed. D. Bell and B. Kennedy, London: Routledge, 396–402.
Brassier, Ray, Iain Hamilton Grant, Graham Harman and Quentin Meillassoux (2007) 'Speculative Realism', *Collapse* 3: 306–449.
Brayton, Sean (2008) 'The Post-White Imaginary in Alex Proyas's "I, Robot"', *Science Fiction Studies* 35.1: 72–87.
Brentano, Franz (1995) *Psychology from an Empirical Standpoint*, London: Routledge.
Brians, Ellen (2011) 'The "Virtual" Body and the Strange Persistence of the Flesh: Deleuze, Cyberspace and the Posthuman', in *Deleuze and the Body*, ed. Laura Guillaume and Joe Hughes, Edinburgh: Edinburgh University Press, 117–143.
Brooker, Will (2002) *Using the Force: Creativity, Community and Star Wars Fans*, London: Bloomsbury.
Brown, William (2009) 'Man without a Movie Camera: Movies without Men: Towards a Posthumanist Cinema?', in *Film Theory and Contemporary Hollywood Movies*, ed. Warren Buckland, Abingdon/New York: Routledge/AFI, 66–85.
Brown, William (2013) *Supercinema: Film-Philosophy for the Digital Age*, Oxford: Berghahn.
Browning, J. E., and C. J. Picart (2009) *Draculas, Vampires, and Other Undead Forms: Essays on Gender, Race, and Culture*, Lanham, MD: Scarecrow Press.
Browning, Mark (2007) *David Cronenberg: Author or Film-Maker?* Bristol/Chicago: Intellect Books.
Brummett, Barry (1984) 'Burke's Representative Anecdote as a Method in Media Criticism', *Critical Studies in Mass Communication* 1: 161–176.
Brummet, Barry (1985) 'Electric Literature as Equipment for Living: Haunted House Films', *Critical Studies in Mass Communication* 2: 247–261.

Brunette, Peter, and David Wills (1989) *Screen/Play: Derrida and Film Theory*, Princeton, NJ: Princeton University Press.
Bryant, Levi R. (2011) 'The Ontic Principle: Outline of an Object-Oriented Ontology', in *The Speculative Turn: Continental Materialism and Realism*, ed. L. Bryant, N. Srnicek and G. Harman, Melbourne: re.press, 261–278.
Buchanan, Allen (2009) 'Moral Status and Human Enhancement', *Philosophy and Public Affairs* 37.4: 346–381.
Buchanan, Allen (2011) *Beyond Humanity? The Ethics of Biomedical Enhancement*, Oxford: Oxford University Press.
Buckland, Warren (2004) *The Cognitive Semiotics of Film*, Cambridge, MA: Cambridge University Press.
Bukatman, Scott (1993) *Terminal Identity: The Virtual Subject in Postmodern Science Fiction*, Durham, NC: Duke University Press.
Bukatman, Scott (2003) *Matters of Gravity: Special Effects and Supermen in the 20th Century*, Durham, NC: Duke University Press.
Buñuel, Luis (1983) *My Last Sigh*, New York: A. Knopf.
Burke, Kenneth (1962) *A Grammar of Motives*, Berkeley, CA: University of California.
Burke, Kenneth (1967) *Philosophy of Literary Form*, revised edn, Berkeley, CA: University of California.
Burke, Kenneth (1969) *Language as Symbolic Action*, Berkeley, CA: University of California Press.
Burt, Jonathan (2001) 'The Illumination of the Animal Kingdom: The Role of Light and Electricity in Animal Representation', *Society & Animals* 9.3: 204–228.
Burt, Jonathan (2002) *Animals in Film*, London: Reaktion.
Butler, Judith (1990) *Gender Trouble: Feminism and the Subversion of Identity*, New York: Routledge.
Butler, Judith (1997) *The Psychic Life of Power*, Stanford, CA: Stanford University Press.
Butler, Judith, Jürgen Habermas, Charles Taylor, and Cornel West (2011) *The Power of Religion in the Public Sphere*, New York: Columbia University Press.
Butler, Octavia E. (2000) *Lilith's Brood*, updated edn, New York: Grand Central Publishing.
Bynum, Caroline Walker (2001) *Metamorphosis and Identity*, New York: Zone Books.
Cadigan, Pat (1991) *Synners*, New York: Bantam.
Callus, Ivan, and Stefan Herbrechter (2007) 'Critical Posthumanism or, the Inventio of a Posthumanism without Technology', *Subject Matters* 3.1: 15–29.
Campbell, Norah, and Mike Saren (2010) 'The Primitive, Technology and Horror: A Posthuman Biology', *Ephemera* 10.2: 152–76.
Campbell, Timothy C. (2011) *Improper Life: Technology and Biopolitics from Heidegger to Agamben*, Minneapolis, MN/London: University of Minnesota Press.
Čapek, Karel (1920/2004) *R.U.R. Rossum's Universal Robots*, New York: Penguin.
Caplan, Arthur (2013) 'Deleting Memory', *MIT Technology Review* 116.4: 10.
Carney, Ray (1994) *The Films of John Cassavetes: Pragmatism, Modernism, and the Movies*, Cambridge: Cambridge University Press.
Carney, Ray (2001) *Cassavetes on Cassavetes*, London/New York: Faber & Faber.
Carney, Ray, and Leonard Quart (2000) *The Films of Mike Leigh: Embracing the World*, Cambridge: Cambridge University Press.
Carrasco, R. C. (2008) 'Gender Representation in U.S. Contemporary Science Fiction Films: The Cyborg Hero', http://www.baas.ac.uk/issue-13-autumn-2008-article-1/.
Carroll, M. (2014) 'Part Human, Part Machine: Cyborgs Are Becoming a Reality', http://www.newsweek.com/2014/08/08/cyborgs-are-walking-among-us-262132.html.
Carroll, Noël (1996) *Theorizing the Moving Image*, Cambridge: Cambridge University Press.
Cartwright, Lisa (1995), *Screening the Body*, Minneapolis, MN: University of Minnesota Press.
Cavalieri, Paola (2001) *The Animal Question: Why Nonhuman Animals Deserve Human Rights*, Oxford: Oxford University Press.

Cavell, Stanley (1979) *The World Viewed: Reflections on the Ontology of Film*, Cambridge, MA: Harvard University Press.
Cecchetto, David (2013) *Humanesis: Sound and Technological Posthumanism*, Minneapolis, MN/London: University of Minnesota Press.
Centers for Disease Control and Prevention (2012) 'CDC Grand Rounds: Prescription Drug Overdoses: A U.S. Epidemic', *Morbidity and Mortality Weekly Report* 61.1: 10–13.
Chatman, Seymour (1985) *Antonioni, or, the Surface of the World*, Los Angeles/Berkeley, CA: University of California.
Chodorow, Nancy (1980) 'Gender, Relation, and Difference in Psychoanalytic Perspective', in *The Future of Difference*, ed. Hester Eisenstein and Alice Jardine, Boston: G.K. Hall, 3–19.
Chris, Cynthia (2006) *Watching Wildlife*, Minneapolis, MN: University of Minnesota Press.
Clark, Andy (2003) *Natural-Born Cyborgs: Minds, Technologies, and the Future of Human Intelligence*, New York: Oxford University Press.
Clark, Andy (2007) 'Re-Inventing Ourselves: The Plasticity of Embodiment, Sensing, and Mind', *Journal of Medicine and Philosophy: A Forum for Bioethics and Philosophy of Medicine* 32.3: 263–282.
Clark, Andy (2009) 'Spreading the Joy? Why the Machinery of Consciousness Is (Probably) Still in the Head', *Mind* 118.472: 963–993.
Clark, Andy (2010) *Supersizing the Mind: Embodiment, Action, and Cognitive Extension*, Oxford: Oxford University Press.
Clark, Andy, and David J. Chalmers (1998) 'The Extended Mind', *Analysis* 58: 7–19.
Clark, Julie (2009) *The Paradox of the Posthuman: Science Fiction/Techno-Horror and Visual Media*, Saarbrücken: VDM Verlag.
Clarke, Arthur (1953) *Childhood's End*, New York: Ballantine.
Clarke, Bruce (2007) 'Posthuman Metamorphosis: Narrative and Neocybernetics', *Subject Matters* 3.1: 31–48.
Clayton, Jay (2003) '*Frankenstein*'s Futurity: Replicants and Robots', in *The Cambridge Companion to Mary Shelley*, ed. Esther Schor, Cambridge: Cambridge University Press, 84–99.
Clough, Patricia Ticeneto (2007) *The Affective Turn: Theorizing the Social*, Durham, NC: Duke University Press.
Clute, John (2011) *Pardon This Intrusion: Fantastika in the World Storm*, Essex: Beccon Publications.
Clynes, M. E., and N. S. Kline (1960) 'Cyborgs and Space', *Astronautics*, September: 26–27, 74–76.
Cochrane, Tom (2008) 'Expression and Extended Cognition', *Journal of Aesthetics and Art Criticism* 66.4: 329–340.
Cohen, Anthony (1985) *The Symbolic Construction of Community*, London: Tavistock.
Cohen, Jon (2013) 'Memory Implants', *MIT Technology Review Magazine*, 18 June, http://www.technologyreview.com/featuredstory/513681/memory-implants/.
Colombetti, Giovanna, and Tom Roberts (2014), 'Extending the Extended Mind: The Case for Extended Affectivity, *Philosophical Studies* 172: 1243–1263.
Connor, James, and Jason Mazanov (2009) 'Would You Dope? A General Population Test of the Goldman Dilemma', *British Journal of Sports Medicine* 43: 871–872.
Cook, Deborah (1987) 'Telesprache', *Philosophy and Literature* 11.2: 292–300.
Cook, John R. (2009) 'Gaming the System: Peter Watkins' *The Gladiators* and *Punishment Park*', *Science Fiction Film and Television* 2.1: 105–114.
Cowan, Doublas E. (2010) *Sacred Space: The Quest for Transcendence in Science Fiction Film and Television*, Waco, TX: Baylor University Press.
Crawford, T. Hugh (2012) 'Screening Science', in *The Educated Eye: Visual Culture and Pedagogy in the Life Sciences*, ed. Nancy Anderson and Michael R. Dietrich, Hanover, NH: Dartmouth College, 141–161.
Creed, Barbara (1993) *The Monstrous-Feminine: Film, Feminism, Psychoanalysis*, London/New York: Routledge.

Crichton, Michael (1972/2002) *The Terminal Man*, New York: Avon Books.
Crow, G., and Allen, G. (1994) *Community Life: An Introduction to Local Social Relations*, Hemel Hempstead: Harvester Wheatsheaf.
Csicsery-Ronay Jr, Istvan (2008) *The Seven Beauties of Science Fiction*, Middleton, CT: Wesleyan University Press.
Cudworth, Erika, and Stephen Hobden (2011) *Posthuman International Relations: Complexity, Ecologism and Global Politics*, London: Zed Books.
Dagognet, François (1992) *Etienne-Jules Marey: A Passion for the Trace*, New York: Zone.
Damasio, Antonio (1994) *Descartes' Error: Emotion, Reason and the Human Brain*, London: Vintage.
Davies, Caroline (2014) 'Conchita Wurst Pledges to Promote Tolerance after Jubilant Welcome Home', *The Guardian*, 11 May 2014. http://www.theguardian.com/tv-and-radio/2014/may/11/conchita-wurst-pledges-to-promote-tolerance.
Davis, Richard Brian (2009) 'Magneto, Mutation, and Morality', in *X-Men and Philosophy: Astonishing Insight and Uncanny Argument in the Mutant X-Verse*, ed. R. Housel and J. J. Wisnewski, Hoboken, NJ: John Wiley, 125–139.
De Garis, Hugo (2005) *The Artilect War: Cosmists vs Terrans. A Bitter Controversy Concerning Whether Humanity Should Build Godlike Massively Intelligent Machines*, Palm Springs: ETC Publications.
De Grey, Aubrey, and Michael Rae (2007) *Ending Aging*, New York: St Martin's Press.
De Kloet, Jeroen (2005) 'Saved by Betrayal? Ang Lee's Translations of "Chinese" Family', in *Shooting the Family*, Amsterdam: Amsterdam University Press, 117–132.
De Kruif, Paul (1945) *The Male Hormone*, New York: Harcourt & Brace.
De Landa, Manuel (1991) *War in the Age of Intelligent Machines*, New York: Zone Books.
De Landa, Manuel (2006) *A New Philosophy of Society: Assemblage Theory and Social Complexity*, London: Continuum.
Deleuze, Gilles (1992) 'Ethology: Spinoza and Us', in *Incorporations*, ed. Jonathan Crary and Sanford Kwinter, New York: Zone Books, 625–633.
Deleuze, Gilles (1988/1993) *The Fold: Leibniz and the Baroque*, Minneapolis, MN: University of Minnesota Press.
Deleuze, Gilles (2001a) *Difference and Repetition*, London: Continuum.
Deleuze, Gilles (2002/2004) *Desert Islands and Other Texts 1953–1974*, Los Angeles: Semiotext(e).
Deleuze, Gilles (2005a) *Cinema 1*, London: Bloomsbury.
Deleuze, Gilles (2005b) *Cinema 2: The Time-Image*, London: Continuum.
Deleuze, Gilles, and Anne Boyman (2001) *Pure Immanence: Essays on a Life*, New York: Zone.
Deleuze, Gilles, and Félix Guattari (1986) *Nomadology: The War Machine*, New York: Semiotext(e).
Deleuze, Gilles, and Félix Guattari (1980/1987) *A Thousand Plateaus: Capitalism and Schizophrenia*, London: Continuum.
Deleuze, Gilles, and Félix Guattari (2000) *Anti-Oedipus: Capitalism and Schizophrenia*, London: Athlone.
Deleuze, Gilles, and Claire Parnet (2007) *Dialogues II*, New York/Chichester: Columbia University Press.
Dempsey, Michael (1981) 'Lost Harmony: Tarkovsky's "The Mirror" and "The Stalker"', *Film Quarterly* 35.1, 12–17.
Dennett, Daniel C. (1993) *Consciousness Explained*, new edn, New York: Penguin.
Department of Defense (2007) *Unmanned Systems Roadmap 2007–2032*, https://www.fas.org/irp/program/collect/usroadmap2007.pdf.
Derrida, Jacques (1967/1974) *Of Grammatology*, Baltimore, MD: The Johns Hopkins University Press.
Derrida, Jacques (1972/1981) *Dissemination*, Chicago: University of Chicago Press.
Derrida, Jacques (1982) 'The Ends of Man', in *Margins of Philosophy*, Chicago: University of Chicago Press, 109–136.

Derrida, Jacques (1987) *Post Card: From Socrates to Freud and Beyond*, Chicago: University of Chicago Press.
Derrida, Jacques (1988) 'Telepathy', *Oxford Literary Review* 11: 3–41.
Derrida Jacques (1991/1993) 'Circumfession', in *Jacques Derrida*, ed. Geoffrey Bennington and Jacques Derrida, Chicago: University of Chicago Press, 3–315.
Derrida, Jacques (1993/1994) *Specters of Marx: The State of the Debt, the Work of Mourning, and the New International*, New York: Routledge.
Derrida, Jacques (1995) 'The Rhetoric of Drugs', in *Points: Interviews 1974–1994*, Chicago: University of Chicago Press, 228–254.
Derrida, Jacques (1995/1996) *Archive Fever: A Freudian Impression*, Chicago: University of Chicago Press.
Derrida, Jacques (1999) 'Word Processing', *Oxford Literary Review* 21: 3–17.
Derrida, Jacques (1998/2000) 'Demeure: Fiction and Testimony', in *The Instant of My Death/Demeure: Fiction and Testimony*, ed. Maurice Blanchot and Jacques Derrida, Stanford, CA: Stanford University Press, 14–103.
Derrida, Jacques (2001a) 'Above All, No Journalists!', in *Religion and the Media*, ed. Hent de Vries and Samuel Weber, Stanford, CA: Stanford University Press, 56–94.
Derrida, Jacques (2001b) 'Specters of Media', in *Deconstruction Engaged, the Sydney Seminars*, ed. Paul Patton and Terry Smith, Sydney: Power Publications, 43–53.
Derrida, Jacques (2003) 'And Say the Animal Responded?', in *Zoontologies: The Question of the Animal*, ed. Cary Wolf, Minneapolis, MN: University of Minnesota Press, 121–146.
Derrida, Jacques (2003a) 'Autoimmunity: Real and Symbolic Suicides – Dialogue with Jacques Derrida', in *Philosophy in a Time of Terror*, ed. Giovanna Borradori, Jacques Derrida and Jürgen Habermas, Chicago: University of Chicago Press, 85–136.
Derrida, Jacques (2008) *The Animal That Therefore I Am*, New York: Fordham University.
Derrida, Jacques (2010) *Copy, Archive, Signature: A Conversation on Photography*, Stanford, CA: Stanford University Press.
Derrida, Jacques, and Bernard Stiegler (1996/2002) *Echographies of Television*, Cambridge: Polity Press.
Dery, Mark (1996) *Escape Velocity: Cyberculture at the End of the Century*, New York: Grove Press.
Descartes, Rene (1960) *Meditations on First Philosophy*, 2nd revised edn, New York: Liberal Arts Press.
De Val, Jaime, and Stefan Sorgner (2011) 'A Metahumanist Manifesto', *The Agonist* 4.2.
De Waal, Frans (2009) *The Age of Empathy: Nature's Lessons for a Kinder Society*, London: Souvenir Press.
Dick, Philip K. (1968) *Do Androids Dream of Electric Sheep?* New York: Ballantine Books.
Dijkhuizen, Jan Frans van (2009) 'Religious Meanings of Pain in Early Modern England', in *The Sense of Suffering: Constructions of Physical Pain in Early Modern Culture*, ed. Jan Frans van Dijckhuizen and Karl E. A. Enenkel, Leiden: Brill, 189–220.
DiSilvestro, Russell (2012) 'The Ghost in the Machine Is the Elephant in the Room: Souls, Death, and Harm at the End of Life', *Journal of Medicine and Philosophy* 37: 480–502.
Dittmer, Jason (2013) *Captain America and the Nationalist Superhero: Metaphors, Narratives, and Geopolitics*, Philadelphia, PA: Temple University Press.
Doane, Mary Ann (1990) 'Technophilia: Technology, Representation, and the Feminine', in *Body/Politics: Women and the Discourses of Science*, ed. M. Jacobus, E. Fox Keller and S. Shuttleworth, New York: Routledge, 163–176.
Dolby, R. G. A. (2006) 'The Possibility of Computers Becoming Persons', in *The Person: Readings in Human Nature*, ed. William O. Stephens, Upper Saddle River, NJ: Pearson, 352–364.
Doležel, Lubomír (1998) *Heterocosmica: Fiction and Possible Worlds*, Baltimore, MD: Johns Hopkins University Press.
Doležel, Lubomír (2010) *Possible Worlds of Fiction and History: The Postmodern Stage*, Baltimore, MD: Johns Hopkins University Press.

Dollimore, Jonathan (2004) *Radical Tragedy: Religion, Ideology and Power in the Drama of Shakespeare and His Contemporaries*, 3rd edn, Durham, NC: Duke University Press Books.

Döring, Nicola M. (2000) 'Feminist Views of Cybersex: Victimization, Liberation, and Empowerment', *Cyber Psychology & Behavior* 3.5: 863–884.

Dowler, Kevin (2013) 'Dismemberment, Repetition, and Working-Through: Keeping Up in Treme', *Canadian Review of American Studies* 43.1: 145–163.

Drexler, Eric (1986) *Engines of Creation: The Coming Era of Nanotechnology*, New York: Anchor Books.

Dreyfus, Hubert L., and S. E. Dreyfus (1999) 'The Challenge of Merleau-Ponty's Phenomenology of Embodiment for Cognitive Science', in *Perspectives on Embodiment: The Intersections of Nature and Culture*, ed. G. W. Haber and H. Fern, Routledge, New York: Routledge, 103–120.

Eagleman, David (2009) *Sum: Tales from the Afterlives*, New York: Pantheon Books.

Eberl, Jason T. (ed.) (2008) *Battlestar Galactica and Philosophy: Knowledge Here Begins*, Malden, MA: Wiley-Blackwell.

Ebersberger, Ingo, Dirk Metzler, Carsten Schwarz and Svante Pääbo (2002) 'Genomewide Comparison of DNA Sequences between Humans and Chimpanzees', *American Journal of Human Genetics* 70: 1490–1497.

Ebert, Roger (2007) 'The Fountain Movie Review & Film Summary (2007) | Roger Ebert', 13 September. http://www.rogerebert.com/reviews/the-fountain-2007.

Economist (2012) 'March of the Robots', *Economist Technology Quarterly*, 2 June: 11–12.

Egan, Greg (2002) *Schild's Ladder*, New York: Eos.

Eldredge, Niles, and S. J. Gould (1972), 'Punctuated Equilibria: An Alternative to Phyletic Gradualism', in *Models in Paleobiolog*, ed. T. J. M. Schopf, San Francisco: Freeman, Cooper, and Company, 82–115.

Ellerman, Evelyn (2007) 'The Internet in Context', in *Psychology and the Internet: Intrepersonal, Interpersonal, and Transpersonal Implications*, ed. J. Gackenbach, 2nd edn, Burlington, MA: Elsevier/Academic Press, 11–33.

Ellul, Jacques (1967) *The Technological Society*, New York: Vintage Books.

Engel, Susan (2005) 'The Narrative Worlds of What Is and What If", *Cognitive Development* 20: 514–525.

Esposito, Roberto (2012) *The Third Person*, Cambridge: Polity.

Evans, C. Stephen (2009) 'Why Should Superheroes Be Good? Spider-Man, the X-Men, and Kierkegaard's Double Danger', in *Superheroes and Philosophy: Truth Justice and the Socratic Way*, ed. T. Morris and M. Morris, Chicago: Open Court, 161–176.

Evans, Marion Williard, H. Ndetan, M. Perko, R. Williams and C. Walker (2012) 'Dietary Supplement Use by Children and Adolescents in the United States to Enhance Sport Performance: Results of the National Health Interview Survey', *Journal of Primary Prevention* 33.1: 3–12.

Evens, Aden (2006) 'Object-Oriented Ontology, or Programming's Creative Fold', *Angelaki: Journal of the Theoretical Humanities* 1.11: 89–97.

Fairweather, Elizabeth (2012) 'Andrey Tarkovsky: The Refrain of the Sonic Fingerprint', in *Music, Sound, and Filmmakers: Sonic Style in Cinema*, ed. James Wierzbicki, Hoboken, NJ: Taylor & Francis, 32–44.

Fawaz, Ramzi (2011) ' "Where No X-Man Has Gone Before!" Mutant Superheroes and the Cultural Politics of Popular Fantasy in Postwar America', *American Literature* 83.2: 355–388.

Ferrando, Francesca (2012) 'Towards a Posthumanist Methodology. A Statement', *Frame, Journal for Literary Studies* 25.1: 9–18.

Ferrando, Francesca (2013) 'Posthumanism, Transhumanism, Antihumanism, Metahumanism, and New Materialisms: Differences and Relations', *Existenz* 8.2: 26–32.

Ferrando, Francesca (2014) 'Is the Post-Human a Post-Woman? Robots, Cyborgs and the Futures of Gender', *European Journal of Futures Research* 43.2: 1–17.

Ferrando, Francesca, and Kevin Warwick (2010) 'Is Science-Fiction a Source of Inspiration for Scientists?', transcript, TV cyborg, conversation, 15 January 2010. https://www.youtube.com/watch?v=sb9TxqhCjKM.
Ferraris, Maurizio (2013) 'Silvaplana: 14 August 1881: Eternal; Recurrence', *New Nietzsche Studies* 9.1/2 (Fall 2013/Fall 2014): 155–166.
Fielding, Julien R. (2003) 'Reassessing the Matrix/Reloaded', *Journal of Religion and Film* 7.2. http://www.unomaha.edu/jrf/Vol7No2/matrix.matrixreloaded.htm.
Finney, Jack (1954) *The Body Snatchers*, New York: Dell.
Fisher, Philip (2002) *The Vehement Passions*, Princeton, NJ: Princeton University Press.
Fitzgerald, Timothy (1999) *The Ideology of Religious Studies*, New York: Oxford University Press.
Foss, Martin (1946) *The Idea of Perfection in the Western World*, Princeton, NJ: Princeton University Press.
Foucault, Michel (1970) *The Order of Things*, New York: Vintage Books.
Foucault, Michel (1995) *Discipline and Punish: The Birth of the Prison*, New York: Vintage.
Foucault, Michel (2003) *'Society Must Be Defended': Lectures at the College de France, 1975–1976*, New York: Picador.
Frank, Arthur W. (2013) 'Biovaluable Stories and a Narrative Ethics of Reconfigurable Bodies', in *After the Genome: A Language for Our Biotechnological Future*, ed. M. J. Hyde and J. A. Herrick, Waco, TX: Baylor University Press, 139–156.
Freedman, Yacov (2012) 'Is It Real…or Is It Motion Capture? The Battle to Redefine Animation in the Age of Digital Performance', *The Velvet Light Trap* 69: 38–49.
Freud Sigmund (1907/1941) *Der Wahn und die Träume in W. Jensens Gradiva*, Gesammelte Werke VII, London: Imago, 29–122.
Freud, Sigmund (1900/1942) *Die Traumdeutung*, Gesammelte Werke II/III, London: Imago.
Freud, Sigmund (1919/1947) *Das Unheimliche*, Gesammelte Werke XII, London: Imago, 227–268.
Freud, Sigmund (2002) *Civilization and Its Discontents*, London: Penguin.
Freyermuth, Gundolf S. (2004) 'Designermutanten und Echtzeitmigranten. Mit der Digitalisierung eskaliert der Prozess neuzeitlicher Individuierung zur Utopie des virtuellen Menschen', in Maresch, Rudolf, and Florian Rötzer (eds.) Renaissance der Utopie. Zukunftsfiguren des 21. Jahrhunderts, Frankfurt am Main: Suhrkamp, 65–91.
Fried, Michael (1988) *Absorption and Theatricality: Painting and Beholder in the Age of Diderot*, Chicago: University of Chicago Press.
Fried, Michael (1998) 'Art and Objecthood', in *Art and Objecthood: Essays and Reviews*, ed. Michael Fried, Chicago: University of Chicago Press, 148–172.
Friedman, Marilyn (1986) 'Autonomy and the Split-Level Self', *Southern Journal of Philosophy* 24.1: 19–35.
Frow, John (2014) *Genre*, New York: Routledge.
Fuchs, Cynthia (2012) ' "Neighboring Sounds": Urban Unease', *PopMatters*, 27 August.
Fukuyama, Francis (1992) *The End of History and the Last Man*, New York: Free Press.
Fukuyama, Francis (2002) *Our Posthuman Future*, New York: Farrar, Straus & Giroux.
Fukuyama, Francis (2004) 'Transhumanism', *Foreign Policy* 144: 42–43.
Gallagher, Shaun (2005) *How the Body Shapes the Mind*, Oxford: Oxford University Press.
Gallagher, Shaun (2013) 'The Socially Extended Mind', *Cognitive Systems Research* 25–26: 4–12.
Gallagher, Shaun, and A. Crisafi (2009) 'Mental Institutions', *Topoi* 28.1: 45–51.
Gatens, Moira (1988) 'Towards a Feminist Philosophy of the Body', in *Crossing Boundaries: Feminisms and the Critiques of Knowledges*, ed. Barbara Caine, E. A. Grosz and Marie de Lepervanche, Sydney: Allen & Unwin, 59–70.
Geertz, Clifford (1973) *The Interpretation of Cultures*, New York: Basic Books.
Gehlen, Arnold (1940/1962) *Der Mensch. Seine Natur und seine Stellung in der Welt*, Frankfurt: Athenäum.

Gelin, Rodolphe (2013) 'Robotics Supporting Autonomy: 5th French Japanese Conference on Bio-Ethics', *Journal International de Bioéthique* 24: 59–70, 180–181.
Genette, Gérard (1983/1988) *Narrative Discourse Revisited*, New York: Cornell University Press.
George, Susan A. (2008) 'Fraking Machines: Desire, Gender, and the (Post) Human Condition in *Battlestar Galactica*', in *The Essential Science Fiction Television Reader*, ed. J. P. Telotte, Lexington: University Press of Kentucky, 159–175.
Geraci, Robert M. (2007) 'Robots and the Sacred in Science and Science Fiction: Theological Implications of Artificial Intelligence', *Zygon* 42.4: 961–980.
Geraci, Robert M. (2011) 'There and Back Again: Transhumanist Evangelism in Science Fiction and Popular Science', *Implicit Religion* 14.2: 141–172.
Gibbs, Raymond W. (2005) *Embodiment and Cognitive Science*, Cambridge: Cambridge University Press.
Gibson, William (1982) 'Burning Chrome', in *Burning Chrome*, ed. William Gibson, New York: HarperCollins Publishers 2003, 179–205.
Gibson, William (1984) *Neuromancer*, New York: Ace Books.
Gierzynski, Anthony (2013) *Harry Potter and the Millennials: Research Methods and the Politics of the Muggle Generation*, Baltimore, MD: JHU Press.
Gilbert, Scott F. (2002) 'The Genome in Its Ecological Context: Philosophical Perspectives on Interspecies Epigenesis', *Annals of the New York Academy of Sciences* 981: 202–218.
Glynn, Alan (2001) *The Dark Fields*, New York: Little, Brown & Company.
Glynn, Alan (2011) *Limitless*, London: Faber & Faber.
Goicoechea, María (2008) 'The Posthuman Ethos in Cyberpunk Science Fiction', *CLCWeb: Comparative Literature and Culture* 10.4: http://dx.doi.org/10.7771/1481-4374.1398.
Goldin-Meadow, Susan (2003) *Hearing Gesture: How Our Hands Help Us Think*, Cambridge: Belknap Press.
Goldman, Steven L. (1989) 'Images of Technology in Popular Films: Discussion and Filmography', *Science, Technology & Human Values* 14.3: 275–301.
Goleman, Daniel (1995) *Emotional Intelligence*, New York: Bantam Books.
Grace, Victoria (2008) 'Fluid, Mutable, Plural, Posthuman Subjectivities: A Radical Project for Feminism?' *International Journal of Baudrillard Studies* 5.2: http://www.ubishops.ca/baudrillardstudies/vol-5_2/v5-2-brgrace.html.
Graham, Elaine (1999) 'Cyborgs or Goddesses? Becoming Divine in a Cyberfeminist Age', *Information Communication & Society* 2: 419–438.
Graham, Elaine (2002) ' "Nietzsche Gets a Modem": Transhumanism and the Technological Sublime', *Literature & Theology* 16: 65–80.
Graham, Elaine L. (2002) *Representations of the Post/Human: Monsters, Aliens, and Others in Popular Culture*, Manchester: Manchester University Press.
Graham, Elaine L. (2013) *Between a Rock and a Hard Place: Public Theology in a Post-Secular Age*, London: SCM Press.
Grandin, Temple (2006) *Thinking in Pictures: My Life with Autism*, 2nd edn, New York: Vintage Books.
Grau, Christopher (ed.) (2009) *Eternal Sunshine of the Spotless Mind (Philosophers on Film)*, New York: Routledge.
Grebowicz, Margret, Helen Merrick and Donna J. Haraway (2013) *Beyond the Cyborg: Adventures with Donna Haraway*, New York: Columbia University Press.
Greenberg, Clement (1988) *The Collected Essays and Criticism*, vol. 1: *Perceptions and Judgments, 1939–1944*, ed. John O'Brian, Chicago: University of Chicago Press.
Griffiths, Alison (2014) 'Tableaux Morts: Execution, Cinema, and Galvanistic Fantasies', *Republics of Letters: A Journal for the Study of Knowledge, Politics, and the Arts* 3.3: 1–32.
Gross, E. (2011) *The Bionic Woman*, *SciFiNow*, Bournemouth: Imagine Publishing.
Grosz, H. E. A., and Marie De Lepervanche (1988) 'Feminism and Science', in *Crossing Boundaries: Feminisms and the Critiques of Knowledges*, ed. Barbara Caine, E. A. Grosz and Marie de Lepervanche, Sydney: Allen & Unwin., 5–27.

Gunning, Tom (1993) ' "Now You See It, Now You Don't": The Temporality of the Cinema of Attractions', *Velvet Light Trap* 32, 3–12.

Gunning, Tom (2006) 'The Cinema of Attraction[s]: Early Film, Its Spectator and the Avant-Garde', in *The Cinema of Attractions Reloaded*, ed. Wanda Strauven, Amsterdam: Amsterdam University Press, 381–388.

Gunning, Tom (2009) '1902–1903: Movies, Stories, and Attractions', in *American Cinema 1890–1909: Themes and Variations*, ed. Andre Gaudreault, New Brunswick, NJ: Rutgers University Press, 112–132.

Habermas, Jürgen (2003) *The Future of Human Nature*, London: Blackwell.

Habermas, Jürgen (2008) 'Religion in the Public Sphere: Cognitive Presuppositions for the "Public Use of Reason" by Religious and Secular Citizens', in Jürgen Habermas, *Between Naturalism and Religion: Philosophical Essays*, London: Routledge, 114–148.

Hables-Gray, Chris, Steven Mentor and Heidi J. Figueroa-Sarriera (1995) 'Cyborgology: Constructing the Knowledge of Cybernetic Organisms', in *The Cyborg Handbook*, ed. Chris Hables-Gray, New York: Routledge, 1–14.

Halberstam, Judith (2011) *The Queer Art of Failure*, Durham, NC/London: Duke University Press.

Halberstam, Judith, and Ira Livingstone (eds.) (1995) *Posthuman Bodies*, Bloomington, IN: Indiana University Press.

Haldane, J. B. S. (1924) *Daedalus, or Science and the Future: A Paper Read to the Heretics, Cambridge on February 4th, 1923*, London: Kegan Paul, Trench, Trubner & Co.

Hamman, Robin B. (1996) 'Cyborgasms: Cybersex amongst Multiple-Selves and Cyborgs in the Narrow-Bandwidth Space of America Online Chat Rooms', Master's Thesis, University of Essex, Colchester, http://www.cybersoc.com/.

Haraway, Donna (1985) 'A Cyborg Manifesto: Science, Technology and Socialist-Feminism in the Late Twentieth Century', in *The Feminism and Visual Culture Reader*, ed. A. Jones, London/New York: Routledge, 475–496.

Haraway, Donna J. (1991) *Simians, Cyborgs, and Women: The Reinvention of Nature*, London: Free Association Books.

Haraway, Donna J. (2000) 'A Manifesto for Cyborgs: Science, Technology, and Socialist Feminism in the 1980s', in *The Gendered Cyborg: A Reader*, ed. G. Kirkup, L. Janes, K. Woodward and F. Hovenden, London: Routledge, 50–57.

Haraway, Donna J. (2004) *The Haraway Reader*, ed. Donna Haraway, New York: Routledge.

Haraway, Donna J. (2008) *When Species Meet*, Minneapolis, MN: University of Minnesota Press.

Harbou, Thea von (2001) *Metropolis*, Rockville, MD: Sense of Wonder Press.

Harman, Graham (2002) *Tool-Being: Heidegger and the Metaphysics of Objects*, Chicago: Open Court.

Harman, Graham (2005) *Guerrilla Metaphysics: Phenomenology and the Carpentry of Things*, Chicago: Open Court.

Harman, Graham (2007) 'Aesthetics as First Philosophy: Levinas and the Non-Human', *Naked Punch* 9: 21–30.

Harman, Graham (2010) *Towards Speculative Realism: Essays and Lectures*, Winchester: Zero Books.

Harman, Graham (2011) *The Quadruple Object*, Winchester: Zero Books.

Harman, Graham (2014) 'Art without Relations', *ArtReview* 66: 144–147.

Hart, David Bentley (2014) *The Experience of God: Being, Consciousness, Bliss*, New Haven, CT: Yale University Press.

Hassan, Ihab (1977) 'Prometheus as Performer: Toward a Posthumanist Culture?' *Georgia Review* 31.4: 830–850.

Hatfield, Charles, Jeet Heer and Kent Worcester (2013) *The Superhero Reader*, Jackson: University Press of Mississippi.

Hauskeller, Michael (2009) 'Making Sense of What We Are: A Mythological Approach to Human Nature', *Philosophy* 84: 95–109.

Hauskeller, Michael (2011) 'Forever Young: Life Extension and the Ageing Mind', *Ethical Perspectives* 18.3: 385–406.
Hauskeller, Michael (2012) 'My Brain, My Mind, and I: Some Philosophical Assumptions of Mind-Uploading', *International Journal of Machine Consciousness* 4.1: 187–200.
Hauskeller, Michael (2014) 'Utopia', in *Post- and Transhumanism: An Introduction*, ed. Robert Ranisch and Stefan Sorgner, New York: Peter Lang, 101–108.
Hawk, Julie (2011) 'Objet 8 and the Cylon Remainder: Posthuman Subjectivization in *Battlestar Galactica*', *Journal of Popular Culture* 44.1, 3–15.
Hayles, N. Katherine (1991) 'The Borders of Madness', *Science-Fiction Studies* 18.3: 321–323.
Hayles, N. Katherine (1999) *How We Became Posthuman: Virtual Bodies in Cybernetics, Literature, and Informatics*, Chicago: University of Chicago Press.
Hayles, N. Katherine (2002) 'Escape and Constraint: Three Fictions Dream of Moving from Energy to Information', in *From Energy to Information: Representation in Science and Technology, Art, and Literature*, ed. B. Clarke and L. Dalrymple Henderson, Stanford, CA: Stanford University Press, 325–354.
Heidegger Martin (1957) 'Der Ursprung des Kunstwerkes', in *Holzwege*, Frankfurt am Main: Klostermann, 7–68.
Heidegger, Martin (1962) *Being and Time*, New York: Harper & Row.
Heidegger, Martin (1977) *The Question Concerning Technology and Other Essays*, New York: Garland Publications.
Heidegger, Martin (2008) *Towards the Definition of Philosophy*, London: Continuum.
Heidegger, Martin (2012) *Bremen and Freiburg Lectures*, Bloomington, IN: Indiana University Press.
Heise, Ursula K. (2008) *Sense of Place and Sense of Planet: The Environmental Imagination of the Global*, New York/Oxford: Oxford University Press.
Herbert, Frank (1973) *Hellstrom's Hive*, New York: Doubleday.
Herbrechter, Stefan (2006) 'The Posthuman Subject in *The Matrix*', in *The Matrix in Theory* (Critical Studies Volume 29), New York: Rodopi, 249–289.
Herbrechter, Stefan (2013), *Posthumanism: A Critical Analysis*, London: Bloomsbury.
Herbrechter, Stefan, and Ivan Callus (2008) 'What Is a Posthumanist Reading?', *Angelaki* 13.1: 95–111.
Heyck, Hunter (2011) 'Embodiment, Emotion, and Moral Experiences: The Human and the Machine in Film', in *Science Fiction and Computing: Essays on Interlinked Domains*, ed. David L. Ferro and Eric G. Swedin, Jefferson, NC: McFarland, 230–248.
Hiebert, Ted (2012) *In Praise of Nonsense: Aesthetics, Uncertainty, and Postmodern Identity*, Montreal: McGill-Queen's University Press.
Hirose, Naoya (2002) 'An Ecological Approach to Embodiment and Cognition', *Cognitive Systems Research* 3.3: 289–299.
Hitchcock, Peter (2010) 'Oil in an American Imaginary', *New Formations* 69.4: 81–97.
Hobson, Janell (2011) 'Rise of the Planet of the Apes Provides Lesson in Liberation', *Ms. Magazine*, 14 August, http://msmagazine.com/blog/2011/08/14/rise-of-the-planet-of-the-apes-provides-lessons-in-liberation/.
Hollinger, Veronica (2009) 'Posthumanism and Cyborg Theory', in *The Routledge Companion to Science Fiction*, ed. M. Bould, A. Butler, A. Roberts and S. Vint, Oxford: Routledge, 267–287.
Hong, Sungook (2004) 'Man and Machine in the 1960s', *Google Scholar*, n.p.
Horikawa, T. (2013) 'Neural Decoding of Visual Imagery During Sleep', *Science*, 3 May.
Houellebecq, Michel (1998) *Les particules élémentaires*, Paris: Flammarion.
Hughes, James (2004) *Citizen Cyborg: Why Democratic Societies Must Respond to the Redesigned Human of the Future*, New York: Basic Books.
Hughes, Thomas P. (2004) *Human-Built World*, Chicago: University of Chicago Press.
Humanity+ (2009) 'Transhumanist Declaration', http://humanityplus.org/philosophy/transhumanist-declaration.

Hurley, Susan (1998) *Consciousness in Action*, Cambridge, MA: Harvard University Press.
Husserl, Edmund (1993) 'Intentional Objects', in *Early Writings in the Philosophy of Logic and Mathematics*, ed. Edmund Husserl, Dordrecht: Kluwer, 345–387.
Huxley, Aldous (1932) *Brave New World*, New York: Harper & Row.
Huxley, Julian (1957) 'Transhumanism', in *New Bottles for New Wine*, London: Chatto & Windus, 13–17.
Hyde, Michael J. (2010) *Perfection: Coming to Terms with Being Human*, Waco, TX: Baylor University Press.
Hyde, Michael J., and Nancy King (2012) 'Communication Ethics and Bioethics: An Interface', *Review of Communication* 10.2: 156–171.
Ihde, Don (1990) *Technology and the Lifeworld: From Garden to Earth*, Bloomington, IN: Indiana University Press.
Ihde, Don (2003) 'Beyond the Skin-Bag', *Nature* 424.6949: 615.
Irigaray, Luce (1974/1985) *Speculum of the Other Woman*, New York: Cornell University Press.
Jackson, Rosemary (1981) *Fantasy: The Literature of Subversion*, Cheltenham: Routledge.
Jameson, Fredric (1991) *Postmodernism, Or, the Cultural Logic of Late Capitalism*, Durham, NC: Duke University Press.
Jameson, Fredric (2005) *Archaeologies of the Future: The Desire Called Utopia and Other Science Fictions*, London: Verso.
Jancovich, Mark, and Derek Johnston (2009) 'Film and Television, the 1950s', in *Routledge Companion to Science Fiction* 71, London/New York: Routledge, 71–79.
Japp, Phyllis, and Lynn M. Harter (2001) 'Technology as the Representative Anecdote in Popular Discourses of Health and Medicine', *Health Communication* 13.4: 409–425.
Jeffords, Susan (1994) *Hard Bodies: Hollywood Masculinity in the Reagan Era*, Brunswick, NJ: Rutgers University Press.
Jenkins, Henry (2006) *Convergence Culture: Where Old and New Media Collide*, New York: New York University Press.
Jenkins, Tricia (2011) 'Nationalism and Gender: The 1970s, *The Six Million Dollar Man*, and *The Bionic Woman*', *Journal of Popular Culture* 44.1: 93–113.
Jindra, Michael (1999) ' "*Star Trek* to Me Is a Way of Life": Fan Expressions of *Star Trek* Philosophy', in *Star Trek and Sacred Ground: Explorations of Star Trek, Religion, and American Culture*, ed. J. E. Porter and D. McLaren, New York: SUNY, 217–230.
Johnson, Derek (2013) *Media Franchising: Creative License and Collaboration in the Culture Industries*, New York: New York University Press.
Johnson, Vida T., and Graham Petrie (1994) *The Films of Andrei Tarkovsky: A Visual Fugue*, Bloomington, IN/Indianapolis: Indiana University Press.
Johnson-Smith, Jan (2005) *American Science Fiction TV: Star Trek, Stargate, and Beyond*, Middletown: Wesleyan University Press.
Johnston, Jessica R. (2001) *The American Body in Context: An Anthology*, Wilmington, DE: Scholarly Resources.
Jordan, Miriam, and Julian Jason Haladyn (2010) ' "Simulation, Simulacra, and Solaris", *Film Philosophy* 14.1: 253–273.
Kang, Minsoo (2011) *Sublime Dreams of Living Machines*, Cambridge, MA: Harvard University Press.
Kant, Immanuel (1964) *Groundwork of the Metaphysic of Morals*, New York: Harper & Row.
Kean, Hilda (1998) *Animal Rights: Political and Social Change in Britain since 1800*, London: Reaktion.
Keeling, Diane Marie (2012) 'History of (Future) Progress: Hyper-Masculine Transhumanist Virtuality', *Critical Studies in Media Communication* 29.2: 132–148.
Kennedy, Barbara (2000) 'Introduction: Cyberfeminisms', in *The Cybercultures Reader*, ed. David Bell and Barbara M. Kennedy, London/New York: Routledge, 283–290.
Keyes, Daniel (1994) *Flowers for Algernon*, Orlando, FL: Harcourt Books.
King, E. Francis (2010) *Material Religion and Popular Culture*, London: Routledge.

King, Geoff, and Tanya Krzywinska (2010) *Science Fiction Cinema: From Outerspace to Cyberspace*, New York: Wallflower Press.

Kinghorn, Kevin (2009) 'Questions of Identity: Is the Hulk the Same Person as Bruce Banner?', in *Superheroes and Philosophy: Truth, Justice and the Socratic Way*, ed. T. Morris and M. Morris, Chicago: Open Court, 223–236.

Kishkovsky, Sophia (2014) *Drag Queen Winner of Eurovision Contest Condemned by Russian Orthodox Church*, on Religion News Service, 12 May, http://www.religionnews.com/2014/05/12/transgender-eurovision-contest-winner-condemned-russian-orthodox-church/.

Kohanski, Daniel (1998) *The Philosophical Programmer: Reflections on the Moth in the Machine*, New York: St Martin's Press.

Kouvaros, George (2004) *Where Does It Happen? John Cassavetes and Cinema at the Breaking Point*, Minneapolis, MN/London: University of Minnesota Press.

Kracauer, Siegfried (1969) *From Caligari to Hitler: A Psychological History of the German Film*, Princeton, NJ: Princeton University Press.

Kristeva, Julia (1980/1982) *Powers of Horror: An Essay on Abjection*, New York: Columbia University Press.

Kroker, Arthur (2014) *Exits to the Posthuman Future*, Cambridge: Polity Press.

Krueger, Joel (2014a) 'Affordances and the Musically Extended Mind', *Frontiers in Theoretical and Philosophical Psychology* 4.1003: 1–13.

Krueger, Joel (2014b) 'Varieties of Extended Emotions', *Phenomenology and the Cognitive Sciences* 13.4: 533–555.

Krueger, Joel, and D. Legrand (2009) 'The Open Body', in *Enacting Intersubjectivity: Paving the Way for a Dialogue between Cognitive Science, Social Cognition, and Neuroscience*, ed. A. Carassa, F. Morganti and G. Riva, Lugano: Universita della Svizzera Italiana, 109–128.

Krueger, Olive (2005) 'Gnosis in Cyberspace? Body, Mind and Progress in Posthumanism', *Journal of Evolution & Technology* 14.2: 77–89.

Kuhn, Thomas S. (1962) *The Structure of Scientific Revolutions*, Chicago: University of Chicago Press.

Kurzweil, Ray (1999) *The Age of Spiritual Machines: When Computers Exceed Human Intelligence*, New York: Viking.

Kurzweil, Ray (2005) *The Singularity Is Near: When Humans Transcend Biology*, New York: Penguin.

Kurzweil, Ray (2012) *How to Create a Mind: The Secret of Human Thought Revealed*, New York: Viking.

Kurzweil, Ray, and Terry Grossman (2004) *Fantastic Voyage: Live Long Enough to Live Forever*, Emmaus, PA: Rodale Books.

Lacan, Jacques (1977) *Écrits: A Selection*, New York: W.W. Norton & Company.

Lacan, Jacques (1998) *The Four Fundamental Concepts of Psychoanalysis*, New York and London: W.W. Norton & Co.

Lacan, Jacques (2004) *Le Séminaire X: L'Angoisse*, Paris: Éditions du Seuil.

Lacan, Jacques (2006) *Le Séminaire XVI: D'un Autre à l'autre*, Paris: Éditions du Seuil.

Laird, James D. (2007) *Feelings: The Perception of Self*, Oxford: Oxford University Press.

Landon, Brooks (2012) 'That Light at the End of the Tunnel: The Plurality of Singularity', *Science Fiction Studies* 39.1: 2–14.

Lanier, Jaron (2010) *You Are Not a Gadget: A Manifesto*, New York: Alfred A. Knopf.

Larson, D. (1997) 'Machine as Messiah: Cyborgs, Morphs, and the American Body Politic', *Cinema Journal* 36.4: 57–75.

Latour, Bruno (1983) 'Give Me a Laboratory and I Will Raise the World', in *Science Observed*, ed. K. Knorr and M. Mulkay, Beverly Hills: Sage, 141–170.

Latour, Bruno (1987) *Science in Action: How to Follow Scientists and Engineers through Society*, Cambridge, MA: Harvard University Press.

Latour, Bruno (1988) *The Pasteurization of France*, Cambridge, MA: Harvard University Press.

Latour, Bruno (1993) *We Have Never Been Modern*, Cambridge, MA: Harvard University Press.

Latour, Bruno (2007) *Reassembling the Social: An Introduction to Actor-Network-Theory*, Oxford: Oxford University Press.
Latour, Bruno (2007a) 'Can We Get Our Materialism Back, Please?', *Isis* 98: 138–142.
Latour, Bruno (2011) 'Reflections on Étienne Souriau's *Les Différents Modes D'existence*', in *The Speculative Turn: Continental Materialism and Realism*, ed. Levi R. Bryant, Nick Srnicek and Graham Harman, Melbourne: re.press, 304–333.
Latour, Bruno (2013) *An Inquiry into Modes of Existence*, Cambridge, MA: Havard University Press.
Latour, Bruno, and Steve Woolgar (1979) *Laboratory Life: The Social Construction of Scientific Facts*, Beverly Hills: Sage Publications.
Lauro, Sarah Juliet, and Karen Embry (2008) 'A Zombie Manifesto: The Nonhuman Condition in the Era of Advanced Capitalism', *Boundary* 235.1: 85.
Lauzen, Martha M. (2014) 'The Celluloid Ceiling: Behind-the-Scenes. Employment of Women on the Top 250 Films of 2013', White Paper, The Center for the Study of Women in Television and Film, San Diego State University, San Diego, CA, http://womenintvfilm.sdsu.edu.
Lawrence, John Shelton, and Robert Jewett (2002) *The Myth of the American Superhero*, Grand Rapids, MI: Eerdmans Publishing.
Le Guin, Ursula K. (1969) *The Left Hand of Darkness*, New York: Walker.
Lem, Stanislaw (1961/1970) *Solaris*, London: Faber & Faber.
LeMenager, Stephanie (2014) *Living Oil: Petroleum Culture in the American Century*, Oxford/New York: Oxford University Press.
Levinas, Emmanuel (1976/2000) *God, Death and Time*, Stanford, CA: Stanford University Press.
Levy, Titus (2011) 'Human Rights Storytelling and Trauma Narrative in Kazuo Ishiguro's *Never Let Me Go*', *Journal of Human Rights* 10: 1–16.
Lewis, David (1976) 'Survival and Identity', in *The Identities of Persons*, ed. Amelie Oksenberg Rorty, Berkeley, CA: University of California Press, 17–40.
Leyda, Julia (2012) 'This Complicated, Colossal Failure': The Abjection of Creighton Bernette in HBO's *Treme*, in *Yeah You Rite: The* Treme *Issue*, ed. Vicki Mayer, *Television & New Media* 13.3: 243–260.
Lippit, Akira Mizuta (2000) *Electric Animal: Toward a Rhetoric of Wildlife*, Minneapolis, MN: University of Minnesota Press.
Lipshin, Jason, and Simon Wiscombe, 'Demolition Man and Cybersex: Sexual Repression as a Tool to Control Underground Culture', http://www.criticalcommons.org/Members/JLipshin/clips/DEMOLITION_MAN_cybersex.mp4/view.
Lock, Margaret M. (2002) *Twice Dead: Organ Transplants and the Reinvention of Death*, Berkeley, CA: University of California Press.
Locke, John (1690) *Essay Concerning Humane Understanding*, http://www.gutenberg.org/cache/epub/10615/pg10615.html.
Locke, Simon (2005) 'Fantastically Reasonable: Ambivalence in the Representation of Science and Technology in Super-Hero Comics', *Public Understanding of Science* 14: 25–46.
Loftus, E. F. (1995) 'The Formation of False Memories', *Psychiatric Annals* 25.12: 720–725.
Luckhurst, Roger (2005) *Science Fiction*, Cambridge: Polity.
Luhmann, Niklas (1989) *Ecological Communication*, Chicago/London: University of Chicago Press.
Luhmann, Niklas (2000) *Art as a Social System*, Stanford, CA: Stanford University Press.
Lumsden, Charles (2004) 'Das posthumane Zeitalter: das Spiel der Werkzeuge und das genomische Vergessen einer utopischen Spezies', in Maresch, Rudolf, and Florian Rötzer (eds.) Renaissance der Utopie. Zukunftsfiguren des 21. Jahrhunderts, Frankfurt am. Main.: Suhrkamp, 132–155.
Lunceford, Brett (2013) 'Telepresence and the Ethics of Digital Cheating', *Explorations in Media Ecology* 12: 7–26.
Lundblad, Michael (2013) *The Birth of a Jungle: Animality in Progressive-Era U.S. Literature and Culture*, Oxford: Oxford University Press.

Lykke, Nina, and Rosi Braidotti (1996) *Between Monsters, Goddesses and Cyborgs: Feminist Confrontations with Science, Medicine and Cyberspace*, London: Zed Books.
Lykke, Nina, and A. M. Smelik (eds.) (2008) *Bits of Life: Feminism at the Intersections of Media, Bioscience, and Technology*, Seattle: University of Washington Press.
Lyotard, Jean-Francois (1979/1984) *The Postmodern Condition: A Report on Knowledge*, Manchester: Manchester University Press.
Lyotard, Jean-Francois (1991) *The Inhuman: Reflections on Time*, Oxford: Blackwell.
Lyotard, Jean-Francois (1993/1997) *Postmodern Fables*, Minneapolis, MN: University of Minnesota Press.
Lyotard, Jean-Francois (2003) *The Inhumane: Reflections on Time*, Stanford, CA: Stanford University Press.
McAvan, Emily (2012) *The Postmodern Sacred: Popular Culture Spirituality in the Science Fiction, Fantasy and Urban Fantasy Genres*, Jefferson, NC: McFarland.
MacCormack, Patricia (2012) *Posthuman Ethics*, Farnham: Ashgate.
McLuhan, Marshall (1994) *Understanding Media: The Extensions of Man*, Cambridge, MA: The MIT Press.
McNeill, David (2005) *Gesture and Thought*, Chicago: Chicago University Press.
McRae, Shannon (1995) 'Coming Apart at the Seams: Sex, Text, and the Virtual Body', in *Wired Women*, ed. Lynn Cherney and Elizabeth Reba Wise, Seattle: Seal Press, 242–264.
Malafouris, Lambros (2008) 'Between Brains, Bodies and Things: Tectonoetic Awareness and the Extended Self', *Philosophical Transactions of the Royal Society B: Biological Sciences* 363.1499: 1993–2002
Manovich, Lev (1995) 'What Is Digital Cinema?', http://manovich.net/content/04-projects/008-what-is-digital-cinema/07_article_1995.pdf.
Manovich, Lev (2006) 'Image Future', *Animation: An Interdisciplinary Journal* 1.1: 25–44.
Maresch, Rudolf, and Florian Rötzer (eds.) (2004) *Renaissance der Utopie. Zukunftsfiguren des 21. Jahrhunderts*, Frankfurt am Main: Suhrkamp.
Margulis, Lynn (1981) *Symbiosis in Cell Evolution*, San Francisco: W.H. Freeman.
Margulis, Lynn (1998) *Symbiotic Planet: A New Look at Evolution*, New York: Basic Books
Margulis, Lynn, and Dorion Sagan (2000) *What Is Life?* Berkeley/Los Angeles, CA: University of California Press.
Markoff, John (2005) *What the Dormouse Said: How the Sixties Counterculture Shaped the Personal Computer Industry*, New York: Penguin Books.
Marshall, Jonathan (2003) 'The Sexual Life of Cyber-Savants', *Australian Journal of Anthropology* 14.2: 229–248.
Martin, Michael (2005) 'Meditations on Blade Runner', *Journal of Interdisciplinary Studies* 17.1–2: 105–122.
Masini, Eleanora (1999) 'Rethinking Future Studies', in *Rescuing All Our Futures: The Future of Futures Studies*, ed. Z. Sardar, Westport, CT: Praeger, 36–48.
Mason, Carol (1995) 'Terminating Bodies: Toward a Cyborg History of Abortion' in *Posthuman Bodies*, ed. J. Halberstam and I. Livingston, Bloomington, IN: Indiana University Press, 225–243.
Matheson, Richard (1954) *I Am Legend*, Greenwich, CT: Gold Medal Books.
Mayer, Vicki (2012) *Yeah You Rite: The Treme Issue*, ed. Vicki Mayer, *Television & New Media* 13.3.
Mazlish, Bruce (1995) *The Fourth Discontinuity: The Co-Evolution of Humans and Machines*, New Haven, CT/London: Yale University Press.
Mazzotta, Giuseppe (2001) *Cosmopoiesis: The Renaissance Experiment*, Toronto: University of Toronto Press.
Meck, Su and Daniel de Visè (2014) *I Forgot to Remember: A Memoir of Amnesia*, New York: Simon & Schuster.
Melton, Jeffrey, and Eric Sterling (2013) 'The Subversion of Happy Endings in Terry Gilliam's Brazil', in *The Cinema of Terry Gilliam: It's a Mad World*, ed. Jeff Birkenstein, Anna Froula and Karen Randell, New York: Columbia University Press, 66–78.

Menary, Richard (ed.) (2010) *The Extended Mind*, Cambridge: The MIT Press.
Mendlesohn, Farah (2003) 'Religion and Science Fiction', in *The Cambridge Companion to Science Fiction*, ed. E. James and F. Mendlesohn, Cambridge: Cambridge University Press, 264–275.
Merrill, Miles (2004) 'Where's Massive?: Past, Present and Future for *The Lord of the Rings*' Crowd Software', *Metro* 139: 142–145.
Metz, Christian (1984) 'Profile of Étienne Souriau', *On Film* 12: 5–8.
Metz, Christian (1997) *Le signifiant imaginaire. Psychanalyse et cinéma*, Paris: UGE.
Miccoli, Anthony (2010) *Posthuman Suffering and the Technological Embrace*, Plymouth: Lexington Books.
Midgley, Mary (1992), *Science as Salvation: A Modern Myth and Its Meaning*, London: Routledge.
Milford, Mike, and Robert C. Rowland (2012) 'Situated Ideological Allegory and *Battlestar Galactica*', *Western Journal of Communication* 76.5: 536–551.
Miller, J. Hillis (2009) *The Medium Is the Maker: Browning, Freud, Derrida and the New Telepathic Echotechnologies*, Brighton: Sussex Academic Press.
Mitcham, Carl Allen (1969) *From Sociology to Philosophy: On the Nature of Criticisms of the Technological Society*, Denver: University of Colorado.
Mitchell, W. J. T. (2005) *What Do Pictures Want?: The Lives and Loves of Images*, Chicago: University of Chicago Press.
Moravec, Hans P. (1988) *Mind Children: The Future of Robot and Human Intelligence*, Cambridge, MA: Harvard University Press.
Moravec, Hans P. (1998) 'When Will Computer Hardware Match the Human Brain? *Journal of Evolutionary Biology* 1, http://www.transhumanist.com/volume1/moravec.htm.
Moravec, Hans P. (1999) *Robot: Mere Machine to Transcendent Mind*, New York: Oxford University Press.
More, Max (1996) 'Transhumanism: Towards a Futurist Philosophy', http://www.max-more.com/transhum.htm.
More, Max (2013) 'The Philosophy of Transhumanism', in *The Transhumanist Reader: Classical and Contemporary Essays on the Science, Pechnology, and Philosophy of the Human Future*, ed. Max More and Natasha Vita-More, Oxford: Wiley-Blackwell, 3–17.
Morton, Timothy (2008) 'Ecologocentrism: Unworking Animals', *SubStance* 37.3: 73–96.
Mullarkey, John (2012) 'The Tragedy of the Object: Democracy of Vision and the Terrorism of Things in Bazin's Cinematic Realism', *Angelaki* 17.4: 39–59.
Mulvey, Laura (1975) 'Visual Pleasure and Narrative Cinema', *Screen* 16.3: 6–18.
Mumford, Lewis (1967) *The Myth of the Machine*, New York: Harcourt Brace Jovanovich.
Muri, Allison (2003) 'Of Shit and the Soul: Tropes of Cybernetic Disembodiment in Contemporary Culture', *Body & Society* 9.3: 73–92.
Murray, Janet (2001) *Hamlet on the Holodeck: The Future of Narrative in Cyberspace*, Boston: The MIT Press.
Naas, Michael (2012) *Jacques Derrida and the Two Sources of Religion, Science, and the Media*, New York: Fordham University Press.
Nagel, Thomas (1971) 'Brain Bisection and the Unity of Consciousness', *Synthese* 22: 396–413.
Nancy, Jean-Luc (1993/1997) *The Sense of the World*, Minneapolis, MN: University of Minnesota Press.
Nasar Sylvia (1998) *A Beautiful Mind*, New York: Simon & Schuster.
Nataf, Isiling (1995) 'Black Lesbian Spectatorship and Pleasure in Popular Cinema', in *A Queer Romance: Lesbians, Gay Men and Popular Culture*, ed. P. Burston and C. Richardson, London/New York: Routledge, 57–80
Nathan, Stuart (2011) 'Developing Autonomous Fighting Machines', *The Engineer*, 6 June, http://www.theengineer.co.uk/in-depth/the-big-story/developing-autonomous-fighting-machines/1008888.article.

Nayar, Pramod K. (2014) *Posthumanism*, Cambridge: Polity.
Nayar, Pramod K. (2014a) 'The Fiction of Bioethics: Kazuo Ishiguro's *Never Let Me Go*', *Notes on Contemporary Literature* 44.3: 9–12.
Negroponte, Nicholas (1995) *Being Digital*, New York: Knopf.
Neimanis, Astrida (2013) 'Morning Sickness and Gut Sociality: Towards a Posthumanist Feminist Phenomenology', *Janus Head* 13: 214–240.
Newman, Stan (2002) 'Max Stirner and the Politics of Posthumanism', *Contemporary Political Theory* 1.2: 221–238.
Neyland, Daniel (2006) *Privacy, Surveillance and Public Trust*, London: Palgrave Macmillan.
Niccolai, Ivan (2014) 'Wally Pfister's Transcendence: Prometheus and the Murder of God', http://www.futurecrunch.com.au/blog/2014/10/22/transcendence-movie-review.
Niedenthal, Paula M. (2007) 'Embodying Emotion', *Science* 316.5827: 1002–1005.
Nietzsche, Friedrich (1969) *Thus Spoke Zarathustra: A Book for All and None*, London: Penguin.
Nissenbaum, Dion (2014) 'U.S. Military Turns to Hollywood to Outfit the Soldier of the Future', *Wall Street Journal*, http://online.wsj.com/articles/u-s-military-turns-to-hollywood-to-outfit-the-soldier-of-the-future-1404527893.
Noë, Alva (2004) *Action in Perception*, Cambridge: The MIT Press.
North, Dan (2008) *Performing Illusions: Cinema, Special Effects and the Virtual Actor*, London: Wallflower Press.
Olivier, Bert (2008) 'When Robots Would Really Be Human Simulacra: Love and the Ethical in Spielberg's *AI* and Proyas's *I, Robot*', *Film Philosophy* 12.2: 30–44.
Olson, Eric (1997) *The Human Animal: Personal Identity Without Psychology*, New York: Oxford University Press.
O'Mathúna, D. P. (2009) *Nanoethics: Big Ethical Issues with Small Technology*, London: Continuum Press.
Orbaugh, Sharalyn (2002) 'Sex and the Single Cyborg: Japanese Popular Culture Experiments in Subjectivity', *Science Fiction Studies* 29.3: 418–435.
O'Regan, Kevin (2011) *Why Red Doesn't Sound Like a Bell: Understanding the Feel of Consciousness*, New York: Oxford University Press.
Ornella, Alexander D. (2009) 'Posthuman Pleasures: Transcending the Human–Machine Boundary', *Theology & Sexuality* 15.3: 311–328.
Oxford English Dictionary, Oxford: Oxford University Press 2014.
Panse, Silke (2013) 'Ten Skies, 13 Lakes, 15 Pools: Structure, Immanence and Eco-Aesthetics in *The Swimmer* and James Benning's Land Films' in *Screening Nature: Cinema Beyond the Human*, ed. Anat Pick and Guinever Narraway, Oxford: Berghahn, 37–59.
Panshin, Alexei, and Cory Panshin (1989) *The World beyond the Hill: Science Fiction and the Quest for Transcendence*, Los Angeles: J.P. Tarcher.
Parfit, Derek (1971) 'Personal Identity', *Philosophical Review* 80.1: 3–27.
Parfit, Derek (1987) *Reasons and Persons*, New York: Oxford University Press.
Parikka, Jussi (2010) *Insect Media: An Archaeology of Animals and Technology*, Minneapolis, MN: University of Minnesota Press.
Parker, Ian (1992) *Discourse Dynamic*, London: Routledge.
Parrinder, Patrick (2000) *Learning from Other Worlds Estrangement, Cognition and the Politics of Science Fiction and Utopia*, Liverpool: Liverpool University Press.
Partington, John S. (2002) '*The Time Machine* and *A Modern Utopia*: The Static and Kinetic Utopias of the Early HG Wells', *Utopian Studies* 13.1: 57–68.
Penley, Constance (1997) *NASA/Trek*, Verso.
Pepperell, Robert (2003) *The Posthuman Condition: Consciousness beyond the Brain*, new edn, Bristol: Intellect.
Perdomo, Daniela (2010) '100,000 Americans Die Each Year from Prescription Drugs, While Pharma Companies Get Rich', http://www.alternet.org/health/147318/100,000_americans_die_each_year_from_prescription_drugs,_while_pharma_companies_get_rich/.

Persson, Ingmar, and Julian Savulescu (2008) 'The Perils of Cognitive Enhancement and the Urgent Imperative to Enhance the Moral Character of Humanity', *Journal of Applied Philosophy* 25.3: 162–177.

Persson, Ingmar, and Julian Savulescu (2010) 'Moral Transhumanism', *Journal of Medicine and Philosophy* 35.6: 656–669.

Peterson, Christopher (2011) 'The Posthumanism to Come', *Angelaki: Journal of the Theoretical Humanities* 16.2: 127–141.

Pettman, Dominic (2013) *Look at the Bunny: Totem, Taboo, Technology*, Blue Ridge Summit, PA: Zero Books.

Philbeck, Thomas (2014) 'Ontology', in *Post- and Transhumanism: An Introduction*, ed. Robert Ranisch and Stefan Lorenz Sorgner, Bern: Peter Lang, 173–184.

Pick, Anat (2011) *Creaturely Poetics: Animality and Vulnerability in Literature and Film*, New York: Columbia University Press.

Pickering, Andrew (1995) *The Mangle of Practice: Time, Agency, and Science*, Chicago/London: University of Chicago Press.

Pinker, Steven (1997) *How the Mind Works*, New York: W.W. Norton & Co. Inc.

Polidori, John (1819) 'The Vampyre', *New Monthly Magazine and Universal Register*, Vol. 1, No. 63.

Pomerance, Murray (2011) *Michelangelo Red Antonioni Blue: Eight Reflections on Cinema*, Los Angeles/Berkeley, CA: University of California Press.

Pordzik, Ralph (2010) 'Closet Fantasies and the Future of Desire in E. M. Forster's "The Machine Stops"', *ELT* 53.1: 54–74.

Pordzik, Ralph (2012) 'The Posthuman Future of Man: Anthropocentrism and the Other of Technology in Anglo-American Science Fiction', *Utopian Studies* 23.1: 142–161.

Porter Peter (1987/1999) *Collected Poems Vol. II*, Oxford: Oxford University Press.

Possamai, Adam, and Murray Lee (2010) 'Religion and Spirituality in Science Fiction Narratives: A Case of Multiple Modernities?', in *Religions of Modernity: Relocating the Sacred to the Self and the Digital*, ed. S. Aupers and D. Houtman, Leiden: Brill, 205–217.

Prince, Stephen (2012) *Digital Visual Effects in Cinema: The Seduction of Reality*, New Brunswick, NJ: Rutgers University Press.

Quine, W. V. O. (1972) 'Review of Milton K. Munitz (ed.), *Identity and Individuation*', *Journal of Philosophy* 69: 488–497.

Ramirez, Steve, X. Liu, P.-A. Lin, J. Suh, M. Pignatelli, R. L. Redondo, T. Ryan and S. Tonegawa (2013) 'Creating a False Memory in the Hippocampus', *Science* 341: 387–391.

Rankin, Ian (ed.) (2006) *Douglas Gordon: Superhumanatural*, Edinburgh: National Galleries of Scotland.

Rasch, William (2000) *Niklas Luhmann's Modernity: The Paradoxes of Differentiation*, Stanford, CA: Stanford University Press.

Raulerson, Joshua (2013) *Singularities: Technoculture, Transhumanism, and Science Fiction in the Twenty-First Century*, Liverpool: Liverpool University Press.

Redmond, Sean (2009) 'Film since 1980', in *Routledge Companion to Science Fiction*, London/New York: Routledge, 134–143.

Reid, Elizabeth M. (1996) 'Communication and Community on Internet Relay Chat: Constructing Communities', in *High Noon on the Electronic Frontier: Conceptual Issues in Cyberspace*, ed. P. Ludlow, Cambridge, MA: The MIT Press, 397–412.

Reid, Roddey (1998) 'UnSafe at Any Distance: Todd Haynes' Visual Culture of Health and Risk', *Film Quarterly* 51.3: 32–44.

Reid, Thomas (1785) *Essays on the Intellectual Powers of Man*, https://archive.org/details/essaysonintellec02reiduoft.

Reynolds, Richard (1992) *Super Heroes: A Modern Mythology*, Jackson, MS: Mississippi University Press.

Rice, Anne (1985) *The Vampire Lestat*, New York: Alfred Knopf.

Ricoeur, Paul (1981) *Hermeneutics and the Human Sciences: Essays on Language, Action and Interpretation*, Cambridge: Cambridge University Press.

Ricoeur, Paul (1984, 1985, 1988) *Time and Narrative*, 3 vols, Chicago: University of Chicago Press.
Rieder, John (2010) 'On Defining SF, or Not: Genre Theory, SF, and History', *Science Fiction Studies* 37.2: 191–209.
Riley v. California (2014) *573 Supreme Court of the United States*.
Rizzolatti, Giacomo, and Corrado Sinigaglia (2008) *Mirrors in the Brain: How Our Minds Share Actions and Emotions*, Oxford: Oxford University Press.
Robert, Jason S. and Francoise Baylis (2003) 'Crossing Species Boundaries', *American Journal of Bioethics* 3.3: 1–13.
Robichaud, Christopher (2009) 'With Great Power Comes Great Responsibility: On the Moral Duties of the Super-Powerful and Super-Heroic', in *Superheroes and Philosophy: Truth Justice and the Socratic Way*, ed. Tom Morris and Matt Morris, Chicago: Open Court, 177–193.
Rockwell, W. Teed (2005) *Neither Brain Nor Ghost: A Nondualist Alternative to the Mind-Brain Identity Theory*, Cambridge: The MIT Press.
Roden, David (2008) 'Cylons in the Original Position: Limits of Posthuman Justice', in *Battlestar Galactica and Philosophy: Knowledge Here Begins Out There*, ed. J. Eberl, New York: Wiley Blackwell, 141–151.
Roden, David (2012) 'The Disconnection Thesis', in *The Singularity Hypothesis: A Scientific and Philosophical Assessment*, ed. A. Eden, J. Søraker, J. Moor and E. Steinhart, London: Springer, 281–298.
Roden, David (2014) *Posthuman Life: Philosophy at the Edge of the Human*, London: Routledge.
Ronen, Ruth (1994) *Possible Worlds in Literary Theory*, Cambridge: Cambridge University Press.
Rorty, Richard (1989) *Contingency, Irony, and Solidarity*, Cambridge: Cambridge University Press.
Rowlands, Mark (2003) *Externalism: Putting Mind and World Back Together Again*, Montreal: McGill-Queen's University Press.
Royle, Nicholas (2005) 'Blind Cinema', in *Derrida: Screenplay and Essays on the Film*, Manchester: Manchester University Press, 10–21.
Royle, Nicholas (2008) 'Telepathies', *Oxford Literary Review* 30.2: v–x.
Rushing, Janice Hocker, and Thomas S. Frentz (1995) *Projecting the Shadow: The Cyborg Hero in American Film*, Chicago: University of Chicago Press.
Russell, Bertrand (1924) *Icarus, or The Future of Science*, New York: E. P. Dutton & Co.
Saler, Benson (2008) 'Conceptualizing Religion: Some Recent Reflections', *Religion* 38.3: 219–225.
Sandison, Alan (1974) *The Last Man in Europe: An Essay on George Orwell*, New York: Barnes & Noble.
Sartre Jean-Paul (1943) *L'être et le néant. Essai d'ontologie phénoménologique*, Paris: Gallimard.
Savulescu, Julian, and Ingmar Persson (2012), 'Moral Enhancement, Freedom and the God Machine', *The Monist* 95.3: 399.
Schaab, Benjamin (2012) 'Metastases of Capitalism: Humanism as Exploitation in *District 9*', *Humanitas. Beiträge der Geisteswissenschaften* 1: 99–115.
Schechtman, Marya (2003) 'Empathic Access: The Missing Ingredient in Personal Identity', in *Personal Identity*, ed. R. Martin and J. Barresi, Malden, MA, and Oxford: Blackwell, 238–259.
Schechtman, Marya (2010) 'Personhood and the Practical', *Theoretical Medicine and Bioethics* 31: 271–283.
Scheer, Edward (2012) 'Posthuman Scenarios and Performative Media', *Performance Research: A Journal of the Performing Arts* 17.3: 23–32.
Scherer, Derek Carl (2014) 'Movie Magic Makes Better Social Robots: The Overlap of Special Effects and Character Robot Engineering', *Journal of Human-Robot Interaction* 3.1: 123–141.
Scholes, Robert (1967) *The Fabulators*, New York: Oxford University Press.
Seaman, Myra J. (2007) 'Becoming More (Than) Human: Affective Posthumanisms, Past and Future', *JNT: Journal of Narrative Theory* 37: 246–275.

Seeley, Thomas D. (2010) *Honeybee Democracy*, Princeton, NJ: Princeton University Press.
Seidel, Asher (2010) *Immortal Passage: Philosophical Speculations on Posthuman Evolution*, Lanham, MD: Rowman & Littlefield.
Serres, Michel (1982) *The Parasite*, Baltimore, MD/London: The Johns Hopkins University Press.
Shaheen, Jack G. (1987) 'The Documentary of Art: "The Undersea World of Jacques Cousteau" ', *Journal of Popular Culture* 21.1, 93–101.
Shapin, Steven (1988) 'The House of Experiment in Seventeenth-Century England', *Isis* 79.3: 373–404.
Shapin, Steven, and Simon Schaffer (1985) *Leviathan and the Air-Pump: Hobbes, Boyle, and the Experimental Life*, Princeton, NJ: Princeton University Press.
Shapiro, Lawrence A. (2014) *The Routledge Handbook of Embodied Cognition*, London/New York: Routledge.
Sharkey, Noel (2008) 'Computer Science: The Ethical Frontiers of Robotics', *Science* 322: 1800–1801.
Sharon, Tamar (2014) *Human Nature in an Age of Biotechnology*, New York: Springer.
Shaviro, Steven (2002) 'The Erotic Life of Machines', *Parallax* 8.4: 21–31.
Shaviro, Steven (2010) *Post Cinematic Affect*, Winchester: Zero Books.
Shaviro, Steven (n.d.) 'Safe', in *Stranded in the Jungle*, http://shaviro.com/Stranded/02.html.
Simmons, Laurence (2011) 'Jacques Derrida's Ghostface', *Angelaki* 16.1: 129–141.
Simon, William, and John H. Gagnon (1986), 'Sexual Scripts: Permanence and Change', *Archives of Sexual Behavior* 15: 97–120.
Simpson, David (2009) *Post-Human*, Bloomington, IN: iUniverse.
Singer, Peter W. (2011) 'Military Robotics and Ethics: A World of Killer Apps', *Nature* 477: 399–401.
Skakov, Nariman (2012) *The Cinema of Tarkovsky: Labyrinths of Space and Time*, London/New York: I.B. Taurus.
Slaby, Jan (2014) 'Emotions and the Extended Mind', in *Collective Emotions*, ed. M. Salmela and C. Von Scheve, Oxford: Oxford University Press, 32–46.
Sloterdijk, Peter (2014) 'Anthropo-Technology', *New Perspectives Quarterly* 31.1: 12–19.
Smith, Barry (1995) *Austrian Philosophy: The Legacy of Franz Brentano*, Chicago: Open Court.
Smith, David C. (1996) 'A Critical Appreciation of John Milius' *Conan the Barbarian*', http://www.barbariankeep.com/ctbds.html.
Smith, Matthew J. (2001) 'The Tyranny of the Melting Pot Metaphor: Wonder Woman as the Americanized Immigrant', in *Comics and Ideology*, ed. Matthew P. McAllister, Edward H. Sewell, Jr. and Ian Gordon, New York: Peter Lang, 129–150
Smith, Paddy (2014) 'Behold the Bionic Man', *Open Skies*, September: 84–92, http://issuu.com/motivatepublishing/docs/openskies_sept_2014.
Smith, Richard G. (2010) *The Baudrillard Dictionary*, Edinburgh: Edinburgh University Press.
Smithers, Tim (1997) 'Autonomy in Robots and Other Agents', *Brain Cognition* 34: 88–106.
Sobchack, Vivian (1988) *Screening Space: The American Science Fiction Film*, New Brunswick, NJ: Rutgers University Press.
Sobchack, Vivian (2004) 'Postfuturism', in *Liquid Metal: The Science Fiction Film Reader*, ed. Sean Redmond, London: Wallflower Press, 220–227.
Sobchack, Vivian (2004a) *Carnal Thoughts: Embodiment and Moving Image Culture*, Berkeley, CA: University of California Press.
Sobchak, Vivian (2014) 'Sci-Why? On the Decline of a Film Genre in an Age of Technological Wizardry', *Science Fiction Studies* 41.2: 284–300.
Sontag, Susan (1965) 'The Imagination of Disaster', *Commentary* October: 42–48.
Sorgner, Stephan (2012) 'Zarathustra 2.0 and Beyond: Further Remarks on the Complex Relationship between Nietzsche and Transhumanism', *The Agonist* 4.2.
Souriau, Étienne (1943) *Les Différents Modes D'existence*, Paris: PUF.

Southworth, Jason (2009) 'Amnesia, Personal Identity, and the Many Lives of Wolverine', in *X-Men and Philosophy: Astonishing Insight and Uncanny Argument in the Mutant X-Verse*, ed. R. Housel and J. J. Wisnewski, Hoboken, NJ: John Wiley, 17–26.

Sparkes, Matthew (2014) 'Should We be Spooked by the Ghosts in the Machine?' *Times Live*, 4 December, http://www.timeslive.co.za/lifestyle/2014/12/04/should-we-be-spooked-by-the-ghosts-in-the-machine.

Stacey, Jackie (2010) *The Cinematic Life of the Gene*, Durham, NC: Duke University Press.

Stapledon, William Olaf (1930) *Last and First Men; A Story of the Near and Far Future*, London: Methuen & Co. Ltd.

Steiff, Josef, and Tristan D. Tamplin (eds.) (2008) *Battlestar Galactica and Philosophy: Mission Accomplished or Mission Frakked Up?* Chicago: Open Court.

Stelarc (1991) 'Prosthetics, Robotics and Remote Existence: Postevolutionary Strategies', *Leonardo* 24: 591–595.

Sterelny, Kim (2004) 'Externalism, Epistemic Artefacts and the Extended Mind', in *The Externalist Challenge*, ed. R. Schantz, Berlin: Walter de Gruyter, 239–254.

Stevenson, Robert Louis (1968) *The Strange Case of Dr Jekyll and Mr Hyde*, London: Magnum Books.

Stiegler, Bernard (1998) *Technics and Time*, vol. 1, Stanford, CA: Stanford University Press.

Stoker, Bram (1897) *Dracula*, Westminster: Archibald Constable & Company.

Strawson, Peter (1963) 'Carnap's Views on Constructed Systems versus Natural Languages in Analytic Philosophy', in *The Philosophy of Rudolf Carnap*, ed. Paul Schilpp, La Salle, IL, Open Court, 503–519.

Stross, Charles (2004) *Singularity Sky*, London: Penguin.

Sublette, Ned (2009) *The Year before the Flood: A Story of New Orleans*, Chicago: Chicago Review Press.

Sullivan, Heather I. (2012) 'Dirt Theory and Material Ecocriticism', *Interdisciplinary Studies in Literature and Environment* 19.3: 515–531.

Suvin, Darko (1979) *Metamorphoses of Science Fiction: On the Poetics and History of a Literary Genre*, New Haven, CT: Yale University Press.

Tarantino, Matteo (2012) 'Toward a New "Electrical World": Is There a Chinese Technological Sublime?' in *New Connectivities in China. Virtual, Actual and Local Interactions*, ed. Pui-lam Law, New York: Springer, 185–200.

Tasker, Yvonne (1993) *Spectacular Bodies: Gender, Genre, and the Action Cinema*, London: Routledge.

Taylor, Nik (2011) 'Rise of the Planet of the Apes: "Human, all too human"', *The Guardian*, 19 August, http://www.theguardian.com/science/blog/2011/aug/19/rise-planet-apes-animal-rights.

Telotte, J. P. (1991) 'The Tremulous Public Body', *Journal of Popular Film & Television* 19.1: 14.

Telotte, J. P. (1992) '*The Terminator*, *Terminator 2*, and the Exposed Body', *Journal of Popular Film & Television* 20.2: 26.

Telotte, J. P. (1995) 'Enframing the Self: The Hardware and Software of Hardware', *Science Fiction Studies* 22.3: 323–332.

Telotte, J. P. (1995a) *Replications: A Robotic History of the Science Fiction Film*, Urbana, IL: University of Illinois Press.

Telotte, J. P. (1999) *A Distant Technology: Science Fiction Film and the Machine Age*, Hanover: Wesleyan University Press.

Telotte, J. P. (2001) *Science Fiction Film: Genres in American Cinema*, Cambridge: Cambridge University Press.

Telotte, J. P. (2008) 'Introduction: The Trajectory of Science Fiction Television', in *The Essential Science Fiction Television Reader*, ed. J. P. Telotte, Lexington, KY: University Press of Kentucky, 1–34.

Telotte, J. P. (2009) 'Film, 1895–1950', in *The Routledge Companion to Science Fiction*, ed. M. Bould, A. Butler, A. Roberts and S. Vint, London: Routledge, 42–51.

Telotte, J. P. (2014) 'Introduction: Why Science Fiction Television (SFTV)?' in *Science Fiction TV*, ed. J. P. Telotte, New York: Routledge, 1–20.
Thacker, Eugene (2003) 'Data Made Flesh: Biotechnology and the Discourse of the Posthuman', *Cultural Critique* 53: 72–97.
Thacker, Eugene (2004a) *Biomedia*, Minneapolis, MN: University of Minnesota Press.
Thacker, E. (2004b) 'Networks, Swarms, Multitudes: Part Two', *CTheory*(a142b), ctheory.net, http://www.ctheory.net/articles.aspx?id=423.
Thacker, Eugene (2010) *After Life*, Chicago: University of Chicago Press.
Thacker, Eugene (2011) 'Necrologies: Or, the Death of the Body Politic', in *Beyond Biopolitics: Essays on the Governance of Life and Death*, ed. Patricia Ticeneto Clough and Craig Willse, Durham, NC: Duke University Press, 139–162.
Theiner, Georg, Colin Allen and Robert L. Goldstone (2010) 'Recognizing Group Cognition', *Cognitive Systems Research* 11.4: 378–395.
Thompson, Kirsten Moana (2006) 'Scale, Spectacle and Movement: Massive Software and Digital Special Effects in *The Lord of the Rings*', in *From Hobbits to Hollywood: Essays on Peter Jackson's Lord of the Rings*, ed. E. Mathijs and M. Pomerance, Amsterdam: Rodopi, 283–299.
Thweatt-Bates, Jeanine (2012) *Cyborg Selves: A Theological Anthropology of the Posthuman*, London: Ashgate.
Thweatt-Bates, Jeanine, J. W. van Huyssteen and E. P. Wiebe (2011) 'Posthuman Selves: Bodies, Cognitive Processes, and Technologies', in *In Search of Self: Interdisciplinary Perspectives on Personhood*, Grand Rapids, MI: William B. Eerdmans Publishing Co., 243–255.
Tirosh-Samuelson, Hava (2012) 'Transhumanism as a Secularist Faith', *Zygon* 47.4: 710–734.
Todorov, Tzvetan (1975) *The Fantastic: A Structural Approach to a Literary Genre*, Ithaca, NY: Cornell University Press.
Toffler, Alvin (2000) 'What Moral Standards Will We Have?' *USA Today*, 7 January.
Toffoletti, Kim (2007) *Cyborgs and Barbie Dolls: Feminism, Popular Culture and the Posthuman Body*, London: I.B. Tauris.
Tönnies, Ferdinand (1887/1963) *Community and Society*, New York: Harper & Row.
Trollope, Anthony (1975/2008) *The Way We Live Now*, Oxford: Oxford University Press.
Tuana, Nancy (2008) 'Viscous Porosity: Witnessing Katrina', in *Material Feminisms*, ed. Stacy Alaimo and Susan Hekman, Bloomington, IN/Indianapolis: Indiana University Press, 189–213.
Tuggy, Dale (2010) 'Trinity', in *Stanford Encyclopaedia of Philosophy*, ed. Edward N. Zalta, http://plato.stanford.edu/archives/fall2009/entries/trinity.
Turkle, Sherry (1995) *Life on the Screen*, New York: Simon & Schuster.
Turkle, Sherry (2007) 'Authenticity in the Age of Digital Companions', *Interaction Studies* 8.3: 501–517.
Turkle, Sherry (2011) *Alone Together: Why We Expect More from Technology and Less from Each Other*, New York: Basic Books.
Turner, Fred (2006) *From Counterculture to Cyberculture*, Chicago: University of Chicago Press.
Turpin, Etienne (ed.) (2013) *Architecture in the Anthropocene: Encounters among Design, Deep Time, Science and Philosophy*, London: Open Humanities Press.
TV Tropes (2014) 'Transhuman', http://tvtropes.org/pmwiki/pmwiki.php/Main/Transhuman (accessed 6 September 2014).
Twardowski, Kasimir (1977) *On the Content and Object of Presentations*, The Hague: Martinus Nijhoff.
Uhlenhaut, Christine, R. Burger and L. Schaade (2012) 'Biological Security and Dual-Use Dilemma in the Life Sciences: Status Quo and Options for the Future', *EMBO Reports* 14: 25–30.
Ulmer, Gregory (1989) *Teletheory*, New York: Routledge.
Uzgalis, William (ed.) (2011) *The Correspondence of Samuel Clarke and Anthony Collins 1707–1708*, Ontario: Roadview Editions.
Van der Tuin, Iris (2014) 'Diffraction as a Methodology for Feminist Onto-Epistemology: On Encountering Chantal Chawaf and Posthuman Interpellation', *Parallax* 20.3: 231–244.

Van Est, Rinie, M. Smits, M. Schuijff and P. Klaassen (2008) *Future Man – No Future Man: Connecting the Technological, Cultural and Political Dots of Human Enhancement*, The Hague: Rathenau Instituut. http://www.rathenau.nl/publicaties/future-man-no-future-man.html.

Varela, Francisco, Evan Thompson and Eleanor Rosch (1992) *The Embodied Mind*, Boston: The MIT Press.

Verbeek, Peter-Paul (2008) 'Cyborg Intentionality: Rethinking the Phenomenology of Human–Technology Relations', *Phenomenology and the Cognitive Sciences* 7.3: 387–395.

Vezzali, Loris, Sofia Stathi, Dino Giovanni, Dora Capozza and Elena Trifiletti (2014) 'The Greatest Magic of Harry Potter: Reducing Prejudice', *Journal of Applied Social Psychology* 45.2: 105–121.

Vidler, Anthony (1992) *The Architectural Uncanny*, Boston: The MIT Press.

Vinge, Vernor (1993) 'The Coming Technological Singularity', https://www-rohan.sdsu.edu/faculty/vinge/misc/singularity.html.

Vint, Sherryl (2007) *Bodies of Tomorrow: Technology, Subjectivity, Science Fiction*, Toronto: University of Toronto Press.

Vint, S. and M. Bould (2006) 'All that Melts into Air Is Solid: Rematerialising Capital in Cube and Videodrome', *Socialism and Democracy*, 20.3: 217–243.

Vonnegut, Kurt (1968) *Welcome to the Monkey House: A Collection of Short Works*, New York: Dial Press Trade Paperbacks.

Wachowski, Lana (2012) 'Lana Wachowski Receives the HRC Visibility Award', YouTube, 24 October, https://www.youtube.com/watch?v=crHHycz7T_c.

Waid, Mark (2009) 'The Real Truth about Superman: And the Rest of Us Too', in *Superheroes and Philosophy: Truth Justice and the Socratic Way*, ed. T. Morris and M. Morris, Chicago: Open Court, 3–10.

Ward, Dave (2012) 'Enjoying the Spread: Conscious Externalism Reconsidered', *Mind* 121.483: 731–751.

Warwick, Kevin (1998) *In the Mind of the Machine: The Breakthrough in Artificial Intelligence*, London: Arrow Books.

Warwick, Kevin (2000) 'Cyborg 1.0', *Wired* 8.2, http://archive.wired.com/wired/archive/8.02/warwick.html.

Warwick, Kevin (2002/2004) *I, Cyborg*, Urbana, IL: University of Illinois Press.

Waskul, Dennis D. (2002) 'The Naked Self: Being a Body in Televideo Cybersex', *Symbolic Interaction* 25.2, 199–227.

Waskul, Dennis D. (2003) *Self-Games and Body-Play: Personhood in Online Chat and Cybersex*, New York: Peter Lang.

Weber, Max (2001) *The Protestant Ethic and the Spirit of Capitalism*, London/New York: Routledge.

Weber, Max 2004) *The Vocation Lectures*, ed. D. Owen, Cambridge: Hackett.

Weil, Kari (2012) *Thinking Animals: Why Animal Studies Now?* New York: Columbia University Press.

Weiner, Bernard (1972) 'Review of *Punishment Park*', *Film Quarterly* 25.4: 49–52.

Welesko, Brian (2014) 'Interstitial Reality: Service Tunnels, Steam Pipes, and Glitches in Constructed Worlds', *Journal of Popular Culture* 47.1: 3–20.

Whissel, Kristen (2010) 'The Digital Multitude', *Cinema Journal* 49.4: 90–110.

Whitehead, Alfred North (1920) *The Concept of Nature*, Cambridge: Cambridge University Press.

Wiener, Norbert (1948) *Cybernetics: Or Control and Communication in the Animal and the Machine*, New York: The Technology Press.

Wiener, Norbert (1960) 'Some Moral and Technical Consequences of Automation', *Science*, New Series 131/3410: 1355–1358.

Williams, A. R. (2015) 'Canned Dreams: On Neoliberalism, Nostalgia and Captive Futures in the US Social Imaginary (and *Iron Man 3*)', *Mediations* (forthcoming).

Williams, Bernard (1973) 'The Self and the Future', in *Problems of the Self*, Cambridge: Cambridge University Press.

Williams, Bernard (1973a) 'The Makropulos Case: Reflections on the Tedium of Immortality', in *Problems of the Self*, Cambridge: Cambridge University Press, 82–100.

Wills, David (1995) *Prostheses*, Stanford, CA: Stanford University Press.

Wills, David (2008) *Dorsality: Thinking Back Through Technology and Politics*, Minneapolis, MN: University of Minnesota Press.

Wilson, Samuel, and Nick Haslam (2009) 'Is the Future More or Less Human? Differing Views of Humanness in the Posthumanism Debate', *Journal for the Theory of Social Behaviour* 39.2: 247–266.

Winner, Langdon (1988) *The Whale and the Reactor: A Search for Limits in an Age of High Technology*, Chicago: University of Chicago Press.

Wolfe, Cary (2003) *Animal Rites: American Culture, the Discourse of Species, and Posthumanist Theory*, Chicago: University of Chicago Press.

Wolfe, Cary (2008) 'The Digital, the Analog, and the Spectral: Echographies from My Life in the Bush of Ghosts', *Angelaki* 13.1: 85–94.

Wolfe, Cary (2010) *What Is Posthumanism?* Minneapolis, MN/London: University of Minnesota Press.

Wolfe, Cary (2013) *Before the Law: Humans and Other Animals in a Biopolitical Frame*, Chicago/London: University of Chicago Press.

Wolfe, Gary K. (2011) *Evaporating Genres Essays on Fantastic Literature*, Middletown, CT: Wesleyan University Press.

Wolff, Janet (2008) *The Aesthetics of Uncertainty*, New York: Columbia University Press.

Woodhead, Linda (2011) 'Five Concepts of Religion', *International Review of Sociology* 21.1: 121–143.

Worden, Daniel (2012) 'Fossil-Fuel Futurity: Oil in *Giant*', *Journal of American Studies* 46.1, 441–460.

Wright, Bradford W. (2003) *Comic Book Nation: The Transformation of Youth Culture in America*, Baltimore, MD: Johns Hopkins University Press.

Wright, Peter (2009) 'Film and Television, the 1960–1980', in *Routledge Companion to Science Fiction* 71, London/New York: Routledge, 90–101.

Wyndham, John (1957) *The Midwich Cuckoos*, London: Michael Joseph.

Yancy, George, and Susan Hadley (2005) *Narrative Identities: Psychologists Engaged in Self-Construction*, Philadelphia, PA: Jessica Kingsley Publications.

Yeager, Patricia (2010) 'Editor's Column: Sea Trash, Dark Pools, and the Tragedy of the Commons', *PMLA* 125.3: 523–545.

Yeats, William Butler (1996) *The Collected Works of W.B. Yeats*, ed. R. Finnerman, New York: Scribner.

Young, Stephen Dine (2000) 'Movies as Equipment for Living: A Developmental Analysis of the Importance of Film in Everyday Life', *Critical Studies in Media Communication* 17.4: 447–468.

Žižek, Slavoj (2001) *Enjoy Your Symptom: Jacques Lacan in Hollywood and Out*, New York: Routledge.

Zwart, Hub (1998) 'Medicine, Symbolization and the "Real Body": Lacan's Understanding of Medical Science', *Medicine, Healthcare and Philosophy: A European Journal* 1.2: 107–117.

Zwart, Hub (2014a) 'Limitless as a Neuro-Pharmaceutical Experiment and as a *Daseinsanalyse*: On the Use of Fiction in Preparatory Debates on Cognitive Enhancement', *Medicine, Health Care & Philosophy: A European Journal* 17.1: 29–38.

Zwart, Hub (2014b) 'The Donor Organ as an "Object A": A Lacanian Perspective on Organ Donation and Transplantation Medicine', *Medicine, Health Care & Philosophy* 17.4: 559–571.

Index of Films and TV Shows

Films:

A Beautiful Mind (Ron Howard, 2001), 223
A Clever Dummy (Ferris Hartman and others, 1917), 113
A Clockwork Orange (Stanley Kubrick, 1971), 156, 393
A.I. Artificial Intelligence (Stephen Spielberg, 2001), 46, 129, 131, 135, 276, 335, 397
Al di là del bene e del male (Liliana Caviani, 1977), 50
Alfie (Lewis Gilbert, 1966), 48
Alien (Ridley Scott, 1979), 80, 117, 121, 155, 273, 380, 393
Aliens (James Cameron, 1986), 63, 132, 394
Aliens, 3 (David Fincher, 1992), 63
Alien Resurrection (Jean-Pierre Jeunet, 1997), 79, 83, 156
Alphaville (Jean-Luc Godard, 1965), 94, 131
Amour (Michael Haneke, 2012), 189
Apocalypse Now (Francis Ford Coppola, 1979), 52
Avatar (James Cameron, 2009), 48, 64, 132, 189, 242, 276, 333, 337, 398
Avengers: Age of Ultron (Joss Whedon, 2015), 400
A Woman Under the Influence (John Cassavetes, 1974), 301, 302, 306

Barbarella (Roger Vadim, 1968), 274
Batman Begins (Christopher Nolan, 2005), 48, 51
Being John Malkovich (Spike Jonze, 1999), 357
Bicentennial Man (Chris Columbus, 1999), 276, 356, 367
Blade (Stephen Norrington, 1998), 76, 241
Blade Runner (Ridley Scott, 1982), 46–48, 51, 78–79, 85, 94–6, 112, 121, 129, 132, 135, 146, 148, 155–6, 189, 243, 279, 332, 345, 368, 374, 393–4
Body Snatchers (Abel Ferrara, 1993), 293
Brave New World (Burt Brinckerhoff, 1980), 261–2
Brave New World (Leslie Libman, 1998), 261–2
Brazil (Terry Gilliam, 1985), 159–60

Captain America: The First Avenger (Joe Johnston, 2011), 240
Captain America: The Winter Soldier (Anthony and Joe Russo, 2014), 17, 240, 398
Casino Royale (Martin Campbell, 2006), 292
Casshern (Kazuaki Kiriya, 2004), 77, 79, 82–6
Chappie (Neill Blomkamp, 2015), 400
Children of Men (Alfonso Cuaron, 2006), 273
Christine (John Carpenter, 1983), 408
Close Encounters of the Third Kind (Steven Spielberg, 1977), 155
Cloud Atlas (Lana and Andy Wachowski, 2012), 132, 277
Cocoon (Ron Howard, 1985), 210
Colossus: The Forbin Project (Joseph Sargent, 1970), 94, 122, 128, 131
Conan, the Barbarian (John Milius, 1982), 45, 48, 52
Conceiving Ada (Lynn Hershman Leeson, 1997), 272
Contact (Robert Zemeckis, 1997), 274
Crash (David Cronenberg, 1996), 263–4
Cyborg (Albert Pyun, 1989), 61
Cyborg, 2087 (Franklin Adreon, 1966), 172

D'ailleurs Derrida [Derrida's Elsewheres] (Safaa Faathy, 1999), 29
Dark City (Alex Proyas, 1998), 137
Dawn of the Planet of the Apes (Matt Reeves, 2014), 158, 321–2, 325–7, 329
Daybreakers (Michael and Peter Spierig, 2009), 158, 208–10, 239
Demon Seed (Donald Cammell, 1977), 122, 128
Der Untergang [Downfall] (Oliver Hirschbiegel, 2004), 51
Derrida (Kirby Dick and Amy Ziering Kofman, 2002), 29
District, 9 (Neill Blomkamp, 2009), 243, 265–8, 380, 384
Don Jon (Joseph Gordon Levitt, 2013), 17–18
Doom (Andrzej Bartkowiak, 2005), 198
Dorian Gray (Oliver Parker, 2009), 209
Dreamcatcher (Lawrence Kasdan, 2003), 380
Dr. No (Terence Young, 1962), 65
Dr. Strangelove (Stanley Kubrick, 1964), 392
Duel (Steven Spielberg, 1971), 407

436

Eagle Eye (D.J. Caruso, 2008), 123
Easy Rider (Dennis Hopper, 1969), 135
Edge of Tomorrow (Doug Liman, 2014), 132
Electric Dreams (Steve Barron, 1984), 376
Electrocuting an Elephant (Thomas Edison, 1903), 312–18
Elysium (Neil Blomkamp, 2013), 45, 241, 279
Enders Game (Gavin Hood, 2013), 132
Epsilon (Rolf de Heer, 1995), 274
Escape from New York (John Carptenter, 1981), 125
Eternal Sunshine of the Spotless Mind (Michael Gondry, 2004), 212, 215, 349, 357
Execution of Czolgosz with Panorama of Auburn Prison (Thomas Edison, 1901), 317
eXistenZ (David Cronenberg, 1999), 137, 190, 196, 200, 260, 274, 293–4, 334

Face/Off (John Woo, 1997), 293
Fantastic Voyage (Richard Fleischer, 1966), 46–7, 53
Fight Club (David Fincher, 1999), 15–16
Forbidden Planet (Fred M. Wilcox, 1956), 131
Frankenstein (J. Searle Dawley, 1910), 77
Frankenstein (James Whale, 1931), 4, 112, 135, 147–8, 156
From Dusk Till Dawn (Robert Rodriguez, 1996), 206
Futureworld (Richard T. Heffron, 1976), 393

Gattaca (Andrew Niccol, 1997), 23, 45, 79–80, 86, 274, 280, 290–2, 396
Gibel sensatii (Alexsandr Andriyewsky, 1935)
Ghost in the Shell (Mamoru Oshii, 1995), 129, 274
Ghost in the Shell, 2: Innocence (Mamoru Oshii, 2004), 275
Godzilla (Gareth Edwards, 2014), 77
Gravity (Alfonso Cuarón, 2013), 189
Groundhog Day (Harold Ramis, 1993), 52
Guardians of the Galaxy (James Gunn, 2014), 67, 356

Hackers (Iain Softley, 1995), 131
Hannah and her Sisters (Woody Allen, 1986), 48, 51
Hannibal (Ridley Scott, 2001), 214–15, 218
Hardware (Richard Stanley, 1990), 61
Hellboy (Guillermo del Toro, 2004), 241
Her (Spike Jonze, 2013), 17–18, 46, 64, 92, 125, 129–30, 132, 139–40, 157, 167, 186, 277, 283, 286, 335, 338, 377

Highlander (Russell Mulcahy, 1986), 356
Hugo (Martin Scorsese, 2011), 99
Hulk (Ang Lee, 2003), 67, 74–6

I Am Legend (Francis Lawrence, 2007), 158
Inception (Christopher Nolan, 2010), 23, 398
I, Frankenstein (Stuart Beattie, 2014), 242
Inspector Gadget (David Kellogg, 1999), 173
Interstellar (Christopher Nolan, 2014), 98
I, Robot (Alex Proyas, 2004), 103, 132, 144–7, 263, 335
In Time (Andrew Niccol, 2011), 23, 208, 295
Interview with the Vampire: The Vampire Chronicles (Neil Jordan, 1994), 207–8, 239
Invaders from Mars (William Cameron Menzies, 1953), 237, 260
Invasion of the Body Snatchers (Don Siegel, 1956), 25, 46, 51, 237, 293, 331, 354, 380
Invasion of the Body Snatchers (Philip Kaufman, 1978), 46, 293
Iron Man (Jon Favreau, 2008), 53, 71–3, 241, 386, 397
Iron Man, 2 (Jon Favreau, 2010), 71, 397
Iron Man, 3 (Shane Black, 2013), 71, 73, 75
It Came from Outer Space (Jack Arnold, 1953), 237

Jaws (Steven Spielberg, 1975), 408
Jobs (Joshua Michael Stern, 2013), 138
Johnny Mnemonic (Robert Longo, 1995), 131, 215

Kick-Ass (Matthew Vaughn, 2010), 67
Koyaanisqatsi: Life out of Balance (Gofrey Reggio, 1982), 277

Last Night (Don McKellar, 1998), 189
Last Year in Marienbad (Alain Resnais, 1961), 190
Lawrence of Arabia (David Lean, 1962), 52
Life of an American Fireman (Edwin S. Porter, 1903), 313
Limitless (Neil Burger, 2011), 217, 219–20, 224–5, 227, 229, 231–4, 244, 398
Liquid Sky (Slava Tsukerman, 1982), 273
Logan's Run (Michael Anderson, 1976), 131, 190, 393
Looper (Rian Johnson, 2012), 23
Lucy (Luc Besson, 2014), 194, 398

M (Fritz Lang, 1931), 408
Mad Max (George Miller, 1979), 47
Making Mr. Right (Susan Seidelman, 1987), 377
Marvel's The Avengers (Joss Whedon, 2012), 71, 383
Mary Shelley's Frankenstein (Kenneth Branagh, 1994), 147, 368
Max Headroom (Annabel Jankel and Rocky Morton, 1984), 125
Melancholia (Lars von Trier, 2011), 15
Memento (Christopher Nolan, 2000), 177–8, 181, 212, 295
Metropolis (Fritz Lang, 1927), 79, 91, 113, 115, 119, 131, 155, 189, 195, 276
Mickey's Magical Christmas (Rick Calabash, 2001), 53
Minority Report (Steven Spielberg, 2002), 23
Moon (Duncan Jones, 2009), 112, 131, 374, 376
Mr. Nobody (Jacob van Dormael, 2009), 211–12
Mulholland Drive (David Lynch, 2001), 23

Naqoyqatsi: Life as War (Godfrey Reggio, 2002), 277
Neighboring Sounds (Kleber Mendonca Filho, 2012), 305–6
Nemesis (Albert Pyun, 1992), 58, 61
Never Let Me Go (Mark Romanek, 2010), 64, 79, 81, 85, 132, 260, 274, 384–5
Nineteen Eighty-Four (Michael Radford, 1984), 261, 263
Nosferatu (Fritz Murnau, 1922), 206
Nosferatu the Vampyre (Werner Herzog, 1979), 206
Nuts in May (Mike Leigh, 1976), 302

Pacific Rim (Guillermo del Toro, 2013), 132
Paradise Trilogy (Ulrich Seidl, 2012, 2012, 2013), 246–55
Parts: The Clonus Horror (Robert S. Fiveson, 1979), 81
Pitch Black (David Twohy, 2000), 397
Planet of the Apes (Franklin J. Schaffner, 1968), 104, 325
Planet of the Apes (Tim Burton, 2001), 260, 397
Play Dead; Real Time (Douglas Gordon, 2003), 312–20
Powaqqatsi: Life in Transformation (Godfrey Reggio, 1988), 277

Prometheus (Ridley Scott, 2012), 53, 117–18
Punishment Park (Peter Watkins, 1971), 300

Red Planet Mars (Harry Horner, 1952), 331
Rise of the Planet of the Apes (Rupert Wyatt, 2011), 103–4, 321–5, 329, 384
RoboCop (Paul Verhoeven, 1987), 5, 47, 53, 58, 61–3, 73, 131, 172–3, 243, 279, 349–50, 357, 395
RoboCop, 2 (Irvin Kirshner, 1990), 61
RoboCop, 3 (Fred Dekker, 1993), 61
RoboCop (José Padilha, 2014), 336, 398
Robot & Frank (Jake Schreier, 2012), 336, 398
Russian Ark (Alexander Sokurov, 2002), 189–90

Safe (Todd Haynes, 1995), 304, 307
Salo, or the, 120 Days of Sodom (Pier Paolo Pasolini, 1975), 247
Seconds (John Frankenheimer, 1966), 211
Serenity (Joss Whedon, 2005), 279, 282, 397
Shane (George Stevens, 1953), 52
Sneakers (Phil Aldon Robinson, 1992), 136–8
S1m0ne (David Niccol, 2002), 23–4
Solaris (Andrei Tarkovski, 1972), 132, 189, 303–4
Source Code (Duncan Jones, 2011), 23, 190, 212
Soylent Green (Richard Fleischer, 1973), 262
Species (Roger Donaldson, 1995), 194, 380
Spider-Man (Sam Raimi, 2002), 67, 70, 76, 157
Spider-Man, 2 (Sam Raimi, 2004), 58
Spider-Man, 3 (Sam Raimi, 2007), 280
Splice (Vincenzo Natali, 2009), 157, 260, 267, 274
Stalker (Andrei Tarkovsky, 1979), 304, 407
Starship Troopers (Paul Verhoeven, 1997), 132
Star Trek: First Contact (Jonathan Frakes, 1996), 64, 79, 134
Star Trek II: The Wrath of Khan (Nicholas Meyer, 1982), 279, 393
Star Trek IV: The Voyage Home (Leonard Nimoy, 1986), 394
Star Wars (George Lucas, 1977), 48, 131, 155, 172, 189, 332, 393
Star Wars Episode V: The Empire Strikes Back (Irvin Kershner, 1980), 393
Strange Days (Kathryn Bigelow, 1995), 137, 272, 375

Super (James Gunn, 2011), 67
Surrogates (Jonathan Mostow, 2009), 51, 156, 333

Taskafa, Stories from the Street (Andrea Luka Zimmerman, 2013), 16
Taxi Driver (Martin Scorcese, 1976), 407
Teknolust (Lynn Hershman Leeson, 2002), 272
Terminator, 2: Judgment Day (James Cameron, 1991), 4, 61, 63, 90, 94, 395, 397
Terminator, 3: Rise of the Machines (Jonathan Mostow, 2003), 63
Terminator Salvation (McG, 2009), 59, 146, 149, 397
The Amazing Spider-Man (Marc Webb, 2012), 280
The Amazing Spider-Man, 2 (Marc Webb, 2014), 280
The Astronaut's Wife (Rand Ravich, 1999), 273, 380
The Birth of a Nation (D.W. Griffith, 1915), 313
The Blob (Irvin Yeaworth, 1958), 25
The Bourne Identity (Doug Liman, 2002), 397
The Boys from Brazil (Franklin J. Schaffner, 1978), 132
The Colossus of New York (Eugene Lourie, 1958), 65, 172–3
The Dark Knight (Christopher Nolan, 2008), 51, 156
The Dark Knight Rises (Christopher Nolan, 2012), 51–2
The Day the Earth Stood Still (Robert Wise, 1951), 116
The Elementary Particles (Oskar Roehler, 2006), 216
The Fantastic Four (Tim Story, 2005), 386
The Fifth Element (Luc Besson, 1997), 274
The Fly (Kurt Neumann, 1958), 331
The Fly (David Cronenberg, 1986), 100, 156
The Fountain (Darren Aronofsky, 2006), 160–1
The Fountainhead (King Vidor, 1949), 49
The Great Gatsby (Baz Luhrmann, 2013), 49
The Great Train Robbery (Edwin S. Porter, 1903), 313
The Handmaid's Tale (Volker Schlöndorff, 1990), 273

The Hunger Games (Gary Ross, 2012), 272
The Incredible Hulk (Kenneth Johnson, 1977), 393
The Incredible Hulk (Louis Leterrier, 2008), 241
The Invasion (Oliver Hirschbiegel, 2007), 293
The Island (Michael Bay, 2005), 64, 79–81, 86, 132, 374, 376
The Lawnmower Man (Brett Leonard, 1992), 170
The Lord of the Rings (Peter Jackson, 2001–2003), 103–7
The Lost Boys (Joel Schumacher, 1987), 206
Them! (Gordon Douglas, 1954), 25
The Machine (Caradog W. James, 2013), 129, 172, 399
The Machine Stops (Philip Saville, 1966), 261–2
The Man from Earth (Jerome Bixby, 2007), 208
The Matrix (Lana and Andy Wachowsksi, 1999), 23, 46, 122, 132, 137–9, 155–6, 189, 190, 192, 260, 263, 272, 349, 369, 376, 380, 383, 396
The Matrix Reloaded (Lana and Andy Wachowski, 2003), 167–8, 170
The Matrix Revolutions (Lana and Andy Wachowski, 2003), 376–7
The Net (Irwin Winkler, 1995), 131
The Pervert's Guide to Cinema (Sophie Fiennes, 2006), 307
There Will Be Blood (Paul Thomas Anderson, 2007), 305
The Shop Around the Corner (Ernst Lubitsch, 1940), 131
The, 6th Day (Roger Spottiswoode, 2000), 352
The Skin I Live in (Pedro Almodovar, 2011), 296
The Social Network (David Fincher, 2010), 138
The Stepford Wives (Bryan Forbes, 1975), 197, 293, 393
The Stepford Wives (Frank Oz, 2004), 197, 293
The Terminator (James Cameron, 1984), 5, 189, 393–5
The Thief of Bagddad (Arthur Lubin, 1961), 52
The Thing (John Carpenter, 1982), 156

The Thirteenth Floor (Josef Rusnak, 1999), 137
The Time Machine (Simon Wells, 2002), 388
The Truman Show (Peter Weir, 1998), 23
The Twilight Saga (various, 2008–2012), 207, 239
The War of the Worlds (Byron Haskin, 1953), 25, 260
The Wind (Victor Sjöström, 1928), 16
The Wizard of Oz (Victor Fleming, 1939), 113
The Wolf of Wall Street (Martin Scorcese, 2013), 49
The Wonderful Wizard of Oz (Otis Turner, 1910), 113
The Village of the Damned (Wolf Rilla, 1960), 237
They Came Back (Robin Campillo, 2004), 344–7
The Zero Theorem (Terry Gilliam, 2014), 160
THX, 1138 (George Lucas, 1971), 117
Things to Come (William Cameron Menzies, 1936), 261
30 Days of Night (David Slade, 2007), 206
Titanic (James Cameron, 1997), 49
Total Recall (Paul Verhoeven, 1990), 374–5
Transcendence (Wally Pfister, 2014), 4, 23, 90, 98, 101, 123, 125, 127–8, 132, 135, 157–8, 239–40, 244, 280, 337, 366, 398–9
Transcendent Man (Barry Ptolemy, 2009), 46
Transformers (Michael Bay, 2007), 45
Tron (Steven Lisberger, 1982), 124–5, 131, 190, 193
Tron: Legacy (Joseph Kosinski, 2010), 124–5
Turin Horse (Bela Tarkov, 2011), 15
Triumph des Willens (Leni Riefenstahl, 1935), 45, 51, 53
12 Monkeys (Terry Gilliam, 1995), 52
28 Days Later (Danny Boyle, 2002), 189
2001: A Space Odyssey (Stanley Kubrick, 1968), 2, 46, 97, 121–2, 130, 144–5, 161, 199, 376, 392, 407
2010: The Year We Make Contact (Peter Hyams, 1984), 376

Ubermensch (Simon Temple, 2009), 53
Un Chien Andalou (Luis Bunuel, 1929), 290
Under the Skin (Jonathan Glazer, 2013), 17–18
Underworld (Len Wiseman, 2003), 239
Universal Soldier (Roland Emmerich, 1992), 61, 279
Upstream Color (Shane Carruth, 2013), 354–5

Vampyr (Carl Theodor Dreyer, 1932), 190
Vanilla Sky (Cameron Crowe, 2001), 349
Videodrome (David Cronenberg, 1983), 72–3
Virtuosity (Brett Leonard, 1995), 166, 170

WALL-E (Andrew Stanton, 2008), 266–7, 273
Watchmen (Zack Snyder, 2009), 53, 156, 241, 286
WarGames (John Badham, 1983), 5, 123, 131
Westworld (Michael Crichton, 1973), 117, 190
When Nietzsche Wept (Pinchas Perry, 2007), 50
World War Z (Marc Forster, 2013), 103

X-Men (Bryan Singer, 2000), 76, 157, 279–80, 283–7, 388
X, 2 (Bryan Singer, 2003), 396
X-Men: First Class (Matthew Vaughn, 2011), 242, 281, 283

Yomigaeri (Akihito Shiota, 2002), 342
Young Frankenstein (Mel Brooks, 1974), 47
You've Got Mail (Nora Ephron, 1998), 131, 166, 170, 331

Zabriskie Point (Michelangelo Antonioni, 1970), 300, 302, 306
Zardoz (John Boorman, 1974), 131

TV Films:

Ghost Dance (Ken McMullen, 1983), 29–30
Man and Superman (Patrick Dromgoole & Alex Kirby, 1982), 45
Monty Pythons Fliegender Zirkus (Alfred Biolek, 1972), 48
R.U.R. (Jan Bussell, 1938), 113–16
Temple Grandin (Mick Jackson, 2010), 177, 179
Zenon: Girl of the, 21st Century (Kenneth Johnson, 1999), 274

TV Series:

Adventures of Superman (Whitney Ellsworth, 1951–1958), 51
Aeon Flux (Peter Chung, 1991–1995), 279
Almost Human (J.H. Wyman, 2013–2014), 63, 119, 276, 332, 336, 398
Alphas (Zak Penn, 2011–2012), 241, 243
Andromeda (Gene Roddenberry, 2000–2005), 239, 279
Angel (Joss Whedon and David Greenwalt, 1999–2004), 241
Ark II (Martin Roth, 1976–1979), 302
Battlestar Gallactica (Glen A. Larson, 1978–1979), 4, 23, 393, 397
Battlestar Gallactica (Ronald D. Moore, 2004–2009), 4, 23, 64, 90–1, 94–5, 118, 126–7, 132, 156, 239, 283–5, 305–6, 334, 356, 368, 397
Bewitched (Sol Saks, 1964–1972), 240, 274
Bionic Woman (David Eick, 2007), 63
Black Mirror (Charlie Brooker, 2011–2013), 332, 336
Breaking Bad (Vince Gilligan, 2008–2013), 185
Buffy the Vampire Slayer (Joss Whedon, 1997–2003), 193, 206, 240, 243, 274
Buried (Rodrigo Cortés, 2010), 190
Caprica (Remi Aubuchon, 2009–2010), 64, 91, 96, 126, 239–40
Carnivale (Daniel Knauf, 2003–2005), 48
Chuck (Josh Schwartz and Chris Fedak, 2007–2012), 241
Continuum (Simon Barry, 2012–), 58, 63, 241
Creamy Mami, the Magic Angel (Osamu Kobayashi, 1983–1984), 274
Dark Angel (James Cameron, 2000–2002), 243, 279
Desperate Housewives (Marc Cherry, 2004–2012), 168, 170
Doctor Who (various, 1963–), 64, 91, 131, 172, 185, 238, 352–4
Dollhouse (Joss Whedon, 2009–2010), 212, 243, 332, 337
Extant (Mickey Fisher, 2014–), 129, 273, 349, 356
Firefly (Joss Whedon, 2002–2003), 156, 279, 397
Fringe (J.J. Abrams, 2008–2013), 280–1
Futurama (Matt Groening, 1999–2014), 244
Heroes (Tim Kring, 2006–2010), 241
Homeland (Howard Gordon, 2011–), 142
In the Flesh (Dominic Mitchell, 2013–2014), 368
Iron Man (1994–1996), 241
Jekyll (Steven Moffat, 2007), 357
Late Night with David Letterman (David Letterman, 1982–1993), 408
Lost (Jeffrey Lieber, J. J. Abrams and Damon Lindelof, 2004–2010), 184
Lost in Space (Irwin Allen, 1965–1968), 47, 131
Married with Children (Michael G. Moye and Ron Leavitt, 1987–1997), 167, 169–70
Max Headroom (Annabel Jankel and Rocky Morton, 1987–1988), 125
My Favorite Martian (John L. Greene, 1973–1976), 240
Orphan Black (Graeme Manson and John Fawcett, 2013–), 64, 157
Penny Dreadful (John Logan, 2014–), 242
Person of Interest (Jonathan Nolan, 2011–), 123
Queer as Folk (Ron Cowen and Daniel Lipman, 2000–2005), 166, 168, 170
Red Dwarf (Grant Naylor, 1988–1993, 1997–1999), 165, 169–70
Resurrection (Aaron Zelman, 2014–), 342, 344
Sex and the City (Darren Starr, 1998–2004), 166, 168
Sliders (Tracy Tormé, 1995–1999), 166, 170
Smallville (Alfred Gough & Miles Millar, 2001–2011), 45, 51
Star Trek (Gene Roddenberry, 1966–1969), 4, 45, 47, 57, 61, 77, 93, 131, 134, 172, 185, 355, 377
Star Trek: The Next Generation (Gene Roddenberry, 1987–1994), 61, 64, 93, 129, 132–3, 156, 165, 168–9, 239, 349, 354, 365, 395
Star Trek: Deep Space Nine (Rick Berman, 1993–1999), 239, 355, 365
Star Trek: Voyager (Rick Berman, 1995–2001), 58, 64, 134, 156, 185, 239, 365
Star Trek: Enterprise (Rick Berman, 2001–2005), 64
The Addams Family (Charles Addams, 1964–1966), 240
The Big Bang Theory (Chuck Lorre and Bill Prady, 2007–), 168, 170
The Bionic Woman (Kenneth Johnson, 1976–1978), 60–1, 274
The Incredible Hulk (Kenneth Johnson, 1978–1982), 393

The Jetsons (William Hanna & Joseph Barbera, 1962–1963), 47, 244, 392
The Munsters (Allan Burns, 1964–1966), 240
The Outer Limits (Leslie Stevens, 1963–1965), 116
The Prisoner (Patrick McGoohan, 1967–1968), 131
The Returned (Fabrice Gobert, 2012–), 339, 343–4
The Six Million Dollar Man (various, 1974–1978), 59–61, 173, 241, 393
The Sopranos (David Chase, 1999–2007), 48
The Tomorrow People (Greg Berlanti, 2013–2014), 243
The Undersea World of Jacques Cousteau (Jacques Cousteau, 1968–1976), 303
The Vampire Diaries (Kevin Williamson, 2009), 207
The Walking Dead (Frank Darabont, 2010–), 49, 189, 266–7
The X-Files (Chris Carter, 1993–2002), 196, 200
Torchwood (Russell T. Davies, 2006–2011), 365
Treme (David Simon and Eric Overmyer, 2000–2013), 299–300, 308
True Blood (Alan Ball, 2008–2014), 49, 240–1, 243, 367
Wonder Woman (Charles Moulton, 1975–1979), 274
Xena: Warrior Princess (Robert Tapert, 1995–2001), 274

General Index

Note: Locators in bold refer to chapter title.

Adorno, Theodor W., 51, 98
advanced morality, 387–8
affective turn, 276
Agamben, Giorgio, 84, 267–8, 300–1, 325–7
agency, 3, 5, 34, 69, 77, 92–3, 99, 104–5, 107, 137, 175, 192, 195–6, 198–9, 247–50, 253, 302, 304, 314, 326, 351, 373, 391, 393, 395–6, 399
  animal, 318
  cybernetic, 197
  digital, 99, 102–6, 124
  material, 253–5, 303
  moral, 149, 389
  non-human, 6, 88, 90, 103, 105, 121, 196, 247–8, 277, 299, 312, 314, 392–3, 396, 399
Alaimo, Stacy, 300, 302–3, 307
Allen, Woody, 48, 51–2, 407
amnesia, 177–9, 212
Anders, Günther, 5, 291
android, 48, 58, 79, **111–19**, 129, 158, 242, 276, 336, 368, 377
Do Androids Dream of Electric Sheep (Philip K. Dick), 95, 146
and slavery, 111, 113, 115–16, 118–19
animals, 15–16, 20, 77–8, 84, 89, 92, 100, 108, 115, 154, 157, 172, 179–80, 196, 205–6, 211, 215–16, 246, 248–51, 266, 274, 286, **311–20**, **321–9**, 337, 341, 346, 351, 362, 368, 382–4, 389, 401, 404
anthropocentrism, 16, 34, 36, 66, 75, 79, 84, 86, 88, 90, 118, 153–4, 156, 158, 259, 262–5, 267, 270, 273, 298, 319, 327, 347, 368, 377, 405
archive, 29, 32–3
artificial intelligence (AI), 2, 13, 20, 46, 62, 64, 89, 103, 120, 129, 132–3, 141–7, 157, 167, 173, 186, 198, 269, 276, 283, 335, 337, 354, 366, 376, 392, 399
assemblage, 32, 78, 83, 85, 87, 96, 107, 311
  assemblage theory, 277
autism, 179–80
autoaffection, 34
autobiography, 29

autonomy, 13, 77, 83, 86, 91–5, 101, 106, 142–9, 226, 248, 262–3, 267, 318, 343, 355–6, 366, 382, 384, 403, 406–7
  of machines, 5, 94, 98, 102, 106, 111–12, 120, 123, 141–9
  of spectral images, 32
  see also machines, autonomous fighting machines

Bach-y-Rita, Paul, 175
Barabasi, Albert-László, 132–5
bare life, 84, 184, 267–8
Baudrillard, Jean, **19–27**, 58–9, 62, 155, 196–7, 234
bifurcation of nature, 37, 40–1
bioconservatism, 7
biological machines, 331, 396
biopolitics, 68, 84, 95, 267, 299–304, 306, 312, 339–40, 345–7
biopower, 25, 157, 248, 252–3, 314
biotechnology, 20, 80, 87, 148, 225–7, 229–33, 246, 260, 269, 278, 293, 333, 362, 394, 397
body, *see* embodiment
  body doubles, 48
  body natural, 344–5, 347
  body politic, 284, 340–1, 344–5, 347
Bostrom, Nick, 47, 98, 141, 143, 147–8, 205, 246–7, 366, 394, 396, 399, 404, 409
Braidotti, Rosi, 14–17, 19, 79, 81, 84, 86, 112, 120, 189, 195–6, 200, 273, 277, 321–2, 327–8, 362, 404–6
brain anatomy, 215
Brentano, Franz, 401–2
Burke, Kenneth, 226–30, 232
Butler, Judith, 226, 322, 325, 364

capitalism, 11–12, 14, 48, 50–1, 68, 78–9, 81, 84–6, 155, 157, 220, 223, 242, 264, 321
  cognitive capitalism, 216–17
  commodity capitalism, 266
  patriarchal capitalism, 325
  technocapitalism, 95

Cartesian, 2, 14, 40, 59, 61, 94, 96, 144, 157, 250, 289, 371, 404–5
  Cartesianism, 248
cartoons and comic books, 47, 52–3, 173, 240–2, 266, 274, 333, 388, 396
chimeras and hybrids, 20, 37–9, 59, 68, 70–3, 75, 77, 83–4, 95–6, **99–108**, 112, 118, 123, 126, 128, 153, 156–7, 159–61, 170, 243, 269, 273, 275, 278, 314, 332, 335, 362, 365, 368–9, 380, 388, 398, 404
cinema of attractions, 313–15, 319
cinematic animal, 311–12, 314, 316
circular time, 305–6
Clark, Andy, 94, 176–7, 374, 396, 399, 404
Clark, Julie, 77–80, 83, 86
class conflict, 50
clones, 16, 20, 24, 64–5, 78–81, 83–4, 86, 96, 115, 122, 132, 157, 237–8, 244, 371, 374, 385, 393, 399
coevolution, 183, 264
cogito, 196
colonialism/postcolonialism, 11, 14, 96, 242, 321
communication, 63, 68, 82, 131–2, 134, 138, 144, 194, 248, 261, 275, 301–2, 337, 375–6, 386
  communication technology, 103, 216, 332, 362
  limitations of, 371, 375, 378
  telecommunication, 58, 130, 293–4, 334
community, 24, 105, 114, 148, 241, 262, 283–8, 323, 325–8, 332, 335, 337, 367, 388
composite image, 99–100, 102–3
computer and neural networks, 20, 22, 26–7, 30, 44, 66, 93, 106–7, 120, 127–8, **130–40**, 153, 163, 222, 334, 354, 366, 371, 377, 386, 394, 396, 398
consciousness, 1–2, 11, 13, 15, 41–2, 44, 69, 80, 100–1, 107–8, 120, 125, 127, 130, 133, 141, 143–4, 146, 191, 216, 221, 259, 290, 295, 342, 346, 352, 356, 366–7, 369, 373–4, 382, 388, 398, 402–3
  collective/distributed consciousness, 130, 134, 237, 350, 354, 365–7, 395, 399
  perceptual consciousness, 174, 177
  planetary consciousness, 306, 389
  see also uploading
constructed worlds, **182–91**

consumer/consumerism, 24, 66, 196–7, 201, 228, 263–4, 300, 305
  consumer society, 264
containment, 93, 200–1, 340–1, 343–4
control, 16, 18, 24, 29, 32–4, 46–7, 62, 70, 72–3, 75–6, 85, 89, 94–5, 105–6, 114, 116–17, 119, 122–4, 127, 130–1, 136–7, 139, 142–4, 147, 164, 167, 169, 171–2, 180, 185, 190, 198, 223, 233, 238–40, 243, 249, 252, 275, 279–81, 283, 301, 314–19, 325, 330–1, 351, 357, 374–5, 386, 393, 398–9
  remote control, 112, 142, 333, 335, 337, 392
  self-control, 221
cosmetic surgery, 211
cosmopoiesis, 186–7, 189, 191
counterculture, 131, 136–8
critical posthumanism, 7, 70–1, 73, 88, 94, 153, 290, 296–7, 362, 366
critical theory, 3, 192, 396
Cronenberg, David, 72, 100, 263–4
crowd simulation, 99, 102–4, 106
culture industry, 46, 51
cybernetic/cybernetics, 57, 60, 62, 77, 134, 144, 155, 165–7, 172–3, 181, 193, 197–9, 235, 237, 241, 244, 246, 271, 281, 330, 337–8, 350, 362, 392, 396
cybersex, **163–71**, 335
cyberspace, 21, 27, 35, 126, 155, 163–4, 166, 221, 271
cyborg, 5, 20, 32, **57–65**, 66, 68–9, 71–4, 79, 88, 94, 96, 100, 107, 131, 149, 153, 155–7, 165, 172–4, 178, 181, 183, 190, 194–8, 216, 231, 237, 239, 241, 243–4, 246, 260, 269, 271–6, 285–6, 293, 303, 305, 322–9, 368, 373, 377, 385, 391–5, 397, 399
  cyborgization, 31–3
  cyborg rights, 383

death and immortality, 45, 48–50, 52–3, 57, 60, 80–1, 85, 96, 148, 158, 161, 192, 197, **205–13**, 260, 277, 292, 311, 314, 316, 333, 336, **339–48**, 349, 367, 369, 375, 403
  death of animals, 317–19, 323, 327, 329
  death of God, 52
  see also eternal youth; life extension
deconstruction, 28, 30–1, 33–6, 188, 248, 250, 265, 269–70, 275, 278, 298

Deleuze, Gilles, **11–18**, 42–4, 78, 81–2, 85–7, 108, 187–8, 199, 249, 294–5, 405
democracy, 33, 125, 135, 234, **235–45**, 282–4, 303, 312, 364, 384–7, 397
  cosmetic, 383–6
  trans-species, 390
Derrida, Jacques, 26, **28–36**, 189–90, 262, 285, 289, 295, 322–3, 325, 346, 404
desire, 1, 12, 17–18, 33–4, 46, 67, 78–9, 93, 99, 104–7, 122, 148, 161, 163, 166–7, 169–71, 174, 177, 195, 198–200, 206, 212, 215, 217–22, 224, 249–52, 260, 262–5, 270–1, 277, 303–4, 307, 316, 325, 341, 343–4, 347, 366, 373, 381, 392–4, 396, 398
  desiring machines, 11–12
  for perfection, 226, 234
digital agents, *see* agency
digitalization, 20, 32–3, 36, 217
digital multitude, 103–8
digital sentience, *see* sentience, digital
digital visual effects, 101–2, 106
dirt theory, 299, 303, 306, 308
disconnection thesis, 91, 95, 97
disembodiment, *see* embodiment
Doležel, Lubomír, 182–3, 186–7, 191
dominance, 15, 279–80, 281–2
dramatism, 227–8
dystopian/utopian, 6, 23, 26, 47, 49, 63, 68, 71, 79–80, 99–102, 105–6, 124, 131, 137, 139–40, 148, 153, 158, 160, 163–4, 167, 169, 193–7, 236–8, 241, **259–68**, 269, 272–4, 277–8, 290, 294–5, 297, 302, 328, 332–3, 338, 380, 384, 395–6
  bio-utopianism, 237

Edison, Thomas, 311–20
Elitism, 115
Ellul, Jacques, 5, 98, 366, 393
embodiment, 5, 13–15, 58, 60–1, 89, 92, 96, 100–2, 105, 107, 123–9, 153, 156, 158, 165–6, **172–81**, 190, 214, 239, 246–54, 259, 276–8, 332, 335–8, 343, 363, 367, 371–4, 377–9, 392, 394–6, 398–400, 403
  embodied cognition, 14, 174–7
emergence narratives, 132–5, 140
emotion, 72, 74–5, 92–4, 115–19, 122, 128, 137, 141, 147, 171, 174, 176–80, 233, 237, 242, 269, 276, 280–2, 287, 289–90, 330, 332, 335–6, 340–2, 345–6, 354–5, 363, 366, 368, 371, 375–9, 392, 395, 407
  absence of, 17–18, 61, 115, 147, 179, 237, 354
  see also enhancement, emotional
empiricism, 41, 263, 402
  radical, 41
  transcendental, 42–4
enhancement/augmentation, 3, 16, 53, 60–4, 70–1, 73–8, 80, 112, 128, 139, 141, 143, 145, 157, 172–81, 194–5, 197–8, 200, 205, 207, 209, 217, 225–6, 229–34, 237–9, 241–2, 244–5, 264, 267, 270, 274, 281–2, 285, 296, 333, 349, 357, 362, 366–7, 381–2, 387–8, 390, 392, 396–7
  bodily, 45, 290, 334, 338, 383
  chemical, 50, 296
  cognitive/psychic, 156, **214–24**, 230–4, 240, 244, 281, 389
  cybernetic, 60, 173, 241, 244
  emotional, 179, **245–55**
  genetic, 74, 119, 239, 280, 282, 291, 403
  memory enhancement, 178, 241
  moral, 143, 281, 387–9
  nanotech, 128
  perceptual, 173, 175
  see also life extension
enlightenment, 3, 39–41, 66, 101, 153, 236, 240, 244, 250, 372, 391, 404
entropy, 192
environment, 16, 24, 34, 36, 63–4, 89, 99, 101, 103–5, 121–2, 128, 175, 177–9, 216, 222, 261, 263–4, 266, 277, 281, **299–308**, 321, 327, 337, 362–3, 366, 405–6
epidermal readings, *see* skin
epistemic understanding, 304, 385–6
equipment for living, 227–9, 233
eternal recurrence, 51–3, 212
eternal youth, 208–9
ethics, 17, 35, 61, 77–8, 84, 90, 127, 140–9, 364, 372, 381, 403
  cyber-ethics, 199
  ethics and ontology, 313
  ethics of difference, 389
  ethics of response-ability, 247, 249, 251
  machine ethics, 121
  medical ethics/bioethics, 153, 238, 273, 382
  narrative ethics, 148

eugenics, 23, 45, 79–81, 83–4, 237, 239, 291
evolution, 2–5, 13–14, 33, 79, 118–19, 120, 122–4, 126, 128, 130, 133, 135, 147, 165, 171, 183, 186–7, 189, 194, 199, 209, 226, 238, 240, 242–3, 246, 259–60, 264, 268–9, 275, 277–8, 280, 283–4, 287–8, 297, 315, 366–8, 373, 377, **380–90**, 406
execution films, 313–14, 316–19
extended mind thesis, 176–7, 404–5

fantasy, 4, 16, 23, 45–6, 51, 53, 66, 69, 73, 76, 77, 100, 106, 121, 125–7, 153–4, 158–62, 163, 171, 192–3, 200, 304, 380–1, 388–9, 392, 396
Forster, E.M., 261
Foucault, Michel, 2, 26, 95, 155, 299, 317, 319
Frankenstein/Frankenstein's Monster, 24, 47, 59, 79–80, 83, 85, 147, 186, 214, 221, 240, 242, 286, 369
see also monster
Fried, Michael, 406–9
Fukuyama, Francis, 238–9, 282, 397

gaming, 51, 123, **192–201**
gender, 3, 5, 20, 59, 62–3, 69–72, 74–5, 77, 91–2, 112, 131, 154, 167, 194–6, 201, 216–17, 262, **269–78**, 289, 297, 319, 321, 332–6, 368, 373
 bisexuality, 297, 368
 intersex, 368
 transsexual/transgender, 20, 26, 157, 159, 368
genetic/genetics, 17, 19, 23, 69, 77–82, 86–7, 94, 100–1, 157, 235, 264, 274, 276, 280–1, 284–5, 290–1, 304, 322–3, 362, 373, 381–2, 387, 393
 genetic determinism, 282, 291–2
 genetic engineering/manipulation, 23, 25, 64–5, 66, 68–70, 74–5, 77–82, 85–6, 100–1, 112, 208, 237–9, 243, 273–4, 281–2, 291, 294, 326, 391, 396, 399
 genetic identity, 290, 292
 see also enhancement, genetic
genius, 38, 48, 52, 126, 180, 223, 230, 239, 383, 392
God/gods, 2, 13, 38, 59, 69, 85, 89, 97–8, 117, 126, 135, 156, 193, 196, 199, 205, 210, 229, 232–3, 273, 275, 287, 356, 362–3, 366–70, 374, 379, 404
 death of, 52, 229
 false gods, 365, 369

God machine, 281
 Playing God, 366
Gordon, Douglas, 311–12, 315–16, 318, 320
governance, **279–88**
Grandin, Temple, 179–81
Grief, 127, 295, 336
Grosz, Elisabeth, 322, 326
Guattari, Felix, 11–15, 43, 78, 81, 85–7, 108, 276

hackers, 123–4, 126, 131, 137–8, 198, 200
Halberstam, Judith, 66, 68, 259, 266–8
Haraway, Donna, 20, 31, 59, 62, 68, 88, 94, 96, 155, 172, 194–6, 198, 259, 268, 275, 286, 312, 322–7, 329, 362, 373, 389, 394, 396, 404
Hassan, Ihab, 1–2, 393
Hayles, N. Katherine, 5, 11–12, 14, 18, 26, 88, 101, 107–8, 125, 155, 163, 165–6, 173, 189, 191, 226, 268, 337, 372, 396
Heidegger, Martin, 5, 48, 98, 153, 214, 325, 366, 402–3, 406
Hermeneutics, 270, 273, 289–90, 293, 297
Hollywood, 15, 25, 51, 61, 67, 71, 74, 78, 81–2, 104, 131–2, 135–9, 198–9, 223, 259, 262, 270–2, 380–1, 389
homeostasis, 165–6
homosexuality/heterosexuality, 50, 71, 77, 201, 235, 275–8, 297, 328, 368
 see also gender
horror, 4, 46, 59, 79–81, 84, 153–4, 158–9, 166, 198, 215, 232, 239, 254, 260, 266, 273, 294, 305, 312, 333, 339, 344, 408
human enhancement, see enhancement/augmentation
human exceptionalism, 6, 111, 113, 115, 118, 153, 263, 326, 384–6
humanism, 1–3, 6, 13, 25–6, 36–7, 40, 68, 76–8, 81, 84, 86–7, 88, 101, 141, 153, 157, 194, 199, 262–3, 266–7, 301, 321, 325–9, 361, 392, 395, 403–5
 end of, 270, 372
 Enlightenment humanism, 101
 liberal, 39, 71–2
humiliation, 248–9, 251–2, 263
Husserl, Edmund, 402, 406
hybrids, see chimeras and hybrids
Hyperreality, 20–1, 23, 26, 58–9, 155, 190, 197, 218

Icarus, 224, 232, 237
identity, see personal identity
immortality, see death and immortality

information, 19, 21, 29, 32, 78, 100–2, 107–8, 122, 124–5, 137–8, 153, 160, 163, 165–7, 173, 175–6, 178, 196, 200, 216, 221–3, 226, 234, 260, 299, 337, 343, 362, **371–9**, 386, 396, 399
instauration, 43–4, 45, 47, 52–3
interspecies attraction, 315

James, William, 41
Johansson, Scarlett, 11, 16–18, 46, 81, 125, 131, 335

Kundera, Milan, 234
Kurzweil, Ray, 2, 46, 53, 133, 194–5, 199, 226, 278, 366, 373–5, 378

Lacan, Jacques, 21, 49–51, 199, 214–24, 260, 265
  Lacanian psychoanalysis, 217
Latour, Bruno, 5, **37–44**, 311, 393, 395–6, 404
life experience, 371, 374–76, 379
life extension, **205–13**
Locke, John, 351–2
Lumsden, Charles, 262, 264

machines, 6, 12–13, 15, 18, 20, 22, 24, 27, 32, 46–7, 57, 59, 62, 83–4, 88–9, 94, 96–7, 100, 108, 112, 114–15, 117–19, 120–9, 131–3, 138–9, 156, 159, 164–8, 170, 172, 196, 198, 201, 215, 237, 246, 251, 259–63, 265–6, 270, 275, 284–6, 291, 293, **330–8**, 349, 362, 366–7, 371, 373–4, 376–9, 385, 388, 392, 394–7
  autonomous fighting machines, **141–9**
  desiring machines, 11–12
  God machine, 281
  squeeze machine, 179–80
Marey, Etienne-Jules, 40, 316
masculinity, 48, 53, 70–2, 74, 95, 170, 271, 297, 301, 343
  hypermasculinity, 62, 71, 156–7, 222
Massive software, 99, 103–5, 107
materiality, 101, 128, 182, 190, 220, 251, 311
Mazzotta, Giuseppe, 186–7
mediated posthumanism, 7
memory, 26, 29, 32–4, 58, 75, 176–9, 211–12, 215, 222, 231, 241, 295, 346, 349–58, 371, 374–5, 378–9
  biopolitics of, 304
  implantation of, 374–6

Merleau-Ponty, Maurice, 175, 191, 393
metahumanism, 7
Metz, Christian, 41, 44
mind uploading, *see* uploading
miracle drugs, 219
modernity and postmodernity, 11, 14, 20, 37, 57–9, 62, 112, 155, 187, 190, 226, 229, 231, 270, 286, 364–5, 369, 372–3
molecurality, 77–8, 81–2, 85
monsters, 4, 49, 75, **77–85**, 100, 103, 155, 159, 206–7, 209–10, 221, 236, 239–40, 242, 265, 270, 273, 278, 296, 393
  see also Frankenstein/Frankenstein's monster
Moravec, Hans, 13–14, 121, 226, 334, 337, 373–4, 378
More, Max, 334, 366
mutants, 15, 69, 77, 91, 241–3, 260, 266, 280–1, 283–5, 288, 385–8, 396, 399

Nancy, Jean-Luc, 188
National Socialism, 45, 51, 86, 114, 119, 240, 242, 385
naturalization of technology, 337
necrology, 340
neo-humans, 79, 86
networks, *see* computer networks
new materialism, 269, 277
Niccol, Andrew, 19, 23–7, 45, 79, 290, 292, 294
Nietzsche, Friedrich, 25, **45–53**, 78, 80, 155, 229, 239, 260, 279, 295

Object-Oriented Ontology (OOO), **401–409**
obsolete bystander, 5
ontology, 2, 3, 6, 14, 18, 30, 41–2, 71, 153, 155, 174, 184, 188, 191, 194, 225, 228, 234, 275, 289, 295, 312–13, 321–2, 324, 327, 329, 340, 343, 362, 374, 381–3, 391–400
  flat ontology, 312, 319, 402, 404
  ontological ambiguity, 297
  ontological hygiene, 154, 362, 369
  ontological uncertainty, 156, 381–3
  see also Object-Oriented Ontology (OOO)
overpopulation, 49, 122, 262

paradigm shift, 3, 391–2, 394–400
Parfit, Derek, 351–2, 358
peak oil, 305, 307

Pepperell, Robert, 14, 68, 70, 75, 372, 376
personal identity, 59, 212, 296, **349–58**, 368, 383
phenomenology, 32, 100–1, 174–8, 180, 186, 190, 293, 395, 402
plasticity, 20, 174–6, 220–1, 338, 362
popular culture, 1, 3, 25, 47, 66, 79, 101, 135, 153, 155, 159, 163, 185, 194–5, 225, 227, 231, 235–7, 242, 244, 330, 333, 365, 372, 392–3, 398
possible worlds, 42, 182–4, 187, 191
postcolonialism, *see* colonialism/postcolonialism
posthumanous subjects, **339–48**
posthumous, 49–50, 83, 207, 366
postmodernity/postmodernism, *see* modernity and postmodernity
postmortality, *see* life extension
post-scarcity, 96, 305–6
post-secular, 361–2, 364–5, 367–70
power, 32, 34, 49, 68, 70, 72, 75, 80, 83–4, 86, 89, 93, 97–8, 104, 112, 114, 116–17, 119, 123–4, 128, 130, 135–7, 139, 145, 148–9, 166, 171, 190, 193, 200, 205, 217, 219–20, 222–4, 226, 229, 232–3, 237, 239–40, 243, 253, 262, 267, 269, 271, 273, 276, 279–82, 286–7, 290, 292, 304, 312–14, 319, 322–3, 326, 328, 331, 336–7, 361, 366, 371–2, 380, 385–7, 392–3, 395, 399, 407
  superpower/supernatural power, 192, 206, 235, 240–1, 243–4, 274
  unlimited, 125, 128, 173, 221, 366–70
  see also biopower
primitivity, 26–7, 77, 83, 128, 135, 158, 286, 315, 333–5
prosthesis/prosthetics, 19, 22, 33–5, 47, 66, 68, 72–4, 76–7, 79, 108, 112, 115, 148, 163, 167, 173, 175, 178, 194, 216, 239, 260, 262–5, 267, 350, 362, 380–1, 397–8, 404
psychoanalysis, 29, 33–4, 44, 50, 78, 195, 217, 275

queer, 68, 264, 272–3
Quine, Willard van Orman, 350

racism, 83–4, 96, 235, 240–4, 250, 269, 272, 280, 321, 326, 328
religion, 22, 36, 45, 57, 91, 97, 119, 126–7, 160, 176, 194–5, 214, 236, 251, 268, 297, 304–5, 330, 337, 355, **361–70**, 374

representation, 1, 4, 18, 21, 24, 28, 31–2, 34, 42, 65, 69–70, 91, 97, 106–7, 115, 125, 132, 135, 137–8, 153–8, 160, 167, 173–4, 186, 188, 193–5, 197, 199, 214, 217, 260, 273, 297, 311, 315, 330, 333–4
  of animals, 317
  of cybersex, 163–171
  of the posthuman, 4, 58–9, 67, 76, 78, 90, 113, 120, 122, 130, 156–9, 190, 193, 197, 235, 240, 290, 292–3, 328, 335, 344, 362, 368–9, 391, 393, 399
  of subjectivity, 278
  of the supernatural, 269
  of technology, 271
robot/robotics, 5, 19, 46, 57, 59, 62, 65, 68–9, 71, 73, 79, 86, 89–96, 94, 111–19, 121, 123, 126–9, 130–2, 141–9, 158, 172–3, 198, 216, 240, 244, 247, 260, 262, 265–6, 269–71, 273, 275–8, 330, 332–4, 336, 354, 356, 367, 376–7, 391, 393, 395, 397–9
  nanorobots, 46, 239
  Rossum's Universal Robots (R.U.R.) (Karel Capek), 113, 275
  social robots, 330, 335–6
  three laws of, 145–7
Ronen, Ruth, 182, 184

Schaab, Benjamin, 263, 265
Schechtman, Marya, 351–3, 355
science fiction (SF), 4, 19, 46, 57, 89, 115, 133, 144, 153, 163, 172, 189, 192, 240, 259, 270–1, 285, 330, 334, 340, 349, 361, 371, 380, 391
Scopophilia, 215, 217–8
secularism/secularization, 86, 361–2, 364–5, 367
  see also post-secular
self, 12–13, 15, 20, 119, 153–4, 157, 265, 269, 275, 292, 304, 351, 353, 373–4, 378
sentience, 5, 64, 94, 96, 111, 116–18, 123, 130, 247, 356, 371–2, 376, 378, 384, 393, 397, 399–400
  digital sentience, **120–9**, 130
sex/sexuality, 3, 18, 45–6, 48, 50, 63, 71–4, 92, 115, 126, 129, 162–71, 211, 216–17, 222, 232, 248–50, 253–4, 262–4, 271–2, 274–5, 282, 286–7, 296, 334–5, 367, 377
  cybersex/virtual sex, 125, **162–71**, 335
sexism, 269–72

shame, 239, 247–9
  Promethean Shame, 291
Silicon Valley, 131–2, 135–9
simulation, 19–24, 26–7, 58, 92–3, 99, 102–4, 107, 120, 125, 138, 146, 163, 192, 196–8, 254, 265, 318, 320, 373
singularity, 19, 21–3, 25–7, 78
  technological singularity, 26, 46, **88–98**, 107, 120, 124, 128, 133, 157, 189–90, 194, 240, 278, 286, 332, 337–8, 343, 366
skin, 17–18, 50, 74, 94, 96, 132, 172, 175–8, 181, 231, 249, 285, **289–98**, 334–5, 399
  epidermal readings, 289–90, 295
  skin clock, 290, 294–5
  skin-job, 96, 285, 335
soul, 34, 52, 91, 95, 146, 207, 216, 305, 315, 337, 369, 373–4, 393, 395
Souriau, Etienne, 38, 40–4
speciecism, 115, 235, 248, 318, 325, 389
species cosmopolitanism, 380–1, 388–90
species diversity, 266
spectrality, 29–32, 34–5, 190, 343–4, 347
speculative posthumanism, 7, 88
Stacey, Jackie, 77, 80, 84–5, 274
Stiegler, Bernard, 28, 31, 33–6
subjectivity, 6, 11–12, 20, 29, 32, 40, 58, 60–1, 63–4, 69, 71, 78, 100–1, 129, 165, 275–6, 278, 285, 294–5, 325, 389, 391–400, 405
  a-subjective consciousness, 42, 44
  cyborgian, 61
  human, 62, 78, 160, 284, 286, 389, 392, 394, 398–9
  modern, 37
  posthuman/non-human, 153–4, 156, 159–62, 285, 287–8, 294, 344, 391–2, 396–8
  social, 59
  transhumanist, 108
subversion, 11, 48, 67, 78, 93, 104, 218, 334, 340, 407
superheroes, 18, **66–76**, 83, 156–7, 241–2, 269, 273–4, 332, 380, 382, 385–9
Superman/superman, 44, 46–7, 51–3, 69, 80, 83, 157, 282, 380, 386–7
superpower, *see* power
systems theory, 183
  second-order systems theory, 299–303, 305–6

tactile visual sensory substitution system (TVSS), 175–6
technoscience, 3, 19, 60, 88, 153, 157, 160, 217, 260–1, 264, 391, 396
technosocial, 155, 391–3, 395–400
teletechnology, 30–5
Telotte, J.P., 58, 62, 64, 148, 311, 331–3
Thacker, Eugene, 101, 106, 264, 268, 340, 343–5
theatre of proof, 37–40, 44
though experiments, 4, 144, 176, 182, 191, 194, 351, 362
Topsy the elephant, 313–19
transcendence, 3, 15, 72, 79, 91, 97–8, 100–2, 105, 107, 121, 123, 126, 130, 158, 173, 181, 192, 194–5, 205, 226–7, 229, 231–2, 234, 264–5, 280, 292–5, 303, 319, 361, 363, 365, 369–70, 372–3, 403
transhumanism, 1–2, 4, 6–7, 45, 47–9, 52–3, 70–6, 79–80, 100–2, 107–8, 112, 120, 125, 127, 141, 148, 153, 157, 161, 182, 184, 186, 189, 191, 194, 205, 226, 231, 233, 235–8, 241, 244–5, 246–7, 259–60, 267, 270, 282, 297, 334, 338, 357, 366–7, 372, 388, 396–7, 399, 403–4
  moral, 388–9
Turing machine, 46
Twardowski, Kazimierz, 402

uncanny, 51, 80, 85, 96, 132, 215, 219, 221, 274, 317–19, 336–8, 342–3, 346
unmanned aerial vehicles (UAVs), 142
uploading, 98, 100, 120, 127, 170, 191, 334, 337, 350, 373–4, 398–9
utopian, *see* dystopian/utopian

vampire, 49, 53, 153, 158–9, 206–10, 213, 235, 239–40, 242–3, 269, 273, 339, 367, 374, 398
video art, 52
Vinge, Vernor, 22, 46, 89–91, 120, 124, 133, 332
virtual reality, 15–16, 19–27, 34–5, 64, 77, 82, 93, 99, 102–3, 105, 108, 124–5, 127, 155, 159, 164–70, 187–8, 192–3, 197, 201, 240, 260, 278, 293–4, 336–7, 362, 365, 367, 375
  virtual sex, *see* cybersex
Vitruvian man, 196, 201
Vivisection, 80, 84, 86, 215, 315, 317

vulnerability, 48, 59, 72, 74, 84–5, 121, 134, 177–9, 216, 222, 229, 300, 311–13, 322, 342
    animal vulnerability, 314–15, 318–19

Welesko, Brian, 190–1
Whitehead, Alfred North, 37, 40
Wiener, Norbert, 337, 392

Wolfe, Cary, 1, 14, 19, 28, 33, 101, 112, 189, 246, 248, 267–8, 299, 304–5, 318, 382, 389, 398, 403–4

Žižek, Slavoj, 49–50, 53, 307
zombie, 32, 49, 53, 62, 77, 83, 85, 99, 103, 153, 158, 189, 206, 242, 265–6, 298, 339, 344, 348, 368

Printed and bound by CPI Group (UK) Ltd, Croydon, CR0 4YY